The Archaeology of
William Henry Holmes

The Archaeology of William Henry Holmes

Edited with an Introduction by
David J. Meltzer and Robert C. Dunnell

SMITHSONIAN INSTITUTION PRESS
WASHINGTON AND LONDON

Holmes's articles originally published in 1894, 1897, 1886, 1903
New material for this edition edited by Eileen D'Araujo

Library of Congress Cataloging-in-Publication Data
Holmes, William Henry, 1846-1933.
   The archaeology of William Henry Holmes / David J. Meltzer and
   Robert C. Dunnell, editors.
      p.   cm.—(Classics of Smithsonian anthropology)
   Includes bibliographical references.
   Contents: Natural history of flakes stone implements—Stone implements
of the Potomac-Chesapeake Tidewater Province—Origin and development
of form and ornament in ceramic art—Aboriginal pottery of the eastern
United States.
   ISBN 1-56098-152-0
   1. Indians of North America—Pottery. 2. Indians of North America—
Implements. 3. Indians of North America—Antiquities. 4. North America—
Antiquities. 5. Holmes, William Henry, 1846-1933. I. Meltzer, David J., 1955-.
II. Dunnell, Robert C., 1942- . III. Title. IV. Series.
E98.P8H63   1992
973'.01—dc20   91-27847

British Library Cataloging-in-Publication data available

Manufactured in the United States of America
96 95 94 93 92   5 4 3 2 1

♾The paper used in this publication meets the minimum requirements
of the American National Standard for Permanence of Paper for Printed
Library Materials Z39.48-1984.

CONTENTS

Note: In the interest of scholarly consistency, original page numbers of the Holmes articles have been retained.

PUBLISHER'S NOTE

William Henry Holmes's articles appearing in this edition are photographic reprints from the original publications. "Natural History of Flaked Stone Implements" is reprinted from *Memoirs of the International Congress of Anthropology*, Chicago, 1893 (Chicago: Schulte Publishing, 1894). "Stone Implements of the Potomac-Chesapeake Tidewater Province" is reproduced from the *Fifteenth Annual Report of the Bureau of Ethnology to the Secretary of the Smithsonian Institution, 1893–94* by J. W. Powell (Washington: Government Printing Office, 1897). "Origin and Development of Form and Ornament in Ceramic Art" was originally published in the *Fourth Annual Report of the Bureau of Ethnology to the Secretary of the Smithsonian Institution, 1882–83* by J. W. Powell (Washington: Government Printing Office, 1886). "Aboriginal Pottery of the Eastern United States" is reprinted from *Twentieth Annual Report of the Bureau of American Ethnology to the Secretary of the Smithsonian Institution, 1898–99* by J. W. Powell (Washington: Government Printing Office, 1903). The original text pagination, spelling, and punctuation have been retained throughout. All illustrations have been reproduced; in a few instances, the order of the plates has been changed to accommodate two-page and color illustrations.

INTRODUCTION

David J. Meltzer and Robert C. Dunnell

William Henry Holmes (1846-1933) has been described as "perhaps the greatest artist-topographer and man of many talents that the West ever produced" (Goetzmann 1966:512). Although known to historians of the field, the "next generation [of archaeologists] would know little of [Holmes's] work" (Mark 1980:163; Goetzmann 1966:512). Why has Holmes's work been largely lost to contemporary archaeology? Why should it command attention today?

In answer to the first question, Holmes's archaeological career was, except for a few years, in government service where he had but modest connections with the developing university system and its students who became the next generation of archaeologists (Darnell 1969; Meltzer 1985:256). Further, Holmes was often at odds with Franz Boas, and it was Boas and his students who would come to dominate American anthropology to a degree unimaginable today. In Boasian histories, Holmes was often neglected (the most exaggerated instance is Benedict [1943], but see the trenchant response by Lowie [1943]).

Although Holmes was an energetic scholar and published widely, a significant part of his effort was devoted to anonymous museum duties—specimen illustration, arrangement, and exhibit. The focus there and in his writing on geographical distribution of material culture, and the relative inattention to chronology, that characterized much of his work fell out of fashion in American archaeology in the 1930s (Guthe 1952; Trigger 1989:122-123).

Much of his professional effort was dedicated to the vigorous, and ultimately successful, debunking of the American Paleolithic, and although "men seldom attain permanent fame for their negative accomplishments" (Swanton 1937:237), in this case Holmes did, and it had the effect of overshadowing much of his other work. His enthusiasm for this thesis led him to take a reactionary position on the antiquity of New World occupation generally, a stance later tinged with private regret (e.g., Holmes to Osborn, March 28, 1924, WHH/SIA).[1]

Finally, our view of history tends to downplay the kind of subtle but fundamental intellectual contributions Holmes made (cf. Clarke 1973). As practitioners of a historical discipline, archaeologists are accustomed to think of our history in terms of a sequence of "discoveries," a string

of empirical turning points, that subsequently condition the development of the discipline (e.g., Heizer 1959, 1962; Willey and Sabloff 1980).
It is easy to acknowledge such empirical precedents. Many events shape
scientific disciplines but often they are new ways in which the subject
matter or problems of a field are conceived (Gould 1988; Mayr 1982).
We seem less inclined to acknowledge precedent when it comes to intellectual matters, yet this is precisely where Holmes's contributions
were manifest. And this is why his work deserves our attention today.

The essential questions of a field are usually specified by the first
competent thinkers to enter it (Gould 1977a:1), and Holmes was a competent thinker par excellence. His work, more than that of any other
scholar in the field before or since, bridges the gap between archaeology
as natural history and as a fledgling natural science. The programmatic
and polemical tone of much of Holmes's writing (replete with references
to the "old" archaeology, e.g., Holmes 1893e:135), itself a symptom of
modernization, testifies to Holmes's intent to change the methodology
of archaeology. His contemporaries saw his work in a similar light: Otis
Mason (1886:818), writing as Holmes's immediate superior at the U.S.
National Museum (hereafter USNM, part of the Smithsonian Institution), noted that Holmes was specially valued for his "philosophic approach" to archaeology. This approach often placed Holmes at odds with
other scholars, even his colleagues in Washington, and saw him partici-
pate in most of the "great debates" of his day. Although the position
Holmes advocated did not always prove correct in the long run, his
"philosophic approach," including stern insistences on the separation of
observation from speculation, on the need for large, representative
samples, and, above all, on what constituted proper evidence, did take
the day and gives his work a modern aura—not surprising, since it is
the basis of our own. Holmes rose to the top of his profession in the first
quarter of the twentieth century and in spite of being an articulate,
trenchant critic of archaeological practice he seems to have been unusually well-liked and respected (Swanton 1937). Historic accounts and
oral tradition agree: Holmes was a "gentleman" (H. B. Collins, J. B. Griffin,
personal communications).

Holmes's novel "philosophic approach" to archaeology often resulted
in the first integrated understandings of particular regions. This impact
is nowhere better expressed than by Willey:

> W. H. Holmes was the first man of considerable intellectual stature to bring
> his talents to bear on the problems of Florida Gulf Coast archaeology. Not
> primarily a field investigator, not a Florida area specialist, his impress has,
> nevertheless, been the greatest of any of those of his time upon later
> generations of archaeologists. . . . He was one of the first to visualize Flor-
> ida prehistory as but a part of the larger fabric of the Indian past of the

eastern United States. With him, Florida archaeology, for the first time, moved away from a consideration of discrete phenomena toward a comprehension of broad categories of related phenomena (Willey 1949:26).

Willey's observations on Holmes's impact in Florida archaeology might be repeated for nearly every area that caught Holmes's attention, and few areas in North America did not.

Still, even Willey's tribute indulges a common misconception—that Holmes was not a "field investigator." It is true that Holmes was not an explorer of the caliber of John Wesley Powell (though he participated in those great adventures) nor an excavator of Cyrus Thomas's (1894) rapacious appetites (though much of Thomas's excavation was done by part-time employees of the Bureau and only visited, if seen at all, by Thomas). However, Holmes spent virtually every season in the field during his prime years and conducted and supervised many excavations, particularly in the Middle Atlantic region and in quarries and mines wherever they were found, to say nothing of his fieldwork in Mexico. More important, Holmes's fieldwork was modern; it was not the exploratory surgery of Thomas, Putnam, or Moorehead. Holmes's fieldwork was designed frequently to answer specific questions—in modern jargon, to test hypotheses. Further, it was carried out with a care to association and recording, which if not fully modern, certainly departed in a modern direction from that of many of his contemporaries. Indeed, the first of two Loubat prizes he was to receive was awarded for his careful fieldwork and the interpretation it allowed of Washington, D.C., area quarries (Swanton 1937:229).

Holmes's "philosophic approach" was expressed in fundamental contributions to ceramic analysis and artifact classification, and played a major role in debunking claims of an American Paleolithic (Meltzer 1983; Willey and Sabloff 1980:49). Curiously, although Holmes's work set the tone of Americanist ceramic analysis for the next fifty years, he repeatedly pointed out (1886a:265; 1886b:367; 1903a:15) that his involvement with the study of ceramics was at the behest of John Wesley Powell, the director of the Bureau of Ethnology (after 1894, the Bureau of American Ethnology, both denoted hereafter as BAE), as part of Powell's largely unrealized plans for a comprehensive treatment of American technology. Nonetheless, Holmes obviously warmed to the task. Even so, Holmes's real passion was lithic analysis, most particularly quarrying. He traveled widely and seemingly at every opportunity to examine and excavate quarries (e.g., Holmes 1890a, 1890b, 1890c, 1891, 1892a, 1892b, 1892c, 1892d, 1894a, 1897a, 1900, 1903b, 1919). His contributions in that field have had lasting, substantive value (Johnson 1978).

Holmes insisted that "proper" classification was a requisite to scientific study in archaeology and outlined the general parameters for same (precociously distinguishing what we would today call functional, stylistic, and technological classification [e.g., 1888:189]), although he contributed almost nothing of substance to that field. (The broad outlines of his work, however, had a decided influence on his colleagues.) Indeed, when Holmes talked about classification, he was usually referring to schemes for the arrangement of museum specimens, a genuine passion (Swanton 1937:237), more akin to the work of Wilson (1899) than modern classification (Dunnell 1986b:161).

Thus, William Henry Holmes played a preeminent role in the early development of American archaeology, though one that is easy to underestimate or, because of the currents of history, to overlook. Yet, as an archaeologist Holmes grappled with many of the fundamental questions that still confront the discipline. The answers he provided may not be (by our standards) correct ones, but understanding them gives us a foundation for comprehending the roots of twentieth-century archaeology, and thus ultimately why we think what we think today (Binford 1981:4; Meltzer 1989a:12–16). This volume, in reprinting four of his works, opens a window into the archaeology of William Henry Holmes and, indeed, the origins of American archaeology.

A context for these papers is supplied here by a biographical sketch of Holmes's professional life, a discussion of his theoretical stance, as well as brief introductions to each of the specific works. There was, of course, far more to Holmes than what we can discuss or reprint here. Nowhere is that more apparent than in our biographical sketch, which out of necessity focuses on Holmes the archaeologist and geologist, paying less attention to his career as an artist, his role as a major figure in the Washington scientific community at a time when Washington science was the center of American science, and his rich personal life. These and other aspects of his professional and personal life receive attention in other works (e.g., Hinsley 1981; Mark 1980; Nelson 1980; Swanton 1937; Thoresen 1977), and especially in the twenty-volume "Random Records of a Lifetime in Art and Science" (Holmes 1932), a collection of his letters, manuscripts, photographs, sketches, and recollections of personal history that Holmes meticulously compiled in his last years and on which we (and others) have depended heavily. The definitive biography that Holmes deserves has yet to be written, however.

A BIOGRAPHICAL SKETCH OF
WILLIAM HENRY HOLMES, ARCHAEOLOGIST

Holmes was born in Cadiz, Ohio, the youngest son of a farm family of English descent, whose two older sons were more willing or able to take on farm duties than the youngest boy, who mostly liked to draw—much to his father's disapproval (Holmes 1932, 1:12; Mark 1980:132; Nelson 1980:254). Unable to secure formal training in art, he turned to education, received a teaching certificate in 1865, graduated (in 1870) from McNeely Normal School in Hopedale, Ohio, and resigned himself to a teaching career (Holmes 1932, 1:12; Nelson 1980:254; Swanton 1937:224). That career was to begin with further study at the State Normal School in Salem, Massachusetts (Swanton 1937:224), but it was derailed before it ever started. Holmes had a chance meeting with a War Department clerk at a Cadiz bookstore, who suggested that if Holmes truly wanted training in art he should go to Washington, to study with painter Theodor Kaufmann (Holmes 1932, 1:24; Nelson 1980:254). With $200 in hand—a gift from his father that was intended to support his studies in Salem—Holmes went to Washington in the spring of 1871. Higher degrees would come later.[2]

Enrolling in Kaufmann's class, Holmes met Mary Henry, daughter of Joseph Henry, the first secretary of the Smithsonian Institution. She told him about the natural history collections on display at the Smithsonian and perhaps—if Holmes had not already known—that the Institution regularly employed scientific illustrators (Holmes 1932, 1:25). Whether or not Holmes went to the Smithsonian hoping to be discovered, he was: an ornithologist passed by as Holmes was sketching two birds on display and invited him into the research area to see illustrations in a monograph on hummingbirds (Nelson 1980:255; Stegner 1954:186). There, Holmes met a number of scientists, among them Fielding Meek and William H. Dall (Holmes 1932, 1:25). Meek was impressed by Holmes's artistic abilities and potential and hired Holmes on the spot for piecework (Stegner 1954:186). Over the next year, except for the summer of 1871 when Meek was in the field and Holmes returned to Hopedale, Meek instructed Holmes in scientific illustration, mostly drawing fossil specimens. Holmes continued his lessons with Kaufmann (Nelson 1980:262).[3]

Holmes took up residence in one of the Smithsonian towers. Sketching ammonites and echinoderms, his skills were refined, and his reputation spread among the corps of scientists who wintered at the Smithsonian, then left every spring to decipher the geology and natural history of the still largely unexplored American West. One of those was Meek's old friend and collaborator, Ferdinand V. Hayden. In 1869 Hayden had successfully lobbied Congress to establish the United States Geological Survey of the Territories, with him in charge. Thus it came about that in May of 1872 Hayden appointed Holmes as artist to the survey (Holmes 1932, 1:29). Holmes joined a remarkable assembly of people that included photographer William Henry Jackson; paleontologists Meek and Edward Drinker Cope; botanist Leo Lesquereux; geologists Joseph

Leidy, John Newberry, and James Stevenson; painter Thomas Moran; zoologist C. Hart Merriam; and a middle-aged entomologist, botanist, and, later, archaeologist, Cyrus Thomas (Bartlett 1962; Goetzmann 1966).

Holmes's initial appointment as an artist with a salary of $1,800 was extended to 1874 (Holmes 1932, 1:55). He first went west (to Yellowstone) with the Hayden survey in 1872, and beginning with the survey's Annual Report of that year, "scarcely a Hayden survey publication on geology lacks illustrations by Holmes" (Nelson 1980:265); for good reason: in the West Holmes first realized his astonishing gifts as a landscape artist.

Now buried in government reports and monographs of the Hayden and later geological surveys, Holmes's majestic panoramas of the Front Range, the Wind Rivers, the Tetons, and the Grand Canyon were unrivaled works of art and science (Stegner 1954:187–191). His technique, as Goetzmann noted, was like no other's: "He could sketch panoramas of twisted mountain ranges, sloping monoclines, escarpments, plateaus, canyons, fault blocks and grassy meadows that accurately depicted hundreds of miles of terrain. They were better than maps, and better than photographs because he could get details of stratigraphy that light and shadow obscured from the camera" (Goetzmann 1966:513). But these were more than mere stratigraphic profiles. To see his panoramas "is to step to the edge of forty miles of outdoors" (Stegner 1954:190; also Bartlett 1962:63). This was art without metaphor, on a scale to rival the subject. Works of contemporary artists, such as Thomas Moran, appeared in galleries, magazines, and expositions and evoked strong images of the West (Stegner 1954:188). It was Holmes, however, who captured the landscape without sacrificing its geological detail (Dutton 1882:ix; Goetzmann and Goetzmann 1986:188).

This ability was partly testimony to his growing skill as a geologist, recognized by Hayden in his appointment of Holmes as assistant geologist in May of 1874 at a salary of $2,400 (Holmes 1932, 1:29, 55). Holmes retained that position until 1879, when the Hayden survey along with the competing independent surveys (under Clarence King, John Wesley Powell, and George Wheeler) were dissolved and replaced by one organization: the United States Geological Survey (hereafter USGS). Many of the personnel from the separate surveys were joined in the USGS.

The field training in geology that the years with the Hayden survey provided was valuable to Holmes. Also, it was during geological reconnaissance of the Southwestern Division of the survey in 1875 that Holmes first encountered the "remarkable [Anasazi] ruins" of the San Juan Valley of New Mexico and Arizona, "thus making his entry into the fascinating realm of archaeology" (Holmes 1932, 1:30; Holmes

1878b:383). This experience kindled a lifelong interest in American archaeology (Judd 1967:23; Mark 1980:136) and provided one of his earliest publications, complete with what would become his trademark: careful and detailed drawings and paintings of artifacts, architecture, site plans, and features (such as rock art) (Holmes 1878b). Holmes and William Henry Jackson took on the task of preparing exhibits on the Puebloan cliff houses for the 1876 Centennial Exposition in Philadelphia (Holmes 1932, 2:127; Swanton 1937:225). Perhaps most important of all, in the summer of 1878 Holmes spent two months working on the geology of Yellowstone; while examining Obsidian Canyon, and seeing the ground littered with worked obsidian nodules, he wrote, "It occurred to [me] . . . that the various Indian tribes of the neighboring valleys had probably visited this locality for the purpose of procuring material for arrow points and other implements" (Holmes 1879:250; also 1883:31). He found many artifacts among the obsidian debris, but "nearly all . . . are imperfect, as if broken or unfinished" (Holmes 1879:250; 1883:32). At the time, Holmes did not accord any particular significance to this episode, but those initial observations of stone tool manufacture would serve as the foundation for one of the leitmotifs of his archaeological career.

With the Hayden survey Holmes was, however, nominally a geologist. His primary function was the creation of geological panoramas, maps, and illustrations, which occupied his time, although he produced a few interpretive pieces. In one of the latter, Holmes (1878a) nearly stumbled on the concept of a laccolith, codified by Powell survey geologist Grove Karl Gilbert in his report on the geology of the Henry Mountains (1877). In those years when the independent geological surveys were competing for federal dollars, Holmes's piece became a minor rallying point for the Hayden group, who, "self-aggrandizing as ever" (Pyne 1980: 93), felt that credit was due them for this interpretive breakthrough (Peale 1877). Holmes himself did feel slighted in the priority issue but never blamed Gilbert (who recognized Holmes's earlier work), only those who wrote about the history of the events: "Merrill [1906] gives credit to Gilbert that really belongs to me" (Holmes 1932, 2:77). For his part, Gilbert named a peak in the Henry Mountains (Utah) after Holmes (Holmes 1932, 1:40, 2:68). Holmes took great pride in that honor and the "unique distinction" of having two mountains (the other in Yellowstone) named for him (Holmes 1932, 1:39).

During late 1879 and early 1880, as the individual surveys were dissolved and partly reconstituted as the USGS, Holmes toured European museums and lived for a time in the American artists' colony in Munich (Holmes 1932, 1:32; Mark 1980:137; Swanton 1937:225–226). He returned to America in August of 1880 to join the USGS as an assistant geologist and within three weeks was again out West, teaming up with

Clarence Dutton in a geological survey of the Grand Canyon. It was a fruitful collaboration, of a "poetic and speculative geologist and [an] artist with geological training and a genius for the literal" (Stegner 1954:189). Dutton produced the monograph, *Tertiary History of the Grand Canon District* (1882), Holmes the accompanying folio-size *Atlas*. The *Atlas* has often been called, without overstatement, "the most beautiful government report ever produced" (Goetzmann and Goetzmann 1986:186; Stegner 1954:189).

Although Holmes was employed as a geologist by the USGS throughout the 1880s, this is hardly noticeable from his activities or publications. While a USGS staff member, he was appointed (in 1882) as honorary curator of aboriginal pottery at the USNM and given supervision of all illustrations for BAE reports (Powell 1886:l; Swanton 1937:226-227). The vignette that appears on the title page of all BAE publications is Holmes's illustration (Swanton 1937:233). From 1880 until 1889, when he was officially appointed to the BAE, Holmes examined and published extensively on archaeological collections in various media (shell, textile, ceramic) pouring in to the USNM from the BAE's mound survey excavations and expeditions throughout the country—particularly the Southwest (e.g., Holmes 1884). Under the auspices of the BAE, he visited collections throughout the eastern United States and undertook archaeological fieldwork in the Valley of Mexico in 1884 and in the Jemez Valley, New Mexico, in the fall of 1887 (Powell 1892:xxix). In the work in Mexico, he undertook what one historian identified as the first sophisticated stratigraphic excavations in the New World (Mark 1980:138-142). He also prepared and installed exhibits for expositions at New Orleans, Louisville, and Cincinnati (Holmes 1932, 1:33). All together in those years he published thirty-seven papers, thirty of which were archaeological and produced using only those "portions of his time as were not absorbed in work pertaining to the U.S. Geological Survey" (Powell 1891:xxv). The remaining geological papers were mostly brief administrative summaries of illustrations his division of the USGS made each year.

Obviously, there was an indistinct administrative seam between the BAE and the USGS (Mark 1980:144). Indeed, both organizations shared a single director, John Wesley Powell. Powell took a populist view of science (Pyne 1980:114) and surrounded himself with those, like Holmes, who had earned their scientific credentials "the hard way," climbing the mountains of the American West and mapping its sun-baked plains. He had little regard for academic (theoretical) geologists, who came bearing Ph.D.'s from laboratories in European universities and who worked mostly in geophysics and geochemistry, arcane disciplines of no special interest to Powell. In Powell's USGS, allegiance was to the service of science as natural history as an organic whole and not to a specific science; many of Powell's employees moved with startling (and often resented) ease among various fields (Hinsley 1976; Mark 1980:144; Meltzer 1985:251).[4]

In the late 1880s, Cyrus Thomas's highly visible, congressionally mandated mound survey was winding down; the widely scattered field operations ceased, and Thomas settled into the BAE's offices in Washington to devote his time to writing the massive report (Thomas 1894) that would justify the congressional appropriation. Powell, no babe in the woods of Washington politics (Swanton 1944:35), looked to move the bureau's archaeological research in another direction (Powell had been opposed to the mound survey, and it was carried out only because of congressional earmarking of his budget), but one with an equally high profile. On June 30, 1889, Powell appointed Holmes to take charge of the "archaeologic fieldwork of the Bureau" (Powell 1894:xxvi). Holmes's first task was to resolve a vexing problem of nineteenth-century American archaeology: the question of the American Paleolithic.

To accomplish that, Holmes began fieldwork at the Piney Branch site, in Washington, D.C., just three miles north of the White House. The selection of Piney Branch was quite deliberate. At this location there was a gravel outcrop, involving two different horizons, one Tertiary and the other Cretaceous, associated with numerous rude artifacts. In the 1880s, Piney Branch had been interpreted as an American Paleolithic site, Pleistocene in age, in recognition of the similarity of the artifacts to European paleoliths, and overall "rude" form (Wilson 1889). Others saw it differently. Proudfit was the first to suggest that the Piney Branch "paleoliths" were merely "the resultant debris of Indian workshops [and not attributable] to paleolithic man" (Proudfit 1889:245; see also Holmes 1897a:17; Putnam 1889).[5]

Perhaps mindful of the lessons of a decade before at Obsidian Canyon in Yellowstone, Holmes took up Proudfit's refrain:

> . . . my first entry into the controversy over paleolithic man resulted from a visit to the Salem Museum where [Frederic W.] Putnam had two cases filled with American paleoliths—so labelled. This was in the late 'eighties. I had already differed with Dr. [Thomas] Wilson on the interpretation of these stones, since among all treasured in the Museum there was not a single specimen that showed definite specialization or signs of use (Holmes to N. Nelson, December 2, 1921, SUB/NAA).

Holmes's careful excavation at the Piney Branch quarries over the fall and winter of 1889–1890 established that the association was with the Cretaceous, not Tertiary gravel. The site itself proved to be a quarry and the "paleoliths" little more than rejects of the manufacturing process.

These investigations had an unambiguous message for Paleolithic proponents: artifact form had no "chronological significance whatever"
(Holmes 1890a:25). These specimens "were all mere rejectage of manufacture of Indian arrowheads, spearpoints, knives, etc.," and so he "felt
justified in challenging the whole American Paleolithic 'evidence'"
(Holmes to Nelson, December 2, 1921, SUB/NAA).

    In the small archaeological community of the time, word of Holmes's
research and its implications for an American Paleolithic traveled fast
(Meltzer 1983:16). Charles C. Abbott, whose Trenton (New Jersey)
gravels discoveries had triggered the search for paleolithic implements, visited Piney Branch, but came away unconvinced that it had
any bearing on "the question of man's antiquity in America" (Abbott
1890:9). Lucien Carr, F. W. Putnam's assistant at the Peabody Museum,
thought the same: "how are you going to get around the Trenton gravels
and California cement wh[ere] implements have been found? The only
way to discredit them is to say 'the boy lied'" (Carr to Henshaw, December 2, 1889, BAE/NAA). Holmes would soon expand his range, ultimately discrediting not only Abbott's Trenton gravels (Holmes 1893b),
but also virtually all others. Between 1890 and 1903, Holmes personally
visited—and criticized—nearly every North American site said to be of
Pleistocene age and/or contain Paleolithic artifacts (e.g., Holmes 1892c,
1893a, 1893b, 1893c, 1893d, 1893e, 1893f, 1897b, 1899, 1902a, 1902b).

    American Paleolithic proponents rose to defend their position, and
there ensued a bitter dispute. Yet, although Holmes participated fully,
his participation was "always quiet and reserved, [and he] argued calm-
ly, but [Holmes's colleague] McGee, so tradition has it, supported his
beliefs with much table pounding" (Judd 1967:15). Nowhere is that
better expressed than in a letter by George Frederick Wright, whose
Newcomerstown (Ohio) Paleolith had come under critical scrutiny by
Holmes (1893d) and whose volume *Man and the Glacial Period* (1892)
had triggered withering and often highly personal attacks by W J McGee
and glacial geologist Thomas C. Chamberlin (of the USGS and the University of Chicago). In the midst of all this, Wright remarked in a quiet
note to Holmes, "I wish all the controversialists would be as courteous
as you and I have been" (Wright to Holmes, April 12, 1893, WHH/SIA;
see also Wilson to Holmes, December 5, 1894, WHH/SIA).

    The controversy over human antiquity in America would last another
three decades (see Meltzer 1983, 1991), but it took far less time for
Holmes's efforts to bear results: although the question of whether human
groups had come to the Americas in the Pleistocene would remain open
(Holmes 1897b:824–825), the American Paleolithic was lost. By the turn
of the century, new "discoveries" of American paleoliths had virtually
ceased (Meltzer 1991).

As an old man looking back over his life, Holmes would identify the period from 1889 to 1894 as "one of the most important periods of my career in the field of science, and one of the most important, perhaps, in the history of American archaeological research" (Holmes, MAP/NAA; see also Holmes 1932, 1:35; Swanton 1937:237). The Piney Branch site was a "sacred spot" and his discoveries there "have done more to clear up the story of man in America than any single piece of research within the United States" (Holmes to Sherrill, April 6, 1925, Holmes 1932, 6:56). He was obviously proud of his role in bringing about "the end of the Paleolithic Man in America" (Holmes, MAP/NAA). However, in a candid letter to Henry Fairfield Osborn, he would also admit that although he found it necessary to attack the whole body of the so-called evidence for the American Paleolithic, "Possibly I went too far" (Holmes to Osborn, March 28, 1924, SUB/NAA; see also Holmes to Nelson, December 2, 1921, SUB/NAA; Swanton 1937:228).[6]

At the time, however, his accomplishments were lauded, at least in non-Paleolithic circles (Meltzer 1983, 1990). On the strength of that work, in August of 1892 Holmes was appointed nonresident professor of anthropologic geology at the University of Chicago, a position engineered by Thomas Chamberlin (Holmes 1932, 7:16). Beginning in December of 1892, Holmes was placed in charge of the BAE exhibits for the World's Columbian Exposition in Chicago (Holmes 1932, 6:68), which included ethnographic and archaeological collections, and—in what was then a novel approach to exhibits (Hinsley 1981:108)—life-size plaster figures engaged in quarrying and artifact manufacture (Holmes 1932, 6:69; Mark 1980:155).

Holmes's work for the BAE in Chicago attracted attention, and in May of 1894, a few months after the exposition ended, he was offered and accepted a permanent appointment in Chicago as curator in the Department of Anthropology in the newly established Field Museum. This was the position a young Franz Boas, temporarily employed at the exposition, had desperately wanted, and Boas was bitterly disappointed not to receive it (the episode is traced in Hinsley [1981: 250-251] and especially in McVicker [1989]). Boas had been especially rankled by the fact that the offer had been made to Holmes "behind my back" (Boas to Jacobi, September 2, 1909, FB/APS [reprinted in Stocking 1974:303-306]; also Boas to Putnam, February 18, 1894, FB/APS), while Boas was still—in his own eyes, at least—"in charge of the Anthropological Department" (Boas to Skiff, February 16, 1894, FB/APS).

Boas received assurances from Holmes (Holmes to Boas, February 21, 1894, FB/APS) and independently from W J McGee (Boas's only close friend within the BAE) that Holmes had not "knowingly [been] a party to any arrangement prejudicial to you," and that in fact Holmes had

hesitated to accept the appointment owing to the "uncertainty as to how
you would be affected should he accept" (McGee to Boas, March 21, 1894,
FB/APS). McGee assured Boas—though Boas already knew (Boas to
Putnam, February 18, 1894, FB/APS)—that Thomas Chamberlin had
engineered the Holmes appointment. Chamberlin, in fact, boasted pri-
vately to Holmes that it came about "almost wholly through my influence" (Chamberlin to Holmes, January 27, 1894, Holmes 1932, 7:8). Even
though "little blame should be attached . . . to Holmes" (McGee to Boas,
March 21, 1894, FB/APS), this was the first strain in Holmes and Boas's
relationship, and it would reverberate over the next three decades
(Stocking 1968:281).

But that was in the future. In May of 1894, Holmes had also just
finished the text of his "Stone Implements of the Potomac-Chesapeake
Tidewater Province" (one of the works reprinted here), later published
in the *Fifteenth Annual Report of the BAE* (Holmes 1897a). W J McGee,
who was then ghostwriting Powell's annual administrative reports (see
below), remarked in the one that preceded Holmes's paper, "In extent
and thoroughness of study, in wealth of material examined, in thoroughness and scientific character of the investigation, Professor Holmes' work
on the quartzite quarries and their products may safely be considered
to stand unrivaled, at least so far as the Western Hemisphere is concerned" (Powell [McGee] 1897:xcvi).

The work was awarded the 1898 Loubat Quinquennial Prize for the
most important work in American archaeology and anthropology in the
preceding three years. It is perhaps not irrelevant to observe that the
judges on the Loubat Committee were H. Peck, D. Brinton, and W J
McGee. Their citation for Holmes's Loubat Prize stated that the volume:

> may be held to mark an epoch in American archaeological research, by
> interpreting the remarkably abundant artifacts of a typical region in the
> light of previous studies of actual aboriginal handiwork, and thus es-
> tablishing a basis for the classification of the stone art of the entire Western
> Hemisphere. It is the result of many years of personal study, numerous
> experiments, and close typological analysis, and is supplied with a wealth
> of illustrative material that gives it most exceptional interest and value
> (Report of the Loubat Prize Committee, to Seth Low, President of Columbia
> University, May 21, 1898, Holmes 1932, 1:83).

The prize was $1,000, a startling amount of money in those days (it
amounted to one-third of Holmes's annual salary). The committee re-
commended the second prize be given to Franz Boas (again!) for "The
Social Organization and Secret Society of the Kwakiutl Indians" (Boas
1897).

In May of 1894 Holmes was given a farewell banquet in Washington, attended by sixty-four of his colleagues in the Smithsonian, the BAE, and the USGS. The details of the banquet were carefully preserved (Holmes 1932, 5:144--158), along with a commendatory letter from Powell, who credited Holmes's "genius and enthusiasm" as the force by which "American archaeology has been revolutionized" (Powell to Holmes, June 8, 1894, Holmes 1932, 5:138).

Holmes's stay in Chicago proved to be pleasant, productive, but very short-lived. There was a trip to Yucatan in the winter of 1894-1895, which Holmes described as "one of the most gratifying and important events of my life" (Holmes 1932, 7:17). After that, his situation deteriorated. There were poor relations with the museum director and conflicts between Holmes's scientific and curatorial aspirations and the business-first attitude of the museum. All Holmes could see ahead were "years of crudeness, struggle and uncertainty" (Holmes to Walcott, January 28, 1897, Holmes 1932, 7:153). In January of 1897, tipped off by McGee that a position might be had in Washington, Holmes wrote C. D. Walcott (then assistant secretary of the Smithsonian) to say that if a position did develop he would be gratified to return to Washington (Holmes to Walcott, January 28, 1897, Holmes 1932, 7:152-153; cf. Swanton 1937:229 [who implies that the initiative was taken by Walcott, not Holmes]).

In April of 1897, Holmes accepted the position of head curator of the Department of Anthropology of the USNM, but the appointment was not official until "the Civil Service matter" was taken care of. As Walcott explained it, "Under the law, some kind of examination must be held," and then moved quickly to assure Holmes—who had been "disturbed" by the need for an exam (Walcott to Holmes, April 7, 1897, Holmes 1932, 7:159)—that any qualifying test would be based on the "publications and positions held by the candidates" (Walcott to Holmes, April 20, 1897, Holmes 1932, 7:161). Holmes passed, "at probably the highest ratio of any one who has ever had any form of examination. The [examining] committee consisted of Major Powell, an officer of the [Civil Service] Commission, and myself" (Walcott to Holmes, June 11, 1897, Holmes 1932, 7:164). Times were indeed less complicated then.

The next five years were uneventful but highly productive. By decade's end Holmes had completed his massive study on aboriginal pottery of the eastern United States (1903a), which is reprinted here. He had begun work on the volume in 1890, originally intending it to be a companion to Thomas's (1894) mound survey (Holmes 1903a:15). However, the two studies did not mature simultaneously, and Holmes subsequently expanded his study to include all eastern pottery regardless of any relation to mounds. This pathbreaking study (Mark 1980:145; Willey and Sabloff 1980:49) turned out to be his last major work on the "fictile arts," because his later plans to complete a general volume on ceramics (as a companion piece to Holmes 1919) were never realized (Swanton 1937:232).

Holmes was involved with museum exhibition work in Omaha, Buffalo, and Charleston (Holmes 1898a, 1898b) and (with the help of Gerard Fowke) was active in archaeological fieldwork during this period, visiting prehistoric stone quarries in California, Mexico, Illinois, Michigan, and Indian Territory (Oklahoma). He also examined the infamous Calaveras (California) site, the Lansing (Kansas) "Loess Man" locality, and a site in Kimmswick (Missouri), where Holmes went to determine "whether there was satisfactory evidence that man was contemporaneous with the mammoth and the mastodon in that region" (Holmes 1932, 9:34; on his research, see Holmes 1897b, 1899, 1901a, 1901b, 1902a, 1902b, also Graham 1980).

Farther afield, Holmes accompanied Powell on a geological and archaeological reconnaissance of Cuba in 1900. This included a side visit to Jamaica with Samuel P. Langley, secretary of the Smithsonian, to "aid him in a study of the flight of the turkey buzzard with a view of learning something of the possibilities of flight" (Holmes 1932, 7:166).

Powell died on September 23, 1902, and his death was followed by a brief but fierce public and private campaign—fueled by Franz Boas— to replace Powell with W J McGee (e.g., Boas 1902a, 1902b; Stocking 1974:305). McGee had been Powell's protege, and as Powell's health declined he turned over the daily operations of the BAE to McGee (McGee claimed that after 1894 he wrote every one of Powell's reports and official papers [Hinsley 1981:246]). Naturally, McGee felt that he deserved to be named Powell's successor. Boas, still resentful of Holmes and desperate to keep the BAE on its course of pure research and beyond the grasp of Langley and a "museum man" (Holmes), joined to help his friend McGee (Hinsley 1981:251). Their campaign failed.

Langley, whose decision it was, had long detested McGee and his brand of science and believed that McGee was unqualified to administer a scientific bureau (Hinsley 1981:248-249). Langley had been under great pressure from Congress to elicit practical results from the BAE, traditionally a low priority for McGee and Powell. By virtue of the administrative independence of Powell's BAE, there was little Langley could do to force them into action. It is not surprising, then, that Langley told Holmes that, after Powell, the relationship between the BAE and the Smithsonian would "materially differ" from what it had been (Hinsley 1981:249).

Holmes had been a close friend of Langley for years and was "the only one at hand personally congenial to the Secretary" (Holmes 1932, 9:8). Even so, when Langley broached the subject of Powell's successor in February of 1902, Holmes argued that McGee should be appointed, not himself. To Langley's insistent overtures, Holmes replied, "I am well suited in and to the place I now hold and have no desire to assume greater responsibilities, besides, I am somewhat afraid of my capacity to stand the strain of the new work" (Holmes 1932, 9:10). Langley, however, had made his decision and, when Powell died, duly appointed Holmes the new chief of the BAE, on October 15, 1902 (Holmes elected to take a lower salary and the title of "Chief," rather than "Director," in deference to Powell's accomplishments [Holmes 1932, 9:7]).

McGee was bitterly disappointed and resentful. His campaign escalated into a general attack on Langley's administration and only ended a couple of months later when the Smithsonian regents made Holmes's appointment official. Langley fired the parting shot: in the summer of 1903, a minor BAE official of the Powell years was put on trial for forgery and embezzlement, though the investigation seemed mostly to focus on McGee's failings as an administrator. Boas thought the whole case a witch-hunt, and "the records tend to confirm his impression" (Hinsley 1981:253). McGee was finished in Washington: in August of 1903 he resigned from the BAE, left the city, and a few years later left anthropology altogether. An angry Boas retreated to New York.

Holmes, as he himself knew, was not the type of administrator to fight for his bureau against Langley (Hinsley 1981:277; Noelke 1974:231). Indeed, Holmes was hardly the administrative type at all:

> he lacked entirely that mixture of tolerance and firmness demanded of an executive. To be sure he had tolerance enough. That was his bane. Firmness was the element wanting. This was due evidently to his highly sensitive artistic nature. He could not bear rows. . . . He could be imposed upon easily by anyone who understood his weakness. . . . He usually gave in at once if any of his staff chose a different line of action from the one he thought should have been taken. . . . He was thoroughly unhappy as an executive (Swanton 1944:35; Judd 1967:24 offers a similar assessment).

Thus, during the Holmes years the Smithsonian secretary was making final decisions on virtually all aspects of the BAE's operation: research direction, publication, and administrative and personnel matters. Even BAE correspondence had to pass first through Smithsonian offices (Hinsley 1981:277-279; Noelke 1974:231-234).

Despite this surrender of control and Holmes's lack of administrative aggressiveness, his accomplishments as chief of the BAE were not insignificant (Hinsley 1981:282). He oversaw the completion of the long-delayed and immensely popular two-volume "Handbook of American Indians North of Mexico" (Hodge 1907, 1910). The project had been initiated by Powell, but it was sped along by Holmes and Langley to appease a Congress demanding practical products of BAE research

(Noelke 1974:238). Holmes himself wrote more than one hundred of the entries for the handbook (Mark 1980:156).

Holmes also played an influential role in the passage of the Antiquities Act of 1906, ensuring the active participation of Smithsonian archaeologists in the permitting process (see Section 8 of the Uniform Rules and Regulations of the Act of 1906) despite vigorous protest by nonfederal archaeologists, who resented the idea of their qualifications being evaluated by Smithsonian archaeologists. This idea was, they argued, "altogether too much for human nature" (Baum to Lacey, February 25, 1904, ANT/NAA). Holmes, however, working largely behind the scenes and with access to the committee's correspondence, effectively rebutted those arguments (Holmes to Lacey, February 27, March 16, 1904, ANT/NAA).

But there were two achievements in his administration in which Holmes took particular pride: his classification and installation in the museum of "the great collections of American Archaeology," and the establishment of a new Division of Physical Anthropology at the USNM under Aleš Hrdlička (Holmes 1932, 1:38). There is no small irony in the latter, for Holmes captured some of Hrdlička's salary and the new division expenses from money made available by the death of longtime Paleolithic advocate and USNM curator Thomas Wilson (Holmes to Langley, November 5, 1902, Holmes 1932, 8:111).

In short order, Hrdlička ably carried the flag against a great human antiquity in the Americas (Meltzer 1983, 1989b; see, e.g., Hrdlička 1903, 1907, 1912, 1918) and became Holmes's closest and most loyal friend. That bond was visible twenty years later when Holmes, hearing that Hrdlička had been given a low efficiency rating in his yearly evaluation, fired off a letter to Charles Walcott, by then secretary of the Smithsonian:

> I regard Dr. Hrdlička as the strongest force in the field of Anthropology that the Institution has had since Powell. He is the foremost physical anthropologist in America, if not in the world. . . . For twenty odd years he has labored faithfully, and in ability, diligence and work accomplished he has no superior in the Institution. . . . Please excuse the liberty I take, but the Doctor is one of my boys and I am proud of him and his remarkable career (Holmes to Walcott, February 11, 1925, AHP/NAA).

Holmes's tenure as chief of the BAE left him little time for archaeological research and no time for writing (Judd 1967:24-25, 38; Swanton 1937:231). But during that period, the honors began to flow in; among the most prized by Holmes was election to the National Academy of Sciences in 1905, an election he attributed to "my geological work in the Survey of the Territories, and to the leading part taken by me in the archaeological researches of the period" (Holmes 1932, 9:135).

Of course, the best tonic for one averse to administrative work is to be reassigned, and it is no surprise that Swanton reported, "One of the happiest days of Holmes' life, it seemed to me, was in 1910 when he retired from the headship of the Bureau (BAE) and returned to head the Division of Anthropology in the National Museum and became Curator of the American Gallery of Art" (Swanton 1944:37). Holmes did not, of course, leave archaeology in 1910. With his resumed status as curator in the USNM (an appointment that would extend to August 1920), he devoted his time to the installation of museum exhibits, perhaps a mundane contribution in the view of some, but one that Holmes himself viewed as his most important work of the period (Swanton 1937:232, 237).

Naturally, in reaching an age when most now consider retirement, Holmes cut back his field efforts. He was content to have others undertake the work (Swanton 1944:36). Hrdlička was sent to South America and Florida to examine the claims of great antiquity there (Hrdlička 1912, 1918); trusted colleagues from other disciplines—Thomas Chamberlin, Chamberlin's son Rollin (a geologist in his own right), John C. Merriam—were also called on to examine the latest evidence from Trenton and new claims from Vero, Los Angeles, and Lone Wolf Creek (e.g., Holmes to Kummell, November 15, 1915, WHH/SIA; Holmes/Hrdlička to Merriam, May 1924, JCM/LC; Holmes to Merriam, November 23, 1925, WHH/SIA). There were also occasional private and public outbursts against the proponents of great human antiquity in the Americas (Holmes 1918, 1925), especially geologists and vertebrate paleontologists, whom Holmes regarded as unqualified to write on archaeological subjects (Holmes to Hay, ca. February 1919, OPH/SIA; Holmes to Loomis, September 24, 1925, WHH/SIA; paleontologist Oliver Hay, who made a sport of baiting Holmes and Hrdlička [e.g., Hay 1918, 1920], was a perennial target).

These outbursts were somewhat balanced by his substantive contributions, among them his "Handbook of Aboriginal American Antiquities" (Holmes 1919). The volume, on lithics, was the first of a planned two-volume set that was never finished (Judd 1967:38; Swanton 1937:232). This publication brought Holmes his second Loubat Prize, though this time it was the lesser Loubat (*The War with Mexico* by J. H. Smith won first prize). Over the first forty years that the Loubat prize was awarded (1893-1933), Holmes was one of only four anthropologists ever to win and the only individual to win twice.

Through the late teens of this century Boas and Holmes became de facto spokesmen for American anthropology, and they were repeatedly called upon to work together on issues and committees related to anthropology. Given their uneasy past relationship, this meant opportunities to clash, and on occasion they did: over control of the *American Anthropologist* (which in 1914 was transferred from Washington to New York and put in the editorial hands of a Boasian); in 1918-1919 over the composition of the Committee on Anthropology for the National Research Council; and in October 1919 over the nominations of Hrdlička and Kroeber to the National Academy of Science (Stocking 1968:285-292).[7]

Matters came to an explosive head in December of 1919, when Boas published a letter in *The Nation* (Boas 1919). It branded Woodrow Wilson a hypocrite and American democracy a fraud, then attacked four unnamed anthropologists (although Boas was free with their names in correspondence) for using their cover for spying in unnamed foreign countries [Mexico], an activity Boas believed jeopardized all anthropologists who might wish to work in a foreign country (Boas 1919, in Stocking 1974:336-337; Boas to Swanton, January 15, 1920, FB/APS). In the heat of patriotism, the letter "triggered a flood of pent-up personal resentment and institutional antagonism" (Stocking 1968:292). Washington anthropologists, led by Holmes, moved swiftly:

> You have doubtless seen the traitorous article by Boas in the last Nation, and I want to say to you and to Saville and others who do not favor Prussian control of Anthropology in this country that we are determined now to end the Hun regime. [Boas's] position of Honorary Philologist in the Bureau of Ethnology has been abolished, and this, I am sure, is not the final step in the official assault upon the Hun positions (Holmes to Hodge [and others], December 24, 1919, SUB/NAA).

A week later Neil Judd, representing Holmes and the Washington anthropologists, engineered the censure of Franz Boas at the annual meeting of the American Anthropological Association in Cambridge (details are given in Stocking 1968). Boas was stripped of his membership in the AAA governing council, threatened with expulsion, pressured into resigning from the National Research Council, then denied the opportunity of a public explanation (ostensibly because to do so would have allowed the identification of the alleged spies, Judd noted, December 1919, HBC/NAA). Holmes was pleased, but not with certain of his colleagues, who apparently did not share his antagonism toward Boas: "I have your recent favor and am surprised that you should wish the continuance of the Prussian regime, the vicious, scheming, minority of the association has ruled long enough, and if it is to continue I shall close my connection with anthropology for good" (Holmes to Hodge, reprinted in Sturtevant 1975:6).

Holmes did, in fact, resign the next year as head curator of anthropology at the USNM, although the timing was apparently coincidental.

He was understandably anxious to be relieved "of much routine work [to allow] a chance to do something more in the way of scientific writing" (Holmes to Hewett, June 25, 1920, NMJ/NAA). In fact, most of his energies were directed to art. He had become involved in writing and helping edit a new journal, *Art and Archaeology*. His watercolors were exhibited in Washington galleries (Mark 1980:158). And he was named director of the newly created National Gallery of Art.

Despite his age, the amputation of his lower left leg as a result of blood poisoning, and the death (in 1925) of his wife, Kate Clifton Osgood (which brought to an end a union that had lasted since the fall of 1883 and had produced two sons), Holmes stayed on as director of the National Gallery for over a decade (Holmes 1932, 1:189). He wrote with obvious satisfaction, "I have been on duty at the Gallery every day, save Sunday, 1929 and 1930. Jan 1931, I am still at my desk. July 1932" (Holmes 1932, 1:189). But his age finally caught up with him, and he retired from the National Gallery post in mid-1932 and went to live with one of his sons in Michigan (Mark 1980:158).

In January of 1933, Holmes suffered a slight stroke (Mary Holmes to Hrdlička, January 22, 1933, AHP/NAA), for which his son's family received some long-distance medical advice from Hrdlička (Hrdlička to Mary Holmes, February 2 and 13, 1933, AHP/NAA). Holmes died on April 20, 1933.

William Henry Holmes and his wife were buried in the Rock Creek Cemetery in Washington, D.C., scarcely two miles from the Piney Branch quarries where he forged his reputation. They were reserved but proud in death as in life; their unassuming marker reads, "They gave to art and science."

HOLMES'S "PHILOSOPHIC APPROACH"

Holmes's work was preceded by more than a century of argument about when and from where the first Americans had come and why they were the savages of early European description. Even though some of the answers had gone through cycles of acceptance and rejection between the 1770s and the 1870s and most were continuously embellished with observational anecdotes designed to convince, the nature of the arguments themselves changed little.

In calling Holmes's distinctive style of archaeological investigation "philosophic," Mason (1886) drew attention to Holmes's unerring predilection, both implicit and explicit, to view observations as the consequence of, and only understandable through, the agency of an abstract view of the nature of history—in modern terms, theory. Further, he discussed these issues in his publications and linked them to the pragmatics of archaeology. In modern terms, he gave his theory methodological and epistemological interpretation. It is because Holmes differed from his predecessors and most of his contemporaries in these most fundamental ways that so much of his work spanning diverse areas and topics turns out to have been of pathbreaking significance.

First and foremost, Holmes was convinced that archaeology ought to be science, so much so that he not infrequently began articles with reference to the scientific status of archaeology or a brief "lecture" on the attributes of being scientific (e.g., Holmes 1892d, 1893c, 1917). Holmes was by no means unique in arguing that archaeology and anthropology ought to be science. This was the common view, not only, as one might expect, among archaeologists and anthropologists, but also more generally in the academic community. For example, W. I. Thomas (1909:4) urged social scientists to draw upon the biological sciences and "the researches of anthropology and ethnology" in their effort to become more scientific. Anthropology was, as just suggested, still classed as a natural rather than a social discipline.

Not too much should be read into these assessments and exhortations to science. For most writers, "science" meant only that the particular discipline was grounded in observation; in the case of anthropology, it recognized that the "arm chair" approach was rapidly giving ground to an observational one. Robinson's essay on "History" (Thomas 1909:11) makes this simple meaning clear when anthropology is classed with physics: ". . . history can never become a science in the sense that physics, chemistry, physiology or even anthropology is a science." All that was requisite for being scientific was the replacement of anecdotal speculation with a systematic foundation in observation and measurement.

In part, that systematic foundation was developed in a frankly uniformitarian fashion: "The first step in acquiring a knowledge of the past is to seek to understand the present. An acquaintance with the historic peoples of a region is the best key to the prehistoric peoples" (Holmes 1897b:825). In practice, Holmes began investigations "with the known peoples and their culture, following the story downward in the successive formations until all traces of occupation disappear" (Holmes 1925:256).

Holmes consistently and vigorously embraced this view of science. It was a cornerstone of his assault on the advocates of Pleistocene occupation of North America (Holmes 1892c, 1893b:35; 1893c, 1897a). He praised it in the work of others (e.g., Holmes 1889). It also led him to evaluate ethnographic and historical testimony critically, not because of disagreeable implied conclusions but because of qualities of evidence. For example, although he initially (Holmes 1886b) accepted Mason's

(1877) earlier account, derived from unpublished descriptions by E. A. Dalrymple, of Pamunkey (Virginia) pottery making as reflecting aboriginal methods as claimed, he later (1903a:152-153) concluded that the residents of nineteenth-century Pamunkey did not have any knowledge of aboriginal ceramic technology and were producing pottery solely to meet the demand of curiosity collectors. Pottery made in the manner described could not have functioned in the manner of aboriginal vessels nor could it have survived the ravages of time. He reached similar conclusions about the efforts of the Moki (American Southwest) in making corrugated ware (1886a:273, 299). Further, in using historical accounts, he cautioned that Europeans familiar with a particular technique of manufacture in their own culture ". . . were prone to discover traces of similar customs here" [in the Americas] (1903a:37). He recognized that illustrations of aboriginal life often Europeanized and romanticized the Indian. With respect to experimental research, including his own efforts, Holmes (1897a:81) pointed out the limitations that arise from equifinality. Such sophisticated matters as sample size, distribution, and quality were frequently cited as mitigating against firm conclusions, even salubrious ones (Holmes 1897a:36, 1903a:19). For example, he routinely questioned whether pottery samples represented the whole of the art, or some subsample, such as mortuary goods, that would skew his conclusions (e.g., Holmes 1886b:370-372; 1903a:23, 27, 40, 83, 104, 132-133). In short, Holmes distanced himself from the anecdotal evidential tradition of the natural historians at every possible turn.

For Holmes, however, there was more to science than simply a commitment to systematic measurement and observation. In science, phenomena were law-governed, even in such seemingly intractable areas as aesthetics: "The science of the beautiful must deal with actual phenomena, with facts as hard, with principles as fixed, and laws as inflexible as do the sciences of biology and physics" (Holmes 1892d:240). Further, "the creations of art are growths as are the products of nature and are subject to the same inexorable laws of genesis and evolution" (Holmes 1892d:243). He held a failure to appreciate this as responsible for the sorry state of explanation, noting that a "war of words has been kept up for generations and the battle still goes on without being won or lost" (1892d:240). In spite of this vision of science as it was to apply to archaeology, Holmes conceived of laws not in the fashion of physics, but as empirical generalizations that captured some observed "regularity" (e.g., Holmes 1890d:141; 1893a:6-7). Consequently, Holmes never cited or supplied any of the "laws" that govern cultural phenomena.

However ambiguous Holmes may have been on the precise structure of law in archaeology, the kind of theory those laws were supposed to affect is abundantly clear. The proper models were evolutionary. For example, in speaking about technology Holmes said, "The laws of evolution correspond closely in all arts, and . . . are traceable with comparative ease throughout all of the succeeding stages of civilization" (1888:196). In his commitment to a general evolutionary view of human history, Holmes was very much a product of his age (Dunnell 1986b; Hinsley 1981; Stocking 1987). But as in the case of his commitment to science, his involvement went deeper and was more complex than the superficial evolutionism of the late nineteenth century. These subtle differences are the germ of Holmes's particular genius.

Holmes accepted the general progressivist notions of Victorian society. This is apparent in virtually everything he wrote (e.g., 1897a:53-61). Human history was, in a general way, a sequence from simple to complex, from horrid to happy, and from bad to good. Not infrequently, he saw archaeology as forecasting a rosy future for mankind: ". . . we are led to comprehend the true relations of the striking present to the marvelous future . . . that future generations will be privileged to enjoy" (Holmes 1892d:255). The process was even likened unto one of "purification" (Holmes 1909:236). Further, Holmes was embued with anthropological evolutionism, particularly the cultural evolutionism of Lewis Henry Morgan. Holmes, like many of his colleagues, employed the Morgan stages of humanity (i.e., savagery, barbarism, etc.) as if they were matters of fact. Holmes wrote the National Academy of Science Biographical Memoir for Morgan (Holmes 1909), and his genuine admiration of Morgan and *Ancient Society* (Morgan 1877) is apparent. He characterized Morgan as "opening a new field of research" and as having formulated the very first, coherent scheme for the history of human social organization. On the other hand, in typical Holmesian fashion, he demurred on the specifics: "it is not claimed that Morgan has said the last word regarding the diversified and intricate subject [human history] . . . . but that he said the first word on many problems that may not be fully solved for generations to come" (Holmes 1909:236). In fact, much of Holmes's writing is characterized by a deep-seated ambivalence toward Morgan's evolution. On the one hand, he saw the general pattern of simple to complex, confirmed generally by experience, everywhere contravened in details. For example, he acknowledged that the ancient pottery of the Southwest was superior in design and manufacture to contemporary products (1886a:269). This he attributed here and in the eastern United States to the influence of contact (1903a:152). In the end, he came to deny the universal linear structure altogether, retaining it only for particular arts, each free to change independently of the other (Holmes 1886c:444, 461; 1894b:300). Even then there were the exceptions.

Holmes deep commitment to progress independent of particular theories probably demanded an accommodation to this aspect of Morgan's evolution. Not so with the concept of *stage*. Although Holmes continued to use stage and terms like *culture grade* as well as specific stage names like *savagery* throughout his career in a didactic sense (e.g., Holmes 1905:552), they carried none of the empirical connotations that they did (and still do) for cultural evolutionists like Morgan. In his address to the American Association for the Advancement of Science (Holmes was twice vice-president of AAAS for Section H), he completely undermined the notion: "There can really be no line of demarcation separating the phenomena of one stage from those of another and there is a danger of the change being thought of as a definite and restricted episode, as marking a complete ending of one phase of existence, and as being a datum point from which to begin the study of the succeeding phase" (Holmes 1892d:248-249). Stages were tools of observation, not facts of human history. The source of the gradualism seen in this quotation seems to have been biology, particularly its evolutionary theory.

It would be a mistake to suppose that Holmes adopted biological evolution in its entirety as a model for human development or even that he understood all of the key tenets; however, it is clear that his attempts to use this theory set him apart from his colleagues and is responsible for the distinctiveness of his "philosophic approach."

His commitment to evolution was, if not the product of, then at least consonant with, his belief that people should not be set apart from nature but considered part of the natural world. Attempting to rectify this notion with the Morgan scheme led Holmes to posit two additional "stages," a prehuman and a presavage stage, the last of which may have occupied as much time as all of Morgan's stages in human history (1892d:246-247). These stages were created only for pedagogic purposes, because Holmes was in the process of undermining the stage concept as a whole. The implied gradualistic view of change is, in fact, the most pervasive evolutionary element in Holmes's work. Gradualism, although not inherent in evolutionary theory, was commonly associated with evolution, even regarded as a hallmark, throughout the nineteenth and most of the twentieth centuries (Dunnell 1980:58-59).

Holmes's most striking appropriation from biological evolution was his use of von Baer's (1828) law relating embryonic development to evolutionary history, particularly in its vulgar interpretation forwarded by Ernst Haeckel (1877:6-7): "Die Keimesgeschichte ist ein Auszug der Stammesgeschichte; oder mit andern Worten: Die Ontogenie ist eine Recapitulation der Phylogenie." The principal difference between the two versions of this "great law" (Gould 1977b) of evolution lay in von Baer's insistence that the process of embryonic growth was a matter of tissue differentiation, specialization, and not that embryos passed through adult states of phylogenetic precursors. Holmes used Haeckel's ontogeny recapitulates phylogeny version in his demolition of the American Paleolithic (Holmes 1890a:23; 1892c, 1894c). Holmes did not simply adopt Haeckel's view to outmaneuver his opponents in a debate; what made his argument so effective is that it was advanced as a general theory of technology and technological change applicable everywhere to everything and under all conditions (see esp. Holmes 1894c). Although the issues inherent in the Paleolithic debate compelled Holmes to make much greater use of the theory than in his other studies, he plainly saw it as applying to all branches of the arts (e.g., Holmes 1894b, l903a).

On the other hand, when emphasizing technological change, Haeckel's "Stammesgeschichte," he consistently took von Baer's more conservative approach. Change is a matter of specialization and differentiation. He saw contemporary technology in exactly those terms; all specialized artifacts are products of differentiation from an original artifact (Holmes 1894b). Further, the environment played a significant role in determining the course of the process (Holmes 1894b:299; 1894c:137; 1903a:24).

There is a tendency today to view the "ontogeny recapitulates phylogeny" idea in evolution as an anachronism (but see Gould 1977b for an enlightened analysis and defense). In the late nineteenth century, however, this concept, particularly the Haeckel popularization, was a prominent element of biological thought and at its peak in general popularity (Gould 1977b:85–86). The leading evolutionist of the day, August Weismann (Mayr 1985), made an only slightly hedged version of the Haeckel principle a central feature of his work (Weismann 1882:270). In the United States, Edward Drinker Cope was a notable exponent of the Haeckelian doctrine (e.g., Cope 1887, 1896). Holmes knew Cope and knew Cope's work (and vice versa, though Cope disagreed with Holmes's views on human antiquity: Cope to Holmes, July 23, 1895, WHH/SIA). So in fixing upon a version of the Haeckelian doctrine, Holmes was thoroughly in tune with contemporary biological thought in the United States and abroad.

Apart from his view that the "environment" strongly influenced the development of technologies and culture generally, Holmes never really adopted any other of the key tenets of biological evolution. Selection, the sine qua non of evolution, never entered any of Holmes's arguments. As close as he came (and the only time he actually ever cited Darwin) was in his suggestion that decorative art may well have begun as a product of sexual selection operating on personal body decoration and that later the concept was extended to other, first personal, then public, objects (Holmes 1892d:250–251). The reason for his aversion to selection as the motor of human cultural changes seems to be quite straightforward. Experience dictated that the motor of cultural change was the human intellect (or lack thereof).

Holmes did not leave this aspect of his "philosophic approach" implicit. He elaborated on how the intellect acted in producing cultural change, first by differentiating origins from modification (a new idea versus elaborations of it). Both were in turn the products of "adventition," by which Holmes meant accident, imitation of forms, both natural (e.g., gourds and pottery) and artificial (e.g., basketry designs on pottery); and invention to satisfy needs or suit fancy (see esp. Holmes 1886c). The inclusion of the notion of adventition may well belie the biological element in his otherwise ethnocentric approach to cultural change. Certainly accident was no more a major mechanism of contemporary cultural evolutionary theory than it is today. Holmes did not separate the generation of variation, basically the subject of his overt theory of change, from the transmission of that variability. This last was left up to the effects, albeit sub rosa, of the innate, progressive drive of the human intellect and the race's increasing tendency toward rationality. Holmes's theory of change quite naturally had a greater appeal to social scientists (e.g., Ellwood 1927; Thomas 1909) than did other aspects of his "philosophic approach."

The incomplete wedding and contradictory character of the main ingredients of Holmes's philosophic approach—nineteenth-century biological evolution, the cultural evolution of nineteenth-century anthropology, and the Victorian progressivism of his own cultural background—doomed the approach as such to a brief academic life. Evolutionism itself, partly based on the kind of criticisms that Holmes himself delivered of anthropological evolutionism, succumbed to the relativistic critique inspired by Boas. By the 1930s a new paradigm founded in chronological methodology, a potential plainly envisioned but not pursued by Holmes, cleared away the last vestiges of the Holmesian "philosophic approach" (Dunnell 1986a; Guthe 1952; Trigger 1989). By the 1940s any suggestion of a link to biology, let alone strong analogies, was decidedly out of favor (e.g., Brew 1946; Krieger 1944). Thus, Holmes's contribution lies not in his particular "philosophic approach" but in giving philosophic approaches—theory—a role in archaeology.

A NEW LOOK AT SOME CLASSIC WORK

Selecting pieces to reissue from the many Holmes published over his lifetime is a daunting task because of the diversity of his contributions. Naturally, no single paper captures the essence of Holmes's archaeology. In this volume we have chosen to reprint four works, two of which

examine Holmes's lithic interests combined with fieldwork; the other two
display his interests in ceramics combined with his talent for integrative
interpretation. All four importantly serve to exemplify Holmes's truly
unique contribution, his "philosophic approach" that forever changed
the character of American archaeology.

THE LITHICS PAPERS

Among the many works of Holmes devoted to lithics and quarrying, we
have selected two complementary works for reprinting here: one
avowedly evolutionary and theoretical—"Natural History of Flaked
Stone Implements" (Holmes 1894c); the other substantive—"Stone Implements of the Potomac-Chesapeake Tidewater Province" (Holmes
1897a). Both were finished in early 1894, at the end of four years of
relatively concentrated work (field, experimental, and analytical) on
stone tool technology. His later works on the subject (e.g., Holmes 1919)
did not benefit from such sustained attention, for by then Holmes's
energies were directed elsewhere. Thus, these two works are the epitome
of Holmes's thoughts on the "origin, manufacture and distribution of
primitive forms of stone implements" (Holmes 1894c:120). The combination of the two show, more precisely than any descriptions we could
muster, how and why Holmes conceived of the subject the way he did,
the assumptions necessary to its execution, the means by which he
carried it out, and why his work was so valued by his peers—and is of
interest today.

Holmes's "Stone Implements of the Potomac-Chesapeake Tidewater
Province"—his Loubat-winning monograph—has, of course, particular
historic value, representing as it does what was considered the best in
archaeological thinking a century ago. Yet, despite their age, both of
these are surprisingly modern works. Holmes distinguished between
local and exotic sources of stone (1897a:29, 73); the movement of stone
by direct acquisition, exchange, or natural processes (1897a:21–23); the
differential "distribution" (we would term it curation) of "domestic" and
"chase" implements by type of site in relation to distance from the stone
source (1897a:139–143). He grappled with problems of equifinality, of
differentiating artificial from naturally flaked stone tools and patterns
of wear (1894c:123); of sorting finished from unfinished implements
(1894c:124). He spoke of direct percussion, indirect percussion, and
pressure flaking (1897a:59–61); of refitting cores (1897a:56); of what we
now term the "Frison effect" (1894c:124); and, of preform ("blade")
caches (1897a:78). He appreciated and detailed the effects of different
raw material types on stone tool production (1894c:125–126). He made
careful (but, ultimately, limb-disabling [1897a:61, 151]) use of experimental stone tool replication (see also Hinsley 1981:104–105).

There is, of course, no mistaking this as a century-old work. Some of the terms and topics may look familiar, but their meaning is not: he used "Archaic" (1897a:31) as a rough synonym for the Paleolithic—some occupation (the existence of which he doubted) that predated the historic one. There are, as well, obvious factual gaps. But in most cases, little effort is required to translate his century-old usage of the language of archaeology and geology (our descendants should be so lucky). What requires brief remark is the theoretical context in which these works are embedded.

As noted in the earlier biographical sketch, the impetus for Holmes's study was the claim that so-called "rude" objects found in Washington—and elsewhere—were products of an earlier and unrelated Paleolithic "race" (e.g., Wilson 1889). The idea of an earlier, unrelated Paleolithic "race" was anathema to BAE archaeologists (Meltzer 1991). From the BAE's founding, bureau archaeologists began with the assumption that the American archaeological record was the product of the American Indian. Methodologically, they started with the material remains of historic tribes and traced them backward, "gradually and without sensible break," to their prehistoric ancestors (Powell 1890:500; see also Holmes 1897a:20). An unrelated Paleolithic occupation was not compatible with that view.

Paleolithic proponents' primary argument was typological. They noted many point-to-point similarities between Paleolithic implements of the Old World and rude tools found in the New. These similarities warranted the conclusion that both groups of artifacts were of similar grade and age (e.g., Wilson 1889). Holmes's view of change, as developed in his "Natural History of Flaked Stone Implements" reprinted here, allowed that the same forms occurred as both finished tools and as unfinished stages in the manufacture of more specialized forms. This meant that no chronological interpretation could be given New World rude tools solely on the basis of formal similarity. Rude tools might be ancient, but they might also be rejectage from the manufacture of more elaborate forms in recent times.

The study reported in "Stone Implements of the Potomac-Chesapeake Tidewater Province" is an empirical effort to determine which of the two possibilities was represented by the New World tools. These results resolved the case in favor of quarry refuse. This led Holmes to argue that proponents of the Paleolithic view everywhere misconstrued embryonic forms, quarry rejects, and preforms for finished, fully functional tools of quite recent age (Holmes 1892c, 1894c, 1897a:31, 53). As he put it, "Every implement resembling the final form here described, and every blade-shaped projectile point made from a bowlder or similar bit of rock not already approximate in shape, must pass through the same or nearly the same stages of development, leaving the same wasters, whether shaped today, yesterday, or a million years ago; whether in the hands of the civilized, the barbarous, or the savage man" (1897a:61). This, coupled with his view that "the history of flaked stone implements, as developed by these studies, is their history everywhere" (1897a:15), he saw as making it easy for the unwary to confound an object rejected early on in the manufacturing process with a genuinely ancient one (Holmes 1894c:123–125). Of course, Paleolithic proponents claimed to have no such trouble (e.g., Abbott 1907).

Holmes used empirical testing to resolve one of the major problems of his time. That testing involved extensive, careful fieldwork, remarkable for its attention to excavation detail, local geology and topography, site stratigraphy (and the problem of delineating natural from artificial deposits), and recording techniques. All of this was supplemented by his own experimental work in stone tool manufacture and well-informed by his knowledge of native lithic technologies (Holmes himself never undertook ethnographic fieldwork, but relied instead on the first-hand reports of his BAE colleagues, among others [Mark 1980:157]).

The result was a substantial body of data that enabled him to draw general conclusions about the processes of manufacture and use of stone tools, conclusions whose empirical foundations made them widely acceptable. His study of the stone quarries of the Tidewater region was a coherent and consonant view of stone tool technology, one that was not only well-founded empirically, but that also articulated exceedingly well with a broader theoretical framework then current in scientific circles generally.

In the process, Holmes also produced an invaluable study of prehistory in a region where the archaeological record has now been either destroyed or buried beneath asphalt and concrete. Holmes, in fact, often looked past his sites, located in what were then the suburbs of Washington, D.C., and saw the city growing in the distance. He spoke wistfully of their settings—of "primitive forest . . . penetrated by obscure trails only" (1897a:63)—and foresaw the day in the not-too-distant future when they would be overrun by development. So he purposefully left behind for us—the "future generations"—"numerous phases of suburban scenery presented in . . . photographic views" (1897a:16). These show us, as he knew they would, views of Washington almost unimaginable today. But, astonishing as it may seem, at least a couple of Holmes's sites are still intact. The Piney Branch quarry—Holmes's "sacred spot"—survives in what is now Rock Creek Park, just west of and below the 16th Street bridge crossing Piney Branch; his "ravines" and "rivulets" look little different today than they do in photographs he took in 1889–1890 (Holmes 1897a, Plates III–V).

So too, Holmes's work on stone tool technology endures. What began as a critical examination of the American Paleolithic became a pioneering venture into our understanding of stone tool technology and function—one that will reward the contemporary reader immensely.

THE CERAMICS PAPERS

The papers selected to represent Holmes's ceramics work parallel those chosen for his lithic contribution, one expressing a theoretical position and the other a major substantive study. As he did with lithics, Holmes devoted much attention to technology; although he considered stylistic and functional issues, they were treated as secondary and derivative. This is, however, the extent of direct parallels between his work in ceramics and lithics. His interest in ceramics stemmed in large measure from his role as the curator of aboriginal pottery in the USNM (Baird 1885), and thus his investigations were based on the study of museum specimens rather than on fieldwork. In his early works on ceramics, Holmes (1886a, 1886b) relied mostly on USNM collections, but for his major treatise reprinted here (Holmes 1903a) he incorporated important collections outside the Smithsonian, including the new materials then being reported by Clarence B. Moore, the major collections of the Davenport Academy of Science (Griffin 1981) and Harvard University, and Thruston's collections from Tennessee. Furthermore, although both his lithics and ceramics studies took place within a general evolutionary framework, his lithics papers drew upon an established biological principle (ontogeny recapitulates phylogeny), whereas his ceramics analysis was guided by more general theory largely of his own manufacture. He used this more general theory, which subsumes that employed in his lithics studies (Holmes 1892d:243), outside the realm of ceramics proper as well (e.g., Holmes 1888).

"Origin and Development of Form and Ornament in Ceramic Art" (Holmes 1886c), the theoretical paper reprinted here, was developed in concert with his first two substantive papers on ceramics, "Pottery of the Ancient Pueblos" (1886a) and "Ancient Pottery of the Mississippi Valley" (1886b). In the former he lays out a general evolutionary position:

> In the transmission of a nation's art inheritance from generation to generation, all the original forms of ornament undergo changes by alterations, eliminations, or additions. At the end of a long period we find the style of decoration so modified as to be hardly recognizable as the work of the same people; yet rapid changes would not occur in the uninterrupted course of evolution, for there is a wonderful stability about the arts, institutions, and beliefs of primitive races. Change of environment has a decided tendency to modify, and contact with other peoples, especially if

of a high grade of culture, is liable to revolutionize the whole character
of the art (Holmes 1886a:303).

"Origin and Development of Form and Ornament in Ceramic Art" is a
detailed effort to explain how such modification occurs and the mechanisms responsible in pottery vessel ornamentation and form. Although
Holmes never presented a comprehensive statement of his theoretical
position in a single place, he came as close as he ever did in this one.
In spite of conceiving evolution as a transmission process and his use
of frankly biological principles in his lithics studies, Holmes took an
anthropocentric view. He posited three mechanisms: adventition, by
which he meant accident; imitation of both the works of man and nature;
and invention proper, something wholly new (Holmes 1886c:445). Human rationality and intention are causative: "The desires of the mind
constitute the motive power, the force that induces all progress in art
. . . "(1890d:139). This compelled Holmes to cast his arguments as speculations about "reasonable" actions on the part of primitive artisans.
Nonetheless, he did reject symbolic approaches, noting that the same
ornamental form might be associated ethnographically with different
symbols in different places (Holmes 1886c:459–460). He also rejected
C. F. Hartt's (1875) biomechanical hypothesis (certain designs are pleasing to the eye muscles to scan). Copying and errors in copying, Holmes
insisted, are sufficient to bring about known variations and their se-
quences. The sort of gradualism implied by the copying mechanism is
a major theme of Holmes's evolutionary theory (see esp. 1892d:246–247).
As noted earlier, his commitment to gradualism was so strong as to
require continuity with nonhuman ancestors and rejection of stage-type
constructs (1892d:248–249).

The other major tenet of Holmes's evolution was "progress." This, of
course, was wholly congruent with a Morgan or Tyler view of evolution
(Dunnell 1980). He was, however, quite ambivalent about its precise
direction and form. Precociously, he recognized that evolution, even
biological evolution, was a different kind of science than physics and
thus that its "laws" were of a different character. Prediction, the hallmark of classical science, was not possible: "The attempt to give more
than a possible or probable genesis of a particular example of design
must therefore be futile. Here, as in biotic evolution, we must be content
to point out general tendencies and to discover general laws" (Holmes
1890d:141). Although Holmes depicted the general tendencies of scientific archaeology as empirical, only his a priori evolutionary tenets are
in evidence. So in the realm of ornamentation, the subject of "Origin and
Development of Form and Ornament in Ceramic Art," evolutionary direction or "progress" is either based on speculation (e.g., geometric

design precedes delineative or ideographic design [see also Holmes 1890d, 1892d]) or is referred to an unexplicated "aesthetic idea" (but see Holmes 1892d). It is probably for this reason that that paper is restricted to a consideration of geometric forms. In functional spheres, however, change arises through differentiation of form, much as developed in his lithic studies.

Even in 1886 Holmes has his doubts about the documentation of "progress" archaeologically or ethnographically (e.g., 1886b:373, 460–461). By the time Holmes published his ceramics magnum opus, "Aboriginal Pottery of the Eastern United States" (1903a), he was even less certain about progress. He spent considerable effort in providing a background and theoretical rationale for the study of pottery (1903a:15–79), but this section is a series of warnings rather than directives. The investigation of pottery was conceived as having one of two ends, as a tool for the investigation of the "histories of peoples" and as the development of a particular technology (art). For the first purpose, though limited to the upper savages and barbarian grades, Holmes saw pottery as second only to readable written records because of the near universality of pottery (near universal availability of materials and a universal need for containers), its chemical stability, and its ability to reflect different cultural elements in its manufacture (1903a:18). He warned against strictly homologous interpretations, pointing out the possibility for parallelisms as well as accidental resemblances (1903a:19). Similarly, although he adopted geographic groupings as his main structure from his earlier work in the Mississippi Valley (Holmes 1886b), he cautioned against regarding such groupings as having ethnic or cultural significance (1903a:21, 81), a caution he frequently forgot later in the work (e.g., 1903a:130, 145, 159, 178). Holmes appreciated that ceramics had the potential for providing chronology: "We may reasonably anticipate that in time the ceramic evidence will materially assist in determining the succession of peoples and also in arriving at a somewhat definite chronology of events" (Holmes 1903a:116). Yet Holmes did not explore such avenues himself. To the extent that ceramics were used for chronology, he relied almost exclusively on C. B. Moore's stratigraphic observations and arguments. When secure chronological comparisons were possible, as in contrasting prehistoric and historic periods, he frequently found it difficult to see the evident change as progressive (1903:83–84, 152). Consequently, he was forced to seek other (e.g., racial, environmental, and difussionist, 1903a:145) explanations for the differences.

Because Holmes was a scientist, insisting on the one hand that there be empirical evidence and on the other that phenomena be orderly and law-governed, he found himself in a quandary. His theory led him to believe that the passage of time would necessarily be reflected in material progress. Yet try as he might, the changes he could document in ceramics were as often at odds with a progressive expectation as consonant with it. The only choice open to Holmes was to regard the observed differences as responsive to other forces acting on a body of materials that were all substantially of an age. The impact of Holmes's theoretical position was to convince him, and many others at the time, that the American archaeological record represented only a brief period of time. It is for this reason, one suspects, that Holmes adopted the pedestrian and only loosely defined regional organization of "Aboriginal Pottery of the Eastern United States."

There is, of course, much more to Holmes's synthesis of eastern North American ceramics. He provided the first big picture of aboriginal American pottery; recognized regional variations that, in spite of them being partly chronological in origin, would persist as organizing tools for more than fifty years (e.g., Caldwell 1958; cf. Smith 1984); and assembled the ethnographic accounts that ultimately came to form the basis for describing American ceramics technology. His keen insights into data characteristics (e.g., the effects of mortuary pottery on interpretations, 1903a:27), interpretative potentials (e.g., the inference of status from mortuary offerings, 1903a:24), and technological and functional correlates (e.g., 1903a:46–47, 157), to name but a few areas of modern interest, make "Aboriginal Pottery of the Eastern United States" useful as well as fascinating reading today.

Perhaps even more instructive is the opportunity, in all of these works, to observe Holmes's struggle to free archaeology from an anecdotal, natural history mode of operation, a battle he carried on not only with his colleagues and predecessors, but also with himself. In reading Holmes one also comes to appreciate that it is a war not yet won.

ACKNOWLEDGMENTS

We would like to express our thanks to Daniel Goodwin, editorial director of the Smithsonian Institution Press, for soliciting this work long ago and for steadfastly believing we would one day complete it. Goodwin, James B. Griffin, and Bruce D. Smith contributed valuable advice on the structure of the volume (the advice was often given over lunches at the Smithsonian Castle during Meltzer's frequent trips to Washington—he will long remember these pleasant and interesting meetings and will never forget that Goodwin always picked up the tab). Griffin and Mary D. Dunnell also made helpful comments and editorial suggestions on the manuscript, for which we are most grateful.

The archival research reported herein was supported by grants to Meltzer from the National Endowment for the Humanities (FE-21370–

87) and the National Science Foundation (DIR-8911249), and by a
Faculty Research Fellowship Leave from Southern Methodist University—spent at the Smithsonian, thanks to the good offices of their Department of Anthropology, and Bruce Smith. The archival research was
eased by the unstinting cooperation of archivists from many institutions.
Given the amount of Holmes material in two of those—where many long
yet productive days were spent—special thanks are due the cordial
staffs of the National Anthropological Archives and the Smithsonian
Institution Archives.

NOTES

1. In many instances we cite unpublished correspondence. Our citations use
    the following acronyms:

    AHP/NAA = Aleš Hrdlička Papers, National Anthropological Archives,
    Smithsonian Institution
    ANT/NAA = American Antiquities Preservation 1897–1915 Files (Re-
    cord Group 2604), National Anthropological Archives,
    Smithsonian Institution
    BAE/NAA = Bureau of American Ethnology, Letters Received, National
    Anthropological Archives, Smithsonian Institution
    FB/APS =   Franz Boas Papers, American Philosophical Society
    HBC/NAA = Henry B. Collins Papers, National Anthropological Ar-
    chives, Smithsonian Institution
    JCM/LC =   John C. Merriam Papers, Library of Congress
    MAP/NAA = Holmes Miscellaneous Archaeological Papers (Record
    Group 4695), National Anthropological Archives, Smith-
    sonian Institution
    NMJ/NAA = Neil M. Judd Papers, National Anthropological Archives,
    Smithsonian Institution
    OPH/SIA = Oliver P. Hay Papers, Smithsonian Institution Archives
    SUB/NAA = Subjects File, Department of Anthropology, National An-
    thropological Archives, Smithsonian Institution
    WHH/SIA = William Henry Holmes Papers (Record Group 7084),
    Smithsonian Institution Archives

2. In 1889, the Board of Trustees of Hopedale Normal College conferred upon
    Holmes an A.B., in recognition of his successes. Holmes was assured that
    "The diploma for your degree is a regular classical diploma. The text is in
    Latin." It was also tactfully pointed out that "The Board expects from all
    who are honored a fee of five dollars, as a matter of courtesy" (Jamisson?
    to Holmes, June 28, 1889, Holmes 1932, 1:100). Three decades later, the
    Board of Trustees of George Washington University awarded Holmes the
    degree of "Doctor of Science" (Stockton to Holmes, April 8, 1918, Holmes
    1932, 1:116), this time without fee.

3. In later years, Holmes apparently told a reporter a slightly different but more charming version of this story:

> "Fate plays curious pranks in the lives of men," said he. "When I was about 20 years old I decided to leave my father's farm in Ohio and locate in Salem. While en route to that flourishing metropolis I stopped off in Washington to see the sights. The first place of interest I visited was the Smithsonian Institute [sic]. I became deeply interested in the bird collection there. I had a pencil and piece of paper and, being somewhat of an artist, I drew sketches of some of the birds. While thus engaged a man stood behind me watching me draw. Presently he placed his hand on my shoulder. He said: 'I'm Prof. Elliot. I'm connected with the Smithsonian. I'm going to Alaska and they will need someone here to make drawings during my absence. Do you want the place?' I took it. That was in 1871, and I have been with the Smithsonian ever since. I don't know whether or not the people of Salem are still expecting me" (from an undated newspaper clipping in the Ales Hrdlicka Reprint files, Box 107, Department of Anthropology, Smithsonian Institution).

4. The USGS's European-trained Ph.D.'s belittled this view of science (no surprise, since Powell was actively dismantling their laboratories). They resented the free exchange of personnel between the organizations and heaped scorn on those geologists—such as W J McGee—who had pretensions of success in both (Pyne 1980:126–130). They bluntly suggested to Powell that he put his ethnologists in some other building. He didn't, and in a budget-cutting frenzy in 1892 he rid the USGS of most of its foreign-trained geophysicists.

5. In later years, Powell assumed the credit for recognizing the implications of the Piney Branch site for the Paleolithic dispute and directing Holmes toward it (Powell 1895). Powell reported that while out West in the late 1860s and early 1870s he watched native peoples manufacture stone tools, some of which were "paleolithic," others "neolithic" in appearance (Powell 1895:3). Powell also reported that he had wandered over the Piney Branch locality, where he saw that many of the artifacts identified as Paleolithic were "strangely like the forms found near the Shoshoni village site" (Powell 1895:3–4). He did not, however, publish these observations before Proudfit's work, or Holmes's, for that matter.

6. Of course, such admissions were rare and entirely private, and this was the same Holmes who just a year later would write—in what Wilmsen (1965:180) described as "one of the low points in American archaeology"—that the researches of Loomis at Melbourne and of Sellards at Vero "are not only inadequate but dangerous to the cause of science" (Holmes 1925:258).

7. We are emphasizing the conflicts between the two, and without doubt

there was a certain tension that permeated their dealings with one another (Mark 1980:159–160). On the other hand, Holmes contributed to the Boas Anniversary Volume in 1906, and Boas in turn contributed to the Holmes Anniversary Volume in 1916. Boas even attended the seventieth birthday dinner for Holmes in December 1916 (Holmes 1932, 10:102–106). Obviously, they were able to maintain a civil relationship; it does not appear, however, that there was any but the most formal communication between the two after the emotional events of late 1919.

REFERENCES

Abbott, C. C.
  1890   Report of the Curator of the Museum of American Archaeology, University of Pennsylvania. *Annual Report* 1:1–54.

  1907   *Archaeologia Nova Caesarea*. MacCrellish and Quigley, Trenton.

Baer, K. E. von
  1828   *Entwicklungsgeschichte der Thiere: Beobachtung und Reflexion.* Borntrager, Konigsberg.

Baird, S. F.
  1885   Report of the Secretary. *Annual Report of the Smithsonian Institution for the Year 1884*: 1–98.

Bartlett, R.
  1962   *Great Surveys of the American West.* University of Oklahoma Press, Norman.

Benedict, R.
  1943   Franz Boas. *Science* 97:60–62.

Binford, L. R.
  1981   *Bones: Ancient Men and Modern Myths.* Academic Press, New York.

Boas, F.
  1897   The Social Organization and Secret Societies of the Kwakiutl Indians. *Report of the United States National Museum for 1895*: 315–738.

  1902a   The Bureau of Ethnology. *Science* 16:676–677.

  1902b   The Smithsonian Institution and Its Affiliated Bureaus. *Science* 16:801–803.

  1919   Scientists as Spies. *The Nation* 109:797.

Brew, J. O.
  1946   The Archaeology of Alkali Ridge, Southwestern Utah. *Papers of the Peabody Museum of Archaeology and Anthropology* 24.

Caldwell, J. R.
  1958   Trend and Tradition in the Prehistory of the Eastern United States. *American Anthropological Association, Memoir* 88.

Clarke, D.
  1973   Archaeology: The Loss of Innocence. *Antiquity* 47:6-18.

Cope, E. D.
  1887   *The Origin of the Fittest.* MacMillan, New York.

  1896   *The Primary Factors of Organic Evolution.* Open Court, Chicago.

Darnell, R.
  1969   "The Development of American Anthropology 1879-1920: From the Bureau of American Ethnology to Franz Boas." Ph.D. dissertation, University of Pennsylvania.

Dunnell, R. C.
  1980   Evolutionary Theory and Archaeology. *Advances in Archaeological Method and Theory* 3:38-99.

  1986a   Five Decades of American Archaeology. In *American Archaeology Past and Future,* edited by D. J. Meltzer, D. D. Fowler, and J. A. Sabloff, 23-49. Smithsonian Institution Press, Washington, D.C.

  1986b   Methodological issues in Americanist artifact classification. *Advances in Archaeological Method and Theory* 9:149-207.

Dutton, C.
  1882   Tertiary History of the Grand Canon District with Atlas. *United States Geological Survey, Monograph* 2.

Ellwood, C. A.
  1927   *Cultural Evolution, A Study of Social Origins and Development.* Century, New York.

Gilbert, G. K.
  1877   *Report on the Geology of the Henry Mountains.* U.S. Geological and Geographical Survey of the Rocky Mountain Region, Washington, D.C.

Goetzmann, W.
  1966   *Exploration and Empire: The Explorer and the Scientist in the Winning of the American West.* W. W. Norton, New York.

Goetzmann, W., and W. Goetzmann
  1986   *The West of the Imagination.* W. W. Norton, New York.

Gould, S. J.
  1977a   Eternal Metaphors of Palaeontology. In *Patterns of Evolution as Illustrated by the Fossil Record,* edited by A. Hallam, 1-26. Elsevier, Amsterdam.

  1977b   *Ontogeny and Phylogeny.* Harvard University Press, Cambridge.

1988   "Boundaries and Categories: A Taxonomist Looks at History." Paper presented at the 1988 Annual Meeting of the American Association for the Advancement of Science, Boston.

Graham, R.
1980   The Kimmswick "Bone Beds": A Historical Perspective. *The Living Museum* 42:40-44.

Griffin, J.
1981   The Acquisition of a Little Known Pottery Haul from the Lower Mississippi Valley. *Geoscience and Man* 22:51-55.

Guthe, C.
1952   Twenty-five Years of Archaeology in the Eastern United States. In *Archaeology of Eastern United States*, edited by J. B. Griffin, 1-12. University of Chicago Press, Chicago.

Haeckel, E.
1877   *Anthropogenie oder Entwickelungeschichte de Menschen.* Third edition. Engelmann, Leipzig.

Hartt, C. F.
1875   Evolution in Ornament. *Popular Science Monthly* 6:266-275.

Hay, O. P.
1918   Doctor Aleš Hrdlička and the Vero Man. *Science* 48:459-462.

1920   Bulletin 60, Bureau of American Ethnology. *Anthropological Scraps* 3:9-12.

Heizer, R. F. (editor)
1959   *The Archaeologist at Work. A Source Book in Archaeological Method and Interpretation.* Harper and Brothers, New York.

1962   *Man's Discovery of His Past: Literary Landmarks in Archaeology.* Prentice-Hall, Englewood Cliffs, N.J.

Hinsley, C. M.
1976   Amateurs and Professionals in Washington Anthropology, 1879 to 1903. In *American Anthropology: The Early Years*, edited by J. Murra, 36-68. West Publishing Company, St. Paul, Minn.

1981   *Savages and Scientists. The Smithsonian Institution and the Devlopment of American Anthropology 1846–1910.* Smithsonian Institution Press, Washington, D.C.

Hodge, F. W.
1907   Handbook of American Indians North of Mexico. Part 1. *Bureau of American Ethnology Bulletin* 30.

1910   Handbook of American Indians North of Mexico. Part 2. *Bureau of American Ethnology Bulletin* 30.

Holmes, W. H.
  1878a   Report on the Geology of the Sierra Abajo and West San Miguel
          Mountains. *Tenth Annual Report, U.S. Geological and Geographical
          Survey of the Territories, 1876*: 187-195.

  1878b   Report on the Ancient Ruins of Southwestern Colorado, Examined
          during the Summers of 1875 and 1876. *Tenth Annual Report, U.S.
          Geological and Geographical Survey of the Territories, 1876*: 383-
          408.

  1879   Notes on an Extensive Deposit of Obsidian in the Yellowstone National
          Park. *American Naturalist* 13:247-250.

  1883   Report on the Geology of the Yellowstone National Park. *Twelfth An-
          nual Report, U.S. Geological and Geographical Survey of the Terri-
          tories, 1878*, 2:1-57.

  1884   Illustrated Catalogue of a Portion of the Collections Made by the
          Bureau of Ethnology during the Field Season of 1881. *Third Annual
          Report, Bureau of Ethnology, 1881–1882*: 427-510.

  1886a   Pottery of the Ancient Pueblos. *Fourth Annual Report, Bureau of
          Ethnology, 1882–1883*: 257-360.

  1886b   Ancient Pottery of the Mississippi Valley. *Fourth Annual Report,
          Bureau of Ethnology, 1882–1883*: 361-436.

  1886c   Origin and Development of Form and Ornament in Ceramic Art.
          Fourth Annual Report, Bureau of Ethnology, 1882–1883: 437-465.

  1888   A Study of the Textile Art in Its Relation to the Development of Form
          and Ornament. *Sixth Annual Report, Bureau of Ethnology, 1884–
          1885*: 189-252.

  1889   Review of Pitt Rivers' Excavations in Cranborne Chase, near Rush-
          more, on the Borders of Dorset and Wilts, 1880-88, Volume 2. *Amer-
          ican Anthropologist* 2:172.

  1890a   A Quarry Workshop of the Flaked-stone Implement Makers in the
          District of Columbia. *American Anthropologist* 3:1-26.

  1890b   Recent Work in the Quarry Workshops of the District of Columbia.
          American Anthropologist 3:224-225.

  1890c   Excavations in an Ancient Soapstone Quarry in the District of Colum-
          bia. *American Anthropologist* 3:321-330.

  1890d   On the Evolution of Ornament, an American Lesson. *American An-
          thropologist* 3:137-146.

  1891   Aboriginal Novaculite Quarries in Garland County, Arkansas. *Amer-
          ican Anthropologist* 4:49-58.

1892a Sacred Pipestone Quarries of Minnesota and Ancient Copper Mines of Lake Superior. *Proceedings, Forty-first Meeting, American Association for the Advancement of Science, Rochester, 1892*: 239-255.

1892b Aboriginal Quarries of Flakable Stone and Their Bearing upon the Question of Palaeolithic Man [abstract]. *Proceedings, Forty-first Meeting, American Association for the Advancement of Science, Rochester, 1892*: 279-280.

1892c Modern Quarry Refuse and the Paleolithic Theory. *Science* 20:295-297.

1892d Evolution of the Aesthetic. *Proceedings, Forty-first Meeting, American Association for the Advancement of Science, Rochester, 1892*: 239-255.

1893a Distribution of Stone Implements in the Tidewater Country. *American Anthropologist* 6:1-14.

1893b Are There Traces of Man in the Trenton Gravels? *Journal of Geology* 1:15-37.

1893c Gravel Man and Palaeolithic Culture: A Preliminary Word. *Science* 21:29-30.

1893d Traces of Glacial Man in Ohio. *Journal of Geology* 1:147-163.

1893e A Question of Evidence. *Science* 21:135-136.

1893f Vestiges of Early Man in Minnesota. *American Geologist* 11:219-240.

1894a An Ancient Quarry in Indian Territory. *Bureau of Ethnology Bulletin* 21.

1894b Order of Development of the Primal Shaping Arts. *Proceedings, Forty-second Meeting, American Association for the Advancement of Science, Madison, 1893*: 289-300.

1894c Natural History of Flaked Stone Implements. *Memoirs, International Congress of Anthropology, Chicago, 1894*: 120-139.

1897a Stone Implements of the Potomac-Chesapeake Tidewater Province. *Fifteenth Annual Report, Bureau of Ethnology, 1893-1894*:13-152.

1897b Primitive Man in the Delaware Valley. *Science* 6:824-829.

1898a Anthropological exhibit of the U.S. National Museum at the Omaha Exposition. *Science* VIII:37-40.

1898b Museum Presentation of Anthropology. *Proceedings, Forty-seventh Meeting, American Association for the Advancement of Science, Boston, 1898*: 485-488.

1899   Preliminary Revision of the Evidence Relating to Auriferous Gravel Man in California. *American Anthropologist* 1:107–121, 614–645.

1900   Obsidian Mines of Hidalgo, Mexico. *American Anthropologist* 2:405–416.

1901a   Use of Textiles in Pottery Making and Embellishment. *American Anthropologist* 3:397–403.

1901b   Aboriginal Copper Mines of Isle Royale, Lake Superior. *American Anthropologist* 3:684–696.

1902a   Flint Implements and Fossil Remains from a Sulphur Spring at Afton, Indian Territory. *American Anthropologist* 4:108–129.

1902b   Fossil Human Remains Found near Lansing, Kansas. *American Anthropologist* 4:743–752.

1903a   Aboriginal Pottery of the Eastern United States. *Twentieth Annual Report, Bureau of American Ethnology, 1898–1899*: 1–201.

1903b   Traces of Aboriginal Operations in an Iron Mine near Leslie, Missouri. *American Anthropologist* 5:503–507.

1905   Contributions of American Archaeology to Human History. *Smithsonian Institution Annual Report for 1904*: 551–558.

1909   Biographical Memoir of Lewis Henry Morgan, 1818–1881. *Biographical Memoirs of the National Academy of Sciences* 6:219–239.

1917   The Place of Archaeology in Human History. *Proceedings of the Nineteenth International Congress of the Americanists, Washington, D.C.*: 5–11.

1918   On the Antiquity of Man in America. *Science* 47:561–562.

1919   Handbook of Aboriginal American Antiquities. Part I. *Bureau of American Ethnology Bulletin* 60.

1925   The Antiquity Phantom in American Archaeology. *Science* 62:256–258.

1932   "Random Records of a Lifetime in Art and Science, 1846–1931." 20 volumes. Unpublished. On file, National Museum of American Art, Smithsonian Institution, Washington, D.C.

Hrdlička, A. H.
1903   The Lansing Skeleton. *American Anthropologist* 5:323–330.

1907   Skeletal Remains Suggesting or Attributed to Early Man in North America. *Bureau of American Ethnology Bulletin* 33.

1912   Early Man in South America. In collaboration with W. Holmes, B. Willis, F. Wright, and C. Fenner. *Bureau of American Ethnology Bulletin* 52.

1918   Recent Discoveries Attributed to Early Man in America. *Bureau of American Ethnology Bulletin* 66.

Johnson, L. L.
1978   A History of Flint-knapping Experimentation, 1833-1976. *Current Anthropology* 19:337-372.

Judd, N.
1967   *The Bureau of American Ethnology: A Partial History.* University of Oklahoma Press, Norman.

Krieger, A. D.
1944   The Typological Concept. *American Antiquity* 9:271-288.

Lowie, R.
1943   Franz Boas, His Predecessors and His Contemporaries. *Science* 97:202-203.

McVicker, D.
1989   "Buying a Curator: Establishing Anthropology at Field Columbian Museum." Paper presented at the 88th Annual Meeting, American Anthropological Association, Washington, D.C.

Mark, J.
1980   *Four Anthropologists: An American Science in Its Early Years.* Science History Publications, New York.

Mason, O. T.
1877   Anthropological News. *American Naturalist* 11:623-627.

1886   Anthropology. In *Annual Report of the Smithsonian Institution for 1885*: 815-870.

Mayr, E.
1982   *The Growth of Biological Thought.* Harvard University Press, Cambridge.

1985   Weismann and Evolution. *Journal of the History of Biology* 18:295-329.

Meltzer, D.
1983   The Antiquity of Man and the Development of American Archaeology. *Advances in Archaeological Method and Theory* 6:1-51.

1985   North American Archaeology and Archaeologists, 1879-1934. *American Antiquity* 50:249-260.

1989a   A Question of Relevance. In *Tracing Archaeology's Past: The Historiography of Archaeology*, edited by A. Christenson, 5-20. Southern Illinois University Press, Carbondale.

1989b   Why Don't We Know When the First People Came to North America? *American Antiquity* 54(3): 471-490.

1991 On "Paradigms" and "Paradigm Bias" in Controversies over Human Antiquity in America. In *The First Americans: Search and Research*, edited by T. Dillehay and D. Meltzer, 13–49. CRC Press, Boca Raton, Fla.

Merrill, G. P.
1906 Contributions to the History of American Geology. *Report of the United States National Museum for 1904*: 189–733.

Morgan, L. H.
1877 *Ancient Society*. World Publishing, New York.

Nelson, C.
1980 William Henry Holmes: Beginning a Career in Art and Science. *Records of the Columbia Historical Society* 50:252–278.

Noelke, V.
1974 "The Origin and Early History of the BAE, 1879-1910." Ph.D. dissertation, University of Texas, Austin.

Peale, A. C.
1877 On a Peculiar Type of Eruptive Mountains in Colorado. *Bulletin of the United States Geological and Geographical Survey of the Territories* 3:551–564.

Powell, J. W.
1886 Report of the Director. *Fourth Annual Report, Bureau of Ethnology, 1882–1883*: xxvii–lxiii.

1890 Prehistoric Man in America. *The Forum* 8:489–503.

1891 Report of the Director. *Eighth Annual Report, Bureau of Ethnology, 1886–1887*: xvii–xxxvi.

1892 Report of the Director. *Ninth Annual Report, Bureau of Ethnology, 1887–1888*: xxiii–xlvi.

1894 Report of the Director. *Eleventh Annual Report, Bureau of Ethnology, 1889–1890*: xxiii–xlvii.

1895 Stone Art in America. *American Anthropologist* 8:1–7.

1897 Report of the Director. *Fifteenth Annual Report, Bureau of Ethnology, 1893–1894*: xvii–cxxi.

Proudfit, S. V.
1889 Ancient Village Sites and Aboriginal Workshops in the District of Columbia. *American Anthropologist* 2:241–246.

Putnam, F. W.
1889 Discussion. "The Aborigines of the District of Columbia and the Lower Potomac." *American Anthropologist* 2:266–268.

Pyne, S.
    1980   *Grove Karl Gilbert: A Great Engine of Research.* The University of
            Texas Press, Austin.

Smith, B. D.
    1984   Mississippian Expansion: Tracing the Historical Development of an
            Explanatory Model. *Southeastern Archaeology* 3:13–32.

Stegner, W.
    1954   *Beyond the Hundredth Meridian: John Wesley Powell and the Second
            Opening of the West.* Houghton Mifflin, Boston.

Stocking, G. W.
    1968   *Race, Culture and Evolution.* Free Press, New York.

    1974   *A Franz Boas Reader: The Shaping of American Anthropology, 1883–
            1911.* University of Chicago Press, Chicago.

    1987   *Victorian Anthropology.* Free Press, New York.

Sturtevant, W. C.
    1975   Huns, Free-thinking Americans, and the AAA. *History of Anthro-
            pology Newsletter* 2(2): 4–6.

Swanton, J. S.
    1937   Biographical Memoir of William Henry Holmes, 1846–1933. *Biographi-
            cal Memoirs of the National Academy of Sciences* 17:223–252.

    1944   "Notes Regarding My Adventures in Anthropology and with Anthro-
            pologists." Manuscript on file, National Anthropological Archives,
            Smithsonian Institution, Washington, D.C.

Thomas, C.
    1894   Report of the Mound Explorations of the Bureau of Ethnology. *Twelfth
            Annual Report, Bureau of Ethnology, 1890–1891*: 1–742.

Thomas, W. I.
    1909   *Source Book for Social Origins.* University of Chicago Press, Chicago.

Thoresen, T.
    1977   Art, Evolution, and History: A Case Study of Paradigm Change in
            Anthropology. *Journal of the History of the Behavioral Sciences*
            13:107–125.

Trigger, B. G.
    1989   *A History of Archaeological Thought.* Cambridge University Press,
            Cambridge.

Weismann, A.
    1882   *Studies in the Theory of Descent.* Translated by R. Mendola. Preface
            by C. Darwin. Sampson, Low, Martson, Searle, and Rivington, London.

1 Introduction

Willey, G. R.
    1949   Archaeology of the Florida Gulf Coast. *Smithsonian Institution Miscellaneous Collections* 113.

Willey, G. R., and J. A. Sabloff
    1980   *A History of American Archaeology.* Second Edition. Freeman, San Francisco.

Wilmsen, E.
    1965   An Outline of Early Man Studies in the United States. *American Antiquity* 31:172-192.

Wilson, T.
    1889   The Paleolithic Period in the District of Columbia. *American Anthropologist* 2:235-240.

    1899   Arrowheads, Spearheads, and Knives of Prehistoric Times. *Report of the United States National Museum for 1897*, Part I:811-988.

Wright, G. F.
    1892   *Man and the Glacial Period.* D. Appleton, New York.

NATURAL HISTORY OF FLAKED STONE IMPLEMENTS.

BY W. H. HOLMES.

A S a result of investigations carried on under the auspices of the Bureau of Ethnology I have accumulated a large body of material relating to the origin, manufacture and distribution of primitive forms of stone implements. Series of the articles collected have been placed on exhibition in the Government building, and it seems appropriate that something should be said in this congress relating to them and to their bearing upon the archæologic questions of the day.

I do not, however, desire to deal with these collections specifically, to describe them or review their history, but to present an analysis of the group of phenomena to which they belong. Thorough analysis of the subject matter of investigation is at the basis of its intelligent consideration. Inferences and conclusions based on a given body of data are unsafe if all the available elements of these data have not been properly considered, and they must still be unsatisfactory if through necessity or oversight any of the elements have been omitted. When analysis is complete classification is easy, consideration is simple, and results are safe, even if not final.

The very general incompleteness and obscurity of the available phenomena of archæologic science, especially in the earlier stages, are well known, and students find it necessary to go over and over again the meager and heterogeneous array of material and to redouble the precautions against misinterpretations and hasty conclusions. History is difficult to read correctly even when the peoples and the whole range of their cultural creations are in full view. Historical investigations based on the scattered relics of a vanished people must be entered upon with the greatest caution. We focus all the light of the present and of the past upon the minutest fields of the remote past, striving thus to read more clearly the obscure characters of the record. No apology is necessary, therefore, for assuming to present here a somewhat exhaustive analysis of that particular group of art remains upon which we must mainly depend for our knowledge of primeval days.

OUTLINE OF STUDY.

In a paper read at Madison, a few days ago, I attempted to give flaked stone art its proper place among the shaping arts, to trace its history from the earliest beginnings up through the stages that mark the progress of culture evolution. It was shown that the flaking of stone was a primal art and that flaked implements are probably the most ancient and elemental existing representatives of human handicraft. If other forms preceded them, they were of destructible materials, and have long since disappeared. The first flake was probably made by casting one stone against another without premeditation or design. From that primal step, once observed and designedly utilized, there has been a gradual progress by infinitesimal advances in technique, through the stages and the ages, ending in the manifold and wonderful works of the present day.

In the study of flaked stone implements the first necessary step is their identification as *implements* as distinguished from the many allied forms, natural and artificial, that have no claims to be called such. The second step is a consideration of their natural history, which embodies two distinct lines of development, one of the individual from its inception in the raw material, through a series of steps of technical progress, to the finished result; the other of the species or group from a primal culture germ through countless generations of implements; with these goes the evolution of form and function. The third step consists in regarding implements as historic records, first, with reference to questions of time; second, with regard to questions of culture, and, third, with respect to the history of peoples. A grouping of these topics and their subdivisions, approximately as treated in these pages, is given in the accompanying synopsis.

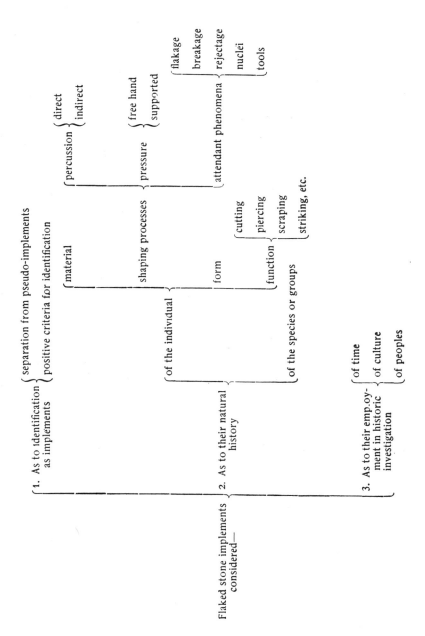

IDENTIFICATION OF IMPLEMENTS.

Separation from analogous forms.   The simpler implements of primitive peoples are often natural forms of stone, or natural forms but slightly altered by human agency.   These must be distinguished where possible from natural forms never used or intended to be used. Natural processes sometimes act in such ways as to produce effects closely resembling the simpler artificial phenomena.   In cases where much depends on a single specimen of simple form likely to be adventitiously duplicated, discrimination becomes a matter of great importance.

Again, flaked implements of any considerable degree of elaboration pass through progressive stages of specialization, and failures, necessarily very frequent in the fracturing of stone, take place at all steps of advancement.   These failures resemble the finished object more or less closely as they happen to have been rejected nearer to or farther from the final shaping stage.   Still again, these abortive forms are liable to resemble somewhat closely finished tools of less elaborate pattern or inferior specialization, belonging to other times or intended for distinct uses.   Most careful discrimination is called for with these possibilities in view.

Still another point must be considered.   The operations of shaping certain classes of tools are not continuous, part of the work being done on the site furnishing the raw material, and part on finishing sites at more or less distant points, and considerable time may elapse between the beginning stages and the final stages of the work, transportation and storage intervening.   Thus many specimens representing a stage of manufacture midway between the first and last shaping acts find their way into collections.   These have generally been called implements.   They are really *unfinished implements*, although they *may not have even a remote resemblance* to the implement in its final shape.   To classify and use in historic studies any of these pseudo-implements as actual implements is to introduce error and pave the way to a falsification of the record.

Positive criteria for identification.   There are numerous means of identification by which the true implement may be separated from the false.   Chief among these criteria may be mentioned (1) degree of elaboration, (2) indications of specialization, (3) signs of use, (4) manner of occurrence and (5) association of other articles.   If form is highly elaborated, a strong presumption is created that the implement is finished, yet this evidence must not, when standing alone, be relied upon implicitly. The same may be said of indications of specialization, which generally imply adaptation to definite use, and hence finish; yet appearances of specialization are in many cases false, as is clearly shown by the study of quarry-shop refuse, where we find most extraordinary recurrent shapes resulting from accident, as, for example, the abortive blade with a high hump on one side, or with a decided bulb near one end. It is not unusual to see in the vicinity of flaking-shops specimens of flakes and rejects that have been flaked upon the brittle edges by passing feet until they present most deceptive appearances of elaboration and even of specialization.

Evidences of use are generally reliable indices of the finished character of the specimen showing them, and where implement-like objects possessing slight indications of elaboration exhibit in repeated instances corresponding marks of application to manual use, the implication is very strong that they are finished implements. Yet appearances of use are sometimes deceptive, as where decay or wear by rolling in water or in roadways has modified the sharp conchoids of original fracture. There are, no doubt, many cases in which specimens rejected by the original flaker, and having pronounced reject characters, are taken up by others and applied to uses like or unlike those contemplated by the original workman. These objects thus become actual implements, but, being sporadic, they do not constitute a class of implements.

The occurrence of similarly shaped stones in numbers on dwelling sites or on other ordinary sites of implement utilization is generally an excellent test of their status; yet if the site is also one producing raw material subject to shaping on the spot, forms often repeated may be only rejects.

Implement-like specimens associated with evidence of work done, as in ancient quarries and mines, or with refuse of shaping operations in which they may have been employed, as on sites where steatite vessels were rudely roughed out, may be safely identified as implements. A stone without artificial shaping or without signs of use, if repeatedly found under the above conditions, may, perhaps with risk, be classed as an implement or article of use. A combination of conditions of shape, surface appearance and occurrence may serve a good purpose in identification.

The importance of full identification of the implement as such should never be lost sight of. It is the first vital point to be considered by the archæologist who wishes to consider questions of comparative culture.   Questions of age and comparative age are settled mainly by other criteria.

Having identified the implement as such, we may proceed to study it, classify it as to material, manufacture, shape and use, and apply it with safety to the solution of the problems of anthropology.

NATURAL HISTORY OF IMPLEMENTS.

Of the individual.   The work of art must be studied pretty much as the biologist studies the living creature.   Each implement has its individual history—its inception, development, form and functions. The naturalist studies the creature with respect to its physical development, tracing its history back through the stages of growth to the embryonic inception.   The archæologist must study the flaked stone with reference to its origin, the morphologic changes that take place under the flaking hammer and the flaker of bone, and the range of its functions when finished.   In this way the life-story of the individual is told.

Of the species.   There is also a family history with the implement as with the living creature.   It has an evolution that begins with the first stone implement shaped by the hand of man and advances through the ages, changing, specializing and differentiating until the various groups of forms, the species, orders and families, are developed.   Each species of implement of to-day is connected by an infinite series of progressive genetic links with the inceptive germ of art, and thus is related to all art.

Accompanying the immediate phenomena of development there are varied attendant phenomena, including the evolution of arts, industries and practices related to or forming a part of the history of implements.

MATERIAL OF IMPLEMENTS.

The nature of the materials available to the implement-maker has much to do with the results reached.   The form-elaboration of the individual object and the development of the species of implement are conditioned by the shaping qualities of the stone.   The processes employed and the development and differentiation of these processes are likewise governed by the characteristics of the materials. Each implement has its origin in a more or less inchoate mass of the raw material.   If the stone is massive one group of processes is employed and one set of results is reached; if it is slaty in character other processes and other results follow its use, and if it is in the form of water-worn stones or concretionary nodules, still other processes are employed and still other results are attained.   The full elaboration of this to ic will not be entered into here.

SHAPING PROCESSES.

The history of implements, both as individuals and as species, must be studied largely through the channels of technique, and especially through the processes employed in manufacture.   There are four groups of processes by means of which the forms of implements are developed, namely, fracturing, battering, abrading, and incising. Fracturing appears to be the most elemental of these, and was probably the first to develop into importance as a shaping art.   With the other processes I have nothing to do in the present study.   The fracturing operations are known as breaking, splitting, flaking, chipping, spalling and knapping, the term flaking being commonly employed to express the act most utilized in the shaping of primitive tools.

The flaking processes are now so well understood in a general way that their employment in art may be studied and discussed without danger of serious error or misinterpretation.   There is in detail, however, great variety of procedure, and all these details can never be fully known.   Each people develops peculiarities in shaping-devices and each region furnishes varieties of shaped results, but all these phenomena come within well defined general lines, and details are not absolutely essential to a full understanding of the subject.   Fracture is accomplished by two classes of processes, distinguished by the manner in which the shaping force is applied; these are known as *percussion* and *pressure.*   The percussive method implies (1) the use of a hard and heavy implement with which the stone to be shaped is struck, producing direct fracture in its simplest form, and (2) the use of two tools, a punch-like implement, set upon the stone at the point to be fractured, and a heavy tool with which this implement is struck, producing fracture indirectly.   This process has been mentioned by a number of observers, but is apparently not well understood by any one.   The pressure process consists in the use of a tool by means of which pressure is applied to the brittle stone in such a way as to fracture it.

Many of the simpler flaked tools of all tribes and times are shaped exclusively by percussion, and in the earliest times flaking by pressure was probably unknown.   In its simplest form fracture by percussion is accomplished by striking with the hammer a given point chosen through a knowledge of the fracturing qualities of the stone. In this work a convex-surfaced hammer is required.   It appears that in somewhat advanced stages of the work the serrated edges of the implement shaped were probably struck across the projecting serrations by a hammer-stone having a wide, flat periphery, a number of minute flakes being removed at one blow.   This is suggested by the occurrence of discoid hammers with flat peripheries on shop-sites and is confirmed by experiment with them.

Flaking by pressure is accomplished in a number of ways indicated by observations made among the savage tribes of both continents.   Pointed or edged implements of bone are generally used, but I will not enter into details, as the present occasion does not call for a fully amplified study of this branch of the subject.

A word may be said in regard to the relations of the two classes of operations in their practice.   Each may be used unaccompanied by the other, the one making large or rude forms, the other shaping forms such as flakes already too delicate for percussive treatment. When both are employed on the same specimen percussive processes take the initiative, breaking up the stone and reducing the pieces, when large, to approximate shape, and to a degree of tenuity and a relation of surfaces such as to make the other methods readily operative.   Smaller hammer-stones are used as the forms become more delicate.   The pressure processes are the elaborating and finishing processes, taking up the work when the ruder processes are compelled to leave off.   The change from percussion to pressure does not necessarily take place at uniform stages of the work.   With tough stone the hammer must go farther than with brittle stone, as the pressure tool cannot so soon be made effective.

In the making of some forms of implements the flaking operations are followed by pecking, grinding and polishing.   The tool shaped by flaking may have its edge or point finished by grinding, and many of the implements whose shapes are blocked out by flaking are largely or entirely worked over by the other methods.   The flaked tools here considered are limited to varieties shaped wholly by the fracturing processes, or but rarely or to a very slight extent subjected to modification by other means.

DEVELOPMENT OF THE INDIVIDUAL.

The simplest possible artificial stone tool is the result of a single blow.   Thus a stone is split or flaked, yielding one (the flake) or perhaps two (the flake and piece flaked from) edged or pointed tools of possibly high efficiency.   The individual history in such cases is exceedingly brief.   By multiplying the blows and directing them intelligently, successive degrees of elaboration are reached and the higher forms are produced.

Synoptic statement.   To understand the individual morphology of flaked stone implements it is only necessary to examine type examples of the several well-defined groups, and these may be arranged in tabular form for comparative study, as in Diagram I.   The flaked implements of the entire world would make a long list, and an attempt to present all varieties in this place would greatly complicate the study. Most of the more important truths can be brought out by considering the flaked products of a limited region, and I have chosen that region with which I am just now particularly familiar, the Chesapeake-Potomac tide-water country.   The synoptic chart includes examples from nine leading groups of implements, extending from the most simple to the most complex forms.   They are placed as nearly as may be in the order of increasing complexity or elaboration and are as follows: The unnotched ax, a sharpened bowlder; the notched ax, a sharpened bowlder; the pick, a pointed and notched tool used in rough-shaping soapstone; the chisel, used in carving soapstone; the knife, a blade notched or plain; the scraper, a blade with beveled edge; the drill point, a blade with slender shaft; the spear point and the arrow point.

Other flaked articles are found in this region, but they are sporadic or do not occur as well developed groups and need not be considered here.   Those selected have the advantage of derivation from a single form of material, the bowlder, the analogies of morphology and the variations of specialization being more easily observed than where varied materials and forms of materials are used.

As the diagrammatic statement expresses clearly the main features of morphology and comparative morphology, the various points need be but briefly sketched.   Beginning at the base with the bowlder, the form of material most used in this region, we pass up through the gradually expanding series to the arrow-point, the most highly specialized form.   The relations of the finished implements, placed at the right, to the successive steps of their morphology, represented by rejected forms filling up the triangle, and to the bowlders in which they have their origin, are apparent at a glance.   It will be seen that the course of procedure in the simplest shapes is repeated more or less closely in the earlier steps of the more elaborate shapes, and that the

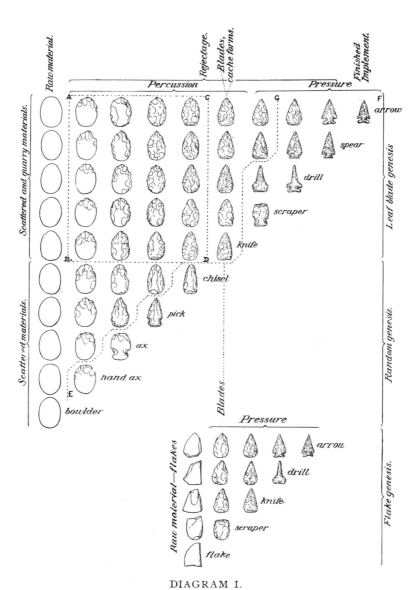

DIAGRAM I.

divergence of specialization takes place toward the end of the process in each case, usually not covering more than one step (as here formulated) in the simpler forms, and not more than three in the higher forms.   Analogies between the rejects, especially in the earlier portions of the various lines, are thus very close.   The finished implement in a given case, if not definitely specialized, may not be distinguishable from rejects of corresponding elaboration belonging to the more elaborate implements above.   Later on examples will be given illustrating the dangers of imperfect identification and careless placing and use of doubtful forms by students of prehistoric archæology.

I may call attention to two other points brought out by the diagram.   First, that the five more highly specialized forms pass through the percussion stage to be further elaborated and finished by the pressure processes, while the four ruder implements are finished by percussive methods alone.   Second, that the former are all based on the leaf-shaped blade as a blank form through which they pass at about the point of transition from the percussive to the pressure methods, and that the latter, although approaching that form, never attain it. The former are of both quarry and random origin; the latter are, so far as I have observed, of random origin only, having been made from scattered pieces or masses of material.

It is worthy of especial notice that nearly all varieties of implements produced and used in great numbers by the aborigines are largely of the leaf-blade genesis, and it follows that the production of these blades was a most important function of the worker in stone. The great demand for projectiles, knives, drills and scrapers, led to the systematic quarrying of flakable stone and gave character to the work done in these quarries and the roughing-out shops with which they are always associated.   A study of these quarries and shops has afforded a key to the history of the blade and thus to the first step in the morphology of all tools of leaf-blade genesis.

The blades from which these five classes of implements are made are largely of quarry-shop production, and that part of the diagram indicated by *A*, *B*, *C*, *D*, is made up entirely of rejected forms, and these, together with the successful blades placed next at the right, represent and define the ordinary range of quarry-shop work.   Operations of like character were carried on, however, wherever the raw material, whether in quantities or in scattered pieces, was obtained and worked. The elaboration of the blade into the various specialized forms is illustrated by the rejects included in the space between the blades and the finished implements at the end of the lines.

It may be noted that all implements of leaf-blade genesis,—the arrow-point, spear-point, drill, scraper, knife, etc.,—do not necessarily pass through the full range of operations here indicated. Many of the smaller specimens are elaborated from flakes and splinters so approximate in shape that they do not require elaboration by percussion, or so delicate that percussion could not be employed. Flaking by pressure is alone required, and an auxiliary diagram is added to Diagram I. that these forms may be properly placed in the scheme of morphology.

It may be further noted here that all implements of a given class are not necessarily of one genesis or of like form and appearance. Simple unmodified flakes with sharp edges are utilized as knives forming a class distinct fiom the ordinary leaf-blade knife. Heavy flakes unmodified are used as scrapers or are rounded and beveled at one end for scraping, giving a type of tool distinct from that shaped from the leaf-like blade.

Of leaf-blade genesis other regions furnish groups of implements not found in the Chesapeake region. In the middle Mississippi province there is a large and important group of agricultural implements, blades either unmodified or variously specialized to facilitate hafting. There are also in this district some not very well-defined groups of fanciful flaked forms and a group of animal shapes that have their development, as a rule, through the leaf-blade blank. The shaping of fanciful forms was often suggested and encouraged on shopsites by the occurrence of accidental flaked forms of peculiar shape.

Morphology of the spear-point. The complete plan of development of leaf-blade groups of implements with attendant phenomena may be illustrated to advantage by a single example taken from the more fully elaborated forms, as, for example, the spear-point. This is a highly specialized implement of highly differentiated use. In Diagram II. I present two examples illustrating its development from two distinct forms of stone, one the irregular, inchoate mass broken from the body of rock in place, the other of the rounded form common to the bowlder and nodule.

The order of morphologic change is the same in both cases. With a hammer-stone of suitable size the original mass was attacked, blows being delivered according to the judgment and desires of the workman so that portions were successively flaked away; the form being gradually reduced to that of a leaf-shaped blade. When the hammer-stone had developed the blade to a certain degree of tenuity its functions were ended. It was not capable of trimming and notching the specimen, and the work was taken up by the more delicate manual processes known as flaking by pressure.

This history is epitomized in the figure, which gives expression to a number of distinct and important groups of facts. The distinction between the use of material derived from the inchoate mass of rock and that having the rounded form of bowlders, pebbles and concretionary nodules is indicated. The general trend and character of the morphology is the same in both cases, and the results, the finished points, are not distinguishable.

Rejects or "not implements" extend from the second to next to the last member of the series, those up to the blade or cache form being the quarry-shop rejects, and those beyond that stage rejects found on sites of specialization. Rejection was more common in the earlier than in the later stages of shaping, as percussion is more liable to produce deformation or undesirable fracture than pressure; still breakage was frequent under the flaking point. The practice of removing a few flakes to test the material resulted in adding much to rejectage in early stages.

The data for a large part of this diagram were obtained from a study of the quarry-shops, where alone the operations of shaping can be studied to advantage, the work there having been confined almost exclusively to roughing out the blank blades. The exact point in the series at which percussion left off and pressure took up the work cannot be determined with exactness; it probably varied with the material, and perhaps with the worker or the occasion. The change occurred at or beyond the close of the quarry work. The quarry work naturally ended and transportation took place when the percussive method had completed the thin blade. The "not transported" forms are those left in the quarry-shops, and the "transported" include the thin blades and all the forms beyond that stage.

Transportation. An interesting episode in the history of implements produced in numbers in localities remote from the sites of utilization is their transportation. As long as implements were mere random products made where scattered material was found their transportation was a matter of little consequence, but when demand grew and manufacture became an industry requiring the opening of great quarries and the working of extensive factories, the carrying industry developed to very considerable importance. It was customary, no doubt, before the white man's materials and implements were introduced, for families or groups of families — possibly whole tribes — to make long journeys to the great flint quarries and to spend weeks or months quarrying the stone and shaping the tools. This is illustrated to-day of·the Yankton Sioux, who, in large parties, journey two hundred miles each summer to work the red pipestone quarries and to make pipes or prepare the stone for trade.

A study of the great flint quarries has demonstrated the fact that the shaping operations in them and about them consisted almost wholly in roughing out leaf-shaped blades—the blank forms for many varieties of tools. At the end of the working season the stock of blades produced, together with such flakes and masses as were desired, were packed up and carried away, largely, no doubt, on the backs of the women.

Storage; the Cache. Following transportation came storage. The discovery of hoards of flaked stones, mainly of blade-like form, has been a matter of much notoriety for many years.   So uniform is the character of these objects that the name "cache blades" or "cache implements" has become attached to them.   The true status of the great body of these objects is sufficiently explained by the discovery that the almost exclusive shaped product of the quarries and great shops is a blade of identical character.   As a rule, therefore, the cache "implement" is the transported and stored product of the great shops—the blank form intended for further distribution and for final shaping into the various tools of leaf-blade genesis.   Although cache forms are mainly blades, hoards of very rude shapes are sometimes found, for transportation in numbers may take place at any stage in the shaping process.   Flakes, fragments and masses of stone were at times gathered and transported in numbers and were thus subject to caching; and finished implements comprising one or more varieties may be assembled, representing the property of some thrifty hunter or the stock in trade of an aboriginal speculator. The manner of storage was usually in compact clusters or piles, the pieces being laid up in neat order and covered with earth.   In cases a mound of earth was thrown up over them, as in the noted instance near Chillicothe, Ohio, where nearly eight thousand discoid blades were obtained from a single mound.

Specialization. Following transportation and storage came trade and specialization. Dissemination was no doubt by the ordinary

channels well known to students of the native tribes.   Specialization
of the blank forms—the blades, flakes and masses—took place probably pretty much as necessity was felt for the implements.   Perhaps in
cases the workmen, often old and skilled hands, shaped and finished
large numbers of those forms most used, ready to be hafted or shafted
for immediate use.   Preceding the going forth of a war party, for example, much activity would be shown.   A party of one hundred men
would require perhaps not less than twenty-five hundred or three
thousand arrow and spear-points for fair equipment; and a notion of
the needs that led to such undertakings as the opening and working of
great quarries can be formed when it is remembered that with the
great nations a thousand or more warriors had to be equipped and kept
on a war footing from year to year and generation to generation.

Specialization takes varied directions, as in producing an edge, a
point, a means of hafting, a sawing edge, a beveled edge, a slender
shaft, a curved blade, a gouge-shaped edge, etc.   In Diagram I. I have
drawn a dotted line which indicates approximately where the work
of specialization began.   The unnotched ax is specialized at the first
step; the specialization being the result on the average of half a dozen
blows removing as many flakes and leaving an irregular cutting edge.
The first step in the shaping of the notched ax in the line above gives
precisely the same result; as does also the first step in each case in the
remainder of the series.   The notched ax is specialized in the second
step by breaking two notches in the sides.   In the shaping of the pick
there are two steps in specialization: first, the flaking of a rude point,
and, second, the making of notches or a rude groove to facilitate hafting.   The flaking of the chisel is more complete than in the pick and
approaches closely that of the knife blade, from which form it differs
in having greater thickness.   The term *knife* is here applied to the unspecialized blade only, because it is difficult or impossible to separate
it, when specialized for hafting, from the other highly elaborated
forms.   This and other like shortcomings of the diagram will not de-
tract from its value in expressing the general truths of morphology.

The second and third steps in shaping the chisel are repeated in
all the series above.   The second, third and fourth steps in the knife
blade are repeated in like manner in the remainder of the series, and
so on.   It is seen that the length of the series indicates approximately
the degree of elaboration.   The arrow-head has a greater variety of
shapes, and, therefore, passes through more steps of morphology than
the spear-point; the spear-point has the same relation with the next in-

ferior form, and so on down the scale.   The steps of the series could be increased to the full number of flakes removed in each case.

In the supplementary diagram flakes take the place occupied by the blades in the main diagram.   They are placed in the percussion column directly under the blades, their entire elaboration being in the pressure column and ranking as specialization, although the first step in each case was probably that of reducing the flake to a leaf-like outline. As to the details of specializing processes and the final forms produced by them nothing need be said in this place.

Function.   The function and manner of use of flaked implements, matters of much importance in their history, must be passed over here for lack of space for their consideration.

INCIDENTS OF MORPHOLOGY.

Now, beside the products of shaping operations in their varied forms, finished and unfinished, there are divers accompanying phenomena which may be briefly referred to in this place.   These phenomena are to be observed mainly on the shop-sites where the shaping was carried on, the shops themselves, where extensively used, being among the most striking features connected with the work.

Flakage.   Fracture by percussion produces fragments, flakes and chips broken from the specimen shaped and cast aside as waste. Pressure, employed in the more delicate manipulations, also gives rise to like results of smaller size, and generally quite minute.   The former are found largely on the great shop-sites where the incipient tools were reduced to approximate size and shape, and the latter on sites where trimming and specializing were carried on.   By a study of flakage much is learned of the nature of the work done.

Breakage.   Breakage of the incipient forms, under the blows of the hammer or the spasmodic application of the pressure tool, takes place at all stages of manufacture, and the pieces, broken at divers angles and shattered in numberless ways, constitute a large portion of the refuse of the shops and, rightly studied, afford an excellent key to the nature of the shaping operations, the progress of morphology and the nature of the final product.   Where operations were extensive every form made is represented by the pieces which may be picked up and joined again.   One variety of fragment is liable to deceive the unwary. When an incipient implement has been flaked all around it sometimes splits in such a way that one or both of the pieces appear to have been themselves the subject of the shaping operations.

Rejectage. The reject proper is a failure resulting not from pronounced breakage, but from abortive shaping operations, which result in the development of some fatal eccentricity of contour. It is typified most fully by the turtleback, a form characterized by a thick body and having conchoid facets resulting from lack of carrying power in the flake-producing impact. In America by far the greater portion of flaked implements are flat to thinness, and usually somewhat leaf-shaped in outline, or are produced by elaborations of a leaf-shaped outline, as the spear-point, arrow-point and drill. In making these forms all that could not be reduced readily to the required degree of tenuity were either broken in the attempt to reduce them or became hopelessly deformed under repeated abortive blows. The thick-bodied flaked stone of approximately leaf-shaped outline is the reject *par excellence,* and probably outnumbers the successful forms— the implements produced—two to one. It is widely distributed, occurring in greatest numbers on or near the sites yielding the raw material and especially, in countless numbers, in the shops surrounding the great quarries of quartzite, flint, jasper, chert, novaculite, argillite and rhyolite. It happened in some cases that the raw material or the more rudely outlined forms were carried away from the quarries to be shaped at leisure on distant sites; turtlebacks are, therefore, occasionally found widely scattered, but in the nature of things this is exceptional. Economy of labor in transportation would require that the material be tested for workability, and reduced as much as possible in weight before removal began.

All of our American flaked tools are, however, not thin and blade-like in outline; picks, chisels, celts, adzes, hatchets and axes are thick intentionally, and the rejects of their manufacture and they themselves should not be confused with rejects of the thin forms. Such tools were, however, seldom made in great numbers, and in many sections are rare or wanting, and, so far as the great quarries already studied are concerned, they constitute no considerable feature. When found scattered over the fields such forms cannot readily be distinguished from the refuse of blade-making, save where specialization has taken place, use has left its mark, or distribution or association affords clues. Rejectage as well as breakage varies with each implement, with the variety of implement and with the material.

Nuclei. Another usual consequent of manufacture, especially where the finer qualities of flint and the glassy rocks were worked, are the nuclei or cores left after the removal of successive flakes for knives or for subsequent shaping.   Generally these objects are readily distinguished from other classes of refuse by the number and uniformity of their facets, which give a fluted effect.

Hammer-stones.   Associated with the refuse of shaping are the various tools utilized in the work.   These are mainly hammers of stone, globular or discoidal in shape and bearing marks of the manner of their use.   It often happens that the periphery of the disk is so worn as to indicate clearly whether the workman was right or left-handed.   In size there is wide range.   The larger specimens, used in breaking up the stone where massive, are as much as ten inches in diameter.   The smaller, used in finishing the more delicate blades, are not above an inch in diameter.   The hammers are usually of heavy, compact rock, and are often bowlders and pebbles from outcrops or stream beds near the quarries; not infrequently they were re-shaped by flaking.

EVOLUTION OF SPECIES.

That nothing springs into being without cause and that no highly-developed form comes into existence without predecessors and ancestry, may be as safely maintained of art as of nature.   The existence of a highly-specialized group of implements implies a long line of antecedent groups reaching back to an original primal form having no such phenomena as variation or specialization.   This necessary relation of the last to a first and the order of procession from the one to the other may be readily expressed in diagrammatic form.   I present two diagrams, the first illustrating the evolution of a single species of implement with phenomena of shaping at successive steps of progress, and the other indicating the morphologies of specialization and differentiation of the whole group of species.   Assuming that in Diagram III. we have at the base *A* the inceptive point of the shaping arts, or, better, the first step in the manipulation of stone, and that the series *B, C,* at the top, represents the development of an individual,—the arrow-head,—we may fill up the interval between by any number of developmental series representing successive steps in the history of the arrow-head species.   The intervals between the lines may be regarded as representing the period of time necessary to the accomplishment of a step in differentiation and specialization.   The number of steps may be large or small, but I have introduced about as many as there are varieties of flaked implements in use by an ordinary community of people.   We can have little definite knowledge of the shape of the ancestral implement or of its particular functions at any given step of

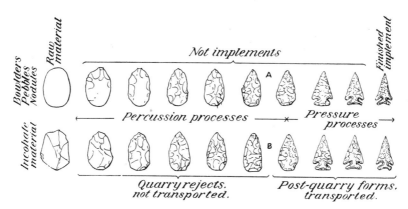

DIAGRAM II.—MORPHOLOGY OF THE SPEAR POINT

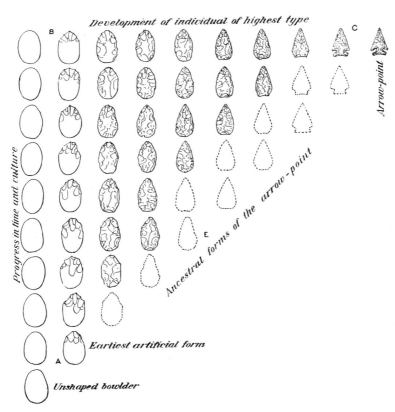

DIAGRAM III.—STEPS IN THE EVOLUTION OF SPECIES.

progress. I, therefore, leave indefinite the final shapes at the right. The arrow may include in its ancestry one or all of the species of flaked implements. It may have had a mixed parentage, as, for example, through a wood or bone tool as to hafting features, and through the stone knife as to its incisive shape. I have not ventured to give any of the ancestral steps or implement groups a name, but if the arrow is the outcome of the less simple devices in stone preceding it, the order of progress would repeat somewhat closely that indicated in Diagram I., the order being that of increasing complexity.

The manner here adopted of representing the evolution of a group or species of implements by a succession of manipulative series is intended to aid in a comparative study of the rejected forms, a matter of much importance in the discussion of questions of progress and time. It will be seen that the steps of progress in manufacture represented by rejected forms pertaining to each implement in Diagram I. necessarily duplicate somewhat closely the corresponding steps of manufacture in Diagram III., although the steps in the former are all of one time, and the latter represent all times.

The facts to be especially brought out are these: The conditions of art in stone are such that the simpler forms of flaked implements employed in cutting, picking, scraping and striking are necessarily shaped by like processes, pass through like changes of form and reach closely identical results, whether made by a people of low culture grade doing their best work, or by a people of high culture doing their rudest work. The early shapes will be repeated in the later shapes, and the refuse of rejection will, in the nature of things, up to the stage where specialization begins to take effect, be largely identical. The finished implement belonging at A in Diagram III., a paleolithic position, may be practically duplicated through all the ages along the vertical line A, B, in Diagram I. So the blade appearing first as an ancestor of the arrow, say at E in Diagram III., is repeated practically in all the blade forms of subsequent ages and in all the blank forms of all implements of blade genesis.

The evolution of species of implements, as of species of animals or plants, is a progress accompanied by specialization and differentiation of form. An implement of the simplest type under stress of human needs is elaborated to increase its efficiency and is specialized to fit it more fully for a particular use. Uses multiply and the specialization takes different directions, diverging and differentiating until the results are complex and numerous species of implements exist.

This process may be expressed to the eye, but it is impossible with our limited knowledge of the details of morphology at the various stages of development to give concrete examples covering the whole ground.   We know that progress of certain kinds took place and that advancement was along certain general lines reaching well-known results, and the general truths of this progress are expressed in Diagram IV.   In this diagram the idea of individual morphology and the whole group of phenomena incident to manufacture are entirely omitted, the relations of genetic succession of the various groups of implements being alone kept in view.   The diagram is made to include the full range of primitive work in stone, as none of the processes by means of which the groups are developed are independent of the others throughout their history.   The more typical flaked groups are placed on the left, the pecked, abraded and incised following to the right.   It is not possible to determine definitely the order of procession, the parting, crossing and intercrossing of lines.   The radical shaping processes, fracturing, battering, abrading and incising, each give rise to species and groups of species of implements, partially enumerated and tentatively placed in the diagram.   The attempt to trace a particular final form back to the beginning would be futile, although in some cases a probable course of progress can be made out, as with the arrow-point, which connects back no doubt through the spear-point and the knife with the primal sharpened stone.   A notion of the comparative complexity of the phenomena at succeeding periods of time and stages of progress may be obtained by comparing the groups of radiating lines at the points crossed by the four concentric lines *A, B, C, D.*

Evolution of implements carries or has associated more or less closely with it other groups of evolutional phenomena which could be given separate consideration to good advantage; these include the evolution of processes, of form, of function, of trade, of transportation, etc., but the discussion of these topics would extend this paper beyond the limits set for it.

Attention has been called to the great importance of thorough analysis of the phenomena of art, and especially to the most exhaustive study of the fragmental materials of archæology.   An analysis, not yet fully perfected, of flaked stone art has been attempted, in which much weight is given to the idea that art should be studied as natural history is studied, that objects of art must not be treated as independent individuals merely, or as groups of individuals associated

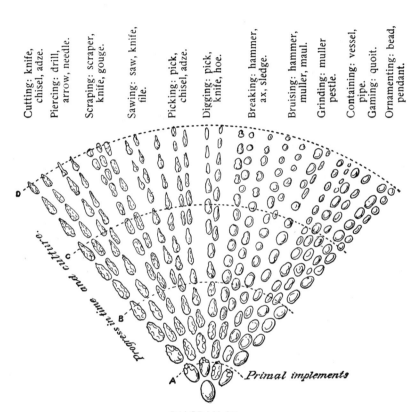

Cutting: knife, chisel, adze.

Piercing: drill, arrow, needle.

Scraping: scraper, knife, gouge.

Sawing: saw, knife, file.

Picking: pick, chisel, adze.

Digging: pick, knife, hoe.

Breaking: hammer, ax, sledge.

Bruising: hammer, muller, maul.

Grinding: muller pestle.

Containing: vessel, pipe.

Gaming: quoit.

Ornamenting: bead, pendant.

Progress in time and culture

Primal implements

D

C

B

A

DIAGRAM IV.

EVOLUTION OF SPECIES OF STONE IMPLEMENTS BY DIFFERENTATION
AND SPECIALIZATION.

by superficial characters for convenience of description, but as phenomena to be rightly understood only through their relationships with the whole scheme of nature, viewed in the light of evolution. It has been shown that the utilization of works of art as the materials of history is unsafe until the whole group of phenomena has been considered with respect to origin, genesis and all the details of morphology and development.

STONE IMPLEMENTS

OF THE

POTOMAC-CHESAPEAKE TIDEWATER PROVINCE

BY

WILLIAM HENRY HOLMES

GROUP IN PLASTER ILLUSTRATING THE WORK CARRIED ON IN AN ABORIGINAL QUARRY WORKSHOP

Prepared by the author for the World's Columbian Exposition at Chicago.   See Supplementary Note I, page 150

CONTENTS

ILLUSTRATIONS

[NOTE.—In cases of inconsistency in the sizes of the illustrated objects as given in the descriptive titles thereof and in the following list the sizes given in the latter should govern.]

9

STONE IMPLEMENTS OF THE POTOMAC-CHESAPEAKE TIDEWATER PROVINCE

By WILLIAM HENRY HOLMES

PREFATORY NOTES

I

The Indian tribes inhabiting the great province drained by the tide-water tributaries of the Chesapeake were simple fishermen, hunters, and warriors whose art aimed at little beyond the supply of passing needs, and the district now furnishes almost nothing in the way of art remains to attract the popular eye. Little has been preserved beyond the simplest varieties of stone implements; but inconspicuous and elementary as these objects are, they have attracted much attention on the part of archeologists, and are now eagerly studied because of their bearing, not only on the history of the region and its people, but on questions of general import in the history of primitive progress. The explorations and studies recorded in the present paper were undertaken for the purpose of determining, if possible, the precise status of these remains, thus making them safely available to the historian of the race who seeks first of all a safe basis on which to found his structure. But some special questions have arisen that for the time overshadow the more general features of the investigation.

The earlier studies of the stone implements of the province developed decided differences of opinion as to the significance of a peculiar class of rudely flaked stones found in vast numbers about the head of tide-water in James, Potomac, and Susquehanna valleys. The main question at issue may be stated as follows: Do these rude objects form part of the remains left by the peoples of the region known to us historic-ally—the Algonquian tribes and their neighbors—as their associations in a general way indicate; or do they belong to an earlier race of much lower culture as suggested by the fact that somewhat analogous forms, found in other parts of the world, characterize the art of very ancient and primitive peoples?

The most extensive deposits of the rudely flaked stones are found along the bluffs in and about the city of Washington. The careful investigations so fully recorded in these pages have proved beyond the shadow of a doubt that the great deposits are on the sites of workshops connected with extensive quarries where the raw material (Cretaceous bowlders) was obtained. It was further found that the widely scattered specimens of the same class were on sites (village-sites or otherwise) yielding less plentiful supplies of the available raw material where manufacture had been conducted on a smaller scale. That the vast body of the rudely flaked stones of the province are rejects of manufacture was readily shown.

As a second step in the investigation it was deemed necessary to determine the exact relations of these objects with the real implements of the region. This was accomplished by first determining by most careful studies of the rejectage of the great flaking shops just what the product of the flaking operations was. This product, so far as the progress of specialization of form on the shop sites indicates, was found to be a leaf-shape blade. A third step in these explorations was then undertaken for the purpose of determining the destiny of these blades—where they were carried and how and by whom used. Many specimens of identical form were found on Indian village-sites in all parts of the surrounding region, and in several cases on sites of historic Algonquian settlements, where they were intimately intermingled with the midden refuse, pottery, and neolithic implements. It was further discovered that a large percentage of the countless stone implements—knives, spearheads, arrowpoints, etc—found in the broad valley below, were of leaf-blade genesis; that before they received their final shapes by trimming, stemming, and notching, they had been blades, corresponding exactly with those produced in the multitude of shops. The shops are, therefore, a necessary complement of the implements of the region and the implements are a necessary complement of the shops. The shops, great and small, are thus definitely connected with the great body of implements of the region, and these implements are directly connected with the dwelling sites of the historic peoples. The practical unity of the stone art of the region is in this way fully established, no type of implement or shaped stone not being fully accounted for by the well-established facts and necessary conditions of recent Indian occupancy.

That these demonstrations should be complete and satisfactory, studies were made of quarries of other materials in the neighboring highland, where the conditions proved to be the same in every respect. Similar leaf-shape blades were made and carried out to the surrounding valleys where they and the implements specialized from them are found closely associated with the more local art products.

That the subject should be further rounded out and completed, all known classes of implements have been studied and relegated to their proper categories, and the history of their manufacture and the classes of rejectage pertaining to them have been determined. In all this work there has not been found a single feature of the art remains or industrial phenomena of the region suggesting the presence of other than the known peoples.

The full series of illustrations presented in this paper will enable the student to make comparisons and arrive at his own conclusions. Great care has been taken to arrange these illustrations so that they will tell the story clearly and fully.

It is fortunate for those who may wish to verify or question the results reached in this study that the full range of phenomena is still well within their reach, and need only to be properly consulted to reveal the whole truth.

It is not attempted in the present paper to apply the results reached to the settlement of controversies arising elsewhere. The same is true of the preliminary paper published while the investigations were under way. Contrary to statements repeatedly made by writers on the subject, the question of the existence of a paleolithic period in Europe is not believed by me to be in any way involved. The verity of the determinations of Boucher de Perthes and his followers has never been questioned, and it is held that, where average conditions prevail, the paleolithic step, as usually defined, is the reasonable and natural first step in human progress. The proper settlement of local questions, and especially the question whether local evidence points toward a paleolithic or other early man in Potomac valley, is all that is directly sought.

The student, however, should not lose sight of the fact that the history of flaked stone implements, as developed by these studies, is their history everywhere, and that the lessons to be learned are of primary importance to the science of archeology. The chief lessons are those of the need of a full and proper discrimination of all the varied phenomena connected with the making, the using, and the distribution of the implements, and the impartial application of these phenomena to the elucidation of the history of culture and race.

II

It must be regarded as a striking circumstance that a large part of the varied phenomena considered in this paper are assembled within 2 or 3 miles of the capitol of the nation, much of it being within the capital city or within the area over which the city streets are now laid out. The greatest aboriginal bowlder quarry known, and the most important implement shops yet observed on the Atlantic slope, are located on Fourteenth street 2½ miles from the President's house. One of the most interesting native soapstone quarries in the great series extending along the eastern base of the highland from Massachusetts to Georgia is on Connecticut avenue extended, barely beyond the city limits; and the most important ancient village-site in the whole tidewater province is situated on Anacostia river within the city and little more than a mile from the capitol. Partly within the city limits and extending up the Potomac to Little falls, we have a great native fishing ground surrounded by a multitude of inhabited sites from which our collectors have filled their cabinets with curious objects of art. The spot now the political center of the nation was thus in prehistoric times a chief resort of the native peoples of the region.

It may not then be too much to expect that the glimpses of aboriginal life afforded by this study will prove of interest to the student of history, and the numerous phases of suburban scenery presented in the photographic views will doubtless be appreciated by future generations of Washingtonians.

III

Until recently it was hardly suspected that the Potomac-Chesapeake province was so rich in ancient remains. The arts and industries of the historic aborigines were extremely simple, and no striking monuments or remains of any kind are found to tell of vanished peoples. Careful exploration has, however, developed evidences of an intelligence and enterprise hardly to be expected of tribes of indolent savages. The use of stone by the prehistoric aborigines was limited to the manufacture of implements and utensils, but their knowledge of the mineral resources of the region was so extensive that no deposit of bowlders, no ledge of flakable stone, no deposit of available stone of any kind, seems to have escaped their attention. Quarrying and manufacture were extensive, and the distribution of the product extended in several cases for a hundred miles or more beyond the source of supply.

The historic tribes of the region were mainly of the Algonquian linguistic stock, the stock of Powhatan and King Philip, and this notable people may be connected by means of the art remains of their numerous village-sites with the great body of ancient inhabitants whose domain extended from South Carolina to Nova Scotia. There are some traces of departure from ordinary Algonquian types of art, but these are not decided enough to warrant the assumption that other peoples of independent culture were directly concerned. The culture status indicated by the remains here brought to the attention of students is precisely that of the historic inhabitants encountered by John Smith.

IV

The explorations embodied in this paper began in 1889 and continued with much interruption until 1894. It is evident from this that the field has been but imperfectly covered, for the tidewater Chesapeake country comprises upward of 20,000 square miles of territory, nearly every mile of which abounds in important traces of ancient aboriginal occupancy. To visit all and examine all would require a good part of a lifetime. Realizing this, the method was adopted of passing rapidly over the various sections and selecting a few typical examples of each class of sites or groups of phenomena for minute examination. The detailed studies made of these sites serve in a great measure to illustrate the whole subject, and though imperfect in many ways, form nuclei about which additional details can be assembled as they are acquired.

V

There are many students of the aboriginal history of the Potomac-Chesapeake province to whom I am indebted for assistance and who should be mentioned in connection with the archeologic study of the region. Prominent among the collectors who have gathered and preserved the fast disappearing relics are Mr J. D. McGuire, of Ellicott, Maryland. The collection of this gentleman, now installed in his charming home in Ellicott, represents a large part of the province, and includes notable series of objects from the soapstone quarries and from the village-sites and shell banks of the Potomac and Chesapeake. Mr McGuire's writings include an important paper on the quarrying of soapstone as indicated by surface phenomena, and various other articles in which more or less specific references are made to the general archeology of the province.

Among the numerous collections of Potomac river material that of Mr W. Hallett Phillips, of Washington, takes first rank. It affords the student more satisfactory opportunities for study than any other collection, as the various sites were systematically visited and the specimens properly cared for and labeled. Many of the illustrations presented in this paper are from his well-stocked cabinets.

Mr Elmer R. Reynolds has for many years been an enthusiastic collector of local relics, and his various accumulations have largely gone to supply the museums of Europe. He has written valuable papers on the Potomac shell deposits and the soapstone quarries of the District of Columbia.

The historian of the Potomac valley is also deeply indebted to the efforts of Mr S. V. Proudfit, of Falls Church, Virginia, whose extensive collections, consisting of many thousands of specimens, were generously donated to the National Museum. Mr Proudfit's paper on local archeology is among the most important issued up to the beginning of systematic work by the Bureau of Ethnology.

Few students of the region have contributed more largely and successfully to the exposition of our local antiquities than Mr Louis A. Kengla, formerly of West Washington, whose collections are preserved by the Georgetown University and whose valuable pamphlet on the archeology of the District was published as a Toner prize essay by that institution.

Another collector, later in the field than the others yet hardly less persistent and successful, is Mr Thomas Dowling, junior, whose aid I have sought on various occasions. Many specimens from his collections appear in the illustrations of this paper.

Mr William Hunter, of Fairfax county, Virginia, made extensive collections along the banks of the Potomac in the Mount Vernon region, and on the opposite side of the river Mr O. N. Bryan gathered many things of value, both series of objects having found a resting place in the National Museum. Mr John Bury made a valuable collection from the Anacostia village-sites, which was acquired recently by the Bureau of Ethnology.

Baltimore has contributed her share to the work of preserving historic materials through her well-known citizen Colonel W. H. Love, whose large collections of specimens and extensive knowledge of sites have been of much service in the preparation of the present memoir. Among the many others who have taken an active part in the work of collecting are Mr J. C. Lang, of Washington, Mr C. M. Wallace, of Richmond, Mr M. H. Valentine, of Richmond, Mr H. M. Murray, of West River, Maryland, and Prof. Thomas Wilson, of Washington.

There are still others to whom acknowledgments must be made: To Mr Frank Hamilton Cushing, who a few years ago made a careful study of the Amelia county, Virginia, soapstone quarry; to Mr F. W. Von Dachenhausen, whose collections from the vicinity of Washington have been drawn upon for illustration, and to Mr De Lancey W. Gill, of the Geological Survey, who has been closely associated with me in the work of collecting and elaborating, I am greatly indebted.

I wish especially to acknowledge the assistance given by Mr William Dinwiddie, who has been almost constantly associated with me in field work and in the office, and who was intrusted with much of the laborious task of quarry excavation; by Mr Gerard Fowke, who conducted the exploration of the Piedmont regions of Virginia and Maryland; and by Major J. W. Powell and Mr W J McGee, to whom I am greatly indebted for encouragement, sympathy, and support at all times and in all places.

The artists whose work adds so much to the effectiveness and scientific value of this publication are Miss Mary M. Mitchell, Mr H. C. Hunter, and Miss Frances Weser. The landscape photographs are largely the work of Mr Dinwiddie, and the series of plates of flaked stones are from the studio of Mr T. W. Smillie, of the National Museum.

CHAPTER I

INTRODUCTORY

THE FIELD OF INVESTIGATION

Previous to the year 1889 little archeologic work was done by the Bureau of Ethnology in the Atlantic coastal region, save, perhaps, in North Carolina, where a number of mounds had been opened under the direction of Dr Cyrus Thomas. A vast, though not an especially attractive field, extending from New Jersey through Delaware, Maryland, Virginia, the Carolinas, Georgia, and Florida, had never received careful or systematic attention. In 1890 the Director of the Bureau decided to begin the survey of this zone, and the first work undertaken was an examination of the tidewater Potomac. Work was begun in the District of Columbia; and with Washington as the initial point, exploration was carried westward into the Piedmont region and eastward and southward to the Atlantic coast.

The great artificial shell fields scattered along the brackish and salt water shore-lines appeared to be the leading feature of interest, and toward these attention was at first directed; but another and somewhat distinct field of investigation soon sprang into prominence. Within the decade ending with 1890 much interest had arisen in regard to the significance of certain rudely flaked stones found in great numbers in the region about Washington. These objects were thought to be of archaic type, and consequently to have an important bearing on two questions of great interest to archeologists, the first relating to the development of art in its early stages, and the second to the nature of the beginnings of man's prewritten history in this country.

A preliminary examination of the subject made it apparent that a solution of the problems thus suggested could be obtained only by a systematic study of the origin, manufacture, distribution, and geologic relations of the articles in question. It was decided to take up this study, and thus the field of investigation was greatly enlarged. The period required for exploration was lengthened indefinitely, and it became necessary to complete certain sections of the work for publication before the whole field could be covered. Division of the subject-matter of investigation into at least two parts was found to be easy and convenient. The main problems of the stone implements separated themselves readily from the history of the peoples and the ordinary traces of their prehistoric and historic presence.

It appeared also that there were convenient geographic subdivisions of the subject, and that in one case at least the geographic unit corresponds very closely with a well-marked ethnologic unit, and strangely enough also with an important unit of colonial history. The great Potomac-Chesapeake province, with its system of tidewater inlets, constitutes a natural subdivision of the coastal zone. Formerly the Susquehanna flowed southward through a restricted valley, entering the sea outside of capes Henry and Charles. By subsequent depression of the land this valley and its tributaries were submerged, and the floods rose until the tide reached Richmond on the James, Washington on the Potomac, and Havre de Grace in the main valley, and one-third of the land became sea, the tortuous shore line following the contours of the hills and valleys in and out in a marvelous maze. Tens of thousands of square miles of upland were transformed more or less completely into a maritime province, and this became the seat of a native confederacy, ruled over by the renowned Powhatan at the period of colonization. This district was thus a native ethnologic unit—a unit in race and culture—and the circumstances of colonization made it a unit in the history of civilization: it is the territory explored, conquered, and mapped by the intrepid John Smith; it is therefore a unit of exploration, conquest, and cartography.

It further appears, from what has been learned of the past of the region, that the historic peoples and conditions pass back without break into the prehistoric era, no traces of distinct occupation or culture phenomena having been found. Archeology but supplements history, and the archeologist works to great advantage in a unique and charming field illumined by the graphic records of the Roanoke, the Jamestown, and the Saint Mary colonies.

In treating the history of this province, it would seem the natural order to present, first, the historical phases of aboriginal occupancy, passing afterward back into the archeologic field; but this order proves inconvenient (as just indicated), and special studies of certain phases of art must receive first attention. The present paper is therefore devoted to examination of the derivation, manufacture, nature, and place in time and culture of the stone implements of the tidewater province—the province of John Smith. This will be followed by other studies, or by a single paper, on the aboriginal history and general archeology of the same area.

The Chesapeake tidewater province lies to the eastward of the heavy dotted line on the map presented in plate I. This is the fall line, where the streams descend from the Piedmont plateau to the tidewater lowland.

THE ART REMAINS STUDIED

The art remains of a vanished people available for the archeologist comprise all material forms shaped or in any way modified by their hands, whether from design or from the incidents of use. There are

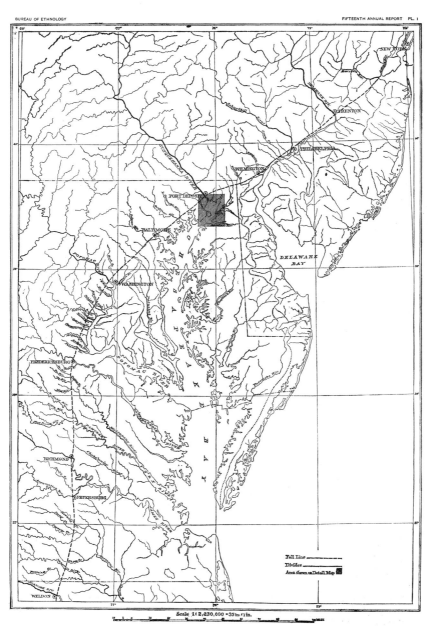

Scale 1:2,230,000 =35 mi. 1 in.

MAP OF THE POTOMAC-CHESAPEAKE TIDEWATER PROVINCE
Extending from the heavy broken line (the fall line) on the west to the dotted line on the east

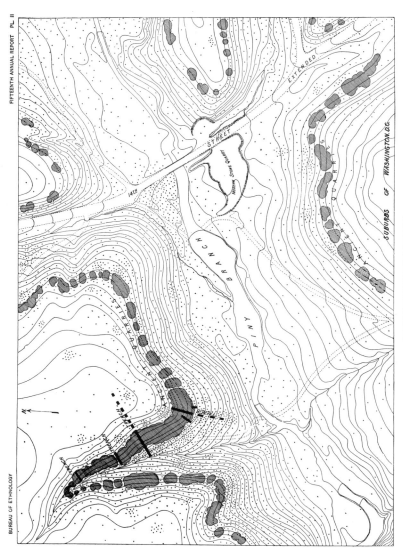

MAP OF THE PINY BRANCH QUARRIES

The shaded areas indicate the quarries approximately and the dotting indicates the distribution of the shops and refuse of manufacture.   Scale about 270 feet to the inch; contour internal, 5 feet

(1) fixed works, consisting of structures—mortuary, defensive or other-wise—dwelling sites, stone hearths, pits, cemeteries, quarries, implement shops, and refuse deposits. There are (2) portable works, including implements, utensils, weapons, and articles of dress, ceremony, and diversion. The subject chosen for this paper, the stone implements, includes but a small section of this great field, but nevertheless a most important one. It will be necessary to deal not only with the things themselves which belong to the second group mentioned, but with their origin and manufacture, leading thus to an investigation of the quarries and workshops, which are fixed remains, and to a study of the industries arising from their operation.

The materials used by a great group of tribes like that occupying the tidewater country in colonial and precolonial times were numerous, and the forms given them in art were naturally extremely varied, but the visible remains today are confined to a few materials, and conse-quently to a limited number of forms. The consideration of these tangible evidences is of the utmost importance to archeology, and their study leads naturally to inquiries into the various arts and industries concerned in their production. Besides this, much may be learned and much more may be surmised with respect to arts and industries of which no material traces remain, and correct inferences may be drawn regarding the customs, habits, and culture of the peoples.

The materials utilized in art were sought and obtained at much expense of time and labor, and the industries to which this search gave rise were no doubt of great moment to the people, although little attention has been paid to the subject by students. Clay was used for pottery, and ocher was obtained for paint. Vegetal and animal sub-stances also were sought and fully utilized. Stone was most exten-sively used by the primitive inhabitants of the tidewater region, and on account of its durability it is by far the most important material with which we have to deal in the prehistoric study. We can but con-jecture as to the beginnings and progress of this search. When men first appeared they found vast supplies of water-worn stones suited to immediate use scattered over the country. These, however, did not serve for all classes of needs, and the energetic savages penetrated the hills, laid bare the rocky deposits, and little by little acquired a mastery of the geologic resources of the province.

CHARACTER OF THE STONE IMPLEMENTS

MATERIALS AND THEIR DISTRIBUTION

Stone exists in many varieties, forms, and conditions, which differ greatly in the various sections of the country, thus giving much diver-sity to the manner of its utilization and to the forms employed in art, and many local peculiarities of art phenomena have arisen. Moreover, the tribes of this region were not fully sedentary and the materials acquired in one section were carried into another, giving rise to much variety in the materials employed by a single people or assembled in a given place. This complexity was also increased to some extent by trade, and no doubt by the undertaking of long journeys for the purpose of securing desired materials. Transportation was confined mainly to the smaller and more laboriously finished articles of use. Unshaped raw materials were not extensively transported, and the large body of the heavier tools and utensils made where material was plentiful were deserted when the locality was abandoned.

The peculiarities of the materials procurable in the tidewater region are very marked. The geologic formations found within this area include only limited portions of the crystalline or older sedimentary rocks, but are derived from them by erosive forces and consist of fragmental deposits, such as sands, clays, gravels, and beds of bowlders. The great rivers of Mesozoic and Cenozoic times swept down from the highlands, bearing fragments of all varieties of rocks and depositing them in beds along the margin of the sea. These transported fragments were, when first taken up by the water, sharp and rugged, but by constant rolling they were reduced to rounded forms, and included all sizes from grains of sand and minute pebbles to bowlders and even to great masses. All classes of rocks were thus seized by the floods and carried seaward; but all varieties did not reach the sea, save perhaps as sand or clay. The softer rocks were reduced to powder before the journey was fairly begun; brittle and much-flawed varieties, and all friable shales and slates, separated into minute fragments and formed beds of sand and gravel; the tough, hard, homogeneous pieces were rolled and rounded and carried ever onward, refusing to break or to be reduced to dust, and finally rested along the seashore and more especially about the mouths of the great rivers.

The primitive inhabitants of the crystalline highland had to make use of massive forms of rock or of rude angular or slightly water-worn fragments, and the reduction of these to available sizes and forms was a difficult work. But the inhabitants of the lowlands were born to more fortunate conditions. The agents of nature—the floods—had with more than human intelligence and power selected the choice bits of rock, the tough quartzite, the flinty quartz, the tough and brittle lavas, the indurated slates, the polished jasper, and the beautiful flints, from all the cliffs and gorges of the mountains, and had reduced them to convenient sizes and shapes, and had laid them down in the beds of the shallow estuaries, where through the subsequent rising of the land and the cutting of valleys they were found at the door of the tidewater lodge, ready or almost ready for immediate use in the arts. Each river coming from a different section of the highland secured and transported the varieties of rock most prevalent in its drainage basin, so that the great tidewater region is divided into mineralogic areas corresponding somewhat to those of the mountain valleys supplying the material.

It will readily be seen that these conditions of mineral resources must have had a marked effect on the art of the region, and thus on the culture of the natives inhabiting it. One drainage area supplies quartz mainly, and the art is quartz art; another supplies quartzite, and the art is quartzite art, and so on. All of these and other conditions will be considered in the discussion of the distribution of the remains of the region, to which subject a subsequent chapter is devoted.

All kinds and conditions of rock in both lowland and highland were exposed to some extent on the surface of the ground and were thus readily obtained, but the more desirable varieties occur in the main beneath the surface, and when the demand for them was great they had to be sought and quarried, thus giving rise to one of the most important of primitive industries.

QUARRYING

Quarrying begins with the removal of a fragment or mass of material partially buried in the ground. It is but a step further to the uncovering and removal of portions wholly buried, and only another step to quarrying on a large scale. The methods and extent of the quarrying necessarily differed with the peoples and their circumstances, with the nature of the material, and with the conditions under which it existed.

Of the details of quarrying operations our knowledge is yet imperfect, though much has been learned in certain directions; and of the tools used in quarrying, aside from those made of stone and left on the sites, no definite information has as yet been obtained. It is quite likely that implements of wood, buckhorn, and bone were used as in foreign stone-age quarries, but traces of these have wholly disappeared from the sites thus far examined. Fire may have been used in some localities as an agent in fracturing masses of stone, but the tidewater region furnished little material, save perhaps quartz, suitable for manipulation by this means. Massive forms of rock are found west of the fall-line or western border of the tidewater country. Flint, jasper, and rhyolite were quarried far back in the highland, and vein quartz was found, and, no doubt, to some extent quarried, in a multitude of places over the whole Piedmont region, and down to and even below the margin of the tidewater area. Steatite or soapstone is a tough, massive rock interbedded with gneissic formations, and rarely occurs in detached masses. In the beginning of its use it was secured where exposed on the surface by prying off small masses. When its compactness made this impracticable it was removed by cutting out roundish masses with stone picks. The lumps thus secured were ready for the sculptor's chisel. In time quarrying developed and was extensively carried on in many parts of Virginia and Maryland beyond the tidewater border.

In the tidewater province proper, quartzite occurs in the shape of bowlders or cobbles only, which, mainly during the Potomac and

Lafayette periods, were derived by erosive forces as fragments from heavy strata in the mountainous region to the northwest. Heavy deposits of these stones accumulated about the mouths of the rivers; by subsequent erosion they were exposed to view in many places and most advantageously for human use in the steeper bluffs that border the streams. Countless numbers, loosened from the well-compacted beds by erosion, descended to the lower slopes and into the streams to be again deposited at lower levels. The surface or float cobbles were extensively used, but the aborigines came to need more than could thus be obtained, and resorted to digging them from their places in the bluffs. The implement makers seem to have found that the freshly removed stones were more easily worked than surface finds, and quarrying, thus encouraged, was carried, in at least two places, over acres of ground. The bowlders were not always easily loosened and removed, as the rounded stones were held together by a matrix of sand and clay which had assumed almost the consistency of a sandstone; but the miners did not always penetrate the formation from above or even directly from the face of the outcrop. It happened that in many cases the bowlder beds rested on a surface of disintegrated gneiss exposed in bluff slopes, and by removing the upper surface of this with such pikes as were at hand the bowlders were undermined and easily knocked down. So far as observed, the bowlder deposits containing workable stone in any considerable quantity rest on the gneissic surfaces where they were laid down by the waters of the ancient sea.

Quartz, which was more generally if not more extensively used than any other material, is found in two forms. It occurs in countless veins which penetrate the gneissic rocks over a large district west of the fall-line. Being much less destructible than the gneisses, it weathers out in dike-like ridges and breaks up into blocks and angular pieces which spread over the ground in vast numbers. Choice varieties of this vein rock were, without doubt, quarried to some extent, but it was so plentiful on the surface that quarrying was not generally necessary. Carried down by the streams of all periods, it occurs plentifully as pebbles and bowlders in all formations in the tidewater region, and was selected or quarried along with the quartzite.

Jasper, flint, rhyolite, and other varieties of stone were rather rare within the tidewater districts, occurring sparingly as pebbles, small bowlders, and worn fragments in gravel deposits and in the beds of rivers. They were procured, however, by the tidewater tribes from masses in place in the uplands and mountains, the quarries being quite extensive, as will be shown subsequently.

MANUFACTURE

INITIAL STAGES

Having secured the raw materials from the surface or by quarrying, the next step was either to utilize them unchanged or to shape them for use. Sharp-edged and pointed stones were used for cutting,

digging, etc, and rounded cobbles from the river or from gravel beds
were well suited for striking, pounding, grinding, etc, but with these
unmodified forms we have little to do, as it is not easy to say that any
given specimen was used at all unless it bears decided marks of use;
and decided marks of use may be regarded as giving the object an
artificial form, as in the case of the improvised mortars, mullers, and
hammerstones so common in the Chesapeake-Potomac region.

SHAPING PROCESSES

The shaping processes by means of which stone was made to assume
artificial forms adapted to human needs are varied and ingenious and
their mastery is of the greatest importance to all primitive peoples.
These processes are distinguished by such terms as breaking, flaking,
cutting, drilling, scraping, pecking, grinding, and polishing. All are
purely mechanical; none are chemical, save a possible use of fire to
induce changes in the rock in some parts of the quarry work. A wide
range of manual operations is represented, and these may be conveniently arranged in four groups: 1, *fracturing*, represented by the terms
breaking, flaking, and chipping; 2, *incising*, including cutting, picking, and scraping; 3, *battering*, including such acts as bruising, pecking,
and hammering; 4, *abrading*, as in rubbing, drilling, boring, sawing,
and polishing. These acts are employed according to the nature of the
stone or the results desired; as, for example, fracture is employed where
the stone to be shaped is brittle, like flint, jasper, or quartz; incision is
employed where the stone is relatively soft, such as soapstone, serpentine, and the like; battering is applied to tough materials, capable of
resisting the shocks of percussion, like granitic rocks and many of
the eruptives. Nearly all varieties are capable of being shaped by
grinding and rubbing.

The processes employed in a given case were determined by the
nature of the material, by the intelligence and skill of the workman,
by the character of the object designed, and by a number of minor con-
siderations. Ninety percent of the stone implements produced in the
tidewater country were shaped by the fracturing processes. For convenience of treatment, I shall present the implements in groups determined by the processes mainly employed in their production as follows:
1, fractured or flaked implements; 2, battered or pecked implements,
and, 3, incised or cut implements. Abrading processes were mainly
auxiliary to the others and will not be presented at length.

Fracturing or flaking—The art of flaking stone was very extensively
practiced in the tidewater region, and ample opportunity is furnished
for observing the work in all its phases. The first step in the process,
where masses were dealt with, consisted in breaking the material by
heavy blows into somewhat approximate shapes and sizes; the second
step was roughing out by free-hand percussion the blank forms of the
various classes of tool desired; the third step was the specialization of
forms by direct or indirect percussion, or by pressure. As to the order

and the manner of conducting these steps, many observations have been made. The finished objects were often produced at once by carrying the work without interruption through all the stages of progress. This was true of sporadic work, where materials were scattered or where the implement was needed at once; but where materials were plentiful and demands not pressing, the workshops became factories and there was an opportunity for, and no doubt a tendency toward, specialization of labor. It was more convenient and profitable for certain individuals to give exclusive attention to the separate steps—first, to quarrying, breaking up the material and selecting pieces in large numbers; second, to roughing-out the blank forms in numbers; and, third, to the work of trimming, specializing, and finishing. These three well-defined steps gave rise to separate industries, carried on by the same individuals at different times or places or by distinct groups of experts at convenient times and places. It would seem that the first and second steps, whether performed by one or by two groups of workmen, were generally accomplished on the spot yielding the raw material; it would be unprofitable to transport masses of material of which nine-tenths would finally have to be consigned to the refuse heap. The blank forms of the articles to be shaped, worked out so far as thoroughly to test the material and its capacity for specialization, were removed from the source of supply to be finished when convenient or when need demanded.

Where disseminated materials were utilized, and especially in cases of immediate need, all the steps were frequently taken and the perfect implement produced at once; but it is observed that in many cases where the material was sparsely scattered as bowlders or nodules over the face of the country, the work of collection and blocking out was first attended to and the hoards of blanks thus produced were transported and stored, subject to final distribution for specialization or use.

Details of these steps in the art of flaking and the variations in process, resulting from differences in material and in articles designed, will, so far as possible, be given in connection with the investigation of the sites affording the observations.

As has been indicated, flaking was employed almost exclusively in the production of projectile points, knives, scrapers, perforators (or drills), hand axes or choppers, notched axes. hoes, and picks; it served to aid in roughing out the forms of various articles finished by pecking and grinding; these are mortars, pestles or mullers, axes, celts, chisels, pipes, ornaments, and diversional and ceremonial objects.

Battering or pecking processes—The acts employed in this class of operations were generally percussive, the impact resulting in a bruising and crumbling of minute portions of the surface of the stone. The hammer used was hard and tough, and the stone shaped was sufficiently tough practically to preclude fracture by the ordinary blow. No specialized tool was necessary, though such came to be made, the result being reached by striking one stone against another of proper relative durability. The several acts are known as battering, bruising, and pecking, the latter term being in common use for the act by which shaping was mostly accomplished. Materials suitable for shaping by this process are plentiful and widely distributed. They occur in the tidewater country wherever flakable stones abound, but the most favorable localities, so far as observed, are along the river banks about the head of tidewater. Village-sites located on the lower terraces about Washington and Georgetown furnish many specimens illustrating failures in all stages of the shaping of celts, grooved axes, pestles, and ceremonial articles from bowlders of diorite and various of the denser varieties of crystalline metamorphic rocks. An examination of certain inhabited sites farther up the river, and in various parts of the highland, develops the fact that extensive work of this class was carried on, and it is probable that a large part of the lowland supply of pecked tools was derived from these distant sources. Such a site and its products are described in detail further on. There is no evidence that the stone used was obtained by quarrying. The ordinary practice seems to have been to select water-worn stones of suitable texture that already approximated the form desired. Battering processes, and the tools produced by them, are presented systematically in a subsequent section.

Abrading processes—Shaping by abrasion in its most elemental form consists in rubbing one object against another with such force as to remove minute particles from one or both. The operations are generally expressed by such terms as grinding, sawing, boring, rubbing, and polishing. All stones are abradable, and all hard stones can be made to serve in the active operations of abrading. These processes were usually supplementary to those of flaking or battering, and were suited especially to sharpening edges and points already approximate in shape, and to giving smooth finish to surfaces. Their employment was very general but not confined to particular localities to such an extent as to leave extensive evidences of the work done. Stones modified in shape and surface characters from use in grinding and polishing are found on many sites in the tidewater country. The products of this group of processes are properly treated for the most part in connection with those of pecking.

Incising processes—This important class of operations shape materials by cutting, piercing, scraping, etc. They imply the use of a hard edged or pointed tool, and a substance to be shaped of somewhat less hardness. The presence of steatite in large bodies and often in exposed situations along the western border of the tidewater country from the Susquehanna to the Savannah led to the extensive utilization of cutting processes by the later aboriginal inhabitants of the region. Our extensive exploration of the quarry sites has given us a clear comprehension of methods of procuring and shaping, and of the results achieved. Rudely shaped stone picks were employed in cutting out the masses, and neatly flaked, pecked, and ground chisels of hard stone served to rough out and trim the bowls and other articles. A subsequent section of the present memoir is devoted to this division of the subject.

Chapter II

MANUFACTURE OF FLAKED STONE IMPLEMENTS

INTRODUCTORY STATEMENT

The discussion of flaked implements comprehends a study of all that pertains to the procuring of flakable stone by means of search, collection, and quarrying, and of everything pertaining to the manufacture of implements by fracture, as in breaking and in flaking or chipping by percussion or pressure; it includes also a classification and descriptive presentation of the finished products and a reference to their respective uses. In the final section the distribution of the raw materials is treated in connection with the study of the distribution of implements.

It is most convenient in treating this complex subject to begin at once with the study of the great industries of quarrying and manufacture, taking up the regions studied or the sites examined in approximately the order of their exploration.

Five materials were extensively used for flaking by the tidewater peoples: quartzite, quartz, rhyolite, jasper, and flint. Several other materials occur less abundantly, among which may be mentioned sandstone, limestone, slate, argillite, basic eruptive rocks, iron quartzite, chalcedony, and quartz crystal. Quartzite and quartz were obtained largely in the form of water-worn pebbles and cobbles from the fragmental deposits of the tidewater region. These materials in this form are closely associated in distribution, and their examination will, in the main, be taken up conjointly. The most extensive deposits of fragmental quartz and quartzite occur about the head of the tidewater Potomac, and their most extensive utilization was confined to the vicinity of Washington. Surface deposits were worked wherever found on the Potomac, James, and other rivers. Rhyolite, argillite, jasper, and flint were obtained from quarries in the mountains, and to some extent along the rivers in fragments, bowlders, and pebbles.

The great quarries about Washington will be described and discussed in detail. Most of them were opened in the littoral deposits abounding in pebbles of quartz and quartzite; many others in veins of steatite or soapstone. They may be taken as types of this class of phenomena observed in and about the tidewater province as well as over the whole Atlantic slope.

Of the exotic materials—rhyolite, jasper, argillite, flint, etc—rhyolite is by far the most important, and the South mountain quarries of this stone may be taken as a type of the great class of quarries furnishing rock from the mass.

QUARRY-WORKSHOPS OF THE DISTRICT OF COLUMBIA

HISTORY OF THE RESEARCH

From time to time during the decade ending with 1890, the attention of archeologists was called to a class of rudely worked stones found in great numbers in the vicinity of the city of Washington; all are shaped exclusively by flaking, and are of forms so simple and rude that the idea prevailed that they were very ancient, this idea being strengthened by the assumption that they are somewhat closely related in form to typical European paleolithic implements. The best-known variety is the so-called "turtleback," a bowlder slightly flaked on one side, giving somewhat regularly arranged conchoid facets suggesting the plates of a turtle's back; but more highly developed forms of varying stages of elaboration are almost equally numerous. The materials are mainly quartzite and quartz, the former very largely predominating.

These objects are pretty generally scattered over the surface of the country, and are found to some extent throughout the tidewater region, being less numerous toward the sea. They occur in greatest abundance, however, as shown by recent discoveries, along the steep faces of the terraces bordering Washington city on the north and west. So plentiful are these rude objects in certain of the suburbs that they are brought in with every load of gravel from the creek beds, and the laborer who sits by the wayside breaking stones for the streets passes them by thousands beneath his hammer each year; the capital city is paved with the art remains of a race who occupied its site in the shadowy past, and whose identity has been a matter of much conjecture.

The first discussion of these objects within my memory occurred at a meeting of the Anthropological Society of Washington in the winter of 1878. A paper on the turtlebacks was read by Dr W. J. Hoffman, in which their character and manner of occurrence, their age and probable relations to the Abbott finds of New Jersey, were discussed, the conclusion reached being that they were probably paleolithic, and that they had, therefore, a purely adventitious association with the relics of Indian art with which they were intermingled on various sites. Later Mr S. V. Proudfit engaged in the collection and study of these forms, and in 1888 published a short paper relating thereto in the journal issued by the Anthropological Society, the *American Anthropologist*. His views of their nature, so far as elaborated, were opposed to those of Dr Hoffman, and have stood the test of later research.

Mr Thomas Wilson, on his return from a long sojourn in Europe in 1887, having been appointed curator of the department of prehistoric archeology in the National Museum, took up the subject afresh, and published a series of papers on the general subject of paleolithic man, making reference to and giving numerous illustrations of these finds. The view taken by Mr Wilson was that they are paleolithic; and as such they were labeled, distributed, and published. His assignment of these objects to this period of human progress was, I understand, based entirely on their supposed analogies of form with the paleolithic implements of Europe.

A somewhat elaborate discussion of the subject took place at a meeting of the Anthropological Society of Washington, held in the month of April, 1889. In the discussion of the archeology of the District of Columbia, three papers, by W J McGee, Thomas Wilson, and S. V. Proudfit, respectively, bore directly on these rude objects. Up to this time, however, no one had essayed to do more than study the surface finds and phenomena, and consequently little was definitely known of the true history and relationships of the objects in question.

My own investigation began in 1889, and the results of the first few months' work in the bluffs of Piny branch, in the northern suburbs of the city, were published in the *American Anthropologist* for the year 1890. The work was resumed in the same place in the spring of 1890, and during that year several other localities were examined. The only sites extensively explored are one on Piny branch and another in the vicinity of the new Naval Observatory, on the western side of Rock creek.

Quite early in the progress of the investigations, which were carried on by means of trenching the deposits yielding the objects, it became apparent that the sites were ancient quarries, where the aborigines had obtained the material and manufactured implements of quartzite and quartz, and that the supposed implements were only the failures, rejects, or wasters unavoidably produced in shaping brittle stone by percussion, and having no significant relationship with archaic or paleolithic art. The work had been very extensive, and consisted in quarrying the bowlders from the heavy beds of Potomac age and in roughing out the implements to be made. On account of the dual nature of the work carried on, I have called these sites quarry-workshops. The important bearing of these investigations on a number of the problems of archeologic science makes it advisable to present them in considerable detail.

GEOLOGY OF THE LOCALITY

As a preliminary step to a study of the evidence of human industry on these sites, it is important that the geology of the vicinity be carefully reviewed. Fortunately this is an easy task, as the identification and relationships of the various formations have been recently made out thoroughly by Messrs McGee and Darton, of the Geological Survey. It is found that the only clastic formations with which the quarry phenomena are directly associated are Cretaceous, and we are therefore not called on to trouble ourselves about the significance of this relationship, since the association is necessarily purely adventitious. It is further ascertained that the other sedimentary rocks of the surrounding region are all older than those with which the works of man are known to be contemporaneously associated. The deposits with which remains of human handiwork are directly associated are mainly talus accumulations, the formation and modification of which have been going on for a long period and are still in progress.

The broad plateau bordering the city on the north is cut by Rock creek and Anacostia river and their tributaries. It is capped with sedimentary formations which extend far eastward and southward, covering the tidewater country; these are underlain by crystalline rocks, gneisses, granites, schists, etc (figure 1), well exposed by the deep scoring of Rock creek and its branches. On the western side of that stream the latter rocks rise to and form the surface of the country. The sedimentary rocks were laid down along the crystalline shore, which sloped gently eastward, in approximately horizontal strata, two formations in Mesozoic time and the Cretaceous period, known as the Potomac

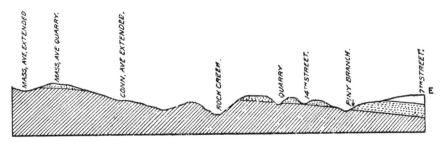

FIG. 1—General section across Rock creek and Piny branch valleys, showing gneissic formations and their relation to the overlying beds of Potomac gravels.

and Severn formations; two in the Eocene period, named in order of deposition the Pamunkey and the Chesapeake; one in the Neocene period, known as the Lafayette formation; and one in the Pleistocene, named after the Federal District the Columbia formation.

The Potomac formation rests on the uneven surface of the gneissic rocks exposed in Rock creek valley, and is composed to a great extent of coarse sediment and fragmental rocks, brought down mainly by the great streams that drained the highland. The lower members of this formation are usually of very coarse materials, and in the Rock creek region they consist largely of pebbles and bowlders of quartz and quartzite, well rounded by water action. The Lafayette formation, resting on the upper surface of the Potomac series in this region, is not to any extent concerned in the present study, although in some sections of the Potomac valley the heavy bowlder deposits included in it were utilized by the aborigines.

Especially heavy accumulations of bowlders occur along that portion of the old shore-line bordering the exit of the ancient Potomac

river from the highland and its entry into the sea, now the District of
Columbia; and as the streams draining this shore-line after its elevation from the sea cut down through the sedimentary formations, these
bowlders were exposed, and are now found outcropping in the sides of
the valleys at the base of the sedimentaries and resting on the gneisses.
Other beds of bowlders are found higher in this section, but none
happen to be so well suited to the use of the primitive implement maker
as those representing the work of the waves along the crystalline
beach. The surface of the gneisses was somewhat uneven, sloping
gently beneath the waves, and the bowlder beds laid down on this surface are of uneven thickness and not of uniform character when followed out horizontally, coarseness decreasing with distance from the
river channel. The aboriginal inhabitant, seeking for stone suitable
for his use, discovered these outcrops of bowlders along the bluffs of
the Potomac and its tributaries, and soon ascertained that the deposits
were heavier and the quality of the material better and more uniform
in Rock creek valley than in any other section. This discovery led in
time to subterranean search on the more favorable sites and finally to
extensive quarrying, the evidences of which are now brought to light.

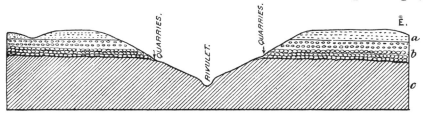

Fig. 2—Section of the ravine, showing formations and position of quarries.

Owing to the friable nature of the bowlder beds and of the gravels
and sands overlying them, the terrace slopes bordering the streams
(save where erosion had recently been particularly active) offered no
good exposures of the bowlders in place, but were covered with deposits, often many feet in thickness, of gravelly talus derived from the
crumbling edges of the strata. The bowlders contained in this overplaced deposit were the first to be utilized, and the work then extended
to the bowlder beds proper, and the refuse of the quarrying was added
to the creeping slope gravels or talus.

The section given in figure 2 shows the relation of the gneisses, the
bowlder beds, and the superficial deposits of sand and gravel outcropping in the quarry ravine.

PINY BRANCH QUARRIES

LOCATION OF THE QUARRIES

In passing out of the city by way of Fourteenth street extended, the
bridge over Piny branch of Rock creek is reached at a point 1⅓ miles

15 ETH——3

beyond the present city boundary, Florida avenue. Here we are already in the midst of the quarry-shop sites, and the rudely worked stones may be picked up on all sides.

The quarries occur about half way up the wooded slopes north and south of the branch, on both sides of Fourteenth street, but the refuse has descended to the stream beds and is found everywhere in the over-placed gravels of the lower levels. The most extensive evidences of ancient working occur on the northern side of the stream west of the road. Here the terrace is upward of 100 feet in height and its faces extremely steep. The map presented in plate II serves to indicate the distribution of quarries over an area of about half a mile square. The bluffs at this point are capped with about 40 feet of the Potomac formation, clays, sands, gravels, and bowlder beds, the Neocene deposits of the Lafayette formation which forms the higher levels of the region having disappeared from the outer promontories, or being but slightly represented by obscure remnants. Beneath the Potomac beds the gneisses are exposed (figures 1 and 2) and may be seen at several

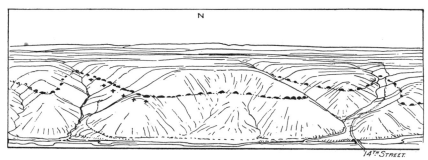

FIG. 3—Panoramic view of Piny branch quarry sites, looking north. The irregular dotted line indicates position of the quarries and the crosses mark the principal points of study.

points, especially about the bridge. They are more fully exposed farther down toward Rock creek, into which the branch flows half a mile below. The gneisses, as well as the Potomac beds resting on them, disintegrate and crumble on and near the surface through the action of various agencies, thus giving rather smooth though steep slopes on which the forest maintains itself with much uniformity. The surfaces are usually covered with a veneering of slope deposits composed of the disintegrated rocks and of vegetal mold, and this over-placed material abounds, up to the quarry level, in artificial débris. It was at first thought that this association of the worked stones with deposits of gravel might be of value as a means of determining the age or period of occupancy, but examination developed the fact that the gravel represented no definite period, its deposition extending from the present back indefinitely into the past.

In figure 3 a generalized view of the Piny branch quarry sites is depicted; it will give a comprehensive idea of the configuration of the locality. The view looks northward across the valley of the branch; a dotted line half way up the slopes separates the sedimentary and crystalline rocks, and in connection with it the quarry sites are indicated by dark figures. The sites examined by trenching are indicated by small crosses.

OPERATIONS ON THE SITE

DISCOVERY AND RECONNOISSANCE

So far as known the first discovery of worked stones on the site of our excavations at Piny branch was made about 1880 by Mr De Lancey W. Gill, of the United States Geological Survey, who was engaged in sketching on the bank of the stream and by chance observed a flaked stone in the gravel at his feet. Subsequently Mr Gill came upon a number of heaps of quarry-shop refuse in the second ravine west of Fourteenth street, at the point selected in 1889 for our trenching operations.

In September, 1889, I visited Mr Thomas Blagden, owner of the property, to obtain permission to work on the premises, and learned from him that about the year 1878 a street contractor had been permitted to collect material for paving from these bluffs, and that various piles of refuse found by us on the surface were gathered together at that time, a portion only of the material collected having been carried away. At that time a narrow roadway was cut leading from the creek up the little ravine to the site of our recent labors. Mr Blagden subsequently informed me that while a boy, some twenty-five years ago, he had observed the great quantities of bowlders at this point, and desiring to know something of the reasons for their accumulation, had secured help to dig a trench, which was abandoned, however, before the bed of bowlder refuse was fully penetrated. I have no doubt that the evidences of former excavation discovered at the fiftieth foot of our first trench, and which caused us no little perplexity at first, is thus fully accounted for.

In beginning the examination of this site the first step taken was a careful examination of its topographic features with especial reference to such eccentricities of contour as might be due to the agency of man. Extensive working over of surface deposits, especially if the pitting were deep, would leave inequalities of profile which, if not obliterated or obscured by natural agencies, would be easily recognized as artificial. Such inequalities were readily found; indeed, they are so well defined in places that even the inexpert observer could not fail to detect them. It was partly on account of peculiarities of profile that excavations were undertaken at the spot selected, and the results have shown that these surface indications were not deceptive.

Toward the upper end of the ravine the elevations and depressions resulting from the ancient quarry work are more pronounced. Either the disturbances here are more recent than below or else the leveling agencies of nature have been less active.

In selecting the position and course for a section through a series of deposits so extensive, and of which so little was known as to depth and mode and order of occurrence, there was considerable danger of missing the most instructive and vital spot. It seemed clear, however, that the section should cut the face of the slope from base to summit, and if necessary extend across the level surface of the spur and continue down the opposite side. This would in all probability reveal the true character of the art-bearing deposits; their relations to the geologic formations of the terrace, ancient and modern; the conditions of original deposition, and the effects of natural causes acting for an unknown period on distribution.

After looking over the ground carefully it was decided to go well up the ravine and rather beyond the apparent middle of the heavier deposits, so that other sections could be run if found necessary, or so that other investigators following should find a large portion of the area untouched. The sequel showed that a better selection could hardly have been made, and the results are so satisfactory, so far as the main points at issue in the investigation are concerned, as to make unnecessary the cutting of other complete sections.

The point selected for the beginning of the section was in the bed of the ravine, a few hundred feet from its junction with Piny branch, and where a line could be drawn from base to summit of the hill without serious embarrassment from the forest trees. This line crossed slightly to the left of the center of a gentle convexity in the profile of the lower half of the slope, thought to be due in a measure to deposits of artificial nature.

After a preliminary surface exploitation of the section, made to ascertain whether or not any considerable excavation would be necessary, a line was stretched on the surface of the ground, and to this numbered tags were fixed at intervals of one foot, to facilitate the accurate recording of data. To further serve the same purpose, a section of the hillside was drawn and divided into squares. For convenience of reference, this section was divided transversely into parts of 10 feet each. It was also arranged to make cross sections at intervals of 10 feet, representing the conditions exhibited in the front wall of the excavation; these were to be divided into square feet for record. This plan was substantially carried out, though modifications were made to suit various exigencies of the case. Sections were made at frequent intervals where increased interest demanded, all being scaled in the same manner. At every available point photographs of the vertical exposures were taken; and in connection with them detailed drawings were made recording character of soil and formations and manner of occurrence of relics.

Before describing the excavation, the conditions existing within the immediate channel of the rivulet at the base of the section may be sketched. The channel was about 6 feet deep and 10 feet wide at this point; the section across it, including both banks, is shown in figure 4. The slopes of the terrace rise from the steep banks of this inner channel at an angle of from 20 to 25 degrees through a vertical distance of 60 feet, giving a distance (measured on the slope) to the summit of about 160 feet on either side. This notch-like ravine is the result of a long period of erosion, which possibly extends far back into early Cenozoic or even Mesozoic time. It had much its present outline, and no doubt a greater part of its present depth, before man made his appearance in the region.

The area drained through this ravine is quite restricted, and, if wholly wooded, the work of erosion would be extremely slow, the refuse descending from the opposite sides so freely as to clog the channel, save at the time of great freshets. The clearing of the fields at the head of the basin has, in recent times, given some additional power to the floods, and the channel is now not only quite clear, but bears evi-

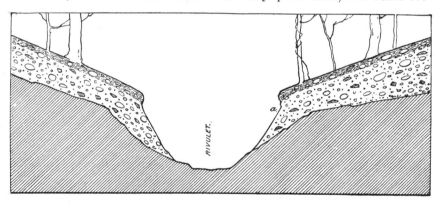

Fig. 4—Section across bed of rivulet at base of quarries.

dence of considerable recent deepening. The gneisses are exposed on the bottom and in the sides of the channel at the point crossed by our section, save where covered by the half-compacted art-bearing talus. The latter deposit is in places as much as 8 or 10 feet deep, and contains innumerable relics from the great shops along the slopes above on the right and left. An excellent illustration of the appearance of the art-bearing débris, from a photograph taken at a point about 30 feet below the initial point of the section, is given in plate III. Partially shaped implements and broken fragments project from the bank in great numbers. The exposure here is 8 feet in depth, but the deposits do not extend far into the bank, forming only a veil over the irregular surface of the gneiss. The latter is exposed beneath the left foot of the standing figure and slopes back from the rivulet bed at a lower angle than does the bank, as shown in the section, figure 4.

A general view of the ravine looking up from the beginning of the section is given in plate IV, and will serve to convey a clear impression

QUARRY-SHOP REFUSE EXPOSED IN THE BANK OF THE RIVULET

The gneiss appears in the bed of the stream beneath the left foot of the figure

VIEW LOOKING NORTH UP THE RIVULET AT THE FOOT OF THE QUARRY SLOPE

The left hand of the figure is placed to indicate the beginning of the first trench

of the scenic characteristics of this retired and charming spot soon to be overwhelmed by the growing city. The left hand of the standing figure rests on the spot at which the excavation in the bank began; here the art-bearing talus deposit covered the gneiss with a veneering hardly more than a foot thick; its character and contents are shown in figure 5. This is the first of the series of crosscuts or transverse sections, and represents the front wall of the excavation within a foot of the beginning of the trench. Partially shaped implements and artificial refuse, which may have come from any part of the slopes above, occur throughout the deposits at this point. Near the surface a leaf-shape blade of ordinary type was found, and at 15 inches in depth three others, more or less perfect, together with typical turtle-backs, were encountered.

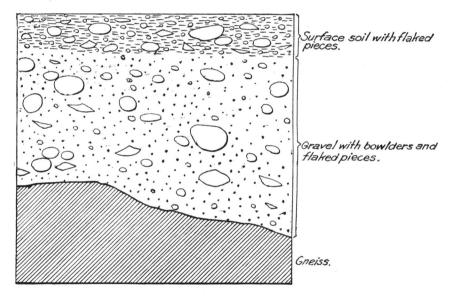

FIG. 5—Cross section at beginning of the first trench.

The exploitation pits (plate V), intended to determine something of the probable nature and extent of the work to be undertaken, were dug along the line of proposed excavation from the starting point in the ravine to the top of the terrace. It was observed that in the lower half the profile of the slope was convex, and that in the upper it was slightly concave. The convexity of the lower part, from the first figure leaning against the young tree to 20 feet beyond the third figure, is due to accumulations of refuse along the lower margin of the quarries, while the depression above (beyond the limit of the picture) is due to the pits left along the quarry face when the site was abandoned.

Continuing the excavation beyond the point at which the first cross section (figure 5) was taken, the art-bearing deposits became quite shallow. The dark mold of the surface was about 4 inches deep, and between the first and tenth foot of the section yielded numerous flaked stones and many artificial fragments and flakes; beneath this and resting on the uneven surface of the gneiss was a foot or more of quite compact gravelly clay, containing a few pebbles and occasionally a small bowlder; at the base the deposit contained much mica, derived from the decaying gneiss on which it rests. In this lower gravel there were no traces of art. Up to the twentieth foot these conditions remained practically unchanged. It will be seen, however, by reference to the longitudinal section (plate VI), that the surface of the gneiss rises less rapidly than the surface of the slope, and that the talus gravels increase in thickness to 3 feet. These pass down into a layer of pink and white clay, which rests on the gneiss. Worked specimens were found as before in the top soil, and artificially broken bowlders occurred in the gravel a foot deep. In the lower part of the dark soil a small pocket or cluster of chips was found, and between the tenth and twentieth foot several chipped stones in various stages of elaboration were unearthed. The cross section at the twentieth foot is shown in figure 6. Throughout the gravel occa-

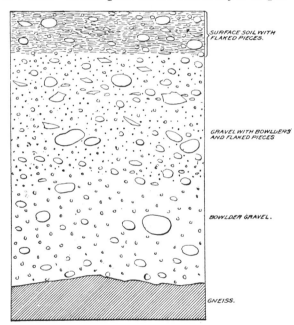

SURFACE SOIL WITH FLAKED PIECES.

GRAVEL WITH BOWLDERS AND FLAKED PIECES

BOWLDER GRAVEL.

GNEISS.

FIG. 6—Cross section at the twentieth foot.

sional bowlders were found, some reaching 6 inches in diameter. From the twentieth to near the twentyfifth foot the conditions and the contents of the section showed no important change. The dark soil reached a thickness of 8 inches, and was underlain by a bed of light sandy subsoil, not before differentiated, about a foot thick. Many partially shaped stones were found in these beds. Beneath this again were gravels and gravelly clays.

At about the twentyfifth foot the conditions of the deposits were observed to change. The limit of the compact gravels and clays forming the base of the deposit was reached, and a mass of rather loose heterogeneous material was encountered. The edge of an ancient excavation had been reached, though this fact was not at first appre-

VIEW FROM THE BED OF THE RIVULET, SHOWING EXPLOITATION PITS

The first figure is at the beginning of the trench, and the third figure is at about the fortieth foot

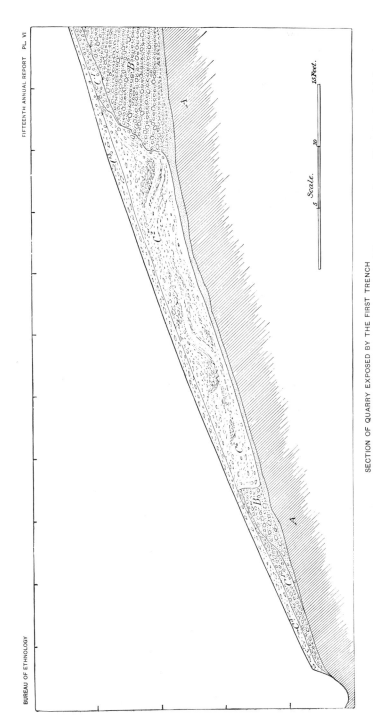

SECTION OF QUARRY EXPOSED BY THE FIRST TRENCH

a, Mica schists; *b*, Potomac (Mesozoic) bowlder beds; *c¹*, Preartificial slope gravels; *c²*, Deposits of shop refuse, showing traces of pits; *c³*, Materials rearranged by natural forces since the period of quarrying

ciated; for the idea of aboriginal quarrying had not yet been more than suggested, and the changes observed in the deposits were at first attributed to natural distributing agencies. In the light of facts subsequently observed, this body of heterogeneous material came to be recognized as part of the débris accumulated in an ancient trench, which was cut obliquely by our trench. The ancient trenching had been 4 or 5 feet deep at this point, and the side wall was quite broken and irregular, sloping at a low angle in some places and in others being vertical or even undercut. The digging had not penetrated to the gneiss surface at this point. The margin of the old trench is seen at *b*, plate VI. From this point (the twentyfifth foot) the work of excavation was carried through the quarry refuse and little by little many novel and striking features were brought to light, until at the eightythird foot the upper quarry face was reached.

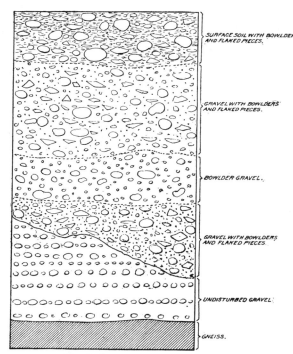

FIG. 7—Cross section at the fortieth foot.

Near the lower margin of the ancient digging a small percentage of artificial material was encountered, but before the thirtyfifth foot was reached the heterogeneous nature of the deposits began to be apparent. It became clear that nearly the entire mass from the surface of the ground to the gneiss floor, a thickness of from 6 to 12 feet, had been worked over by the primitive quarrymen. There was abundant evidence of the nature of the operations carried on both in securing and in working up the bowlders.

The cross section exposed in the front wall at the fortieth foot is given in figure 7. As might be expected in the refuse heaps of such a quarry there was little regularity and slight continuity in the deposits, so that the section exposed along the left wall of our excavation seldom corresponded closely with that along the right. The running section given in plate VI is not literal, but is drawn to express in a somewhat generalized way the conditions observed.

Between the fortieth and the fortyeighth foot the trench crossed, at about 3 feet from the surface, what had been a pit or transverse trench with sloping sides, between 2 and 3 feet deep. This had been filled with material previously worked over and containing much shop refuse. The character and relations of the deposits are well shown in the sections and photographs presented herewith.

The upper figure in plate VII represents a detailed study of the contents of the ancient pit as seen in the left wall of the excavation. Of this interesting exposure it was impracticable to obtain photographs, since the cutting was too narrow to permit the use of the camera; but the drawing was carefully made, and being supplemented by photographs of the face of the cutting at the fortieth and also at the fortyfourth foot, serves to assist in giving a satisfactory idea of the leading characteristics of the deposits. The bottom of the depression had been somewhat uneven when the filling-in began. The material, most of which consisted of fractured or partially flaked bowlders, had accumulated rapidly, and for a depth of 3 or 4 feet contained only a very small percentage of sand, clay, and gravel. Scattered over the bottom and sides was a layer of light, coarse sand which had descended from above and partially filled in the spaces between the bowlders and fragments; and throughout the mass, where the interspaces were filled at all, it was chiefly by coarse sand, small pebbles, and the flakes from the manufacture of implements.

A very decided bedding of these coarse materials was apparent, its curves following and repeating those of the bottom of the depression, but diminishing toward the surface. In the stratum of finer material overlying the coarser contents of the pit and in the dark loam of the surface there was also a slight sagging and thickening, indicating that the obliteration of the pit had been but recently accomplished.

It was observed that the distribution of the filling materials was unequal, the coarser gravel and larger bowlders being lodged at the left in the section, which was the lower side of the ancient pit (*a*, plate VII). This was to be expected, for the source of supply of filling débris was from above, and as the tool maker worked over the material upon the slope the heavier pieces rolled down until stopped by irregularities of the surface. It was also noticed that the percentage of flakes and failures was greatest at the left side of the depression from the fortyfirst to the fortysixth foot, where the flakers, it would appear, must have occupied the pit margins.

That the work was done on this spot, and that little subsequent distribution has taken place, is clearly seen, as the failures and broken tools often lie together with the flakes struck from them. It is safe to conclude also that the accumulation was rapid. The accumulation of the finer and more compact bed overlying the contents of the pit was probably slower and was no doubt due partially to natural slope agencies, though it contains a large percentage of worked material; the darker

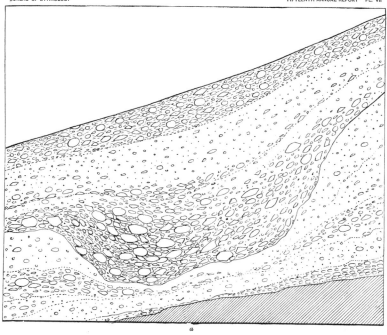

a

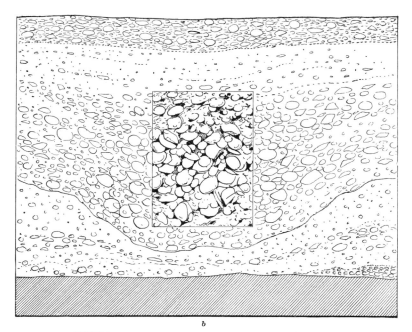

b

SECTION OF ANCIENT PIT FILLED WITH QUARRY-SHOP REFUSE FROM ABOVE

The rectangle elaborated in the lower figure indicates approximately the area included in the photograph reproduced in plate VIII

CHARACTER OF QUARRY-SHOP REFUSE AT THE FORTYFOURTH FOOT

The bowlders have nearly all been broken and many pieces are partly shaped

soil of the surface was filled with shop refuse, most of which has not
been far removed from the spot of manufacture. The cross sections are
too limited in extent to show clearly the bedding of the accumulations,
but they serve to illustrate the nature of the contents of the pits.

The conditions at the fortyfourth foot are given in (*b*) plate VII. By
carrying the excavation to the right and left the outlines of the old
depressions were found to be irregular and extended so far that I did
not undertake to define them fully. It appeared, however, that our
section had cut the deepest part of this particular depression. A photograph covering the rectangular space outlined by a dotted line in the
section is reproduced in plate VIII. I am fortunate in being able to
present such an illustration of the composition of the refuse at this
point, as it affords evidence that can not be gainsaid, and the student
may study the nature, conditions, and relations of the component parts
with ease. The picture covers a space about 2 feet wide by 3 high,
the top being 2½ feet below the surface of the ground and the bottom
within a few inches of the deepest part of the ancient excavation. The
unusual number of large bowlders is a notable feature, but it will be
found that the broken and worked ones far outnumber the unbroken,
and that several partially shaped tools are in sight, occupying positions
no doubt very much the same as when dropped by the workman. A
turtleback appears near the base beneath the large split bowlder; others
are seen to the left and a little higher, while numbers are seen to be
dropping out of the loose, open mass of refuse near the middle of the
picture. The section abounds throughout with artificial material.

After passing the fiftieth foot the deposits exhibited the usual phenomena, and no features of exceptional interest were encountered until
the seventieth foot was reached. The bottom of the old pits continued
at about the same level, so that the artificial deposits became gradually
deeper as we advanced. Occasionally small masses of the Potomac
gravel (small bowlders and pebbles held together by an indurated sand
matrix) were encountered, indicating the proximity of the ancient
quarry face. The pitting had been carried down almost to the gneiss
floor, which was here nearly level, being covered with a bed of sharp
yellow sand from an inch to a foot thick. It was afterward ascertained that this layer of sand formed a part of the original Potomac
deposits and separated the gneisses from the beds of bowlders above,
as shown in the section. The artificial deposits, about 7 feet deep at
the sixtieth foot, deepened to 10 or 11 feet at the quarry face 20 feet
farther on.

Between the fiftieth foot and the sixtieth the refuse was distributed
in alternating beds of gravelly earth and shop deposits, as shown in
the general section. These beds constituted the refuse derived from
extensive operations along the quarry face. After passing the seventieth foot the layers of refuse were inclined toward the quarry face, as
indicated in the section.

The quarry face (plate XIII) was encountered at about the eightieth foot, but sloped back in steps to the ninetieth foot and beyond. It showed a stratum, 10 feet or more in thickness, consisting largely of medium size quartzite bowlders embedded in a matrix of nearly pure sand, so indurated that the bowlders were extremely difficult to remove, and considerable masses of the conglomerate could be knocked down and removed without breaking up. The face was extremely irregular, indicating that when deserted the ancient quarrymen had penetrated to greatly varying depths; they had descended to the gneiss surface in excavations from 10 to 12 feet deep, had removed the bowlders by direct attack from above, from the front, and by undermining, and had selected and thrown out those best suited to the purpose of the flaker. Few of those left in the pits and dump had been more than tested by the removal of a flake or two. The work of shaping was in the main carried on about the margins of the pits out of the way of the quarryman. The earth, gravel, and undesirable bowlders were thrown back against the lower side of the pits, lodging in irregular beds sloping into the pits, as shown in the section.

Between the seventythird foot and the seventyeighth our trench passed through large pockets or masses of shop refuse. The largest body, consisting of tons of chips, failures, and broken bowlders, was confined to a space extending from 3 to 7 feet from the surface; smaller pockets of the same character were found as deep as 9 feet. The exposure in the sides and front of our trench showed these deposits clearly, and illustrations are selected from the fine series of photographs taken. Plate IX represents nearly the full height of the front of our trench at the seventyseventh foot, and plates X and XI illustrate the composition of the refuse in detail, showing a preponderance of rather large bowlders, most of which have been partially worked or broken to test the material. The portion shown in plate XI belongs lower in the section, extending down from the seventh nearly to the ninth foot in depth. Several shaped pieces are in sight. In plate XII we have a fine illustration of the clusters of shop refuse at about the eightieth foot. The clinging wet earth obscures many of the fine flakes, but enough is seen to indicate the very great amount of work done on this spot. The mass was made up of unshaped refuse and of shaped specimens, illustrating the whole range of quarry-shop work from the first flake to the rude thin blade; the latter, it was gradually learned, being the almost exclusive product of the flaking operations. A section showing the quarry pit and the face of Potomac bowlders is presented in plate XIII. This terraced face, receding in irregular steps, appears to have undergone little change since it was deserted by the prehistoric quarrymen. The bowlders are compactly bedded and retain their places with great tenacity.

The deepest work of which evidence was discovered was about 11 feet beneath the present surface. It is probable that when deserted the pit at the quarry face was much deeper, as considerable degra-

FACE OF THE TRENCH AT THE SEVENTYSEVENTH FOOT, SHOWING POCKETS OF
ARTIFICIAL REFUSE

CHARACTER OF REFUSE DEPOSITS AT THE SEVENTYSEVENTH FOOT AND FROM TWO TO FOUR FEET BENEATH THE SURFACE

POCKET OF REFUSE DEPOSITS AT THE SEVENTYSEVENTH FOOT AND FROM FIVE TO NINE FEET BENEATH THE SURFACE

PORTION OF AN EXTENSIVE DEPOSIT OF SHOP REFUSE NEAR THE QUARRY FACE

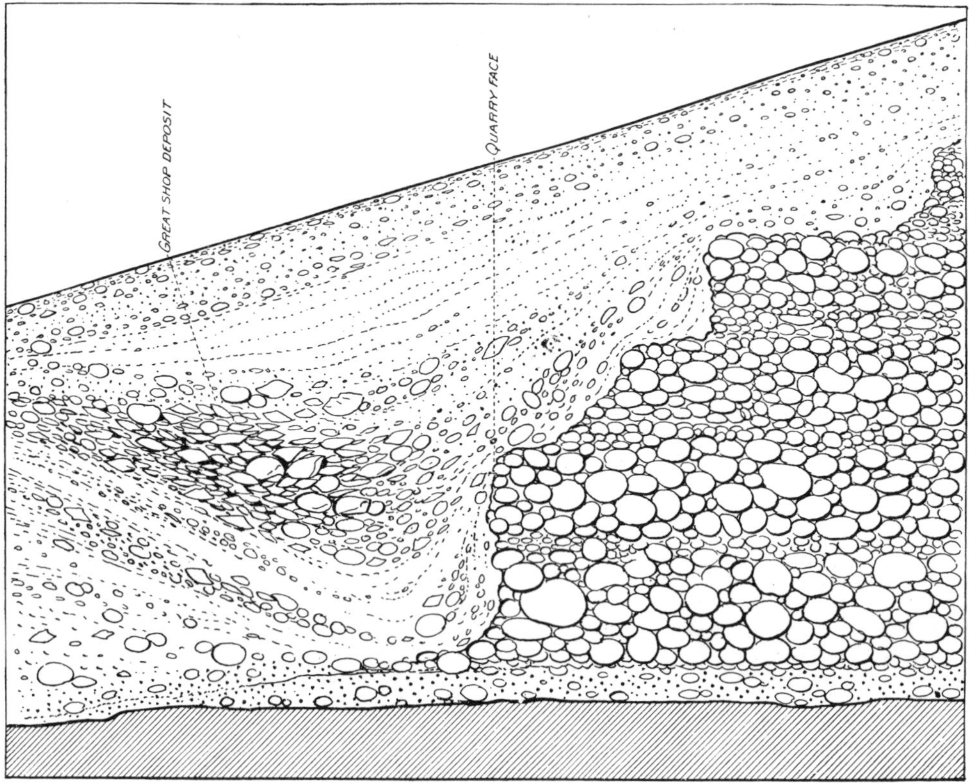

QUARRY FACE

GREAT SHOP DEPOSIT

SECTION SHOWING THE IRREGULAR QUARRY FACE, THE BOWLDER BEDS AT THE RIGHT AND A DEPOSIT OF SHOP REFUSE AT THE LEFT

ROOTS OF A CHESTNUT TREE GROWING IN A BED OF SHOP REFUSE SEVEN FEET DEEP.
Few pieces have not been broken or shaped by the hammer, and numerous thick leaf shape forms are in sight

dation of the slope must have taken place since the desertion of the quarries.   In another trench farther up the ravine the quarry face was exposed to a depth of from 12 to 15 feet.

Plate CIII and the frontispiece, described in the supplement, serve to illustrate the probable conditions under which the work was carried on by the savage quarrymen.   The miner with a strong wooden pike is seen dislodging bowlders from the bed; a second workman is breaking up a large mass of quartzite, and the flaker engaged in roughing-out the blades is seated near at hand.   The life-size group from which these views were taken was prepared under the writer's direction for the World's Fair, in Chicago.   The figures were modeled by U. S. J. Dunbar, sculptor, and were costumed after drawings published in the works of Hariot and John Smith, the assumption being that this work on Piny branch was done by the Algonquian tribes known to the colonists of Jamestown and Roanoke.   However this may be, the work of procuring and working the bowlders is, I am convinced, correctly indicated by this group.

The quarry was about 60 feet wide where crossed by our trench, and was 3 or 4 feet deep at the lower margin and 11 feet deep at the quarry face.   The bowlders, forming a large part of the mass worked over, had nearly all been tested for flakability by the removal of a flake or two, or had been more or less fully worked.   All of the material removed from the trench was carefully assorted and studied by us, and the important results reached through its consideration will be given further on.

If we allow that the ancient operations were somewhat uniform in extent along the terrace face, say for a distance of 500 feet, the material worked over on this side of the ravine would amount to 100,000 cubic feet or more, and the number of bowlders secured and worked or partly shaped would reach millions.

THE TREE PIT

Lateral excavations from the first trench were made wherever the appearance of the refuse encouraged it, but the deposits did not vary in any important respect.   About 10 feet north of this trench, opposite the sixtieth foot, stands a chestnut tree some 3 feet in diameter and rather massive at the base.   For the purpose of determining the relation of this tree to the artificial deposits, an excavation was made uncovering nearly one-half of the roots to the depth of about 7 feet.   The main root penetrated the refuse and passed through the undisturbed gravel and into the decayed gneiss beneath.   The roots had made their way through the deposit of compact quartzite fragments, inclosing many of them almost completely (plate XIV) and assuming irregular distorted forms imposed by the angular stones.   As a matter of course, the tree postdates the quarry period, as do other trees much older.   In one of the ravines near Fourteenth street a white oak, at least 200 years old, grows in the same manner in a mass of shop refuse.

The refuse about the roots of the chestnut tree contained more than the usual percentage of partially shaped tools, and several bushels of these, showing rude leaf-shape outlines, were collected. A photograph made shortly after beginning the excavation shows the inclosure of worked stones in the base of the tree and their prevalence in the mass of refuse (plate XIV).

THE SECOND TRENCH

A second trench carried across the old quarry in the spring of 1890 failed to furnish features of especial interest and added little to the fund of information acquired from the trench made the previous year. It was not expected, however, that this second excavation would expose extensive deposits of refuse or well marked quarrying. The site was chosen in a depression, or incipient gulch in the slope, where no marks of disturbance could be detected, whereas the first trench was carried across a convexity in the face of the hill, which convexity bore every indication of being the result of artificial disturbance and accumulation. Having determined that surface appearances in the first case really indicated the conditions beneath the surface, the second trench was made where no indications of artificial disturbance could be noted. This trench was 100 feet north of the first. No well-defined shop sites were discovered, and evidences of ancient quarrying were quite meager. Artificial refuse was evenly distributed throughout the overplaced gravels to a depth of about 3 feet. These conditions would seem to indicate that the shallow depression in which the trench was dug had been filled from shops and quarries at the right and left, or perhaps from random working at higher points on the slope.

Excavation was begun in the rivulet bank, here about 6 feet high. The immediate bank was found to consist of a mass of refuse, well filled with broken bowlders and rejects and chips which exhibited a sort of rude bedding as if rearranged by the action of the rivulet or as if deposited on its successive though very narrow flood plains. Our trenching soon passed through these deposits. The gneiss which formed the bed of the stream rose rapidly beneath the loose mass forming the bank, and at 10 feet from the stream approached within 3 feet of the surface. From the tenth to the thirtieth foot the gneissic surface followed the slope of the hill at a pretty uniform depth of 3 feet; beyond this it passed horizontally beneath deposits of Potomac bowlders. Overplaced gravels from the tenth foot to the end of our trench contained but few artificial objects, and these did not occur at a greater depth than about 3 feet. These gravels for the most part were made up of a heterogeneous mixture of clay, sand, and pebbles, with occasional bowlders. Near the bottom they consisted principally of material derived directly from the disintegrating surface of the Potomac bowlder beds.

THE THIRD TRENCH

The site for a third trench was chosen with the view of securing evidence on two questions of especial interest. The first was the question of the relation of the ancient quarrying to the present bed of the rivulet; the second related to the significance of a series of depressions observed along the upper part of the slope a little above the quarry level (as determined at other points) and immediately below the upper margin of the terrace slope. The place selected was about 200 feet farther up the gulch than the second trench, and where the length of the slope was only 80 feet and the height about 40 feet. At this point the Potomac bowlder bed outcrops at or but little above the level of the stream bed, and it was thought that evidence of ancient excavation might be found so near the present bottom of the gulch as to indicate the comparative recentness of the work. Observations on this point are given in detail further on.

As to the other question, it was surmised that the depressions along the upper part of the slope marked the sites of ancient pits, and investigation showed that this surmise was not far wrong. The depressions are in all cases a little higher up than the old pits and above the bowlder bed level, and are apparently the result of miniature landslides, by means of which the original quarry pits were filled up.

The phenomena disclosed in this trench are quite interesting and may be given in some detail. Entering the bank on the level of the stream bed, we followed the surface of the gneiss for a number of feet. Within the first 10 feet patches of undisturbed Potomac bowlder gravel remained on the gneiss surface. At about the twentieth foot the bowlder bed began to thicken, and its upper surface rose with the slope of the talus. The bank of the rivulet was between 4 and 5 feet in height, and was composed of loose heterogeneous refuse, which, as the excavation advanced, was found to be rudely bedded with the slope as indicated in the section (plate xv). The loose refuse was from 5 to 7 feet deep, and rested on the gneiss or the uneven surface of the bowlder bed. Broken cobbles, rude rejects, broken embryo implements, and chips were pretty evenly distributed throughout the mass. At the twentyseventh foot the floor of the quarry made an abrupt descent of 3 or 4 feet.

In advancing beyond the twentyseventh foot the bottom of the ancient quarry rose but slightly, and at the fortieth foot it was 10 feet beneath the surface. The deeper parts were filled with loose material—clay, gravel, and bowlders—intermingled with which were a number of fragments including chips and broken, unfinished tools, but there was not here or in the vicinity any very decided evidence of chipping on the spot. The lowest point of this ancient pit was only 2 feet above the present bed of the gulch at the nearest point.

Between the thirtieth and the fortieth foot no features of particular interest were encountered. As shown in the longitudinal section, a number of pockets of shop refuse occurred between the twentyeighth foot and the thirtyfifth. These may have been shop sites, but had more the character of refuse descended from above into depressions or pits. The mass of material about these pockets and beyond, up to the fortyfifth foot, was comparatively barren of artificial refuse. The middle parts of the mass of filled-in material, as indicated in the section, is quite homogeneous, as if never worked over by man, and must have descended into the quarry pit en masse as a miniature landslide from above. It consists of loose, crumbling, sandy clay of reddish color—a characteristic of the higher-level beds—containing some gravel and occasional bowlders. Rather high up in the sides of the trench could be seen indications of old overplaced débris containing shop refuse and coarse materials, all of grayish color. Near the surface the overplaced gravel was again reddish and barren of art.

In approaching the fiftieth foot, pockets of shop refuse began to appear, and at from 4 to 6 feet deep and beyond the fiftysixth foot characteristic quarry-shop phenomena were encountered. Beds of clay and refuse of varying colors were seen dipping into the hill as the quarry face was approached. Nature distributes her materials with the slope, but art reverses this; as the earth is thrown out of a quarry pit it forms layers con-

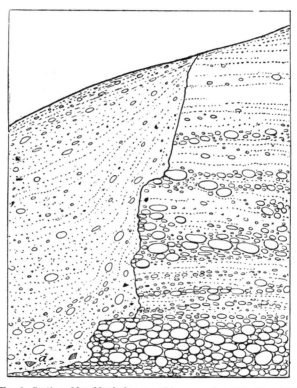

FIG. 8—Section of bowlder beds exposed in quarry face 13 feet in height.

forming roughly to the slope into the pit. The section exposed in this trench is given in plate xv.

At the fiftyseventh foot a descent of 2 feet was made into a deeper portion of the ancient quarry as shown in the section. At the sixtieth foot the bottom of the old quarry was 13 feet beneath the present surface, and at about the sixtythird foot the quarry face was encountered. When this was uncovered to the full width of our trench, the section shown in figure 8 was disclosed. Beginning at the top there were about 3 feet of overplaced slope material, dark above from the presence of vegetal mold and composed of sandy clay below; beneath this were

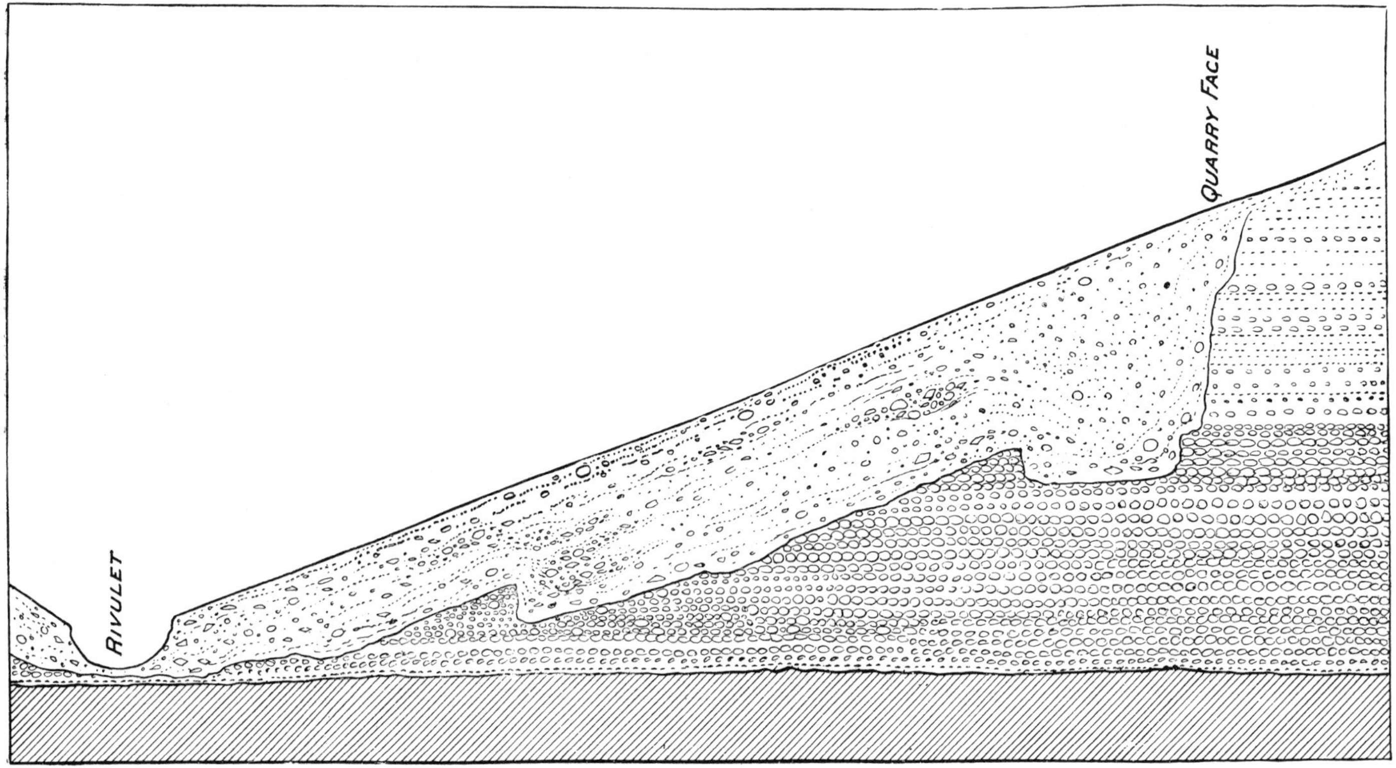

QUARRY FACE

RIVULET

SECTION SHOWING DEPOSITS FILLING THE QUARRY EXPOSED BY THE THIRD TRENCH.   QUARRY FACE 13 FEET IN HEIGHT

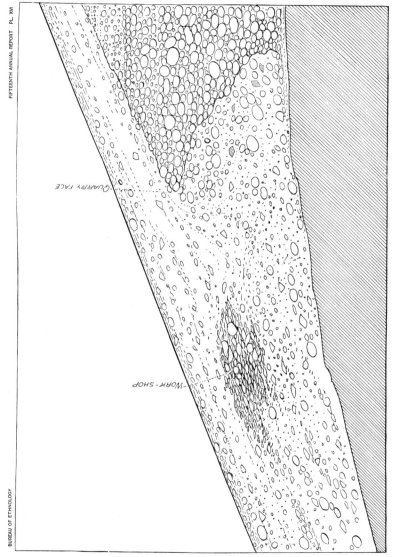

QUARRY FACE

WORK-SHOP

SECTION SHOWING THE QUARRY FACE EXPOSED BY THE FIFTH TRENCH

Bowlder bed undercut by ancient quarrymen at the right and stop-refuse deposit at the left

the Potomac beds in place, comprising, first, about 3 feet of coarse loose-bedded sands of varied kinds, then alternating layers of sand, gravel, and bowlders, and at the base a compact layer of bowlders. The ancient workmen had penetrated this latter bed at this point only to the depth of a foot or two. On the bottom and against the quarry face were a few chips and chipped bowlders, but the mass of material filling up the ancient excavation was barren of art and consisted of a mixture of clay with sand and gravel, derived from the margins of the ancient pit chiefly by sliding from the overhanging front wall. This wall or quarry face as uncovered by us was only 12 or 13 feet high, but when the ancient miners deserted the spot it must have been very much higher, probably 20 feet if the period was recent and perhaps more if the time was remote. As already stated, the configuration of the slope showed that a slide had taken place, leaving a hollow just under the crest of the slope and giving a rounded mass on the site of the ancient digging. Beneath the highest part of this mass our trench disclosed the deepest point reached by the aborigines. The filling up by sliding en masse was thus shown by the surface configuration of the site as well as by the character of the filling material.

It appears that the bottom or floor of the ancient quarry was quite uneven, but its full conformation could not be made out from the disclosures of a trench 3 feet wide. In examining the sides of our trench in the vicinity of the ancient quarry face I discovered that our left wall had for several feet coincided here and there with the steep side wall of the ancient excavation.

The digging of this trench amply repaid the labor expended, as answers were obtained to a number of the questions presenting themselves. It was found, first, that the ancient quarrying was carried on at a level only 2 or 3 feet above the present bed of the rivulet, and second, that the trenches had been filled by sliding masses in such manner as to produce inequalities of the surface not yet effaced. In addition, the conclusions reached by a study of the other trenches were confirmed: 1, that there were well-defined quarries with quarry faces of considerable vertical extent in the Potomac bowlder deposits; 2, that little shaping was done in the deeper pits save that required in testing the quality of the stone; 3, that the only work in the shops about the excavations consisted in the roughing-out of leaf-shape blades; 4, that the ancient diggings were extremely irregular, much labor having been expended in exploitation and in reaching the heavier deposits of workable bowlders; and, 5, that undermining was by no means the exclusive method of reaching and securing the bowlders.

Study of this trench afforded a remarkable instance of the confusion possible in the association of works of art with gravel bluffs where workable stone was sought. Had the cutting for a roadway or other modern improvement been made along the side of this gorge the exposures in the walls would have shown "implements" embedded under unaltered gravels at a depth of 13 feet (*a*, figure 8), and it is thus seen that in such a cutting the detection of the true conditions might be next to impossible without careful and extensive excavation.

A number of trenches were opened about the southwestern point of the promontory as indicated on the map. It was expected that these would throw light on various peculiar features of the topography, and also add to the information regarding quarrying and manufacture. The results are all that could be desired.

The fourth trench was opened on the rounded point of the promontory 300 feet south of the first trench, while the fifth was made a little farther around toward the east. The phenomena observed in these trenches were so nearly identical that I shall omit detailed mention save of the latter and more interesting.

The fifth trench furnished much of the evidence necessary to complete the story of the ancient quarries. The general conditions were uniform with those revealed in the first trench. At the thirtyfifth foot a pocket of shop refuse of unusual interest was encountered. As exposed by the trench (plate XVI) it was 4 or 5 feet in horizontal extent and perhaps 3 feet deep, and its upper surface was 2 or 3 feet beneath the surface of the ground. No part of the quarries, 30 feet across (measured on the slope) and from 6 to 9 feet deep, was entirely free from flakes and flaked stones, but the work of shaping had been carried on most extensively on this one spot. From the deposit upward of 40 blades, broken near the finishing stage, were recovered, though the search made was by no means exhaustive; fully one-fourth of the shaped pieces remained in the excavated débris. This pocket of refuse was not essentially different in any of its features from those encountered in the first trench, but it had somewhat more the appearance of a trimming or finishing shop than any yet seen. There were few large or rude pieces and the flakes averaged small; still no traces were found of specialized shapes, or even of well-trimmed edges or points. The highest form made was a roughed-out blade such as a majority of those found in caches.

The most interesting feature of this trench was its quarry face, which was encountered at about the fortieth foot. It was discovered that extensive undercutting had been done by the ancient quarrymen, and, as we advanced, the overhanging face was found to extend forward several feet, as shown in plate XVI. The phenomena of this quarry face are instructive in one important direction. They reveal, with more than usual clearness, a favorite method of the ancient quarrymen. The massive bowlder bed all around this promontory had been deposited on the gneiss. Entering the face of the bluff on the surface of this rock, rendered friable by decay, the overplaced stratum of compacted bowlders and sand was undermined, so that the quarrying of the bowlders became a comparatively easy matter. They were easily loosened and fell into the hand of the workman from the matrix of compacted sand, as clean and fresh in color as when deposited by the sea in Mesozoic times. By thus working on the gneiss surface, antler picks or wooden stakes sharpened by fire would serve to perform the work of undermining and knocking down, whereas our men found it a difficult task to penetrate the closely compacted conglomerate from its upper surface or from the front, even with the aid of steel picks.

THE SIXTH TRENCH

The examination of the third trench made it clear that in certain cases the ancient pits had been filled, or partially filled, by the sliding of sand and gravel from the quarry wall and from the bluff above. This fact led to the opinion that some of the unique features of conformation observed about the outer point of the terrace were, in a measure at least, due to slides brought about by quarrying operations. To one familiar with the ancient quarrying in this locality, the concavity on the horizon of the bowlder outcrop and the convexity of profile just below, as seen in the sections, would at once be attributed to human agency. In this case, however, the deformation is on such a scale that natural agencies could alone have accomplished the result.

On the southwestern angle of the spur, and at a level about 60 feet below the crest, there is a roundish hump or shoulder 100 feet or more across and rising perhaps 15 feet above what would seem to be a normal profile. This occurs just beneath the level of the bowlder outcrop, and thus has the appearance of a great dump heap to the quarries.

The character of the rocks forming the bluff is such that they disintegrate very gradually, and with ordinary activity of the erosive forces a slope of sufficient declivity to invite landslides would not occur. The question arose as to whether extensive quarrying on the face of the bowlder bed and the consequent undermining of the superposed beds of gravels and sands, here some 40 feet in thickness, might have brought about the sliding of a mass from above sufficient to produce the hump observed. The only possible means of arriving at a satisfactory solution of the question was by trenching. A series of excavations was made covering the profile of the spur from near the summit to the outer base of the convexity that gave rise to the inquiry. The section shown in figure 9 serves to indicate the position of these pits as well as the nature of the profile. The light portions represent the excavations made, and the dotted line at the top indicates the position of the mass supposed to have descended to form the hump. The results of the pitting may briefly be given: The pit at a was in shop refuse similar to that usually found in the quarry dumps higher up. The pit b was carried 13 feet deep through a mass of sand and gravel more or less disturbed, but apparently not by human agency. The material corresponded closely to that of the beds above the quarry level. Near the base, at 12 feet deep, numerous quartzite chips and fragments evidently of artificial origin were found. Analogous conditions were observed in pit *c*. Pit *d* on the quarry level passed through thin slope gravels, containing some artificial material, into the normal bowlder beds. Pit *e* disclosed the sands and gravel of the upper slopes.

Although the observations were not so complete as could be desired, the evidence secured supports the theory that sliding took place as a result of the quarrying operations, and that the protuberance on the slope below represents the transported mass. The presence of shop refuse in the lower pit, the occurrence of artificial flakes near the bottom of the mass of sand and gravel forming the hump, the absence of normal dump heaps and of quarry excavations along the bowlder outcrop above, all tend to confirm this conclusion. The movement of a large mass from the upper wall of the quarries would obliterate the quarries and carry the quarry refuse down in front of it to the position of pit *a*. These evidences, taken together with the apparently abnormal conformation of the spur, seem to be sufficient warrant for the conclusion reached.

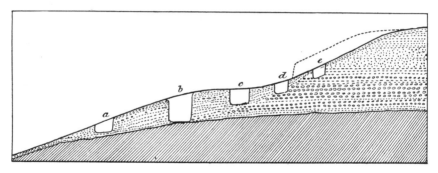

FIG. 9—Section exposed by trenching on outer angle of terrace. Flaked stones were found in pits *b* and *c* near the surface and near the bottom only.

OTHER PINY BRANCH SITES

East of the point just described the broad end of the terrace spur facing Piny branch is very steep, and few traces of quarry or shop work are to be seen; but lower down the slope, near the base, are masses of material that must have descended by sliding and creeping. Shop refuse is distributed through these masses and is found in the floodplain of the creek at the base. By stream action the flaked stones and refuse of flaking have been scattered through the recent floodplains of the whole valley below. On the eastern point or corner of the spur overlooking the Fourteenth street bridge over Piny branch there are numerous indications of ancient pitting on the bowlder-bed level, and shop refuse is plentiful. Following this level around the slopes of the ravines just west of Fourteenth street and across to the eastern side, the same phenomena are observed. The slopes of the bluff west of that in which the first trenching was done also bear evidence of having been extensively worked, and all around the bluffs as we approach Rock creek valley proper, rising gradually to the crests of the terrace spurs, flaked stones are found.

On the southern side of the branch quarries occur both east and west of Fourteenth street at nearly the same level. Much work was done near a spring at a point beneath the "house in the tree" and opposite Spring road, which extends eastward from Fourteenth street.

East of Fourteenth street the only quarry of importance is on the place of Mr W. J. Rhees. This is on Spring road, a few hundred yards from Fourteenth street, as indicated on the map. It is probable that in this vicinity many evidences of ancient quarrying have been destroyed by building, cultivation, and landscape gardening. In this direction the bowlder beds, dipping gently eastward, descended beyond the reach of primitive quarrymen.

PINY BRANCH SHOPS

GENERAL FEATURES

As indicated in describing the quarry phenomena, shops in which the bowlders were flaked were established at convenient points about the pits, and the piles or clusters of flakes, failures, and fragments are very numerous. The undisturbed clusters are often lenticular in form as originally accumulated, and occur within the body of the refuse just as they were covered by quarry refuse in the progress of the work. Some of those exposed by the trenches have been described and illustrated incidentally in the description of the quarries, and something may now be said of such as were scattered over the surface of the site.

In the bank of the rivulet, about 100 feet higher up the stream than the initial point of our first trench, the caving in of the bank has exposed a large deposit of shop débris. It consists in parts of exceptionally small flakes, fragments, and failures, and was evidently a favorite shop to which much of the selected material from the adjacent pits was carried.[1] Other similar shops are found near by, but in most cases the spots are obscured by refuse from above, or are partially obliterated by the sliding or creeping movements constantly acting on the steep declivities.

Farther away from the pits are what I have termed trimming shops. These are on high points, on bits of level terrace, or on the level upper surface of the plateau. To these places bowlders and fragments, after testing or partial working, were carried to be further trimmed and possibly, in some cases, fully specialized. Small flakes and well-advanced broken blades characterize these spots. It is probable that lodges were pitched on some of these sites, and it would seem reasonable that

---

[1] During the examination of the site many scientific men visited the spot and examined the trenches and masses of fragmental quartzite, observing for themselves the nature and extent of the operations carried on by the ancient peoples. Among these were J. W. Powell, D. G. Brinton, Henry Balfour, T. C. Chamberlin, W J McGee, J. A. Holmes, G. K. Gilbert, C. H. Hitchcock, G. Brown Goode. O. T. Mason, Thomas Wilson, H. C. Mercer, and F. W. Putnam.

the quarrymen should have established a considerable community in the vicinity. A dwelling site is said to have been observed on the level ground, now a meadow, at the head of the ravine, and there are some evidences of primitive dwelling on the terrace overlooking Rock creek west of Mount Pleasant.

The terrace-like spurs bordering the ravine in which the trenches were dug are covered with flakes and broken blades left by the workmen. These are not now in clusters, as must have been the case originally, but are distributed rather evenly over the surface, as if the growth of forests and other disturbing agencies had been long at work shifting them about.

The distribution of shops and shop refuse is shown on the map forming plate II.

SPECIAL FEATURES

THE QUARRY-SHOP PRODUCT

Examination of the phenomena of the quarries and shops is naturally followed by a study of the articles produced in them. This is a subject of the deepest interest, and no pains have been spared to obtain full and wholly reliable determinations.

At first it was supposed that the rudely flaked stones found scattered over the sites of these quarries were bona-fide implements, and as such they found their way into literature, much speculation having been indulged in with respect to their age, to their use, and to the grade of culture to which they probably pertained. These and similar articles from the surface are still regarded by some as implements, and numerous specimens are still (1894) exhibited as paleolithic implements without any reason save that they somewhat resemble certain rude forms of European paleoliths.

Viewed in the light of the studies recorded herein, however, the roughly flaked stones are seen to be not implements at all, but the refuse of implement making, including many rejects or failures which, being partially shaped, indicate or suggest more or less fully the ruder forms of flaked implements used by primitive peoples, but which may not have even a remote resemblance to the final form to be made. It was observed that the work on the site was extremely limited in range; that it consisted in reducing the bowlders, or parts of bowlders, by flaking processes to thin leaf-shape blades, which were no doubt intended either for use as simple blades for cutting and scraping, or designed to be specialized, as occasion demanded, into arrowpoints, spearheads, perforators, and the like. So simple are the conditions that a dozen specimens may be made to illustrate the entire range of shaping work.

In plate XVII is shown a series of flaked stones, taken from this site, which includes all the ordinary forms of rejects and epitomizes the full range of shaping operations. Beginning with the bowlder *a*, from which two chips have been taken, we pass through successive stages of

elaboration, reaching the most highly developed forms in *k*, *l*, and *m*—
long leaf-shape blades. Profiles of type specimens representing three
stage of progress are placed at the right. The upper is the true
turtleback, the second the double turtleback or incipient blade, and
the third the well-advanced blade. As would be expected, no good
examples of the fully finished (roughed-out) blades were found entire
on the site, and illustrations of approximately finished work had to be
selected from broken specimens of which both halves happened to be
recovered, or from the many single halves. In nearly all cases these
blades have a broad and a pointed end, and an examination of many
specimens indicates that these features were generally foreshadowed in
the earlier stages of shaping and were kept in view throughout the progress of the work. The blades of most advanced type, represented by
broken pieces only, vary from 2 to 5 or 6 inches in length, and are generally under 2 inches in width and less than one-half an inch in thickness. It was apparently requisite that blades to be acceptable should
be measurably straight and symmetric, that they should have an oval
lanceolate outline, that they should be within a certain limit of weight,
and that the edges should have a bevel adapted to further elaboration
by flaking processes. Only one piece was found that had certainly
been carried beyond this simple stage; in this piece a rude stem had
been worked out at the broad end, as in the ordinary spearhead. This
specimen (*a*, plate XVIII) was found near the surface of a mass of shop
refuse, but was without reasonable doubt part of the original deposit.
Two other pieces (*b* and *c*) found at considerable depths exhibit slight
indications of specialization of form. The specimen shown in *d* is hardly
more than an ordinary failure, rejected on account of too great thickness or other eccentricity of shape.

For the purpose of conveying a clear notion of the nature of the
final quarry form—the leaf-shape blade—I have brought together in
plates XIX, XX, XXI, and XXII a number of the rejects that seem to
approach the form striven for by the quarry-shop flaker. Some are
entire blades, all of which exhibit more or less palpable defects of
form (as judged by the standards made out by a study of the quarry-
shop work and by the ordinary blades found so plentifully on village-
sites). Others were broken near the final stage of the shaping, and in
numerous cases both pieces were found where they had been dropped
by the workman and covered up by the accumulating débris. It will
be noticed that nearly all the whole pieces are excessively thick in some
part, while some are crooked or defective in outline, and we may conclude that they were rejected on account of some of these shortcomings.
We are, in my judgment, sufficiently warranted in concluding that most
of those specimens now in fragments were broken in vain efforts to
reduce the excessive thickness (as in *a*, plate XX) or to correct some
defect in outline. Breakage was liable to take place at any stage of
the work, the danger increasing, however, as the form increased in
tenuity.

The excessive thickness so fatal to success results from the failure of flakes to carry sufficiently far back from the margin to overlap opposing flakes. In the process of shaping stones of varying degrees of availability by fracture, many eccentric forms are necessarily developed; and these peculiarities of failures, being due to common defects in the flaking qualities of the stone, are often repeated, giving to the superficial observer the impression that the particular form was the result of design. Thus, for example, there are many specimens having one flat side and one convex or pyramidal side. It happened in such cases that one side was reduced readily to the flattish or slightly convex surface desired, but that the other worked badly, giving a high peak which could not be removed. This form and the double-peaked variety are constantly repeated because the tendency of the flaking from a bowlder is strongly toward high apexes, great skill being required to prevent this result and to obtain just the proper convexity. To attempts to remove these high humps by violent strokes is due much of the breakage in all stages of the work. Examples of this class of failures are found on every shop site and need not be mistaken for finalities in shape.[1]

The incipient tools have very considerable range in size, the blade shown in *b*, plate XXI, being 5½ inches in length, while others reach upward of 6 inches. The smallest specimens found in the quarry-shops are a little under 2 inches in length. Plate XXIII is intended to indicate the relation of the roughed-out blade to the bowlder from which it was derived. Two examples are given, the profile being added in each case that the conditions may be understood fully. In the specimens chosen for illustration, both ends retain small areas of the original surface of the bowlder. The relation of the blade to the original bowlder is not at all uniform. The fracture was sometimes such that three-fourths or more of the mass was removed all from the one side before the desired degree of convexity of that side was obtained, so that the blade was finally derived from very near one surface of the bowlder, as indicated in the profiles. The occurrence of such specimens as this has led to the supposition that in some cases a number of blades were made from a single bowlder by splitting, and this is no

[1]During the period intervening between the completion of the work on Piny branch and the date of the present writing (five years), I have examined many other quarries in various parts of the country and close analogies were observed everywhere and even identical results where conditions were identical. I have also encountered in this period numerous illustrations of the baneful results flowing from a lack of appreciation of the nature of the quarry and shop work and of the rejectage always associated with it. One very earnest and intelligent gentleman, who had dwelt for many years in a flint-producing district where the fields were filled with refuse of manufacture, had spent a great deal of time in gathering and classifying the varied forms of rejectage, supposing all to be implements. The result was truly astonishing. He had grouped similar forms together as so many varieties of tools and had worked out suppositious uses and was able to decide how some forms were shaped to fit the hand and others were designed for hafting. He had made excellent drawings and was ready to issue an elaborate and costly work. In his mind every shape was significant, and all fractures, such as come from necessity in all broken stones and are often remarkable, were indications of design, and the more eccentric accidents of fracture were evidences of consummate skill on the part of the workman.

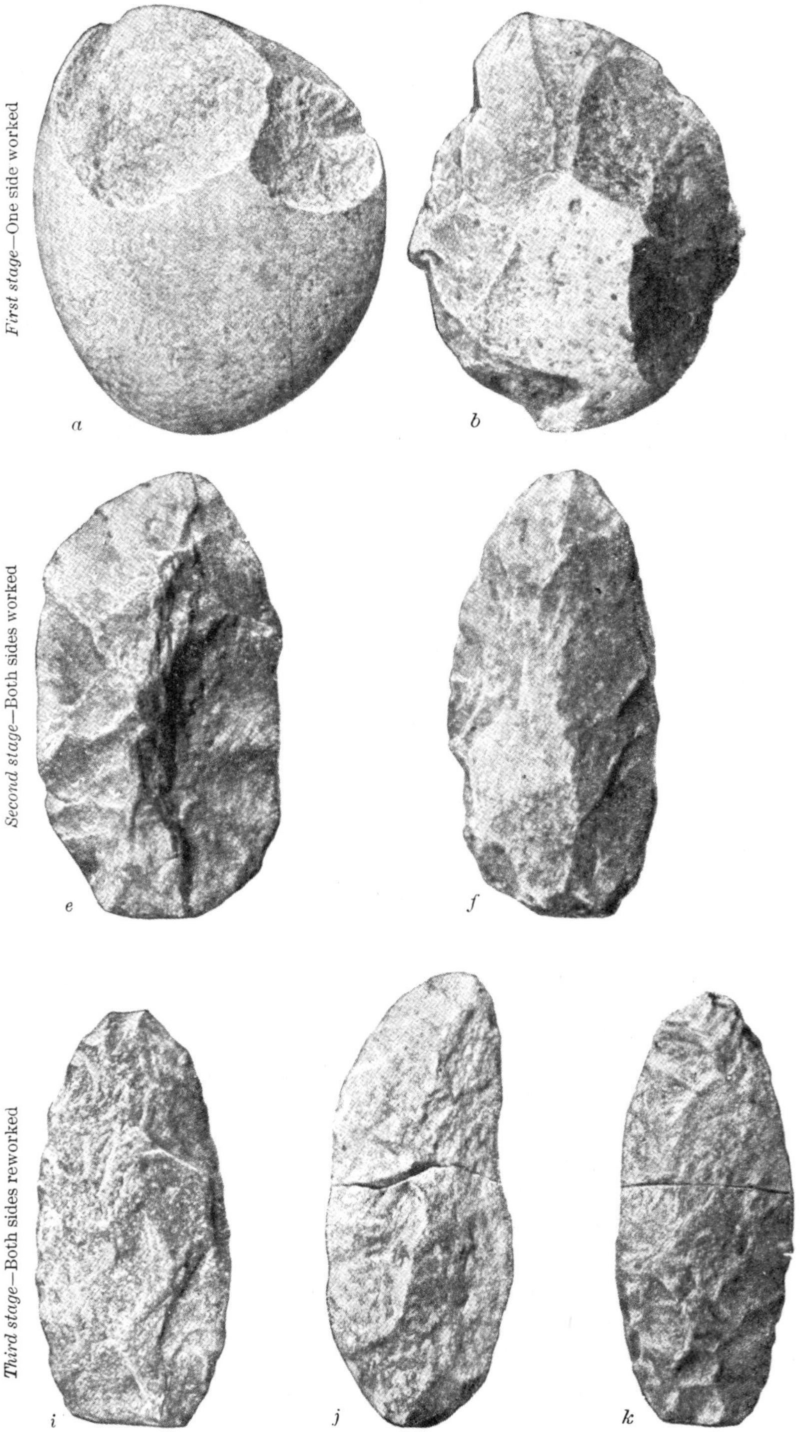

First stage—One side worked

a

b

Second stage—Both sides worked

e

f

Third stage—Both sides reworked

i

j

k

QUARRY-SHOP REJECTS—PROGRESSIVE SERIES, BEGINNING WITH

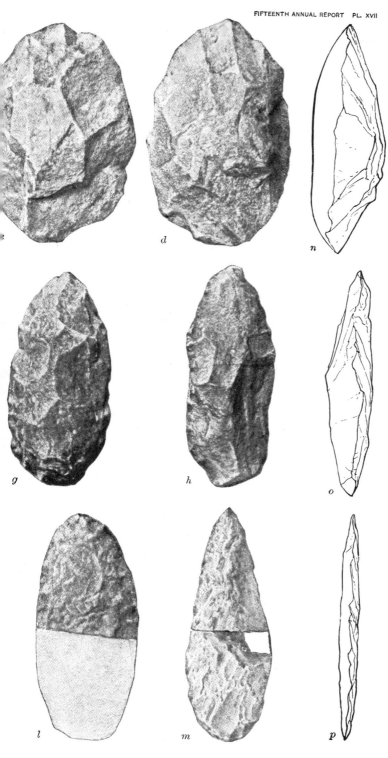

THE BOWLDER AND ENDING WITH THE THIN BLADE

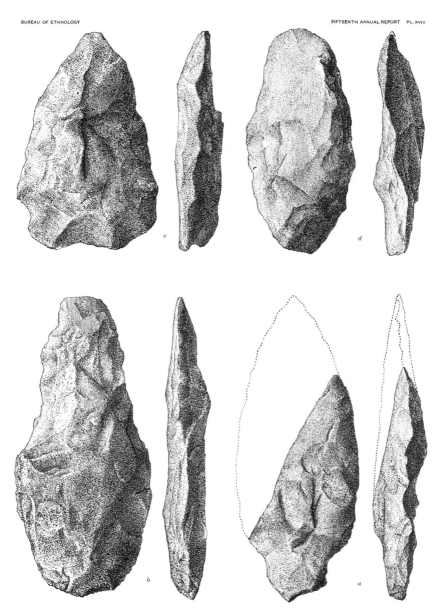

BLADE LIKE REJECTS FROM THE QUARRY-SHOP REFUSE— *a*, *b*, AND *c* SHOWING SLIGHT SPECIALIZATION   (ACTUAL SIZE)

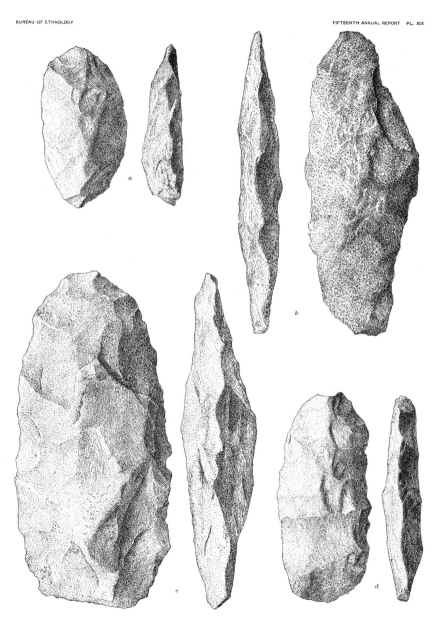

REJECTED BLADES OF MOST ADVANCED FORM FOUND IN THE QUARRY-SHOP REFUSE (ACTUAL SIZE)

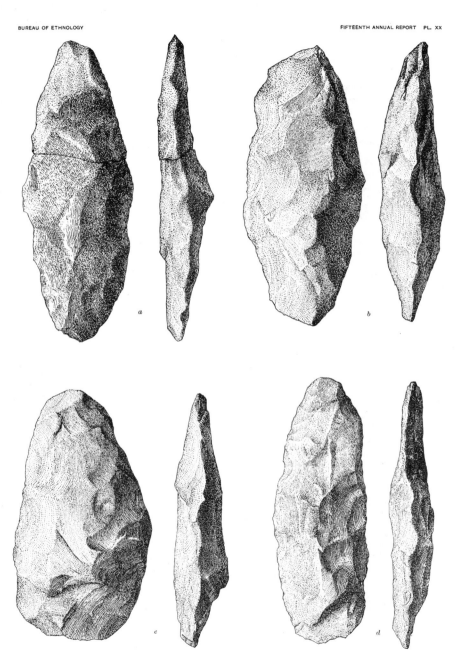

REJECTED BLADES OF MOST ADVANCED FORM FOUND IN THE QUARRY-SHOP REFUSE (ACTUAL SIZE)

BROKEN BLADES REPRESENTING THE MOST HIGHLY ELABORATED FORMS MADE IN THE QUARRY SHOPS   (ACTUAL SIZE)

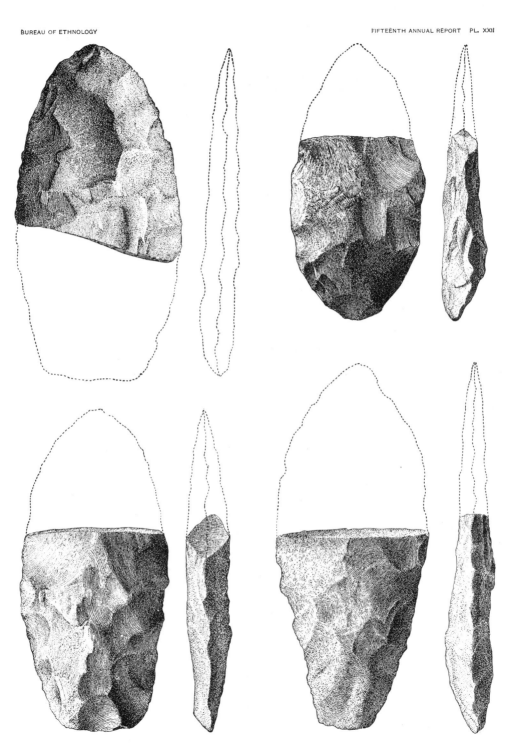

FRAGMENTS OF BLADES REPRESENTING THE MOST HIGHLY ELABORATED FORMS MADE IN THE QUARRY SHOPS

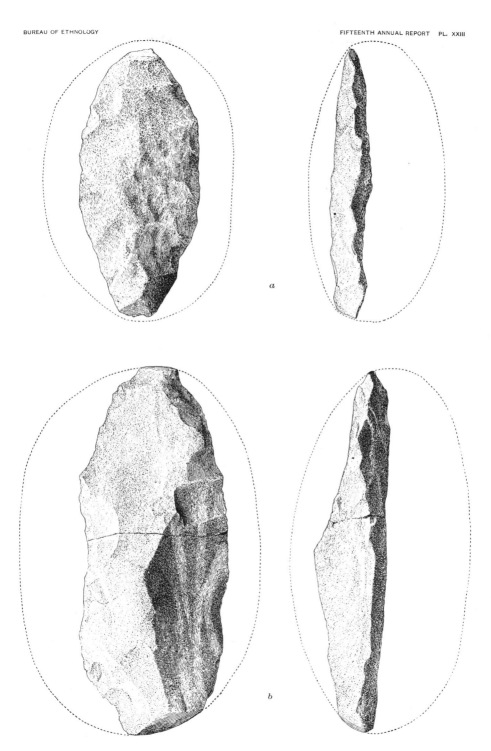

a

b

RELATION OF THE FLAKED BLADE TO THE PARENT BOWLDER (ACTUAL SIZE)

doubt correct where fracture was exceptionally favorable, but a bowlder did abundantly well in yielding a single specimen of the class roughed-out on the quarry site.

In a majority of cases the completed blade retains no trace of the original surface of the bowlder, as the great number of blows necessary to obtain the desired shape removed it altogether; and in most cases, no doubt, the specimen was reduced to two-thirds or one half of the length and width of the bowlder. It is probable that the projectile point, 1½ or 2 inches in length, was often the entire result of flaking up a bowlder 3 or 4 inches long.

The various forms of worked stones are distributed throughout the mass of refuse, as would be expected in a quarry-shop. In many cases clusters of flakes are found, and with them the fragments and failures produced during a single sitting or by a series of sittings on the one spot. In b, plate XXIII, and in a and b, plate XXIV, three pieces are presented, illustrating three stages of progress, the first-mentioned specimen belonging between the other two. These were found, with the flakes derived from them, in a small cluster in the first trench.[1] The large specimen was rejected after having received a few blows from the hammer, the relief of the side flaked remaining too pronounced to warrant continuation of the work; the second piece was broken when both sides had been roughly reduced to approximate contour; while the third example was splintered after having reached almost the requisite thinness and contour. Thus we have, as the result of a few minutes' flaking, a series of forms representing the whole range of quarry-shop shaping operations and extending from the rudest to the most elaborate stage.

Occasionally we encounter specimens in which the flaking was carried all around the margin of the stone in such a manner as to give a number of steeply sloping facets. These have a close resemblance to what are known as cores, that is, masses of raw material from which flakes have been removed to be used as knives, etc. It is difficult to draw the line between the steep-faceted failure and the typical core form, as the one shape grades into the other. Four of these core-like pieces, the best and nearly the only specimens collected, are represented in plate XXV. It is impossible to determine whether or not they are really cores rather than mere failures of the blade maker. Certainly no use was made on the quarry or shop sites of flakes such as would be derived from them, for had such flakes been worked up on the site traces of the operations would have been left among the refuse. True, the flakes may have been carried away, as were the blades produced in the quarry, to be utilized or specialized elsewhere, but I have not

---

[1]It is quite possible that by a little careful work all the pieces of the bowlders used on this spot could have been recovered and the original form restored by fitting the bits together, but the true conditions were so patent that this was not considered essential. In subsequent years such restorations have been made in a number of cases, and notably by Dr W. A. Phillips, of Evanston, Illinois, who has in two or three instances restored the bowlder so fully that each part can be taken off in the order in which it was flaked by the ancient arrow maker of the gravelly shores of Lake Michigan.

been able to learn that the primitive inhabitants of the Potomac region often used flakes such as were taken from these objects, either in their original form as cutting or scraping tools or in the manufacture of projectile points, scrapers, and drills; nearly all specialized quartzite implements are fairly thick bodied and substantial. The great rarity of typical core shapes on these shop sites should also be noted as indicating the probability that ordinary high-peaked specimens are mere accidents of blade-making operations.

In some cases large bowlders have been broken and flaked in such manner as to suggest the notion that the detached pieces were intended to be used in implement making; but howsoever this may be, much experience has taught me that irregular masses of quartzite are much more difficult to manage—to reduce to the symmetric blade—than are the bowlders when the latter are of convenient size. It is different with more brittle materials, which may be worked up to good advantage from the angular mass.

In my very careful and prolonged efforts to determine the object of the quarry-shop work and the character of the product I studied the numerical relations of the various forms of rejectage with excellent results, which may be given in some detail.

In shaping implements by flaking there are necessarily failures at all stages of the work from beginning to end, as already shown, and these failures are susceptible of grouping into four classes: The first class includes tested bowlders, rejected in early stages of the work because of unfavorable material, adverse fractures, flaws, etc, which occur in countless numbers on the site; the second stage includes those considerably worked on one side and rejected because of palpable defects developed or brought out by that work; the third group includes such specimens as were flaked somewhat fully on both sides before it became apparent that further effort was useless; and the fourth class comprises the well-defined leaf-like blade. Now it was found by study of the shaped refuse that breakage under the heavy blows of the hammer took place at all stages of the work, and that nearly as many failures had resulted from breakage into halves or approximate halves as from imperfectly developing contour. I found, however, by segregating and comparing the varieties, that one group of halves had no corresponding group of unbroken forms, and I concluded that this group of halves represented the true quarry product.

The observations may be formulated as follows (the first series—the tested bowlders—being omitted because they were practically innumerable): In the first trench I found, of the second class (n, plate XVII), 380 whole specimens and 460 halves; of the third class (o), 250 whole specimens and 320 halves; and of the fourth stage (p), no whole specimens and 380 halves. The latter were halves of comparatively thin, well-shaped blades, and were not represented by any whole blades of like proportions. In other words, there were 380 half blades of a grade of advancement superior to that of the best entire blade. From

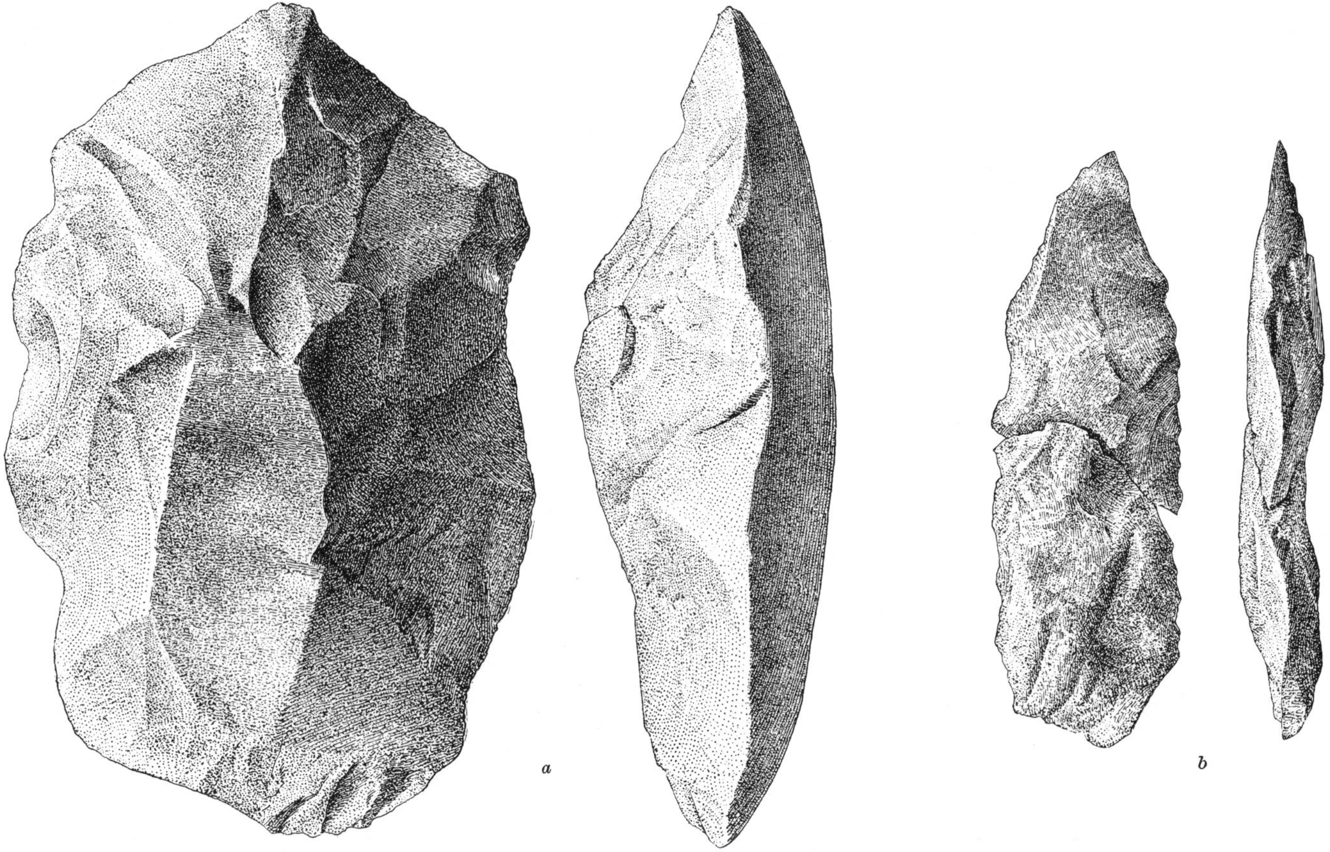

a

b

TWO SPECIMENS OF FLAKED STONE THAT, TOGETHER WITH THE LOWER SPECIMEN OF PLATE XXIII AND THE FLAKES MADE IN SHAPING THEM, WERE FOUND IN A SINGLE CLUSTER (ACTUAL SIZE)

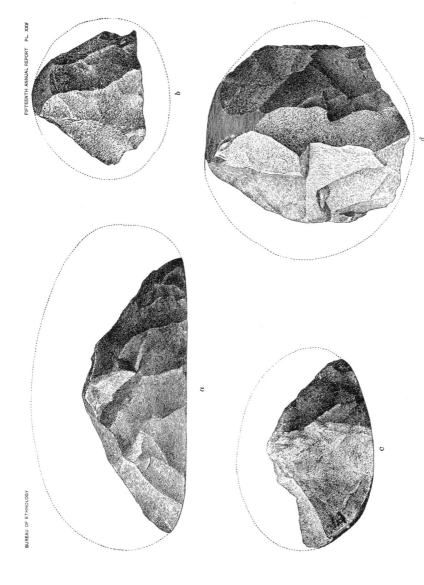

CORE-LIKE FORMS FROM WHICH FLAKES HAVE BEEN TAKEN EITHER IN FUTILE ATTEMPTS AT SHAPING AN IMPLEMENT OR FOR USE AS IMPLEMENTS

this the inference was reached that all unbroken blades of this class were carried away. It would appear, also, that of the shaped stones no other varieties were carried away, since no other variety is without a full percentage of unbroken specimens, the presence of these in the refuse being sufficient evidence that they were not desired or removed from the site.

The determination that the leaf shape blade was the exclusive shaped product of these great quarries is of greater importance than at first appears. It affords the key to many of the most puzzling problems of flaked stone art. It settles the status of multitudes of rudely flaked stones formerly of enigmatical status, and enables us to tell the story of the cache and write for the first time the full history of the countless flaked implements scattered over the land.

TOOLS USED IN FLAKING

As has already been indicated, the flaking tools were probably bowlders selected for the purpose from the multitude of available examples. Though few were found that show any considerable evidence of wear, many specimens occur which are more or less battered, apparently by use. With multitudes of natural hammers of choice shapes and assorted sizes at hand, it was manifestly useless to shape special tools or to bring in shaped tools from the outside. The scarcity of well-shaped and much-used hammers in this quarry is a very notable fact, and has been the subject of much speculation. It is found that in other quarries, subsequently examined, these objects are very numerous, and this has led to the surmise that possibly hammers made of other material, such as buckhorn, were employed in flaking the bowlders. This, we must admit, is possible, but as the evidence stands today the matter must be left largely to conjecture.

PROCESSES OF MANUFACTURE

Discussion of the processes of manufacture, of the destiny of the shaped product, and of other general topics might be left until the other quarries and shop sites are described, but can as well be taken up here, since the results obtained by a study of this group of quarry-shops are repeated in the other cases.

It has been mentioned elsewhere that the first step, after the removal of the bowlders from the bed by the quarrymen, was to test them for quality of material. As a rule, the removal of a single flake, or at most a very few flakes, enabled the expert workman to determine whether or not the stone was reasonably tractable. The selected material was removed to the shop sites, where the flaker took up the work.

The process employed in flaking appears to have been exclusively fracture by free-hand percussion, the act being a quick, firm stroke, regulated in force by the nature of the resistance to be overcome and by the result desired; no trace or suggestion of other kind of procedure was observed. The bold but unsymmetric outline of the forms produced and the rather haphazard arrangement of the percussion points preclude the idea that any process capable of accurately adjusting the point of contact between the tool used and the article shaped could have been employed. At best such a method would certainly not be readily applicable to a stone of the refractory nature of quartzite. Though the manner of delivering the stroke seems sufficiently determined, the precise method of holding the stone shaped is left to conjecture. My own experiments have been conducted on the assumption that it was held in the hand. The account of flaking processes given in the following paragraphs is based on the belief that free-hand percussion with hammers of stone or other hard and heavy material was the exclusive or principal quarry-shop process.

Referring to the series of graded rejects illustrated in plate XVII, we observe that the process of manufacture and the steps of development

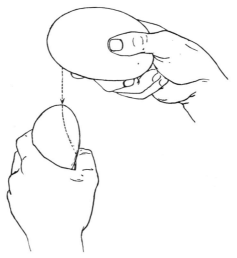

FIG. 10—First step in bowlder flaking.

were essentially as follows: Grasping a bowlder in either hand (supposing bowlder hammers to have been used), the first movement was to strike the edge of one against that of the other at the proper angle to detach a flake (figure 10). The second movement and the third were similar, and so on until the circuit was completed. If no false stroke was made and the stone had the right fracture, these few blows, occupying but as many seconds, gave as a result a typical turtleback—a bowlder with one side faceted by artificial flaking, the other side, save through accident, remaining smooth. If the removal of a single row of flakes was not sufficient, the work was continued until the one side was reduced to the proper degree of convexity, and the availability of the stone for further elaboration was made apparent. A type profile is illustrated in *n*, plate XVII. If the results thus far reached were satisfactory, the stone was turned in the hand, and by a second series of blows the remaining smooth side was flaked away (figure 11), when the result was a two-faced stone or double turtleback—the incipient blade. With perhaps a few additional strong strokes the rough stone began to assume the appearance of the final form. A type profile is seen in *o*, plate XVII. If at this stage, and, I may say, if at any preceding stage, the stone developed defects or unmanageable features (such as too great thickness, crookedness, or humps that could not be removed), it was thrown away, and thus became part of the refuse; and it would appear that all the entire specimens collected, since they were taken by us from the refuse, did develop some of these short-comings. If, however, the form developed properly, the work was continued into the final stage, which consisted in going over both sides a

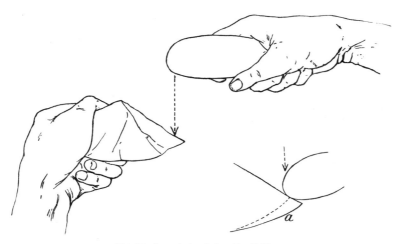

FIG. 11—Second step in bowlder flaking.

second and perhaps a third time, securing, by the use of small hammers and by deft and careful blows upon the edges, a thin, symmetric blade. A profile is given in *p*, plate XVII. Four broken specimens that must have been all but complete, for they are apparently more perfect than any whole pieces left on the site, are shown in *j*, *k*, *l*, and *m* of the same plate. It is important to observe that when the thin blade represented by these halves was realized, the work of the quarry-shop (and the only work of the quarry-shop, so far as shaping is concerned) was ended. The process and the machinery had accomplished all that was asked of them, and all that they were capable of accomplishing. The neat, but withal rude, blades, and these only, of the shaped products were carried away. Further work, additional shaping—and such there was in most cases, no doubt—employed other processes and was carried on in other fields. Flakes and fragments suitable for elaboration into implements may have been selected for transportation, but no evidence of this is procurable.

The course of procedure just described I have investigated in the most careful manner, and by experiment have followed every step of the process, and have achieved almost every result. I have found that in reaching one final form I have left many failures by the way, and that these failures duplicate, and in proper proportions, all the forms found on the quarry sites. I was unfortunately prevented from carrying out these experiments as fully as desirable by permanently disabling my left arm in attempting to flake a bowlder of very large size.

I further find by these experiments—and the conclusion is a most important one—that every implement resembling the final form here described, and every blade-shaped projectile point made from a bowlder or similar bit of rock not already approximate in shape, must pass through the same or nearly the same stages of development, leaving the same wasters, whether shaped today, yesterday, or a million years ago; whether in the hands of the civilized, the barbarous, or the savage man.

It may be well here to define with some care the apparent limitations of the classes of procedure concerned in the manufacture of flaked tools. Direct or free-hand percussion by means of unhafted or hafted implements is the natural method of reducing large amorphous masses to something approximating the special shapes reached in the advanced stages of the art. It was probably the leading method utilized in very early times; but this process, even in the most skillful hands, has its limitations in certain directions. For example, blows can not be given with sufficient regularity to produce great symmetry of outline and desirable uniformity of flaking; and, again, when implements under treatment become attenuated, the sharp blow is extremely liable to shatter them. The skill of the artificers being equal, these limitations vary with the degree of brittleness and homogeneity of the material used.

Quartzite is extremely refractory, and the skill of the workman must have been tried to the utmost to carry the manufacture by the free-hand process to a stage of elaboration where the other methods would be operative. It is possible that some method employing indirect percussion may have followed that of direct percussion. By indirect percussion I mean the use of two tools, one the hammer and the other the punch, the latter being set on the exact spot to receive the impact or blow, thus eliminating the element of uncertainty characteristic of the free-hand blow, although necessarily lacking in percussive power. By one or both of these methods the blades were carried to such a degree of symmetry and attenuation that the artist was able to employ pressure to advantage. Then, by skillfully using a bit of bone or antler, he could carry the tool to the highest possible degree of specialization and finish. That the latter method was employed by the

Chesapeake tribes is clearly indicated by John Smith, who, speaking of a Powhatan warrior, says, "His arrow head he quickly maketh with a little bone, which he ever weareth at his bracert, of any splint of a stone, or glasse in the forme of a heart, and these they glew to the end of their arrowes."[1] This could not apply, of course, save where the bit of stone already approximated the proportions and especially the thickness of the article to be made.

DESTINY OF THE QUARRY BLADES

Now, although the blades produced in the quarry-shops may without modification have been used for cutting, scraping, perforating, and other purposes, I am decidedly of the opinion that as a rule they were intended for further elaboration; this is rendered almost certain, first, by the fact that the most fully shaped broken pieces found on the quarry-shop sites are but rudely trimmed on points and edges, specimens of like grade being little fitted for use in cutting and scraping; and, second, that all the tens of thousands of specialized forms—spearheads, arrowpoints, and perforators—are necessarily specialized from such blades, as shown in a subsequent section. The quarry-workshop was naturally not a place for finishing tools, but one for roughing-out the material and selecting that fitted to be carried away for final shaping. A laborer engaged in such work in a pit in the forest would not be likely to throw aside the rough hammer used in fracturing cobble stones to take up and operate an entirely different kind of machinery, involving a distinct and delicate process. Being a reasoning and practical creature, he would carry away the roughed-out tools, the long, thin blades, to be disposed of or to be finished at his leisure and by whatsoever method experience placed at his disposal.

The quarries, being extensive, were worked somewhat systematically and the product was naturally of great importance to the people concerned. The blades made during a prolonged season's work were numerous and were carried to village-sites far and near for use, specialization, or trade. There would be in their history a period of transportation attended by storage, and this would explain the cache, an interesting feature of stone-implement phenomena, and one which involves just such blades as were produced in the quarry-shops.

THE DUMBARTON HEIGHTS QUARRY-SHOPS

LOCATION

The second group of quarry-workshops to receive attention is located on the western side of Rock creek, a quarter of a mile north of the new Naval Observatory and a mile and a half southwest of the Piny branch site already described. The quarries occupy a narrow, heavily timbered spur of the Tennallytown ridge and overlook a deep and picturesque

---

[1] History of Virginia, Richmond, 1819, vol. I, p. 132.

ravine. On the plats of the new city subdivisions bordering Massachusetts avenue extended this locality is called Dumbarton heights.

Although hardly beyond the city limits, this site still retains the extreme wildness of a primitive forest and is penetrated by obscure trails only. The sound of the hammer is now constantly heard, however, even in the wildest spots, and suburban avenues threaten it on all sides. It will probably not be many years before the illustration given in plate XXVI, from a photograph taken early in the spring of 1891, will be the only memento of the primal wilderness now covering these hills. A fine rivulet, tributary to Rock creek, meanders the deep ravine, overlooked on the north by the quarry promontory and on the south by the observatory.

GEOLOGY OF THE SITE

In its geologic features this locality corresponds very closely with the Piny branch site. A bed of Potomac bowlders caps the summit of the ridge, extending to a depth of from 1 to 25 feet, and resting on the somewhat uneven surface of the gneissic rocks. The main ridge, with which this spur connects by a narrow and very slightly depressed saddle, rises toward Tennallytown, nearly 200 feet higher, and is composed of sands, gravels, and bowlder beds of more recent age. The outcrops of bowlders in the gulches and slopes have been worked in many places by the ancient quarrymen. On the spur or promontory examined the bowlders outcrop at a level of 280 feet above tidewater, which is 50 feet higher than the exposures on Piny branch. This difference is probably to some extent an index of the slope of the ancient gneissic beach or sea bed on which the Potomac bowlders were laid down. The bed resting on the gneissic surface seems to have contained a larger percentage of workable bowlders than any of the superposed deposits. This led to the almost exclusive working of this bed by the ancient peoples, who must have familiarized themselves with all exposed deposits of material.

The beds containing quartzite bowlders are at this point upward of 20 feet in thickness, but the workable material is confined to a few feet at the base, with scattering specimens in gravel deposits at higher levels. The bowlders sought and worked here are almost identical in every respect with those quarried on Piny branch. The deposits, however, present some points of difference. At the latter point the bowlders were pretty uniformly bedded, and the sands and gravels associated with them exhibited distinct traces of horizontal bedding; but on Dumbarton heights the bowlders are distributed pretty uniformly throughout a matrix of tough argillaceous sand, presenting the appearance of heterogeneous dumping, rather than of regular bedding by aqueous agencies.

Portions of the deposits were here in a most favorable condition to be worked, as they occupied the summit of the ridge and were exposed to view over the surface of the entire crest. The bowlders were obtained by entering the hillside on the gneissic floor as well as by pitting the bowldery surface at various points. The latter method was extensively followed at the western end of the outstanding ridge, which is nearly flat for a width of 75 feet or more. This relation of the bowlder deposits to the surface of the ground had an important bearing on the preservation of the evidences of ancient work. On the sloping surfaces the pits are entirely obliterated by the descent of refuse from above, but on the upper surface they are still distinctly visible.

The worked-over surface is everywhere irregular, but the depressions are in no case more than a few inches in depth. It is probable that as a rule they were not deep when deserted by the ancient workmen, as one pit would be filled by refuse from another as the work went on. Such pits as were left open on the upper surface of the ridge would at first fill rapidly by falling in from the sides, but the rate of filling would decrease with the decrease of depth, and when a degree of shallowness like that observed at present had been reached, the compacted cobbles would have something of the stability of an artificial pavement; and where the position did not admit the accumulation of vegetal mold, centuries might pass without perceptible change. On steep sites, as in some parts of Piny branch, the friable overhanging deposits must have descended rapidly into the old quarries, obliterating all traces of the pits in a very short time.

DISTRIBUTION OF QUARRY PITS

On the map the crest of the promontory resembles the human foot in profile. The ancient quarries were located mainly on the heel, where they covered an acre or more. A little work was done along the sole of the foot, and several pits 2 or 3 feet deep had been dug at other points.

As the ancient work was prosecuted along the crest and margins of this promontory, the shop and quarry refuse is largely distributed over the slopes and has descended to the bed of the creek on the south and into the ravines and depressions on the other sides. The most striking feature of the promontory is its mantle of broken bowlders, admirably shown in plate XXVI. The whitish bowlders appear in strong contrast with the somber hues of the forest and its carpet of brown leaves and dark mold.

TRENCHING

The western projection of the quarry spur bore the most decided traces of ancient operations, and was therefore chosen as the best place to begin the work of trenching. Beginning near the extreme southwest end of the crest, near the upper surface of the gneiss rocks and at the base of the capping of bowlders, a trench 3 feet wide was carried horizontally into the gently sloping hillside. Beyond the first 10 feet the digging was not continuous, but consisted of a line of short trenches with intervals of a few feet. For about 40 feet but little of particular interest was encountered. The mass, to a depth gradually increasing to 8 feet as we advanced, consisted of earth and gravel, intermingled with shop refuse. This rested on the uneven floor of the old quarry, composed of the undisturbed, firmly compacted bowlder-bearing gravels. The ancient workmen rarely penetrated, save on the outer margins of the quarry, to the gneiss bed.

At the fortyfifth foot a pocket of refuse, containing broken bowlders, failures, broken blades, and flakes, in considerable quantities, was exposed. This was at a depth of about 3 feet. The conditions were identical with those of the Piny branch sites as the quarry wall was approached. The characteristics of the exposures in the trenches may be summed up in a few words. The quarry débris consists of a heterogeneous mass of sandy clays, sand, gravel, bowlders of quartz and quartzite, and shop refuse, all well compacted and difficult to penetrate and remove with pick and shovel. The shop refuse includes broken bowlders up to a foot in greatest dimension, rejects representing all varieties of failures, unfinished tools broken at various stages of development, and numberless flakes. These are generally distributed throughout the mass of quarry débris, but at intervals clusters or pockets were encountered, where considerable shaping had been done at a single sitting or on a particular spot.

The quarry face was reached at a distance of about 55 feet from the beginning point of the trenching. It was, at the point reached, quite abrupt, being nearly vertical for about 5 feet. The full depth was about $7\frac{1}{2}$ feet. At other points, exposed in various lateral trenches, the old quarry face was found to be very poorly defined. It would appear that the ancient quarrymen did not work with any considerable regularity or system. Numerous excavations had been carried into the sloping face of the hill, and had been abandoned near the crest. The series of terminations constitute an irregularly scalloped and variously inclined quarry face. A detailed description of the numerous short trenches, opened at various points along the margin of the promontory crest, need not be given. The conditions are uniform, and at no point was the ancient work so extensive as where the first two trenches were dug.

In one of the side trenches a good deal of charcoal was found, and at the depth of about 6 feet a charred log more than 10 feet long and in places a foot in diameter was encountered. It rested on or near the bottom of the ancient excavation, and consisted of a shell of charcoal, the interior uncharred portion having been entirely replaced by sand, which had found its way through the crevices. There is no reason to suppose that it was used by the ancient quarrymen in their work, or that it was anything more than a log which, having fallen into the deserted pit, was burned by forest fires. Charred wood and small masses of charcoal were found, but man's agency was not necessarily involved in their production.

15 ETH——5

SITE OF THE DUMBARTON QUARRY, SHOWING REFUSE-COVERED SLOPES DESCENDING FROM THE QUARRIES ALONG THE MARGIN OF THE CREST

POTOMAC BOWLDER BED RESTING ON THE SURFACE OF DISINTEGRATED GNEISS EXPOSED IN GRADING U STREET, BELAIR HEIGHTS, WASHINGTON CITY

The nature of the quarrying, the processes of implement shaping, and the quarry product correspond closely with those of the Piny branch site, and a description would but repeat what has been already said in the previous section.

OTHER ROCK CREEK SITES

North of the Dumbarton heights quarries the bowlder beds occur near or on the summits of the hills, and traces of ancient manufacture are occasionally seen. On a high point less than a quarter of a mile west of the crossing of Connecticut avenue and Pierce mill road, much shop refuse is found. This is within a few hundred yards of the Rose hill soapstone quarry, and represents the extreme limit of the Potomac bowlder deposits in this direction.

The new Naval Observatory on the ridge south of the quarry just described is built on an ancient quarry site. Quarrying, apparently on a limited scale, was carried on in the banks of the ravine now occupied by the power house, as the excavations for foundations and drainage exposed quantities of the chipped bowlders.

The bluffs of Rock creek within the suburbs of the city are lined with sites on which the ancient bowlder worker established his shops. The work was everywhere the same, save that as a rule quarrying was not carried on to such an extent as to leave traces of the pitting. On both sides of the creek at the crossing of Massachusetts avenue the refuse of bowlder flaking is strewn over the slopes from base to summit of the bluffs. The cutting of U street at a point overlooking the Massachusetts avenue bridge on the east has exposed an excellent section of the base of the Potomac bowlder beds. A portion of the exposure is shown in plate XXVII. Beneath the bowlders is the crumbling surface of the micaceous gneiss. Considerable flaking was done on the surface at this point, and clusters of flakes and failures occur on the slope back of the seated figure. Beyond is the valley of Rock creek and the heights on the west. In the Zoological park, a little farther up the valley and connecting around the faces of the Mount Pleasant bluffs to the Piny branch site, are numerous spots on which considerable work was done.

It may be added that on the level upper surfaces of the plateau occupied by Mount Pleasant and by neighboring suburbs there are traces of aboriginal occupation, consisting chiefly of finished, often broken flaked implements of ordinary varieties, and rarely of pecked and polished tools.

SHOP SITES OF THE MIDDLE POTOMAC VALLEY

FALLS SECTION OF THE POTOMAC

A study of the manufacture of stone implements in the Potomac region would properly include an examination of the thousands of

sites up and down the river and in the affluent valleys on the east and
west, but there is a great degree of sameness in the materials employed
and in the work done. While a few typical localities thoroughly studied illustrate the whole subject, the presentation will not be complete
without a brief sketch of the whole field.

Investigations in the ancient bowlder quarries of the Rock creek
valley were concluded in June, 1890, and attention was at once turned
to the study of related phenomena in the surrounding region. That
portion of the Potomac between the head of tidewater and Great
falls—about 10 miles of the most interesting and picturesque part of
its course—possesses very considerable archeologic interest. The natural phenomena are quite distinct from those of Rock creek, and as a
consequence there is a distinct class of archeological phenomena. The
falls portion of the Potomac was evidently a great fishing resort for
the aborigines, where at one time or another every available site was
occupied for more or less permanent dwelling. The section was rich in
the materials most utilized in native art. All kinds of rocks were
found; there were bowlders of quartz, quartzite, and slate; fragments
of these and other rocks; veins of quartz suitable for use in arrow making; rounded masses of traps and metamorphosed slates, the favorite
materials for making grooved axes and celts; soapstone in extensive
beds; clay, and occasional bits of rare stones brought down from the
distant mountains. The deposits of bowlders were not of a nature
to encourage extensive quarrying as on Rock creek, but the varied
resources were fully and constantly drawn on by the dwellers by the
river. In cases the villages were distributed over beds of river drift
which furnished nearly every variety of stone and in many forms; and
the art products of such a site, as picked up by the archeologist, are
varied in the extreme. There were considerable deposits of bowlders
on the northern terraces from Georgetown to above Cabin John bridge,
and quartz was everywhere.

The most notable sites of the fishing villages are in the vicinity of
Little falls. Some are on the terraced bluffs overlooking the river on
both sides, while others are on the floodplain, only a few feet above
high tide or above the ordinary river current, being swept freely by every
spring freshet.

On the left bank of the river, almost at the foot of Little falls and
about a quarter of a mile below the bridge, is a site that may receive particular attention. The floodplain is here several hundred feet in width,
extending from the river, at the point where tide and cascade meet, back
to the canal. This floodplain has been carved by the river out of the
gneiss rocks, the scarred surface of which retains enough soil to encourage vegetation; the young growth develops during the summer, to be
torn up by the freshet of the following spring. A portion of this plain,
over against the canal and just above the antiquated Eades mill, half
a mile below the bridge, was so free from invasion by the waters and had

accumulated so much soil that a small patch has been plowed and planted during recent years. In the spring of 1880 the great flood swept the site, tearing out pits and trenches and denuding the field of its soil. This spot was soon after this event visited by collectors who obtained numerous spearheads and arrowpoints, with some other well-fashioned relics. In the spring of 1890 I visited the site and found many objects of art and observed some interesting facts. Mainly the objects found were rude, representing that part of the art products not desired by collectors of specimens, but such as are essential, along with the more finished things, to the story of the occupancy of the site and the pursuit thereon of native arts and industries. The river had in former years deposited on the corrugated surface of the plain numbers of worn and partially worn stones of every variety. At one point was a bed of well-rounded bowlders containing many flakable pieces. Living on this site, surrounded by banks of gravel and heavy beds of bowlders, the savage artisan did not need to quarry the material from which to flake his projectile points and his knives. He gathered them at his lodge door, and with deft hand carried them through all the stages of manipulation from the first flake to the finished implement. Quartz and quartzite were freely used, and the soil is filled with the refuse of manufacture. The rejects are identical in every essential respect, so far as the rude stages are concerned, with those of the Piny branch quarries. But here at home the work was carried further; here the various forms were specialized, the points were affixed to the arrowshafts and spears, and here, within the limits of the village at which they were made, they were used and lost. Knives and scrapers and perforators and drills were made and used, and were lost or broken and left with the other village refuse.

On this site were found the fine-grain tough stones utilized for axes and chisels. They were selected by the primitive artisans from the heaps of drift, in shapes resembling the art form desired. They were broken and flaked, if need be, into approximate shape, and were then battered or pecked into final form and ground and polished according to custom or need. Specimens were collected illustrating every step from the beginning to the end of the process. Along with the other forms, several picks and chisels of the variety used in cutting soap-stone were discovered. Their presence is explained by the fact that near at hand occur outcrops of soapstone, and an ancient quarry has been observed near the Virginia end of the bridge and within a stone's throw of Little falls. Hammerstones, whetstones, pestles, mortars, as well as fragments of ordinary Potomac pottery and pieces of soapstone ornaments and vessels, were found. It would seem that every form of relic known in the Potomac region, from the rudest turtleback to the most finished tool of polished stone, occurs on this site—a site, it should be remarked, so modern in its period of occupancy that it is still swept by the annual freshets. Numerous illustrations of articles from this site will appear in subsequent sections of this paper.

An important village-site occurs on the high terrace overlooking the northern end of the bridge, formerly occupied by Freeman's greenhouses, now the property of the Baltimore and Ohio railway company, and another site yielding great numbers of relics is situated on the Donaldson place, high above the river on the southern side.

In June, 1890, my attention was called to a series of chipped stones obtained from the farm of Thomas Dowling, about a mile above Cabin John bridge and 8 miles from Washington. The collection was made by Thomas Dowling, junior, and included many of the rude forms common on the quarry-shop sites already examined, as well as a number of well-finished implements. During a visit to the locality it became apparent that this was an ordinary shop site, which bore also considerable evidence of having been occupied for dwelling. The site is a hundred yards beyond the Dowling gate, on a terrace, the summit of which is about 20 feet above the Conduit road and 160 feet above the Potomac. Back of the terrace, which is but a few acres in extent, the hills rise gradually to their full height of some 350 feet above the river. The surface of the terrace is somewhat uneven, and is covered with rocks of varying sizes, including many bowlders and masses of quartzite with irregularly shaped remnants of other varieties of stone. Much of this material was utilized by the aborigines. It is to be noted that the available material supplied by this site does not correspond closely to that of the great quarry sites of Rock creek. The hills above furnish but few workable bowlders until we go far back from the river. During the early Pleistocene Columbia period these lower terraces were subject to river overflow and thus received accessions of bowlders and fragments of rock from the up-river country, but this material is inferior, both in quantity and in quality, to that of the Potomac formation. It does not appear that extensive quarrying was carried on in this locality, as the deposits would not warrant it.

ANACOSTIA VALLEY

The estuary of Anacostia river varies from one-quarter to three-quarters of a mile in width in its lower course, but just above Bennings bridge it becomes quite narrow. It is bordered for the most part by low alluvial terraces which rise from the water to the base of the slopes of the plateau, here reaching nearly 300 feet in maximum height. In places low bluffs composed of Columbia gravels approach the river banks, and in the angle between the Anacostia and the Potomac the Columbia formation occurs in terraces varying from a few feet to nearly 100 feet in altitude; on these in the main the city of Washington is built.

The only members of the Columbia formation of particular interest in this study are the bowlder-bearing gravels. These are extensively exposed in places, and in the vicinity of the navy yard reach a thickness of 20 feet or more, though the bowlders are not generally suited to the use of the implement maker. They are often of quartzite and of a suitable size for flaking, but the material is not sufficiently glassy, and they are so scattered throughout the great mass of gravel that quarrying was not encouraged. Workable bowlders were weathered out in considerable numbers, however, and these were used by the aborigines. Quartz bowlders and pebbles were also found in plenty, and in some localities were sufficiently abundant to lead to extensive manufacture. Such a locality occurs on the left bank of the river near the Pennsylvania railway bridge. Here the terrace gravels are filled with workable pebbles, and many rejects and also many finished points are found on the sites, which were dwelling places as well as implement factories. The turtlebacks are often very minute, being in many cases less than an inch in length. Although the inhabitants of the tidewater section of Anacostia river were thus well supplied near at hand with the ordinary varieties of stones, they probably found it advantageous to visit the hills higher up when an unusual supply was called for.

The Potomac bowlder beds, which furnish the best materials in the region, outcrop around the slopes of the hills bordering the north-western branch of the Anacostia, 10 miles up. In the vicinity of Riggs mill, $3\frac{1}{2}$ miles above Hyattsville and a mile northwest of the Maryland Agricultural College, the manufacture of quartzite tools was carried on quite extensively. It has not been ascertained definitely that quarrying was resorted to, but there is a strong probability that such was the case. The bowlder beds are very heavy at this point, and agriculture is much impeded by the millions of rounded stones that come to the surface in the fields. A small percentage of quartz pebbles are intermingled with those of quartzite. The heaviest deposits of bowlders occur in the middle slopes about the mill, and the refuse of manufacture is found everywhere. The conditions are much the same as on the Rock creek sites. Here, however, all stages of the shaping process are represented, from the tested bowlder with one or two flakes removed to the finished arrowpoint and spearhead. Many pieces have one side worked, others have both sides rough flaked, and a very large number are reduced almost to the typical quarry blade. There are here more broken blades—that is, of those apparently almost completed—than at any other point yet examined. At least a hundred were found in an hour's search.

It is worthy of special note that on these sites a considerable amount of specialization was carried on, and some finished points are found, while there are many fragments of those evidently broken in trimming the edges and tips and in adding the notches; this was not true of the Rock creek quarries. This difference is accounted for by the fact that the Anacostian sites were habitable in places, and traces of encampments where finishing shops were probably established are found at a number of points. The occurrence of implements and projectile points of exotic materials on several of these sites is satisfactory proof of the presence of dwellings.

Many similar sites occur at corresponding localities on the other branches of the Anacostia. There is little doubt that the inhabitants of Nacochtank resorted to the quarries of Rock creek and Piny branch; for great numbers of leaf-shape blades of quartzite, as well as of quartz and rhyolite, are found on the chain of sites extending all the way from Bennings to a point opposite Alexandria.

THE TIDEWATER POTOMAC

The Potomac formation, which yields the great body of workable bowlders, extends far down the river, but is found to yield smaller amounts of available materials as the distance from Washington increases. The outcrops are generally at considerable altitude above the river, and at many points on the lower levels there are deposits of bowlder-bearing material derived from the erosion of the Potomac beds. This redistribution is now going on, so that everywhere there are more or less extensive accumulations of workable bowlders. The superior formations, the Lafayette and Columbia, also yield considerable workable stone, which is reassorted and redistributed by the river. There are in places deposits of exceptionally heavy bowlders of limited extent as far down as the confluence with Chesapeake bay. About the mouth of the Wicomico, for example, bowlders are found in large numbers. On Popes creek and along Port Tobacco river the gravels furnish many bowlders of all sizes, which were extensively used by the shell-bank peoples for mortars and mullers, and for shaping both small and large implements. The valley of Zakiah creek, in Charles county, is noted for the great number of arrowpoints and spearheads to be found on its banks; while the gravels are well supplied with workable pebbles of quartz and quartzite, suitable for the implement maker.

On the western side of the river, from Rosslyn to Potomac creek, and extending far back into the hills, extensive deposits of bowlders are exposed. In all of this district no quarries have been observed, although it is probable that in hundreds of places bowlders have been obtained by excavation; but it would appear that the deposits outside of the immediate vicinity of Washington were nowhere sufficiently rich in workable material to encourage quarrying on a large scale. Workshops are, however, found throughout this region, and refuse corresponding in every respect to that of the great quarries is widely distributed.

Especially notable sites are the high terraced points about Mount Vernon and on the island of Chopawomsie, several miles below. From the former Mr William Hunter has made extensive collections, now for the most part owned by the National Museum, and it is not unusual to see collections of quartzite and quartz points from the neighboring fields offered for sale to visitors at Mount Vernon. At Chopawomsie a bed of bowlders outcrops near the upper end of the island only a few feet above low water. The débris of manufacture of quartz and quartzite tools is very plentiful on the island, and large collections have been made of these, and of finished implements as well, by Mr W. H. Phillips, of Washington. The débris of flaking duplicates the refuse of the quarries in character.

There is hardly a village-site on tidewater Potomac where quartz pebbles were not found and worked, and the workshops are innumerable. It is evident that manufacture was carried on wherever the proper material was obtained, and it is equally clear that the processes employed and the articles produced were uniform throughout.

SITES IN JAMES RIVER VALLEY

The manufacture of quartzite and quartz implements was carried on very extensively in all the principal valleys draining into the Chesapeake on the west. They are found scattered over the country, and on the more fully occupied sites along the rivers the store of arrowpoints and spearheads seems next to inexhaustible. The great collections made by M. S. Valentine, esquire, and his sons, in the James and neighboring valleys; of Mr C. M. Wallace, mainly about the falls of the James, and of J. H. Wrenshall, on Dan river, bear testimony to this.

Nearly all of the stones along Moccasin and Gillys creeks below Richmond are of sandstone or soft quartzite, unsuitable for arrow making, and very few chips are found along the banks of either. The banks of Shockoe creek are composed mostly of quartz and hard quartzite pebbles, and the bed of the creek is filled with them. If any quarrying was ever done here, no traces of such work have survived the changes due to grading for various improvements. It is probable that the aborigines did very little digging, as the creek would wash out more stone than they could well utilize. On the surface, and especially on the slopes of the park of "Chimborazo," quartz and compact quartzites exist in great plenty, but it is useless to seek for evidences of aboriginal work now.

Near the ocher mills, about 5 miles above the mouth of the Appomattox, as also at points on the opposite side of the river, pebbles of quartz occur in the greatest profusion. On the bluff back of the mills the ground is covered with flakes and spalls, and it appears that much work was done here.

On a bluff 30 feet high between Gravelly run and the mouth of Baileys creek the ground in the few places where it is exposed is covered with small flakes and chips. It seems to have been a village-site, or at least a place where the implements were finished after being blocked out elsewhere.

QUARRIES OF THE HIGHLAND

MATERIALS QUARRIED

In a brief and necessarily imperfect manner the history of stone flaking within the valleys of the tidewater region has been sketched in the foregoing pages. Incidentally it was shown that much of the material employed in the tidewater region for stone implements was not indigenous. It will now be desirable to study the origin and manufacture of the exotic materials so extensively employed by the natives of the lowland.

The local materials were not of the best varieties, including little else, as I have shown, than brittle quartz and refractory quartzite. The other materials sought in the highland at distant points are rhyolite, jasper, argillite, and flint. All are found in limited quantity as pebbles in the tidewater portions of the valleys in which they occur in place in the highland, and the refuse left by arrow makers is found sparsely scattered over the valleys. This refuse is closely analogous in its forms with corresponding refuse resulting from the shaping of quartz and quartzite pebbles. In some manner the natives of the lowland acquired a knowledge of the location of the deposits of these materials in the highland, and quarries were opened and worked and transportation of the material, shaped or partly wrought, became an important industry.

LOCATION AND PRODUCT

RHYOLITE QUARRIES

First in importance of the exotic materials used by the inhabitants of the lowland is a variety of rather coarse-grain rock found in South mountain, a high group of ridges extending from near the Potomac at Harpers Ferry to the southern side of the Susquehanna at Harrisburg, Pennsylvania. It is an ancient eruptive rock of the acidic class, occurring interbedded with other formations and outcropping in narrow belts parallel with the trend of the range. It is generally bluish gray in color, though sometimes purplish, and is often banded and mottled by what may be regarded as flow lines. Dark varieties closely resemble slate, and the structure is often somewhat slaty. Generally it is flecked with light-colored crystals of feldspar, by which character it is easily recognized. Its fracture is often uncertain on account of a shaly or laminated structure, but it is capable of being worked more readily into large and long implements than any other of the several varieties of rock found in the upper Potomac valley.

The history of the discovery of this material may be of interest to archeologists. On taking up the study of the tidewater region it was observed that at least one-fourth of the implements collected were made of a gray slaty stone. These objects were in the main knife-like blades, projectile points, drills, etc, of usual types of form, though occasional ruder pieces and flakes were found. In a very few cases larger masses of the rock were reported, one weighing several pounds having been obtained from the banks of the Potomac opposite Mount Vernon. It was of compact flakable stone, and although of turtleback type had somewhat the appearance of a core or mass from which flakes had been removed for shaping small implements. It may have been

used or intended for use as an implement, although this is not probable. It is shown in figure 12. A much larger piece, an oblong blade-
like mass, was found by Mr J. D. McGuire in the Patapsco valley.
Such shapes are very common in the quarries, and are often mere
rejects of the blade maker.

For several years the source of this stone remained unknown.
Members of the Geological Survey were engaged in examining parts
of the Piedmont plateau drained by the Potomac, and I appealed to
them to keep a lookout for the stone. In the summer of 1892 Professor

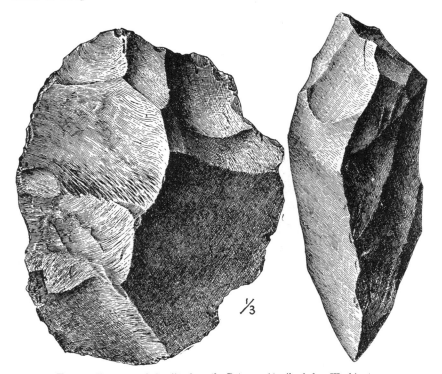

Fig. 12—Fragment of rhyolite from the Potomac, 10 miles below Washington.

G. H. Williams, of Johns Hopkins university, an assistant geologist
on the Survey (whose untimely death in 1894 was a serious loss to
science), reported its occurrence in South mountain, and in the autumn
he and Mr Arthur Keith, of the Geological Survey, furnished me with a
map of the formations so far as outlined at that time. The outcrops
extended in broken narrow belts through Maryland and Pennsylvania,
as already mentioned.

Early in November, 1892, I set out in search of the quarries. Taking
a team at Keedysville, Maryland, I crossed the mountain ridge at several points, finding excellent outcrops of the rock at many points, but
no trace of aboriginal operations appeared until I reached Maria

Furnace, Pennsylvania, on a branch of the Monocacy, 10 miles south-west of Gettysburg. Here the mountains rise abruptly and to great heights from the narrow stream bed, and the rhyolite forms a large part of the rocky mass. A cluster of flakes was observed on the road-side some 2 miles above the railway crossing, and extensive aboriginal quarries were soon found on the mountain side half a mile up the northern slope.

During the first visit only a preliminary examination was made. The ancient workings observed cover several acres of the wooded mountain side. The pitting is not pronounced, although traces of disturbance are readily recognized and the entire soil is filled with broken masses of the rock and the refuse of blade making. Near the lower margin of the quarries a small patch had recently been cleared and planted in peach trees. Here countless numbers of the partially shaped pieces were to be seen, and in an hour I had my wagon loaded with turtlebacks, broken blades, and hammerstones. The rock tends to break in flattish forms, and the rejects indicate that the blades made here averaged long and thin as compared with the shapes made from the compact bowlders of the tidewater region.

As in all the quarries so far examined, blade making was, so far as the refuse indicates, the almost exclusive work of the shops. Plate XXVIII is devoted to the illustration of specimens of successive grades of development, from the mass of raw material reduced to convenient size for beginning shaping operations to the long slender blades almost as fully developed or advanced as are the blades found in the caches and on the village-sites of the lowland.

No evidence was found of attempts at specialization of form, and there is not the least doubt that finishing operations were conducted subsequent to transportation to the villages in the valleys. Shops where many small flakes were found contained fragments of unspecialized blades only. The hammerstones were not numerous, and were as a rule rather unsymmetric globular masses of greenish-gray eruptive rock—probably a diabase.

These and probably other quarries of South mountain were the centers from which the natives distributed rhyolite over a vast area including 20,000 square miles or more of the Chesapeake-Potomac region. The quarry examined is 75 miles northwest of Washington, and was readily accessible to the inhabitants of Potomac and Patuxent rivers. The amount of material transported was very great, and the industry must have been a most important one, frequent journeys to the mountains of Pennsylvania being a necessary feature.

By a study of the range of quarry elaboration it is readily determined that the chief product was a blade corresponding to the products of other quarries, and differing only as a result of the difference in material. It has already been mentioned that multitudes of specimens derived from this or other similar quarries in the mountains are scattered over the tidewater province. In a few cases flaked masses have been seen weighing a number of pounds, much larger than would ordinarily be carried to points distant from the quarry. It is possible that in cases they are derived from water-transported masses.

As would naturally be expected, a great many blades of the roughed-out type are found in the lowland. Several caches have been reported, and in plates XXIX, XXX, and XXXI examples from a number of these are given. Through the kindness of Colonel W. H. Love, of Baltimore, I am able to present the remarkable set of blades given in plate XXIX. The cache, plowed up in a garden on Frogmore creek, near Baltimore, contained eight pieces, three of them being broken. The entire blades range from 7 to nearly 11 inches in length, and in form are very narrow and thin, with straight sides, and with the usual broad base and acute point.

The boldly flaked and handsome blade presented in a, plate XXX, was obtained, with several others like it, by Mr Brewer on South river, Maryland, from a few inches beneath the surface of the ground in a grove near his house. The two specimens b and c are of very different type, and the former is slightly specialized, rude notches having been broken in the sides near the base. These are from a cache of about a dozen pieces found near a village-site on the floodplain of the Potomac a few hundred yards below Chain bridge.

Very much like the preceding, though ruder, were a number of blades found by Colonel W. H. Love on an island at Point of Rocks, Maryland. I introduce these specimens here, as they clearly indicate what must have been a common practice with the South mountain quarry-men—the carrying away from the quarries of hoards of bits and roughly trimmed blades of rhyolite. The island has in recent years suffered much from the great floods that now and then devastate the valley, and a few years ago an ancient village-site of considerable extent was exposed by the removal to a few feet in depth of the surface soil. Pottery and stone implements of usual types were found, and at one point Colonel Love discovered what appeared to be a flaking shop, as many bits of broken rock flakes and chipped pieces were scattered about. Partly buried in the soil was a flattish stone a foot or more across and 2 or 3 inches thick, on and about which, as well as scattered through the soil near by, were numerous bits of rhyolite, a dozen or two being of the type shown in c, plate XXX, while others were ruder and some were mere flakes and fragments. Scattered about were a few finished and partially finished arrowpoints. The relation of these to the squarish stone, the presence of hammerstones, and the fact that the upper surface of the stone was considerably roughened and picked into holes by sharp points led to the surmise that possibly this was a shop, the stone being the anvil on which the fragments of rhyolite were placed to be shattered or shaped. I am at a loss, however, to understand just how such appliances could be utilized in the work of flaking. A sketch indicating approximately the relation of the cluster of partially shaped fragments to the large stone is presented in figure 13.

FLINT QUARRIES

Flint does not occur in any considerable bodies within convenient reach of the tidewater region. Pebbles are found in limited numbers in the various bowlder deposits and along the stream courses. Limited masses of the rock occur in the limestone formations of the Piedmont plateau; and one considerable outcrop of the rock in Highland county, Virginia, is known to have been worked by the natives. In May, 1893, Mr Gerard Fowke, of the Bureau of Ethnology, at my request made a reconnoissance in the region to verify the reports of extensive aboriginal quarries in Crabapple bottom, Highland county, and furnished the following notes:

"On a spur that rises to a height of 200 feet, just west of the village of New Hampden, a large amount of flint has been released by the decomposition of the limestone in which it was embedded. It is mostly in the form of small nodules or fragments, although some of it is interstratified with the limestone. Over a considerable area on the

FIG. 13—Supposed anvil stone and cluster of slightly shaped bits of rhyolite.

northern end and at the top of the ridge, the earth has been much dug over by the aborigines for the purpose of procuring the stone. Most of the pits remaining are quite small, few larger than would contain a cartload of earth. The largest are on top of the ridge, where a few have a depth of 2 to 3½ feet, with a diameter of 20 to 30 feet. The latter cover an area of about an acre; the others are so scattered that it is difficult to estimate their extent. There is no outcrop of stone at any point where digging has been done, and it appears that the searchers for the material had learned that the flint nodules and fragments were distributed through the soil excavated for them in such spots as proved to contain them in greatest abundance, making no effort to quarry out the stone in which they occur. At various places on the summit of the ridge the flint projected above the ground, and

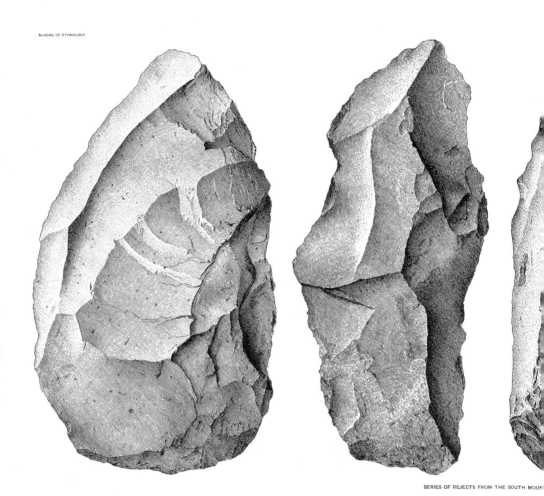

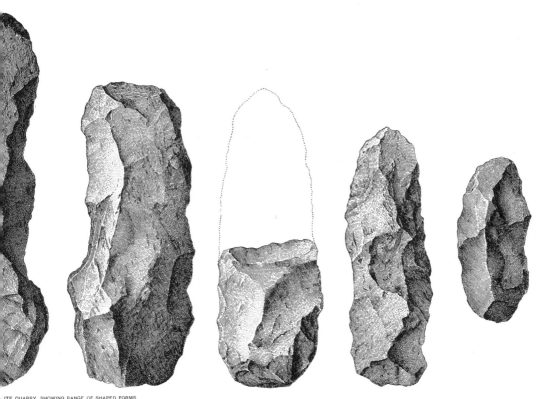

RHYOLITE CACHE BLADES FROM A GARDEN ON FROGMORE CREEK, NEAR BALTIMORE (ONE-HALF ACTUAL SIZE)

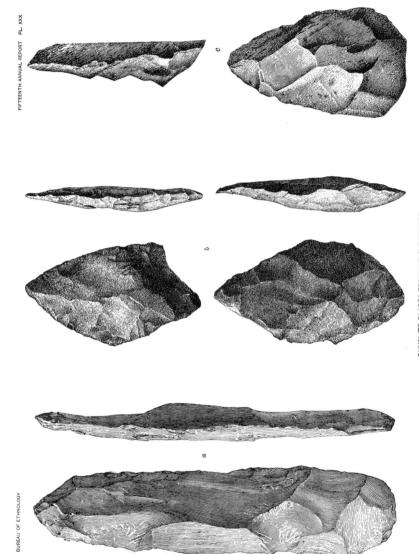

RHYOLITE BLADES FROM VARIOUS CACHES

a, Cache on South river, Maryland; b, Cache at Little Falls of the Potomac; c, Cache near Point of Rocks, Maryland

there it had been battered off with stones; but there is no evidence that quarrying was resorted to.

"Such portion of the hill as is not in timber has a heavy blue-grass sod, and the ground is visible only in a few small spots where animals have burrowed. Flint chips and flakes were found at several of these. At the foot of the spur at its northwestern terminus is a spring, around which these indications of manufacture are abundant; and it is reported that before the grass had become so thick a great many broken or unfinished implements were picked up. Spalls and chips are abundant in the face of the bank around the spring, but it can not be ascertained except by excavation how far they extend. So far as could be learned the space covered by this workshop seems too limited to have been utilized for flaking more than a small part of the flint that could have been obtained by the amount of digging apparent; it may, however, be more extensive than reported, or there may be others in the vicinity which have been overlooked. This can be determined only by researches at such points as seem favorable for the location of arrowpoint factories."

It is a notable fact that the existence of these quarries was known and recorded at a very early date, as the following extract from Maxwell's Historical Register, Richmond, 1850, will show:

On the lands of Mr John Sitlington, in Crabbottom, Highland county, there is an area of perhaps 100 acres all dug over in pits. This was the great treasury of that dark clouded flintstone out of which the Indians made those arrowheads of that color found all over our state. The rock there is in great perfection, and in inexhaustible quantity. It would surprise anyone to see what labor had been expended here and what vast quantity of the rock obtained. Here was the red man's California.

Flint implements occur so sparingly over the great tidewater areas that it seems hardly likely that extensive quarries existed within easy reach of the lowland peoples. No caches have been recorded, and it seems unnecessary to illustrate the forms of implements, which do not differ in type from those of other materials. In the Potomac valley above Harpers Ferry the village-sites yield flint arrowpoints and spearheads, mostly black in color, in very considerable numbers.

JASPER AND ARGILLITE QUARRIES

Although these materials were used by the tidewater peoples, and although some of the articles found were undoubtedly derived from quarries, the exact location of these sources of supply can not be determined. It is not improbable, however, that the quarries in Berks and Lehigh counties, Pennsylvania, furnished the material. Implements and other articles of these materials are later referred to.

CACHES

It will be observed that the leaf-shape blades made in the quarries are identical in character with the hoard or cache blades so well known all over the country. There can be little doubt that these hoards are deposits of blades produced in the quarry-shops or on sites furnishing supplies of the raw material and transported and stored for utilization or trade. Few caches of the quartzite blades have been reported from the tidewater country. It is much more common to find deposits of blades of other materials not obtained in the region, and therefore brought from a distance by quarry workers or traders. At the mouth of South river, Maryland, near the banks of Selby bay, four hoards have been found, and are now for the most part in the collection of Mr J. D. McGuire. Two are of argillite and one of jasper, brought, no doubt, from workshops in Pennsylvania, some 150 miles away, and one is of rhyolite, probably from the quarries on the head of Monocacy creek, in Pennsylvania. A fifth cluster, consisting of eight fine, long blades, was found in a garden near Baltimore, and is now owned by Colonel W. H. Love of that city. Five examples appear in plate XXIX. Still another hoard, consisting of six long, slender blades of slaty South mountain rhyolite, was obtained by Mr H. Newton Brewer, from his farm on South river, Maryland. An illustration from this cache is given in a, plate XXX. A cache of a dozen blades, found on a village-site at Eades mill, below Chain bridge, is represented in b, plate XXX, and a similar lot from an island in the Potomac, below Harpers Ferry, is illustrated in c of the same plate. Nests of quartzite blades are reported from different parts of the Potomac valley. One, consisting of six pieces, all slightly specialized, was obtained from a village-site in Anacostia by Mr W..H. Phillips (a and b, plate XXXI); a second (c, in the same plate), owned by Mr Thomas Dowling, junior, contains four or five blades, and is from Bennings; and a third, now in the National Museum, is also from the vicinity of Washington. Others reported from Potomac creek and elsewhere have been scattered by collectors who did not appreciate their importance. We can not say in any case that the quartzite blades found in caches had their origin in the Washington quarries, for identical forms were produced on numberless sites throughout the region yielding the raw material, but, in the nature of things, the greater quarries would be more frequently represented in the caches than the smaller.

The quarry-shop type of blade is not confined to the cache or to cache finds. It is found widely distributed over the country on village-sites, fishing stations, etc. These objects are plentiful on village-sites in the region producing the raw material in plenty, and decrease rapidly in numbers as we recede from that region. Thus a village-site on the Anacostia yields hundreds of these blades, while a similar site on the lower Potomac may not yield half a dozen. They are found in considerable numbers in such places as the bluff village-sites about Mount Vernon and the great shell fields of Popes creek, where beds of workable bowlders are convenient. The cache is not a necessary result of the quarry, but the quarry explains the cache.

CHAPTER III

FLAKED STONE IMPLEMENTS

GENERAL FEATURES

The treatment of this division of the subject will be brief, since the object of the present paper is chiefly to develop the history of the great industries connected with quarrying, manufacture, and distribution, rather than to discuss the finished implements and their uses. Up to the present time a rational account of the earlier stages of the work of the aboriginal artisans, of the history of the implement up to the point where its functions as an implement began, has not been given. The finished objects have been voluminously discussed by many authors, but this discussion began in the middle of the subject as now developed and is thus incomplete and unsatisfactory. Unfinished forms and rejects have not been clearly distinguished from implements proper, and much time has been wasted in classifying and finding uses for objects that are not implements at all.

Attention has already been given to the destiny of the blades produced in such great numbers in the quarry-shops and in the workshops scattered over areas affording the raw material. From these sites were distributed, often in unfinished condition, the innumerable specimens found in caches and on dwelling, hunting, fishing, and other sites all over the tidewater country. The processes of elaboration, by means of which the blades are roughed-out and prepared for final shaping, have already been considered at some length.

We are not able to say at just what point in the shaping of the blade or implement from quartzite and each of the other stones (for the point would not be uniform with all varieties) the percussion processes ceased and the pressure processes took up the work. It was certainly later in the quartzite than in any of the others, because of its coarse grain and exceeding toughness and the consequent lack of thin and sharp edges on which the pressure tool must take hold. The pressure methods were applied somewhat as indicated in the following paragraphs.

In the method most readily available for the final steps a blank form or a flake having the approximate shape was held firmly between the fingers and thumb of the left hand. A firm piece of bone having a rather thin edge or angle like that of a three-cornered file was taken in the right hand and set upon the sharp edge of the stone and at right angles to it so firmly that a slight cut or notch was made in the bone, then, with a quick, firm movement of the right hand, met by a similar

80

movement of the left, the bone was made to move across the edge of
the stone (figure 14), in doing which it took with it a flake, varying
in length, width, and depth with the skill and power of the workman,
the nature of the stone, etc. A rapid repetition of this operation,

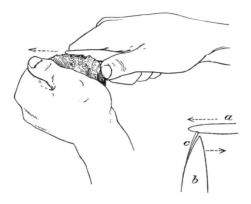

FIG. 14—Flaking by pressure, a bone implement being used.
a the bone tool, *b* the stone, *c* the flake.

accompanied by a proper resetting of the tool, quickly reduced the
piece, if it worked readily, to almost any desired outline. The same
result was obtained in various other ways, but always by means of
suddenly applied or spasmodic pressure. The blank form may have
been held down by the fingers on the edge of a stone, as shown in
figure 15, and the point of the bone held in the other set so as to

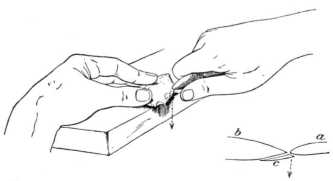

FIG. 15—Flaking by pressure, a bone point being used, the implement to be
shaped resting on a support.

catch the edge of the stone to a width corresponding to that caught
by the notched bone in the other position, when a quick downward
pressure upon the flaking tool would remove the flake. Again, in
larger work, where greater force was required to remove the flakes,
15 ETH——6

a tool long enough to place against the arm or chest of the operator may have been used. In this way much additional force could be thrown into the spasmodic movement. Another device, practiced by some tribes, consisted of a notched or forked bone or pincers, which was set upon the sharp edge of the blank and given a sudden twist, thus removing the flake.

These operations apply exclusively to implements of leaf-blade type and to minute forms of other origin. The various ruder and heavier varieties of tools were shaped by percussion exclusively.

The flaked implements of the province may be arranged in two great groups: One consists of small and well-shaped forms, such as knives, drills, scrapers, and projectile points, almost universally employed by the native tribes; the other comprises heavier and ruder tools, generally made on or near the site of intended use, and probably rarely carried about the person or transported to any great distance. The latter class includes bowlders sharpened at one end by removing a few flakes, giving a cutting edge or a pick-like point; bowlders and other stones, often large, similarly sharpened, and in addition notched at the sides for hafting; as well as quite heavy bowlders, or other compact bits of rock, rudely notched for hafting, designed for use probably as hammers or sledges. A unique group of this class of implements was developed in connection with the quarrying and shaping of steatite. It includes digging tools and picks of large size and often of rude shape, and of cutting tools of chisel-like character, shaped by flaking but often sharpened by grinding. These are fully illustrated in a subsequent chapter. We may also add sledge heads and hammers used for breaking up the rock in rhyolite, jasper, and argillite quarries, and such flaking hammers and other large tools and utensils as are in cases shaped by fracture.

Implements of the first-mentioned class originated in the quarries and in scattered shops, and were not easily made, save from material of good flaking qualities; the latter could be made of ordinary surface bowlders and of coarse, inferior stone. The former are almost universally distributed; the latter are found but little beyond the sites yielding the raw material. The former are light, thin, and symmetric, and have their genesis mainly through the leaf-shape blade; the latter are heavy, thick, and not necessarily symmetric, and never reach a high degree of elaboration.

IMPLEMENTS OF LEAF-BLADE GENESIS

TYPICAL CHARACTERS

Perhaps none of the products of aboriginal art are better known than those which may be grouped under this head and which are referred to as knives, drills, scrapers, and projectile points. Their employment must have been general, as their dissemination is almost universal.

Their number is beyond estimate. Their most important characteristic is their general shape, nearly all being referable to origin through the leaf-shape blade. Fill out the outline of almost any specimen, large or small, and the blade form is restored (plate XXXII). As a rule they are thin, a necessary condition for projectile points (save the most minute forms, which are merely sharp bits of stone) and a convenience in the case of knives, scrapers, and drills, which were carried more or less about the person. The typical scraper, with one side flat and the other sharply beveled, is an exception; it is illustrated in plate XXXIII, *a*, *b*, *c*, and is a rare form in this region. Another form of scraper is of leaf-blade genesis, as seen in the same plate, *e*, *f*, *g*, and in *f*, plate XXXII, which illustrate a prevailing form of scraper made by sharpening the broken end of a spearhead. Other exceptions to the rule are minute drills and other points made from bits of angular stone so small and so approximate in shape that systematic shaping was unnecessary. All of the implements of these several classes are designed to be set in handles or in the ends of shafts.

It is the common practice to speak of spearheads and arrowpoints as if they belong to well-distinguished classes, but the line can not be drawn between them with any degree of clearness. The larger forms were, in general, doubtless used as spearheads and the smaller for arrowpoints; yet it is probable that a large percentage of specimens of medium size were used in either way as occasion required. These implements were also equally serviceable for other purposes, and any of them may have been hafted and used for cutting, scraping, or digging. The slender-shafted perforator or drill, evidently adapted to boring stone, wood, bone, and the like, and in numerous cases bearing evidence of use, may also have served at times as a projectile point. The line separating these classes of objects into functional groups is therefore somewhat arbitrary, although convenient for descriptive purposes. In presenting illustrations I shall not attempt to separate them fully by function or manner of use. It is better to arrange them in groups by shape and size. One group may include simple blades of the larger sizes, unspecialized forms, which may have been used for various purposes; a second, the larger stemmed and notched specimens which served largely as knives, scrapers, and spearheads; a third, the medium-size specimens, mainly spearheads; a fourth, the smaller varieties, used mainly as arrowpoints; a fifth, drills, and a sixth, scrapers. These groups will be reviewed briefly in the order named, but in presenting the numerous illustrations further on the grouping is based principally on material in order that form genesis and peculiarities due to material may be better indicated. The grouping by shape is made secondary.

The materials found in this region did not encourage great elaboration. Quartzite was tough and coarse-grained; quartz was extremely brittle. The forms are, therefore, not elaborate and do not compare in

QUARTZITE CACHE BLADES FROM ANACOSTIA AND BENNINGS SITES, DISTRICT OF COLUMBIA

a, b, Phillips collection; *c,* Dowling collection.

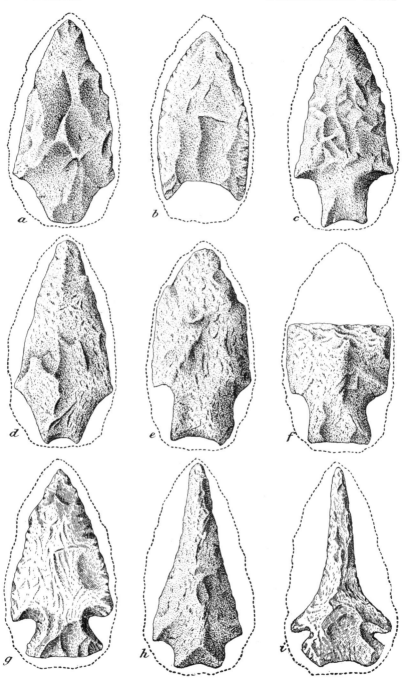

RELATION OF SPECIALIZED LEAF-BLADE IMPLEMENTS OF VARIOUS KINDS TO THE ORIGINAL BLADE

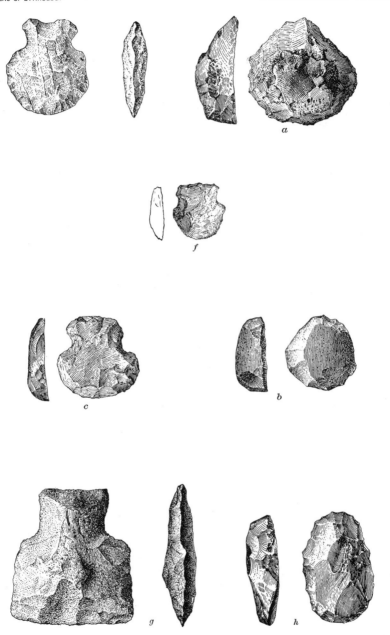

SCRAPING IMPLEMENTS OF QUARTZ AND QUARTZITE (ACTUAL SIZE)

a, b, and *c* have one flat side and a beveled edge; *e, f, g,* appear to be broken projectile points
sharpened at the edge

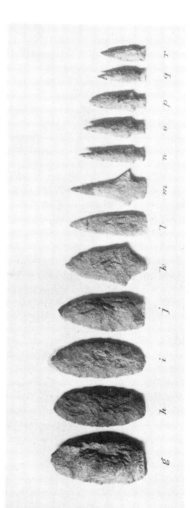

SERIES OF FLAKED FORMS ILLUSTRATING PROGRESSIVE STEPS IN THE MANUFACTURE OF PROJECTILE POINTS, ETC, FROM QUARTZITE BOWLDERS
(ABOUT ONE-THIRD ACTUAL SIZE). OBTAINED FROM SHOPS AND VILLAGE-SITES ABOUT WASHINGTON CITY

refinement with those of the interior where flint was abundant. Rhyolite was hardly less tractable, but flint and jasper admitted of much
higher refinement.

There are somewhat marked variations in the shape of objects of like
class, material, and size, and this is possibly due partly to the presence
of different tribes or families within the district. Though there is some
tendency toward localization of particular shapes, all forms are, so far
as I can learn, pretty well distributed up and down the province. Many
of the differences in detail of shape may have their origin in causes
operating within the limits of a particular district or within a single
tribe. Of possible causes of variation may be mentioned differences in
method of hafting, differences in use, variations in models, or the tendencies of individual taste.

BLADES—BLANKS, CUTTING IMPLEMENTS

It is the fashion to speak of the leaf-shape blades as knives; but no
one can say of any particular unspecialized blade, save where it shows
signs of use, whether it was a finished tool intended to be used in this
form as knife or scraper, or whether it was simply a blank awaiting
the pleasure of the elaborator. It was not necessary to stem or notch
the knife blade for hafting, as the haft could be made the full width of
the blade, but the projectile point had to be trimmed down or notched at
the stem end to accommodate it to the width of the slender shaft in
which it was set. The large size of some of the stemmed and notched
forms would seem to preclude the notion of their use as projectile
points, yet it is not safe to say that any one of these objects was not
used or could not have been used, on occasion, by some of the warlike
natives of the Chesapeake province as heads for their spears or javelins.

It is a matter worthy of note that colonial writers rarely mention
the use of stone knives, while shell and reed knives are many times
referred to. One mention of the former may be given. Smith,[1] speaking of medical practices, makes the following remark: "But to scarrifie
a swelling, or make incision, their best instruments are some splinted
stone." This may, of course, refer either to elaborately shaped implements or to mere flakes or sharp fragments. Plate XXXV illustrates
blades of quartzite; plate XXXIX, blades of quartz, and plate XLIV,
blades of rhyolite.

SPECIALIZED BLADES—PROJECTILE POINTS, ETC

Under this head may be placed, for convenience of description, all
medium and small size points having outlines specialized for hafting,
since all such may have been used for arrowpoints or for heads of
spears or javelins. Colonial writers make frequent mention of the use
of arrows by the Chesapeake peoples, and spears and javelins are
occasionally referred to. Smith describes a variety of forms in the

---

[1] History of Virginia, Richmond, 1819, vol. I, p. 137.

following extracts: "They (the Powhatan Indians) vse also long arrowes tyed in[to] a line, wherewith they shoote at fish in the rivers. But they of *Accawmacke* vse staues like vnto Iauelins headed with bone. With these they dart fish swimming in the water."[1] The Susquehannocks, inhabiting the upper Chesapeake, used arrows "fiue quarters long, headed with the splinters of a white christall-like stone, in forme of a heart, an inch broad, and an inch and a halfe or more long."[2] The Powhatan Indians pointed their arrows "with splinters of christall, or some sharpe stone, the spurres of a Turkey, or the bill of some bird."[3] Father White mentions the use of spears by some of the Maryland Indians.

It appears from the writings of Smith and others that great numbers of arrows were used, and that the natives expended them on occasion without apparent reserve. The manufacture of the points was undoubtedly a matter of great and vital importance to these people, and much time and labor must have been expended in procuring, roughing-out, and transporting the material, and in shaping the implements.

The projectile points of the Chesapeake province have a wide range in form and size. This is due in a measure to the widely diverse nature of the materials used and to the wide range of use, and partly, no doubt, to the fact that numerous tribes of people have occupied the region or have bequeathed to it their peculiar art forms. Projectile points are fully illustrated in subsequent plates.

NARROW-SHAFTED BLADES—PERFORATORS OR DRILLS

The so-called perforator or drilling point is a feature of importance in the flaked-stone art of the Chesapeake. These objects are derived, as are the projectile points, from leaf-shape blades produced in the ordinary workshops, and are of like form in all materials. They were probably used in some sort of hand drill, e. g., the pump drill in use among many tribes; and it is not uncommon to find specimens with the points rounded and worn smooth by use; yet we are not at all certain that they were exclusively used as drills, or that they are not really a variety of projectile points well adapted, on account of their shape, to use in drilling. The delicacy and brittleness of many specimens must have unfitted them for use in the drilling of hard substances. Examples in quartzite, quartz, and rhyolite are presented, along with the projectile points, in accompanying plates.

SPECIALIZED BLADES, ETC—SCRAPERS

Scraping tools were constantly required in the arts of the savage tribes, and the forms developed are uniform over a wide extent of country. In many sections special shapes were made for dressing skins,

---

[1] History of Virginia, Richmond, 1819, vol. I, p. 133.
[2] Ibid, p. 120.
[3] Ibid, p. 132.

shaping wood, and related uses. The most common type is a short, often rather thick, discoid blade or flake with blunt end, beveled by minute flaking from one side, which is usually flat, the other side being convex; this gives a keen and strong scraping edge. This form must have been set in bits of wood or bone after the manner of the woman's knife of Arctic peoples. These objects are, as a rule, not of leaf-blade genesis. Another variety was often made by sharpening the broken ends of projectile points. Implements of this class are usually of leaf-blade genesis. They were set in handles after the manner of ordinary knives, and are notched for that purpose (plate XXXIII, e, f, g). In three years' work in the tidewater region I have not obtained more than two or three well-specialized specimens of each of the classes; other collectors, however, have been more fortunate.

A very few specimens are found of imperfect semilunar shape which may have been hafted as scrapers or knives. Those brought to my attention are so rude that it is not possible to say whether they are designed shapes or only freaks of eccentric flaking.

LEAF-BLADE IMPLEMENTS GROUPED BY MATERIAL

For the reason that satisfactory separation of the various classes of leaf-derived implements—knives, scrapers, drills, arrowpoints, and spearheads—can not be made, I have brought together a series of plates and figures illustrating the whole group as developed in the three materials best representing the native work of the region. In each case plates illustrating successive steps in form development of the individual are given, while the other plates and figures are intended to convey an idea of types of form and range of shape and size.

QUARTZITE IMPLEMENTS

The quartzite implements here represented are derived almost wholly from bowlders, and in the main passed through the leaf-blade stage. The material does not admit of great elaboration or refinement of form. The larger varieties, presumably spearheads, prevail, yet all types of form known in the whole range of material appear. In numbers the quartzite tools, taking the whole Chesapeake-Potomac tidewater area, are perhaps inferior to quartz.

Plate XVII illustrates a series of steps in the individual form development of the average projectile point, beginning with the bowlder and passing forward to the leaf-shape blade—the extent of the quarry-shop elaboration; and plate XXXIV illustrates the complete morphology of the fully specialized implement of this class. It is not assumed that all or any of the seven or eight specialized specimens passed through exactly the forms indicated by the blades and rejects preceding them, these being selected merely to indicate in a general way the course of progress from the raw material to the final forms. The beginnings may have been in large or small bowlders, fragments, or flakes, but all must have passed through kindred transformations.

Plate xxxv contains a few examples of the leaf-shape blades, the outlines varying from the oval to the imperfectly ovoid form, with one point sharp and the other blunt, the ratio of length to width also varying. These are the forms produced in the quarry-shops and in other roughing-out shops. As a rule they show traces of the bold work of the free-hand flaking, and the untrimmed edges and points bear strong evidence that they were not yet ready to be devoted to any use. They are rarely above three-eighths of an inch thick. They are found occasionally in caches, but generally on village-sites where the plow turns them out of the soil along with other classes of relics. Plates xxxvi and xxxvii illustrate many excellent examples of the specialized forms of leaf-blade genesis. They include pretty nearly the full range of what may be, with approximate accuracy, designated projectile points. It happens that none of the scraper or perforator forms are included, but these are rare in quartzite.

QUARTZ IMPLEMENTS

Quartz implements were derived from the raw material, chiefly in two forms: first, vein rock, procured from outcrops or by quarrying; and, second, water-worn pieces in the form of bowlders and pebbles, obtained from surface accumulations, outcrops of gravel, or from quarries. The former was used in the highland and down to the margin of the vein-bearing crystalline rocks—a line somewhat outside of the present fall-line. The latter was the great source of supply to dwellers in the lowland. It is not possible to distinguish implements made from the two forms of the stone save where portions of the water-worn surface are preserved. This rarely occurs in a well-finished piece, but vast areas are sprinkled with the wasters of manufacture, all indicating failures in blade making from pebbles. Notwithstanding the fact that bowlders and pebbles are nature-selected material—that is, those bits least weakened by flaws and seams—they are still extremely liable to shatter under the hammer.

Years of study in the tidewater country have led me to the conclusion that pebbles were the source of at least three-fourths of the quartz implements there found. The vein quartz is much more difficult to use, being hard to reduce to the blade form, while the pebbles are readily reduced. An evolution series is given in plate xxxviii, the upper line showing profiles of the specimens represented in the lower line. Plate xxxix contains a series of blades such as were derived from the working of pebbles. The range of form and size is not great. The largest are rarely so much as 4 inches in length and an inch and a half in width; the smallest are very minute. In shape the ordinary leaf-like blade is most common, some are long and slender, others wide and triangular, while a few are approximately discoid. Some of these may

QUARTZITE BLADES OF VARYING SIZE AND OUTLINE, MAINLY UNSPECIALIZED (ACTUAL SIZE).   OBTAINED
FROM POTOMAC VILLAGE-SITES

SPECIALIZED QUARTZITE BLADES, PROBABLY IN THE MAIN PROJECTILE POINTS, FROM POTOMAC VILLAGE-
SITES (ACTUAL SIZE)

SPECIALIZED QUARTZITE BLADES, PROBABLY IN THE MAIN ARROWPOINTS, FROM POTOMAC VILLAGE-SITES
(ACTUAL SIZE)

SERIES OF FORMS ILLUSTRATING PROGRESSIVE STEPS IN THE MANUFACTURE OF ARROWPOINTS FROM QUARTZ PEBBLES, OBTAINED MAINLY FROM SHOPS AND VILLAGE-SITES NEAR ANACOSTIA (ACTUAL SIZE)

QUARTZ BLADES SHOWING LITTLE OR NO TRACE OF SPECIALIZATION, OBTAINED MAINLY FROM POTOMAC
VILLAGE-SITES (ACTUAL SIZE)

SPECIALIZED QUARTZ BLADES, PROBABLY IN THE MAIN ARROWPOINTS, OBTAINED FROM POTOMAC
VILLAGE-SITES (ACTUAL SIZE)

have been completed implements, for they are well finished and very handsome, while others, as clearly indicated by the crude surfaces, irregular edges, and blunt points, are blanks intended for further elaboration. A few of those illustrated may be rejects, as they are rather thick and clumsy.

If the blades shown in plate XXXIX were elaborated a little more by means of the bone flaker, edges and points trimmed and delicate notches cut, we should have about the series of specialized implements illustrated in plate XL. These represent some large specimens, which may be knives or spearheads, and a number of smaller size, probably arrowpoints.

Plates XLI and XLII include a pretty wide range of the smaller points, and, so far as photographic representation is capable, convey a complete idea of the Potomac valley forms. The majority of the specimens are from the collection of Mr W. H. Phillips. The long lozenge forms, occupying the upper part of plate XLI, are very plentiful and often extremely neat in finish and graceful in outline. Below are triangular forms, also very pleasing in appearance; and in plate XLII notched forms and various eccentric shapes are seen.

RHYOLITE IMPLEMENTS

The South mountain rhyolite quarry and its phenomena, and the transported masses, fragments, and blades referable to it, have received attention on earlier pages. It is now necessary only to present an epitome of the varied and interesting articles of this material that may be classed as finished implements. This brittle stone was shaped almost exclusively by flaking processes, and the final forms were in nearly all cases derived through the leaf-shape blade. The massive, or laminated, free-flaking stone encouraged the making of large blades, and the range of size in the finished objects is considerably above that of any other tidewater material. The texture was too coarse to encourage elaboration, and the specialized forms include very little beyond the simple blades and spearheads and arrowpoints and an occasional perforator. The order and manner of development of the average blade-derived implement of rhyolite are well shown in the series of drawings presented in plate XLIII. The quarry forms extend to d, and the cache and disseminated forms appear in e, f, g, and h (side views below, profiles above).

As shown in a preceding section, the cache blades of this material are often long and highly attenuated, and few examples of flaked blades east of the Appalachian ranges surpass in size the fragmentary specimen shown at the left in plate XLIV. Just what this blade should be called may not be determined, but it seems that such a specimen was more probably designed to be hafted as a symbol of authority or as a ceremonial object than as an implement to be used for any practical purpose. The contour of the fragment preserved would seem to indicate that the original could not have been much short of 12 or 13 inches in length. Blades of this general class are all very thin, rarely exceeding three-eighths of an inch in thickness. The plate contains six other blades of varying length and outline. The two larger specimens are from the Anacostia site, near the Pennsylvania avenue bridge; the others are from various points in the vicinity of Washington.

In plate XLV a number of partially or wholly specialized forms are shown. They may be classed as knives or spearheads. Spearheads are well represented in plate XLVI, and many smaller projectile points of varied form are seen in plate XLVII. They repeat in a great measure the quartz and quartzite shapes.

FLINT AND JASPER IMPLEMENTS

As already remarked of the use of flint in another place, it does not seem necessary to dwell at length on implements of this material, since they are comparatively rare, and but repeat the forms seen in other materials.

Jasper also has a somewhat meager interest in the tidewater province. Although the sources of this material are not definitely determined, it is safe to conclude that certain large and boldly flaked cache forms found in the Chesapeake country were derived from material in the mass and not from the small blocks or pebbles sometimes found in the gravel deposits of the lower Susquehanna and lower Delaware valleys.

The only quarries of jasper so far brought to public notice are those discovered and examined by Mr H. C. Mercer, of the University of Pennsylvania. They are located in Bucks and Lehigh counties, Pennsylvania. In these localities there is evidence of extensive quarrying and of considerable shaping operations. There can be no doubt that much of the jasper and many of the jasper tools found so plentifully in the Delaware and Susquehanna valleys came from these quarries or others of the same mineral belt, and it is highly probable that the hoards of blades and some of the larger flaked implements of the tidewater country came from these distant sources. It was probably difficult to secure jasper sufficiently massive to permit of the manufacture of such blades, and these objects must have represented much labor on the part of the makers. A noteworthy hoard of large jasper blades was obtained from a cache in a field near the mouth of South river, Maryland, 120 miles from the nearest known quarry. It may be noted, however, that no known quarry produces jasper of the dark-green color characterizing these specimens, which are now in the cabinet of Mr. J. D. McGuire, of Ellicott, Maryland.

ARGILLITE IMPLEMENTS

The conditions of the occurrence of argillite objects and implements in the Chesapeake province correspond very closely to those characterizing the occurrence of jasper. The objects are blades, mostly of the

SPECIALIZED QUARTZ BLADES, PROBABLY IN THE MAIN ARROWPOINTS, OBTAINED FROM POTOMAC
VILLAGE-SITES (ACTUAL SIZE)

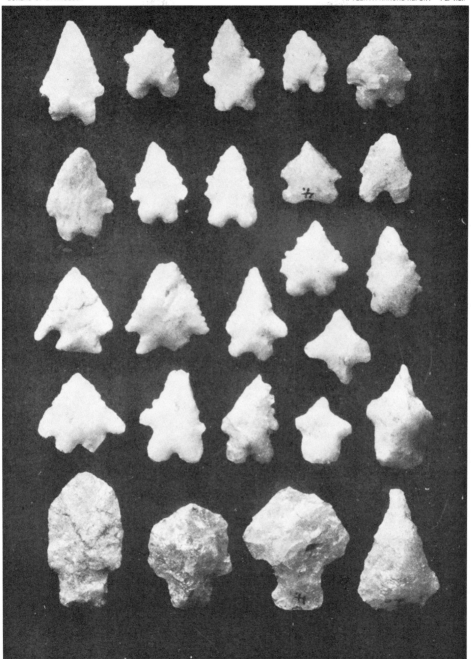

QUARTZ ARROWPOINTS OF ECCENTRIC SHAPES, OBTAINED MAINLY FROM POTOMAC VILLAGE-SITES
(ACTUAL SIZE)

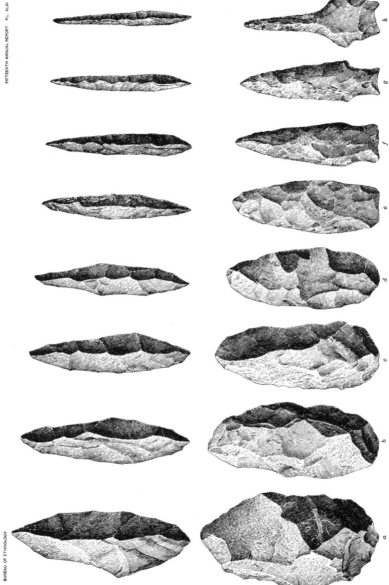

SELECTED FORMS ILLUSTRATING PROGRESSIVE STEPS IN SHAPING RHYOLITE IMPLEMENTS

a, b, c, and d are quarry-shop rejects, e, f, g, and h, are from village-sites in the lowland.   Profiles are shown in the upper line

UNSPECIALIZED RHYOLITE BLADES, MAINLY FROM ANACOSTIA VILLAGE-SITES (ACTUAL SIZE)

SPECIALIZED RHYOLITE BLADES, PROBABLY LARGELY KNIVES AND SPEARPOINTS, MAINLY FROM ANACOSTIA VILLAGE-SITES (ACTUAL SIZE)

SPECIALIZED RHYOLITE BLADES, PROBABLY LARGELY PROJECTILE POINTS, MAINLY FROM POTOMAC
VILLAGE-SITES (ACTUAL SIZE)

cache type, with an occasional specialized implement. The only source of this material known to have been extensively utilized by the ancient peoples is on Delaware river some 25 miles above Trenton. Here there are quarries and roughing-out and specializing shops, and the refuse clearly indicates the manufacture of just such blades as those obtained from caches and on village-sites on the shores of Chesapeake bay. Caches of similar blades are found in many parts of Pennsylvania and New Jersey, and there can be no doubt that the products of the Berks county quarries were extensively disseminated over the Delaware and Susquehanna valleys, and that some of them were owned and stored in the usual hoards, even so much as 150 miles south of the source of supply.

In order that the evidences of manufacture as represented by the argillite quarry refuse may be compared with corresponding features in the other quarries, a series of the rejects from the Point Pleasant (Pennsylvania) shops and associated village-sites is represented in plate XLVIII. An examination of the specimens of cache clusters from South river, Maryland, makes clear their close relationship with the forms produced in the quarry.

RUDE FLAKED IMPLEMENTS

Besides the thin forms of flaked implements which have their genesis through the blade-like blank, or through flakes or fragments of like conformation, there are many heavy forms, some of which may be regarded as extemporized or emergency tools, since they appear to have been made to supply temporary or exceptional wants, or for use largely on or near the spot of manufacture only. They may be grouped for description under the following classes: 1, hatchet-like tools, made of bowlders by striking off a few flakes, thus giving a rude edge or point; 2, ax-like implements, made like the first but having notches broken in the sides to aid in attaching a handle; their uses were probably cutting, hoeing, and the like; 3, picks and digging tools, much like the preceding and used in quarrying soapstone, as well as in other similar uses; 4, slightly notched bowlders, used as hammers and sledges; 5, hammerstones. Where bowlders were not plentiful, implements of corresponding classes were made from ordinary fragments of stone. It seems probable that these ruder implements were in many cases devoted to the same uses subserved by several more highly finished forms, and no doubt specimens could be selected connecting the lower with some of the higher forms by a graduated series. It is the intention to include here only such classes or groups of utensils as are made ready for use mainly by processes of fracturing.

The hatchet-like tool, made mainly of bowlders by striking off a few flakes from one end, is found in great numbers in many parts of the region. Though belonging to late times it is extremely archaic in type. It would seem to approach more nearly the proper idea of a paleolithic tool than any other known form, as hardly more than half a dozen blows were ever expended in elaborating its shape. It is found on fishing village-sites and elsewhere all over the bowlder-yielding districts. At Rock point on the Potomac, 80 miles below Washington, the shell banks and village-sites are literally strewn with these objects, and they are found by hundreds in the great shell bank at the mouth of Popes creek. The bowlders used were obtained in the vicinity in each case. These tools were apparently intended to be held in the hand, as there is usually insufficient space for hafting, and the unmodified end is round and well suited for grasping. Their great number and very wide utilization sufficiently indicate that they served some important function in the arts and industries of the fisher people. To cut up fish, to break bones, to open oysters, and to cut wood may be regarded as possible uses. I have selected several specimens, shown in face and profile in plates XLIX and L, to illustrate the various forms. Typical examples appear in *a* and *b*, plate XLIX. Specimen *a*, plate L, is of medium size and usual shape, and *b* and *c* are more elaborately flaked and have a greater appearance of battering or of use in rough work than is usual; the latter are rather exceptional forms. Many have broader edges and longer bodies. A specimen sharpened at both ends and probably intended for hafting is shown in *c*, plate XLIX. It is not unusual to find implements of other varieties, such as polished axes, which have become much worn or have ceased to be valued, sharpened by a few heavy strokes as are these bowlders. This form grades almost imperceptibly into the notched axes, picks, and hoe-like forms, as will be seen by reference to succeeding illustrations. These tools are identical in shape with thousands of the rejects found in our quarries where a few flakes were removed to test the material of the bowlders. They are identical also with specimens published by some authors as paleolithic implements. The sharpened bowlder tool is distinguished from the bowlder reject by the aid of the following observations: 1, it is found on the sites where implements were used, i. e., on village-sites and in shell heaps; 2, thus found it has evidently been obtained and removed from the deposits of bowlders, generally near at hand; 3, as found on village-sites and in shell heaps it often shows signs of use; 4, the same form in the bowlder-flaking shop is evidently one of the necessary forms of bowlder-flaking rejectage and never shows traces of use. The quarry reject is associated with its complement of refuse and related forms, whereas the implement on the site of use stands alone. The implement also presents suggestions of specialization when studied in numbers, but the quarry reject conforms to no one well-defined type of form. A similar form is found also in the soapstone quarries, where it was employed as a quarrying and cutting tool. It thus appears that objects of this general type, this essentially paleolithic type, may, in the Potomac valley, be either (1) quarry rejects, (2) a common variety of village-site tool, or (3) a quarry tool; but found in the vicinity of Washington,

RHYOLITE ARROWPOINTS, MAINLY FROM POTOMAC VILLAGE-SITES (ACTUAL SIZE)

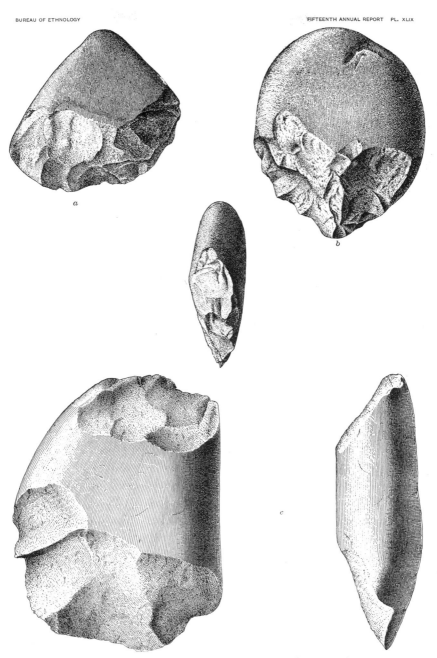

SHARPENED BOWLDERS FROM POTOMAC VILLAGE-SITES (ACTUAL SIZE)

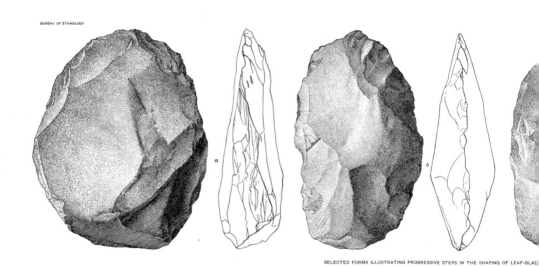

SELECTED FORMS ILLUSTRATING PROGRESSIVE STEPS IN THE SHAPING OF LEAF-BLAD

a, b, c, d,

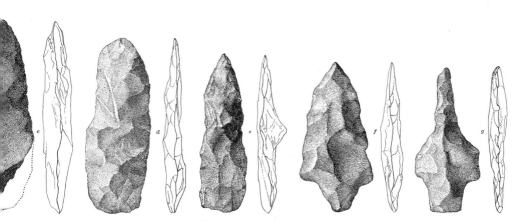

ROM ARGILLITE, FROM VILLAGE- AND SHOP-SITES AT POINT PLEASANT, PENNSYLVANIA
classed as rejects

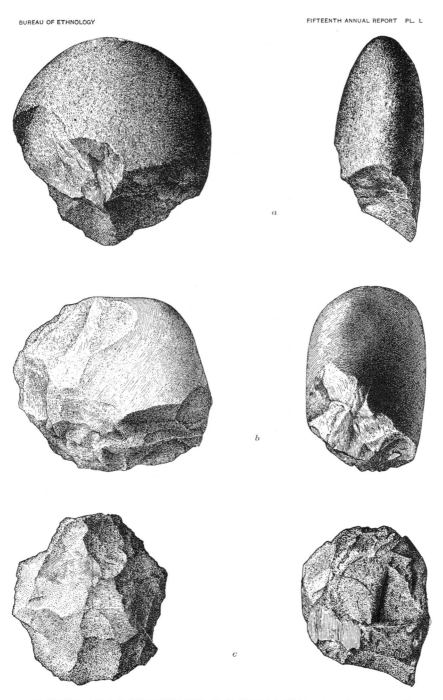

a

b

c

SHARPENED AND BATTERED BOWLDERS FROM POTOMAC SHELL HEAPS (ACTUAL SIZE)

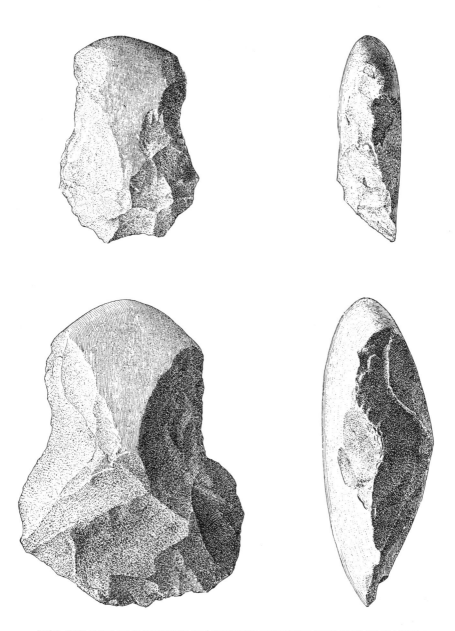

RUDE AXES MADE BY SHARPENING AND NOTCHING QUARTZITE BOWLDERS BY FLAKING,
FROM POTOMAC VILLAGE-SITES (ACTUAL SIZE)

where bowlders were used by tens of thousands in blade making, the chances are a hundred to one that they are rejects of blade making.

It may occur to some that possibly this village-site tool was produced in the quarries and that the rejected forms of like type are the rejects resulting from its manufacture. That this is not the case may be inferred from the facts that it usually occurs in the immediate vicinity of supplies of bowlders, and that it could be made of bowlders of inferior material, such as are found in countless places all over the Potomac region. By those who have studied the various forms on the ground, the idea that it is in any sense connected with the quarry work would not be entertained.

The notched ax is found scattered over an extended area which includes all the western tributaries of the Chesapeake. It is especially abundant in districts which, like portions of the Potomac valley, are supplied with abundance of large bowlders. In some localities these tools are quite numerous, and on sites such as the Popes creek shell heaps they are obtained by scores. As a rule they are extremely rude, and seem like tools intended for temporary rather than permanent use. They were certainly not sufficiently valuable to be transported to any great extent, and I have seen few that show pronounced marks of use. They were usually made by striking off half a dozen chips from one end of a flattish, oblong bowlder and by breaking rude notches in its sides, as shown in plate LI. The appearance is mostly that of a very elementary form of the grooved ax, the notches evidently having served to facilitate hafting. They could have been used for chopping, for digging and hoeing, or for cutting up game and breaking bones. In very many cases the edge is made by removing the flakes from one side of the bowlder only, leaving an adz-like profile. It is hard to say whether the haft was attached with the edge at right angles to the handle, as in our adzes or hoes, or whether the blade was placed as in our ax. Some idea of the variety of forms taken by these tools is conveyed by the specimens shown in plates LII and LIII. Occasional specimens show considerable elaboration, and it is quite possible to assemble a series showing a complete gradation from the simplest notched ax to symmetrically shaped and well-finished forms of grooved axes.

All of the forms referred to as picks, and which pertain largely to the quarrying and working of soapstone, are abundantly illustrated under the head of cut-stone implements, with which they are placed, not because they are themselves in any sense cut stones, but because they were employed in cutting the soapstone and because it seems better that all phenomena pertaining to that interesting and important subject be kept together. To obtain a complete notion of the ruder forms of flaked-stone implements it will therefore be necessary to turn to the pages treating of steatite.

A few other implements of correspondingly rude character are shaped exclusively by flaking, though in many cases continued use has given them the appearance of pecked, abraded, or polished forms. In *a*, plate LIV, we have a hammer or sledge—a flattish bowlder notched on the sides for hafting. The flat face is shown at the left and the profile at the right. The smaller objects of this class may have been used for sinkers and the larger possibly for anchors, for sledges, or even for weapons of war and the chase, and, properly hafted, would have been as highly effective as the more elaborately finished articles. The lower figure in this plate is an oblong bowlder that was probably hafted as a sledge, and the ends have been fractured by use. Examples of this class sometimes show traces of wear by the haft.

The foregoing varieties of rudely flaked stones are those most characteristic of the inhabited sites, including fishing grounds, shell heaps, and village-sites generally, in the Potomac and Chesapeake valleys.

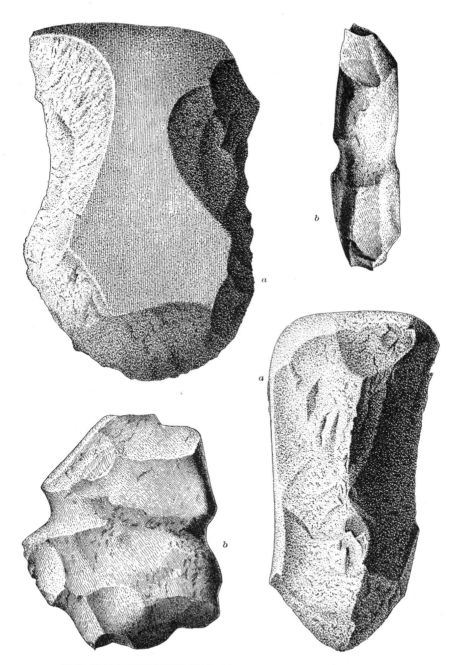

RUDE AX-LIKE IMPLEMENTS FROM POTOMAC VILLAGE-SITES (ACTUAL SIZE)

a, made by sharpening and notching a quartzite bowlder; *b*, made by sharpening a rude grooved ax

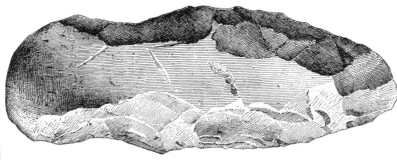

RUDE AXES OR PICKS MADE OF QUARTZITE BOWLDERS SHARPENED AND NOTCHED BY FLAKING, FROM POTOMAC VILLAGE-SITES (ACTUAL SIZE)

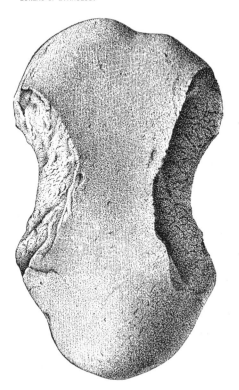

a

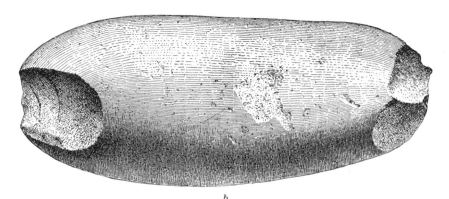

b

SLIGHTLY MODIFIED QUARTZITE BOWLDERS USED AS IMPLEMENTS, FROM POTOMAC
VILLAGE-SITES (ACTUAL SIZE)

GROUP OF CELT-AXES FROM THE TIDEWATER REGION (ABOUT ONE-THIRD ACTUAL SIZE)

CHAPTER IV

BATTERED AND ABRADED STONE IMPLEMENTS

GENERAL PROCESSES OF MANUFACTURE

The term pecked implements is used to designate such articles as owe certain of their more marked characteristics of form to the battering processes of bruising and crushing by successive blows—the bushing or bush-hammering of modern stone workers. The aboriginal stone worker produced this effect largely by means of pecking the object undergoing manufacture lightly with a suitable stone tool. The process is a tedious one, and especially so in the hands of a novice, but the skilled operator with proper stone and suitable tools soon defines a groove or removes an excrescence.

The battering processes do not generally stand alone, but are associated to greater or less extent with (1) flaking, which, when employed, precedes the pecking, and (2) grinding and rubbing which follow it. Percussive drilling of hard stone is a variety of battering, and rotary drilling and sawing go with the auxiliary process of grinding. Implements shaped largely by battering are so often finished by abrasion that the term "polished stone implements" is often applied to the entire group, but as I desire to deal here mainly with the more decidedly dynamic shaping agencies, abrading will not be referred to save as an auxiliary process.

All, or nearly all, primitive peoples with whom we are acquainted understand and practice the art of shaping stone by battering and its auxiliary processes. Archeologists have reached the conclusion, from a study of certain groups of prehistoric remains, that the battering-abrading operations belong to a somewhat advanced stage of human progress, and that their employment was preceded by a period in which fracturing processes alone were practically used. This is probably in a broad way true of the race, and is certainly true of many peoples or nations. The reason for this order must be sought in (1) the nature of the operations involved, (2) in the materials available to primitive artisans, and (3) in the capacities and needs of men.

Of the four leading shaping acts, which may be designated as fracturing, battering, abrading, and incising, it may be hard to say which is the most elemental. However, the ease with which, or the order in which, they would come into actual use would not depend on the simplicity of the single act, but, supposing materials and needs uniform, on the ease with which they could be made to produce desired results. Without going into details, which I have discussed elsewhere,[1] it may be stated that although the flaking act is not more simple or elemental than the others it is not decidedly more difficult, and that it has an enormous advantage over them in being capable by a single operation—a simple blow—of producing effective and constantly needed implements for cutting and piercing, whereas the other acts must be repeated many times without marked results, and repeated in such manner and order as to bring about a result not comprehensible save through long periods of experiment. Therefore, I conclude that where materials are favorable the powers and wants of men will tend most decidedly to the adoption and general practice of the flaking processes in advance of the other stone-shaping processes. At the same time it would seem that there need be assumed no great gulf between the two classes of operations. It is indeed hard to see how one could exist for a long period without the development of the other. Assuming that in general flaking is the first to be utilized, we can understand how the other process would be suggested to man. When a mass of stone is to be broken and flaked into shape, a flaking stone or hammer is called for. This hammer in use becomes bruised and gradually takes upon itself a purely artificial shape—the result of battering. If irregularly ovoid, it is in use turned between the thumb and fingers until its periphery becomes symmetric. Viewing this result it would seem but natural that the workman should understand and apply to producing other shapes the processes by means of which the tool in his hand is reduced to specialized shape. Again, the stone flaked, if it be somewhat tough, is often battered on the edges by the hammer in vain attempts to remove flakes, so that portions of the surface are changed in contour and exhibit the battered character. It seems remarkable that such operations should go on for long ages producing visible results without attempts to utilize the means of modifying shape thus distinctly suggested. At any rate the time did come when primitive men recognized the adequacy of battering as a means of shaping stones. Natural forms were first modified in use and the operations came to be understood and applied. Battering, called in its typical development pecking, was resorted to as a means of increasing the adaptability of available forms to ordinary needs, and a new and important group of shaping operations sprang into existence.

The tidewater country furnishes much evidence on the practice of this branch of the shaping arts among a rude seminomadic people. On ancient sites we find artificially modified water-worn rocks—bowlders and pebbles of hard and tenacious materials—cast away at all stages of the shaping operations from the first traces of pecking, where the

[1] Proceedings of the American Association for the Advancement of Science, Madison meeting, 1893, pp. 289–300.

work of removing an objectionable lobe or projection was just begun, to the stage where the traces of natural contour are all but obliterated. We find also specimens that have passed into the wholly artificial state, into symmetric and perfected tools, as well as others which have been modified by use, reshaped, reused, and practically worn out. Similarly we observe various worked stones of tough and hard varieties in which the pecking has been preceded by flaking. In some cases the whole surface has been flaked over, and in other cases projecting portions only have been removed. Examples are found in which the battering process has been merely commenced, and others on which the work has gone so far that only the deeper flaked conchoids are traceable. Of course many wholly artificial and highly finished articles have passed through this series of operations, preserving no record of their earlier morphology.

SPECIAL PROCESSES

CLASSES OF IMPLEMENTS

With a people so simple and primitive as those inhabiting the tidewater country, the range of pecked and polished implements and other objects is not great. Two standard forms employed by them in common with nearly all the native peoples of America are the celt or hatchet and the grooved ax. These are too well known to call for presentation except in so far as they may be needed in explaining the processes of manufacture or in indicating local peculiarities of shape. Besides the two leading forms there are pestles and mullers, mortars, picks, chisels, pierced tablets, winged ceremonial stones, plummet-like forms, beads, and pipes; to these we may add hammerstones and grinding and polishing stones. Few of these objects occur in large numbers, and a very small percentage only of any variety exhibit high elaboration or neat finish. The artificial shapes of many of these objects are due largely or entirely to the effects of use. Illustrations of several classes of forms are given in the accompanying plates.

So far as I have been able to learn, no example of the carving of a human figure or animal form has been discovered in this whole province, a circumstance confirming the story of the potter's art as well as the records of colonial times, which indicate that although the peoples cultivated maize and were an able and enterprising race they were in many respects not far removed in matters of art from the base of the American culture scale.

MATERIALS USED

The materials employed for shaping by the battering processes must possess a high degree of toughness combined with the hardness necessary to effective use when finished. Quartzite, quartz, flint, chert, and various other brittle forms of rock are ill fitted for reduction by pecking, and were not extensively used for highly finished tools. Granites and certain varieties of eruptive rock were preferred; these are heavy, hard, tough, and fine grained. The tidewater country furnishes none of these rocks save such as were brought down in fragmentary form by the rivers and deposited along their banks. The search for materials was not confined to the tidewater country but extended far up into the hills and ranges on the west. Shapes approaching the form desired were selected when possible, and the water-worn pieces often had the double advantage of being already approximate in shape as well as especially compact and durable. The exact source of the raw material used in any given case is difficult to determine, (1) because the pieces used are commonly erratic, and (2) because the implements and other articles made are of a nature to be treasured and hoarded up and of a size permitting ready transportation. Perhaps 75 percent of the implements made were of the compact basic volcanic rocks of the Piedmont region, and 80 or 90 percent were made from the water-worn masses or bowlders.

EXAMPLES OF THE IMPLEMENTS

The manufacture of pecked implements can not be studied so readily and satisfactorily as can that of flaked stones, for the work was not often so extensive as to lead to the opening of quarries and the development of permanent workshops where evidence could accumulate, yet we are still able to secure full information with respect to the processes and steps of manufacture. Village-sites in the vicinity of deposits of the raw material yield ample evidence as to the nature of the various operations.

Two series of illustrations presented herewith will suffice to show the processes and progress of the shaping of pecked tools. These series (plates LV and LVII) are composed of a number of different specimens selected of a size and shape to represent as nearly as possible the appearance that would be assumed at successive stages of progress by a single specimen undergoing manipulation.

The evolution of the celt is shown in plate LV. The first three specimens are rejects or unfinished forms thrown aside during the process of shaping. We begin with a water-worn stone, 1, approximating in general outline the tool to be made. A few flakes have been removed, making the edges thinner and sharper and thus saving a large amount of pecking. In 2 the surface has been gone over roughly with the pecking hammer, reducing the ruggedness; in 3 the pecking is well advanced, and in 4 the grinding is well under way; 5 represents a specimen well polished and with marks of use, and 6 is a celt that appears to have been much shortened by use and resharpening.

The range of contour is not great in these simple tools, yet there are marked variations in proportion; thus we have cylindrical, flat, pyramidal, and pointed forms, and there are always local variations indicating differences in people, material, functions, etc. In plate LVI a group of celts from the tidewater village-sites is presented.

a
b
c

SERIES OF SPECIMENS ILLUSTRATING PROGRESSIVE STAGES

d   e   f

NG OF CELTS BY FRACTURING, BATTERING, AND ABRADING

A series of forms illustrating the development of a grooved ax is shown in plate LVII. These specimens were obtained from village-sites in the neighborhood of the head of tidewater on the Potomac. On account of the length of the series I have omitted the bowlder which would naturally precede the artificially shaped series. The first figure represents an early stage in the work of shaping. The side shown has been flaked into shape save at the top where a portion of the bowlder surface is still seen. The work of pecking away the irregularities has extended over most of the surface, and the deeper conchoids at the edges, and one or two some distance from the margin, are still visible. The opposite side is less fully worked, the original surface of the bowlder being less than half removed. The groove has not been commenced save perhaps as indicated by a very faint depression at the left. In this rudimentary state it is difficult to determine, save by the general outline, whether a celt or a grooved ax was to be made.

In the second example the bowlder chosen was originally much nearer the general outline desired than in the first case. Little flaking had to be done. The groove is already well under way, although fully one-half of the original surface remains untouched either by the flaking or by the pecking hammer.

In a third specimen, omitted from the series to reduce its length, the battering operations are well advanced, small portions of the original surface only remaining. There is a freshness and crudeness about the work, indicating that the specimen, if regarded as complete, had not yet been devoted to use.

The next example (the third illustrated) bears evidence of use, and was probably finished, though the edge has been broken by accident or flaked for remodeling. It is somewhat crude in surface, and retains small patches of the original bowlder surface.

The fourth specimen figured is apparently a finished implement, though bits of the bowlder surface still appear. The battered surface has been considerably rubbed down and the edge has been ground.

The last specimen of the series is a highly elaborated and well-finished specimen, purely artificial in every part. The battered surface is entirely removed by abrading operations, and the blade and the groove are well polished—first by the finisher and second, no doubt, by use. A final specimen, originally in the series, but omitted for want of space, shows much evidence of use and repeated sharpening of the edge. The blade is shortened and blunted, and the poll is well worn. In size the axes of this region vary from less than 2 inches in width by 3 in length to 6 or 7 inches in width by 12 in length. Their shapes are probably less varied than those of many other regions, yet the extremes of shape are very wide apart. The series of outlines presented in plate LVIII will serve to convey an idea of the range of form.

A broad distinction in shape is based on the manner of hafting. In one group the groove extends entirely around the implement, while in another group one lateral edge is straight, being so arranged as to permit the wedging of the haft band. There are specimens, however, varying so far from the type forms as to bridge the gap between types. The specimen seen in *a*, plate LVIII, is flat and rectangular in outline, with encircling groove in the middle; *b* is similar, but with groove more shallow on one margin, and placed about one-third of the way from the top; *c* has a wide encircling groove near the top and a narrowing toward the point; *d* has the groove very low on the shaft and the blade is wide at the edge; *e* has one straight side for wedge hafting, and a wide projecting shoulder below the groove in the opposite edge; *f* has the groove bordered by low ridges all around.

A very good idea of the appearance and range of form of these implements may be gained from the numerous examples brought together in plate LIX. These specimens belong partly to the National Museum and partly to the collection of Mr W. H. Phillips. Nearly all are from the village-sites of the Potomac valley.

MANUFACTURING SHOPS

Pecked, ground, and polished implements were made in large numbers by our aboriginal tribes, but not in such abundance as were the flaked tools. They were in a measure luxuries, requiring time and skill in manufacture, and serving no purely utilitarian purpose that could not be served almost as well by the products of pure flaking—a shaping process many times more economical of time and labor than the battering-grinding processes. As a result of this relation of the two great classes of processes, the phenomena of manufacture observed by the archeologist present many decided differences.

The manufacture of implements in large numbers required abundance of material, the deposits of which had to be uncovered and then broken up and removed, and this resulted in the opening of quarries and in the accumulation of large bodies of débris. This is true of the manufacture of flaked and cut-stone implements, as we have seen, but the battered-abraded tool used in limited numbers usually had a sporadic or random origin, suitable pieces of stone being picked up and utilized; the amount of the product depended very considerably, no doubt, on the plenitude of convenient pieces of stone. Rarely, therefore, do we find sites where the making of these forms was carried on extensively. The phenomena of manufacture by pecking and grinding, being scattered, have not been so well understood as the phenomena of flaking.

The variety of stone most used for the manufacture of celts and axes is a compact, greenish-gray trap or trap-like rock derived originally from the highlands of Maryland and Virginia, but obtained by the aborigines very largely from the bowlder beds of the tidewater rivers near their exit from the highland or at other points higher up the streams where partly rounded fragments had been deposited in large numbers. A

SERIES OF SPECIMENS ILLUSTRATING PROGRESSIVE STAGES IN THE SH

GROOVED AX BY FRACTURING-BATTERING-ABRADING PROCESSES

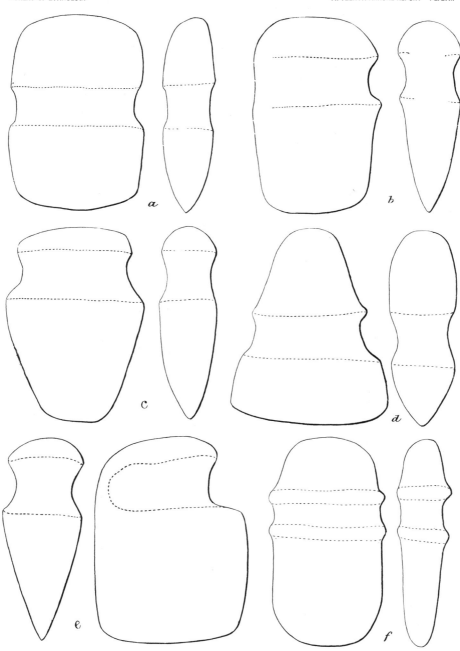

OUTLINES OF GROOVED AXES ILLUSTRATING THE RANGE OF FORM COMMON IN THE TIDEWATER
REGION

GROUP OF GROOVED AXES FROM POTOMAC-CHESAPEAKE VILLAGE-SITES

great deal of shaping was done on the various village-sites about the Little falls of the Potomac and on other streams at the crossing of the fall-line.

The most striking example of this class of site yet observed is located in Page county, Virginia, 2½ miles east of Luray. The spot was first visited by Mr Gerard Fowke in 1892; but his report,[1] dealing with evidences of dwelling and mound building, contains slight mention of the phenomena referred to here. The site, which must be that of an important aboriginal village, occupies several acres of bottom land located on the eastern side of Pass creek, a few hundred yards above its confluence with Hawksbill creek. The only notable topographic feature of the site is a mound some 3 feet high and 200 feet in diameter, in which Mr Fowke found human remains in almost incredible numbers, besides occasional implements and utensils deposited with the dead. There are many graves scattered over the terrace, a row of eight, each containing decayed human bones, together with implements and earthenware, having been freshly disturbed by the plow at the time of my visit. The materials utilized in implement making by the inhabitants were derived from great accumulations of pebbles, bowlders, and partly water-worn fragments of rock occurring in the banks and bed of the stream and now exposed where the floods have torn channels through the alluvial bottom; and probably also from deposits of similar but rather coarser materials outcropping in the face of a terrace which rises to a considerable height from the eastern margin of the narrow bottom. On the village-site about the mound the phenomena of manufacture are more or less confused with those of utilization, but separation of the varied features is in the main possible and easy. The evidence of manufacture consists of large quantities of rejectage, comprising broken masses of stone, tested bowlders and rejects of all stages of development, together with flakes and hammerstones. The phenomena of dwelling are—aside from the mounds and graves—arrowpoints and spearheads, drills, worn celts and axes, pitted stones, mortars, pestles, and pottery.

Two principal materials were utilized and two distinct classes of implements were made, leaving equally distinct varieties of rejectage. Quartzite was utilized in making the ordinary flaked tools, mostly projectile points, and the ground is filled with turtlebacks, flakes, and broken blades of this material, duplicating the rejectage of the well-known tidewater sites. The greenish-gray trap or trap-like rock was employed in the manufacture of battered-abraded tools, mostly celts, and the flat ground about the mound and extending from the stream back to the base of the terrace is strewn with the rejectage. This stone occurs in bowlders and irregularly water-worn masses in the banks of the stream and scattered over the floodplain, but not to any extent in the higher-cut terraces which represent the Lafayette period. It was assumed, therefore, that the implement rock had a local origin

---

[1] Archeologic Investigations in James and Potomac Valleys, Bull. Bur. of Eth., 1894.

somewhere within the drainage of Pass creek. Mr W J McGee, who accompanied me to the spot, undertook to trace the material to its source and met with almost immediate success. Observing that the particular variety of stone did not occur to any notable extent in the beds of neighboring streams, he followed Pass creek to the forks, and there found it confined mainly to the bed of the middle fork. Ascending this, he soon encountered a body of intrusive rock, a rather coarsely crystalline diabase, not identical save in parts with the rock used by the Indians, which is of finer grain and has the appearance of a sedimentary slate or shale altered by contact with the intruded mass. It appears, as remarked by Mr McGee, that the spot occupied by the village was probably the only spot to be found on which this stone could be found in forms well suited to the needs of the implement maker, and at the same time in sufficient quantity to make extensive manufacture possible. It is not improbable that the village came to be located here as a result of the discovery of these conditions.

It was found that in nearly all cases the work of shaping by the battering-abrading processes was preceded by flaking the rounded masses into approximate shape. Rejects representing all stages of the work of flaking, pecking, and grinding are found in numbers. There is the bowlder or mass with a few flakes removed in testing, or the shattered fragments resulting from breakage under the preliminary testing or shaping blows; there are hundreds of rejects representing early stages of manipulation, the thick turtleback forms duplicating in general appearance the corresponding rejectage of projectile-point making; there are the approximate blade-like forms but rarely approaching thinness; there are many pieces broken under the flaking hammer at all stages of the work; there are also many specimens in which the pecking has just begun, and others more advanced, and these stages are represented by much breakage under the pecking hammer; finally, there are the completed implements with ground edges and surfaces, in which the pecking and grinding has to a large degree obliterated the conchoids of flaking.

Although the celt is usually classed with the pecked and polished implements, it is readily seen that on this site flaking was of greatest importance as the main difficulties were encountered, the chief shaping work accomplished, within the flaking stage. The pecking removed excrescences and added to symmetry, and grinding reduced the edge to an even curve and uniform bevel. Grooved axes also were made on this site, but to a less extent, the operations being well represented, however, in the rejectage and in numerous finished implements occurring on the site.

The series of specimens presented in plates LX to LXIV illustrate a progression from incipient stages through a succession of rejects, fragments, and unfinished forms to broken specimens of well-finished tools. The reference letters are continuous through the set of plates.

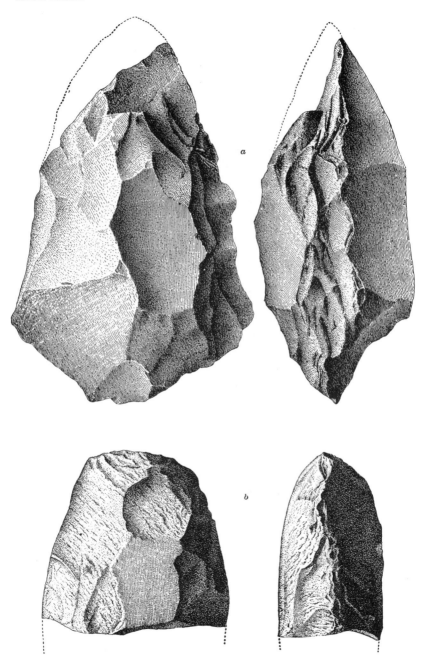

FLAKED SPECIMENS ILLUSTRATING THE REJECTAGE OF CELT MAKING; RUDE FORMS FROM SHOP
NEAR LURAY, VIRGINIA; THREE-FOURTHS ACTUAL SIZE

FLAKED SPECIMENS ILLUSTRATING THE REJECTAGE OF CELT MAKING; THE WORK OF PECKING
NOT BEGUN; FROM SHOP NEAR LURAY, VIRGINIA; THREE-FOURTHS ACTUAL SIZE

SPECIMENS ILLUSTRATING THE REJECTAGE OF CELT MAKING; THE WORK OF PECKING BEGUN;
FROM SHOP NEAR LURAY, VIRGINIA; THREE-FOURTHS ACTUAL SIZE

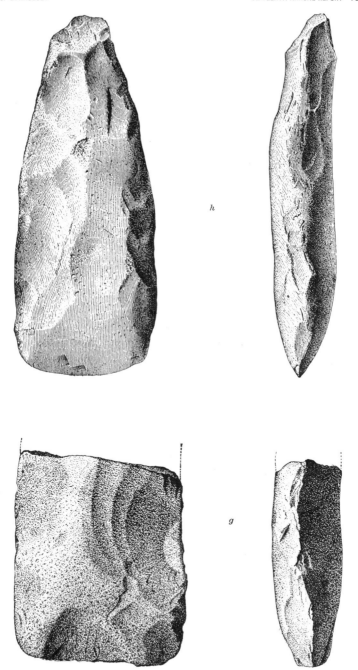

SPECIMENS ILLUSTRATING THE REJECTAGE OF CELT MAKING; THE WORK OF PECKING WELL
UNDER WAY AND GRINDING COMMENCED; FROM SHOP NEAR LURAY, VIRGINIA; THREE-
FOURTHS ACTUAL SIZE

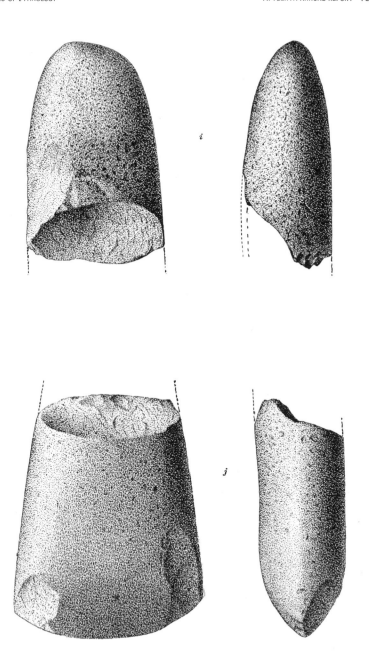

SPECIMENS ILLUSTRATING BREAKAGE IN CELT MAKING; PECKING AND GRINDING WELL
ADVANCED; FROM SHOP NEAR LURAY, VIRGINIA; THREE-FOURTHS ACTUAL SIZE

SPECIMEN ILLUSTRATING ROUGHED-OUT CELT, VERY THICK AT THE LOWER END; FROM
SHOP NEAR LURAY, VIRGINIA; THREE-FOURTHS ACTUAL SIZE

This object might readily be taken either for a reject of leaf-shape blade-making or for a completed implement of one of the larger varieties; but, found on a celt-making site, it may safely be classed as a reject of celt making.   It is a typical celt blank, defective, however, in having insufficient thickness of poll and at the same time too great massiveness at the broader edge.   The latter condition would have made the pecking necessary in producing an edge very prolonged and laborious

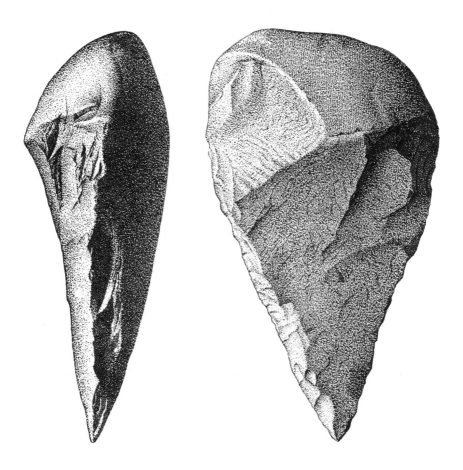

SPECIMEN FROM CELT SHOP NEAR LURAY, VIRGINIA; PROBABLY REJECTED ON ACCOUNT OF
DEFECTIVE WORK WITH FLAKING HAMMER; POSSIBLY AN IMPLEMENT INTENDED FOR
LOCAL USE; THREE-FOURTHS ACTUAL SIZE

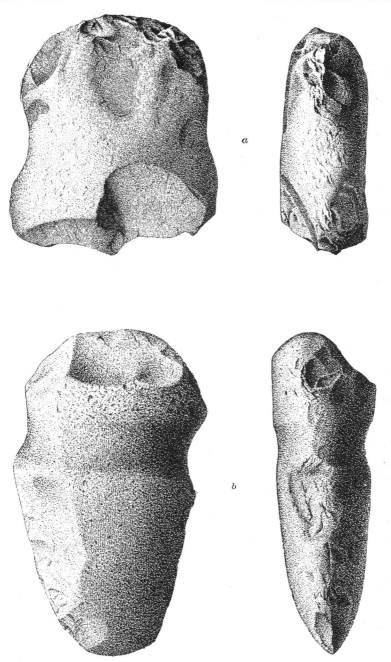

SPECIMENS ILLUSTRATING THE MANUFACTURE OF GROOVED AXES; FROM THE CELT SHOP
NEAR LURAY, VIRGINIA; THREE-FOURTHS ACTUAL SIZE

The first step—the testing and shaping of the crude mass—though represented by much rejectage, is omitted for economy of space. An illustration of a slightly advanced stage is given in *a*, a thick, clumsy form, rejected no doubt on account of the breaking away of portions of the upper end. A half blade representing a somewhat more advanced stage is given in *b*, in which a portion of the water-worn surface remains; and *c* and *d* illustrate further progress in flaking out the thick blade. In *e* and *f* the battering has begun, the former having been rejected probably on account of defective shape at the upper end, and the latter having broken under the hammer. In the fragment *g* the pecking was well under way, and in *h* much of the surface has been pecked and the edge with portions of the sides ground. In this case the flaking seems to have been so successful that little pecking intervened between the roughing-out by the flaking process and the finishing by the grinding process. The specimen shown in *i* is the upper end of a well-advanced specimen, and *j* is the blade of what must have been a perfected implement. It is, of course, impossible to say whether these latter pieces were broken during the finishing operations or in use.

COMPARISON OF CELT MAKING WITH BLADE MAKING

A comparison of the rejected forms produced in celt making as practiced in such shops as that of Pass creek with corresponding forms from the flaked-blade shops such as those of Piny branch will prove instructive. In general appearance the rejects of the two sites are very much alike. At a glance we see that the form constantly kept in view in both cases is of leaf shape, one end being decidedly pointed and the other broad and abruptly terminated. We observe, however, that in the flaked group—the leaf-shape group proper—the *pointed* end was designed to be finished for use, and that in the group shaped by flaking, pecking, and grinding—the celt group—the *broad* end was designed to form the edge of the implement, and this distinction can be traced in the rejectage back toward the inceptive stage by the difference in degree of attention given to the two ends. In the one case the narrow end was to be specialized for use and the broad end for hafting; in the other, the broad end was to be specialized for use and the narrow end for holding or hafting. In general, we may say that rejectage in the one class was the result of too great thickness, and in the other class of (in many cases) too great thinness. Two excellent examples of failure in celt making resulting from too great thickness at the broad end and thinness at the small end are shown in plates LXV and LXVI.

As made on the Pass creek site, the grooved axes were roughed-out by flaking pretty much as were the celts, rude notches being broken in the sides as the only possible contribution of the flaking process to the groove making. In plate LXVII specimens of axes are given, showing traces of the conchoids of flaking, though the implements are well advanced through the subsequent pecking and grinding stages.

Plates LXVIII and LXIX are devoted to the illustration of the hammerstones of this site. They are interesting as representing all the forms used in flaking, as well as pecking and grinding, on a site where nearly every form of tool was made and where every shaping process was employed. I do not consider it probable that any fully satisfactory separation of the specimens used for one purpose from those habitually employed in another can be made, though it is to be expected that each process separately practiced would lead to pronounced specialization. The first specimen of the series (*a*, plate LXVIII) is a water-worn pebble modified by crushing and flaking of the edges, probably in part or wholly by use, while *b* retains little of the natural surface, and at least a part of the flaking was manifestly designed to give shape to the object. The specimen shown in *c*, plate LXIX, is a stage further advanced, the surface being partly battered into roundness, and *d* is still more highly specialized. The last specimen of the series, *e*, has been much reduced by pecking and perhaps, in part, by abrading, and exemplifies the pitted hammerstones characteristic of the eastern United States.

MISCELLANEOUS PECKED IMPLEMENTS

As already remarked, the pecked and abraded implements of the tidewater province comprise few objects aside from the celt and the grooved ax. Several varieties are represented, but the numbers are limited and the shape and finish, save in a few rare exceptions, are rather rude. The accompanying plates, from LXX to LXXV, inclusive, illustrate such varieties as I encountered during the period of my investigations. Numerous more perfect implements of several of the classes have been found, but they are now out of my reach.

Plate LXX contains four examples of perforated tablets, two having two perforations and two having one each. The fragment *a*, made of gray slate, is from the Potomac near Washington and is covered with apparently meaningless engraved figures. The specimen shown in *b* is of red-banded slate and was obtained from the great shell deposit at the mouth of Popes creek, Maryland. The large specimen *c* is of banded slate and was found in the highland in Virginia. The small fragment *d* is from the District of Columbia.

Four examples of winged ceremonial stones are illustrated in plate LXXI. The roughed-out form *a* was obtained from a village-site at Little falls, and the other specimens, all fragmentary, came from the vicinity of Washington.

The pitted stones and mortar shown in plate LXXII are from the great shell heap at the mouth of Popes creek, and are common forms. The same may be said of the upper figure in plate LXXIII. The pestle shown in *b* was found on a village-site at Halls landing, Patuxent river; the pestle *c* was picked up in a field above Little falls, and the sinker came from a village-site near Little falls.

HAMMERSTONES FROM THE CELT SHOP NEAR LURAY, VIRGINIA; THREE-FOURTHS ACTUAL SIZE

HAMMERSTONES FROM THE CELT SHOP NEAR LURAY, VIRGINIA; THREE-FOURTHS ACTUAL SIZE

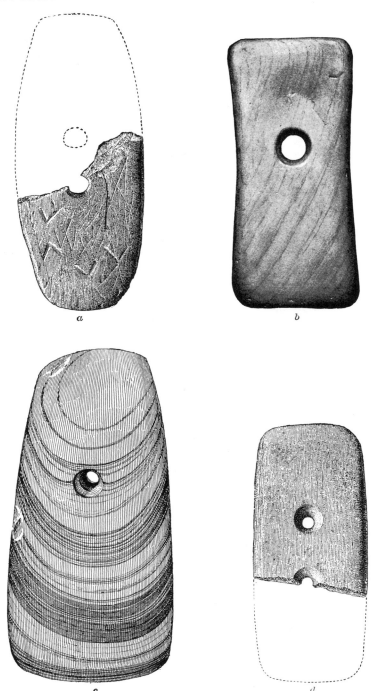

PERFORATED TABLETS OF SLATE; THREE-FOURTHS ACTUAL SIZE

a, *b*, and *d*, from tidewater Potomac, and *c* from middle Potomac

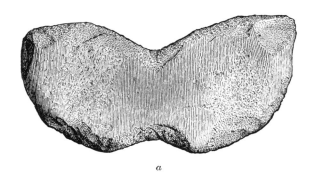

a

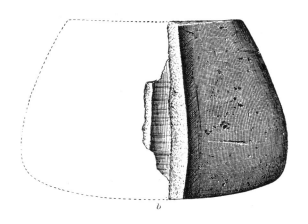

b

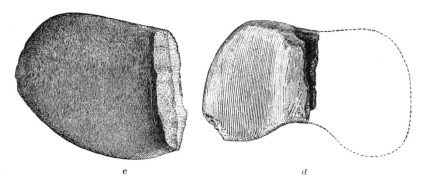

c   *d*

WINGED CEREMONIAL STONES FROM THE VICINITY OF WASHINGTON, D. C.

a, 3¾ inches in length; *b*, 2½ (?) inches in height; *c*, 2 inches in height; *d*, 1½ inch in height

PITTED STONES AND MORTAR FROM TIDEWATER VILLAGE-SITES

a-b, one-third actual size ; *c-d, e*, one-half actual size

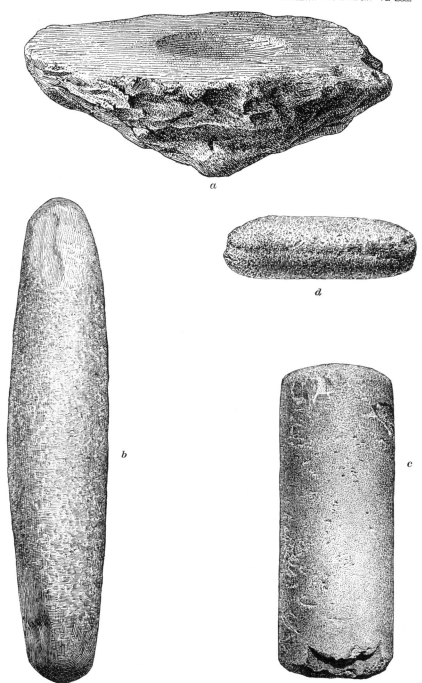

MORTAR, PESTLES, AND SINKER (?) FROM THE TIDEWATER PROVINCE

a, 11⅝ inches in length; *b*, 14 inches in length; *c*, 7 (?) inches in length; *d*, 3 inches in length

ABRADING STONES FROM THE VICINITY OF WASHINGTON, D. C.

a, b, c, three-fourths actual size ; *d,* actual size

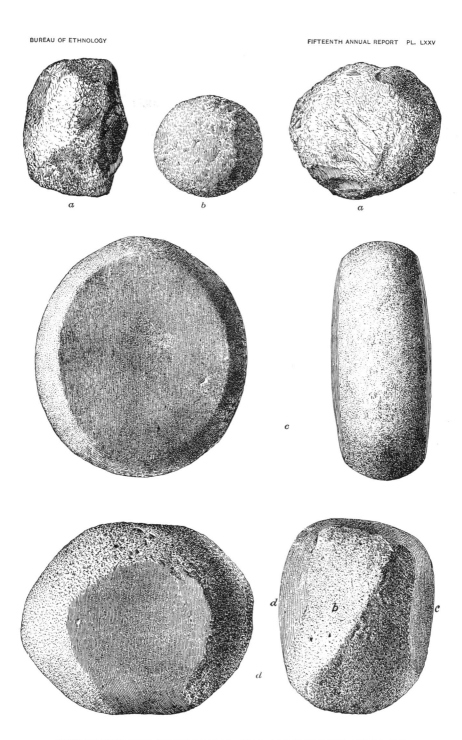

HAMMERSTONES FROM POTOMAC VILLAGE-SITES; THREE-FOURTHS ACTUAL SIZE
a, quartz; *b, c, d*, quartzite

Of the peculiar stones illustrated in the upper figures of plate LXXIV
I will not venture to say more than that they are apparently abrading
implements, but whether they were for the shaping of stone tools or the
dressing of wood, bone, or thongs can not be determined. The material appears to be a dark-gray eruptive rock. The lower specimen is of
a somewhat gritty stone and was probably a simple grindstone. All
are from sites about the head of tidewater on the Potomac.

The hammerstones brought together in plate LXXV represent the
varieties most common on the village-sites of the province. All are
from the tidewater Potomac. The smaller specimens in the upper line
are of quartz and the others are of quartzite.

CHAPTER V

INCISED OR CUT STONE UTENSILS

SCOPE OF THE TOPIC

This chapter is made to include two distinct yet necessarily associated groups of phenomena: 1, all that relates to the origin, manufacture, nature, use, and historic significance of utensils shaped by the incising methods; and, 2, all that relates to the utensils and implements employed in the shaping operations. In order that the whole subject of the manipulation of the softer varieties of stone might appear together as a unit in this place, the various flaked, battered or pecked, and polished implements used in quarrying and carving were passed over with mere mention in the sections to which they strictly belong, and are presented in some detail in the following pages, with a series of illustrations.

PROCESSES AND MATERIALS

Under the head of cut stone we have to deal with but few materials, and only one of these (steatite, or soapstone) was of importance in the native art of the tidewater country. Mica, serpentine, clay-slates, and others of the softer calcareous and argillaceous rocks were sparingly shaped by the process in some sections. The shaping operations were necessarily confined to narrow limits by the lack of effective cutting tools. Steatite and like soft and tough massive substances were cut with pointed pick-like tools and by edged, chisel-like blades, probably in most cases set in some sort of handle for direct free-hand operation, or with other classes of handles, to be operated with the aid of a mallet of bone or of antler or wood. Mica must have been cut with sharp edges or points, such as are furnished by the fracture of glassy varieties of stone.

Subsidiary to the incising processes in the shaping of soft stones are several of the other processes, such as sawing, drilling, scraping, and grinding.

USE OF MICA

So far as we can learn, mica was not extensively used by the Chesapeake-Potomac peoples; but it can not safely be affirmed that it was not used in some quantity in nearly any given locality, since the material is not sufficiently durable to be preserved, save under very favorable conditions. Mica does not occur in forms suitable for working within considerable distances of tidewater sites. It is said to have been worked by the natives in several counties of southern-central Virginia and in Pennsylvania and the Carolinas. The processes of mining, as observed in the mines of North Carolina, appear to have been much the same as in the quarrying of steatite. The deposits were uncovered and the massive crystals were broken up with hammers and the best sheets secured to be used for mirrors, or cut into desired shapes for ornaments. In the spring of 1893 Mr De Lancey W. Gill went to Mitchell county, North Carolina, under my direction, to collect materials representing the ancient mica-quarrying industry for the Columbian Exposition at Chicago. Numerous quarrying implements resembling those used in the soapstone quarries were found, and the excavations are reported to be quite as extensive as in any other class of the aboriginal quarries of the east.

STEATITE UTENSILS

CHARACTER, USE, AND DISTRIBUTION OF THE MATERIAL

Steatite (or soapstone) was used somewhat extensively by the natives of the tidewater country in the manufacture of pots, dishes, and cups, as well as of smaller articles, such as pipes and ornaments. It was obtained along the western border of the tidewater country, either from the surface or by quarrying, and the articles made are scattered over the entire province, occurring somewhat less frequently as we pass outward toward the Atlantic shore-line. The larger objects were extremely heavy and their transportation was necessarily limited largely to the waterways.

Steatite is of common occurrence over a wide belt of territory extending through the New England states and continuing down the Atlantic slope to Alabama. In Maryland and Virginia the best-known deposits occur along the eastern border of the Piedmont highland, often within the border of the tidewater area. Its geologic relations and character are now pretty well made out.

Being a tenacious rock, it resists erosion and is consequently well exposed in stream banks, in cliffs, and on the crests of hills and ridges. The outcrops have been worked by the aborigines in innumerable places in Vermont, New Hampshire, Massachusetts, Rhode Island, Connecticut, New Jersey, Pennsylvania, Maryland, Virginia, the Carolinas, and Georgia. More recently the whites have mined it extensively, and many of the quarries originally worked by the Indians have been reopened for commercial purposes, and the traces of the ancient operations thereby partially or entirely obliterated. At the same time this work has resulted in calling the attention of students of archeology to the subject and in giving them an excellent opportunity for investigating the ancient industry.

SURFACE INDICATIONS OF QUARRYING

As a rule the surface indications of the ancient operations are not distinctly marked. The pittings are commonly not very deep; on slopes where filling-in takes place rapidly they are wholly obliterated. Few instances occur in which the depressions now remaining are more than 2 or 3 feet deep. The diameter of the pittings does not generally exceed 20 or 30 feet, yet in cases they had the form of trenches or chains of pits extending for hundreds of feet along the strike of the deposit. Mr Fowke describes an excavation seen by him near Culpeper, Virginia, which is 150 feet in diameter and of undetermined depth, being filled with water and débris.

SPECIAL INVESTIGATIONS

EARLY KNOWLEDGE OF STEATITE

The use of soapstone by the native races is frequently mentioned by early writers, but no information is given of the acquisition and shaping of the material. One of the earliest accounts of the work in this country is that of Mr Paul Schumacher, who discovered typical quarries in the state of California. His illustration of the quarry face, with its partly developed nodes of the stone, published in the eleventh annual report of the Peabody Museum, would equally well illustrate the operations in our eastern quarries. The vessels and other articles produced are very numerous and differ widely from eastern forms.

Subsequently, Dr Elmer R. Reynolds, of Washington city, made some studies in the Rose hill quarry near Washington, and published a paper on the subject in the thirteenth annual report of the Peabody Museum. About this time Mr F. H. Cushing, representing the Smithsonian Institution, made extensive excavations in an ancient quarry in Amelia county, Virginia, and prepared a model of the exposed quarry surface illustrating the various phases of cutting out the incipient vessels. No report of his work was published, save a note in the *American Naturalist* for 1878.

In 1882 an important paper by Mr J. D. McGuire on the soapstone quarries of Maryland and the District of Columbia was read before the Anthropological Society of Washington, an extract of which is published in the second volume of its transactions. The present writer's preliminary paper on the Connecticut avenue quarries appeared in the *American Anthropologist* for October, 1890.

A very interesting and extensive quarry was discovered in about the year 1877, on the ground of Mr H. N. Angell, near Providence, Rhode Island, and a note describing the phenomena observed appears in the *American Naturalist* for 1878. These phenomena are essentially identical with those of more southern localities.

A like example was observed on the farm of J. T. Case near Bristol, Connecticut, in 1892, and excavations were made therein by Marshall H. Saville for the Peabody Museum. Many interesting specimens were obtained, not differing materially from those of other quarries. Vermont has furnished a similar example, and Pennsylvania abounds in such quarries. According to Charles H. Stubbs, in a note in the Smithsonian Report for 1882, an important quarry is located near Christiana, Lancaster county, in the latter state.

Explorations conducted for the Bureau of Ethnology during the years 1890–1894 extend from the Patuxent valley in Howard county, Maryland, to the southern borders of Virginia. I made it a rule in this as in other departments of field work to visit and examine as many sites as possible, and then to select certain favorable examples for detailed study, making these the types of groups of phenomena too extensive to be fully gone over. Excavation has been undertaken at but two points—the Rose hill or Connecticut avenue quarry, near Washington, and a quarry near Clifton, Fairfax county, Virginia, 22 miles southwest of Washington.

DEVELOPMENT OF THE QUARRYING INDUSTRY

The early occupants of the Potomac region, in their search for materials capable of serving them in their simple arts, probably discovered and attempted to utilize loose masses of the soft and tough stone known to us as steatite or soapstone. The progress toward its extensive utilization was no doubt very slow, and unless previous knowledge of such stone had been gained elsewhere, must have continued for centuries. Step by step the peculiar qualities and adaptabilities of the material were developed and diligent search was made for it throughout the highland. When the convenient loose masses were exhausted, the rock in place was attacked where it outcropped in the stream beds and on the hillsides, and partially detached portions were pried or broken off; then the process of uncovering followed and the quarrying industry was initiated. Sharp stones were employed to cut off projecting pieces, and finally cutting tools were made and improved, so that the solid stone could be removed to considerable depths.

We are not able to discover just what devices were employed in the preliminary quarry work. The earth was probably loosened with wooden pikes and with picks of stone and antler, and was thrown up with the hands or carried out in baskets of bark or cane, or in skins. As the quarrying advanced the older pits were filled with the débris, and evidences of the operations were much obscured. It is only when the pits are fully cleaned out that we come to realize the full nature and extent of the ancient work. Our excavations brought to light surprising evidences of the energy, perseverance, and skill of the native miner, and showed the practice of an art totally distinct from that carried on in the bowlder quarries of Piny branch.

MINING AND SHAPING OPERATIONS

The method of conducting the quarry work was substantially as follows: When a sufficient area of the solid stone had been uncovered, the workmen proceeded with pick and chisel to detach such portions as were desired. If this surface happened to be uneven, the projections or convexities were utilized, and the cutting was not difficult; if the rock was massive and the surface flat, a circular groove was cut, out-lining the mass to be removed, and the cutting was continued until a depth was reached corresponding to the height of the utensil to be made; then, by undercutting, the nucleus was detached or so far severed that it could be broken off by means of sledges or levers. If the stone happened to be laminated, a circular groove was cut through at right angles to the bedding, and the discoid mass was removed without the need of undercutting. If the conditions were favorable, a second disk was cut adjoining the first, and then a third, and so on, pretty much as the housewife cuts up the thin layer of dough in biscuit making.

In cases where the floor and walls of a well-developed quarry are fully exposed, as in the Clifton and Amelia county quarries in Vir-ginia, the details of ancient operations are clearly displayed. In cases it is seen that the task of cutting out the mass was just begun when operations in the quarry closed, while in others it was well under way and the bulbous nuclei stand out in bold relief. In cases where under-cutting has taken place the rounded form resembles a mushroom on its stem and is ready to be removed by a blow; while in many other cases we see only roundish depressions in the quarry surface, in the bottoms of which are stumps or scars indicating that removal of the mass had taken place. It often happened that the work of cutting was stopped by the discovery of defects in the stone. In very many cases defects were not discovered until too late, and the operations of removal at the last moment became abortive; instead of breaking off at the base, as was intended, the cleavage of the stone was such that the body split in two, leaving a portion remaining attached to the stem. The drawing presented in plate LXXVI will give a more satisfactory idea of the whole range of phenomena than can any mere description.

A notable feature of the cutting out of these masses of stone is the attendant shaping of the mass, which was rudely sculptured as the work went on, the contour of the vessel being approximately developed. Although I have seen no good examples of this class, it is confidently stated by others that rude nodes were carved at opposite ends of the mass as incipient handles, and that excavation of the bowl was begun, so that when severed from the stem the vessel was already well under way.

QUARRY PRODUCT

So far as I have observed, the quarries rarely yield evidence of the prosecution of any other shaping work than that of obtaining the rounded bodies of stone and the partial development of vessels. Pipes, sinkers, ceremonial stones, and ornaments were made by the same people, but mostly no doubt from choice bits of stone carried

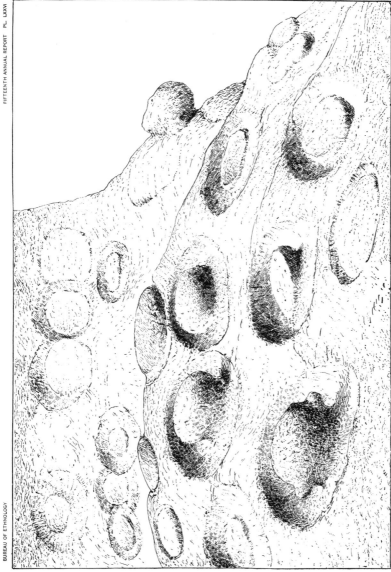

SURFACE OF A SOAPSTONE QUARRY, SHOWING VARIOUS PHASES OF THE CUTTING OPERATIONS

In the Clifton quarry an area of upward of 2,000 square feet is covered with these evidences of ancient industry

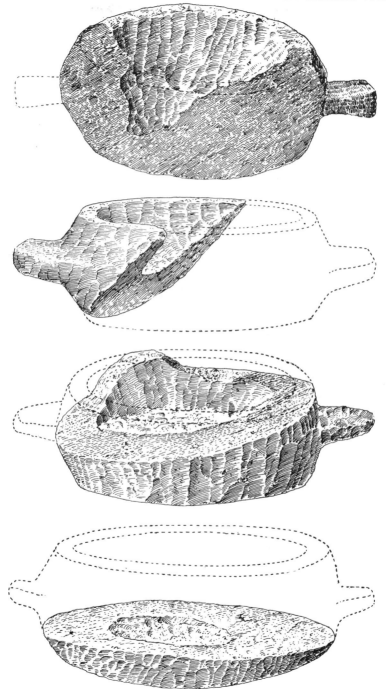

INCIPIENT VESSELS BROKEN DURING THE SHAPING OPERATIONS AND LEFT WITH THE QUARRY
REFUSE; FROM THE CLIFTON QUARRY; ABOUT ONE-THIRD ACTUAL SIZE

away for the purpose, or perhaps often from fragments of vessels broken in use.

About the quarries and in the quarry débris are specimens exhibiting every stage of the vessel-shaping work; irregular fragments and well-rounded masses just as cut from the quarry, but usually showing some defect of texture or shape, explaining their desertion or rejection; other pieces partly shaped before the defects became apparent; and very many specimens broken by the blows of the shaping tools, as illustrated in plate LXXVII; so that every step of the work and every phase of the shaping operations are fully represented. The rough-dressed shapes vary a good deal with the different quarries, though on the whole there is decided uniformity in the work as carried on throughout the soapstone belt. Final forms, as shown by village-site remains, are limited to shallow trays or dishes, trough-like forms, and deep basins. Nowhere in eastern United States were pots made of the deep globular form so common in California.

A prevailing shape in the Potomac-Chesapeake region is an oblong basin with ear-like projections or handles at the ends. The largest specimens are about 25 inches in length. The width is often hardly more than half the length, and the depth averages perhaps one-half the width. This form may have been suggested by wooden dishes or mortars of like shape, examples of which are still in use among some of the Algonquian tribes. Other forms approach more nearly a circular outline, as viewed from above, and these usually have greater depth. In cases the outline is somewhat rectangular. Roughed-out cups of small size are sometimes found.

The handles of steatite vessels differ much in size and shape as well as in position. Some are placed near the margin or rim, but others, where the vessels are deep, occur low on the profile. The accompanying illustrations (plates LXXVIII, LXXIX, and LXXX) convey accurate notions of many details.

The form development of a vessel of ordinary character is illustrated in plate LXXVIII. The ovoid nucleus as cut out of the quarry appears in a, the handles being only slightly suggested. Excavation of the bowls was begun by a series of pick strokes outlining the basin, as seen in b, a core-like elevation remaining in the center until removed by continued cutting, as suggested in c and d. The form of the roughed-out vessel as developed in the quarries is quite fairly indicated in e. In some cases the excavation began with a pit in the center and was carried outward by successive strokes toward the rim; and in very many cases the work was unsystematic and crude, as is well shown in plate LXXIX. In specimens found on the surface of the ground the tool marks are much obscured by weathering, but in those from a depth they are as fresh as if made but yesterday. The cutting implement was in some cases pointed or spike-like, but generally had a chisel-like, though rounded, cutting edge half an inch or more in width, leaving impressions such as are shown in plate LXXIX, which illustrates two somewhat small rejects from the Connecticut avenue quarries. This edge was sometimes rather rough and uneven, leaving scratchy lines, suggesting a flaked rather than a polished tool. The character of the work varies a great deal; in some cases the strokes were bold and professional in appearance, in others timid and uncertain. Three excellent examples of roughed-out vessels are shown in plate LXXX; *a* and *b* are from quarry sites, where they were rejected and deserted, while *c* is from a village-site at College Station, Maryland, several miles from the nearest quarry. These specimens show decided differences in shape of bowl and placement of handles.

IMPLEMENTS USED IN QUARRYING AND CUTTING

CHARACTER OF THE TOOLS

The tools and utensils employed in the quarrying and shaping of steatite may be reviewed with considerable care, since they prove to be, as far as brought to light, largely of classes peculiar to the work and hitherto practically unknown to archeologists.

It is safe to assume that there were many implements of wood as well as bone and antler used in uncovering and removing the stone that have wholly disappeared. These hypothetic utensils would no doubt include levers, pikes, mauls or mallets, picks, hoes, and shovel-like tools.

Naturally very many of the tools used were of stone, and these are found in considerable numbers on the quarry sites and on shop and village sites in the vicinity. There is no clear distinction to be drawn between those used in quarrying and cutting out the raw material and those employed in shaping the vessels, yet it may be assumed that in general the heavy, rude tools were for quarrying and that the more delicate, sharp-edged or pointed tools were for shaping and finishing. The heavier tools consist of rounded sledge-like masses used for driving wedges and for breaking off portions of the stone, of heavy wedge-like stones, often much battered as if from blows by heavy sledges, and of pick-like forms, some rude, others well shaped by flaking and pecking. One variety of the picks is roughly grooved by flaking and pecking, and another has a plain shaft, often a little curved as if to be attached to a handle somewhat as our picks and adzes. In several of the quarries we have found ordinary grooved axes, most of them having been remodeled or resharpened by flaking to make them efficient in picking and cutting; then there is a large class of chisel-like tools of varied sizes and shapes, sometimes improvised from stones of approximate proportions slightly flaked or ground to effective points, sometimes flaked out of the raw material, which is generally a greenish-gray basic eruptive rock obtained from the highland, and possibly by quarrying.

Generally these tools were made by skilled hands and are developed into such highly individualized shapes that we are compelled to allow

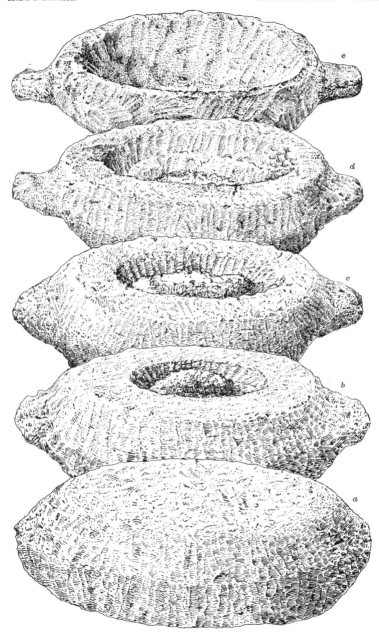

SERIES OF FORMS SHOWING STEPS IN THE STEATITE-SHAPING PROCESS RANGING FROM
THE OVOID MASS CUT FROM THE QUARRY TO THE ROUGH FINISHED VESSEL; FROM
THE CLIFTON QUARRY; ABOUT ONE-THIRD ACTUAL SIZE

QUARRY-SHOP REJECTS SHOWING EARLY STAGES OF THE STEATITE SHAPING WORK AND SHOWING THE
CHISEL OR PICK MARKS WITH PERFECT CLEARNESS. FROM THE CONNECTICUT AVENUE QUARRIES;
ABOUT ONE-HALF ACTUAL SIZE

a

b

c

EXAMPLES OF UNFINISHED STEATITE VESSELS

a and *b* (11 inches and 8 inches, respectively, in length) are from the Cliton quarry, and *c* (11½ inches in length) is from a village-site at College Station, Maryland

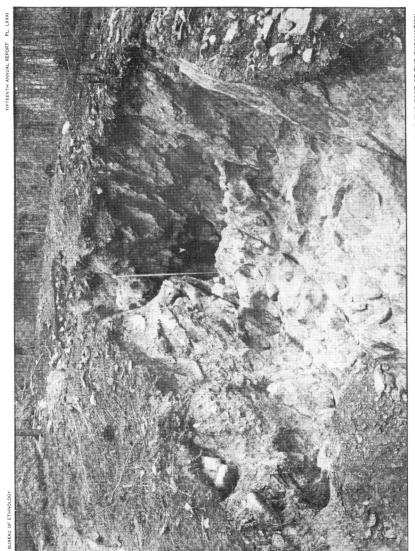

VIEW OF THE CLIFTON QUARRY AFTER CLEARING OUT, AS IT APPEARED FROM A PLATFORM ERECTED IN THE STREAM BED AT THE FOOT OF THE EXCAVATION

that the industry in which they were employed was one of importance and long standing. Nearly all the forms are represented in the several plates accompanying this chapter.

The number of the tools and their importance to the steatite-working peoples is illustrated by the following observations: Around a single pit located in a plowed field on Patuxent river, and nearly obliterated by successive plowings, I found during a single visit some 30 entire and broken implements, and from the excavation in the quarry near Clifton, Virginia, nearly four dozen of the chisel-like tools, some broken and some entire, were found.

MANNER OF USING THE TOOLS

There are three or four ways in which the cutting tools could have been used. The simplest was that of holding the pointed stone in the hand or hands, and thus striking the potstone. This would, however, be a most unsatisfactory method and would hardly be applied where opportunity was afforded for superior methods.

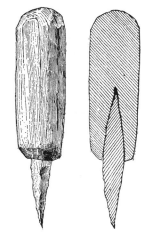

Another manner of use was that of setting the sharpened stone or chisel in a short handle of buckhorn, and striking this with a stone or billet of wood. The chisel marks left in many cases suggest this method very strongly, and the heavy end of the tool as found is usually furnished with a short and rough-flaked point suitable for setting in a handle, as suggested in figure 16. Many specimens of this class are too minute to be utilized in any other way, and some are slightly notched as if mere knives.

FIG. 16—Probable manner of hafting the smaller chisels.

A third method is that of hafting the pointed stone as an adz or ax is hafted. The grooved tools were undoubtedly used in this way, and many of the grooveless forms could have been attached as is the ordinary primitive adz. This would give much greater efficiency in all the work of cutting and roughing-out, and the boldness and irregularity of the stroke marks left on the quarry face and on the detached masses and partly finished vessels make it practically certain that this was the manner of their attachment. With short handles, such as indicated in figure 17, effective and very neat work could be done, and it may be remarked that such a tool could be handled in the cramped quarters in which the cutting was often carried on almost as conveniently as could the chisel driven by a mallet.

Among the chisels there are numerous slightly curved forms, some with one ground point that could have been hafted as in a, figure 17, and others with two points that may have been mounted so as to make both points effective, as in b, figure 17. The shortest two-pointed tool, a very neat and delicate specimen, is hardly more than 3 inches long, while the largest is 11 inches in length.

STEATITE QUARRIES

THE CLIFTON QUARRY

The most interesting example of the soapstone quarries examined by the Bureau during the progress of the work described in the present paper was the Hetzel-Hunter quarry, near Clifton, in Fairfax county, Virginia. Late in the fall of 1893 Mrs Margaret Hetzel, of Clifton and Washington city, communicated to Professor O. T. Mason, of the National Museum, the fact that in prospecting a soapstone deposit near

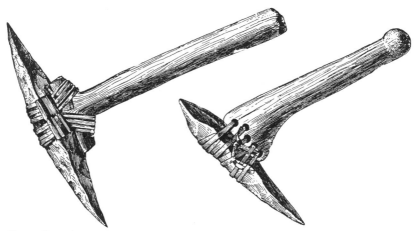

Fig. 17—Probable manner of hafting the single-pointed and the two-pointed chisels or picks.

Clifton the owners had discovered traces of aboriginal operations, and expressed a desire that the Smithsonian Institution should undertake an examination. This was reported to me by Professor Mason, and the quarry was put on the list for examination so soon as the field season of 1894 opened. Late in March the work was taken up, and Mr William Dinwiddie was sent out with instructions to clear out the ancient excavations in such a way that, if possible, the entire floor and the quarry faces would be exposed for study and photography. This was done in the completest possible manner, and in a few weeks a most striking illustration of the enterprise and skill of our aboriginal tribes was exposed to view. A trench or gallery some 25 feet wide and reaching in places a depth of 16 feet had been carried into the face of the hill to a distance of 60 or 70 feet, and a second pit, inferior in dimensions, had been opened beyond this. Almost the entire excavation had been carved out of the solid steatite by means of stone picks and

15 ETH——8

chisels, and all the evidences of the cutting and sculpturing—even the whitened surfaces of the tool marks—were as fresh as if the work of yesterday.

The quarry is located on a small branch of Bull run, 2 miles north-west of Clifton and 22 miles a little south of west of Washington city. The steatite outcrops in the bed and banks of a small rivulet, crossing it at right angles, and seems to be an irregular bed or stratum inter-calated with the gneiss of the Piedmont formation. It varies from 20 to 40 or 50 feet in thickness, and has a nearly north-and-south strike and a dip of from 70° to 80° toward the west.

The ancient peoples probably began work by removing detached or partly detached masses from the stream bed, and then little by little followed the ledge up and into the steep hillside toward the north. This hill is a spur of a low ridge on the west, and is some 40 feet in height. It slopes off rapidly to the junction of the quarry rivulet with another branch two or three hundred feet below. The surface is cov-ered with soil and disintegrated gneiss.

Our investigations developed the fact that there had been two main pits or excavations—a long and wide gallery mentioned above, and higher up a second pit about 20 feet in diameter and 8 or 10 feet deep connecting with the first but lying at the left, as indicated in the accompanying sketch map, figure 18.

So completely were the ancient excavations filled up that inexperi-enced eyes would hardly have detected anything unusual in the appear-ance of the rounded slope of the hill. The main trench was marked by a slight depression toward the upper end, and the débris accumu-lated low down along the sides formed barely perceptible convexities. No doubt the excavations had been largely filled as the work advanced, and material from the upper pit had helped to obliterate what remained of the main final depression.

The location of the upper pit was indicated by a shallow depression some 20 feet in diameter and 2 or 3 feet deep, where modern exploiters had sunk a prospect hole. This pit had been left open, and its position high on the hill had prevented rapid filling.

When the Bureau began its work of excavation the owners of the quarry had already uncovered a portion of the ancient quarry floor, which rises from the stream bed at a low angle, so that at 30 feet it is about 10 feet above the stream and not more than 4 or 5 feet beneath the slope surface. But little stone had been removed by the ancient workmen, although evidences of excavation and cutting were distinctly seen, and a few stumps, scars, and bulbous chiseled masses appeared at the upper edge.

Soon after beginning work the floor was found to descend into numer-ous pits and depressions where the superior quality of the stone had led the quarrymen to persist in their work. The general level of the floor was maintained for a distance of some 70 feet back into the hill, and the deeper pittings at the back reached 15 or 16 feet beneath the

profile of the slope.   Much impure stone had been cut away in efforts
to reach the purer masses, and this was a most laborious work.   But
it is safe to say that one-half or three-fourths of the excavation was
accomplished by cutting out, with chisels and picks, the solid and
massive steatite.   The whole surface, with its nodes and humps and
depressions, covered everywhere with the markings, groovings, and
pittings of the chisel, presented a striking example of the effectiveness

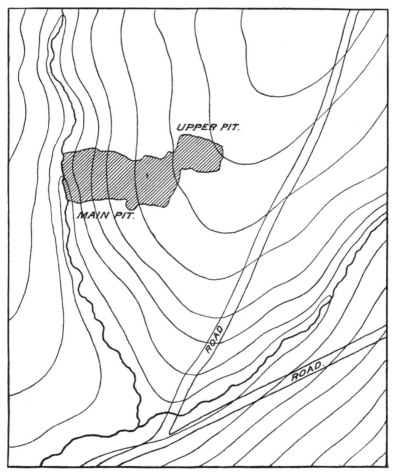

FIG. 18—Sketch map of the Clifton quarry; scale about 50 feet to the inch.

of native methods and the persistence of native efforts.   A view of the
quarry, after it had been thoroughly cleaned out and swept, is shown
in plate LXXXI.   The photograph was obtained by erecting a platform
20 feet in height in the stream bed at the foot of the quarry.   The
deepest part of the pitting is at the back, where the figure of a man
may be imperfectly made out.   The farther extension of the quarry is

indistinctly seen at the left beyond the measuring rod. The irregularly noded and pitted surface is rather imperfectly shown in the picture. The width of the seam of workable stone is indicated by the width of the quarry, and the change in direction at the farther end of the main pit seems to have been due to a change in the character of the stone.

In plate LXXXII I have brought together a number of the cutting implements selected from the two or three score recovered. Many examples are of small size and show varying degrees of finish. Those shown are of a dark-gray eruptive rock and have been carefully shaped and finished. The larger specimen a, a has been ground into nearly symmetrical shape and has a fine conical point. The chisel b, b was flaked into general shape and both ends were reduced by grinding to excellent flattish cutting edges. The smaller specimen c has a neatly sharpened point and is wide at the opposite end, and like the smaller example d, which is obscurely notched near the top, was probably set in an antler handle for use as a chisel. Among the finds was a well-shaped and much-used hammerstone of quartzite, which had probably served to trim and sharpen the cutting tools.

Traces of an old village-site were discovered on the stream bank, a hundred yards or more below the quarry, and here various objects of steatite, including a partially shaped but broken pipe, were found. The more ordinary dwelling sites of the operators of this quarry were doubtless on the larger streams below, and probably extended far down the Potomac. This quarry can not be a great many miles from the "antimony mines" reported by the native guides to the English who first explored the Potomac. The fact that these peoples were enterprising enough to work an "antimony mine" suggests the probable identity of these Indians with the workers of the soapstone mines as well as of the quartzite quarries of the general region.

THE CONNECTICUT AVENUE QUARRIES

Extensive deposits of steatite are found within the limits of the District of Columbia, but only one locality presents abundant traces of ancient operations. This site is by some called the Rose hill quarry and by others the Dumbarton quarry. It is situated on Connecticut avenue extended, 4 miles from the Executive Mansion, three-fourths of a mile east of Tenallytown, and a mile and a half from each of the two great quartzite-bowlder quarries already described.

LITERATURE

The quarries in this locality seem to have been first studied by Dr Elmer R. Reynolds, who in 1878 published[1] a careful description of the

---

[1] Thirteenth annual report of the Peabody Museum, 1878, p. 526.

site and of the articles collected by him. About that time visits to the site were made by Dr Charles Rau, Professor O. T. Mason, Mr F. H. Cushing, and others, and extensive collections of articles, mainly from the surface of the ground, were made. Mention is made by Dr Reynolds of excavations conducted by these gentlemen, but no definite information on this point is on record. Mr Cushing informs me that slight excavations were made on the southern hill. A paper published by Mr Louis A. Kengla, formerly of Washington, gives considerable additional matter, accompanied by illustrations of fragments of vessels obtained in the District of Columbia.[1]

SITE AND SURFACE INDICATIONS

The mass of steatite exposed on this site, being firmer and tougher than the gneisses with which it is associated, gave rise, as erosion progressed, to two very decided prominences, separated by a sharp ravine cut by a small stream, tributary to Rock creek, known as Soapstone creek. The natural exposures are confined to the bed and the steeper banks of the stream and to the crests of the hills, the latter rising in somewhat conical form—the one on the southern side of the ravine to about 80 feet and the one on the northern side to fully 90 feet above the stream.

The northern hill has a rounded, oblong summit, in which the steatite is exposed or approaches very near the surface for a length, nearly north and south, of more than 100 feet and a width of 20 or 30 feet. The rock seems to be bedded with the greatest length of the crest, and consists of nearly vertical, more or less massive layers of steatite. The slopes of the hill are covered with deposits of disintegrated gneiss and vegetal mold, and consequently the gneiss with which the steatite is surrounded and interbedded is in no place visible. The whole site is thickly covered with forest trees and underbrush.

In 1891 the extension of Connecticut avenue led to the removal of the lower portions of both hills, as indicated in the sketch map *a*, plate LXXXIII, the cut in the southern hill exposing portions of the strata to a depth of 60 feet, and obliterating a number of the ancient pits. The steatite brought to light by the grading is, however, of very poor quality and unfit for commercial purposes, which is true also of the entire deposit, as indicated by the cessation of recent quarrying operations conducted by the Hunter brothers. A section of the two hills appears in *c*, plate LXXXIII.

The evidences of ancient pitting are confined chiefly to the summits of the hills, but no one can say to what extent the exposures of soapstone in the sides of the ravine were worked. The southern bank of the stream has recently been excavated to a considerable depth by the Hunter brothers, and the original configuration is somewhat destroyed;

---

[1] Archeology of the District of Columbia, Washington, 1883.

IMPLEMENTS USED IN CUTTING STEATITE ; FROM THE CLIFTON QUARRY

a, two-thirds actual size ; *b, c, d,* actual size

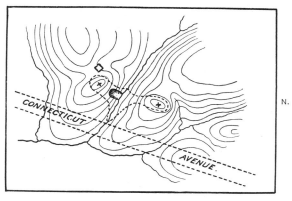

a

Sketch map of the Connecticut avenue quarries. The area of the soapstone
outcrop is inclosed by a dotted line and the tops of the two hails are
marked by crosses

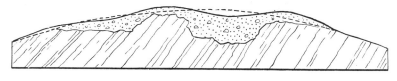

b

Section of the pittings on the northern hill.   The dotted line indicates the original profile

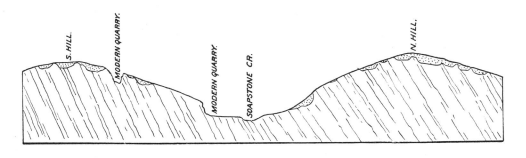

c

Section through the two hills, Connecticut avenue quarries

MAP AND SECTIONS OF THE CONNECTICUT AVENUE STEATITE QUARRIES

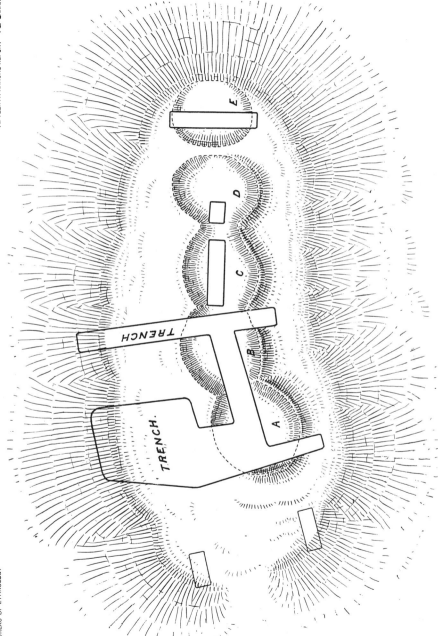

MAP SHOWING TRENCHING OF THE ANCIENT STEATITE QUARRIES ON THE NORTHERN HILL ; SCALE ABOUT 20 FEET TO THE INCH

VIEW IN EXCAVATION ON THE NORTHERN HILL, SHOWING SURFACE OF MASSIVE STEATITE ONLY SLIGHTLY MARKED
BY THE QUARRY IMPLEMENTS

but on the northern side there is an obscure excavation of considerable dimensions that may be at least partially due to aboriginal operations. Pits sunk in the sides of the hills would soon be filled by débris descending from above, but on the crests they would necessarily remain clearly marked for a long period of time; their obliteration in the latter case would depend on the very slow accumulation of vegetal mold or of wind-blown material. In any attempt at estimating age from mere appearances, therefore, the relation of the excavation to the surrounding surface must be considered; this has already been pointed out with some degree of care in describing the quartzite-bowlder quarries.

The excavations undertaken under my supervision were confined largely to the summit of the northern hill, as the ancient quarries had there remained wholly undisturbed save by the normal agencies of nature. A row of pits, forming almost a connected trench, extended along the crest and for a short distance down the northern end of the hill. There were five well-marked depressions in this series, the outlines being irregular (see plate LXXXIV). All were less than 25 feet in diameter, and the greatest depth was not above 2 or 3 feet. Dr Elmer R. Reynolds describes one pit on the southern hill as being over 3 feet deep. The heaps and ridges of débris thrown from the pits by the ancient miners extended along the sides of the row of pits, and were not above a foot in height. This débris consisted for the greater part of earth and irregular masses of steatite. Among the latter were found many fragments of unfinished vessels and rejects of various kinds. Shallow depressions, marking the sites of ancient pits, occur along the sides of the crest on the southern and western slopes of the hill.

EXCAVATIONS MADE

Our examinations of the Connecticut avenue quarries were commenced by carrying a trench across the southern pit of the series on the northern hill. This exposed portions of the ancient quarry face on the southern, eastern, and western sides, while the northern edge of our excavation penetrated the full depth of the ancient quarry, which was here not more than 4 or 5 feet.

Beginning with the deepest part of this first trench, a wide trench was carried northward along the chain of ancient pits. Cross trenches were dug at frequent intervals, and others were subsequently dug on the southern slope. In all, not less than 800 square feet of the ancient quarry floors were exposed and cleared off, and a very good idea of the nature of the ancient quarrying was obtained. The principal pits were worked to a depth of from 2 to 6 feet by the aborigines, and the bottoms and sides present the irregular appearance necessarily produced by prying out such masses of potstone as the quarrymen were able to detach. A view taken in the main trench is shown in plate LXXXV, and a section across one of the pits is given in b, plate LXXXIII. The beds of steatite are quite massive, exhibiting irregular lines of cleavage; the quality is, however, in the main, rather inferior. A sketch plan showing the trenches made on the quarry site is given in plate LXXXIV.

As in the quartzite-bowlder quarries, little evidence remains of the methods of quarrying. Tools of the classes already referred to were no doubt used to loosen and remove the earth and to pry up masses of the stone. Heavy rounded stones and hafted sledges served to break up the larger pieces and to detach projecting portions. In several places on the floor and sides of the quarry the surface of the potstone sl ows the usual pick marks, and in one place a slight grooving was seen where the work of dividing a large block had begun. The exposed surfaces seem for the most part to represent cleavage planes, and until solid massive rock was encountered the laborious process of cutting was uncalled for.

So far as the evidence obtained on the site shows, work was confined almost exclusively to procuring material for use in vessel making, but apparently the pots were not often shaped or even partly shaped in place, to be afterward detached by undercutting and wedging as observed in many other places. It appears that as a rule the rough block was first obtained, then trimmed down to the approximate size and form, and afterward hollowed out ready for the finishing operations, which were in most cases conducted elsewhere. There were naturally many failures from breaking, from splitting along partially developed cleavage planes, and from imperfections in texture; and many hundreds of these failures yet remain on the site, in the pits, in the heaps of débris, and scattered far down the slopes of the hill and along the stream bed.

TOOLS RECOVERED

The tools with which the work of quarrying was accomplished were sought most assiduously. It was expected that they would, in a measure at least, correspond to the tools known to be used by the modern Indians of the region, as many steatite pots are found on ordinary village-sites. This was found to be the case to a limited extent only. It was found that the tools used were, as a rule, made for and especially adapted to the work, which is unlike any other industry of the aborigines. The implements prove, therefore, to be in a measure unique, forming a class of their own.

The remoteness of the site and the rugged conformation of the hills on which the quarries are located render it improbable that the locality was used for dwelling or for any other purpose than that of quarrying and shaping the potstone.

The tools found all pertain to quarrying and to roughing-out the vessels, and may conveniently be divided into three classes: 1, those improvised on the spot for local temporary use; 2, those made for the purpose on distant sites; and, 3, those pertaining originally to other uses, brought from the villages and utilized in the quarries. A major·ity are of the first of these classes. They are, as a rule, quite rude, and were derived from quartz veins and bowlder beds in the vicinity of the quarry. Specimens collected approach as nearly a paleolithic type as any tools found in the Potomac region. Nothing more primi·tive is possible. The hills and slopes in the vicinity abound in out·crops of vein quartz, which breaks up into angular fragments. These are now so plentiful on the neighboring fields as to burden agriculture. Such angular fragments were gathered for use in the quarries. Some were already well adapted to use, while others were slightly trimmed, to give them better points and edges. Illustrations of these tools appear in figures 19 and 20.

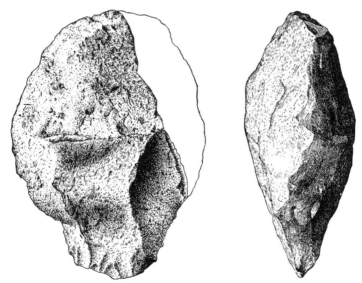

FIG. 19—Rude pick of quartz, slightly sharpened by flaking.

A number of angular masses of quartz were discovered that were not apparently adapted to any use and that showed no signs of having been used. They may be fragments of larger masses broken in use. A few bruised cobbles were found that must have been utilized in some way in the quarry work.

It is not considered necessary to take further notice of specimens showing no decided evidence of design or use, or that do not by their natural conformation show especial adaptation to use. The objects of quartz that show evidence of shaping by percussion are all of one type. They are thick, angular masses, weighing a pound or more; one end is brought to a short, sharp point, and the other is somewhat rounded, as if to be held in the hand or hands for striking. Of the same general shape are two picks made from quartzite bowlders and resembling heavy-pointed turtlebacks (figures 21, 22). In no case

FIG. 20—Rude pick of quartz, slightly sharpened by flaking.

does the form of these tools suggest the attachment of a haft, although such attachment would probably be feasible.

Three chisel-like tools were found in the main trench on the summit of the hill. They are of peculiar types, and we may fairly assume that

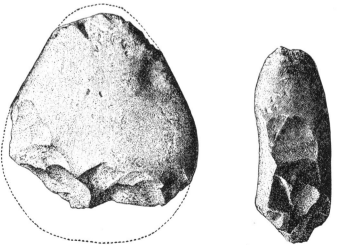

FIG. 21—Rude pick made by sharpening quartzite bowlder.

they were made.for use in the potstone shop. One made of gray eruptive rock is blade-shaped and has a fine chisel-like point or edge. It is shown in *a,a*, plate LXXXVIII.

Another specimen (illustrated in *b,b*, plate LXXXVI) is of greenish-gray slaty-looking eruptive rock, very slightly altered by chemical changes. It is rather rudely chipped along both sides, and the point has been made quite sharp by grinding. Properly hafted as a pick, or as a chisel to be driven by a mallet, this little celt would have been a very effective tool in shaping and trimming the vessels. As it stands, without hafting, it is too small for effective use. A small chisel from the southern hill is given in *c,c* in the same plate.

From the soil that filled one of the shallow pits on the southern margin of the crest of the hill, a chipped tool of unusual shape, given in *a,a*, plate LXXXVII, was obtained. It resembles somewhat the drills or perforators of the same material found on village-sites, but is larger, ruder, and less symmetrical, and was probably made especially for use in the trimming of soapstone vessels.

FIG. 22—Rude pick made by sharpening quartzite bowlder.

Another is made of a blackish argillite-like rock that has become gray on the surface through oxidation of some of its constituent minerals. In its general configuration it is somewhat like the quartzite blades produced in the quarry-shops of the district, but it differs from them in having a chisel-like point or edge. This edge is somewhat oblique and shows but little evidence of use, although chemical changes in the stone may have obliterated such evidence. It is shown in *b,b*, plate LXXXVII.

A quite perfect specimen of this class, having a well-rounded body and neat, sharp edge, was picked up on the southern hill; it is shown in *d,d*. A much larger example of the same class was brought to light by the grading operations along Connecticut avenue, on the eastern slope of the southern hill (plate LXXXVIII). A nest of four well-shaped chisels, two of which appear in plate XCI, was discovered by me near the summit of the hill; all were sharpened by grinding.

One of the most important finds made during the excavations at this place was a large grooved ax of the wedge-hafted type (*a*, plate XCII). It was found in one of the shallow pits on the southern margin of the hilltop, a foot from the surface and resting on the surface of the soapstone in place. There is no doubt that this tool was used by the ancient quarrymen in dislodging, and possibly in trimming, the masses of stone. Its edge shows considerable wear, apparently from use as a pick, and its surface irregularities are filled with steatite. Its weight and shape would make it a very effective tool. If proof that the workers of these quarries were Indians were necessary, the discovery of this object would seem to be satisfactory. Finds on the sites of ancient soapstone quarries in Maryland include many of these grooved axes. In most cases they have been more or less completely remodeled by flaking to fit them more fully for use as picks.

CORRELATION WITH BOWLDER QUARRIES

The question arises as to what correlations can be made out between the steatite quarries and the quartzite-bowlder quarries of the District of Columbia. Are they all probably of one age and the work of one people, or are they separated by long periods of time and by marked differences in art characters? It is observed that the two classes of quarries are located in the same valley and only a mile and a half apart; that they correspond as closely in extent and in appearances as could be expected if worked at one time and by one people; that modern neolithic implements are found in the steatite quarries, and that the products of the steatite quarries are found on many modern village-sites.

It appears that the steatite was not quarried to a depth equal to that of the quartzite bowlders, but it will be seen at a glance that the difficulties attending the working of the former are much the greater. With increasing depth the steatite becomes firmer and more massive, and the difficulty of detaching the necessary masses with primitive tools increases. With the bowlders the difficulty does not increase with the depth in the same degree, and greater depths could be reached with comparative ease.

It is true that the bowlder quarries exhibit more decided evidence of great age than do the steatite quarries in that the pits are much more completely filled up and obliterated. This fact may, however, lead to erroneous conclusions if the conditions under which the two classes of pits existed are not considered. The deepest steatite pits were not over 5 or 6 feet in depth, but they were excavated in solid rock and on the crests of hills where there was little or no material to fall into them save the leaves from the trees. Such of the pits as were not on the summits were entirely or almost entirely filled up. The cobble pits on

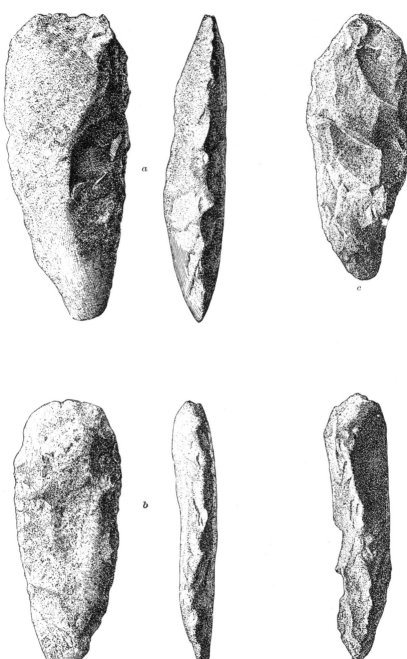

THREE CHISEL-LIKE IMPLEMENTS OF DARK ERUPTIVE ROCK FROM THE CONNECTICUT AVENUE
QUARRIES; ROUGHED OUT BY FLAKING AND SHARPENED BY GRINDING; ACTUAL SIZE

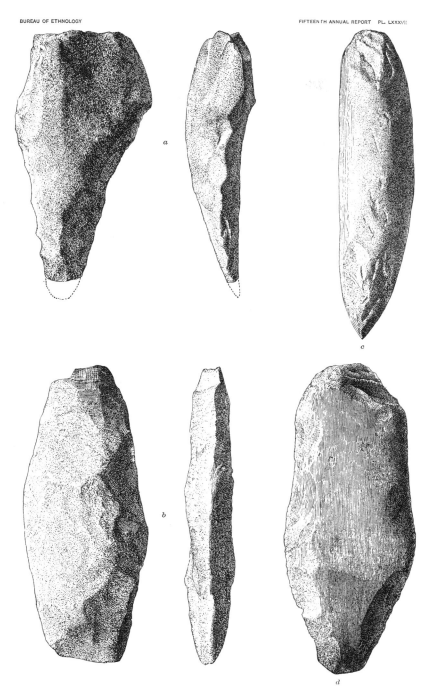

STEATITE-CUTTING IMPLEMENTS OF ERUPTIVE ROCK FROM THE CONNECTICUT AVENUE QUARRIES; ACTUAL SIZE

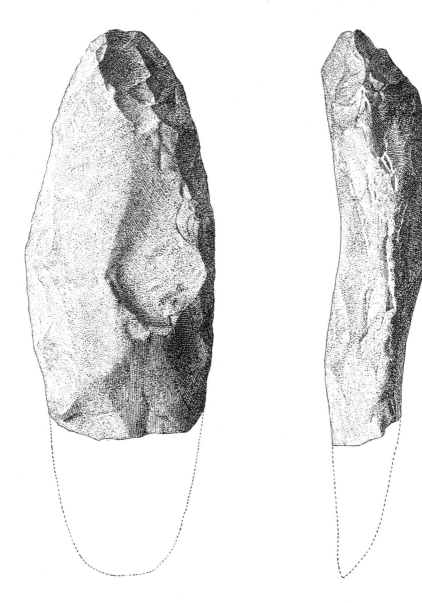

FRAGMENT OF A STEATITE QUARRY IMPLEMENT OF GREENISH-GRAY ERUPTIVE ROCK, EXPOSED
BY GRADING OF CONNECTICUT AVENUE ; THREE-FOURTHS ACTUAL SIZE

IMPLEMENTS USED IN CUTTING STEATITE; FROM A CACHE OF FOUR FOUND NEAR THE SURFACE ON THE SOUTHERN HILL

a, two-thirds actual size; *b*, actual size

Piny branch were in all cases situated on the slope of the hills, and were therefore directly beneath overhanging masses of loosely compacted sands and gravels and may have been more completely filled up in one year than the steatite pits in a century.

The character of the two sites corresponds very closely in the respect that both are in hills so steep as to be quite unsuited for camping or dwelling. Both are therefore naturally free from village refuse, and the tools found, for the most part if not exclusively, consist of those actually used in the work of quarrying and roughing-out the articles produced.

In the cobble quarries no tools of a durable material were needed save the natural bowlders found by thousands in the quarries. Carefully shaped hammerstones, polished celts, and grooved axes had no place in the industries carried on in these localities. A grooved ax, such as that found in the Connecticut avenue quarry, would be an effective tool in the work of quarrying steatite, and could be used without the least danger of breakage. The chisels were especially adapted to, and no doubt made for, the cutting out and carving of the steatite.

The nature and range of the work of shaping carried on in both classes of quarries has a close correspondence. No finished pieces of work of the classes made there were found in either class. In the cobble quarries the blade was roughed-out to a convenient shape for transportation and subsequent elaboration; in the steatite quarries the pots were roughed-out and carried away to be finished elsewhere. It is significant also that on many village-sites in the vicinity the shaped objects of both materials are found freely and intimately associated.

Review of the evidence thus shows many significant correspondences in the work of the two classes of quarries, and no differences that require the assumption of wide distinction either in time, people, or culture. The historical aborigines are probably responsible for all the phenomena observed.

THE SHOEMAKER QUARRY

About 2 miles southwest of the Rose hill quarries, and not far from the grounds of the American University, there are several obscure outcrops of steatite. Numerous partially worked vessels have been found, but if quarries ever existed they are now entirely obliterated by the plow.

THE LITTLE FALLS SITES

A slight outcrop of steatite occurs in the creek bank at the Virginia end of Chain bridge over the Potomac, just below Little falls and at the head of tidewater; but no traces of ancient work have been observed. That the work of quarrying and cutting this rock was prosecuted in the vicinity is indicated by the discovery of steatite picks and chisels, and many articles made of steatite, finished and unfinished, on the village-sites in the vicinity. These are well represented in the collections of Thomas Dowling, junior, and F. W. von Dachenhausen, of Washington. Typical mining and cutting tools are rarely found at any considerable distance from the quarries. Several small chisels of the usual type, shown in plate XC, were obtained from a village-site between Chain bridge and Eades mill, on the northeastern side of the river; and two sinker-like objects of soapstone from this locality, one discoidal with a peripheral groove and the other oblong with a groove passing along the sides and across the ends, are shown in *a* and *b*, plate XCIX. A small, partially finished ring or bead is represented in *c* on the same plate.

THE BRYANT QUARRY

Following the trend of the soapstone belt northeastward from the Tenley quarries, the first observed occurrence of a primitive quarry is at Four Corners, on the estate of Mr Bryant. Near this gentleman's mansion are two clusters of trees, each less than an acre in area, in which the steatite outcrops, and on account of which the land has not been utilized for agricultural purposes. Considerable work has been done on this site. In the first cluster of trees, 100 yards south of the house, a number of shallow depressions are seen marking the sites of ancient pits and trenches. Numerous worked pieces and partially shaped pots are scattered about, and a few tools have been found, mostly by Mr W. H. Phillips, who kindly directed my notice to this site. The material, the nature of the work, and the tools used correspond very closely with the same features of neighboring sites.

QUARRIES OF THE PATUXENT VALLEY

Numerous steatite quarries have been discovered in Montgomery and Howard counties, Maryland, within the limits of the Patuxent valley. Our knowledge of them is due chiefly to the enterprise of two resident archeologists, Mr J. D. McGuire, of Ellicott, and the late Thomas Bentley, of Sandyspring. The former gentleman has an extensive series of the quarry utensils and products, and has published a valuable paper concerning them.[1] I have been permitted to make illustrations of several specimens from the Bentley collection by Mrs E. P. Thomas, the collector's daughter, and additional illustrations have been obtained from the local collections of Mrs Charles Kirk and Miss Frances D. Stabler, of Olney.

Schooley's mill site—At Schooley's mill, on the eastern side of the Patuxent and about half a mile below Snells bridge, steatite of excellent quality outcrops in a number of places. These outcrops have recently been worked to some extent by the residents of the vicinity, but traces of ancient quarrying have not been entirely obliterated. It is difficult in most cases to distinguish the modern from the ancient

---

[1] Transactions of the Anthropological Society, vol. II, 1882, p. 39.

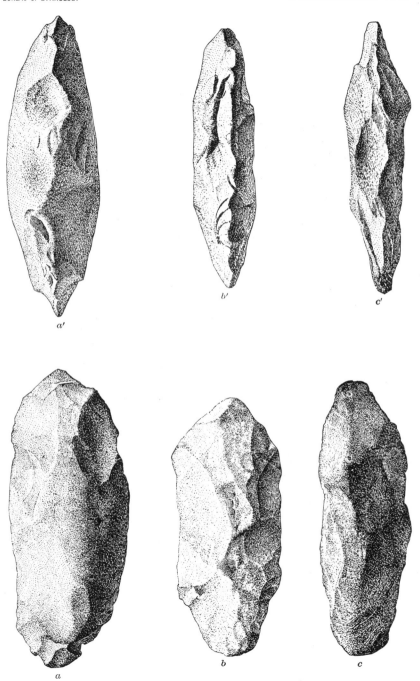

IMPLEMENTS USED IN CUTTING STEATITE; FROM VILLAGE-SITES AT LITTLE FALLS OF THE POTOMAC; ACTUAL SIZE

MASS OF STEATITE PARTIALLY CUT OUT BY MEANS OF STONE CHISELS AND NOW EXPOSED ON THE SITE OF THE
THOMPSON QUARRY

GROOVED AXES USED IN SOAPSTONE QUARRIES

The fine specimen *a* is from the Connecticut avenue quarry, north hill, three-fourths actual size; *b* and *c* are from the Thompson quarry, about one-half actual size

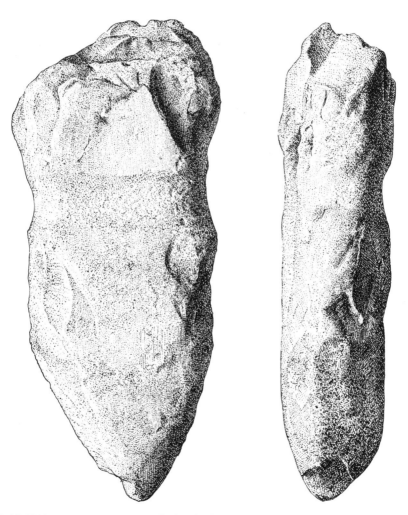

RUDE GROOVED PICK OF DARK ERUPTIVE ROCK FROM THE WILSON QUARRY; THREE-FOURTHS
ACTUAL SIZE

pits, but there are a number of irregular depressions in a grove on the hillside just above the mill that may be regarded as of aboriginal origin. Masses of steatite appear at many points, and some of these bear evidence of the use of stone picks in detaching masses of the rock. A number of broken pots were observed, including several varieties of form. One is a flat-bottom basin or pan of circular outline and vertical periphery, about 13 inches in diameter and from 3 to 4 inches deep, the bowl being roughed-out to about half that depth. The entire surface retains the marks of the roughing-out pick, which has been boldly handled. Another specimen, half of which was found, represents an oblong shallow basin with projections for handles at the ends. Another appeared to be part of a deep, almost hemispherical bowl, neatly worked but retaining no traces of handles.

In an hour's search two fragmentary tools were found. They are ordinary chisel picks, one showing the point and the other the head or rounded end. The surfaces have the appearance and feel of ordinary sandstone, but on examination the material is found to be a very fine-grained argillite. Part of the surface of the larger specimen has been shaped by pecking, the remainder having been flaked.

Thompson quarry—The region about Browns bridge over the Patuxent abounds in deposits of steatite, and the ancient workings are extensive. The first outcrop encountered after leaving the Laurel and Sandyspring pike is on the farm of Mr Benjamin Thompson, midway between the tollgate at Ednor and the bridge. A grove of trees with much undergrowth borders the road on the right, covering an area of 2 or 3 acres. In the grove the soapstone outcrops at many points; numerous large masses protrude from the beds of leaves and mold, and present the deeply excoriated surfaces characteristic of weathered steatite. At the roadside and in the lanes, as well as in the neighboring fields, fragments and protruding masses of the rock are seen. A careful search revealed no very definite traces of ancient pitting, but an interesting feature was encountered near the entrance to the wood at the right. An angular mass of the rock rises about 2 feet above the ground, and the highest corner of this has been partially encircled by a deep, wide groove, which still shows the pick marks as seen in plate XCI. It seems remarkable that pick marks exposed to the weather should have been preserved for so long a period, yet the work must undoubtedly be attributed to the aborigines who disappeared from this region a century and a half ago.

The fragments of pots observed here are of ordinary types. A fine medium-size chisel (*b*, plate XCIV) was found in a field adjoining the grove, and other fragments were picked up at different points in the vicinity. A boy living near by had found two fine picks, made by remodeling grooved axes, illustrated in *b* and *c*, plate XCII.

Brown quarry—On the farm of Mr T. E. Brown, within about half a mile of the last-mentioned bridge over the Patuxent, steatite is quite plentiful. In the fields near the house masses project from the ground and fragments are scattered about in great profusion. A number of worked places were seen, and a grooved pick made from a grooved ax and the point of an ungrooved pick of medium size were collected.

Wilson quarry—The site most productive of implements for working steatite is located within 50 yards of the Patuxent, half a mile below Brown's bridge, on the farm of Mr W. F. Wilson. The quarry sites have been cultivated to such an extent that but slight indications of the ancient pits are seen. A few small outcrops of the steatite are found, and within a radius of 60 feet about one of these over thirty

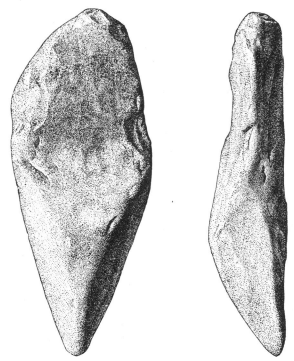

FIG. 23—Implement used in cutting steatite; from quarry in Howard County, Maryland.

tools were picked up. This series includes chisels of ordinary varieties (*c*, plate XCIV) and rude grooved picks of the extemporized variety, one of the latter appearing in plate XCIII.

Fragments of unfinished vessels of various forms were observed on the land of Mr Wilson on the northern side of the river within the limits of Howard county. Several acres of forest land are covered by rough-looking masses of dark steatite. In some places it has been worked and indistinct pits can be traced, and rudely shaped pieces of the material, together with specimens of the tools, were encountered. Beyond this spot, on the farm of Mr Henry Kruhm,

another quarry is located. The outcrops are limited, but characteristic fragments of worked steatite and three rather rude chisels were
found, two of which are shown in figures 23 and 24.

QUARRIES NEAR OLNEY

During a short stay at "Fair Hill," the residence of Mr Richard
Kirk, at Olney, Maryland, my attention was called to a number of rude
soapstone dishes that lay strewn about the grounds, and Mrs Charles

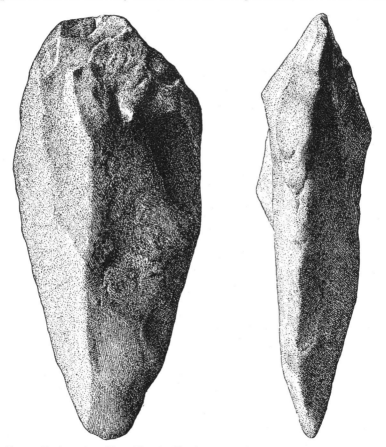

FIG. 24—Implement used in cutting steatite; from quarry in Howard County, Maryland.

Kirk had in her possession an excellent specimen of the two-point
chisel-pick (shown in figure 25). Ancient quarries are located in the
meadows below the house and in the adjoining woods on Brooke grove
farm; they are now almost obliterated by recent quarrying and by
farming over the sites. Worked pieces of steatite and specimens of
the tools used are still occasionally picked up in the vicinity. The
rude vessels are all of usual types, and no example was seen that
approaches at all near a finish.

The chisel pick mentioned above was found by Mr Charles Kirk on the quarry site. It is made of iron-impregnated sandstone, which appears and rings like metal. It has been worked rudely into shape

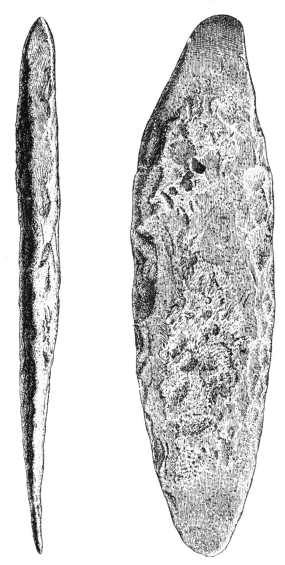

Fig. 25—Implement used in cutting steatite; from the Olney quarry.

by flaking, and then finished apparently by grinding. It is 8 inches long, 3 inches wide, and half an inch thick, and would appear to be one of the most effective tools of its class yet found. I was so fortunate as to find on this site the small chisel shown in a, plate XCIV,

15 ETH——9

IMPLEMENTS USED IN CUTTING STEATITE; FROM QUARRIES IN THE VICINITY OF SANDYSPRING, MARYLAND

a and *b*, actual size ; *c*, two-thirds actual size

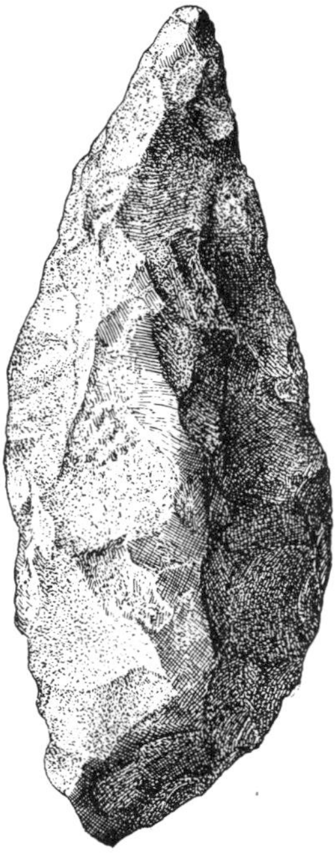

a

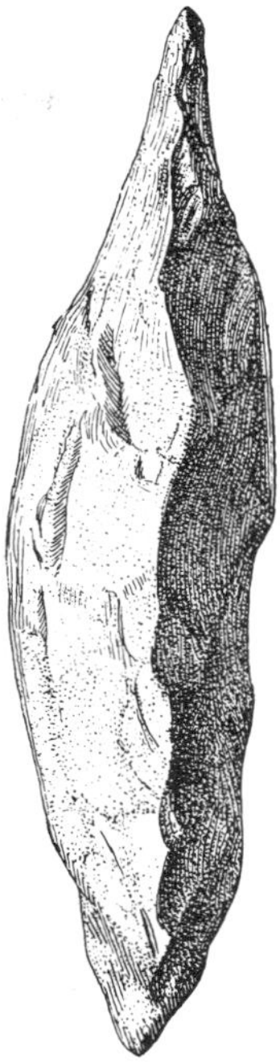

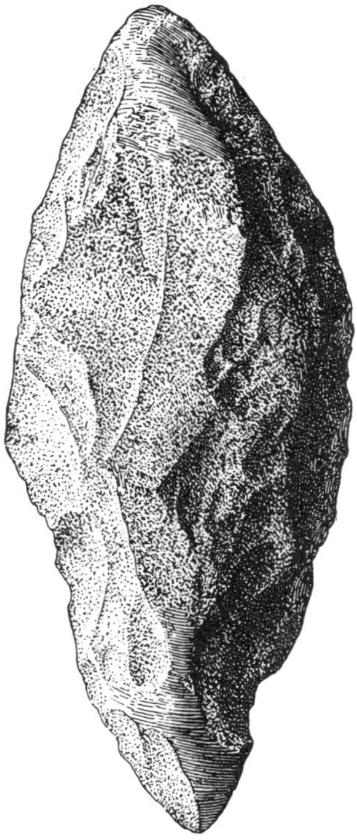

b

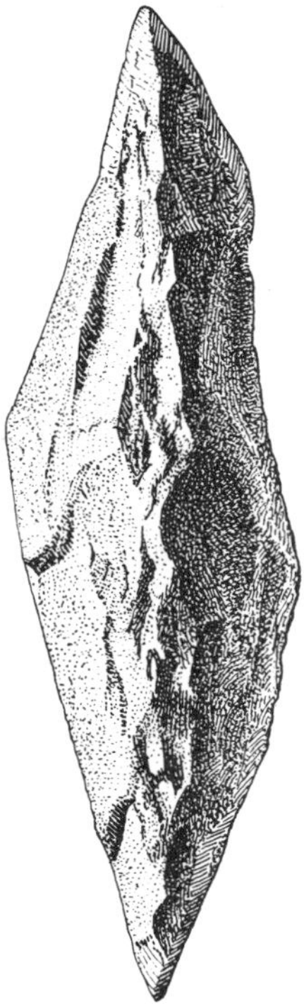

POINTED IMPLEMENTS OF DARK ERUPTIVE ROCK USED IN CUTTING STEATITE

The lower specimen is from the Kirk place, Olney, Maryland; actual size

which is almost identical in size, appearance, and material with one found in the Rose hill quarry in the District of Columbia. The point is well shaped, and shows the effects of use. The head terminates in a sharp edge, which is not worn, and must have been protected by a haft when in use. The material appears to be a fine-grain greenish-gray argillite. A second chisel of small size (a, plate xcv) was subse-

quently picked up in the field near the Kirk residence. Half a dozen fine soapstone tools were obtained from this vicinity by Miss Frances D. Stabler, who resides at Sharon, a neighboring estate.

About a mile south of Olney, on the farm of Mr Mackall, the location of an ancient quarry was noted, and the usual refuse of aboriginal operations was observed. A chisel made of blue-gray porphyry and a very rudely grooved or notched fragment of quartz, once hafted as a pick, were picked up. This quarry is said to extend to the farm of Dr Kirk, which lies south of Mr Mackall's place.

Another site formerly occupied by the aboriginal soapstone worker is situated about 4 miles west of Olney, on the premises of Mr Holland. This place did not yield any form of tool, but the unfinished vessels occur as usual. Other sites are reported in this vicinity.

The collection of Mrs Mary Bentley Thomas, of Sandyspring, was made from the quarries of the vicinity, several of which are mentioned above. There are many specimens of the partially shaped vessels illustrating all phases of the work. The picks comprised in this collection are very fine. Some are modified grooved axes, others are fragments of rock roughed-out by flaking just enough to make them avail-

FIG. 26—Implement used in cutting steatite; from Sandyspring quarry.

able, with the addition of a haft, for working the soft stone. One of the former is shown in plate xcvi, while the latter type is illustrated in figure 26. One of the most striking implements found in this collection, and of wider interest than the other quarry tools, is a gouge of the New England type, which has been roughly grooved by the steatite worker in order that a haft might be attached (figure 27). This specimen serves to add to the force of the remark, suggested by the remodeling of grooved axes for the rough work of the quarries, that the date of this work is comparatively recent. It would seem that older tools from all sources were pressed into service for carrying on a new art.

FIG. 27—Gouge-like implement grooved for hafting and used in a steatite quarry near Sandyspring, Maryland.

FALLS CHURCH AND HOLMES RUN QUARRIES

Near Falls Church, and some 3½ miles southwest of Little falls, Virginia, steatite has been found, and some traces of ancient work have been reported. Similar reports come from several other localities in Alexandria and Fairfax counties.

In 1891 a soapstone mine was opened on what was then the Bassett place, on Holmes run, 7 miles from Alexandria and the same distance from Georgetown. As the work advanced a few shallow depressions

STEATITE PICK MADE BY SHARPENING A GROOVED AX, FROM A QUARRY NEAR SANDYSPRING,
MARYLAND; ONE-HALF ACTUAL SIZE

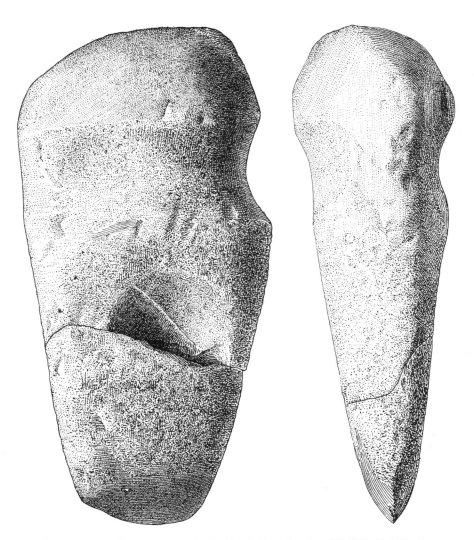

GROOVED AX USED AND BROKEN IN A STEATITE QUARRY IN FAIRFAX COUNTY, VIRGINIA;
TWO-THIRDS ACTUAL SIZE

marking the sites of ancient pits were observed, and in cutting through them several rudimentary vessels and numerous mining and cutting tools, broken and entire, were encountered. The ancient work had extended to the depth in one place of 7 or 8 feet. Several specimens from this site are illustrated in the accompanying plates. An ordinary grooved ax, broken in use, is illustrated in plate XCVII, and two other axes modified by flaking to give them sharper cutting edges (plate XCVIII) are of special interest as further illustrating the subordination of general to special function among the tools of the aboriginal quarrymen.

AMELIA COUNTY QUARRIES

On the southern side of James river, in Amelia county, Virginia, a very interesting site was studied by Mr F. H. Cushing, who conducted extended excavations and made a model of an ancient pit illustrating the manner in which the masses of partially shaped steatite were cut out and removed. The tools recovered and the quarry rejects were identical with those from the more northern sites.

MADISON COUNTY QUARRIES

Between 5 and 6 miles from Orange, on the road to Madison court-house, Virginia, is a negro church, at which a road turns off north-ward. At a point about 200 yards from the church the latter road strikes an outcrop of steatite, along which it runs for 500 or 600 yards. Most of the deposit has been so much worked by residents that it is now impossible to determine whether there is any trace of aboriginal work except at the extreme northern end of the outcrop. Here there are a few small pits that seem due to ancient work.

CULPEPER COUNTY QUARRIES

There is a very extensive quarry of steatite near Waylands mills, on the Orange road, 9 or 10 miles west of Culpeper court-house. At the top of a hill, something over 100 feet high, the steatite outcrops and the pits begin at once. They are all to the right of the road, and vary from a foot to 4 feet in depth, with the exception of one, which is fully 150 feet in diameter, the bottom being filled over an area of 50 or 60 feet across with muck, so that its depth can not be determined. Almost the entire surface has been dug over for half a mile in extent.

On the farm of H. I. Aylor, about $2\frac{1}{2}$ miles from the mill, is another steatite quarry, in which it is reported that aboriginal digging was extensive, and that fragments of pots and the like were plentiful. Specimens may be found at neighboring houses, especially at the negro cabins, where they are used for "chicken troughs."

BRUNSWICK COUNTY QUARRIES

On the farm of Bassett B. Wilkes, at Charlie Hope station, 6 miles west of Lawrenceville, Virginia, there are several pits, extending over an acre in area, where steatite has been quarried by the Indians. The stone crops out near the top of a narrow ridge on which considerable manufacturing seems to have been carried on, as fragments of vessels are numerous.

RELATION OF CLAY AND STEATITE POTTERY

It might appear that peoples employing earthenware would hardly resort to the difficult task of quarrying and working steatite for vessel making, since the uses to which both classes of utensils were devoted must have been nearly identical; but that the historical tribes made pottery and at the same time employed soapstone vessels is known through colonial records, and also from the frequent occurrence together on village-sites and in shell banks of vessels made of both materials. It has also been observed that pulverized steatite was often used in tempering ordinary pottery, and that the vessels so tempered are occasionally modeled in the form of steatite vessels, having the heavy projections or handles at the sides.

The occurrence of grooved axes and celts in the quarries, and the adaptation of these tools by slight modification to use as picks and chisels, indicates with sufficient clearness that the quarrying of steatite was a comparatively recent industry, practiced after all forms of polished implements had been perfected, and in all probability by the Algonquian peoples.

VARIOUS ARTICLES OF STEATITE

The number of miscellaneous carvings of steatite found in the tidewater districts is very limited, and the execution is usually inferior. They are in striking contrast with the work in neighboring districts in North Carolina and Tennessee, which furnish pipes and ornaments of remarkable beauty.

The fragment of a neatly carved platform pipe shown in a, plate XCIX, was found on an Anacostia village-site, near the Pennsylvania avenue bridge. The rudely shaped, channeled, sinker-like objects, b, c, d, are from village-sites near Little falls of the Potomac, and the bit of pipestem e is from a dwelling site near the Clifton quarry, Virginia.

The specimens illustrated in plate C are from village-sites in Virginia, and represent several stages of the shaping operations—a was roughed-out by breaking and sawing; b was reduced to approximate shape by cutting and abrasion, but the bowl is not yet excavated; and c appears to be a finished specimen, though quite rude in appearance. The object shown in d has been carefully trimmed, but the work is not sufficiently advanced to show whether a pipe or an ornament was to be made.

That such a very limited number of miscellaneous steatite carvings should be found in the tidewater country is a matter of some surprise.

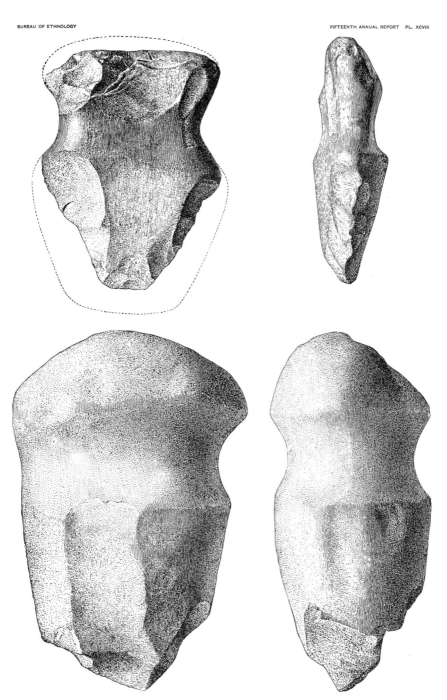

GROOVED AXES SHARPENED BY FLAKING FOR USE IN QUARRYING STEATITE, FROM THE HOLMES RUN QUARRIES;
TWO-THIRDS ACTUAL SIZE

SMALL ARTICLES—PIPES, SINKERS, AND A BEAD—MADE OF STEATITE; ACTUAL SIZE

CHAPTER VI

DISTRIBUTION OF STONE IMPLEMENTS

THE AREA INVESTIGATED

The tidewater portions of Maryland and Virginia have an area nearly equal to that of the state of Maryland. About one-fourth of the area is occupied by broad arms of the sea, chiefly Chesapeake bay and its tributaries, and the land is a much diversified plain, broken by erosion into hills and terraced valleys. It extends inland from the Atlantic seaboard to the base of the highland or Piedmont plateau, which rises on the west to the Appalachian mountains. The curved line separating the two topographic divisions—the lowland and the highland—is marked by falls in all the rivers, and by the location of town and cities through which pass the great highways of travel connecting the north with the south. On this line are located Philadelphia, Havre de Grace, Baltimore, Laurel, Washington, Fredericksburg, Richmond, and Petersburg (see plate I). This was the shore-line of the Atlantic when the formations constituting the lowlands were laid down.

The separation of the lowland from the highland is not a topographic separation only; there are pronounced biologic and geologic distinctions, and these combined in archaic times to produce marked anthropologic distinctions. The tidewater region furnished a plentiful supply of game and fish, and in the brackish and salt water areas an abundance of oysters. The natives lived much on the water, and were perhaps more nearly a maritime people than any other group of tribes in the east. Their peculiar biologic environment had a marked influence on their art, giving it unique forms and exceptional distribution; while their unusual geologic surroundings had a still more pronounced effect on their implements, utensils, and weapons, limiting the forms and sizes and determining to a considerable extent the kinds employed in the various districts, independently of biologic and other conditions.

In early historic times the tidewater country was inhabited by numerous tribes of Indians, mainly of Algonquian stock, subject to the renowned Powhatan. A few other nations were located about the headwaters of Chesapeake bay and others appeared at times along the western and southern borders. The period covered by this occupancy practically closed about the middle of the last century. Its beginning is not determined, but it probably does not date back very many centuries. Of antecedent or prehistoric peoples, if such there were, we have no

134

information, for the art remains are simple and homogeneous, giving no hint of the presence in this region of any other than the historic tribes. The region is nearly identical with that explored by that intrepid and illustrious adventurer and colonist, John Smith, whose accounts of the natives are among our most valuable contributions to the aboriginal history of the Atlantic states.

DISTRIBUTION OF MATERIALS

GEOLOGIC DISTRIBUTION OF STONE

The geology of the tidewater country is wholly unlike that of the highland, and the rocks available to the aborigines in the two regions were not only different in distribution but peculiar in the shapes they took and in other features that affect the character of the utensils made and employed. In the highland, west of the dotted line on the map forming plate I, the varieties of rock occur in massive forms and with definite independent distribution. The workable varieties, such as quartz, quartzite, rhyolite, jasper, and flint, were much sought by the aborigines of the lowland. Fragmental material was to be obtained almost everywhere on the surface, but choice varieties were confined to limited areas and often to distant regions, and where the surface exposures were not sufficient to supply the demand, quarrying was resorted to and the work of extracting, transporting, and trading or exchanging the stone must have become an important factor in the lives of the people. The masses of rock were uncovered, broken up, and tested; the choice pieces were selected and reduced to forms approximating the implements to be made, and in this shape they were carried to the lowland.

In the lowland all varieties of hard stones are fragmental, and the species are intermingled in varied ways. These fragments of rock are not merely broken, angular pieces, such as characterize the surface of the highland, but are rounded masses and bits known as bowlders or cobbles and pebbles, and comprise chiefly such tough, flinty, homogeneous stones as are available in the arts of primitive man. Nature, in her own way, selected from the highland along the stream courses the very choicest bits of the crumbled rocks, reduced them in hundreds of cataract mills and in the breakers of the seashore to rounded forms, and deposited them in what are now the lowlands, in great heaps and beds, ready to the hand of primitive man.

At first it would seem to even the keenest observer that a cobble or ovoid bowlder or pebble would be a difficult form of stone to utilize in making knives, spearheads, arrowpoints, drills, and scrapers. The smooth, rounded mass had to be transformed into a thin blade, every contour of which is incisive or angular. So far apart are the two classes of forms that few people have thought of the bowlder as a prominent source of these objects. But when we look into the matter more carefully we find that nature has not provided any other form of the several tough varieties of stone so perfectly suited to the purposes of the stone-implement flaker as the bowlder or pebble.

Each river brought down from the highland only such varieties of stone as belonged to the drainage of that river, so that in one valley one set of materials prevails and in another a different set of materials appears, varying with the geologic formations of the region drained. Rivers having identical formations have nearly identical bowlders; long rivers crossing numerous formations have many varieties; short rivers crossing but few formations have but a limited number.

There is also a selection as to size by each drainage way. Near the base of the highland, where the force of the current is reduced by meeting tidewater, the larger bowlders are dropped, the smaller ones are deposited farther down, and the pebbles and sand are carried far seaward. Small and weak streams transport fewer pieces and drop them sooner. This selection does not hold good with ice transportation, which agency has carried irregular masses of stone to many widely distributed points. Notwithstanding the fact that all water-transported stones are more or less rounded, there is a selection with respect to degree of roundness. If dropped early in the progress of transportation, the bowlder is imperfectly rounded; if carried far, it is fully rounded. Near the margin of the highland, therefore, there is a large percentage of imperfectly rounded stones, and farther out there is a small percentage of decidedly irregular forms. These conditions are probably considerably modified by the action of the waves along the ancient seashore which skirted the base of the highland. Such fragments as were subjected to wave action became fully rounded and were deposited in beds along the ancient beach-lines. It is not easy to distinguish the beach-rolled material from that rounded by the flow of streams, both agencies having no doubt frequently acted in turn on the same material.

Again, we observe that on river banks near the base of the highland many varieties of rock are present, but with each mile as we descend the number is diminished—the softer species are reduced to sand as they move toward the sea and one after another disappears. Quartz, being the hardest, is last to yield to the erosive agents, and at various points along the ocean beach well-polished quartz pebbles are found.

A comparison of the Potomac and Patuxent rivers with respect to these points is instructive. In ancient times both streams, as they descended from the mountains, gathered fragments of rock and carried them downward until the soft and friable ones were reduced to sand and the tough, flinty varieties became bowlders and pebbles. The latter consisted chiefly of quartz and quartzite. The Potomac was a long stream, heading far in the west and cutting through many ranges of mountains and hills. It crossed heavy beds of quartzite in the region of the Blue ridge. This rock is tough and massive, and breaks up into rather large fragments; thus it is that we have many large quartzite bowlders deposited in the valley about Washington and below, the sizes diminishing toward the sea. Between the Blue ridge and tidewater the river crosses a belt of gneiss rocks intersected by many veins of quartz. This latter rock is hard and brittle, and breaks up into small fragments, which, when rounded, are usually of the size denominated pebbles. These were taken up by the waters in countless numbers and distributed with the quartzite bowlders from Washington to the sea. But the quartz is harder than the quartzite and resisted the erosive agents more successfully, so that after the quartzite disappears there are still quartz pebbles in plenty.

The other stream, the Patuxent, has a limited drainage and does not cross the quartzite belt but drains the quartz-bearing zone. Below the point of its entrance into the tidewater country at Laurel, we find, of the flakable stones, chiefly quartz in small fragments; lower down all are well rounded, forming pebbly gravels. It is thus seen that nature has selected the rocks used by the tidewater peoples and has distributed them in groups varying with original location, with hardness, with toughness, with shape, and with size.

GEOLOGY AND ART

The effect of the natural conditions of distribution on the stone art of the various districts was necessarily pronounced. One community located conveniently to deposits of large bowlders used large stones, and the tools shaped from them average large. Another community located in a pebble-bearing district utilized pebbles, so far as they are capable of utilization, and this people had few large tools and many small ones, the average size being small. Dwellers in quartzite-bearing districts had quartzite tools, those having quartz deposits had quartz tools, and those residing near the base of the highland had many varieties of stone and hence used a much greater diversity of stone tools, since the working qualities or capacities of each stone vary from the rest.

As a result of these conditions the tidewater Potomac is rich in chipped tools, both of quartzite and of quartz, of home production. The Patuxent yields a large percentage of quartz tools, most of which are native. The Potomac yields to the collector a large percentage of large tools, the Patuxent a large percentage of small ones. These remarks relate to the native varieties of material and implements made from them. Exotic materials had their own peculiar distribution, which will be examined further on.

Nearly all rude, bulky implements of chipped stone, and all failures or rejects of manufacture, are, as a matter of course, found on or near the sites from which the raw materials were derived. Rejects are large and clumsy on the upper tidewater Potomac because of the large size of the bowlders available; they are small on the Patuxent because the pebbles utilized were small.

Again, we observe that the percentage of failures—the turtlebacks and other refuse of manufacture—decreases rapidly with the distance from the source of supply of the raw material. This may be illustrated by a suppositious case. In the vicinity of Washington we have a great deposit of quartzite bowlders. In figure 28 the dotted line may be taken as roughly indicating the area yielding workable bowlders, and the angular markings show the distribution of rejects of manufacture. The successful blades and the finished tools produced radiate much more widely, but also diminish with distance from the source of supply, as indicated by the smaller strokes in figure 19, a generalized case also. Favorite routes of travel would receive the fuller supply of these

FIG. 28—Distribution of rejects of manufacture, confined largely to the area yielding the raw material.

objects, and dwelling and important hunting and fishing sites would have large supplies, as indicated by " village-sites " in figure 29. On the source of supply of the raw material, failures and unfinished implements or rejects exceed finished implements in numbers, but beyond this the latter are almost wholly prevalent. So-called paleolithic forms, the rejects of manufacture, are thus confined to certain areas— the areas producing the raw material—and it is easy to see how, in various sections of the country before the true nature of these forms was known, certain localities were thought to have been especially favored by the hypothetic paleolithic man.

It would appear from what has been said that the artificial distribution of materials is limited by, and is indeed a modification of, the natural distribution, and that each class of artificial objects is scattered in a way peculiar to itself. But the human agent is an important factor. Other things being equal, human distribution of small things is far, of large objects near; implements of war and the chase travel far, domestic utensils remain near; improvised articles or devices are near, highly elaborated and valuable objects go far; along thoroughfares distribution is far, across thoroughfares it is near. Again, much-occupied sites are richly stocked with utensils, while slightly occupied spots have but few; sites near the source or sources of supply have a wealth of art, very distant ones have almost nothing; and sites convenient to a plentiful supply of one material have many tools of that material; sites remote from any of the sources

FIG. 29—Distribution of implements, much more general and extensive than the distribution of rejects.

have a limited supply from many sources. So, too, a sedentary people will not distribute widely, while wandering or semisedentary tribes will transport their possessions to many distant places; and sites occupied by numerous tribes in turn will have diversified art remains. It may be further noted that on sites devoted to single or simple industries the range of tools will be small, while on sites where occupations were varied the range will be large; and that where peoples were varied, occupations varied, materials varied, and time was long, we will have the widest range.

The tidewater peoples were by no means content with the materials supplied by the province in which they lived, although these naturally received first attention. Not being favored by nature in the quality and range of their material, they seem to have searched far and near for those finer-grained, homogeneous varieties so much used in other regions. They sought flint in the mountains of Virginia fully a hundred miles beyond the tidewater limit; they discovered the slaty-looking volcanic porphyry called rhyolite in South mountain 75 miles northwest of Washington, and jasper and argillite were obtained from eastern and northeastern Pennsylvania. It is probable that in some cases the tidewater peoples made long journeys in search of these rocks and spent a considerable season quarrying and roughing-out the blank forms and selecting choice bits to be carried home. On the other hand, much of the material from these distant places may have reached the lowland by exchange or trade, and a certain amount, not ascertainable, of the supply of implements of exotic materials was no doubt due to visits and incursions of the peoples occupying the region of the source of supply, as, for example, jasper by the Susquehannocks of the north and flint by the Monacans of the west. It may be that in time, by careful comparison of the forms of implements characterizing various exotic materials, something may be suggested of the presence of neighboring peoples in, or at least of their influence on, the art of the tidewater region. Distribution is really very general, implements made of all of the varieties of stone mentioned being scattered more or less fully over the Chesapeake-Potomac country as far south as James river.

Jasper, the quarries of which have recently been located by Mr H. C. Mercer, of Philadelphia, is most plentiful in the upper Chesapeake and Susquehanna regions. Argillite, which was obtained in the Delaware valley, did not find its way to any great extent into Maryland and Virginia, although several caches of blades have been discovered in the middle Chesapeake region and implements are occasionally found. Rhyolite implements are most plentiful in the Patuxent and Potomac valleys, and especially in those portions of them adjoining South mountain. The quarries of this stone are in Pennsylvania near the head of the Monocacy, and the implements are very numerous on that stream, while fragments of considerable size have been carried far down the Potomac. Transportation was, no doubt, mainly by water. Probably one-fourth of the spearheads and arrowpoints of the Potomac region are made of this rock. Dark or blackish flint was used in making smaller projectile points, and these are rare in the tidewater country, but increase in number toward the west, and prevail in the middle and upper Potomac region.

It should be noted that of these exotic materials we have in the tidewater country very few large or rude implements, and as a matter of course failures of manufacture are rare, save those that result from breakage during such specializing and finishing operations as were conducted subsequently to transportation from the quarry. Of quartz and quartzite, the native flakable stones, there are countless rejects of manufacture of all grades, as described in the foregoing pages.

It may be said of quartzite and quartz that a portion of these materials, perhaps a large portion, especially of the latter, was gathered from the highland beyond the tidewater limit, and no one can say from the examination of ordinary finished implements of these materials whether or not they were made from a native bowlder or pebble or from a foreign mass or flake; yet the presence of countless numbers of the rejects of manufacture from bowlders and pebbles of these materials within the tidewater area, and the rarity, so far as I have been able to discover, of refuse of manufacture in the highland, seem to make the true conditions clear.

Cut, pecked, ground, and polished implements of usual types are common in this region. Steatite, used in making pots, pipes, sinkers, ceremonial stones, and ornaments, was quarried in hundreds of places along the eastern border of the highland. The unfinished objects are found on and about the quarry sites and on dwelling sites near by. The finished utensils and implements are scattered far and wide over the tidewater province, but grow less plentiful as we approach the Atlantic coast. The picks and chisels used in working the soapstone are confined to the quarries and to shop and dwelling sites in the vicinity. Scores of these objects have been gathered from the Chain bridge sites, within an hour's walk of numerous quarries of the stone they were used in shaping.

Grooved axes and celts were made for the most part of tough bowlders of volcanic and rarely of granitic rocks obtained from the stream beds or about the margins of the highland. Failures resulting from the manufacture of these implements are frequently found on village-sites along the banks of the larger streams but rarely very far beyond the range of the raw material. The implements themselves are of the widest distribution.

COMPARATIVE DISTRIBUTION OF IMPLEMENTS

DISTRIBUTION BY CLASSES

The liability of the various stone implements of the tidewater region to transportation is approximately expressed in the partial list given below. Beginning with those least subject to transportation and ending with those most subject to it we have the following tentative order:

Mortars, generally extemporized from large, flattish or ovoid bowlders having at least one concave surface, which was gradually deepened by use or purposely hollowed out, were probably rarely far removed from the site of their first utilization. Many other improvised tools and utensils—mullers, pestles, hammerstones, etc—were equally home stayers, being merely natural shapes picked up and adapted to the needs of a place or occasion.

Sharpened bowlders, embracing extemporized chopping or bone-break-
ing tools, occur on all river sites where bowlders were at hand. The
edge or point was made by removing one or more flakes, which required
but a moment's work. They were not transported far beyond the limits
of the bowlder-producing area.

Notched and sharpened bowlders, used as improvised axes and picks
or hoes, are closely related to the preceding, but intended to be hafted.
Their transportation was but slight, as they are rarely found far beyond
the range of deposits of heavy bowlders. Half a dozen blows with a
hammerstone were sufficient to fashion one of these objects. They were
probably not sufficiently essential or valued to be transported, save in
exceptional cases. Blunt-end hammer-like objects notched for hafting
are distributed sparsely over corresponding areas.

Picks and chisels, used for working steatite, traveled but little beyond
the quarries and the neighboring villages where the finishing was done.
These consist of rude, sharp stones, of axes and celts worked over or
"upset" to secure good points and edges, and of thick leaf-shape chisels
reduced to approximate shape by flaking and then ground to an edge
at one or both ends.

Net sinkers are not common. The rude specimens were probably
carried back and forth to some extent along the streams, and small
well-finished pieces may have been carried everywhere.

Pestles, cylindrical stones symmetrically shaped and well finished by
battering, were apparently carried from place to place and perhaps for
long distances. Ruder specimens were extemporized and not transported.

Hammerstones—Many of these objects are improvised from bowlders
and were quickly cast aside, as already indicated, but others were
carried far out into the bowlderless region.

Soapstone vessels are widely distributed, reaching in rather rare cases
points 50 miles or more from the highland in which the material was
quarried.

Grooved axes, celts, scrapers, drills, knives, spearheads, arrowpoints,
as well as *pipes, ceremonial stones,* and *ornaments* were freely transported, covering the full range of the peoples employing them, and
not infrequently, no doubt, passing from district to district through
other hands.

Rejects resulting from failures in specialization of transported forms
and of attempts at remodeling of worn or broken tools are to be found
everywhere, but rejects of the roughing-out processes are not greatly
affected by the transporting agencies, remaining on the shop sites, as
has been shown.

DISTRIBUTION BY PARTICULAR SITES

Some of the eccentricities of distribution may be illustrated by an
examination of the art contents of sites having varying relations to
the deposits of raw material.

1. On a site of quarrying and manufacture where dwelling was inconvenient, as on the bluffs of Rock creek, the work was confined mainly to roughing-out leaf-shape blades, and the series of art forms comprises a limited range, including turtlebacks and other kinds of rejects, with refuse and implements of manufacture. On the quarry-shop sites of Rock creek nothing exotic, nothing finished, nothing that might not readily be classed as paleolithic, if shape alone were considered, was found in three months' work.

2. On a site of quarrying and manufacture where dwelling was practicable, and where lodges were actually pitched to a limited extent, we find intermingled with the rude forms some specialized implements and a few tools of exotic origin, such as projectile points of rhyolite, with axes and celts, as at Riggs mill, 8 miles northeast of Washington.

3. On a site of manufacture and at the same time of extensive dwelling, as at Anacostia, in the District of Columbia, where much raw material was at hand, all varieties of refuse and of rude forms are found; likewise well-shaped and wholly finished specimens of flaked tools of local origin prevail. There are also all the cut, pecked, and polished tools, and the ceremonial stones and ornaments common to village-sites. Besides these many exotic materials in varied forms are found.

4. On a village-site where no raw material save small quartz pebbles is found there will be a full range of small quartz rejects and of small quartz implements, with a liberal supply of finished implements of exotic materials, averaging small.

5. On a site remote from all sources of raw material, as on the eastern shore, the objects average small and are much varied in material and style, having come far, through numerous peoples, and from many sources.

Typical illustrations of the two last-mentioned varieties of sites are difficult to find, for the reason that in all sections, even far out toward the present ocean beach, there are occasional ice-borne bowlders and fragments of considerable size, and these were collected by the natives and used for mortars and mullers and for various flaked and battered implements; and such objects destroy the entire simplicity of conditions conceived for the sites described.

DISTRIBUTION BY GENESIS AND FUNCTION

A synoptical statement is made in the accompanying plate (CI), which exhibits many of the most striking features of the flaked-stone archeology of this province, and indicates clearly the points most requiring attention in other regions. The stories of the origin and form of the material, of manufacture, rejection, elaboration, transportation, storage, specialization, and use are all expressed or suggested. Four materials are represented—two native and in the form of bowlders, and two exclusively exotic and derived from mass deposits. Each series indicates the course of development through which most of the finished forms passed between the first stroke given to the shapeless stone and the finished work of art. The size is considerably reduced in the drawing.

In the first and second series all the forms from the bowlder to the most minute art shapes are represented in solid lines, being exclusively tidewater art. In the first series, numbers 1, 2, 3, 4, 5, and 6 are shop rejects (turtlebacks, etc) and are not implements. Numbers 7, 8, and 9 are roughed-out forms (blanks or blades ready for further specialization) and are not necessarily implements, although they were perhaps available as knives and scrapers. The numbers from 10 to 18 are specialized forms derived mainly, no doubt, from bowlders, and include knives, spearheads, arrowpoints, and perforators or drills.

The second series comprises forms derived mainly from quartz pebbles; naturally they are smaller than the quartzite forms. They are drawn in solid lines, being of native derivation. Numbers 1, 2, 3, 4, 5, 6, and 7 are shop rejects (turtlebacks) and are not implements. Number 8 is a profile showing an ordinary "peak" or hump of the reject. Numbers 9, 10, and 11 are successful blades, which may have been employed as knives or scrapers, though such forms were usually intended for specialization into arrowpoints, spearheads, perforators, etc, as indicated in numbers 12 to 20.

The third series, consisting of objects of rhyolite, is drawn partly in solid lines and partly in dotted outlines. Those in solid lines comprise transported and specialized objects, which were collected in the tidewater country. Those in dotted lines, a, b, c, d, e, and f, are the rejects of manufacture which are not found in the tidewater country, being obtained only on the quarry-shop sites in Adams county, Pennsylvania. The successful blades, illustrated in g, h, and i, were carried away from the quarry to be used as they are or for specialization into the succeeding forms, j to q, when needed. The tidewater province is abundantly supplied with all the forms from g to q.

The fourth series, composed of articles of jasper, repeats very closely the conditions of the third or rhyolite series. The sizes average smaller on account of the inferior massiveness and minuter cleavage of the rock. The rejects of manufacture, indicated in dotted lines, are obtained mainly from the recently discovered quarries in eastern Pennsylvania. Other quarries nearer at hand may yet be found, and some of our rivers furnish occasional bits and pebbles of this material. The cache and finished objects, g to q, are widely scattered over the tidewater region. Three or four other materials of equal interest with those given could be added, but the lesson would not be made clearer than as it stands.

It is of the utmost importance, in taking up the stone implements of a region, that each leading material be traced back to its source, so that from this point of view a study can be made of the full life history of the implements—the work of quarrying, shaping, transporting, finishing, and use. Each form or class of implement will thus be found to have left in its wake a trail of "wasters" or rejects peculiar to itself. Until these are understood, selected, and set apart, there is necessarily much confusion.

It is seen by a study of plate CI, in conjunction with the representations of actual specimens in preceding plates, that a half or more of the range of native flaked forms are actually not implements. The separation is approximately indicated by the upper brackets marked "not implements" and "implements." It will be observed that this division separates the cache forms or blanks of the middle column into two parts. Portions of this class of objects were mere quarry shapes, distributed to be elaborated when needed, but some of them were probably utilized in their blank shape as knives, etc, and some show a slight degree of specialization (as in number 9 of the first series), and thus properly take their place with implements. Nearly all of the specimens shown in this column are actual cache finds, some being depicted on reduced scale in order to get the entire series within the limits of a plate.

The distribution of cut, battered, ground, and polished stone implements, and of the refuse of their manufacture, is governed by laws similar to those governing the distribution of flaked stone.

15 ETH——10

RÉSUMÉ

Geologic history of the province—The Potomac-Chesapeake tidewater province lies outside or east of what is known as the "fall line"—the base of the highland proper—and is a broad, much broken plateau, nowhere more than a few hundred feet in height. The geologic formations consist in the main of loosely bedded bowlder-gravels and sands derived from the highland at periods when the sea covered the entire area, washing the highland along the fall line. Subsequent elevations of a few hundred feet drove the sea outward beyond its present limit, and erosion carved the exposed land into hills and valleys.

At a later period the land was depressed a hundred feet or more, and the valleys were filled with water from the sea, forming a thousand arms and inlets whose tortuous margins now meander the old hill slopes of the province midway in their height.

Historic peoples—When first visited by the English this district was occupied by numerous Indian tribes, who subsisted largely by hunting and fishing, but engaged to some extent in the cultivation of maize. They were a vigorous, valiant race, but had made but little progress in any of the arts save those of mere subsistence. Today they have entirely disappeared, and students interested in their history gather the scattered remains of their art, seeking thus to supplement the meager records of colonial days.

Art remains—The art remains preserved to our time indicate the prevalence of extremely simple conditions of life throughout the past, and exhibit no features at variance with those characterizing the historic occupancy. While their study throws much light on numerous episodes of the history of the aboriginal tribes, the story they tell of themselves and of the industrial struggles of primitive peoples in general is of profound interest.

Status of art—As indicated by the remains, art in stone—which is the leading art represented—was still almost wholly within the implement-making phase of the stone age, mythology and the esthetic forces not yet having lent their inspiration to the hand of the sculptor.

Utilization of stone—Stone in its various forms was much valued and used by these people and was sought both in the lowland and in the highland beyond. In the lowland it occurred as bowlders and pebbles brought down by the waters and in the highland as original masses and as surface fragments dislodged by natural forces. It was gathered from the surface for various uses, and when the supply was insufficient

146

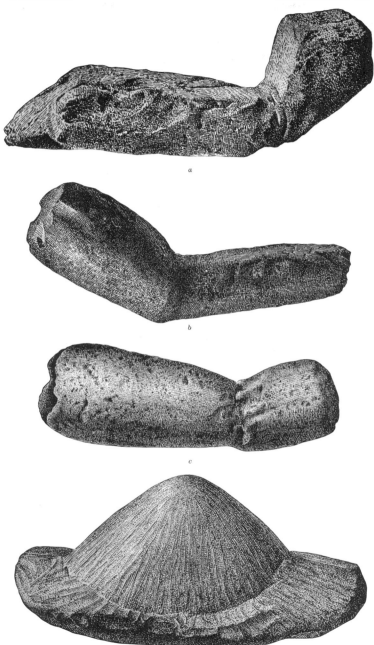

a

b

c

d

SPECIALIZED AND PARTIALLY SPECIALIZED OBJECTS OF STEATITE; ACTUAL SIZE

SYNOPTIC GROUPING SHOWING ORIGIN, FORM GENESIS, AND DISTRIBUTION OF THE FLAKED-STONE IMPLEM

Implements

Transported

Cache forms   Specialized forms

HE CHESAPEAKE-POTOMAC TIDEWATER REGION.   THE SCALE VARIES FROM ONE-THIRD TO ONE-SIXTH

QUARRY GROUP IN PLASTER SET UP ON THE PINY BRANCH SITE, WITH RESTORATION OF HISTORIC ACCESSORIES BY MR F. H. CUSHING

it was dug from the ground; and thereby the quarrying industry developed.

Shaping processes—The implements made were of many forms and served a multitude of purposes. Their history divides itself naturally into two sections, the period of manufacture being sharply separated from the period of utilization. The first stage, the full analysis of which is of the utmost importance, is studied to best advantage through the shaping processes employed in manufacture. These processes were adapted to the kind of material utilized and the nature of the results desired and are grouped under four heads, as follows: (1) Fracturing processes, (2) battering processes, (3) incising processes, and (4) abrading processes.

Fracture processes—Of the implements made and used in this province perhaps 90 per cent were shaped by fracture processes. These deal with all brittle stone, and the shaping is attended by constant breakage and failure, so that for each completed form several abortive forms are produced more or less closely resembling some of the simpler varieties of finished implements. This work was carried on all over the large area furnishing the raw material, and the articles made and used were everywhere intimately intermingled with the rejectage of manufacture. So confusing were the conditions that no definite line could be drawn between the two classes of objects. The discovery of quarries in the hills, entirely isolated from sites and phenomena of specialization and use, made the separation easy, and led to a correct understanding of what may well be called the morphology of flaked implements.

Lowland quarries—The great quarries of the lowland were located in the bluffs about the head of tidewater on the Potomac and yielded quartzite bowlders in vast numbers. These were obtained and partially elaborated on the local shop sites. The bowlders were cast out of the pits and a few flakes removed to test the material; the best stone was selected and the desired implements roughed-out by free-hand fracture. The form almost universally sought was a leaf-shape blade suitable for further elaboration into any of the specialized forms having their genesis through this general form. The blades made—with perhaps unshaped flakes and fragments—were carried away, and the soil soon closed over the pits and the vast bodies of shop refuse; and these latter, now for the first time systematically examined, tell the story of operations and results with absolute certainty and complete uniformity.

Story of rejectage and refuse—The débris of the quarry-shops consists of (1) tested and shattered bowlders, (2) flakes, and (3) broken and abortive incipient implements, the last necessarily illustrating all the steps of implement development from inception to the end of the quarry work. Thinness was an essential feature of the blades made, and failure resulted in a majority of cases from the development of too great thickness along the middle of the form. It is these thick forms, flaked on one or both sides and exhibiting types of conformation necessarily oft repeated, and scattered over the country wherever shaping from bowlders was attempted, that have puzzled and confused archeologists. It was not the practice here or elsewhere to finish the implements on the quarry site. The form was developed just far enough to make transportation easy and the subsequent work of specialization simple and safe.

Destiny of the quarry product—From the quarry-shops the blades were carried away to be specialized, finished, and used. Some are found in hoards or caches, suggesting transportation from the quarries or from place to place in numbers; some are found on village-sites and scattered over the fields, and many examples still retain the crude edges and points just as they came from the roughing-out shops; others are neatly trimmed, probably for use as knives, scrapers, etc, while the vast majority are sharpened and stemmed, or notched for hafting as projectile points. In these objects we have not only the quarry-shop product but the product of all other shops of the province as well.

Rude flaked implements—Numerous heavy flaked implements of the region, found on village-sites, in shell banks, and elsewhere, were shaped from bowlders by striking off a few flakes, giving rude edges and points. They are not of quarry origin as the inferior grades of material, found very generally distributed, were utilized. As scattered about they are not easily distinguished from the ordinary rejectage of blade making.

Highland quarries—Quarries beyond the limits of the tidewater region were extensively worked by implement makers. The stone was in the mass, but the processes employed in shaping it and the results reached closely duplicate corresponding features in the lowland quarries. The blades made were transported to all parts of the lowland and worked up into implements duplicating the local varieties. No rejects of this work are found in the lowland, and rude implements of the materials involved are extremely rare outside of the highland.

Battering and abrading processes—Implements to be shaped by these processes—celts, axes, and the like—were very often reduced to approximate shape by flaking. Tough, heavy, hard stones were preferred, and disseminated water-worn pieces were often chosen. The fracturing processes employed were the same as those concerned in ordinary flaking, but since the objects to be made were of different classes the rejectage presents distinct types of form. The celt, the most numerous class of pecked-abraded tools, has a wide edge and a roundish body somewhat pointed above. Flaked implements of leaf-blade origin have a point instead of an edge, while the bodies are flat and the upper end is broad. These distinctions were necessarily foreshadowed in the incipient forms, and aborted specimens, found intermingled on sites of manufacture, may be distinguished by tendencies, in the one type, to specialization of a broad end, and in the other by tendencies to definition of a pointed end. The celt forms roughed-out by flaking were specialized by pecking processes and completed by grinding and polishing, the rejectage being unimportant, as the processes were not so violent as to lead to frequent breakage.

Incision processes—Softer varieties of stone were shaped by cutting. The rock, chiefly soapstone, was extensively quarried from massive deposits in the highland and worked into vessels, pipes, and a few less important varieties of objects. As with the other groups, the articles made were only roughed-out in the quarries, specializing and finishing being conducted mainly on sites of use. The implements employed in this work form a distinct class. Many of the quarry forms are rude sledges and picks, while the cutting tool proper is a chisel or pick—according to the manner of hafting—made of hard, tough stone and shaped usually by flaking, pecking, and grinding. Sites of manufacture for these tools have not been observed, and are probably scattered and unimportant.

Distribution of implements—Distribution is found to present a number of points of interest, most of which pertain to the relation of the implements as found to the sources of the raw material. Rejectage of manufacture is little subject to transportation, though raw material in convenient form may have traveled a long way. The smaller implements found their way to very distant parts, while the larger and especially the ruder forms remained on or near the sites of original use. Distribution from the great quarries was doubtless in large numbers, and trade as well as use may have assisted in the dissemination. The general distribution over the country was brought about by many minor agencies connected with use. Each province, each district, and site, here and elsewhere, is supplied with art remains brought together by the various agencies of environment—topographic, geologic, biologic, and ethnic—and the action of these agencies is to a large extent susceptible of analysis, and this analysis, properly conducted, constitutes a very large part of the science of prehistoric archeology.

SUPPLEMENTARY NOTES

I

The quarry group presented in the frontispiece and again in another setting in plate CII was prepared as an exposition exhibit rather than as a necessary feature of the studies recorded in the present paper. It may be further stated that it is intended to exemplify a great art of the race—the shaping of stone by flaking processes—rather than to illustrate a satisfactorily established episode in the history of a particular people. After the return of the group from the World's Columbian Exposition at Chicago, where it formed part of a set of exhibits illustrating the various great quarry-shops of the United States, I conceived the notion that the figures could be taken to Piny branch and placed in the actual quarries, thus more graphically portraying the ancient operations. A site was selected for the purpose on the margin of a gulch near Fourteenth street, where some great oaks grow on the beds of ancient refuse; but before the project could be carried out I was called away from the work permanently. I happened, however, to mention my plans to Messrs Cushing and Dinwiddie, of the Bureau of Ethnology, and these gentlemen very generously took up the work, and the result is indicated in the accompanying view, plate CII, which on its receipt was a great surprise to me, as much more had been done than I had contemplated. It seems that Mr Cushing found traces of dwelling on the site selected, and resolved to restore the scenes of the past in all possible detail without deviating from the theoretic historic models. He established a camp, built the lodge of matting, carried out an antique wooden mortar and other appropriate utensils, laid a hearth of bowlders, and constructed the framework of poles for drying fish and game. The scene is altogether complete and realistic though the picture is somewhat lacking in contrast of light and shade.

It remains only to say in this connection that I desire nothing more than that the group should be taken for what it is worth as an illustration of a most important industry carried on in nearly every part of the country. It will, however, I am sure, assist in conveying a definite impression of the work prosecuted so extensively in the District of Columbia, and as it associates with the quarries the only people that have any claim whatsoever to the occupancy of the region and the site, the chances are greatly in favor of the practical correctness of the impressions conveyed.

Since the completion of this group it has been a source of regret that a fourth figure was not added to illustrate the final steps of the work— the specializing of the blades by pressure processes—though it is true that this would be putting together portions of the work not usually associated in the great quarries here and elsewhere. General conditions would have warranted the association, however, for, as has been shown elsewhere, where sites of dwelling or use were closely combined with sites producing the raw material the roughing-out operations were doubtless often followed by the finishing processes in a continuous series.

Copies of the group, as illustrated in the frontispiece, are now set up in the National Museum at Washington and in the Field Columbian Museum at Chicago.

II

While engaged in the work of excavation on the Piny branch quarry site, I took up the matter of the shaping processes employed by the quarrymen, and assuming that bowlders were used for hammerstones, attempted to accomplish by free-hand flaking what had been done by the ancient artisans. For some time I labored at great disadvantage, as I was experimenting as a rule with material already rejected as unfit for use. When the quarry face was reached and the superiority of the bowlders fresh from the bed realized, I took up the work with renewed hope, but an accident to my left arm, resulting from attempts to flake a very large stone held in the left hand, caused the practical discontinuance of the experiments. Although not absolutely sure that I was working as the quarrymen had worked, there can be no doubt that I was not far wrong, for no other known process could take the place of free-hand percussion in fracturing and flaking the firm, smooth, round bowlders. The hammer, even if of other material, would have to be operated in an identical manner.

In taking up the work of flaking stone I fully realized the difficulty of the task. The art is not to be learned in a day any more than are any of the ordinary mechanic arts such as carpentry or the working of metal, yet if savages learned it others can learn it, and no doubt of ultimate success need be felt by any student willing to give liberally of time and labor.

The difficulty of flaking the stone was not great, for a considerable percentage of the bowlders fracture with comparative ease; but the great difficulty was in causing the flakes to carry far enough across the face of the stone to give the necessary low convexity to the surface, and when this result was reached approximately on one side it was extremely uncertain whether it could be repeated on the other side, the requisite form, as indicated in this and all other quarry-shops of the same class, being a thin blade of lens-like profile. The sections shown in figure 29a illustrate phases of successful and unsuccessful flaking.

In the first illustration the left side shows the removal of four flakes and reduction of the surface to nearly the necessary degree of convexity. The work on the other side failed utterly, the flakes did not carry, and a high peak resulted. This is the profile of multitudes of failures.

In the second figure the flaking progressed encouragingly on both sides, but neither was reduced to the requisite flatness. A blade of this degree of convexity was usually rejected. A satisfactory profile was

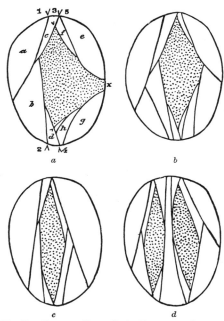

produced in the third case illustrated, and as indicated in the fourth figure a lucky splitting of the bowlder made it possible to produce two successful blades. I found that very often before I had obtained the desired profile some unfortunate blow shattered the stone, but I got very near the desired result in numerous cases, duplicating the best of the rejected forms, but falling a little short of the blade as perfected by the ancient workmen and carried away for use and elaboration.

In plate CIII some of the results of my efforts at blade making are presented. I observed that the rejectage of my work, where falling among the freshly uncovered rejectage of the site, was not to be distinguished from it in any way—not even in many cases by the freshness of the fracture.

FIG. 29a—Cross sections illustrating successive removal of flakes from bowlders. The dotted space is the section of form produced, a and b being failures and c and d successes.

As to the work of specializing the perfected blade into keen-edged knives, slender drills, and stemmed and notched projectile points, it does not seem to compare in difficulty with the making of the thin blades themselves from the bowlders.

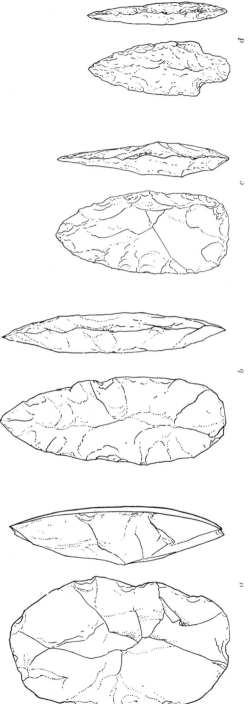

RESULTS OF EXPERIMENTAL FLAKING BY PERCUSSION AND PRESSURE; THREE-FOURTHS ACTUAL SIZE

a, Turtleback with convexity so pronounced as to lead to rejection.   b, Blade approximating desired form, but so thick as to lead to rejection.   c, Blade successful, save for slightly too great thickness near the wider end.   d, Point slightly specialized by use of flaking tool impelled by pressure from shoulder

SMITHSONIAN INSTITUTION——BUREAU OF ETHNOLOGY.

ORIGIN AND DEVELOPMENT

OF

FORM AND ORNAMENT IN CERAMIC ART.

BY

WILLIAM H. HOLMES.

CONTENTS.

ILLUSTRATIONS.

411

ORIGIN AND DEVELOPMENT OF FORM AND ORNAMENT IN CERAMIC ART.

By William H. Holmes.

INTRODUCTORY.

For the investigation of art in its early stages and in its widest sense there is probably no fairer field than that afforded by aboriginal America, ancient and modern.

At the period of discovery, art at a number of places on the American continent seems to have been developing surely and steadily, through the force of the innate genius of the race, and the more advanced nations were already approaching the threshold of civilization; at the same time their methods were characterized by great simplicity, and their art products are, as a consequence, exceptionally homogeneous.

The advent of European civilization checked the current of growth, and new and conflicting elements were introduced necessarily disastrous to the native development.

There is much, however, in the art of living tribes, especially of those least influenced by the whites, capable of throwing light upon the obscure passages of precolumbian art. By supplementing the study of the prehistoric by that of historic art, which is still in many cases in its incipient stages, we may hope to penetrate deeply into the secrets of the past.

The advantages of this field, as compared with Greece, Egypt, and the Orient, will be apparent when we remember that the dawn of art in these countries lies hidden in the shadow of unnumbered ages, while ours stands out in the light of the very present. This is well illustrated by a remark of Birch, who, in dwelling upon the antiquity of the fictile art, says that "the existence of earthen vessels in Egypt was at least coeval with the formation of a written language."[1] Beyond this there is acknowledged chaos. In strong contrast with this, is the fact that all precolumbian American pottery *precedes* the acquisition of written language, and this contrast is emphasized by the additional fact that it also antedates the use of the wheel, that great perverter of the plastic tendencies of clay.

---

[1] Birch: History of Ancient Pottery, 1873, p. 8.

The material presented in the following notes is derived chiefly from the native ceramic art of the United States, but the principles involved are applicable to all times and to all art, as they are based upon the laws of nature.

Ceramic art presents two classes of phenomena of importance in the study of the evolution of æsthetic culture. These relate, first, to *form* and second, to *ornament.*

Form, as embodied in clay vessels, embraces, 1st, *useful shapes*, which may or may not be ornamental, and, 2d, *æsthetic shapes*, which are ornamental and may be useful.   There are also *grotesque* and *fanciful shapes*, which may or may not be either useful or ornamental.

No form or class of forms can be said to characterize a particular age or stage of culture.   In a general way, of course, the vessels of primitive peoples will be simple in form, while those of more advanced races will be more varied and highly specialized.

The shapes first assumed by vessels in clay depend upon the shape of the vessels employed at the time of the introduction of the art, and these depend, to a great extent, upon the kind and grade of culture of the people acquiring the art and upon the resources of the country in which they live.   To illustrate: If, for instance, some of the highly advanced Alaskan tribes which do not make pottery should migrate to another habitat, less suitable to the practice of their old arts and well adapted to art in clay, and should there acquire the art of pottery, they would doubtless, to a great extent, copy their highly developed utensils of wood, bone, ivory, and basketry, and thus reach a high grade of ceramic achievement in the first century of the practice of the art; but, on the other hand, if certain tribes, very low in intelligence and having no vessel-making arts, should undergo a corresponding change of habitat and acquire the art of pottery, they might not reach in a thousand years, if left to themselves, a grade in the art equal to that of the hypothetical Alaskan potters in the first decade.   It is, therefore, not the age of the art itself that determines its forms, but the grade and kind of art with which it originates and coexists.

Ornament is subject to similar laws.   Where pottery is employed by peoples in very low stages of culture, its ornamentation will be of the simple archaic kind.   Being a conservative art and much hampered by the restraints of convention, the elementary forms of ornament are carried a long way into the succeeding periods and have a very decided effect upon the higher stages.   Pottery brought into use for the first time by more advanced races will never pass through the elementary stage of decoration, but will take its ornament greatly from existing art and carry this up in its own peculiar way through succeeding generations.   The character of the ornamentation does not therefore depend upon the age of the art so much as upon the acquirements of the potter and his people in other arts.

ORIGIN OF FORM.

In order to convey a clear idea of the bearing of the preceding statements upon the history of form and ornament, it will be necessary to present a number of points in greater detail.

The following synopsis will give a connected view of various possible origins of form.

Origin of form............ ...... $\begin{cases} \text{By adventition.} \\ \text{By imitation.......... } \begin{cases} \text{Of natural models.} \\ \text{Of artificial models.} \end{cases} \\ \text{By invention.} \end{cases}$

FORMS SUGGESTED BY ADVENTITION.

The suggestions of accident, especially in the early stages of art, are often adopted, and become fruitful sources of improvement and progress. By such means the use of clay was discovered and the ceramic art came into existence. The accidental indentation of a mass of clay by the foot, or hand, or by a fruit-shell, or stone, while serving as an auxiliary in some simple art, may have suggested the making of a cup, the simplest form of vessel.

The use of clay as a cement in repairing utensils, in protecting combustible vessels from injury by fire, or in building up the walls of shallow vessels, may also have led to the formation of disks or cups, afterwards independently constructed. In any case the objects or utensils with which the clay was associated in its earliest use would impress their forms upon it. Thus, if clay were used in deepening or mending vessels of stone by a given people, it would, when used independently by that people, tend to assume shapes suggested by stone vessels. The same may be said of its use in connection with wood and wicker, or with vessels of other materials. Forms of vessels so derived may be said to have an adventitious origin, yet they are essentially copies, although not so by design, and may as readily be placed under the succeeding head.

FORMS DERIVED BY IMITATION.

Clay has no inherent qualities of a nature to impose a given form or class of forms upon its products, as have wood, bark, bone, or stone. It is so mobile as to be quite free to take form from surroundings, and where extensively used will record or echo a vast deal of nature and of coexistent art.

In this observation we have a key that will unlock many of the mysteries of form.

In the investigation of this point it will be necessary to consider the processes by which an art inherits or acquires the forms of another art or of nature, and how one material imposes its peculiarities upon another material. In early stages of culture the processes of art are closely akin to those of nature, the human agent hardly ranking as more than a part of the environment. The primitive artist does not proceed by methods identical with our own. He does not deliberately and freely examine all departments of nature or art and select for models those things most convenient or most agreeable to fancy; neither does he experiment with the view of inventing new forms. What he attempts depends almost absolutely upon what happens to be suggested by preceding forms, and so narrow and so direct are the processes of his mind that, knowing his resources, we could closely predict his results.

The range of models in the ceramic art is at first very limited, and includes only those utensils devoted to the particular use to which the clay vessels are to be applied; later, closely-associated objects and utensils are copied. In the first stages of art, when the savage makes a weapon, he modifies or copies a weapon; when he makes a vessel, he modifies or copies a vessel.

This law holds good in an inverse ratio to culture, varying to a certain extent with the character of the material used.

Natural originals.—Natural originals, both animal and vegetable, necessarily differ with the country and the climate, thus giving rise to individual characters in art forms often extremely persistent and surviving decided changes of environment.

The gourd is probably the most varied and suggestive natural vessel. We find that the primitive potter has often copied it in the most literal manner. One example only, out of the many available ones, is necessary. This is from a mound in southeastern Missouri.

In Fig. 464, *a* illustrates a common form of the gourd, while *b* represents the imitation in clay.

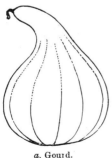 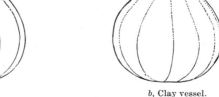

a, Gourd.   b, Clay vessel.

FIG. 464.—Form derived from a gourd.

All nations situated upon the sea or upon large rivers use shells of mollusks, which, without modification, make excellent receptacles for water and food. Imitations of these are often found among the products of the potter's art. A good example from the Mississippi Valley is shown in Fig. 465, *a* being the original and *b* the copy in clay.

In Africa, and in other countries, such natural objects as cocoanut shells, and ostrich eggs are used in like manner.

Another class of vessels, those made from the skins, bladders, and stomachs of animals, should also be mentioned in this connection, as it is certain that their influence has frequently been felt in the conformation of earthen utensils.

In searching nature, therefore, for originals of primitive ceramic forms we have little need of going outside of objects that in their natural or slightly altered state are available for vessels.

a, Shell.   b, Clay.

Fig. 465.—Form derived from a conch shell.

True, other objects have been copied. We find a multitude of the higher natural forms, both animal and vegetable, embodied in vessels of clay, but their presence is indicative of a somewhat advanced stage of art, when the copying of vessels that were functionally proper antecedents had given rise to a familiarity with the use of clay and a capacity in handling it that, with advancing culture, brought all nature within the reach of the potter and made it assist in the processes of variation and development.

Artificial originals.—There is no doubt that among most peoples art had produced vessels in other materials antecedent to the utilization of clay. These would be legitimate models for the potter and we may therefore expect to find them repeated in earthenware. In this way the art has acquired a multitude of new forms, some of which may be natural forms at second hand, that is to say, with modifications imposed upon them by the material in which they were first shaped. But all materials other than clay are exceedingly intractable, and impress their own characters so decidedly upon forms produced in them that ultimate originals, where there are such, cannot often be traced through them.

It will be most interesting to note the influence of these peculiarities of originals upon the ceramic art.

A nation having stone vessels, like those of California, on acquiring the art of pottery would use the stone vessels as models, and such forms as that given in Fig. 466 would arise, a being in stone and b in clay, the former from California and the latter from Arizona.

Similar forms would just as readily come from gourds, baskets, or other globular utensils.

Nations having wooden vessels would copy them in clay on acquiring the art of pottery. This would give rise to a distinct group of forms, the result primarily of the peculiarities of the woody structure.

Thus in Fig. 467, *a*, we have a form of wooden vessel, a sort of winged trough that I have frequently found copied in clay. The earthen vessel given in Fig. 467, *b*, was obtained from an ancient grave in Arkansas.

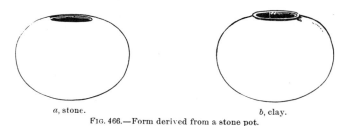

a, stone.   b, clay.

FIG. 466.—Form derived from a stone pot.

The carapace of some species of turtles, and perhaps even the hard case of the armadillo, could be utilized in a similar way.

The shaping of a knot of wood often gives rise to a dipper-shaped

a, wood.   b, clay.

FIG. 467.—Form derived from a wooden tray.

vessel, such as may be found in use by many tribes, and is as likely an original for the dipper form in clay as is the gourd or the conch shell; the familiar horn vessel of the western tribes, Fig. 468, *a*, would have

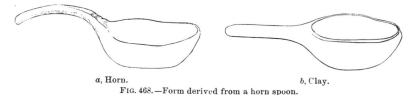

a, Horn.   b, Clay.

FIG. 468.—Form derived from a horn spoon.

served equally well. The specimen given in *b* is from Arkansas. As a rule, however, such vessels cannot be traced to their originals, since

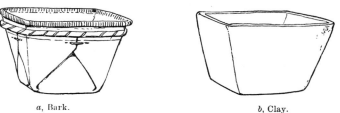

a, Bark.   b, Clay.

FIG. 469.—Form derived from a bark vessel.

by copying and recopying they have varied from the parent form, tending always toward uniform conventional shapes.

A vessel of rectangular outline might originate in wood or bark. In Fig. 469, *a*, we have a usual form of bark tray, which is possibly the prototype of the square-rimmed earthen vessel given in *b*.

Basketry and other classes of woven vessels take a great variety of forms and, being generally antecedent to the potter's art and con-

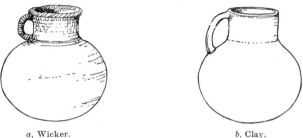

a, Wicker.   b, Clay.
FIG. 470.—Form originating in basketry.

stantly present with it, have left an indelible impression upon ceramic forms. This is traceable in the earthenware of nearly all nations. The clay vessel is an intruder, and usurps the place and appropriates the

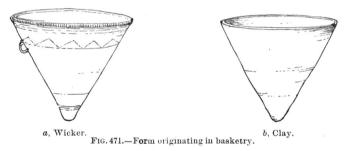

a, Wicker.   b, Clay.
FIG. 471.—Form originating in basketry.

dress of its predecessor in wicker. The form illustrated in Fig. 470, *a*, is a common one with the Pueblo peoples, and their earthen vessels often resemble it very closely, as shown in *b*. Another variety is given

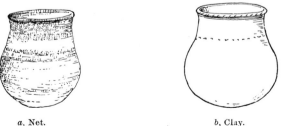

a, Net.   b, Clay.
FIG. 472.—Form originating in basketry.

in Fig. 471, *a* and *b*. These specimens are from southwestern Utah. Fig. 472, *b*, illustrates a form quite common in the Southern States, a

4 ETH——29

section in which pouch-like nets and baskets, *a,* were formerly in use and in which the pots were often modeled.

INVENTION OF FORM.

In the early stages of art, forms are rarely invented outright and I shall not stop to consider the subject here.

MODIFICATION OF FORM.

The acquisition of new materials, the development of new uses, the employment of new processes of manufacture, and many other *agencies* lead to the multiplication of forms through modification. The processes by which highly differentiated forms are reached are interesting throughout and repay the closest study.

A preliminary classification of the various causes that lead to modification is given in the following synopsis:

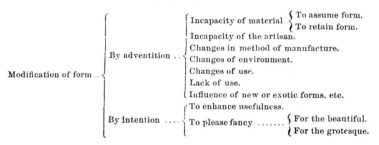

MODIFICATION BY ADVENTITION.

Incapacity of material.—It is evident at a glance that clay lacks the capacity to assume and to retain many of the details of form found in antecedent vessels. This necessarily results in the alteration or omission of these features, and hence arise many modifications of original forms.

The simple lack of capacity on the part of the potter who undertook to reproduce a model would lead to the modification of all but the most simple shapes.

The acquisition of the art by a superior or an inferior race, or one of different habits would lead to decided changes. A people accustomed to carrying objects upon the head, on acquiring earthen vessels would shape the bases and the handles to facilitate this use.

Improvements in the methods of manufacture are of the greatest importance in the progress of an art. The introduction of the lathe, for example, might almost revolutionize form in clay.

As arts multiply, clay is applied to new uses. Its employment in the manufacture of lamps, whistles, or toys would lead to a multitude of distinct and unique forms.

The acquisition of a new vessel-making material by a nation of potters and the association of the forms developed through its inherent qualities or structure would often lead ceramic shapes into new channels.

The contact of a nation of potters with a nation of carvers in wood would tend very decidedly to modify the utensils of the former. One example may be given which will illustrate the possibilities of such exotic influences upon form. In Fig. 473, *a*, we have an Alaskan vessel

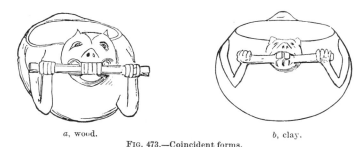

a, wood.   b, clay.

FIG. 473.—Coincident forms.

carved in wood. It represents a beaver grasping a stick in its hands and teeth. The conception is so unusual and the style of vessel so characteristic of the people that we should not expect to find it repeated in other regions; but the ancient graves of the Middle Mississippi Valley have furnished a number of very similar vessels in clay, one of which is outlined in *b*. While this remarkable coincidence is suggestive of ethnic relationships which do not call for attention here, it serves to illustrate the possibilities of modification by simple contact.

A curious example illustrative of possible transformation by adventitious circumstances is found in the collection from the province of ancient Tusayan. A small vessel of sphynx-like appearance, possibly derived more or less remotely from a skin vessel, has a noticeable resemblance to some life form, Fig. 474, *a*. The fore-legs are represented

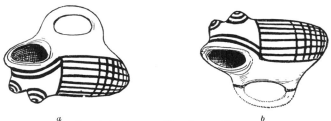

a   b

FIG. 474.—Form resulting from accident.

by two large bosses, the wide-open mouth takes the place of the severed neck, and a handle connects the top of the rim with the back of the vessel. The handle being broken off and the vessel inverted, *b*, there is a decided change; we are struck by the resemblance to a frog or toad. The original legs, having dark concentric lines painted around them, look like large protruding eyes, and the mouth gapes in the most realistic manner, while the two short broken ends of the handle resemble legs and serve to support the vessel in an upright position, completing the illusion. The fetich-hunting Pueblo Indian, picking up this little vessel in its mutilated condition, would probably at once give to it the sacred character of the water animal which it resembles, and it might readily transmit its peculiarities of form to other generations of vessels.

It is not necessary in this study to refer at length to the influence of metallic vessels upon ceramic forms. They do not usually appear until the ceramic art is far advanced and often receive a heritage of shape from earthen forms. Afterwards, when the inherent qualities of the metal have stamped their individuality upon utensils, the debt is paid back to clay with interest, as will be seen by reference to later forms in many parts of the world.

MODIFICATION BY INTENTION.

To enhance usefulness.—There can be no doubt that the desire upon the part of the archaic potter to increase the usefulness and convenience of his utensils has been an important agent in the modification of form. The earliest vessels employed were often clumsy and difficult to handle. The favorite conch shell would hold water for him who wished to drink, but the breaking away of spines and the extraction of the interior whorl improved it immeasurably. The clumsy mortar of stone, with its thick walls and great weight, served a useful purpose, but it needed a very little intelligent thought to show that thin walls and neatly-trimmed margins were much preferable.

Vessels of clay, aside from the forms imposed upon them by their antecedents and associates, would necessarily be subject to changes suggested by the growing needs of man. These would be worked out with ever-increasing ease by his unfolding genius for invention. Further investigation of this phase of development would carry me beyond the limits set for this paper.

To please fancy.—The skill acquired by the handling of clay in constructing vessels and in efforts to increase their usefulness would open an expansive field for the play of fancy. The potter would no sooner succeed in copying vessels having life form than he would be placed in a position to realize his capacity to imitate forms not peculiar to vessels. His ambition would in time lead him even beyond the limits of nature and he would invade the realm of imagination, embodying the conceptions of superstition in the plastic clay. This tendency would be encouraged and perpetuated by the relegation of vessels of particular forms to particular ceremonies.

ORIGIN OF ORNAMENT.

The birth of the embellishing art must be sought in that stage of animal development when instinct began to discover that certain attributes or adornments increased attractiveness. When art in its human sense came into existence ideas of embellishment soon extended from the *person*, with which they had been associated, to all things with which man had to deal. The processes of the growth of the æsthetic idea are long and obscure and cannot be taken up in this place.

The various elements of embellishment in which the ceramic art is interested may be assigned to two great classes, based upon the character of the conceptions associated with them. These are *ideographic* and *non-ideographic*. In the present paper I shall treat chiefly of the non-ideographic, reserving the ideographic for a second paper.

Elements, non-ideographic from the start, are derived mainly from two sources : 1st, from objects, natural or artificial, associated with the arts; and, 2d, from the suggestions of accidents attending construction. Natural objects abound in features highly suggestive of embellishment and these are constantly employed in art. Artificial objects have two classes of features capable of giving rise to ornament: these are *constructional* and *functional*. In a late stage of development all things in nature and in art, however complex or foreign to the art in its practice, are subject to decorative treatment. This latter is the realistic pictorial stage, one of which the student of native American culture needs to take little cognizance.

Elements of design are not invented outright: man modifies, combines, and recombines elements or ideas already in existence, but does not create.

A classification of the sources of decorative motives employed in the ceramic art is given in the following diagram :

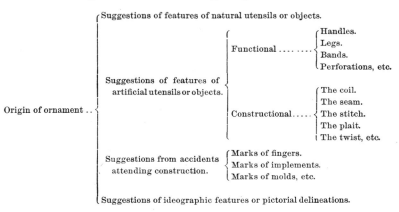

SUGGESTIONS OF NATURAL FEATURES OF OBJECTS.

The first articles used by men in their simple arts have in many cases possessed features suggestive of decoration. Shells of mollusks are exquisitely embellished with ribs, spines, nodes, and colors. The same is true to a somewhat limited extent of the shells of the turtle and the armadillo and of the hard cases of fruits.

These decorative features, though not essential to the utensil, are nevertheless inseparable parts of it, and are cast or unconsciously copied by a very primitive people when similar articles are artificially produced in plastic material. In this way a utensil may acquire ornamental characters long before the workman has learned to take pleasure in such details or has conceived an idea beyond that of simple utility. This may be called unconscious embellishment. In this fortuitous fashion a ribbed variety of fruit shell would give rise to a ribbed vessel in clay; one covered with spines would suggest a noded vessel, etc. When taste came to be exercised upon such objects these features would be retained and copied for the pleasure they afforded.

Passing by the many simple elements of decoration that by this unconscious process could be derived from such sources, let me give a single example by which it will be seen that not only elementary forms but even so highly constituted an ornament as the scroll may have been brought thus naturally into the realm of decorative art. The sea-shell has always been intimately associated with the arts that utilize clay and abounds in suggestions of embellishment. The *Busycon* was almost universally employed as a vessel by the tribes of the Atlantic drainage of North America. Usually it was trimmed down and excavated until

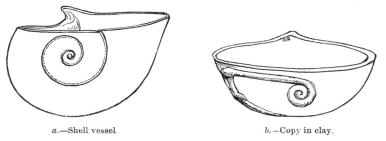

a.—Shell vessel.   b.—Copy in clay.

FIG. 475.—Scroll derived from the spire of a conch shell.

only about three-fourths of the outer wall of the shell remained. At one end was the long spike-like base which served as a handle, and at the other the flat conical apex, with its very pronounced spiral line or ridge expanding from the center to the circumference, as seen in Fig. 475 a. This vessel was often copied in clay, as many good examples now in our museums testify. The notable feature is that the shell has

been copied literally, the spiral appearing in its proper place. A specimen is illustrated in Fig. 475 *b* which, although simple and highly conventionalized, still retains the spiral figure.

In another example we have four of the noded apexes placed about
the rim of the vessel, as shown in Fig. 476 *a*, the conception being that
of four conch shells united in one vessel, the bases being turned inward
and the apexes outward. Now it is only necessary to suppose the addition of the spiral lines, always associated with the nodes, to have the
result shown in *b*, and by a still higher degree of convention we have

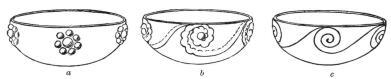

FIG. 476.—Possible derivation of the current scroll.

the classic scroll ornament given in *c*. Of course, no such result as this
could come about adventitiously, as successful combination calls for the
exercise of judgment and taste; but the initiatory steps could be taken—
the motive could enter art—without the conscious supervision of the
human agent.

SUGGESTIONS BY FEATURES OF ARTIFICIAL OBJECTS.

Functional features.—Functional features of art products liable to influence ornament comprise handles, legs, feet, rims, bands, and other
peculiarities of shape originating in utility. Handles, for instance, may
have been indigenous to a number of arts; they are coeval and coex-
tensive with culture. The first load, weapon, or vessel transported by
man may have been suspended by a vine or filament. Such arts as have
fallen heir to handles have used them according to the capacities of the
material employed. Of all the materials stone is probably the least
suited to their successful use, while clay utilizes them in its own peculiar

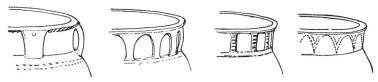

FIG. 477.—Ornament derived through the modification of handles.

way, giving to them a great variety of expression. They are copied in
clay from various models, but owing to the inadequate capacities of the
material, often lose their function and degenerate into mere ornaments,
which are modified as such to please the potter's fancy. Thus, for example, the series of handles placed about the neck of the vessel become,

by modification in frequent copying, a mere band of ornamental figures in relief, or even finally in engraved, punctured, or painted lines, in the manner suggested in Fig. 477. Legs, pedestals, spouts, and other features may in a like manner give rise to decoration.

Constructional features.—Features of vessels resulting from construction are infinitely varied and often highly suggestive of decoration. Constructional peculiarities of the clay utensils themselves are especially worthy of notice, and on account of their actual presence in the art itself are more likely to be utilized or copied for ceramic ornament than those of other materials. The coil, so universally employed in construction, has had a decided influence upon the ceramic decoration of certain peoples, as I have shown in a paper on ancient Pueblo art. From it we have not only a great variety of surface ornamentation produced by simple treatment of the coil in place, but probably many forms suggested by the use of the coil in vessel building, as, for instance, the spiral formed in beginning the base of a coiled vessel, Fig. 478 *a,*

a.—Coiled fillet of clay.   b.—Double coil.

Fig. 478.—Scroll derived from coil of clay.

from which the double scroll *b,* as a separate feature, could readily be derived, and finally the chain of scrolls so often seen in border and zone decoration. This familiarity with the use of fillets or ropes of clay would also lead to a great variety of applied ornament, examples of which, from Pueblo art, are given in Fig. 479. The sinuous forms as-

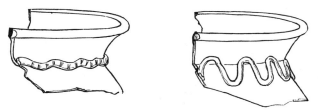

Fig. 479.—Ornamental use of fillets.

sumed by a rope of clay so employed would readily suggest to the Indian the form of the serpent and the means of representing it, and might thus lead to the introduction of this much revered creature into art.

Of the various classes of utensils associated closely with the ceramic art, there are none so characteristically marked by constructional features as nets and wicker baskets. The twisting, interlacing, knotting, and stitching of filaments give relieved figures that by contact in manufacture impress themselves upon the plastic clay. Such impressions come in time to be regarded as pleasing features, and when free-hand methods of reproducing are finally acquired they and their derivatives become essentials of decoration. At a later stage these characters of basketry influence ceramic decoration in a somewhat different way. By the use of variously-colored fillets the woven surface displays figures in color corresponding to those in relief and varying with every new combination. Many striking patterns are thus produced, and the potter who has learned to decorate his wares by the stylus or brush reproduces these patterns by free-hand methods. We find pottery in all countries ornamented with patterns, painted, incised, stamped, and relieved, certainly derived from this source. So well is this fact known that I need hardly go into details.

In the higher stages of art the constructional characters of architecture give rise to many notions of decoration which afterwards descend to other arts, taking greatly divergent forms. Aboriginal architecture in some parts of America had reached a development capable of wielding a strong influence. This is not true, however, of any part of the United States.

SUGGESTIONS OF ACCIDENTS.

Besides the suggestions of surface features impressed in manufacture or intentionally copied as indicated above, we have also those of accidental imprints of implements or of the fingers in manufacture. From this source there are necessarily many suggestions of ornament, at first of indented figures, but later, after long employment, extending to the other modes of representation.

IDEOGRAPHIC AND PICTORIAL SUBJECTS.

Non-ideographic forms of ornament may originate in ideographic features, mnemonic, demonstrative, or symbolic. Such significant figures are borrowed by decorators from other branches of art. As time goes on they lose their significance and are subsequently treated as purely decorative elements. Subjects wholly pictorial in character, when such come to be made, may also be used as simple decoration, and by long processes of convention become geometric.

The exact amount of significance still attached to significant figures after adoption into decoration cannot be determined except in cases of actual identification by living peoples, and even when the signification is known by the more learned individuals the decorator may be wholly without knowledge of it.

MODIFICATION OF ORNAMENT.

There are comparatively few elementary ideas prominently and generally employed in primitive decorative art. New ideas are acquired, as already shown, all along the pathway of progress. None of these ideas retain a uniform expression, however, as they are subject to modification by environment just as are the forms of living organisms. A brief classification of the causes of modification is given in the following synopsis:

Modification of ornament...................................
{
Through material.
Through form.
Through methods of realization.
}

Through material.—It is evident at a glance that *material* must have a strong influence upon the forms assumed by the various decorative motives, however derived. Thus stone, clay, wood, bone, and copper, although they readily borrow from nature and from each other, necessarily show different decorative results. Stone is massive and takes form slowly and by peculiar processes. Clay is more versatile and decoration may be scratched, incised, painted, or modeled in relief with equal facility, while wood and metal engender details having characters peculiar to themselves, producing different results from the same motives or elements. Much of the diversity displayed by the art products of different countries and climates is due to this cause.

Peoples dwelling in arctic climates are limited, by their materials, to particular modes of expression. Bone and ivory as shaped for use in the arts of subsistence afford facilities for the employment of a very restricted class of linear decoration, such chiefly as could be scratched with a hard point upon small irregular, often cylindrical, implements. Skins and other animal tissues are not favorable to the development of ornament, and the textile arts—the greatest agents of convention—do not readily find suitable materials in which to work.

Decorative art carried to a high stage under arctic environment would be more likely to achieve unconventional and realistic forms than if developed in more highly favored countries. The accurate geometric and linear patterns would hardly arise.

Through form.—Forms of decorated objects exercise a strong influence upon the decorative designs employed. It would be more difficult to tattoo the human face or body with straight lines or rectilinear patterns than with curved ones. An ornament applied originally to a vessel of a given form would accommodate itself to that form pretty much as costume becomes adjusted to the individual. When it came to be required for another form of vessel, very decided changes might be necessary.

With the ancient Pueblo peoples rectilinear forms of meander patterns were very much in favor and many earthen vessels are found in which bands of beautiful angular geometric figures occupy the peripheral zone, Fig. 480 *a*, but when the artist takes up a mug having a row of hemispherical nodes about the body, *b*, he finds it very difficult to apply his favorite forms and is almost compelled to run spiral curves about the nodes in order to secure a neat adjustment.

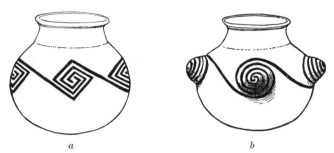

a   *b*

FIG. 480.—Variations in a motive through the influence of form.

Through methods of realization.—It will readily be seen that the forms assumed by a motive depend greatly upon the character of the mechanical devices employed. In the potter's art devices for holding and turning the vessel under manipulation produce peculiar results.

In applying a given idea to clay much depends upon the method of executing it. It will take widely differing forms when executed by incising, by modeling, by painting, and by stamping.

Intimately associated with methods of execution are peculiarities of construction, the two agencies working together in the processes of modification and development of ornament.

I have previously shown how our favorite ornament, the scroll, in its disconnected form may have originated in the copying of natural forms or through the manipulation of coils of clay. I present here an example of its possible origin through the modification of forms derived from constructional features of basketry. An ornament known as the guilloche is found in many countries. The combination of lines resembles that of twisted or platted fillets of wood, cane, or rushes, as may be seen at a glance, Fig. 481 *a*. An incised ornament of this character, possibly derived from basketry by copying the twisted fillets or their impressions in the clay, is very common on the pottery of the mounds of the Mississippi Valley, and its variants form a most interesting study. In applying this to a vessel the careless artist does not properly connect the ends of the lines which pass beneath the intersecting fillets, and the parts become disconnected, *b*. In many cases the ends are turned in abruptly as seen in *c*, and only a slight further change is necessary to lead to the result, *d*, the running scroll with well-developed links. All of these steps may be observed in a single group of vessels.

It may be thought by some that the processes of development indicated above are insufficient and unsatisfactory. There are those who, seeing these forms already endowed with symbolism, begin at what I conceive to be the wrong end of the process. They derive the form of symbol directly from the thing symbolized. Thus the current scroll is, with many races, found to be a symbol of water, and its origin is attributed to a literal rendition of the sweep and curl of the waves. It is more probable that the scroll became the symbol of the sea long after its development through agencies similar to those described above, and that the association resulted from the observation of incidental resemblances. This same figure, in use by the Indians of the interior of the continent, is regarded as symbolic of the whirlwind, and it is probable that any symbol-using people will find in the features and phenomena of their environment, whatever it may be, sufficient resemblance to any of their decorative devices to lead to a symbolic association.

FIG. 481.—Theoretical development of the current scroll.

One secret of modification is found in the use of a radical in more than one art, owing to differences in constructional characters. For example, the tendency of nearly all woven fabrics is to encourage, even to compel, the use of straight lines in the decorative designs applied. Thus the attempt to employ curved lines would lead to stepped or broken lines. The curvilinear scroll-coming from some other art would be forced by the constructional character of the fabric into square forms, and the rectilinear meander or fret would result, as shown in Fig. 482, a being the plain form, painted, engraved, or in relief, and b the same idea developed in a woven fabric. Stone or brick-work would lead to like results, Fig. 483; but the modification could as readily move in the other direction. If an ornament originating in the constructional character of a woven fabric, or remodeled by it, and hence rectilinear, should be desired for a smooth structureless or featureless surface, the difficul-

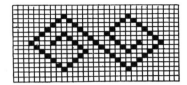

<table>
<tr><td>a, free-hand form.</td><td>b, form imposed by fabric.</td></tr>
</table>

FIG. 482.—Forms of the same motive expressed in different arts.

ties of drawing the angular forms would lead to the delineation of curved forms, and we would have exactly the reverse of the order shown in Figs. 482 and 483. The two forms given in Fig. 484 actually

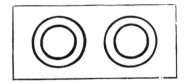
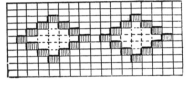

<table>
<tr><td>a, free-hand form.</td><td>b, form imposed by masonry.</td></tr>
</table>

FIG. 483.—Forms of the same motive expressed in different arts.

occur in one and the same design painted upon an ancient Pueblo vase. The curved form is apparently the result of careless or hurried work, the original angular form having come from a textile source.

a   b

FIG. 484.—Variations resulting from change of method.

Many excellent examples illustrative of this tendency to modification are found in Pueblo art. Much of the ornament applied to pottery is derived from the sister art, basketry. In the latter art the forms of decorative figures are geometric and symmetrical to the highest degree, as I have frequently pointed out. The rays of a radiating ornament, worked with the texture of a shallow basket, spring from the center and take uniform directions toward the margin, as shown in Fig. 485. But when a similar idea derived from basketry (as it could have no other origin) is executed in color upon an earthen vessel, we observe a tendency to depart from symmetry as well as from consistency.   I call atten-

Fig. 485.—Geometric form of textile ornament.

tion here to the *arrangement* of the *parts* merely, not to the motives employed, as I happen to have no examples of identical figures from the two arts.

Fig. 486.—Loss of geometric accuracy in painting.

It will be seen by reference to the design given in Fig. 486, taken from the upper surface of an ancient vase, that although the spirit of the decoration is wonderfully well preserved the idea of the origin of all the rays in the center of the vessel is not kept in view, and that by carelessness in the drawing two of the rays are crowded out and terminate against the side of a neighboring ray. In copying and recopying by free-hand methods, many curious modifications take place in these designs, as, for example, the unconformity which occurs in one place in the example given may occur at a number of places, and there will be a series of independent sections, a small number only of the bands of devices remaining true rays.

A characteristic painted design from the interior of an ancient bowl is shown in Fig. 487, in which merely a suggestion of the radiation is preserved, although the figure is still decorative and tasteful. This process of modification goes on without end, and as the true geometric

FIG. 487.—Design painted upon pottery.

textile forms recede from view innovation robs the design of all traces of its original character, producing much that is incongruous and unsatisfactory.

The growth of decorative devices from the elementary to the highly constituted and elegant is owing to a tendency of the human mind to elaborate because it is pleasant to do so or because pleasure is taken in the result, but there is still a directing and shaping agency to be accounted for.

I have already shown that such figures as the scroll and the guilloche are not *necessarily* developed by processes of selection and combination of simple elements, as many have thought, since they may have come into art at a very early stage almost full-fledged; but there is nothing in these facts to throw light upon the processes by which ornament followed particular lines of development throughout endless elaboration. In treating of this point, Prof. C. F. Hartt[2] maintained that the development of ornamental designs took particular and uniform directions owing to the structure of the eye, certain forms being chosen and perpetuated because of the pleasure afforded by movements of the eye in following them. In connection with this hypothesis, for it is nothing more, Mr. Hartt advanced the additional idea, that in unison with

[2] Hartt: Popular Science Monthly, Vol. VI, p. 266.

the general course of nature decorative forms began with simple elements and developed by systematic methods to complex forms. Take
for example the series of designs shown in Fig. 488. The meander *a*
made up of simple parts would, according to Mr. Hartt, by further elaboration under the supervision of the muscles of the eye, develop into *b*.
This, in time, into *c*, and so on until the elegant anthemium was achieved.
The series shown in Fig. 489 would develop in a similar way, or otherwise
would be produced by modification in free-hand copying of the rectilinear

FIG. 488.—Theoretical development of fret-work.

series. The processes here suggested, although to all appearances reasonable enough, should not be passed over without careful scrutiny.
    Taking the first series, we observe that the ornaments are projected in
straight continuous lines or zones, which are filled in with more or less
complex parts, rectilinear and geometrically accurate. Still higher
forms are marvelously intricate and graceful, yet not less geometric and
symmetrical.
    Let us turn to the primitive artisan, and observe him at work with
rude brush and stylus upon the rounded and irregular forms of his

utensils and weapons, or upon skins, bark, and rock surfaces. Is it probable that with his free hand directed by the eye alone he will be able to achieve these rythmic geometric forms. It seems to me that the whole tendency is in the opposite direction. I venture to surmise that if there had been no other resources than those named above the typical rectilinear fret would never have been known, at least to the primitive world; for, notwithstanding the contrary statement by Professor Hartt, the fret is in its more highly-developed forms extremely

FIG. 489.—Theoretical development of scroll work.

difficult to follow with the eye and to delineate with the hand. Until arts, geometric in their construction, arose to create and to combine mechanically the necessary elements and motives, and lead the way by a long series of object-lessons to ideas of geometric combination, our typical border ornament would not be possible. Such arts are the textile arts and architecture. These brought into existence forms and ideas not met with in nature and not primarily thought of by man, and combined them in defiance of human conceptions of grace. Geometric ornament is the offspring of technique.

ABORIGINAL POTTERY OF THE EASTERN UNITED STATES

BY

W. H. HOLMES

INDIAN WOMAN OF FLORIDA, WITH EARTHEN BOWL AND EARS OF CORN(?).
FROM A DRAWING BY JOHN WHITE NOW IN THE BRITISH MUSEUM.

CONTENTS

6 CONTENTS

ILLUSTRATIONS

7

ABORIGINAL POTTERY OF THE EASTERN UNITED STATES

By W. H. Holmes

PREFACE

During the decade beginning with 1880 the writer published a number of detailed studies of the aboriginal pottery of the United States. These were based largely on the Government collections, and appeared mainly in the annual reports of the Bureau of Ethnology. The ware of several localities was described and illustrated in a catalog of Bureau collections for 1881, published in the Third Annual Report, and the same volume contained a paper on "Prehistoric Textile Fabrics Derived from Impressions on Pottery." The Fourth Annual Report contained illustrated papers on "Ancient Pottery of the Mississippi Valley" and "Form and Ornament in the Ceramic Art." In 1885 a paper on the collections of the Davenport Academy of Sciences appeared in the fourth volume of the Academy's proceedings, and several short articles have since appeared in the American Anthropologist. It was expected by the Director of the Bureau that the studies thus made, being preliminary in character, would lead up to a monographic treatise on native fictile art to form one of a series of works covering the whole range of native arts and industries.

The present paper was commenced in 1890, and in its inception was intended to accompany and form part of the final report of Dr Cyrus Thomas on mound explorations conducted for the Bureau during the period beginning with 1881 and ending in 1891. A change in the original plan of publication dissociated the writer's work from that of Dr Thomas, whose report was assigned to the Twelfth Annual, which it occupies in full. Delay in publishing the present paper afforded an opportunity for additional exploration and study, and the work was revised and amplified. Its scope was extended from the consideration of the pottery of the mound builders to that of the entire region east of the Rocky mountains, the volume of matter being more than doubled and the value of the work greatly enhanced.

15

The collections made use of in the preparation of this paper are very extensive, and represent a multitude of village sites, mounds, graves, cemeteries, shell heaps, and refuse deposits in nearly all sections of the great region under consideration. At the same time it should be noted that the material available is far from complete or satisfactory. Much of it was carelessly collected and insufficiently labeled, and some districts are represented by mere random sherds which can not be depended on as a basis for important deductions. The collections made by the Bureau of American Ethnology are the most important, and some recent explorations have added material of a high order scientifically. Of the latter the work of Mr Frank H. Cushing in Florida and of Clarence B. Moore in Florida and other southern states may be specially mentioned.

Details not considered essential to the story of the art have been omitted. Tedious recitals of form, color, size, and use of individual specimens have been avoided, the illustrations being relied on as the most satisfactory means of conveying a full and correct impression of the art. It was intended by the Director of the Bureau, when the preparation of preliminary papers on the various aboriginal arts began, that the illustrations prepared as the work developed should be brought together in final form in the monographic volumes of Contributions to North American Ethnology. It was found, however, that to utilize all of the material thus made available would in this case make the volume excessive, so a careful selection has been made from the earlier illustrations, and typical examples have been brought together in plates. In the main, however, the illustrations here presented are new, as the old work did not extend much beyond the one ceramic group represented in the Middle Mississippi Valley province.

The writer is much indebted to officers and custodians of the following institutions and societies for privileges accorded and assistance given in the preparation of this work: The National Museum, Washington; the Davenport Academy of Sciences, Iowa; the Peabody Museum, Cambridge; the American Museum of Natural History, New York; the Academy of Sciences, Philadelphia; the Free Museum of Science and Art, Philadelphia; the Museum of Art, Cincinnati; and the Canadian Institute, Toronto.

To many individual collectors grateful acknowledgments are due. Chief among them are the following: Mr W. H. Phillips, of Washington, whose cooperation and assistance have been of the greatest service and whose collection of archeologic materials from the Potomac valley is unequaled; Mr Thomas Dowling, jr., whose collections from the same region have always been at the writer's disposal; Colonel C. C. Jones, of Augusta, Georgia, to whom the country and especially the southern states are indebted for so much of value in the departments of history and archeology; General Gates P. Thruston, of

Nashville, whose explorations in Tennessee have yielded an unrivaled collection of valuable relics and whose writings have been freely drawn on in the preparation of this work; Mr W. K. Moorehead, of Xenia, Ohio, whose various collections have been made available for study; Mr Clarence B. Moore, of Philadelphia, whose great collections from the mounds and shell heaps of Florida, Georgia, and Alabama the writer has been called on to describe; Mr Frank Hamilton Cushing, whose technologic skill has been of frequent assistance and whose collections from the central New York region and from Florida have been of much service; Reverend W. M. Beauchamp, of Baldwinsville, New York, who has furnished data respecting the ceramic work of the Iroquois; Mr H. P. Hamilton, of Three Rivers, Wisconsin, a careful collector of the fragile relics of the west shore of Lake Michigan, and Mr E. A. Barber, who kindly supplied a large body of data relating to the tobacco pipes of the region studied.

Mention may also be made of the writer's great indebtedness to those who have assisted him in various ways as collaborators; to Mr W J McGee, whose scientific knowledge and literary skill have been drawn on freely on many occasions; to Mr William Dinwiddie, whose excellent photographs make it possible to present a number of unrivaled illustrations; to Mr John L. Ridgway, Miss Mary M. Mitchell, and Mr H. C. Hunter for many excellent drawings; to Mr DeLancey Gill for his very efficient management of the work of drawing, engraving, and printing illustrations, and to many other members of the Smithsonian Institution, the Bureau of American Ethnology, the Geological Survey, and the National Museum for valued assistance.

20 ETH—03—— 2

INTRODUCTION

Ceramic Art in Human History

Objects of art may be studied with immediate reference to two main lines of investigation. First, they may be made to assist in telling the story of the origin and evolution of art and thus of many branches of culture, and, finally, of man; and second, they may be made to bear on the history of particular groups of people, of communities, tribes, and nations, and through these again on the origin and history of the race, the ultimate object of the whole group of investigations being a fuller comprehension of what man is, what he has been, and what he may hope to be.

The ceramic art takes an important place among the arts of man, and its products, and especially its prehistoric remains, are invaluable to the student of history. Of the lower stages of progress through which all advanced nations have passed—stages represented still by some of the more primitive living peoples—this art can tell us little, since it was late taking its place in the circle of human attainments, but it records much of the history of man's struggles upward through the upper savage and barbarian stages of progress. It preserves, especially, the story of its own growth from the first crude effort of the primitive potter to the highest achievement of modern culture. It also throws many side lights on the various branches of art and industry with which it has been associated.

Of all the movable products of barbarian art it appears that pottery is the most generally useful in locating vanished peoples and in defining their geographic limitations and migrations. The reasons for this may be briefly stated as follows: first, the need of vessels is common to all mankind, and the use of clay in vessel making is almost universal among peoples sufficiently advanced to utilize it; second, since the clay used readily receives the impress of individual thought, and, through this, of national thought, the stamp of each people is distinctly impressed upon its ceramic products; third, the baked clay is almost indestructible, while, at the same time, it is so fragile that fragments remain in plenty on every site occupied by the pottery makers; fourth, vessels are less than all other articles fitted for and subject to transportation, being the most sedentary, so to speak, of all minor artifacts. It follows that, so far as objects of art are capable of so doing, they serve, as has been said, to mark their maker's habitat and indicate his movements.

Still more fully pottery records the history of the decorative arts—the beginnings and progress of esthetic evolution. To a large extent, also, religious conceptions are embodied in it. Mythical beings are modeled and painted, and their strange symbols are introduced into the decorations. Every touch of the potter's hand, of the modeling tool, the stylus, and the brush becomes, through changes wrought in the plastic clay by the application of heat, an ineffaceable record of man's thought and of woman's toil. These fictile products, broken and scattered broadcast over all habitable lands, are gathered and hoarded by the archeologist, and their adventitious records are deciphered with a fullness and clearness second only to that attained in the reading of written records.

Notwithstanding the above-mentioned very decided advantages of the ceramic art over other arts as a record of prehistoric peoples, its shortcomings in this direction are apparent at a glance. The student is embarrassed by the parallelisms that necessarily exist between the arts of widely separated peoples of like grade of culture and like environment. Even the discriminating investigator may be misled in his efforts to use these relics in the tracing of peoples. Other classes of confusing agencies are interchanges by trade, multiple occupation of sites, adoption of pottery-making captives, and the amalgamation of communities; by all of these means works of distinct families of people may in cases be thrown into such close association as to make ethnic determinations difficult and uncertain.

The danger of making erroneous use of prehistoric works of art in the identification of peoples is especially great where the number of available relics is limited, as is very often the case in archeologic collections. Conclusions of importance respecting a given people may in this way be based on evidence afforded by intrusive products or on exceptional conditions or phenomena—conclusions difficult to controvert and increasingly difficult to correct as the years pass by.

ABORIGINAL AMERICAN POTTERY

It is hardly possible to find within the whole range of products of human handicraft a more attractive field of investigation than that offered by aboriginal American ceramics, and probably no one that affords such excellent opportunities for the study of early stages in the evolution of art and especially of the esthetic in art. The early ware of Mediterranean countries has a wider interest in many ways, but it does not cover the same ground. It represents mainly the stages of culture rising above the level of the wheel, of pictorial art, and of writing, while American pottery is entirely below this level, and thus illustrates the substratum out of which the higher phases spring. But it should be noted that not merely the beginnings of the story are represented in the native work. The culture range covered is quite wide, and opportunities of tracing progress upward to the very verge of civilization are afforded. Between the groups of products belonging to the inferior tribes scattered over the continent from Point Barrow to Terra del Fuego, and those representing the advanced cultures of Central America and Peru, there is a long vista of progress. Near the upper limit of achievement is the pottery of Mexico, comprising a wonderful cluster of well-marked groups. Some of the highest examples of the ceramic art are found in or near the valley of Mexico, and a number of striking vases of this region, preserved in the Mexican National Museum, may be regarded as masterpieces of American fictile art. Central and South America furnish a series of superb groups of earthenware, among which are those of Guatemala, Nicaragua, Costa Rica, Chiriqui, Colombia, Bolivia, Peru, Brazil, and Argentina, each disputing with Mexico the palm of merit. Following these in order are various groups of ware whose remains are assembled about the margins of the greater culture centers or distributed widely over remoter districts. The work of the Pueblo tribes in Arizona and New Mexico, all things considered, stands first within the area of the United States; closely approaching this, however, is the attractive ware of the Mississippi valley and the Gulf coast. Below this and at the base of the series is the simple pottery of the hunter tribes of the North.

Numerous tribes have continued to practice the art down to the present time, some employing their original methods and producing results but little modified by the lapse of centuries, while others, coming more directly under the influence of the whites, have modified their work so that it no longer has any particular value to the ethnologist devoted to aboriginal studies. The Pueblo country furnishes the best example of survival of old methods and old ideals. Here numerous tribes are found practicing the art successfully, producing vases and other articles quite equal in many respects to the ancient product. The study of the present practices is highly instructive, and the archeologist may begin his study of the ancient pottery of America with a pretty definite knowledge of the technical and functional status of the art, as well as a clear conception of the manner in which it embodies the symbolic and esthetic notions of a people.

POTTERY OF THE EASTERN UNITED STATES

GEOGRAPHIC GROUPING

In the eastern United States the study of the potter's art is essentially an archeologic study, although something may be learned by a visit to the Catawba and Cherokee tribes of North and South Carolina, and accounts published by those who have witnessed the practice of

the art in past generations, although meager enough, are not appealed
to in vain, as will be amply shown in subsequent sections of this paper.

The first requisite on taking up the study of a field so extensive and
varied is a means of classifying the phenomena. We soon observe
that the pottery of one section differs from that of another in material,
form, color, and decoration, and that groups may be defined each
probably representing a limited group of peoples, but more conveniently treated as the product of a more or less well-marked specialization area. By the aid of this grouping it is easy to proceed with
the examination of the ware, and a reasonably clear idea of the art of
the regions and of the whole field may readily be gained.

First in importance among the groups of ware is that called in
former papers the Middle Mississippi Valley group. Geographically
this group presents some interesting features, which will be considered
in detail later. The margins of the area it occupies are not well defined,
and occasionally pieces of the ware are found far outside its ordinary
habitat and associated with strangers. This area has a central position in the Mississippi valley, and other varieties of pottery lie to
the north, east, and south, with overlapping and often indefinite outlines. On the north is the area characterized by ware to which I
have for convenience given the name Upper Mississippi or Northwestern group. In the Ohio valley we have varieties of ware to which
local names may be attached. The New York or Iroquoian pottery
occupies the states of New York and Pennsylvania, extending in places
into other states and into Canada. We have Atlantic Algonquian
ware, South Appalachian ware, and several groups of Gulf Coast
ware. Many of these groups are so clearly differentiated as to make
their separate study easy. Within the limits, however, of their areas
are numerous subgroups which do not possess such strong individuality and such clear geographic definition as the larger ones, but which
may well be studied separately and may in time be found to have an
ethnic importance quite equal to that of the better-defined groups of
ware. Although they are confined to such definite geographic areas
we are not at all sure, as has been pointed out, that these groups of
ware will be found to have any intelligible correspondence with the
stocks of people that have at one time or another occupied the
region, for varieties of art phenomena are often regional rather
than ethnic. Besides, many important groups of people have not left
great accumulations of art products, and great groups of products
may have been left by comparatively insignificant communities. Separate groups of people may have practiced nearly identical arts, and portions of a single people may have practiced very different arts. In
view of these and other uncertainties hampering the correlation of
archeologic data with peoples, we can not do better than at first

study the ancient ware by itself, and afterward proceed in such special case as may offer encouragement in that direction to connect the art with the peoples, adding such evidence as may be thus secured to our knowledge of the history of families and tribes.

Up to the present time there has been a very imperfect understanding of the character and scope of the fictile products of the whole region east of the Rocky mountains. Some writers have regarded everything indiscriminately as simple, rude, and of little importance; others, going to the opposite extreme, have found marked variations with impassible gulfs between the higher and lower forms—gulfs corresponding to the wide distinctions supposed by some early writers to exist between the cultures of the so-called mound-builder and the common Indian.

Notwithstanding the fact that the ware of eastern North America is easily separable into groups, some of which differ widely from others, when we assume a broader point of view all varieties are seen to be members of one great family, the points of correspondence being so marked and numerous that the differences by means of which we distinguish the groups sink into comparative insignificance. A wide range of accomplishment is apparent, and strong evidences of individuality are discovered in the different groups, but these differences are probably far in excess of the differences existing in the culture status of the peoples concerned in their production. This fact is apparent when we observe the relative condition of progress among the tribes of to-day. It is seen that the arts are not symmetrically and equally developed; the inferior ware of one locality does not indicate that the people of that locality were inferior in culture, for the reverse may be the case, but it may signify that the conditions of life were such that the potter's art was uncalled for, or imperfectly practiced, while other arts took the lead and were highly perfected. The culture status of a given people must be determined by a consideration of the sum of the planes of all the arts and not by the plane of any one art.

It has often been remarked that the pottery of the North is rude as compared with that of the South, but in Florida and on the Gulf coast pottery is now and then found which is quite as low in the scale as anything about the borders of the Great lakes, and occasional specimens from New York, Ohio, Michigan, and Wisconsin fairly rival in all essential features the best products of the southern states. Conditions governing the practice of the art were, however, on the whole, decidedly more favorable in the South, and here it has been practiced more fully and more constantly than in the North.

Climatic conditions, degree of sedentation, nature of food supply, and availability of material have each a marked influence on the condition of the arts. The art that flourishes on the Gulf coast with a

prosperous sedentary people may be undeveloped or entirely neglected by a people wandering from place to place in the barren, icy
regions of the North; yet, could we for a generation exchange the
environments of these peoples, the potter's art would still be found
practiced and flourishing in the more salubrious climate and neglected
and disused in the rigorous one.

QUANTATIVE DISTRIBUTION

Earthenware relics are very generally distributed over the country,
but the distribution is far from uniform. Wherever pottery-making
tribes dwelt, wherever they wandered, camped, sought water, collected
food, conducted ceremonies, or buried their dead, there we find the
relics of this art. Usually, no doubt, localities and regions occupied
by prosperous sedentary peoples are marked by greater accumulations of such remains. The native tribes, no matter whence they
came, distributed themselves along the great waterways, and the more
favorable spots along such rivers as the Ohio, the Tennessee, the
Mississippi, and the Red river possess almost inexhaustible supplies
of ancient ware. A broad region, including the confluences of the
great streams of the Mississippi system, the Missouri, the Ohio, the
Tennessee, the Cumberland, and the Arkansas, seems to be the richest
of all, yet there are less-extended areas in other sections almost equally
rich. The observation has been made that an arid environment encourages the vessel-making arts, but here we have a region abounding in
moisture which is richer than any other section in its supply of clay
vessels.

MANNER OF OCCURRENCE

Since pottery was made very largely for use in the domestic arts,
its remains are everywhere associated with household refuse, and are
found on all village, house, camp, and food-producing sites occupied
by pottery-making peoples. It is plentiful in the great shell heaps
and shell mounds along the Atlantic and Gulf coasts, and abounds in
and around saline springs where salt was procured. Found under
such conditions it is usually fragmentary, and to the superficial
observer gives a very imperfect idea of the nature and scope of the
art, but to the experienced student it affords a very satisfactory
record.

Nearly all peoples have at some period of their history adopted the
practice of burying articles of use or value with their dead, and the
aborigines of this country were no exception. It is to this mortuary
usage that we owe the preservation of so many entire examples of
fragile utensils of clay. They are exhumed from burial mounds in
great numbers, and to an equal extent, in some regions, from common
cemeteries and simple, unmarked graves. The relation of various

articles of pottery to the human remains with which they were associated in burial seems to have been quite varied. It is probable that the position of the vessel was to a certain extent determined by its office; it may have contained food or drink for the dead, personal articles of value, or offerings to deities to be propitiated, and custom or fancy dictated the position it should occupy; but it appears that in many cases the articles were cast in without regard to relative position or order.

CHRONOLOGY

Anthropologists are well agreed that pottery making is not one of the earliest arts practiced by primitive man. Its beginnings probably mark in a general way the step from savagery to the lower stages of barbarism, as defined by Morgan. If the average aborigines of the eastern half of the United States be regarded as occupying, at the time of European colonization, the middle status of barbarism, it would seem that the practice of the art was not new, having probably extended through all of the first stage of barbarism. It is not possible, however, to arrive at any idea of the equivalent of this range of progress in years. From the depth of certain accumulations, from the succession of strata, and from the great mass of the structures in which fictile remains are found in some sections, we are led to believe that many centuries have passed since the discovery or introduction of the art; but that it was still comparatively young in some of the eastern and northern sections of the United States is strongly suggested, first, by the scarcity of sherds, and second, by a comparison of its functional scope with that of the ceramic art of the more advanced nations of Mexico and Central America, among whom it filled a multitude of important offices. With many of our nomadic and semi-sedentary tribes it had not passed beyond the simplest stage of mere vessel making, the only form employed being a wide-mouthed pot. It may be questioned, however, whether degree of simplicity is a valuable index of age. It is possible that in a region where conditions are unfavorable the art could be practiced a thousand years without material change, while in a more favored environment it might, in the same period and with a people of no greater native ability, rise through a succession of stages to a high degree of perfection.

FUNCTIONAL GROUPING

CLASSIFICATION OF USE

The uses to which the earthenware of the aborigines was applied were numerous and important; they may be classed roughly as domestic, industrial, sacerdotal, ornamental, and trivial or diversional. To the first class belong vessels for containing, cooking, boiling (as in sugar and salt making), eating, drinking, etc.; to the second class belong various implements used in the arts, as trowels and modeling tools; to the third class belong vessels and other articles used in funeral rites, as burial urns and offerings; as personal ornaments there are beads, pendants, and ear and lip plugs; and for trivial and diversional uses there are toy vessels, figurines, and gaming articles. Most of the objects may serve a number of uses, as, for example, a single vessel may, with a simple people, answer for culinary, for religious, and for mortuary purposes, and tobacco pipes may have ceremonial as well as medical and diversional uses.

Although the esthetic idea was considerably developed among all classes of our aborigines, and much attention was paid to embellishment, it is not probable that any vessel was manufactured for purely ornamental purposes. Neither can it be shown that in the area covered by the present study earthenware served, as do our terra cottas, for portraiture or for records of any description.

Pottery was probably first used in connection with the employment of fire in culinary work—in heating water and in cooking food—and there is no doubt that the cooking, the storing, and the transporting of food and drink remained everywhere the most important of its functions.

DIFFERENTIATION OF USE

The differentiation of use, which must have taken place gradually, probably began by the setting aside or the manufacture of certain vessels for special departments of domestic work. Afterward, when vessels came to be used in ceremonies—religious, medical, or mortuary—certain forms were made for or assigned to special rites. The vessel that served in one office was not considered appropriate for another, and one that was sacred to one deity and had decorations symbolizing his attributes was not considered acceptable to another. We do not know to what extent special shapes were made for different sacerdotal uses by our eastern aborigines, but it is safe to say that this class of specialization had made decided headway in the west and south.

Differentiation in the functions of vessels was probably to some extent of preceramic development, since art in clay sprang into existence long after other arts had been well perfected, and pottery naturally fell heir to duties previously performed by vessels of bark, wicker, shell, fruit shells, horn, stone, or other more archaic receptacles for boiling, serving, containing, and transporting.

VESSELS FOR CULINARY AND OTHER DOMESTIC USES

Primitive earthen vessels have usually a round or somewhat conical base, which suggests the manner of their use. Among savage races hard, level floors were the exception, while floors of sand or soft earth were the rule, and under such conditions a round or conical base would be most convenient. The pot in cooking was generally set directly on the fire, and was kept in position by the fuel or other supports placed about its sides.   This is illustrated in plate II, a copy of the original of plate XV of Hariot's New Found Land of Virginia, now pre-

FIG. 1—Indian women using earthen vessels in making cassine.   From Lafitau, J. F., Mœurs des sauvages ameriquains, vol. II, plate V, figure 1.

served in the British Museum, London.   A curious specimen of early colonial illustration, depicting a number of women preparing a ceremonial drink called cassine in earthen vessels, is reproduced from Lafitau in figure 1.   Boiling by means of heated stones cast into the vessel may have been practiced for some time after the introduction of pottery as a survival of the preceramic usage, and was probably resorted to on occasion by many primitive peoples.

In cases, probably, the earthen vessel was suspended over the fire by means of poles, vines, and cords, as shown in figure 2, from School-craft's Indian Tribes. This method of suspension is made possible by the attachment of strong ears or handles, by eccentric modeling of the rim—such as accentuated incurving or outcurving—or by perforation of the upper margin. As a rule, however, the vessels show no indications of this kind of use, and the form is seldom such as to warrant the conclusion that suspension was intended. But a small percent-

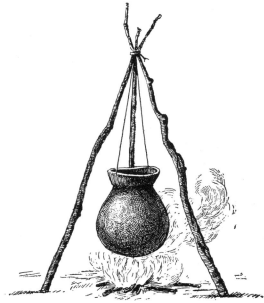

FIG. 2—Suspension of the vessel from a tripod. From Schoolcraft, H. R., Historical and statistical information respecting the . . . Indian tribes of the United States, part 1, plate XXII.

age of prehistoric vessels recovered in the complete state show indications of use over fire. This is accounted for by the fact that entire vessels are mostly obtained from graves and were mortuary rather than culinary utensils. The broken ware obtained from refuse heaps and habitation sites is the débris of cooking, eating, and drinking utensils, and of vessels for carrying and storing, and this very often shows indications of use over fire.

SALT-MAKING VESSELS

The evaporation of saline waters for the purpose of obtaining salt was carried on by the natives in several favorable localities in the Mississippi valley. It is probable that the waters were evaporated by means of heat applied to the vessel in the usual manner, but it is also held by good authorities that the work was sometimes conducted by means of exposure simply to the rays of the sun.

A somewhat remarkable class of earthenware vessels, the remnants of which are found at several points in the Mississippi valley, is believed to have been employed in the manufacture of salt. The localities are scattered over a large area extending as far east as Knoxville, Tennessee, and as far west as White river in north-central Arkansas and southern Missouri. The distinguishing characteristics of the vessels are their large size, their vat-like shape (see plate III a), the great thickness of their walls, and their peculiar surface finish (b, c), which consists largely of impressions of coarse, open-mesh textile fabrics. They are found in most cases in or near the vicinity of saline springs. Perhaps the best known locality is on Saline river, near Shawneetown, Illinois. It is not improbable that similar springs formerly existed at points now marked by the occurrence of this remarkable ware, where no salines now exist. It is definitely stated by the Knight of Elvas that the Indians of the Mississippi valley manufactured salt. He informs us that—

The salt is made along by a river, which when the water goes down leaves it upon the sand. As they can not gather the salt without a large mixture of sand, it is thrown together into certain baskets they have for the purpose, made large at the mouth and small at the bottom. These are set in the air on a ridgepole and, water being thrown on, vessels are placed under them wherein it may fall; then, being strained and placed on the fire, it is boiled away, leaving salt at the bottom.[a]

In another place it is stated that—

They passed through a small town where was a lake and the Indians made salt; the Christians made some on the day they rested there from water that rose nearby from springs in pools.[b]

The above locations must both have been in Arkansas and not far from Hot Springs.

Typical specimens of this ware are found in the suburbs of Nashville, Tennessee; at Shawneetown, Illinois; near Vincennes, Knox county, Indiana; in Knox county, Tennessee; in Alexander and Union counties, Illinois; at Kimmswick, near St Louis, Missouri; at Ste Genevieve, Missouri; at one or more points in Ohio; and probably, as is indicated by Schoolcraft, on White river above Batesville, Arkansas. Schoolcraft says that—

It is common, in digging at these salt mines, to find fragments of antique pottery, and even entire pots of a coarse earthenware, at great depths below the surface. One of these pots which was, until a very recent period, preserved by a gentleman at Shawneetown, was disinterred at the depth of 80 feet, and was of a capacity to contain 8 or 10 gallons. Others have been found at even greater depths, and of greater dimensions. We will not venture to state the surprising capacities of several

[a] Smith, Thomas Buckingham, Narratives of the career of Hernando de Soto, as told by a knight of Elvas, and in a relation by L. Hernandez de Biedma, New York, 1866, p. 124.
[b] Same work, p. 153.

of these antique vessels that were described to us, lest, not having seen them, there may be some error in the statements, which were, however, made in the fullest confidence. The composition and general appearance of this fossil pottery can not be distinguished from those fragments of earthenware which are disclosed by the mounds of the oldest period, so common in this quarter, and evince the same rude state of the arts. In all this species of pottery which we have examined there is a considerable admixture of silex in the form of pounded quartz, or sand, in comparatively coarse grains; which, as is very well known, has a tendency to lessen the shrinkage of the clay, to prevent cracks and flaws in drying, and to enable the mass to sustain the sudden application of heat without liability to burst. The whole art of making chemical crucibles, as well as those employed in a large way in several manufactures where great heats are necessary, is founded on this principle.[a]

Brackenridge states that—

The saline below Ste Genevieve, cleared out some time ago and deepened, was found to contain wagonloads of earthenware, some fragments bespeaking vessels as large as a barrel, and proving that the salines had been worked before they were known to the whites.[b]

In 1901 I visited a village site near Kimmswick, Missouri, where salt had been made by the aborigines from local saline springs. The vicinity of the springs was plentifully supplied with the coarse, net-marked sherds, and many pieces were scattered over the neighboring village site. Specimens restored from the fragments, and now preserved in museums in Kimmswick and St Louis, are shallow bowls, from 20 to 30 inches in diameter. Some specimens are quite plain. A good example of this class is illustrated in plate x.

The great depth at which the ware is sometimes found is recorded by Mr George Escoll Sellers, who has had ample opportunity for personal observation of the Illinois salines. The bed rock in one of the saline river springs worked by the whites is 42 feet below the surface, and pottery was found at this depth by the workmen who sunk the well.

Mr Sellers's views are expressed in the following paragraph:

This, to me, is conclusive evidence that, whoever the people were who left the masses of broken pottery as proof of their having used the salt waters, they resorted to precisely the same means as did their more civilized successors of our time—that is, sinking wells or reservoirs to collect the brine; and the dipper-jug which had been dropped had sunk to the bottom, showing that their reservoirs were down to the rock.[c]

That the aboriginal peoples should have excavated to so great a depth seems almost incredible. Even if there were good reason for such a work native appliances would hardly have been equal to the task of constructing the necessary walls of stone or casing of wood. It is more probable that the spring channels were naturally of dimensions permitting the vessels to sink gradually to these great depths.

[a] Schoolcraft, H. R., Travels in the central portions of the Mississippi valley, New York, 1825, p. 202.
[b] Brackenridge, H. M., Views of Louisiana, Pittsburg, 1814, p. 186.
[c] Sellers, George Escoll, Aboriginal pottery of the salt springs, Illinois, in Popular Science Monthly, vol. XI, New York, 1877, p. 576.

Mr Sellers discovered a village or camp site in proximity to one of these springs, and his observations with respect to it are as follows:

I found the most abundant remains of pottery, not only represented by fragments of the large, coarse salt pans, but by many pieces of small vessels of much finer texture and of superior workmanship, such as would be used for domestic purposes. From these and large quantities of chippings and offal I inferred that this was the site of the old settlement. The broken pottery, the black soil, the waste from long occupancy extending a considerable distance both east and west of the springs, and to the foot of the bluffs on the south, covering an area of about 30 acres, were confirmatory of this view.[a]

A burial place was found on a terrace at no great distance. Some of the stone cists were paved with fragments of the "great salt pans," but these were much decayed. This, Mr Sellers believes, conclusively couples the tenants of these ancient graves with the makers and the users of the salt pans.

In regard to the manufacture of these remarkable vessels it appears that Mr Sellers's observations and theories are in the main correct. That baskets were not used is apparent on the most casual examination. The manner of using the fabrics with which the ware is marked is discussed in the present paper under the head Manufacture. Mr Sellers's identification of the factory is also well supported, and there is nothing improbable in the theory of the use of clay molds or cores to model on, though there is little corroborative evidence on this point.

A remarkable example of this pottery recently found in the suburbs of Nashville, Tennessee, is now in the collection of General Gates P. Thruston, of Nashville. It is a flat-bottomed basin about 31 inches in diameter and 12 inches deep; the walls are nearly an inch in thickness and the surface has the characteristic fabric impressions (see plate III c). A large fragment of this vase is illustrated in his work on the Antiquities of Tennessee, plate X, and the following paragraph relating to it is quoted therefrom:

The large vessel was found within a few yards of the "Sulphur Spring," or the old "French Lick," at Nashville, in excavating for the foundations of the new springhouse. This sulphur and salt spring was doubtless the central feature of a populous aboriginal settlement for centuries. Extensive burial grounds were found on both sides of the "Lick Branch," and many fine implements and specimens of earthenware have been obtained there.[b]

In the discussion of stone graves in the vicinity of Nashville, Tennessee, Mr R. S. Robertson makes the following remarks in regard to fragments of salt vessels:

These graves are found everywhere about Nashville and within the city limits. On the ridges close to the Sulphur Spring the stones inclosing such graves may be seen protruding from the ground, where the earth above has weathered off. Fragments of pottery abound, some of the common sort, and others very thick—about one-half

---

[a] Sellers, Aboriginal pottery of the salt springs, pp. 576–577.

[b] Thruston, Gates P., The antiquities of Tennessee, Cincinnati, 1890, pp. 157–158.

to three-fourths inch—composed of a grayish clay, with large fragments of shells. The vessels of which they were part must have been very large. Traditionally, they are believed to have been used in evaporating salt from the spring. A brief search resulted in finding numerous specimens on the surface and protruding from the sides of the ridges near the surface. It is said that the saline properties of the spring were more noticeable before the deep bore was made which produced the sulphur water, which is so much patronized.[a]

We have from East Tennessee, in Knox county, specimens of this ware identical with that from Nashville and other more western localities. Although this pottery is not correlated with any particular salt lick or spring, we may fairly assume that it was employed in making salt, since there are salt springs in the vicinity.

Referring to explorations of Mr William McAdams, of Alton, the Alton, Illinois, Telegraph speaks of salt springs on Saline creek, Cooper county, Missouri, in the following words:

These springs were also a great resort of the aborigines and mound-builders, and the ground about the oozing brine, to the depth of 3 or 4 feet, is filled with the remains of the peculiar earthen vessels used by the mound-builders in salt making. In the woods about, for the whole vicinity is covered with a forest, are many mounds and earthworks. From one small mound two of the earthen salt kettles were obtained. They were shaped like shallow pans, an inch and a half in thickness and near 4 feet across the rim.[b]

Another site noted for the occurrence of this peculiar earthenware is located in St Louis county, Missouri, near the village of Fenton. Here there are springs, both sulphur and salt. This site has been visited by Mr O. W. Collett, of St Louis, who gives an account of it in the Kansas City Review, vol. IV, p. 104.

The following statement made by Du Pratz is sufficiently definite on the question of native salt making:

About 30 leagues up the Black river on the left side, there is a stream of salt water flowing from the west; about 2 leagues up this stream is a lake of salt water which is nearly 2 leagues in length by 1 in width; 1 league farther up toward the north another lake of salt water is discovered, almost as long and broad as the first.

This water passes without doubt through some salt mines; it has the taste of salt without the bitterness of sea water. The natives come from a long distance to this place to hunt in winter and to make salt. Before the French had traded them kettles they made earthen pots at the place, for this purpose; when they had enough to load themselves, they returned to their country loaded with salt and dried meats.[c]

SUGAR-MAKING VESSELS

In comparatively recent aboriginal times, if not in very ancient times, earthen pots were used for collecting and boiling the sweet sap of the sugar maple. So far as my observations have gone the earliest mention of sugar making by the aborigines is found in Joutel's Journal, writ-

[a] Robertson, R. S., Antiquities of Nashville, Tennessee, Smithsonian Report for 1877, Washington, 1878, pp. 277-278.
[b] See also McAdams, Wm., Prehistoric remains from southeast Missouri, Kansas City Review, vol. VII, Kansas City, 1884, p. 279.
[c] Du Pratz, Antoine Simon Le Page, Histoire de la Louisiane, Paris, 1758, vol. I, pp. 307-308.

ten nearly two hundred years ago.   Lafitau, whose observations began about the year 1700, gives an illustration in which the whole process is indicated—the tapping of the trees, the collecting of sap, the boiling of the water, and the shaping of the soft sugar into cakes, the latter work being conducted by an Indian woman who in the engraving is represented as a handsome Caucasian girl.   It will be seen from the following extract that this author makes the definite statement that the French learned the art from the Indians—no particular nation being mentioned, however.   He writes as follows:

In the month of March, when the sun has acquired a little force and the trees commence to contain sap, they make transverse incisions with the hatchet on the

FIG. 3—Native maple-sugar making.   Reproduced from Lafitau.

trunks of these trees, from which there flows in abundance a liquid which they receive in large vessels of bark; they then boil this liquid over the fire, which consumes all the phlegm and causes the remainder to thicken to the consistency of sirup or even of a loaf of sugar, according to the degree and amount of heat which they choose to give it.   There is no other mystery.   This sugar is very pectoral, excellent for medicine; but although it may be more healthy than that of the canes, it has not a pleasing taste nor delicacy and almost always has a little burnt flavor.   The French prepare it better than the Indian women from whom they learned to make it; but they have not yet reached the point of bleaching and refining it.[a]

The description of Lafitau's plate may be translated as follows:

The women occupied in watching the vessels, which are already full of the liquid that flows from the trees, carry this liquid and pour it into the kettles seen on

[a] Lafitau, Joseph François, Mœurs des sauvages ameriquains, Paris, 1724, vol. II, p. 154

the fire, which are watched by an old woman, while another, seated, kneads with the hands this thickened liquid, now in a condition to acquire the consistency of sugar loaf.[a]

This plate was reproduced in an article on maple-sugar making by H. W. Henshaw, published in the American Anthropologist for October 1890 and is given in figure 3.

The following extract from Hunter indicates that the making of maple sugar by the Indians was very generally practiced. He is speaking of the Osage Indians and their neighbors.

In districts of country where the sugar maple abounds the Indians prepare considerable quantities of sugar by simply concentrating the juices of the tree by boiling till it acquires a sufficient consistency to crystallize on cooling. But as they are extravagantly fond of it, very little is preserved beyond the sugar-making season. The men tap the trees, attach spigots to them, make the sap troughs; and sometimes, at this frolicking season, assist the squaws in collecting sap.[b]

Dr Lyman C. Draper makes the following statement, which sufficiently indicates the nature of the sugar-making industry in recent times:

From twenty-five to thirty years ago, when I resided at Lockport, in western New York, I well remember that large quantities of stirred maple sugar were brought into the country, made by the Indians in the Mackinaw region, and put up in small bark boxes, containing from one to several pounds each.[c]

Sugar is still made by a number of tribes, but earthen vessels have probably not been used in its manufacture for many years.

SPINDLE WHORLS OF CLAY

The state of culture of the eastern tribes had not yet led to the general employment of many earthenware articles beyond the mere vessel for cooking and containing. The clay effigies so common in some sections were generally vessels shaped exteriorly to resemble animal forms, exceptions being noted especially in Florida, where various mortuary figures having no practical function were manufactured. Spindle whorls appear to have been used to a limited extent in the South, and in Adair's time clay was used for weighting the spindle. Speaking of the use of wild hemp, that author remarks that—

The old women spin it off the distaffs with wooden machines having some clay on the middle of them to hasten the motion.[d]

As found on ancient sites, however, there is difficulty in distinguishing such articles from beads, gaming disks, or other perforated bits of clay, and I have discovered few examples of fully authenticated spindle whorls within the area here considered.

---

[a] Lafitau, Mœurs des sauvages ameriquains, vol. II; Explication des planches et des figures, planche VII.

[b] Hunter, John D., Memoirs of a captivity among the Indians, London, 1823, p. 290.

[c] Draper, Lyman C., in Grignon, Augustin, Recollections; Third Annual Report and Collections of the Wisconsin Historical Society, Madison, 1857, p. 255.

[d] Adair, James, History of the American Indians, London, 1775, p. 422.

MUSICAL INSTRUMENTS OF EARTHENWARE

Many early writers mention the use of earthern vessels for drums. Parchment or buckskin was stretched over the mouths of large pots, and this, beaten with sticks, furnished the music for dances and ceremonies and noise for the gratification of savage taste. In Central America and apparently, also, in Florida special forms were modeled for this purpose, the rim being shaped for the convenient attachment of the skin head.

Joutel, speaking of the southern Indians, states that on burial occasions the—

dancers take care to tie calabashes or gourds about their bodies, with some Indian wheat in them, to rattle and make a noise, and some of them have a drum, made of a great earthen pot, on which they extend a wild goat's skin, and beat thereon with one stick, like our tabors.[a]

FIG. 4—Use of earthen vessel as a drum (Potherie).

Potherie has bequeathed us an illustration of an Indian beating a pottery drum (see figure 4)—drawn from description, no doubt, but interesting as a record of facts or statements not embodied, so far as has been noted, in the text of his work.[b]

Lafitau mentions the use of earthenware drums by the Iroquois; and Butel-Dumont makes the following statement, reference being had to the Louisiana Indians:

The next day at dawn all this troop sets out on the march, having at its head the cleverest among them, who carries the calumet, and as they approach the village all begin to sing and dance. One of them carries in the left hand an earthen pot covered with a dressed deerskin stretched tightly over it and fastened to it by a cord, and with a single drumstick in his right hand he beats the time on this pot, which serves

---

[a] Joutel's Journal of La Salle's last voyage, in French, B. F., Historical collections of Louisiana, pt. 1, New York, 1846, pp. 187-188.

[b] Potherie, Bacqueville de la, Histoire de l'Amérique septentrionale, Paris, 1753, vol. I, plate opp. p. 17.

as a drum; all respond by cries, which they utter in time; some carry *Chichicouas* or empty gourds, in which are placed glass beads or little pebbles to make a noise, and they shake them in time with the rest.[a]

Lawson mentions the use of an earthen porridge pot with deerskin head as a drum by Indians of Carolina. Were it considered necessary, many other references could be made to the use of earthenware drums.

Whistles and rattles of baked clay are very common in Mexico, and in Central and South America; but few examples, so far as the writer has learned, have been discovered in the mound region. General Thruston, in his valuable work on the "Antiquities of Tennessee," illustrates an earthenware

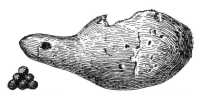

FIG. 5—Earthenware rattle, with clay pellets (Thruston).

rattle and the pellets of clay used in it (see figure 5). A few vases have been found having hollow legs or attached animal features, in which pellets were placed so that when used on festive or ceremonial occasions they would serve as rattles as well as receptacles.

VARIOUS IMPLEMENTS OF EARTHENWARE

Trowel-like objects of baked clay are occasionally found in the central districts of the Mississippi valley, and illustrations are given in figure 6 *a*, and also in a subsequent section. The body is discoidal in shape, and an arched loop or a ridge springing from one side serves as a handle. The other side, which is the working surface, is slightly convex, never flat, and generally shows considerable polish. These objects resemble in a general way our ordinary smoothing or "flat"

a   *b*   *c*

FIG. 6—Earthenware trowels and modeling tools.

iron for laundry work. General Thruston found excellent examples of these implements in graves near Nashville, Tennessee, and he is convinced they were trowels used in plastering and smoothing walls and floors of houses. A similar implement having, instead of a loop handle, an upright stem from 1 to 6 inches in length and 1 inch or more in diameter occurs very generally over the middle Mississippi region (see figure 6 *b*, *c*). The upper end of the handle is sometimes enlarged a little or simply rounded off, and again it is divided into two

---

[a] Butel-Dumont, George Marie, Mémoires sur la Louisiane, Paris, 1753, vol. I, pp. 192–3.

or three lobes or prongs. When placed stem downward these implements very closely resemble an ordinary form of toadstool. They
have been regarded by some as stoppers for bottles, but this was
certainly not their normal use, and General Thruston is probably
right in classing them as modeling tools for pottery making. The
convex surface is smooth, often retaining the peculiar polish that
comes from long use. The form is exactly suited to use in supporting
the wall of the semiplastic vase
from within while the manipulation of the outer surface is
going on with paddles or other
modeling or decorating tools
(see figure 7). It is true that
all forms of these objects may
have been used in rubbing surfaces under manipulation or in
pulverizing substances in mortars, taking the place of mullers
or pestles of wood and stone,
and this was the view of Dr Joseph Jones with respect to the
loop-handled variety. When a

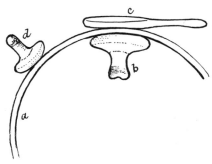

FIG. 7—Probable manner of using earthenware modeling tools: b as an interior support, c as a modeling
or decorating paddle, d as a polishing implement.

number of these objects of both forms are placed together, with the
polished convex surface to the front, all are seen to be identical in
appearance, save that a few of the loop-handled variety are oval in
outline (see plate XXXVI).

BAKED-CLAY OFFERING RECEPTACLES

Another not uncommon use of baked clay was in the construction of
sacrificial basins or altars. Dr Joseph Jones in the following paragraph describes the use of a large shallow receptacle not differing
materially from the salt pans already described:

In the center of the mound, about 3 feet from its surface, I uncovered a large
sacrificial vase or altar, 43 inches in diameter, composed of a mixture of clay and
river shells. The rim of the vase was 3 inches in height. The entire vessel had
been molded in a large wicker basket formed of split canes and the leaves of the
cane, the impressions of which were plainly visible upon the outer surface. The circle of the vase appeared to be almost mathematically correct. The surface of the
altar was covered with a layer of ashes about 1 inch in thickness, and these ashes
had the appearance and composition of having been derived from the burning of
animal matter. The antlers and jawbone of a deer were found resting upon the surface of the altar. The edges of the vase, which had been broken off apparently by
an accident during the performance of the religious ceremonies, were carefully laid
over the layer of ashes, and the whole covered with earth near 3 feet in thickness, and
thus the ashes had been preserved to a remarkable extent from the action of the rains.[a]

---

[a]Jones, Joseph, The aboriginal mound-builders of Tennessee, in American Naturalist, Salem, 1869,
vol. III, p. 68.

The altars found in the mounds of the Ohio valley are usually large shallow basins built in place by applying clay to a basin-like depression in the ground and smoothing the surface roughly with the hands or trowels. The altar fires baked the clay, giving it the consistency of earthenware.

CEMENT AND PLASTER

Native clays and earths were extensively used in the construction of numerous classes of fixed works, and it is found that various mix-

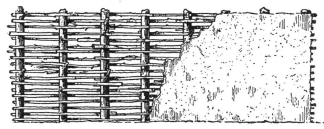

FIG. 8—Use of clay in plastering house wall of interlaced canes, Arkansas. From Thomas, 12th Annual Report of the Bureau of Ethnology, figure 118.

tures—cement-like combinations of clay, sand, gravel, etc.—were employed to add to the firmness of these constructions. In the middle and lower Mississippi valley provinces plastic clay was employed extensively in plastering the walls and roofs of houses of cane and other interlaced vegetal parts, and floors were laid in the same material (see figure 8).

EARTHENWARE USED IN BURIAL

To what extent earthen vessels were used as receptacles for the remains of the dead can not be satisfactorily determined. The whites,

FIG. 9—Rectangular burial casket of earthenware, Tennessee.

FIG. 10—Earthen vessel containing bones of children, Alabama (Moore).

accustomed to the practice of burial of ashes in cinerary urns among eastern nations, were prone to discover traces of similar customs here,

and perhaps made statements on insufficient evidence.   It is true, however, that the dead were burned in many sections of the country, and
that the ashes or rather, perhaps, the charred remnants of bones were
placed in such receptacles as were at hand for burial.   The burial of
the disarticulated bones of the dead, especially of children, in earthen

Fig. 11—Earthen vessel inverted over a skull for protection, Georgia (Moore).

Fig. 12—Earthenware burial urn and bowl cover, Georgia.

vessels, was quite common in the South Appalachian province and
occurred occasionally, at least, in other regions.   To what extent vessels
were manufactured exclusively for mortuary purposes can not be
determined, since no particular form seems to have been considered
necessary.   The larger boiling or containing pots, taken from the
household supply, seem to have been satisfactory.   Occasionally, how-

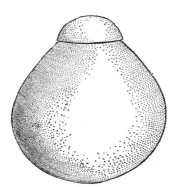

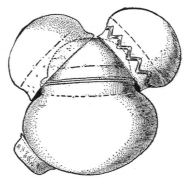

Fig. 13—Earthenware burial urn with cover, Georgia.

Fig. 14—Earthernware burial urn with bowl cover and other vessels, Alabama (Moore).

ever, receptacles appear to have been shaped for the purpose; the
casket shown in figure 9 was of this class.   It was obtained from a
burial mound at Hale's point, Tennessee, and contained the bones of
an infant.   Figure 10 shows the top view of a burial vase from a
mound in Wilcox county, Alabama, containing bones of infants.

In very many cases earthen vessels, especially bowls, are found inverted over the skull of the deceased, as shown in figure 11, and not infrequently large fragments of earthenware were placed over and around the head, probably as a protection.

The commonest form of pot burial is illustrated in figures 12, 13, 14, and 15. The remains were crowded into the vessel and the bowl was fitted over or into the mouth of this receptacle.

Perhaps the most general use of vases in burial was that of containing food, drink, and other offerings intended by friends of the departed to serve some mythical post-mortem purpose. That the deposition of these arti-

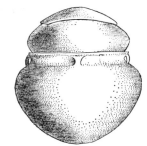

Fig. 15—Earthernware burial urn with bowl cover, Alabama (Moore).

cles with the dead had, however, become a mere form or symbol in many cases is shown by the fact that the vessels were often broken and

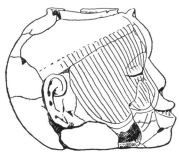

Fig. 16—Mortuary vases imitating the dead face, middle Mississippi valley.

that fragments merely were sometimes used. In one section of the Mississippi valley we find small mortuary receptacles made to repre-

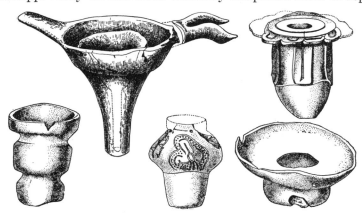

Fig. 17—Toy-like vessels used as funeral offerings, Florida (Moore).

sent the human face as it appears after death. So unusual is the shape that we are justified in assuming that the vessels were made exclu-

FIG. 18—Toy-like funeral offerings imitating vegetal forms, Florida (Moore).

sively for mortuary use and consignment to the tomb. They are too small to have contained bones, and we can only surmise that they were intended to contain food, drink, or other kinds of offerings. An

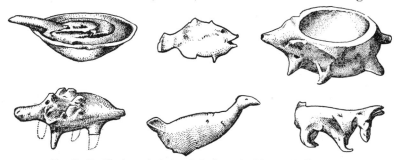

FIG. 19—Toy-like funeral offerings imitating animal forms, Florida (Moore).

example is shown in figure 16, and two excellent specimens appear in plate XLIII. In some other regions, notably in Florida, rude imita-

FIG. 20—Toy-like figurine representing babe in cradle, Tennessee (Thruston).

tions of vessels, hardly capable of bearing up their own weight, were made and cast into the grave (see figure 17). With these were also figurines made in the rudest way, representing many forms of animal and vegetal life, shown in figures 18 and 19.[a] It is possible that these were offerings made after the manner of the ancient Egyptians, who placed images of slaves and various implements and utensils in the tomb, with the idea that they would in some way be of service to the dead in the future existence.

The modeling of various life forms was extensively practiced by

[a] Moore, Clarence B., Certain sand mounds on the St Johns river, Florida, part I, in Journal of Academy of Natural Sciences of Philadelphia, ser. 2, vol. x, pt. 1, Phila., 1894.

the potters of some sections, but almost universally as elaborations and embellishments of vessels, pipes, and other useful articles. Serious attempts at the modeling in clay of human or animal figures for the figure's sake were apparently quite exceptional, although images in stone are common. Nearly all solid figures in clay so far reported have the character of toys or rude votive or mortuary offerings. The collections of Clarence B. Moore contain many specimens of such burial figurines from the

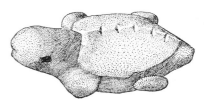

FIG. 21—Small image of a turtle, Tennessee.

mounds of Florida (see figure 19). General Thruston illustrates a small clay figure representing a babe in its cradle from a mound in Tennessee (figure 20); also the image of a turtle from the Noel cemetery near Nashville (figure 21); and recently Dr Roland Steiner, of Grovetown, Georgia, has forwarded to the Museum a number of small figures of reddish terra cotta in which a variety of physiognomy and facial expression appear (see figures 22 and 23). These figures have a more marked resemblance to Mexican work of the same class than any yet found within the territory of the United States. The flattening out of the head, as seen in profile, is especially noteworthy. They are from the Etowah

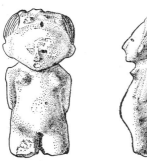

FIG. 22—Small earthenware figures suggesting ancient Mexican work, Georgia.

group of mounds in Bartow county, Georgia.

Strangely enough, the most striking examples of this class of work yet found in the eastern United States are from a region where the ordinary wares are inferior and not very plentiful. I refer to some

FIG. 23—Earthenware heads of Mexican type, Georgia.

specimens of small figurines in clay obtained by Professor F. W. Putnam from a mound in southwestern Ohio. They appear to excel any similar work north of Mexico in the appreciation of form and proportion shown by the makers, but illustrations have not as yet been published.

The occurrence of such unusual features of art as this and the flat-headed figurines mentioned above, adds force to the suggestion afforded by certain unique works in stone, copper, and shell found in the general region, that some of the early people had contact, more or less direct, with the advanced nations of Mexico.

PERSONAL ORNAMENTS OF EARTHENWARE

Clay, colored by a variety of oxides and other substances, was extensively used for painting the person as well as various objects of art, but

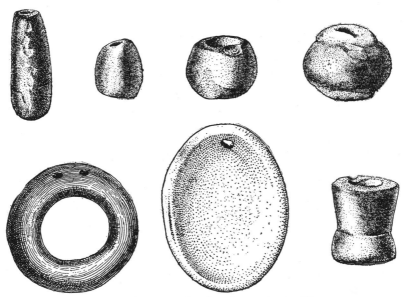

FIG. 24—Earthenware beads and pendants, various localities.

FIG. 25—Ear plugs of earthenware, middle and lower Mississippi valley.

articles of baked clay were rarely utilized for ornament. Occasionally baked clay was employed for beads and pendants (see figure 24), and for ear plugs and labrets (figures 25 and 26), in the same manner as were similar forms in stone and shell, but this use was not common, as the material was not sufficiently attractive in appearance to gratify the savage taste.

FIG. 26—Labrets of earthenware, middle and lower Mississippi valley.

EARTHENWARE DISKS AND SPOOLS

From many sections of the country we have small earthenware disks, generally shaped from potsherds, and in some cases perforated. They average between 1 and 2 inches in diameter, and are in many cases very carefully rounded and finished. They are obtained from dwelling sites, and occasionally from graves. One theory as to their function is that they were used in playing games of skill or chance. The perforate variety may in cases have been used as spindle whorls, but recently Mr Clarence B. Moore has found specimens so related to human remains in burial as to lead to the conclusion that they had served as cores for copper ear disks. Examples are presented in figure 27.

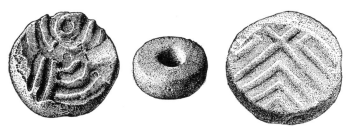

FIG. 27—Pottery disks, probably used in playing some game.

Among the imperfectly understood varieties of earthenware objects are some spool-like forms found in the Ohio valley. Illustrations of two specimens found near Maysville, Kentucky, appear in figure 28. The following notes regarding them are furnished me by Mr Gerard Fowke, of Chillicothe, Ohio:

I have seen a few, probably 15 or 20, of these "spools," though I am at a loss to classify them. A few are drilled [longitudinally] through the center. The figures engraved represent, perhaps, the extremes of slenderness and thickness in proportion to length. So far as my knowledge of them goes they are found only in Lewis, Fleming, Mason (of which Maysville is the county seat), Nicholas, and Bracken counties, Kentucky, and Brown and Adams counties, Ohio—all these counties being contiguous. It is reported that one was found in Ross county and one in Scioto county, Ohio.

While there is considerable variation in the incised lines, they all seem to be modifications of the two systems in the specimens illustrated.

Fig. 28—Spool-shaped articles of clay, containing unusual designs in incised lines. From a photograph furnished by Thomas W. Kinney, Portsmouth, Ohio.

EARTHENWARE TOBACCO PIPES

Pipes for smoking tobacco and other dried plants were generally made of vegetal substances or of stone, but in some sections clay was much used. Smoking as a matter of gustatory gratification was a widespread custom, and many accounts agree in making it an important feature in magic, religious ceremonials, councils, and treaties.

There is probably no good reason to question the general belief that the pipe was in use in America on the arrival of Europeans. Specimens are found in such varied situations and, besides, the shapes are so highly differentiated that any other conclusion must needs be supported by strong evidence. The simplest form of the pipe is a straight tube, found only now and then in the East, but the prevailing form on the Pacific coast. In the northeastern states the fundamental shape is a nearly plain bent tube slightly enlarged at the bowl end, represented in the most elementary form by the pipes of the Chesapeake province, and appearing in more elaborate shapes in the Iroquoian region in Pennsylvania and New York. The short, wide-bowled, bent trumpet of the South Appalachian province is a local development of the same general type, and the clumsy, massive, bent tube of the Gulf and Middle Mississippi states is a still more marked variant. The monitor and platform shapes of the Central states depart widely from the simple tube, and no end of curious modifications of form come from changes in the relative proportions and positions of

Fig. 29—Range in form of tobacco pipes.

stem and bowl, and especially from the addition of plastic life forms in almost infinite variety. A synopsis of the range of form from the straight tube to the platform with discoid bowl is given in figure 29. It is remarkable that the great Ohio Valley province and the Middle South, furnishing stone pipes of the highest grade, yield few and rude pipes of clay. Pipes were smoked with or without stems of other material. Illustrations and descriptions of type specimens will be given as the various groups of ware to which they belong are presented. A comprehensive work on American tobacco pipes has been published recently by the National Museum.[a]

MATERIALS

CLAY

Clay suited to the manufacture of the plain earthenware of the aborigines is widely distributed over the country, and it is not likely that any extended region is without a plentiful supply. The clay used was often impure, and in many cases was probably obtained from

[a] McGuire, J. D., Pipes and smoking customs, Report of the United States National Museum, 1897.

recently deposited alluvial sediments. Clean clays were, however, diligently sought and generally procured, and in many cases they seem to have been carefully prepared by pulverizing, washing, and kneading, as was observed by Dumont and others. Finely prepared washes of clay were made for surface finish. Clay unmixed with any kind of tempering was sometimes used for modeling vessels, pipes, and some of the less important articles. The more advanced potters used paste having degrees of refinement suited to the nature of the object modeled. Utensils to be used over fire were tempered with coarser ingredients.

TEMPERING MATERIALS

Great diversity of tempering materials is observed. This diversity is due to the multiplicity of mineral products brought within the range of experiment. It is apparent that many materials were suited to the purpose. The choice of a single material, where many abounded, must have been due to accident in the incipient stages of the art. It is not uncommon, however, to find several substances used in the work of a single community—or what appears to be such. The ingredients varied to some extent also with the uses to which the vessels were to be devoted. They include pulverized rocks and mineral substances of many kinds, powdered shells of mollusks, powdered potsherds, and perhaps cinders, besides ashes of bark, sponge, and the like. Raw vegetal substances were also used, the fibrous parts being broken or pulverized.

The advantages to be secured by the introduction of foreign particles into the clay may be somewhat diverse. It is fair to assume that tempering was intended to impart some quality or property to the paste that the pure clay did not possess to the desired degree. In building vessels the clay may have been handled with greater facility through the introduction of sand, but this could not be true of the addition of coarse, sharp particles of shell or crystalline rock; their presence must really have added to the difficulty of shaping and finishing the vessel.

Tempering may have served a useful purpose during the drying and baking of the clay. It is well known that pure clay has a strong tendency to shrink and crack in drying, and it is readily seen that the particles of tempering material would in a measure counteract this tendency. The coarse particles would interfere with the progress of the parting movements; the undulations that separate finer particles with ease would produce no effect. The progress of a crack would be impeded, just as a fracture in a glass plate is stopped by boring a hole at the extremity of the flaw. It would thus appear that even cavities in the paste serve a useful purpose, and that sawdust and cut straw, even if reduced to ashes by firing, would have performed in a way the functions of tempering. In a fine-grained paste the flaw would, when

once started, continue through the wall of the vessel in a direct line
without interference.   In the tempered paste it would, in avoiding the
solid particles, or through interference of cavities   take a sinuous
course or be led off in diverging directions.

Again, any condition or ingredient that reduces the amount of contraction resulting from drying out during the baking process must be
advantageous.   It may be possible for a body of clay to contract so
evenly as to suffer no injury, yet, as a rule, there must be considerable
unevenness of contraction, with consequent danger, and it would seem
that the greater the contraction the greater the danger of disaster.
Clay contracts through the evaporation of water held between the minute
particles.   The coarse particles of tempering may contain water, but,
being rigid, they do not contract on drying out.   The amount of contraction would thus be reduced in direct ratio with the increase of tempering material, and this would seem a most important consideration to
the potter.

It may be further surmised that the presence of foreign particles in
the clay may serve some purpose in connection with the distribution of
the heat in firing or in subsequent use over fire.   The points reached
by a given degree of heat in pure clay may be on or close to a particular
line or plane and may thus give rise to distinctly localized strain,
whereas the foreign particles may tend to conduct the heat unevenly
and distribute the strain.

In reference to the function of the tempering material during the
subsequent use of the vessel, it might seem that the presence of large
fragments of hard substances would weaken the wall of the vessel so
that when in use it would readily be fractured by a strain or blow;
but the particles arrange themselves so that strong points alternate
with the weak ones in such a way as to increase strength rather than
to reduce it.   It appears further that the particles of tempering, especially if coarse, must add greatly to the toughness of the paste during
the use of the vessel, much as they do during the drying-out process,
and it is not impossible for a flaw to extend entirely through and across
a vessel, and still not seriously impair its strength, as the particles of
tempering are so interlocked or dovetailed that separation can not
readily take place.   It would appear, therefore, that the offices of the
tempering ingredient are almost purely physical, and not chemical.
In America the heat employed in firing earthenware was not sufficient
to seriously alter any of the mineral constituents.   It rarely happened
that the heat was sufficient to calcine the shell material with which the
clay in many sections was filled.

The favorite tempering materials were powdered shell and pulverized
crystalline rock.   Sand, the grains of which were rounded, and various
other materials, so finely powdered as to be almost impalpable, were
often employed.   In the piedmont regions of North Carolina and

Virginia vessels are found made of paste consisting of coarsely pulverized steatite and barely enough clay to hold the particles together. Mica, iron pyrites, and other crystalline substances were much used in some sections. It is not uncommon to see examples in which the paste contains 75 or 80 per cent of the tempering ingredients.

The use of powdered shell was very general. It is not known that any particular variety of shell was preferred. The shells were pulverized in mortars or by means of such devices as were at hand. Du Pratz observed their use in early times. He remarks that—

Near the Nactchitoches are found banks of shells ["Coquilles de Palourdes"] such as those which form the shell island. This neighboring nation says that ancient tradition teaches them that the sea was formerly extended to this spot; the women of this nation come here to gather them [the shells]; they make a powder of them and mix it with the earth of which they make their pottery, which is considered the best. However, I would not advise the indiscriminate use of those shells for this purpose, because by nature they crack when exposed to fire; I think, therefore, that those which are found among the Nactchitoches have acquired this good quality only by losing their salt during a period of several centuries that they have been out of the sea.[a]

It is rather remarkable that in many, if not in a majority of cases, the bits of shell have not been affected by the heat of baking or use, as their original luster is fully preserved. The Pamunkey Indians of Virginia, who were found practicing the art of pot making only a few years ago, calcined their shells, and, as a consequence, where a large percentage of the material was used in tempering the clay, the vessels are inclined to fall to pieces from the slacking that follows use in water.

MANUFACTURE

THE RECORDS

A careful study of the methods and processes of manufacture employed in the ceramic art of America must furnish much that is of interest to the student of technic evolution. Besides this, the intimate knowledge of the art gained in the study of the technique of manufacture may also be of value when applied to questions of a more purely ethnic nature, for peculiar methods and devices of art characterize the peoples employing them, and in connection with other classes of evidence may be of use in tracing and identifying peoples. Much remains to be done in this branch of the study, for, considering the fact that the ceramic art has been so generally practiced by the natives since the advent of Europeans, our knowledge of the methods of manufacture seems very meager. Those whites who came in contact with the aborigines most intimately took very little interest in the native arts, and, as a rule, made no record of them whatever, and now, when interest is finally awakened, we find these arts in the main superseded and lost.

---

[a] Du Pratz, Antoine Simon Le Page, Histoire de la Louisiane, Paris, 1758, vol. I, pp. 163–164.

Our knowledge of the technic of the art is fortunately not limited to that furnished by literature or by observation of modern practices. An examination of the many relics preserved to our time throws much light on the methods of fictile manipulation. The potter's fingers have left an indelible and easily read record upon every sherd. Slips, enamels, and glazes which tend to obscure evidences of manipulation had not come into use or were sparingly employed, and the firing was so slight as to leave all the ingredients, save in color and hardness, practically unchanged.

First Use of Clay

Clay was probably first employed in the unbaked state as an auxiliary in various arts, but in such a simple manner that traces of the work are not preserved to us. The beginnings of the use of utensils of baked clay by our northern tribes must have been of comparatively recent date, but these incipient stages are necessarily obscure. If the art was of local origin a long series of almost imperceptible steps must have led up to successful methods of shaping and baking. Suitable clays would have to be discovered and brought into use, and it would be long before the intelligent use of tempering materials and advanced methods of manipulation were known.

Shaping Processes and Appliances

The shaping processes employed in vessel making were chiefly modeling and molding. These operations are equally elementary and probably of nearly equal antiquity, or, what amounts to the same thing, they came into use at corresponding stages of culture. If, as has been suggested, the clay vessel originated with the employment of clay as a lining for cooking pits, or in protecting baskets, fruit shells, or other articles from destruction by fire in culinary operations, the clay would be applied to, and would take the form of, the pit or vessel, and the art of molding would be suggested. Modeling began with the first touch of the fingers to a plastic material, but modeling directed to a definite end—the art of modeling—did not begin until some desired form was designedly reproduced. The assumption that the vessel was the first art form in baked clay may or may not be well founded, but that it soon became and always remained the most important product of the potter's art must pass unchallenged.

Although the molding process was much used in archaic times, it alone was never competent to complete a utensil; the plastic clay had to be squeezed into the mold and was therefore shaped, on one side at least, by modeling with the fingers or an implement. On the other hand, modeling alone was capable of accomplishing every necessary part of the shaping and finishing of vessels.

20 ETH—03——4

There has been much discussion regarding the probable nature of the mechanical appliances in use by pre-Columbian potters. It is now well established that the wheel or lathe was unknown in America, and no substitute for it capable of assisting materially in throwing the form or giving symmetry to the outline by purely mechanical means had been devised. The hand is the true prototype of the wheel as well as of other shaping tools, but the earliest artificial revolving device probably consisted of a shallow basket or bit of gourd in which the clay vessel was commenced and by means of which it was turned back and forth with one hand as the building went on with the other. This device is illustrated farther on in connection with studies of textile appliances employed in the art.

Within the United States molds were generally, though not always, improvised affairs and seldom did more than serve as a support for the lower part of the clay vessel during shaping and finishing by the modeling processes. These molds were employed either as exterior or interior supports, to be removed before the baking began or even before the vessel was finished. They consisted of shallow baskets, sections of gourd shell, and vessels of clay or wood shaped for the purpose. The textile markings so often seen on the exterior surfaces of vases are not, however, impressions of baskets employed in modeling and molding, but of pliable fabrics and cords used, possibly, in supporting the vessel while in the process of construction, but in most cases as a means of shaping, texturing, and ornamenting the surface, and applied by successive imprintings or malleations. This topic is presented in detail toward the close of this section.

It is apparent that the actual process of building and shaping an ordinary vessel was in a general way much the same, no matter whether it was supported by a shallow vessel serving as a rudimentary mold or wheel, or whether it was the work of the hands unaided by such mechanical device. The work was commenced at the center of the rounded bottom, either with a small mass of clay, which was flattened out and modeled into the proper curve by pressure of the fingers, or with the end of a strip of clay coiled on itself and welded together and worked into the desired form. In either case the walls were, as a rule, carried upward from the nucleus thus secured by the addition of strips of clay which were often so long as to extend more than once around the growing rim, thus assuming the character of a coil. Coil building was practiced in a very skillful manner by the ancient Pueblos. With these people the strips of clay were cut and laid on with the utmost regularity, and the edges were made to overlap on the exterior of the vessel, forming spiral imbrications. In the eastern United States the strips of clay were wide, irregular, and rude, and were worked down and obliterated, the finished vessel rarely showing traces of their employment. The strips were not systematically over-lapped as they were with the Pueblos, but one turn was set somewhat directly on the edge of the preceding turn and was attached to it by pressure and by drawing down the edges, both exterior and interior. Specimens from many sections fracture along the strip junctions, thus revealing the width of the fillets and the manner of their manipulation. The beginning of a coil is shown in figure 30 *a*. Attachment was accomplished by drawing both edges of the fillet down over the convex edge of the preceding turn, as is seen in *b* and *c*. Commonly the walls were evened up and the form corrected and developed by the aid of modeling tools. A convex-surfaced implement, a piece of gourd, for example, was held on the inner surface to support the wall, while paddles, rocking tools, and scrapers were used to manipulate the exterior surface. When the body of the vessel had been brought into approximately final shape, the margins—or in constricted forms the neck and rim—

a   *b*   *c*

FIG. 30—Use of the coil in vessel building: *a*, beginning of coil; *b*, ordinary superposition of coils or strips; *c*, section.

received attention. Handles, legs, and other relieved features, including ornaments, were shaped and added, and the points of junction were carefully finished off. In the case of compound or even of complex forms the parts were separately shaped and afterward joined by pressure and rubbing. Surface finish was accomplished in a number of ways, varying with the people, the period, and the locality, and with the use to which the vessels were to be applied. The most elementary treatment consisted of rubbing the surface with the hand and finger tips. But various tools were used, each leaving its own characteristic markings, and these in the more ordinary ware served as an ornamental finish. In the better ware the surface was rubbed down and polished with smooth stones or bits of shell.

DECORATING PROCESSES

When the vessel was built and practically complete, attention was turned toward decoration. During the shaping operations features of form and texture very often arose that proved pleasing to the potter, and these were preserved and elaborated. Thus the potters of each community, each nation, developed their own set of devices for decorating, besides acquiring from associated arts and from neighboring peoples additional ideas and facilities by means of which their art was gradually enriched.

The fingers and fingernails were employed to produce many rude effects in relief and in intaglio; tools of many shapes, improvised or manufactured for the purpose, were used; sharp pointed ones to incise, gouge-like forms to excavate, dull and rounded points to trail, and all the varieties for indented designs. Of kindred nature is a species of rude inlaying, which consists of setting into the clay, in patterns, bits of colored mineral, such as mica and quartz.

In some sections of the country engraved stamps, which generally took the form of paddles, were used to cover the plastic surface with diaper-like patterns; in others thin disks with indented or otherwise finished peripheries were rolled back and forth on the plastic surface, producing similar figures. Again, in many places woven fabrics were applied to the clay, leaving artistic patterns, and cords were impressed to produce ornamental figures of textile character. Then again processes of preparing and applying color were known in some sections and extensively employed. Clays of varying hues were ground and prepared in a liquid state to be applied with brushes. The surface was in cases prepared for the color by the addition of a layer or wash of fine paste. No description of the processes of applying the colors has been recorded, but they are probably not unlike those practiced in the Pueblo country today, and may have been borrowed by the people of the lower Arkansas from their Pueblo neighbors or from nations inhabiting the western or southern shores of the Gulf of Mexico.

BAKING PROCESSES

When completed the utensil was dried in the shade, in the sun, or before the fire, according to the needs of the case or to custom; afterward it was baked with greater or less thoroughness. The Catawbas, it would seem, having excellent clay, found baking before the fire quite sufficient. The Cherokees embedded the vessel in bark, which was fired, and the vessel came out red-hot. In no section was a very high degree of heat intentionally applied and the paste remained comparatively soft. The shell material used in tempering was often not calcined, and vitrification rarely took place. Such traces of vitrification as have been observed may have been produced long subsequent to the original baking. It has often been stated that furnaces prepared for the purpose of firing earthenware have been identified, but it is difficult to substantiate this belief, as the phenomena observed may be due to the use of earthenware in connection with fireplaces or with kilns built for other purposes.

Methods of firing observed in use were extremely simple and consisted usually of devices for surrounding the vessels somewhat evenly with burning fuel. By such means the paste was hardened, and, in most cases discolored, taking a variety of hues depending on its mineral ingredients and on the manner of applying the fire and the degree of heat attained. Some of the effects of color observed are undoubtedly due to causes operating at a period subsequent to the original firing. In cases where pigments were used in surface finish or in ornamental designs it can not be determined whether or not changes in hue produced by chemical reactions in baking were anticipated and relied on to produce desired results.

PROCESSES OF MANUFACTURE IN PRESENT USE

Authors from whom information derived from personal observations can be obtained are very few in number, and up to the present time no detailed account of the manufacture of earthenware in the great province covered by this paper has been published. The best accounts are casual notes by writers who sought only to entertain, or who had little conception of the subject with which they were dealing. Perceiving this I sought means of securing detailed and accurate information. In 1888, learning that Mr James Mooney, the indefatigable student of aboriginal history, was about to pay a visit to the Cherokee villages of western North Carolina, I secured his aid. Armed with a list of topics furnished by me he made a careful study of the art as practised among these peoples, and from his notes have been compiled the two valuable accounts which follow:

MANUFACTURE BY CATAWBA WOMEN

Living with the Cherokees were (in 1890) two Catawba women, Sally Wahuhu, an old woman of 80 years, who had come from the Catawba reservation in South Carolina about fifty years before, and Susanna Owl, about 40 years of age, who had been with the Cherokees four years. These women, being skilled potters, were induced to make some vessels, that Mr Mooney might witness the operations. Their methods were probably in the main Catawban, but the manner of baking, by means of which a rich black color was given to the ware, was said by the elder woman to have been acquired from the Cherokees. She also maintained that the Catawbas did not burn their wares in the fire, but baked them before it.

On the Cherokee reservation two kinds of clay are used. They are found mainly on the north bank of the Soco creek, in Jackson county, North Carolina, and are usually closely associated in their deposition. One variety is fine-grained and of dark brown color; this is used for pipes, because it readily takes a high polish. The other variety is light gray or whitish in color and contains sand so coarse as to give it a gritty texture. For the manufacture of ordinary earthenware these clays are mixed in about equal proportions; they are placed together and pounded with a stick or with such tools as happen to be convenient. By adding water a paste of about the consistency of putty is soon produced, which in this state is ready for use; it may, however, be preserved an indefinite period provided it does not freeze.

In making a vessel a sufficient quantity of the paste was placed by the Catawba women on a board and rolled into cylinders about an inch thick, which were cut up into sections eight or ten inches long. A small mass of clay was then taken, from which a disk about five inches in diameter was formed; this, turned up at the edges, served as the bottom of the vessel. It was placed on a board and one of the strips of clay, properly flattened out, was carried around its circumference and broken off on completing the circuit. The margin was bent slightly upward and the junction was rubbed over with the thumb nail to unite it. The process was repeated until the bowl was complete, the last strip being turned slightly outward with the fingers to form the rim. The joints were then rubbed over with the nails, and the whole surface, inside and out, was rubbed with a piece of gourd shell until it became quite even. During the smoothing process the vessel was beaten with the hands and dexterously turned by tossing in the air. The work up to this point had occupied about fifteen minutes. In the case of vessels requiring ears or handles, small cylinders of stiff clay were shaped, set in holes bored through the vessel, and clinched inside, and the joints were carefully smoothed over. The vessel was then allowed to dry until the next day. Having remained in the sun for a number of hours it was again placed on a board which was held in the lap and the surface was scraped with a bit of gourd shell until the walls were sufficiently thin and even. Some parts, including the edges, were pared off with a knife. When the scraping or paring dislodged grains of sand, the holes were filled with bits of clay from the bottom of the vessel and the surface was smoothed over with the fingers. The surface was now rubbed over with the gourd shell and polished with a smooth pebble which, in this case, had been brought from South Carolina by the elder woman. This part of the process, occupying about fifteen minutes, finished the second day's work.

After the vessel had dried until the afternoon of the third day, in the sun, as far as possible, the surface was again rubbed inside and out with the polishing stone. This work occupied half an hour. After this the vase was placed before the fire where not exposed to drafts and dried or baked for an hour; it was then ready for firing, which was conducted indoors. Oak bark was used for firing; Sally Wahuhu stated that poplar bark gave a superior color and finish. Bark was preferred to wood because it was more easily broken up and was more convenient. A heap of bark was laid on a bed of living coals; the vessel was filled with broken bark and inverted over the pile of ignited bark and then completely covered with the same fuel. The exterior bark was fired and the supply renewed for an hour, when the red-hot vessel was taken out. It was kept away from drafts during the burning and the first part of the cooling to prevent cracking. It was allowed to cool near the fire until the red heat had disappeared, when it was removed to the open air. On examination it was found that the inside had been colored a deep, glistening black by the burning, but the exterior, save in spots where the bark had been dense and the fire much smothered, was of grayish and reddish tints.

The Catawba potters excel in the manufacture of pipes. Susanna Owl used only the fine brown clay. In making an ordinary pipe she first rolled out a cylindric cone about five inches long, one end of which was less than half an inch in diameter and the other an inch or more. This cone was broken in the middle and the narrow piece was joined to the other near the smaller end and at right angles, the junction being perfected by the addition of bits of clay and by manipulation with the fingers. The processes of shaping, polishing, and drying were the same as with ordinary pottery. Three other varieties of pipes are made, described severally as cockscomb-shaped, ax-shaped, and boot-shaped. Incised ornamental figures are executed with a needle or a bent pin. This work is done on the evening of the second day or on the morning of the third. The bowl is not bored out until the pipe is nearly ready for firing. The pipes are baked, often several at a time, by embedding in burning bark, and a vessel is inverted over them during the process to impart a uniform glistening black finish.

The work of the Catawba potters was observed by Dr E. Palmer on their reservation in South Carolina in 1884, and somewhat detailed notes were furnished by him to the Bureau of Ethnology. They use a light porous clay containing a large percentage of vegetal matter. It is moistened, then taken in the hands by bits, and kneaded by the fingers until all hard particles are removed and the texture becomes uniform. When enough is thus treated to make a vessel, a small portion is taken up and flattened between the hands and formed into a disk. This is placed on a board, and other portions are rolled out into rolls a foot or less in length. One of these is wrapped about the margin of the disk and worked down and welded with the fingers, and others are added in like manner until the walls rise to the desired height. When the surface is made sufficiently even and the clay becomes firm, smooth quartz pebbles are used to give a polish.

The vessels are carefully dried in the shade and then baked by covering them with bark which is kept burning until they are sufficiently hardened. They are frequently moved about to prevent such constant contact with the burning bark as would blacken them too much. The colors produced are shades of brown mottled with grays and blacks. When the potters desire they produce a black shining surface by covering the articles with some inverted receptacle during the baking process.

MANUFACTURE BY CHEROKEE WOMEN

Mr Mooney found that although the making of pottery had fallen into disuse among the Cherokees, three women were still skilled in the art. The names of these potters are Uhyûñli, then 75 years of age, Katâlsta, about 85 years of age, and Ewi Katâlsta, daughter of the last named and about 50 years old.

Cherokee processes differ from the Catawba, or more properly, perhaps, did differ, in two principal points, namely, *a*, the application of a black glossy color by smother-firing, and, *b*, the application of ornamental designs to the exterior of the vessel by means of figured paddles or stamps. The employment of incised decorations was more common among the Cherokees than among the Catawbas.

Katâlsta used clay of the fine dark variety obtained near Macedonia Church. She prepared it as did the Catawba women, but in building she sometimes used one long coil which was carried spirally from the bottom to the rim after the manner of the ancient Pueblos and the potters of Louisiana. The inside of the vessel was shaped with a spoon and polished with a stone, the latter having been in use in the potter's family, near Bryson City, North Carolina, for three generations. The outside was stamped all over with a paddle, the body of which was covered with a checker pattern of engraved lines, giving a somewhat ornamental effect. The rim was lined vertically by incising with a pointed tool. At this stage of the process the vessel was lifted by means of a bit of cloth which prevented obliteration of the ornaments. When the vessel was finished and dried in the sun it was heated by the fire for three hours, and then put on the fire and covered with bark and burned for about three-quarters of an hour. When this step of the process was completed the vessel was taken outside the house and inverted over a small hole in the ground, which was filled with burning corn cobs. This fuel was renewed a number of times, and at the end of half an hour the interior of the vessel had acquired a black and glistening surface. Sometimes the same result is obtained by burning small quantities of wheat or cob bran in the vessel, which is covered over during the burning to prevent the escape of the smoke.

The implements used by the potters of this reservation are the tool for pounding the clay; the bits of gourd or shell, or other convex-surfaced devices for shaping and polishing; the knife for trimming edges; smooth pebbles for final polishing; pointed tools of wood, metal, etc., for incising patterns; and paddle stamps for imparting a rude diapered effect to the exterior surface of the vessel. The stamp patterns are usually small diamonds or squares, formed by cutting crossed grooves on the face of a small paddle of poplar or linn wood.

Plain pipes of rather rude finish are made by the Cherokees after their ordinary manner of earthenware manufacture.

their meate
of earth

The Seething of
in Potts

USE OF THE EARTHEN POT IN BOILING

DRAWN BY JOHN WHITE, OF THE ROANOKE COLONY, 1585-1588

Heliotype Co. Boston.

a (HEIGHT 6½ INCHES)

Heliotype Co. Boston.

b (HEIGHT 10½ INCHES)

EARTHEN VESSELS FINISHED IN COLOR
MIDDLE MISSISSIPPI VALLEY

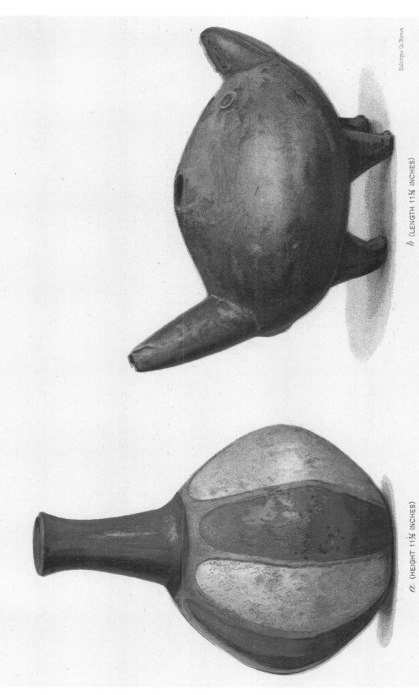

a (HEIGHT 11½ INCHES)

b (LENGTH 11½ INCHES)

EARTHEN VESSELS FINISHED IN COLOR

MIDDLE MISSISSIPPI VALLEY

Heliotype Co. Boston.

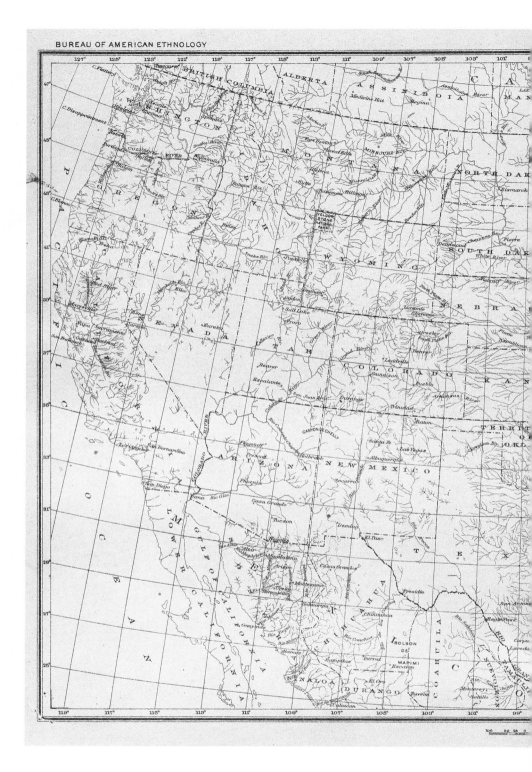

DISTRIBUTION OF ABORIGINAL
POTTERY GROUPS
IN EASTERN UNITED STATES
BY W. H. HOLMES, 1901.

Middle Mississippi
Valley group

South Appalachian
group

Middle and Northern
Atlantic slope group

Iroquois group

North Western
group

a (HEIGHT 11 INCHES)

b (HEIGHT 10 INCHES)

EARTHEN VESSELS FINISHED IN COLOR

MIDDLE MISSISSIPPI VALLEY

b (ARKANSAS, HEIGHT 6 INCHES)

a (ARKANSAS, HEIGHT 4 INCHES)

c (ARKANSAS, HEIGHT 6 INCHES)

d (MISSOURI, HEIGHT 8½ INCHES)

EARTHEN VESSELS FINISHED IN COLOR
MIDDLE MISSISSIPPI VALLEY

a (HEIGHT 6 INCHES)

b (HEIGHT 6¾ INCHES)

EARTHEN VESSELS FINISHED IN COLOR

MIDDLE MISSISSIPPI VALLEY

For the purpose of showing the close general resemblance of the processes here recorded to those of Louisiana Indians witnessed, though inadequately described, by Du Pratz and Butel-Dumont one hundred and fifty years ago, I add the following paragraphs from these authors, quite literally translated.

As soon as these peoples had settled in a fixed dwelling place, it was necessary to find the safest and most convenient method of cooking maize and meats; they bethought themselves of making pottery. This was the work of the women. They sought for greasy earth, reduced it to powder, rejected the gravel which was found in it, made a sufficiently firm paste, and then established their workshop on a flat block of wood on which they formed the pottery with the fingers, smoothing it with a pebble, which was carefully preserved for this purpose. As fast as the clay dried they added more, supporting it with the hand on the other side; after all these operations they baked it by means of a hot fire.[a]

The following is from Butel-Dumont:

Moreover, the industry of these Indian girls and women is admirable. I have already reported elsewhere with what skill, with their fingers alone and without a turning lathe they make all sorts of pottery. This is the method they employ:

After having gathered the earth suitable for this kind of work, and having well cleansed it, they take shells which they grind and reduce to a very fine powder; they mix this very fine dust with the earth which has been provided, and, moistening the whole with a little water, they knead it with the hands and feet, forming a dough of which they make rolls 6 or 7 feet long and of whatever thickness is desired. Should they wish to fashion a dish or a vessel, they take one of these rolls and, holding down one end with the thumb of the left hand they turn it around with admirable swiftness and dexterity, describing a spiral; from time to time they dip their fingers in water, which they are always careful to have near them, and with the right hand they smooth the inside and outside of the vessel they intend to form, which, without this care, would be undulated.

In this manner they make all sorts of utensils of earth, dishes, plates, pans, pots, and pitchers, some of which contain 40 and 50 pints. The baking of this pottery does not cause them much trouble. After having dried it in the shade they build a great fire, and when they think they have enough coals they clear a place in the middle where they arrange the vessels and cover them with the coals. It is thus that they give them the baking which is necessary. After this they can be placed on the fire and have as much firmness as ours. Their strength can only be attributed to the mixture which the women make of the powdered shells with the clay.[b]

A few additional accounts of the making of earthenware by the tribes of the region under review may be quoted. The statements of persons who have not themselves witnessed the processes of manufacture may in cases be vitiated by information derived through unreliable sources and should always be carefully considered with this possibility in view.

---

[a] Du Pratz, Antoine Simon Le Page, Histoire de la Louisiane, Paris, 1758, vol. II, pp. 178–79.
[b] Butel-Dumont, George Marie, Mémoires sur la Louisiane, Paris, 1753, vol. II, pp. 271–73.

Hunter, who is one of the best early authorities on the Osages and other Indians of the Missouri and the upper Mississippi regions, makes the following statement:

In manufacturing their pottery for cooking and domestic purposes, they collect tough clay, beat it into powder, temper it with water, and then spread it over blocks of wood, which have been formed into shapes to suit their convenience or fancy. When sufficiently dried, they are removed from the molds, placed in proper situations, and burned to a hardness suitable to their intended uses.

Another method practiced by them is to coat the inner surface of baskets made of rushes or willows with clay, to any required thickness, and, when dry, to burn them as above described.

In this way they construct large, handsome, and tolerably durable ware; though latterly, with such tribes as have much intercourse with the whites, it is not much used, because of the substitution of cast-iron ware in its stead.

When these vessels are large, as is the case for the manufacture of sugar, they are suspended by grapevines, which, wherever exposed to the fire, are constantly kept covered with moist clay.

Sometimes, however, the rims are made strong, and project a little inwardly quite around the vessels, so as to admit of their being sustained by flattened pieces of wood, slid underneath these projections, and extending across their centers.[a]

These paragraphs appear to apply to the Osage Indians and probably to their neighbors.

Mr Catlin's account of the manufacture of pottery by the Mandans of the upper Missouri is a valuable addition to our knowledge. Although often quoted it should not be omitted from this paper.

I spoke also of the earthen dishes or bowls in which these viands were served out; they are a familiar part of the culinary furniture of every Mandan lodge, and are manufactured by the women of this tribe in great quantities, and modeled into a thousand forms and tastes. They are made by the hands of the women, from a tough black clay, and baked in kilns which are made for the purpose, and are nearly equal in hardness to our own manufacture of pottery, though they have not yet got the art of glazing, which would be to them a most valuable secret. They make them so strong and serviceable, however, that they hang them over the fire as we do our iron pots, and boil their meat in them with perfect success. I have seen some few specimens of such manufacture, which have been dug up in Indian mounds and tombs in the Southern and Middle states, placed in our Eastern museums, and looked upon as a great wonder, when here this novelty is at once done away with, and the whole mystery; where women can be seen handling and using them by hundreds, and they can be seen every day in the summer also, molding them into many fanciful forms and passing them through the kiln where they are hardened.[b]

That the art was very generally practiced even by the less sedentary tribes of the great Missouri basin is attested by the following extract from a very interesting book by Mr George Bird Grinnell:

Years ago, on the sites of abandoned Pawnee villages, on the Loup Fork and on the Platte, fragments of pottery used to be found among the débris of the fallen lodges. The manufacture of this pottery was no doubt abandoned long ago, and has probably not been practiced to any considerable extent since they met the whites.

a Hunter, John D. Memoirs of a captivity among the Indians, London, 1823, pp. 288–89.
b Catlin, George, Letters and notes on the North American Indians, London, 1844, vol. I, p. 116.

A man about fifty years of age stated to me that he had never seen these pots in use, but that his grandmother had told him that in her days they made and used them. He said that they were accustomed to smooth off the end of a tree for a mold. A hot fire was then built, in which stones were roasted, which were afterward pounded into fine powder or sand. This pounded stone they mixed with fine clay, and when the material was of the proper consistency they smeared it over the rounded mold, which was perhaps first well greased with buffalo tallow. After the clay had been made of even thickness throughout, and smooth on the outside, they took a small, sharp stone, and made marks on the outside to ornament it. When the material was sufficiently dry, they lifted it from the mold and burned it in the fire, and while it was baking, "put corn in the pot and stirred it about, and this made it hard as iron." This may mean that it gave the pot a glaze on the inside. In these pots they boiled food of all kinds. Mr Dunbar informs me that these pots were also made in later times within a frame-work of willow twigs. The clay, made very stiff, was smeared on this frame, the inside being repeatedly smoothed with the moistened hand, and but little attention being given to the appearance of the outside. After they had been sun-dried, such pots were baked without removing the frame, which burned away in the fire, leaving the marks of the twigs visible on the outside of the pot.[a]

The following extracts from the writings of Peter Kalm refer to the practice of this art in the eastern portions of the country, and indicate that the art of clay vessel making was entirely abandoned in those sections familiar to that author more than a century ago. The specimens exhibited by Mr Bartram probably came from the South. Mr Kalm wrote:

Mr Bartram shewed me an earthen pot, which had been found in a place where the Indians formerly lived. He who first dug it out kept grease and fat in it to smear his shoes, boots, and all sorts of leather with. Mr Bartram bought the pot of that man; it was yet entire and not damaged. I could perceive no glaze or color upon it, but on the outside it was very much ornamented and upon the whole well made. Mr Bartram shewed me several pieces of broken earthen vessels which the Indians formerly made use of. It plainly appeared in all these that they were not made of mere clay, but that different materials had been mixed with it, according to the nature of the places where they were made. Those Indians, for example, who lived near the seashore pounded the shells of snails and mussels and mixed them with the clay. Others, who lived farther up in the country where mountain crystals could be found, pounded them and mixed them with their clay; but how they proceeded in making the vessels is entirely unknown. It was plain that they did not burn them much, for they are so soft they might be cut in pieces with a knife; the workmanship, however, seems to have been very good, for at present they find whole vessels or pieces in the ground which are not damaged at all, though they have lain in the ground above a century. Before the Europeans settled in North America the Indians had no other vessels to boil their meat in than these earthen pots of their own making, but since their arrival they have always bought pots, kettles, and other necessary vessels of the Europeans, and take no longer the pains of making some, by which means this art is entirely lost among them. Such vessels of their own construction are therefore a great rarity even among the Indians. I have seen such old pots and pieces of them, consisting of a kind of Serpentine stone, or Linnæus's Talcum, Syst. Nat. 3, p. 52.[b]

---

a Grinnell, George Bird, Pawnee hero stories and folk-tales, New York, 1893, pp. 255–56.

b Kalm, Peter, Travels into North America, vol. I, Warrington, 1770, pp 227–29.

In the following extract the author appears to refer to the use of pottery in New Jersey; and sherds now found in so many localities no doubt represent the art of the time referred to.

The old boilers or kettles of the Indians, were either made of clay, or of different kinds of pot stone (Lapis ollaris). The former consisted of a dark clay, mixt with grains of white sand or quartz, and burnt in the fire. Many of these kettles have two holes in the upper margin, on each side one, through which the Indians put a stick and held the kettle over the fire as long as it was to boil. Most of the kettles have no feet. It is remarkable that no pots of this kind have been found glazed, either on the outside or the inside. A few of the oldest Swedes could yet remember seeing the Indians boil their meat in these pots.[a]

Many details of clay manipulation are given in subsequent pages as the various groups of ware are presented.

SIZE

The production of a vessel of clay required much skill, experience, and foresight; it was not a single, simple act of construction that was necessary, but a series of progressive operations of a delicate and difficult nature, extending over a number of days. These difficulties were much increased with the increase in dimensions of the utensil. A vessel so small as to be kept well within the grasp of the fingers could be built at once, and without great danger of failure at any stage of the work, but in building a large vessel the walls had to be carried upward by degrees, time being required to allow the plastic paste to set and thus to become capable of supporting additional weight. The danger of failure in subsequent stages of the work also increased with the size, and a vessel of clay two or more feet in diameter, and three-fourths that height, carried successfully through all the steps of modeling, drying, burning, coloring, and ornamentation may well be regarded as a triumph of barbarian manipulative skill.

The average Indian vase, as seen in our museums, is rather small, having a capacity of a gallon or less, but these surviving vessels do not fairly represent the dimensions of the original products; large vessels are rarely preserved for the reason that as a rule, save in limited districts, they were not buried with the dead, as were the smaller pieces.

The use for which the vessel was intended had much to do with its size. The boiling of messes for feasts where many people were to be served required large pots, as did also storage, and evaporation of water for salt or sugar. The so-called salt pots found in Tennessee, Illinois, and Missouri are among the largest vessels known in any section of the country, and fragments have been found indicating a a diameter of three feet or more. In such vessels the depth usually is not great; indeed, few vessels of any class have been collected having a height greater than twenty-four inches. The thickness of the walls of

---

[a] Kalm, Peter. Travels into North America, vol. II, London, 1770, pp. 41–42.

these large vessels, in many cases, reaches or exceeds three-fourths of an inch, and their weight must have been considerable. The potter undoubtedly found it a difficult task to handle them while the clay was still in a plastic or semisolid state.

As a rule the walls of ordinary vases are surprisingly thin, and we are led to admire the skill of the potter who could execute vessels of large size and fine proportions with walls at no point exceeding three-eighths of an inch in thickness. Size varies from the extreme proportions above mentioned to those of toy vessels not more than an inch in diameter and height.

FORMS

The absence of all suggestiveness of form in the natural clay, together with its plasticity when moist, and its brittleness when dry, must have prevented its early independent use in the shaping arts; but when the means of hardening it by baking, and strengthening it by tempering, came to be understood, a new and ever-expanding field was opened to art.

With primitive peoples the first known use of baked clay is in the construction of vessels. The development of form in vessel making is governed by numerous influences and conditions; first, there are functional influences or requirements; second, inherited suggestions and limitations; third, mechanical agencies; fourth, ideographic requirements; and fifth, esthetic forces.

1. Function is of necessity the leading influence in all that pertains to the selection of models and the determination of size and general contour. Primarily the vessel was intended to contain that which unrestrained would be difficult to hold, handle, and transport, and its shape had to be such as would permit the successful performance of these functions. As uses differentiated and multiplied, the various primal forms underwent many changes. The manner of use also led in many cases to special modifications of shape. A pot to be placed upon the fire differed in base and rim from one that was to be suspended; a vase intended to stand upright on a hard floor was different in shape from the one that was to be set upright in the sand.

2. The duties to which earthen vessels were assigned were originally performed by other classes of vessels, and when a new material, wholly amorphous and offering no suggestions of form, came into use, shapes were copied from antecedent vessels, as men, in constructing, necessarily follow suggestions offered by what already exists. Clay vessels, therefore, took forms depending much on the vessels with which the potter was acquainted, and the potters of different nations having unlike models produced different forms from the very start. These inceptive characteristics were long retained and exercised a lasting influence. No race in the world appears to have made as much use of

natural forms in the art at a corresponding grade of culture as the American Indian, and the striking result is seen at a glance, when any large number of vessels made by the more advanced tribes is brought together.

3. In the use of any material in the shaping arts certain processes and certain mechanical aids are employed, and these vary with the materials and with the acquirements of the potter so that great variation of form results. Clay has limitations of strength unburned and burned, and form is governed by these limitations. If the potter is unskilled of hand and eye, his work will lack in symmetry and grace; and if his appliances are imperfect, its form will as a consequence be unsymmetric and rude. The introduction of each improved device leads to modifications of form. It is readily seen, for example, that the discovery of the wheel must have led to the introduction of many new features of form, consigning many others to oblivion.

4. Ideographic influences are felt but little in early stages of the art, yet in time they become a powerful force in giving shape to articles of clay. If, for example, a vessel is intended for use in connection with rites relating to a particular animal deity, the shape is made to suggest the form of that deity. The idea in such cases governs not only the shape but the color and decoration.

5. Esthetic influence is necessarily weak during the earliest practice of the art, and shape is apparently slow to receive esthetic notice and modification; but, even at this stage, use, model, and technic give much that is regarded as pleasing in form. Certain proportions and something of grace are necessarily embodied in each vessel and it is quite impossible in a given case to determine at just what point the esthetic idea begins to produce its effects. In even the most primitive groups of earthenware there are apparent traces of the action of this force in the modification of margins and in the turning of curves.

The forms produced in the primitive stages of the art are, as a rule, exceedingly simple. We may assume that the most elementary form is the bowl or cup with rounded bottom, wide mouth, and plain margin. There are a number of influences tending to give the base a rounded rather than a flat or concave shape, among which are the available natural forms or models, the manner of use, and the ease and naturalness of construction. Flat and concave bottoms come late, as do also such features as pedestals, annular bases, feet, and legs. These come into use no doubt with the introduction of hard, level floors in the dwelling. As skill increases, the margin of the vessel rises, the outline varies from the globular form, and many causes lead to specialization and elaboration, so that we have oblong and flattened bodies, constricted rims, straight and recurved lips, short and high necks, and many degrees of constriction of opening. Compound and complex forms follow, and finally the potter ventures on the production of natural forms, representing and portraying shells, fruits, birds, beasts, and men, essaying also many fanciful creations. However, for a long time the fundamental purpose of vessels was that of containing, and the various changes rung on their forms do not seriously interfere with this normal function.

After great skill is acquired in the handling of clay other articles are manufactured, and the ceramic field is greatly enlarged; thus we have implements, pipes, figurines, idols, spindle whorls, musical instruments, and personal ornaments.

COLOR
COLOR OF PASTE

The colors observed in primitive earthen vessels are, in a great measure, the result of causes not regulated or foreseen by the potter; the clays employed have different hues, and in the process of baking alterations in color take place through chemical changes or through the deposition of carbonaceous matter on the surfaces. The range of these colors is quite large and varies with materials and processes, but the prevailing colors are dark reddish, yellowish, and brownish grays, often unevenly distributed over the surface of the vessel. Many tribes were not satisfied with the colors produced in this way, but submitted the vessel to special processes to effect desired changes. One method, already referred to and thought to be aboriginal, consisted in covering the vessel with fuel which was burned in such a way as to confine the smoke, thus giving a glossy black finish.

When vessels are broken, it is observed that the color of the paste is not uniform throughout the mass; usually the interior is darker than the surface, which was exposed directly to the heat in baking and lost such portions of its original coloring matter as happened to be most volatile. Possibly this effect may in cases be produced by weathering, or, rather, by the bleaching action of the soil in which the vessels were embedded.

APPLICATION OF COLOR

It was a common practice with some tribes to apply a wash of color to the surface of the vase, generally to the more exposed parts of the exterior only. Little is known of the manner in which the colors were mixed and used. They were usually applied before the baking, and were always polished down with a rubbing stone. Red was the favorite color.

Du Pratz mentions the use of color by the Natchez Indians in the following lines:

On the same hill (White hill) there are veins of ocher, of which the Natchez had just taken some to stain their pottery, which is very pretty; when it was besmeared with ocher it became red after burning.[a]

The preference for particular colors may be due to a number of

---

[a] Du Pratz, Antoine Simon Le Page, Histoire de la Louisiane, Paris, 1758, vol. I, p. 124.

causes, two of which are of especial importance: first, with some peoples colors had peculiar mythologic significance, and on this account were appropriate to vessels employed for certain ceremonial uses; second, most savage and barbarian peoples have a decided fondness for colors, and appreciate their esthetic values, taste being exercised in their selection.   There is good evidence that both superstitious and esthetic motives influenced the potters of the mound region; but it is impossible to say from a study of the vases exactly what part each of these motives took in producing the results observed in the wares studied.   Ordinarily domestic pottery did not receive surface coloring, as subsequent use over fire would entirely obliterate it.   Coloring for ornament is more fully discussed in a subsequent section (page 66).

DECORATION

EVOLUTION OF DECORATION

A volume could be written on this most attractive subject, but a brief outline is all that can be given in this place.   The origin and early development of the idea of embellishment and the manner in which decorative features came to be introduced into the ceramic art can not be examined in detail.   I have dwelt on these topics to some extent in two papers already published, Form and Ornament in the Ceramic Art, Fourth Annual Report of the Bureau of Ethnology, and the Evolution of Ornament, an American Lesson, in the American Anthropologist, April 1890.   It is not essential to the purpose of this paper that I should here do more than characterize and classify the native decorative work of the eastern United States in a somewhat general way, detailed studies being presented in connection with the separate presentation of ceramic groups.

Decoration may be studied, first, with reference to the subject-matter of the ornamentation—its form, origin, and significance—and, second, with reference to the methods of execution and the devices and implements employed.   It may also be examined with reference to such evidence as it affords regarding racial and tribal history.

The subject-matter of primitive ceramic ornament, the elements or motives employed, may be assigned to two great classes based on the character of the conceptions associated with them.   These are nonideographic, that is to say, those having a purely esthetic office, and those having in addition to this function associated ideas of a superstitious, mnemonic, or other significant nature.   Nonideographic elements are mainly derived from two sources: first, by copying from objects having decorative features, natural or artificial, and second, from suggestions of a decorative nature arising within the art from constructive and manipulative features.   Natural objects, such as sea-shells and fruit shells, abound in features highly suggestive of embellishment, and these objects are constantly and intimately associated with the plastic art and are copied by the potter.   Artificial objects have two classes of features capable of giving rise to ornament; these are constructional and functional. Those of the former class are represented by such features as the coil employed in building, and the stitch, the plait, and the twist employed in textile fabrics. Those of the latter are represented by handles, legs, bands, perforations, etc. Suggestions incidental to manufacture, such as finger markings, imprints of implements, and markings of molds, are fruitful sources of nonideographic decorations.

In the primitive stages of the art simple nonideographic elements seem to predominate, but it is difficult to draw a line separating them from the ideographic, for an idea may at any time become associated with even the most elementary design. When, however, we encounter delineative elements or subjects employed in ornamental offices, we may reasonably assume that ideas were associated with them, that they were symbolic. It is pretty generally conceded that life forms were not employed in early art save when they had a peculiar significance and applicability in the connection in which they were used, and it is probable that the associated idea was often retained even though the representation became so conventionalized and formal that the ordinary observer would no longer recognize the semblance of nature. This topic was examined in detail in a recent study of the art of ancient Chiriqui,[a] and is presented in equally definite form in the section of this paper devoted to Gulf Coast ware.

The range of imitative subjects employed in surface decoration is not large. Within the whole area studied, no representation of a plant has been found; birds and the human figure were rarely delineated, and even quadrupeds, so generally employed in modeling, do not appear with frequency in other forms of expression. Ceramic decoration is probably late in taking up the graphic and ideographic art of a people. This conservatism may be due to the fact that in early stages the art is purely domestic, and such delineations would have little appropriateness. It is probably not until the fictile products come to take a prominent place in superstitious usages that significant designs are demanded and employed.

METHODS OF DECORATING

The decoration of earthenware was accomplished in a number of ways which are classified by form characters as relieved, flat, and depressed. The processes employed are modeling with the fingers and with tools, molding in baskets or other vessels having ornamented surfaces, and stamping, paddling, impressing, puncturing, carving, incising, polishing, and painting with such tools as were most convenient. A brief review of the decorating processes has already been given under the head Manufacture.

---

[a] Holmes, W. H., Ancient art of the province of Chiriqui, in Sixth Annual Report of the Bureau of Ethnology, Washington, 1888.

The modeling of animal forms constituted a prominent feature of the potter's art in the Mississippi valley as well as in some other sections. As a rule the figures were modeled, in part at least, in the round, and were attached to or formed essential parts of the vase. Usually, no doubt, they had a symbolic office, but their decorative value was not lost sight of, and the forms graded imperceptibly into conventional relieved features that to all appearances were purely decorative.

Decorative designs of a purely conventional character were often executed in both low and salient relief. This was generally accomplished by the addition of nodes and fillets of clay to the plain surfaces of the vessel. Fillets were applied in various ways over the body, forming horizontal, oblique, and vertical bands or ribs. When placed about the rim or neck, these fillets were often indented with the finger or an implement so as to imitate, rudely, a heavy twisted cord—a feature evidently borrowed from basketry or copied from cords used in mending or handling earthen vessels. Nodes were also attached in various ways to the neck and body of the vessel, sometimes covering it as with spines. In some cases the entire surface of the larger vessels was varied by pinching up small bits of clay between the nails of the fingers and the thumb. An implement was sometimes used to produce a similar result.

The esthetic tendencies of the potters are well shown by their essays in engraving. They worked with points on both the plastic and the sun-dried clay, and possibly at times on the fire-baked surface. Figures thus produced exhibit a wide range of artistic achievement. They illustrate all stages of progress from the most archaic type of ornament—the use of loosely associated dots and straight lines—to the most elegant combinations of curves, and the delineation of life forms and fanciful conceptions.

In many cases when a blunt implement was employed, the line was produced by a trailing movement. The result is quite distinct from that of incision, in which a sharp point is used, and excision or excavation which is more easily accomplished with the end of a hollow reed or bone. The application of textile fabrics giving impressions of the mesh was very general, and engraved paddles were used to give similar effects. These topics are treated at length elsewhere in this paper. Repoussé work, which consisted in punching up nodes by applying a blunt tool to the opposite side of the vessel wall, was common in some localities.

The use of color in decorating earthenware marks a very decided advance beyond the inceptive stage of the art. Vessels to be employed in ordinary culinary work needed no surface ornament, and could not retain it during use. When differentiation of use had made some progress, and neat appearance became desirable, coloring was applied, and when the office became ceremonial or superstitious, elaborate designs were employed. Ornament in color is common in the middle and lower Mississippi regions, and is seen to some extent along the Gulf coast and in Florida; rare examples have been found in the middle Ohio region and east of the Appalachian high land in Georgia and the Carolinas. The most decided prevalence of color in finish and decoration is discovered in the Arkansas region, from which locality as a center this feature is found to fade out and gradually disappear. The reason of this is not determined, but it is to be remarked that Arkansas borders somewhat closely on the Pueblo country where the use of color was general, and this idea, as has already been remarked, may have been borrowed from the ancient Pueblo potter.

The colors used in painting were white, red, brown, and black; they consisted for the most part of finely pulverized clay mixed with ochers and of native ochers alone. Occasionally the colors used seem to have been mere stains. All were probably laid on with coarse brushes of hair, feathers, or vegetal fiber. The figures in most cases are simple, but are applied in a broad, bold way, indicative of a well-advanced stage of decorative art. Skill had not yet reached the point, however, at which ideographic pictorial subjects could be presented with much freedom, and the work was for the most part purely conventional. As would be expected, curvilinear forms prevail as a result of the free-hand method of execution; they embrace meanders, scrolls, circles, spirals, and combinations and grouping of curved lines. Of rectilinear forms, lozenges, guilloches, zigzags, checkers, crosses, and stellar shapes are best known. Many of these figures were doubtless symbolic. Life forms were seldom attempted, although modeled figures of animals were sometimes given appropriate markings, as in the case of a fine owl-shaped vessel from Arkansas, and of a quadruped vase, with striped and spotted body, from Missouri. Examples of human figures from Arkansas have the costume delineated in some detail in red, white, and the ochery color of the paste, and numerous vases shaped in imitation of the human head have the skin, hair, and ornaments colored approximately to life.

In some cases the patterns on vases are brought out by polishing certain areas more highly than others, and an example is cited by C. C. Jones in which inlaying had been resorted to.[a]

USE OF TEXTILES IN MODELING AND EMBELLISHING

RELATION OF THE TEXTILE AND CERAMIC ARTS

Among the tribes of a wide zone in southern British America and northern United States, and extending from the Atlantic to the Rocky mountains, the ceramic art was intimately associated with the textile art,

---

[a] Jones, C. C., Antiquities of the southern Indians, p. 459.

and the earthenware exhibits traces of this intimacy as one of its most constant characteristics. These traces consist of impressions of textile articles made on the plastic clay during manufacture, and of markings in imitation of textile characters traced or stamped on the newly made vessels. The textile art is no doubt the older art in this region as elsewhere, and the potter, working always with textile appliances and with textile models before him, has borrowed many elements of form and ornament from them. Textile forms and markings are thus in this part of America a characteristic of the initial stages of the ceramic art.

It is true that we can not say in any case whether the potter's art as practiced in the northern districts is exclusively of local development, springing from suggestions offered by the practice of simple culinary arts, especially basketry, or whether it represents degenerate phases of southern art radiating from far away culture centers and reduced to the utmost simplicity by the unfriendly environment. We are certainly safe, however, in assuming that this peculiar phase of the art represents its initial stage—a stage through and from which arose the higher and more complex phases characterizing succeeding stages of barbarism and civilization.

Whether with all peoples the art passed through the textile stage may remain a question, because the traces are obliterated by lapse of time, but we observe as we pass south through the United States that the textile-marked ware becomes less and less prevalent. However, sufficient traces of textile finish are still found in Florida and other Gulf states to suggest a former practice there of the archaic art.

CLASSES OF TEXTILE MARKINGS

Textile markings found on pottery are of five classes: first, impressions from the surface of rigid forms, such as baskets; second, impressions of fabrics of a pliable nature, such as cloths and nets; third, impressions from woven textures used over the hand or over some suitable modeling implement; fourth, impressions of cords wrapped about modeling paddles or rocking tools; fifth, impressions of bits of cords or other textile units, singly or in groups, applied for ornament only and so arranged as to give textile-like patterns. In addition, we have a large class of impressions and markings in which textile effects are mechanically imitated.

The several kinds of textile markings are not equally distributed over the country, but each, to a certain extent, seems to characterize the wares of a particular region or to belong to particular groups of ware, indicating, perhaps, the condition and practices of distinct peoples or variations in initial elements affecting the art. There may also be a certain order in the development of the various classes of impressions—a passing from simple to complex phenomena, from the purely mechanical or the simply imitative to the conventionally modified and highly elaborated phases of embellishment.

The extent to which baskets were used in modeling pottery in this great province has been greatly overestimated. Instead of being the rule, as we have been led to believe, their use constitutes the exception, and the rare exception.

The functions of the fabrics and textile elements used in connection with the manufacture of pottery deserve careful consideration. There can be little doubt that these functions are both practical and esthetic, but we shall not be able to make the distinction in all cases. Practical uses may be of several kinds. In modeling a clay vessel a basket may be used as a support and pivot, thus becoming an incipient form of the wheel (see figure 31). It may equally well assist in shaping the bodies of the ves-

FIG. 31—Use of a basket in modeling an earthen vessel (Pueblo Indians, Cushing, in the Fourth Annual Report of the Bureau of Ethnology).

sels, thus assuming in a limited way the functions of a mold (see figure 32). The mat on which a plastic vessel happens to rest leaves impressions rendered indelible by subsequent firing. The same may be true of any fabric brought into contact with the plastic surface, but the impressions in such cases are accidental and have no practical function.

That baskets were used in the East as molds is attested by historical evidence, as may be seen by reference to the citation from Hunter, previously made. I can but regard it as remarkable, however, that in handling thousands of specimens of this pottery I have found no vase the imprints on which fully warrant the

FIG. 32—Use of a basket as a mold for the base of an earthen vessel (Pueblo Indians, Cushing, work cited).

statement that a basket was employed as a mold, or even as a support for the incipient clay form. Many assertions to the contrary have been made, probably through misapprehension of the nature of the

FIG. 33—Vase showing impressions resulting from the use of pliable fabrics in wrapping and sustaining the vessel while plastic.   Height 4 inches.

a   *b*

FIG. 34—Fragment of salt vessel, with cast in clay, showing kind of fabric used in modeling vessels. About one-half actual size.

markings observed. On fragments of imperfectly preserved vessels distinctions can not readily be drawn between disconnected impres sions made by the partial application of pliable fabrics or textile covered stamps and the systematically connected imprintings made by the surface of a basket. The unwary are likely even to mistake the rude patterns made by impressing bits of cords in geometric arrange- ment about the rims of vases for the imprints of baskets.

USE OF PLIABLE FABRICS IN MODELING

Pliable fabrics, such as sacks, nets, and cloth, were made use of as exterior supports in holding or handling the vessel while it was still in a plastic condition. Mr Mooney says that the Cherokees use a rag to lift the pot at one stage in its manufacture, and it is easy to see that cloths or nets wrapped about the exterior surface of the plastic walls would serve to prevent quick drying and consequent cracking of

FIG. 35—Fragment of a cooking pot showing impressions of a net-covered paddle, North Carolina. About three-fourths actual size.

the clay along a weak line. Binding up with cloths or nets would inter- fere with the deforming tendency of pressure during the modeling process and of sinking from weight of the plastic walls. Mr Sellers, a very acute observer, believed that the modeling of certain large salt basins was done on core-like molds of clay. In such a case, or where, as observed by Hunter, blocks of wood were used, the cloth would serve an important purpose in facilitating the removal of the plastic or partly dried clay shell and in supporting it during subsequent stages of the shaping and finishing processes. Such removal would probably be accomplished by turning the mold, with the vase upon it, upside down, and allowing the latter to fall off into the fabric by its own weight or by the means of pressure from the hands. An excellent example of the impressions made on the surface of vases by fabrics applied in the course of manufacture is shown in figure 33. The

FIG. 36—Bowl from a North Carolina mound, showing impressions of a cord-wrapped malleating tool. Diameter 6 inches.

FIG. 37—Bowl made by the author. The surface finished with the cord-wrapped paddle shown in figure 38. Diameter 6 inches.

specimen is a small vessel obtained from a mound in Lenoir county, North Carolina. Figure 34 *a* illustrates an ordinary example of the fabrics used by the makers of salt pans in wrapping the plastic form. The positive restoration, *b*, was obtained by making an impression in clay from the potsherd.

Use of Textiles in Malleating Surfaces

An extended series of experiments, made for the purpose of determining the functions of fabrics in pottery making, has led to the observation that the imprintings were in many cases not made by textiles used as supports, but were applied wrapped about the hand or a modeling tool as a means of knitting or welding together the clay surface. Experiment shows that the deeper and more complex the imprintings, if properly managed, the more tenacious becomes the clay. An example of net-paddled ware is given in figure 35. Scarifying, combing, pinching with the fingernails, or malleating with engraved paddles, served the same purpose.

Use of Flat Cord-wrapped Malleating Tools

It was further observed, as a result of these investigations, that more than half of the textile markings on vases are not really imprints of fabrics at all, but are the result of going over the surface with modeling tools covered or wrapped with unwoven twisted cords. This is well illustrated in figures 36 and 37.

Figure 36 illustrates a small bowl from a mound in North Carolina. The surface is completely covered with deep, sharp markings made by paddling with a cord-wrapped tool applied repeatedly and at various angles.

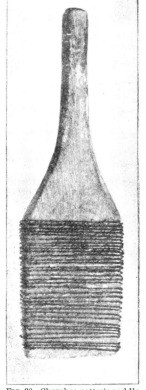

Fig. 38—Cherokee potter's paddle wrapped with cord and used in malleating the bowl shown in figure 37.

Figure 37 shows a similar cup made of potter's clay as an experiment. The malleating implement was a Cherokee potter's paddle which I had wrapped with native cord (see figure 38).

Use of Cord-wrapped Rocking Tools

Of the same general class as the cord-wrapped paddle were other tools, more or less rounded and wrapped with cord. These may have been applied as paddles, but were usually rocked back and forth, the rounder forms being revolved as a roulette. The impressions of the

FIG. 39—Potsherd showing effect produced by rocking a cord-wrapped implement back and forth. About three-fourths actual size.

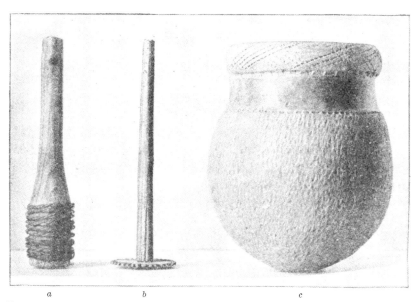

a   b   c

FIG. 40—a, A cylindric modeling tool wrapped with cord (restored); b, a notched wheel or roulette (restored); c, a vessel made by the author; surface finished with a cord-wrapped implement and decorated with the roulette. About one-half actual size.

flat paddle are distinguished by the patchy and disconnected nature of the imprints. The rolling or rocking implement was not lifted from the surface, and gave a zigzag connection to the markings, illustrated in figure 39.

The rolling or rocking modeling tools had an advantage over the

FIG. 41—Potsherds showing simple method of applying cords in decorating vases.
About three-fourths actual size.

flat paddles in treating round surfaces, and especially about the constricted neck of the vessel. I have undertaken to restore this implement, as illustrated in figure 40 *a*, and have used it successfully in

FIG. 42—Small pot with finger-nail markings giving the effect of basket impressions.
One-third actual size.

imitating effects common in the simpler wares of a vast region (see figure 40 *c*). Implements of this class served the triple purpose: (1) of modeling the surface, reducing irregularities; (2) of kneading and knitting the surface, making the walls stronger; and (3) of imparting a

FIG. 43—The roulette (restored) inked and rocked on a sheet of paper.

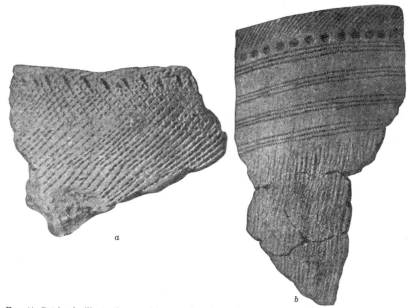

FIG. 44—Potsherds illustrating markings produced by the notched wheel; *a* about three-fourths actual size; *b* about one-third actual size.

texture to the surface that may have been regarded as pleasing to the eye. It is seen, however, that whenever it was desired to add ornamental designs, even of the most simple kind, this cord marking was generally smoothed down over that part of the surface to be treated, so that the figures imprinted or incised would have the advantage of an even ground.

USE OF CORDS IN IMPRINTING ORNAMENTAL PATTERNS

Growing out of the use of cord-wrapped tools in modeling and finishing the clay surfaces is a group of phenomena of great importance in

FIG. 45—Potsherds with stamped markings giving textile-like effects. One-half actual size.

the history of ceramic ornament. I refer to the imprinting of twisted cords, singly and in such relations and order as to produce ornamental effects or patterns. In its simplest use the cord was laid on and imprinted in a few lines around the shoulder or neck of the vessel. Elaborations of this use are imprintings which produce a great variety of simple geometric patterns, differing with the regions and the peoples. Connected or current fretwork and curved figures were not readily executed by this method, and are never seen. A few examples of cord-imprinted patterns are shown in figure 41. Hard-twisted cords were

a   b

FIG. 46—Modeling paddles with faces carved to imitate textile patterns.   One-haf actual size.

FIG. 47—Potsherds showing textile-like effect of finishing with engraved paddles.   About one-half actual size.

in most general use, but their markings were imitated in various ways, as by imprinting strings of beads and slender sticks or sinews wrapped with thread or other unwoven strands.

It would seem that the textile idea in decoration went beyond the imprinting of textiles and cords, and that textile markings were imitated in many ways, indicating possibly the association of ideas of a special traditional nature with the textile work and their perpetuation in ceramics by the imitation of textile characters. A few of these imitations

FIG. 48—Incised designs of textile character. About one-half actual size.

may be mentioned. In figure 42 is shown a small pot to which the appearance of a basket has been given by pinching up the plaster surface with the finger nails.

The notched wheel or roulette, restored in figure 40 b, was used in imitating cord-made patterns, and this was probably an outgrowth of the use of cord-covered malleating tools. This tool was confined rather closely to one great group of pottery, the so-called roulette-decorated ware of the Northwest. Its effective use is shown in figure 40 c, and in illustrations of the ware given in the sections treating of the pottery of the Northwest. The manner of using the implement is well illustrated in figure 43, where an improvised wheel has been inked and rocked back and forth on a sheet of paper. The potsherds shown in figure 44 illustrate these markings as applied by the ancient potters.

Decorative effects closely resembling those produced by the use of cords and the rocking tool were made by narrow, notched stamps applied to the plastic surface in the manner indicated in figure 45. Connecting directly with this simple stamp work, in which a succession of separate imprintings give the textile effects, is the use of the engraved modeling and decorating paddle, so common in the South Appalachian region.

Two Cherokee paddles with engraved surfaces are given in figure 46 *a* and *b*, and the effect of the use of similar implements is shown in figure 47. The sherds illustrated are from Florida mounds.

In figure 48 is presented a bit of ware from a New Jersey village site in which textile-like combinations of lines have been worked out with an incised tool.

Owing to the close association of these rouletted, stamped, and incised effects with the textile-imprinted groups of ware, I feel warranted in speaking of them as in general growing directly out of textile practices, although they are not necessarily always so connected, as the use of the stamp may in cases have arisen from the use of non-textile tools in modeling

It is thus seen from what has been said that the textile art has served in various ways to shape and modify the ceramic art, and the textile technic has bequeathed its geometric characters to the younger art, giving rise to most varied forms of embellishment, and no doubt profoundly affecting the later phases of its development.

POTTERY OF THE MIDDLE MISSISSIPPI VALLEY

In presenting a review of the several groups or varieties of earthenware it seems advisable to begin with that group most fully represented in our collections, as it will exhibit the widest range of those features and phenomena with which we must in all cases deal. By far the most complete in every essential is the great group of utensils representing the middle Mississippi valley region. The descriptions and illustrations of this group will serve as a basis of comparison in presenting all other groups, thus greatly facilitating and abbreviating the work.

Geographic Distribution

The geographic distribution of the ware of this group naturally receives first consideration. Apparently its greatest and most striking development centers about the contiguous portions of Arkansas, Missouri, Illinois, Kentucky, and Tennessee. The area covered is much greater, however, than would thus be indicated; its borders are extremely irregular, and are not as yet at all clearly defined. Typical specimens are found as far north as Chicago, as far northeast as

Pittsburg, and as far southeast as Augusta, Georgia. Closely related forms are found also along the Gulf of Mexico, from Tampa bay to the Rio Brazos. As a result of the segregation of the peoples of this vast province into social divisions—each more or less isolated and independent and all essentially sedentary—there are well-marked distinctions in the pottery found, and several subgroups may be recognized. The most pronounced of these are found, one in eastern Arkansas and western Tennessee, one in southeastern Missouri, one in the Cumberland valley, Tennessee, and a fourth in the lower Mississippi region. Others may be distinguished as collections are enlarged.

The pottery of this great group does not occupy exclusively any large area. Varieties of ware whose typical development is in other centers of habitation may be found in many places within its range. As to the occurrence of occasional specimens of this ware in remote localities, it may be remarked that there are many agencies that tend to distribute art products beyond their normal limit. These have been referred to in detail in the introductory pages. The accompanying map, plate IV, will assist in giving a general impression of the distribution and relative prevalence of this ware.

ETHNIC CONSIDERATIONS

It is not clearly apparent that a study of the distribution of this pottery will serve any important purpose in the settlement of purely ethnic questions. The matter is worthy of close attention, however, since facts that taken alone serve no definite purpose may supplement testimony acquired through other channels, and thus assist in establishing conclusions of importance with respect to tribal or family history.

It is clear that this ware was not made by one but by many tribes, and even by several linguistic families, and we may fairly assume that the group is regional or environmental rather than tribal or national. It is the product of conditions and limitations prevailing for a long time throughout a vast area of country. As to the modern representatives of the pottery-making peoples, we may very reasonably look to any or all of the tribes found occupying the general region when the whites came—Algonquian, Siouan, Muskhogean, Natchesan, and Caddoan.

With respect to the origin of this particular ceramic group we may surmise that it developed largely from the preceramic art of the region, although we must allow that exotic ideas probably crept in now and then to modify and improve it. That exotic features did migrate by one agency or another from Mexico is amply attested by various elements of form and technic found in the ceramic as well as in other arts.

I have sought by a study of the plastic representations of the human

face and figure to learn something of the physiognomy of the pottery-making peoples, but have sought without success. It is evident
that portraiture was rarely, if ever, attempted, and, contrary to what
might be expected, few of the greatly varied representations of faces
suggest strongly the Indian type of countenance.

Chronology

The pottery of this great province is wonderfully homogeneous in its
most essential characteristics, and we are not able to say by its appearance or character that any specimen is older or more primitive than
another. Exploration has been too unsystematic to enable us to reach
any safe conclusions respecting the comparative age of specimens
based on the manner of occurrence or relations to artificial or natural
deposits. There can be no reasonable doubt, however, that the manufacture of this ware began many centuries before the advent of the
white race; it is equally certain that the art was extensively practiced
until quite recent times. The early explorers of the valley witnessed
the manufacture, and the processes and the manner of use of the ware
are, as we have seen in a preceding section, described by several writers.
Notwithstanding the early introduction of metal vessels and other
utensils that naturally superseded those of clay, some of the tribes of
the province seem to have practiced the art continuously nearly to the
present day, and some of the pieces recovered from mounds and graves
are thought to suggest European models. It is certain, however, that
the art had reached its highest stage without the aid of civilized hands,
and in the study of its many interesting features we may feel assured
that we are dealing with essentially aboriginal ideas.

Preservation

It is generally admitted that there is no vital ethnic or other distinction between the pottery found in mounds, that found on village
sites, and that obtained from ordinary graves or stone cists. The condition of the mortuary ware varies with the quality of the terra cotta,
and with the conditions of its inhumation. Considering the porous
character of the paste and the great degree of moisture in the soil of
the Mississippi valley, the state of preservation of many of the vases
is remarkable. In some other sections of the country the pieces of
pottery were perforated or broken before their inhumation took place,
but such was not the practice in this province. The ware of village
sites and middens naturally is largely in fragments, and the plowing
of cemetery sites has broken up vast numbers of the mortuary vessels.

State of Culture of Makers

The simple life of these people is indicated by the absence of such
ceramic forms as lamps, whistles, bricks, and tiles, and by the rare

occurrence of other articles in common use with many barbaric nations. Clay pipes, so neatly shaped even in neighboring districts, are of very rude character over a large part of this district, as is shown in plate XXXIII, at the end of this section. The reason for this is not plain, since the potters of the middle and lower Mississippi region were in advance of all others in the eastern half of the United States in the manipulation of clay, as a comparative study of form, color, and decoration will amply show. In variety and refinement of form this ware excels perhaps even that of the ancient Pueblos, but in almost every other respect the fictile art of the latter was superior. There is nothing to indicate that the culture of the earlier occupants of the valley differed materially from that existing among the historic tribes of the same area.

USES

It is difficult to determine with precision the functions of the various forms of vessels in this group, or, for that matter, in any group where differentiation is well advanced. Certain varieties of rather plain and often rude vessels show traces of use over fire; these were doubtless for boiling and cooking, and for the manufacture of salt. They are usually recovered from midden sites and are in a fragmentary condition. Particular forms were probably intended for preparing and serving food, for storing, carrying, and containing water, oil, honey, salt, paint, fruit seeds, and all articles pertaining to domestic or ceremonial use. Nearly all the better finished and delicate vases are without marks of rough usage, and there can be little doubt that many of them were devoted to sacerdotal and mortuary uses, and that they were made expressly for these purposes. Vases of refined and unusual shape, carefully finished and ornamented, especially those decorated in color, were certainly not generally intended for ordinary domestic use.

Rarely an unusual shape is found suggesting manufacture for burial purposes, and the larger culinary vessels were at times devoted to the burial of children, and probably, also, to the burial of the bones of adults. The presence in the graves of unbaked vases, or what are believed to be such, and of figurines, miniature image vessels, and death's-head vases is suggestive of special making for mortuary use. Probably no other people north of the valley of Mexico has extended its ceramic field as widely as the southern mound-builders. The manufacture of images, toys, rattles, gaming disks, spool-shaped ear ornaments, labrets, beads, pipes, trowels, modeling tools, etc., indicate the widening range of the art.

MATERIALS AND MANUFACTURE

Materials and manufacture have been discussed in the introduction in such detail that little further need be said here. A few features

distinctive of the group may be noted. It is observed that the paste
varies in color from a light yellowish gray to dark grays and browns.
The light colors were used in vases to be decorated in color. The
paste is never vitreous, but is often well baked, firm, and tenacious.
Now and then a specimen is discovered that seems to have been sun-dried
only, disintegrating readily in water. It is not unusual to find examples
of vessels whose paste is quite porous and of low specific gravity.
This may be due partly to the use of combustible tempering matter or
to the decay of portions of the pulverized shell tempering. As a rule
the vases are of medium or heavy weight, and in some cases the walls
are quite thick, especially in the tall bottles.

In the better ware tempering materials were finely pulverized or
were used in comparatively small quantity. Coarse shell was used in
the ruder forms of domestic ware and for the so-called salt vessels.
Fragments of shell fully an inch in greatest dimension have been
observed in the latter ware. In exceptional cases, especially on the
outskirts of the area covered by the group, powdered quartz, mica,
and other minerals in large and sharp grains are observed. The paste
was manipulated after the fashion already indicated in the introductory
pages, and the firing was conducted, no doubt, in the usual primitive
ways. Traces of pottery kilns within the district have been reported,
but sufficient particulars have not been given to enable us to form a
definite notion of their character.

SURFACE FINISH

The finish, as compared with the work of civilized nations, is crude.
The surface was often simply hand-smoothed, while in cases it was
scarified or roughened by the finger nails or by modeling tools. Generally, however, it was more or less carefully polished by rubbing
with an implement of stone, shell, bone, or other suitable material,
the markings of these tools being distinctly visible. There is no reason for supposing that glazing was understood, although pieces having
partially vitrified surfaces are occasionally found. The surface was
often washed with a film of fine light-colored clay, which facilitated
the polishing, and in many cases a coat of thick red ocher was applied;
this also was polished down. The comparatively rare occurrence of
textile finish in the better wares may be due in a measure to the preference for polished or painted surfaces, in producing which original
texturings were necessarily obliterated, but it is also probable that
these potters had risen above the decidedly primitive textile stage
of the art.

COLOR

As has been indicated, the paste of this ware presents two marked
varieties of color—a dark hue, ranging from a rich black to all shades
of brown and gray, and a lighter series of tints comprising warm

ochery grays, rarely approaching the reddish or terra-cotta tones. It is possible that these differences of color were, to some extent, intentionally produced by regulation of the materials or methods of firing. This theory is confirmed by the fact that certain forms of vases are quite generally dark, while other forms are as uniformly light, the latter in nearly all cases having been finished in color or with designs in color.

FORM

RANGE

This ware exhibits great variety of outline, many forms being extremely pleasing. In this respect it is far superior to the other groups of the eastern United States. The vessels are perhaps more varied in shape than those of the Pueblo country, but are less diversified and elegant than those of Mexico, Central America, and Peru. They take a higher rank than the prehistoric wares of northern Europe, but, as a matter of course, lack the symmetry and refinement of outline that characterizes the wheel-made pottery of Mediterranean countries. As the vessels are grouped by forms later, in presenting the illustrations, it is unnecessary to make further reference to this topic here, save to call attention to the accompanying plates of outlines (plates v, vi, and vii), which give in a connected series the full range of form of this group.

ESTHETIC MODIFICATIONS

It can hardly be maintained that the ancient peoples of this region had a very refined appreciation of elegance of outline, yet there are many modifications of shape that indicate a taste for higher types of beauty and a constant attempt to realize them. There is also a very decided leaning toward the grotesque. To such an extreme have the dictates of fancy been followed in this respect that utility, the true and original office of the utensil, has often taken a secondary place, although it has never or rarely been entirely lost sight of. Bowls have been fashioned into the shape of birds, fishes, reptiles, and shells, and vases and bottles into a multitude of animal and vegetal forms, without much apparent regard for convenience. Much of this imitative and imaginative art is undoubtedly the direct offspring of mythologic conceptions and superstitious practices and is thus symbolic rather than esthetic; but it seems to me highly probable that pure fancy, mere playfulness, had a place, as in more southern countries, in the creation of unusual forms.

ANIMAL FORMS

The portrayal of animal forms in one art or another was almost universal among the American aborigines, but with these middle Mis-

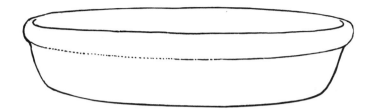

a, USUAL FORM OF LARGE SALT VESSELS OR VATS

b, FRAGMENT OF LARGE SALT VESSEL, SHOWING CORD IMPRESSIONS

c, FRAGMENTS OF SALT VESSEL FROM "SULPHUR SPRING," NASHVILLE, TENNESSEE
(THRUSTON COLLECTION, DIAMETER ABOUT 31 INCHES, HEIGHT 12 INCHES)

EARTHEN VESSELS USED IN SALT MAKING
MIDDLE MISSISSIPPI VALLEY GROUP

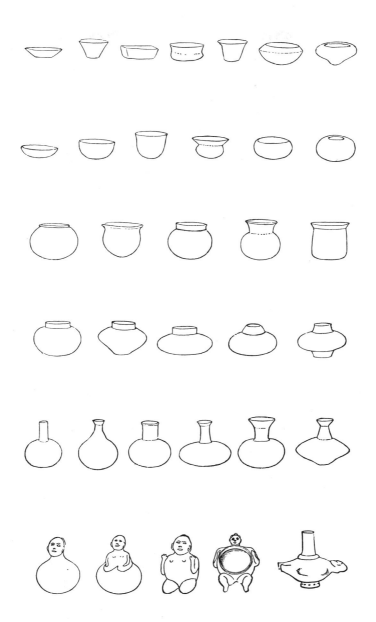

SERIES OF OUTLINES INDICATING RANGE OF FORM OF VASES
MIDDLE MISSISSIPPI VALLEY GROUP

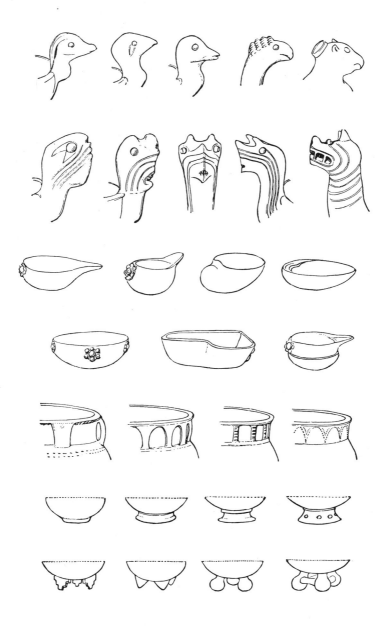

SERIES OF OUTLINES SHOWING VARIOUS FEATURES OF VASE
ELABORATION

MIDDLE MISSISSIPPI VALLEY GROUP

VASES OF COMPOUND FORM

MIDDLE MISSISSIPPI VALLEY GROUP

sissippi valley peoples it was more prevalent, perhaps, than elsewhere. Not only are many animal forms recognizably represented, but a considerable number of the grotesque shapes already referred to probably originated in representation of animals.

ORNAMENT

The ancient potter of the middle Mississippi valley province gave particular attention to the embellishment of his ware, and the results are much more varied and mature than those of the northern and eastern sections. Nearly all methods known in the country were employed, but the higher types of linear and plastic design prevailed much more fully here than elsewhere.

The method of execution was usually by incision, a more or less sharp point being used. Finger-nail marking and indentation with a point were favorite decorations, and ridges and nodes were set on in decorative arrangements. Decoration in color was common in this province, though rare in others. The colors used in painting were white, red, brown, and black, and generally consisted of clays, white or tinted with iron oxides. Occasionally the colors used seem to have been mere stains—possibly of vegetal origin. All were probably laid on with coarse brushes of hair, feathers, or vegetal fiber. The color designs are in most cases quite simple, and are applied in broad, bold lines. The figures are, to a great extent, curvilinear, and embrace meanders, scrolls, circles, and combinations and groupings of curved lines in great variety. Rectilinear forms, lozenges, guilloches, zigzags, checkers, crosses, and stellar forms are usual, and the stepped figures so characteristic of Pueblo work are sometimes seen.

The decided prevalence of curved forms is worthy of remark. With all their fertility of invention, the inhabitants of this valley seem not to have achieved the rectangular linked meander, or anything more nearly approaching it than the current scroll or the angular guilloche, while with other peoples, such as the Pueblos of the Southwest and the ancient nations of Mexico and Peru, it was a favorite device. The reasons for this, as well as for other peculiarities of the decorative art of the province as embodied in pottery, must be sought in the antecedent and coexistent arts of the province. These peoples were probably not so highly accomplished in the textile arts as were the Pueblos, and had not felt the influence of advanced architecture as had the Mexicans. The practice of highly developed forms of these arts gives rise to and encourages angular geometric styles of decoration.

DISTINGUISHING CHARACTERS OF THE GROUP

If asked to point out the one feature of this ware by which it could most readily be distinguished from all other groups, I should select the bottle shape as the most satisfactory. There is no group of primitive ware in America, save possibly in Peru, in which the slender-necked carafe or decanter-like bottle is so marked a feature. In most of the native groups it is unknown. This, however, is not the only marked characteristic of the ware. The range of shape is very wide, and several features are strikingly unique. There are many effigy vases of remarkable character; of these may be mentioned those representing hunchback human beings, cups or vases imitating heads of men and beasts and grotesque, nondescript creatures or conceptions. Again, the use of color in surface finish and decoration is a strong characteristic of the ware. Colored ware is found in many sections, especially in the South, but in no other part of the region considered in this paper was color so generally or so fully applied to the execution of ornamental designs and realistic delineations, as in depicting wings and feathers of birds, spots of animals, costume on human figures, and in effigy vases even the color of hair, skin and face-paint—features of decoration practically unknown elsewhere in the area considered. Head-shaped vases are rather rare in North America, although common in Peru. Excellent examples are found in the center of the Middle Mississippi province, and in cases are so well modeled as to have lead to the suggestion that they may be actual casts from the human face.

SOURCES OF INFORMATION

Owing to the wide range of form and character exhibited by the vessels of this group it will be impossible fully to illustrate them within the limits of this paper. The student may, in a great measure, supply the need for fuller illustration by referring to the following works: Explorations of the Aboriginal Remains of Tennessee, by Joseph Jones, Washington, 1876; Reports of the Peabody Museum, by F. W. Putnam; and Antiquities of Tennessee, by General Gates P. Thruston. These works for the most part illustrate the ware of Tennessee. Edward Evers, in Contributions to the Archeology of Missouri, presents a large number of vases of the southeast Missouri district; and an extended series of illustrations of the wares of Arkansas was published in the Fourth Annual Report of the Bureau of Ethnology.

EXAMPLES

The illustrations brought together in the accompanying plates comprise examples of almost every type of the earthenware of this province, but they still fail to give a satisfactory idea of the very wide range of form and ornament.

PLATTERS, CUPS, AND BOWLS

Platters and bowl-shaped vessels exhibit great diversity of size, shape, and ornament. In size they range from less than 1 inch in diameter and depth to upward of 20 inches in diameter and a foot or more in depth.   If we include under this head the so-called salt pans, described in the introduction, the greatest diameter will reach perhaps 40 inches.   In material, color, and surface finish they are generally uniform with vessels of other classes.   Their uses were doubtless chiefly domestic.

Many of these bowls are simply segments of spheres, and vary from a shallow platter to a hollow, perforated globe.   Others have elongated, compressed, or conic bodies, with round or flattened bases. The horizontal outline or section may be round, oval, waved, rectangular, or irregular.   Some have flattish projections at opposite sides or ends, imitating a common form of wooden tray or basin.   Stands and legs are but rarely attached; handles, except those of grotesque character, are rarely seen.   A dipper or ladle shape is encountered now and then.

The ornamentation of bowls was accomplished in a variety of ways. Rim modifications constitute an important feature.   In section the margin or lip is square, oblique, round, or grooved.   The scallop was often employed, and notched and terraced forms, resembling the sacred meal bowls of Zuni, are not uncommon.   Relief ornaments such as fillets and nodes and various horizontal projections were also employed, and pleasing effects were produced by the use of incised lines and indentations.

The potter was not satisfied with these varied forms of decoration, and his fancy led him to add embellishments of elaborate and extraordinary character.   The nodes and ridges were enlarged and prolonged and fashioned after a hundred natural and fanciful forms. Shapes of shells, fish, birds, beasts, human and imaginary creatures were utilized in a multitude of ways.   Especial attention was given to the heads of animals.   These were modeled in the round and attached to the rim or side, while other parts of the animal were placed upon different portions of the vessel.

The body of the bowl was somewhat less profusely ornamented than the rim.   The interior as well as the exterior received painted, relieved, and intaglio designs.   In the painted bowls the favorite idea for the interior was a series of volutes, in broad lines, radiating from the center of the basin.   Groups of festooned lines, either painted or engraved, and arranged to give the effect of imbricated scales, formed also a favorite motive.   The exterior surface of the incurved rims of globular vessels offered a tempting surface to the artist and was often tastefully decorated in varied styles.

As a rule the bowls and platters of this region are fairly uniform in material, surface finish, and decorative treatment with the other vessels of the region.   A somewhat unique group of bowls was obtained from a small domiciliary mound near Arkansas Post, Arkansas, two illustrations appearing in plate VIII *g* and *h*. The most striking characteristic of these vessels is their ornament, which embodies some unusual combinations of lines deeply and rather boldly incised. Many of the pieces are new-looking, but a small number have been blackened by use over fire. The hemispheric shape is most common, although there are some shallow forms, and a few of the vessels have flaring rims. The paste is yellowish and the surface is roughly finished. A very large percentage of shell has been used in tempering. Other bowls of simple though varied form, and having a variety of incised decorations, are shown in the same plate. All are from graves or mounds in Arkansas, except *e* and *f*, which are from a mound in southeastern Missouri.

A second group of bowls is given in plate IX. All these are from Arkansas except *b*, which is from a contiguous locality in Missouri. An exceptionally fine piece of work is illustrated in *e*. An example of the deep cauldron-like boiling vessels found in some sections is presented in plate X *a*. A curious casket used for burying the bones of a child is given in plate X *b*. It is preserved in the collection of the Davenport Academy of Sciences, and was found in a grave at Hales point, Tennessee. One of the largest examples ever recovered in a complete state is shown in plate X *c*. It was obtained from a mound in Jefferson county, Missouri, and is 29½ inches in diameter. Most of these specimens have been described in the annual reports of the Bureau of Ethnology.

POTS

Plate XI serves to illustrate a very large class of wide-mouthed vessels of pot-like character. They are generally darkened by use over fire, and more than any other form probably served as ordinary culinary utensils. The size varies from that of a drinking cup to that of a cauldron of 15 or 20 gallons capacity. Two large and fine specimens are given in plate XII. The frequent occurrence of strong handles confirms the theory of their use for boiling and handling food. The specimens illustrated are from Tennessee and Arkansas.

The rims of these vessels were modified for decorative purposes very much as are the rims of the bowls. The bodies are sometimes elaborately ornamented, mostly with incised figures, but often with punctures, nodes, and ribs. The incised lines, curved and straight, are arranged to form simple patterns encircling the upper part of the vessel. The punctures, made with a sharp point, form encircling lines and various carelessly executed patterns. A rude sort of ornamentation was produced by pinching up the soft clay of the surface between the nails of the fingers and thumb. Relief ornament consists chiefly of applied fillets of clay arranged to form vertical ribs. Rows of nodes are sometimes seen, and in a few cases the whole body is covered with rude nodes or spines (see plate XI).

a (ARKANSAS, DAVENPORT ACADEMY
COLLECTION, ONE-THIRD)

b (ARKANSAS, DIAMETER OF BOWL 6 INCHES)

c (ARKANSAS, DAVENPORT ACADEMY
COLLECTION, ONE-THIRD)

d (ARKANSAS, LENGTH 8¾ INCHES)

e (MISSOURI, DIAMETER 5¾ INCHES)

g (ARKANSAS, DIAMETER 11¼ INCHES)

f (MISSOURI, DIAMETER 6 INCHES)

h (ARKANSAS, DIAMETER 12¾ INCHES)

CUPS AND BOWLS

MIDDLE MISSISSIPPI VALLEY GROUP

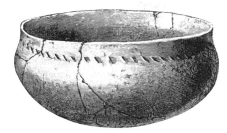

b (MISSOURI, DIAMETER 8¼ INCHES)

a (AKANSAS, DIAMETER 7 INCHES)

c (ARKANSAS, DIAMETER 8 INCHES)

l (ARKANSAS, DAVENPORT ACADEMY COLLECTION,
ONE-THIRD)

e (ARKANSAS, LENGTH 14 INCHES)

f (ARKANSAS, DAVENPORT ACADEMY COLLECTION,
ONE-THIRD)

g (ARKANSAS, DIAMETER 10¼ INCHES)

CUPS AND BOWLS
MIDDLE MISSISSIPPI VALLEY GROUP

a (ARKANSAS, DIAMETER 19 INCHES)

b (TENNESSEE, DAVENPORT ACADEMY COLLECTION, ONE-FOURTH)

c (MISSOURI, M. C. LONG COLLECTION, DIAMETER 29½ INCHES)

LARGE BOWL, BURIAL CASKET, AND CALDRON

MIDDLE MISSISSIPPI VALLEY GROUP

a (TENNESSEE, DAVENPORT ACADEMY
COLLECTION, ONE-THIRD)

b (ARKANSAS, DAVENPORT ACADEMY
COLLECTION, ONE-THIRD)

c (ARKANSAS, DAVENPORT ACADEMY
COLLECTION, ONE-THIRD)

e (ARKANSAS, DAVENPORT
ACADEMY COLLECTION,
ONE-THIRD)

d (ALABAMA (?), DAVENPORT ACAD-
EMY COLLECTION, ONE-THIRD)

f (ARKANSAS, DAVENPORT ACADEMY
COLLECTION, ONE-THIRD)

g (ARKANSAS, DAVENPORT ACAD-
EMY COLLECTION, ONE-THIRD)

h (ARKANSAS DAVENPORT ACADEMY COLLECTION, ONE-THIRD)

i (MISSOURI, DIAMETER 4¼ INCHES)

COOKING POTS, ETC.

MIDDLE MISSISSIPPI VALLEY GROUP

a (TENNESSEE, DAVENPORT ACADEMY COLLECTION, ONE-THIRD)

b (ARKANSAS, DAVENPORT ACADEMY COLLECTION, ONE-THIRD)

LARGE COOKING POTS
MIDDLE MISSISSIPPI VALLEY GROUP

a (ARKANSAS, DAVENPORT ACADEMY COLLECTION,
ONE-THIRD)

b (ARKANSAS, DAVENPORT ACADEMY COLLECTION,
ONE-THIRD)

d (ARKANSAS, HEIGHT 7 INCHES)

c (ARKANSAS, HEIGHT 8 INCHES)

e (ARKANSAS, DAVENPORT ACADEMY COLLECTION,
ONE-THIRD)

f (ARKANSAS, DIAMETER 9 INCHES)

BOTTLES

MIDDLE MISSISSIPPI VALLEY GROUP

BOTTLES

Of all the forms of vessels found in this province the bottle is the most varied and interesting, and is more suggestive of the advanced taste of the potter than is any other class of vessel. In plate XIII some fine examples of bottles are shown. Two neat specimens are illustrated in *a* and *b*. The surface finish is excellent in both cases. The lines of the figures are carefully drawn, and seem to have been produced by trailing a smooth, rather blunt point, under even pressure. It is difficult to get a line so even and nicely finished by simple incision or by excavating the clay. The design in *a* consists of groups of curved lines arranged in pairs, which are separated by plain vertical bands. It might be considered an interrupted or imperfectly connected form of the running scroll. This grouping of lines is frequently met in the decorative designs of the southern states. The design on the other vase, *b*, is still more characteristic of the South. It consists of an encircling row of round, shallow indentations, about which are linked series of imperfectly developed incised scrolls, and of two additional rows of depressions, one above and the other below, through which parallel lines are drawn. The handome vase shown in *c* was obtained, along with many other fine specimens, from mounds near Little Rock, Arkansas. It is of the dark polished ware with the usual fire mottlings. The form is symmetric and graceful. The neck is ornamented with a band of incised chevrons, and the sloping upper surface of the body is encircled by a series of stepped figures engraved in the plastic clay. The vessel shown in *d* has a wide annular base and a body apparently compounded of a large flattish form and a smaller kettle-like form set upon it. The latter is furnished with handles and decorated with encircling lines of indentations. The vessel shown in *e* may be taken as a type of a very large class. It is most readily described as a short-necked, widemouthed bottle. It is symmetric and nicely finished. The lip is supplied with a narrow horizontal rim. The body expands somewhat abruptly from the base of the upright neck to the squarish shoulder, and contracts below in an even curve, giving a hemispheric base. We have in *f* a good example of a class of bottle-shaped vessels, the necks of which are wide and short and the bodies much compressed vertically. It is a handome vase, symmetric, quite dark in color, and highly polished. The upper surface of the body is ornamented with a collar formed of a broad fillet of clay, or rather of two fillets, the pointed ends of which come together on opposite sides of the vase.

As skilled as these people were in modeling life forms and in engraving geometric devices, they seem rarely to have attempted the linear representation of life forms. We have, however, a few good examples of such work. The engraved design covering the body of a small vase, figure 49, is one of the most remarkable ever obtained from the mounds.　It consists of two winged and crested rattlesnakes which encircle the expanded part of the vessel, and of two sunflower-like figures alternating with them.　These designs are carefully engraved with a needle-like point and are adjusted to the form of the vase in a way that suggests forethought and experience and an

Fig. 49—Bottle decorated with serpent designs, Arkansas.　Three-fourths actual size.

appreciation of the decorative value of the figures.　By dint of rubbings, photographs, and sketches, a complete drawing of the various figures has been obtained, and they are given in figure 50 on a scale of about one-third actual size.　The rosette figures probably represent the sun.　There can be little doubt that the figures of this design are derived from the mythologic art of the people.

Fig. 50—Winged serpents and sun symbols from the vase illustrated in figure 49.

The ancient potter of the central districts did not venture, save in very rare cases, to delineate the human figure graphically, and such attempts as have come to hand do not do much credit to the artistic capacity of the people.　A specimen is shown in figure 51, the four figures in simple lines occupying the periphery of the body of a large plain bottle of the usual dark-colored ware of eastern Arkansas.

In plate XIV we have selections from the very large group of high-necked bottles. The piece shown in *a* is a good illustration of a type of form common to Missouri and Arkansas. The neck is high and cylindric and the body resembles a slightly flattened globe. Set about the shoulder are four medallion-like faces, the features of which are modeled roughly in low relief. The ware is of the ordinary dark, slightly polished variety. There are few vases from the mound region more pleasing in appearance than that shown in *b*. It is a black, well-polished bottle with neck expanding below and body peculiarly flattened beneath. The body is encircled by a band of chaste and elaborate scroll work.

A handsome bottle-shaped vase with flaring lip is shown in *c*. The neck widens toward the base and the body is subglobular, being slightly conical above and rather abruptly expanded at the periphery. The

FIG. 51—Bottle ornamented with four engraved human figures, Arkansas. One-fifth actual size.

surface is only moderately smooth. The body is ornamented with a handsome design of incised lines, which consists of a scroll pattern, divided into four sections by perpendicular lines.

The vase shown in *d* is compound, and represents a bottle set within the mouth of a pot. The neck is high, wide, and flaring, and rests on the back of a rudely-modeled frog, which lies extended on the upper surface of the body. The notched encircling ridge, beneath the feet of the creature, represents the rim of the lower vessel, which is a pot with compressed globular body and short, wide neck. This vase is of the dark, dead-surfaced ware and is quite plain. Four vertical ridges take the place of handles.

One of the most striking of the bottle-shaped vases is shown in *e*. It is symmetric, well-proportioned, and well-finished. The color is dark and the surface is roughened by a multitude of pits which have resulted from the decay of shell particles used for tempering. The paste crumbles to a brownish dust when struck or pressed forcibly. The most remarkable feature of the piece is the broad, convex, hood-like collar that encircles the neck and spreads out over the body like an inverted saucer. This collar is curiously wrought in incised lines and low ridges, by means of which grotesque faces, suggesting owls, are produced. The eyes are readily detected, being indicated by low knobs with central pits, each surrounded by three concentric circles. They are arranged in pairs on opposite sides. Between the eyes of each pair an incipient nose and mouth may be made out. The face is outlined below by the lower edge of the collar and above by a low indented ridge crossing the collar tangent to the base of the neck. The most expanded part of the body is encircled by an incised pattern consisting of five sets of partially interlocked scrolls.

A step in differentiation of form is illustrated in the vessels presented in plate xv. A flat bottom would serve to keep a tall bottle in an upright position on a hard, level floor, but a ring was still better, and could be added without deformation of the vessel. Annular bands of varying heights and shapes were used, several forms being illustrated in this plate.

The tripod afforded even better support than the ring, and had come into common use with these people; four legs, in imitation of the legs of quadrupeds, were occasionally employed. The form of these supports is extremely varied, and some of the more usual types are illustrated in plate xvi. The first, *a*, is a large-necked, rather clumsy vessel of ordinary workmanship, which rests on three globular legs. These are hollow, and the cavities connect with that of the body of the vessel. The whole surface is well polished and dark in color.

The vessel depicted in *b* has a number of noteworthy features. It resembles the preceding in shape with the exception of the legs, which are flat, and have stepped or terraced margins. The whole surface of the vessel is a warm gray, and is decorated with characteristic designs in red and white. A stepped figure encircles the neck, and semicircular figures in white appear on opposite sides at the top and base. The body is covered with scroll work in broad, red lines, the spaces being filled in with white. Each leg is half red and half white. The bottle *c* is from Missouri, and is of the plain dark ware. The specimen shown in *d* is finished in plain red.

For the purpose of conveying an idea of the great variety of shape characterizing the simple bottles of this group and the boldness of the painted decoration the series presented in plate xvii have been assembled. The four pieces in the first group are of the plain, dark ware and have annular bases. Those of the second group are supported on tripods; the series beneath shows variations in the form of the body; and the specimens in the third line illustrate the use of designs in white, red, and black.

ECCENTRIC AND COMPOUND FORMS

Three vessels are shown in plate xviii *a*, *b*, and *c* which in form resemble the common teapot. The specimen shown in *b* is well made and carefully finished. A spout is placed on one side of the body and a low knob on the other. The latter is not a handle but represents, rather, the head of an animal. These characters are repeated in most of the specimens of this type that have come to my notice. Two small circular depressions occur on the sides of the vessel alternating with the spout and the knob, and these four features form centers about which are traced four volutes connecting around the vessel. In

b (ARKANSAS, HEIGHT 7 INCHES)

c (ARKANSAS, HEIGHT 9 INCHES)

a (ARKANSAS, DAVENPORT ACADEMY
COLLECTION, ONE-THIRD)

d (ARKANSAS, DAVENPORT ACADEMY
COLLECTION, ONE-THIRD)

e (ARKANSAS, HEIGHT 10½ INCHES)

BOTTLES
MIDDLE MISSISSIPPI VALLEY GROUP

a (ARKANSAS, HEIGHT 8 INCHES)

b (ARKANSAS, DAVENPORT ACADEMY
COLLECTION, ONE-THIRD)

c (ARKANSAS, DAVENPORT ACADEMY COLLECTION,
ONE-THIRD)

d (ARKANSAS HEIGHT 7½ INCHES)

BOTTLES

MIDDLE MISSISSIPPI VALLEY GROUP

a (ARKANSAS, DAVENPORT ACADEMY COLLECTION,
ONE-THIRD)

b (ARKANSAS, DAVENPORT ACADEMY COLLECTION,
ONE-THIRD)

c (MISSOURI, HEIGHT 9½ INCHES)

d (MISSOURI, HEIGHT 8½ INCHES)

BOTTLES
MIDDLE MISSISSIPPI VALLEY GROUP

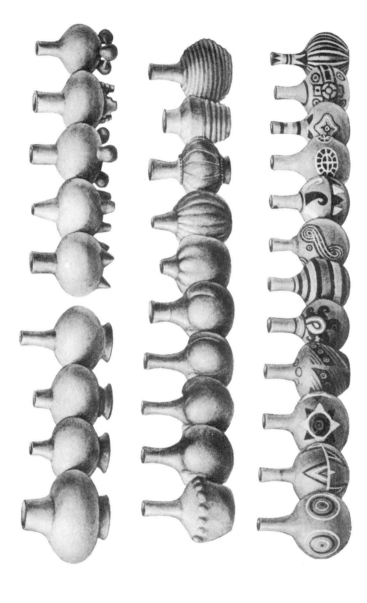

VARIOUS FORMS OF BOTTLES

MIDDLE MISSISSIPPI VALLEY GROUP

a (ARKANSAS, HEIGHT 3¾ INCHES)

d (ARKANSAS, DAVENPORT ACADEMY COLLECTION, ONE-THIRD)

b (ARKANSAS, DAVENPORT ACADEMY
COLLECTION, ONE-THIRD)

c (ARKANSAS, HEIGHT 4 INCHES)

e (ARKANSAS, DIAMETER 7 INCHES)

f (ARKANSAS, DAVENPORT ACADEMY
COLLECTION, ONE-THIRD)

BOTTLES OF ECCENTRIC SHAPE

MIDDLE MISSISSIPPI VALLEY GROUP

c (MISSOURI, DIAMETER 4 INCHES)

a (MISSOURI, DIAMETER 5 INCHES)

d (ARKANSAS, DAVENPORT ACADEMY
COLLECTION, ONE-THIRD)

b (MISSOURI, LENGTH 5¼ INCHES)

e (MISSOURI, LENGTH 7¼ INCHES)

f (ARKANSAS, HEIGHT 5 INCHES)

g (ARKANSAS, HEIGHT 7 INCHES)

VESSELS IMITATING SHELL AND GOURD FORMS
MIDDLE MISSISSIPPI VALLEY GROUP

a fine red piece from Mississippi, now in the National Museum collection (plate XL b), the knob is replaced by the head of a turtle or other reptile and the spout becomes the creature's tail. In connection with the teapot-like vessels it will be well to describe another novel form not wholly unlike them in appearance, an example being shown in d, plate XVIII. The shoulder is elongated on opposite sides into two curved, horn-like cones, which give to the body a somewhat crescent-shaped outline. The vessel is of the ordinary plain, dark ware and has had an annular base which is now broken away.

Vases with arched handles, like those shown in e and f, are quite common. In some cases the handle is enlarged and the body reduced until the vessel assumes the appearance of a ring. Similar forms are common in other parts of the American continent, especially in Peru.

Vases of compound form are of frequent occurrence in this region. A number of examples in outline have been assembled for convenience of comparison in plate VII, and many others could be added.

LIFE FORMS

Clay vessels imitating in form marine and fresh-water shells are occasionally obtained from the mounds and graves of the Mississippi valley. The conch shell appears to have been a favorite model, especially as modified for a drinking cup by the removal of one side of the walls and all the interior parts (plate XIX, a and b). A two-story cup of the same class is shown in c. The clam shell is also imitated. The more conventional forms assumed by these vessels are especially interesting as illustrating the varied ways in which life forms modify the normal conventional shapes of vessels, thus widening the range of the art.[a]

A very good illustration of this class of vessel is given in d. It is evidently intended to imitate a trimmed conch shell. The apex and a few of the surrounding nodes are shown at the right, while the base or spine forms a projecting lip at the left. A coil of clay forms the apex, and is carried outward in a sinistral spiral to the noded shoulder. Excellent examples in clay, imitating clam shells, are illustrated in General Thruston's work on the Antiquities of Tennessee, plate VI (plate XLVII of this paper).

In many countries the shape of earthen vessels has been profoundly influenced by vegetal forms and especially by the hard shells of fruits.[b] The gourd, the squash, and the cocoanut are reproduced with great frequency. In many cases the shape of the body of vases not at once suggesting derivation from such forms may finally be traced to them. Thus the lobed bottles of Tennessee probably owe their chief characteristic to a lobed form of the gourd. In plate XIX f and g

---

[a] For studies of shell vessels and their influence on ceramic forms, see Second Annual Report, Bureau of Ethnology, p. 192, and Fourth Annual Report, Bureau of Ethnology, pp. 384 and 454.

[b] This subject is discussed in a paper on form and ornament in the ceramic art, Fourth Annual Report, Bureau of Ethnology, p. 446.

two examples of gourd-shaped vessels from Arkansas are given. The Tennessee forms are fully illustrated by General Thruston (work cited).

Plates XX, XXI, XXII are intended to illustrate the treatment of animal forms by the ancient potter. The animals imitated cover a wide range, including probably a large percentage of the more important creatures of the Mississippi valley. The manner of applying the forms to the vessel is also extremely varied, making a detailed account quite impossible. The degree of realism is far from uniform. In many cases birds, fishes, and quadrupeds are modeled with such fidelity that a particular species is forcibly suggested, but the larger number of the imitations are rude and unsatisfactory. Many forms are grotesque, sometimes intentionally so. In plate XX are several illustrations of the manner of applying bird forms to the elaboration and embellishment of bowls. Specimens *a* and *b* are from southeastern Missouri. The peculiar form of head seen in *a* is found all over the lower Mississippi and Gulf regions, while the example *c* has the head turned inward, and resembles a vulture or buzzard. In *d* two heads are attached, both grotesque, but having features suggestive of birds. A finely modeled and finished bird-shaped bottle is shown in *e*. It is finished in red, black, and white, the wings being striped with red and white. The heads in *b* and *f* appear to have human features, but it is not improbable that the conception was of a bird or at most of a bird-man compound.

A very striking specimen is shown in plate XXI*a*, the neck of the bird being unusually prolonged. In *b* the bird is placed on its back, the head and feet forming the handles of the vessel. The wings are rudely represented by incised lines on the body of the vessel. Other bird forms are shown in plate XXII. The delineation of the painted specimen *c* is unusually realistic, and the general appearance recalls very forcibly the painted owl vases of the Tusayan tribes and the more ancient occupants of the valley of the Rio Colorado.

The usual manner of treating forms of fish is shown in plate XXIII *a*, *b*, and *c*. The exceptional application of the fish form to a bottle is illustrated in *d*. The frog or toad was a favorite subject for the aboriginal potter, and two ordinary examples are presented in *e* and *f*. The originals of *g* and *h* are not readily made out.

The use of mammalian forms in vase elaboration is illustrated in plates XXIV and XXV. There can be but little doubt that the potter had a deer in mind when plate XXIV*a* was modeled, while *b* suggests the opossum. But the originals for the specimens presented in plate XXV are not readily identified, and the head in *e* is decidedly grotesque, although it is not impossible that the particular species of animal intended in this and in other cases may finally be made out.

Plates XXVI, XXVII, and XXVIII serve to illustrate some of the varied methods of employing the human figure in ceramic art. In plate XXVI five bottles are shown; *a* represents the entire figure, and *b* the entire

a (MISSOURI, DIAMETER 8 INCHES)

b (MISSOURI, DIAMETER 4¼ INCHES)

c (ARKANSAS, DAVENPORT ACADEMY COLLECTION,
ONE-THIRD)

e (ARKANSAS, DAVENPORT ACADEMY
COLLECTION, ONE-THIRD)

d (ARKANSAS, DAVENPORT ACADEMY COLLECTION, ONE-THIRD)

f (ARKANSAS, DAVENPORT ACADEMY COLLEC-
TION, ONE-THIRD)

BOWLS IMITATING BIRD FORMS
MIDDLE MISSISSIPPI VALLEY GROUP

a (ARKANSAS, DAVENPORT ACADEMY COLLECTION, ONE-THIRD)

c (MISSOURI, LENGTH 2 INCHES)

b (ARKANSAS, DAVENPORT ACADEMY COLLECTION, ONE-THIRD)

VESSELS IMITATING BIRD FORMS
MIDDLE MISSISSIPPI VALLEY GROUP

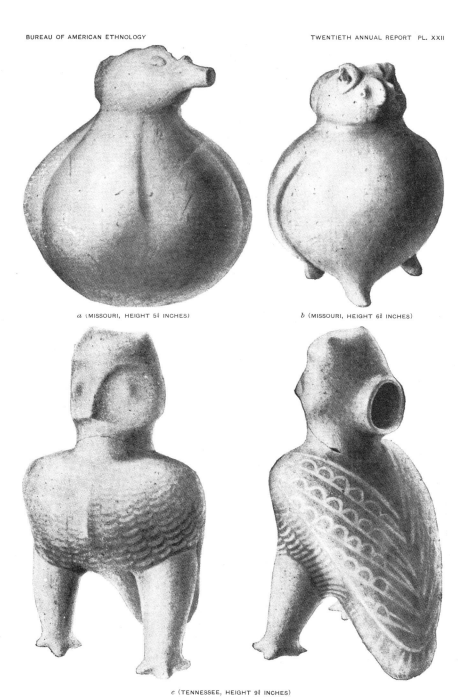

a (MISSOURI, HEIGHT 5⅞ INCHES)

b (MISSOURI, HEIGHT 6⅞ INCHES)

c (TENNESSEE, HEIGHT 9⅞ INCHES)

VESSELS IMITATING BIRD FORMS
MIDDLE MISSISSIPPI VALLEY GROUP

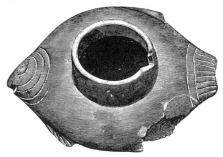

a (ARKANSAS, DAVENPORT ACADEMY COLLECTION,
ONE-THIRD)

b (MISSOURI, LENGTH 7¾ INCHES)

c (MISSOURI, LENGTH 8 INCHES)

d (ARKANSAS, DIAMETER 3¼ INCHES)

e (ARKANSAS, DAVENPORT ACADEMY COLLECTION,
ONE-THIRD)

g (ARKANSAS. DAVENPORT ACADEMY COL-
LECTION, ONE-THIRD)

f (MISSOURI, DIAMETER 5¼ INCHES)

h (ARKANSAS, DAVENPORT ACADEMY COLLECTION,
ONE-THIRD)

VESSELS IMITATING FISH AND BATRACHIAN FORMS
MIDDLE MISSISSIPPI VALLEY GROUP

a (ARKANSAS, DAVENPORT ACADEMY COLLECTION, ONE-THIRD)

b (ARKANSAS, DAVENPORT ACADEMY COLLECTION, ONE-THIRD)

VESSELS IMITATING ANIMAL FORMS
MIDDLE MISSISSIPPI VALLEY GROUP

a (ARKANSAS, DAVENPORT
ACADEMY COLLECTION,
ONE-THIRD)

e (ARKANSAS, DAVENPORT ACADEMY COLLECTION, ONE-THIRD)

b (TENNESSEE, DAVENPORT
ACADEMY COLLECTION,
ONE-THIRD)

f (ARKANSAS, DAVENPORT ACADEMY COLLECTION, ONE-THIRD)

c (ARKANSAS, DAVENPORT ACADEMY
COLLECTION, ONE-THIRD)

d (ARKANSAS, DAVENPORT ACADEMY COL-
LECTION, ONE-THIRD)

g (ARKANSAS, LENGTH 10¼ INCHES)

VESSELS IMITATING ANIMAL FORMS
MIDDLE MISSISSIPPI VALLEY GROUP

a (MISSOURI, HEIGHT 5¼ INCHES)

c (ARKANSAS, DAVENPORT ACADEMY COLLECTION, ONE-THIRD)

d (ARKANSAS, DAVENPORT ACADEMY
COLLECTION, ONE-THIRD)

b (MISSOURI, HEIGHT 9½ INCHES)

e (ARKANSAS, DAVENPORT ACADEMY
COLLECTION, ONE-THIRD)

VESSELS IMITATING THE HUMAN FORM
MIDDLE MISSISSIPPI VALLEY GROUP

a (MISSOURI, EVERS COLLECTION, HEIGHT 6 INCHES)

c (TENNESSEE, HEIGHT 7¾ INCHES)

c (ARKANSAS, DIAMETER 5¾ INCHES)

d (ARKANSAS, LENGTH 11 INCHES)

b (ARKANSAS, WIDTH 7 INCHES)

f (ARKANSAS, HEIGHT 8¾ INCHES)

VESSELS IMITATING THE HUMAN FORM
MIDDLE MISSISSIPPI VALLEY GROUP

figure seated upon the globular body of the vessel, while *c* and *d* are average examples of the hunchback figures so common in the art of this region. It seems probable that persons suffering from this class of deformity were regarded as having certain magic powers or attributes. A small blackish bottle, capped with a rudely modeled human head, is illustrated in *e*. The opening in all of these figurines is at the top or back of the head.

A number of novel forms are given in plate XXVII. In *a* the heavy figure of a man extended at full length forms the body of the bottle. The treatment of the figure is much the same in *b*, and other forms are shown in *c*, *d*, *e*, and *f*. A very interesting specimen is shown in plate XXVIII. The figure represents a woman potter in the act of modeling a vase.

In plate XLIII we have two examples of the remarkable head vases, probably mortuary utensils, found in considerable numbers in graves in eastern Arkansas and contiguous sections of other states. The faces have been covered with a whitish wash well rubbed down, the remainder of the surface being red. Fuller descriptive details are given in preceding pages and in the Fourth Annual Report of the Bureau of Ethnology. Additional specimens are shown in plates XXIX, XXX, XXXI, and XXXII. Specimen *a* of plate XXIX has two owl-like faces modeled in low relief on opposite sides of the body, and *b* is embellished with a well-suggested human mask painted white and having closed eyes. The striking vessel presented in *c* and in plate XLIII *b* and plate XXX serves well as a type of the mortuary death's-head vases, and the various illustrations will serve to convey a very complete idea of their character. So well is the modeling done and so well is the expression of death on the face suggested that some students have reached the conclusion that this and other specimens of the same class are bona fide death masks, made possibly by coating the dead face with clay and allowing it to harden, then pressing plastic clay into this mold. Mr Dellenbaugh[a] has urged this view, but it is difficult to discover satisfactory evidence of its correctness. Most of the heads and faces of this group are so diminutive in size and so eccentric in shape that ordinary modeling was necessarily employed, and this implies the skill necessary to model the larger specimens. This head (plate XXX), which is the largest of the group, is only 6 inches in height, and if cast from the actual face, would thus represent a young person or one of diminutive size. My own feeling is that to people accustomed to model all kinds of forms in clay, as were these potters, the free-hand shaping of such heads would be a less difficult and remarkable undertaking than that of molding and casting the face, these latter branches of the art being apparently unknown to the mound-building tribes.

---

[a] Dellenbaugh, F. S., Death mask in ancient American pottery. American Anthropologist, February 1897.

In form this particular vessel is a simple head, 6 inches in height and 6 inches wide from ear to ear. The aperture of the vase is in the crown, and is surrounded by a low, upright rim, slightly recurved. The cavity is roughly finished, and follows pretty closely the contour of the exterior surface, except in projecting features such as the ears, lips, and nose. The walls are from one-eighth to one-fourth of an inch in thickness, the base being about three-eighths of an inch thick. The bottom is flat, and on a level with the chin and jaw.

The material does not differ from that of the other vessels of the same locality. It contains a large percentage of shell, some particles of which are quite large. The paste is yellowish gray in color and rather coarse in texture. The vase was modeled in the plain clay and permitted to harden before the devices were engraved. Afterward a thick film of fine yellowish-gray clay was applied to the face, partially filling up the engraved lines. The remainder of the surface, includ-ʃ the lips, received a thick coat of dark red paint. The whole sur-face was then polished.

The illustrations will convey a more vivid conception of this strik-ing head than any description that can be given. The face can not be said to have a single feature strongly characteristic of Indian physi-ognomy; instead, we have the round forehead and the projecting chin of the African. The nose, however, is small and the nostrils are narrow. The face would seem to be intended for that of a young person, perhaps a female. The features are well modeled, and the artist must have had in his mind a pretty definite conception of the face to be produced, as well as of the expression appropriate to it, before begin-ning his work. It is possible even that the portrait of a particular face was intended. The closed eyes, the rather sunken nose, and the parted lips were certainly intended to give the effect of death. The ears are large, correctly placed, and well modeled; they are perfo-rated all along the margins, thus revealing a practice of the people whom they represented. The septum of the nose appears to have been pierced, and the horizontal depression across the upper lip may indicate the former presence of a nose ornament.

Perhaps the most unique and striking feature is the pattern of incised lines that covers the greater part of the face. The lines are deeply engraved and somewhat "scratchy," and were apparently exe-cuted in the hardened clay before the slip or wash of clay was applied. The left side of the face is plain, excepting for a figure somewhat resembling a grappling hook in outline, which partially surrounds the eye. The right side is covered with a comb-like pattern, placed ver-tically with the teeth upward. The middle of the forehead has a series of vertical lines and a few short horizontal ones just above the root of the nose (see plate XXX). In plate XXIX c an outline of the front face is given, and the engraved figure is projected at the

VESSEL REPRESENTING THE POTTER AT WORK (INDIANA)

MIDDLE MISSISSIPPI VALLEY GROUP

(HEIGHT 7 INCHES)

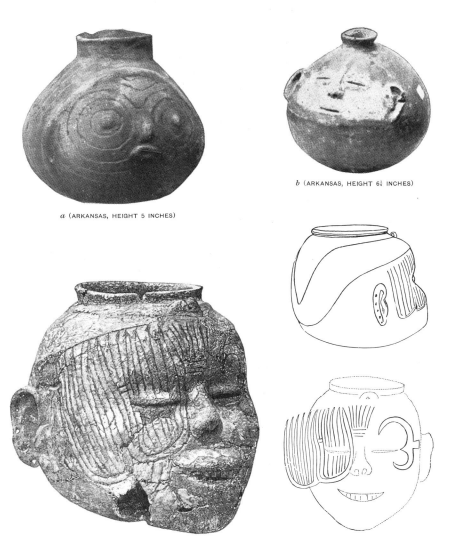

a (ARKANSAS, HEIGHT 5 INCHES)

b (ARKANSAS, HEIGHT 6¼ INCHES)

c (ARKANSAS, DAVENPORT ACADEMY COLLECTION, HEIGHT 6⅞ INCHES)

VESSELS IMITATING THE HUMAN HEAD

MIDDLE MISSISSIPPI VALLEY GROUP

VESSEL IMITATING THE HUMAN HEAD (ARKANSAS)

MIDDLE MISSISSIPPI VALLEY GROUP

(HEIGHT 6¼ INCHES)

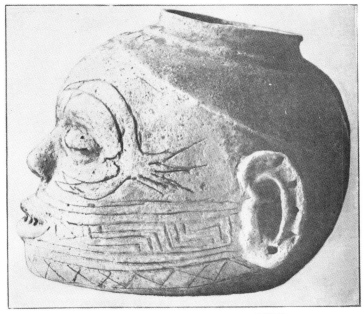

VESSEL IMITATING THE HUMAN HEAD, ARKANSAS

MIDDLE MISSISSIPPI VALLEY GROUP

(HEIGHT 6½ INCHES)

side. The significance of these markings, which no doubt represent tattooed or painted figures, can only be surmised in the most general way. It happens that some rather indistinct markings at the corner of the mouth have been omitted in the engraving.

It is observed that on the forehead, at the top, there is a small loop or perforated knob. Similar appendages may be seen on many of the clay human heads from this valley. A Mexican terra-cotta head, now in the Museo Nacional, Mexico, has a like feature, and, at the same time, has closed eyes and an open mouth.

A head covering, possibly the hair conventionally treated, extends over the forehead and falls in a double fold over the back of the head, terminating in points behind, as is seen in plate XXIX c.

Another vase of a very similar character, now in the Davenport, Iowa, Museum, is about one-half the size of this. The face is much mutilated. A third specimen, also in the Davenport collection, is somewhat larger than the one illustrated in plates XXIX c and XXX, but is nearly the same in finish and color. The face has the same semblance of death, but the features are different, possessing somewhat decided Indian characteristics, and there is no tattooing.

The specimen shown in plate XLIII a, and again in plate XXXI, was exhumed at Pecan point by agents of the Bureau of Ethnology. In size, form, color, finish, modeling of features, and expression, this head closely resembles the one first described. The work is not quite so carefully executed and the head probably has not such pronounced individuality. The curious engraved device that, in the other example, appeared near the left eye here occurs on both sides. The lower part of the face is elaborately engraved. Three lines cross the upper lip and cheeks, reaching to the ear; a band of fret-like devices extends across the mouth to the base of the ears, and another band, filled in with oblique, reticulated lines, passes around the chin and along the jaws. The ears are perforated as in the other case, and the septum of the nose is partly broken away as if it had once held a ring. A perforated knob has occupied the top of the forehead as in the other examples. The face is coated with a light yellowish-gray wash, and the remainder of the surface is red.

Four additional examples of the death's head vases are shown in plate XXXII. They present varied characteristics in detail, but all correspond closely in the more important features of form and expression.

TOBACCO PIPES

In the East and Northeast the clay tobacco pipes of the aborigines were often superior in execution, design, and decoration to the ordinary utensils of clay associated with them. In the central and southwestern sections pipes were for the most part remarkably rude and without grace of outline, and generally without embellishment, while

tne earthenware of the same territory was well made and exhibits pronounced indications of esthetic appreciation on the part of the potters.

A number of the pipes of the middle Mississippi province are illustrated in plate XXXIII. Generally they are made of the same admix-
tures of clay and pulverized shell as are the associated vessels. The
colors are the ordinary dark and yellowish-gray shades of the baked
clay. Traces of blackening by use are observed, and the bowls in a
few instances are still partly filled with the compacted black ash left
presumably by the native smoker. The shapes are simple, being as a
rule slight modifications of a heavy bent tube somewhat constricted at
the elbow and expanding toward the ends. Both openings are large and
conic and are often nearly equal in capacity and closely alike in shape.

Without modification of the fundamental outlines, many varieties of
shape were produced, the most common being a flattening of the base
as though to permit the bowl to rest steadily on the ground while the
smoking was going on, probably through a long tube or stem. This
flattening is in many cases accompanied by an expansion at the margins, as in plate XXXIII *a*, *b*, or by a flattish projection beyond the
elbow, as in *e*. Occasionally the shape is elaborated to suggest rudely
the form of some animal, the projection at the elbow being divided and
rounded off as though to represent the knees of a kneeling figure, and
in rare cases various features of men or other creatures are more fully
brought out. In one instance the projection at the elbow becomes an
animal head, in another medallion-like heads are set on around the
upper part of the bowl. In *a* and *c* incised figures have been executed
in a rather rude way, the motives corresponding with those found on
the earthen vessels of the same region. The specimen shown in *a* was
lent by Mr Warren K. Moorehead. Other variations of the type are
illustrated in McGuire's Pipes and Smoking Customs, pp. 530–535.
Typical as well as variously modified forms of this variety of pipe are
found in Tennessee. Alabama, Georgia. Florida, and, more rarely, in
other states.[a]

MISCELLANEOUS ARTICLES

The art of the modeler was directed in the main toward the making
and embellishing of vessels, yet solid figurines of men and animals and
heads of men, mostly small and rude as though merely toys or funeral
offerings, are now and then secured by collectors. Specimens are
illustrated in the introduction and in connection with various groups
of ware.

In plates XXXIV and XXXV several articles are brought together to
illustrate the use of clay in the manufacture of implements, personal
ornaments, and articles of unknown or problematic use or significance.
The specimens shown in plate XXXIV represent a rather rare variety of

[a] For southern pipes see the various papers of Clarence B. Moore.

a (HEIGHT 6¾ INCHES)

b (HEIGHT 4⅝ INCHES)   *c* (HEIGHT 4 INCHES)

d (HEIGHT 5¼ INCHES)

VESSELS IMITATING THE HUMAN HEAD, (ARKANSAS)

MIDDLE MISSISSIPPI VALLEY GROUP

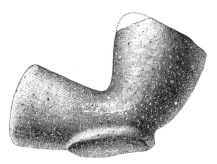

a (ARKANSAS, MOOREHEAD COLLECTION,
LENGTH OF BASE 2¼ INCHES)

b (ARKANSAS, LENGTH OF BASE 2½ INCHES)

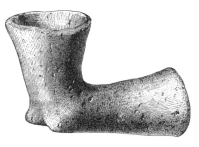

c (ARKANSAS, LENGTH OF BASE 2¾ INCHES)

d (ARKANSAS, LENGTH OF BASE 2¾ INCHES)

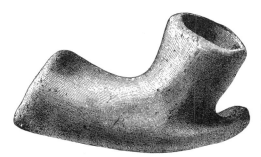

e (ARKANSAS, LENGTH OF BASE 4¼ INCHES)

f (ARKANSAS, LENGTH OF BASE 2¾ INCHES)

TOBACCO PIPES
MIDDLE MISSISSIPPI VALLEY GROUP

a (KENTUCKY, DIAMETER 4⅜ INCHES)

b (TENNESSEE, DIAMETER 4⅜ INCHES)

c (TENNESSEE, LENGTH 6 INCHES)

TROWELS OR MODELING IMPLEMENTS
MIDDLE MISSISSIPPI VALLEY GROUP

MODELING IMPLEMENTS

MIDDLE MISSISSIPPI VALLEY GROUP

(ONE-HALF)

implement, already described in the introduction. They seem to be adapted to use as trowels or finishing tools for plastered walls or floors. They are found mainly in Tennessee. The discoidal smoothing surface shows generally a decided polishing by use, and the looped handle is manifestly intended for grasping, in the manner of a common smoothing iron. These implements could have served, however, in the modeling of large earthenware vessels, or as crushers or pulverizers of foods or paints. Illustrations of a large class of stopperlike or mushroom-shaped forms that may have been used as modeling or smoothing tools in pottery making, as indicated in the introductory section, are included in plate xxxv. That the functions of these objects and those given in the preceding plate are similar or identical is indicated by the character of the convex polishing surface shown in plate xxxvi. Illustrations of earthenware earrings, labrets, a small rattle and the pellets derived from it are given in the introduction.

DECORATIVE DESIGNS

Plate xxxvii is introduced for the purpose of conveying an idea of the character and range of the decorative designs most usual in this region. Many of the more elementary forms are omitted. The more elaborate meanders, twined designs, and scrolls are incised. Another group of designs, embodying many symbolic devices, is given in plate xxxviii. These are executed usually in red and white paint.

From the beginning of my rather disconnected studies of the ornamental art of the native tribes, I have taken the view that, as a rule, the delineative devices employed were symbolic; that they were not primarily esthetic in function, but had a more serious significance to the people using them. When vases were to be devoted to certain ceremonial ends, particular forms were made and designs were added because they had some definite relation to the uses of the vessels and were believed to add to their efficacy. The studies of Dr J. Owen Dorsey, Mr Cushing, Mrs Stevenson, Miss Fletcher, Dr Fewkes, and others have little by little lifted the veil of uncertainty from the whole group of aboriginal delineative phenomena, and the literal significance and function of a multitude of the designs are now known. We thus learn that the devices and delineations on the Mississippi valley pottery are symbols derived from mythology. Stellar and lobed figures and circles probably represent the stars, the sun, or the horizon circle. The cross, the various forms of volutes and scrolls, and the stepped figures represent the four winds, the clouds, and rain; and the reptiles, quadrupeds, birds, men, and monsters are connected with the same group of phenomena. The vessels marked with these figures were no doubt devoted to particular functions in the ceremonial activities of the people. Plate xxxvii presents a series of the purely formal designs. Speculation as to the significance of particular forms of these figures is probably quite unnecessary, since the general nature of all is so well understood. Definite explanations must come from a study of the present people and usages, and among the Mississippi valley tribes there are no doubt many direct survivals of the ancient forms.   Mr C. C. Willoughby has discussed this topic at length in a paper published in the Journal of American Folk-Lore.   The same region furnishes many similar symbols engraved on shell, bone, and stone.

PAINTED VASES

Several specimens, selected to illustrate the interesting color treatment so characteristic of this group of pottery, are presented in plates XXXIX, XL, XLI, XLII, and XLIII.   The flattish bottle, plate XXXIX a, is by no means as handsome or elaborate in its designs as are others in our collections, but it serves quite well to illustrate the class.   The red color of the spaces and figures is applied over the light yellowish ground of the paste and is carefully polished down.   The specimens reproduced in plates XL, XLI, and XLII have been referred to and sufficiently described in preceding pages.   An exceptionally fine example of the colored human figure is given in plate XXXIX b.   Parts of the head and body are finished in red, other parts and the necklace are in white, while certain spaces show the original yellowish gray color of the paste.

POTTERY OF TENNESSEE

I am so fortunate as to be able to add a number of plates (XLIV, XLV, XLVI, XLVII, XLVIII, XLIX, and L) illustrating the wares of the Cumberland valley, Tennessee, and especially of the Nashville district. These plates appeared first in Thruston's Antiquities of Tennessee, and I am greatly indebted to this author for the privilege of reproducing them here.

POTTERY OF THE LOWER MISSISSIPPI VALLEY

Archeologic investigation has not extended into the central southern states save in a few widely separated localities, and enough material has not been collected to permit a full and connected study of the primitive art of the province.   It would seem from present information that the region of the lower Mississippi is not so rich in fictile products as are many other sections; at any rate our museums and collections are not well supplied with material from this part of the South, and literature furnishes but brief references to the practice of the ceramic art (see Introduction).   Some fugitive relics have come into the possession of museums, and on these we must mainly rely for our present knowledge of the subject.   Much of the earthenware appears to be nearly identical with, or closely allied to, that of the middle Mississippi region, as well as with that of the Gulf coast farther east.

CONVEX SURFACES OF TROWELS AND MODELING IMPLEMENTS

MIDDLE MISSISSIPPI VALLEY GROUP

(ABOUT ONE-HALF)

DECORATIVE DESIGNS

MIDDLE MISSISSIPPI VALLEY GROUP

DECORATIVE DESIGNS

MIDDLE MISSISSIPPI VALLEY GROUP

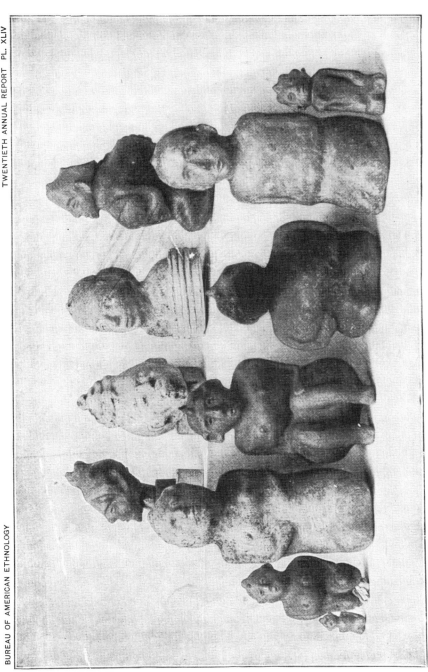

EARTHENWARE OF TENNESSEE

MIDDLE MISSISSIPPI VALLEY GROUP

(THRUSTON COLLECTION)

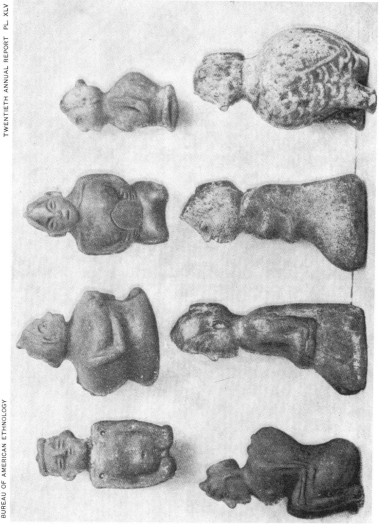

EARTHENWARE OF TENNESSEE
MIDDLE MISSISSIPPI VALLEY GROUP
(THRUSTON COLLECTION)

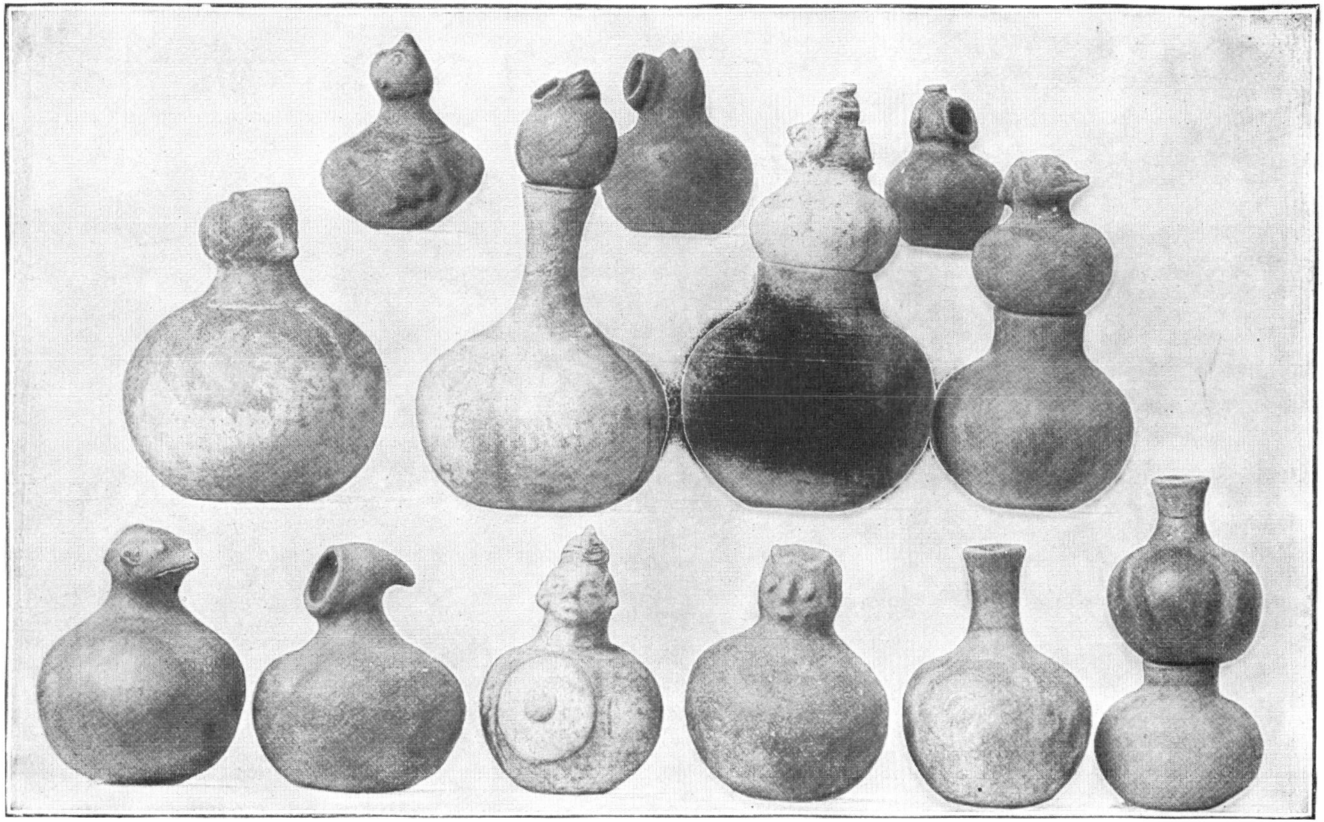

EARTHENWARE OF TENNESSEE

MIDDLE MISSISSIPPI VALLEY GROUP

(THRUSTON COLLECTION)

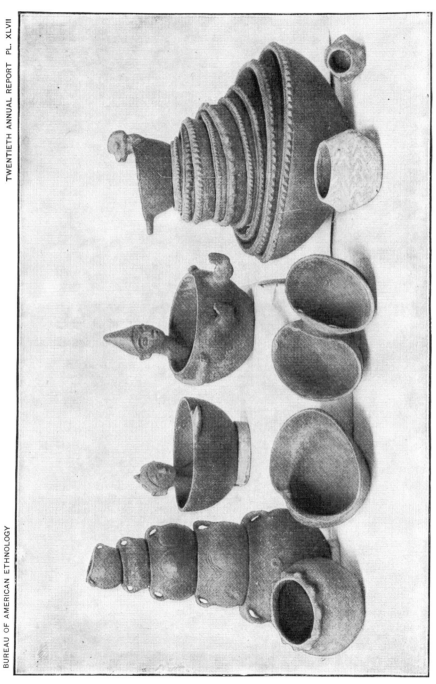

EARTHENWARE OF TENNESSEE

MIDDLE MISSISSIPPI VALLEY GROUP

(THRUSTON COLLECTION)

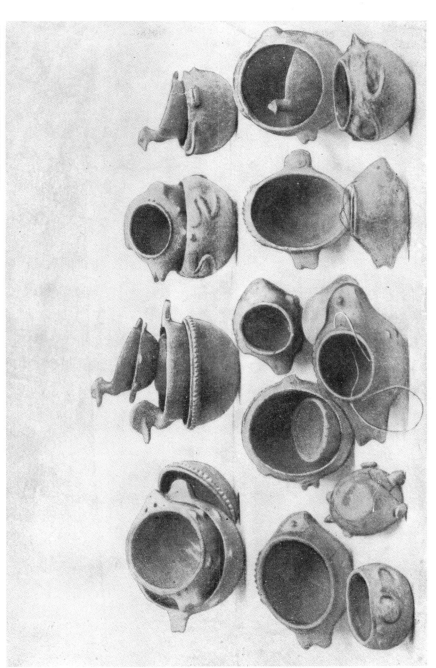

EARTHENWARE OF TENNESSEE

MIDDLE MISSISSIPPI VALLEY GROUP

(THRUSTON COLLECTION)

EARTHENWARE OF TENNESSEE

MIDDLE MISSISSIPPI VALLEY GROUP

(THRUSTON COLLECTION)

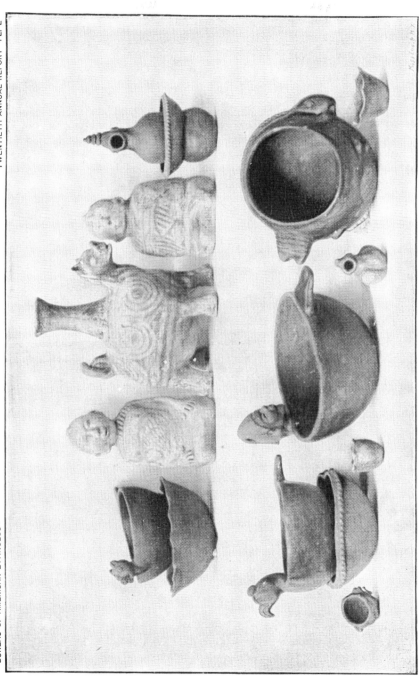

EARTHENWARE OF TENNESSEE

MIDDLE MISSISSIPPI VALLEY GROUP

(THRUSTON COLLECTION)

A large series of the vases from Louisiana and Texas would, if they were brought together, undoubtedly yield many points of interest with respect to the influence of Mexican and Pueblo art on that of this province. Such a series would also be of much value in connection with the history of the various tribes occupying the valley when it was first visited by the French. Du Pratz and Butel-Dumont have left us brief but valuable records of the practice of the art in this section, but we are not definitely informed which of the various peoples were referred to in their accounts. In those days no distinction was made between the linguistic families, although Natchesan, Tonikan, Caddoan, Muskhogean, and Siouan peoples were encountered. So far as the evidence furnished by the collections goes, there is but one variety of the higher grade of products. Citations regarding the practice of the art in this province have been made under the head Manufacture, and need not be repeated here.

FIG. 52—Bowl made by Choctaw Indians about 1860 (diameter 9½ inches).

The only specimen of recent work from this province which is preserved in the national collections is a blackish bowl, well polished and ornamented with a zone of incised lines encircling the body. It is illustrated in figure 52. The record shows that it was made by the Choctaw Indians at Covington, St Tammany parish, Louisiana, about the year 1860. It is said that the art is still practiced to a limited extent by these people.

The highest types of vases from Louisiana and Mississippi have but slight advantage over the best wares of the St Francis and Cumberland valleys. The simpler culinary wares are much the same from St Louis to New Orleans. Some localities near the Gulf furnish sherds of pottery as primitive as anything in the country, and this is consistent with the early observations of the condition of the natives. The Natchez and other tribes were well advanced in many of the arts, while numerous tribes appear to have been, at times at least, poverty-stricken wanderers without art or industry worthy of mention. It is possible that the primitive forms of ware found on some of these southern sites may represent the art of the archaic ancestors of the more advanced peoples of the valley, but at present we seem to have no means of settling such a point. It is well known, however, that single communities produced at the same time a wide range of ware, the style, material, shape, and finish depending on the uses of the vessels or on the haste with which they were prepared. At Troyville, Catahoula county, Louisiana, for example, a mound examined by agents of the Bureau of Ethnology yielded almost every variety and grade of ware known in the South and Southwest, including coarse shell-tempered ware, silicious ware, fine argillaceous ware, stamped ware, red ware, fabric-marked ware, and incised ware.

Of great interest, on account of the perfection of its finish, is a variety of pottery found in graves and mounds on the lower Mississippi and on Red river. Daniel Wilson published a cut representing some typical specimens of this ware from Lake Washington, Washington county, Mississippi.[a] Several years ago a number of fine examples of the same ware, labeled "Galtneys," were lent to the National Museum by the Louisiana State Seminary at Baton Rouge. Photographs of some of these vessels were kept, but the Curator made no definite record of their origin or ownership. A small number of pieces of the same ware are to be found in the various collections of the country, notably in the Free Museum of Science and Art, Philadelphia.

The most striking characteristics of the better examples of this ware are the black color and the mechanical perfection of construction, surface finish, and decoration. The forms are varied and symmetric. The black surface is highly polished and is usually decorated with incised patterns. The scroll was the favorite decorative design, and it will be difficult to find in any part of the world a more chaste and elaborate treatment of this motive. In plate LI a a photograph of a small globular vase or bottle marked "Galtneys" is reproduced. The design is engraved with great precision in deep, even lines, and covers nearly the entire surface of the vase; it consists of a double row of volutes (plate LIII d) linked together in an intricate and charming arrangement, corresponding closely to fine examples from Mycene and Egypt. A skilled draftsman would find the task of executing this design with equal precision on a plane surface extremely trying, and we can but marvel at the skill of the potter who could produce it, properly spaced and connected in every particular, on the surface of the globular vase. Farther up the Mississippi there are examples embodying the same conception of compound volutes, but the combinations are much less complex and masterly.

In plate LI four other vases, all presumably of this group, have been brought together. They do not differ widely from the pottery of the

---

[a] Wilson, Daniel, Prehistoric man, London, 1862, vol. II, pp. 21–22.

a

b

e (MISSISSIPPI, DAVENPORT ACADEMY
COLLECTION, ONE-THIRD)

c (LOUISIANA, DIAMETER 5 INCHES)   d (LOUISIANA, HEIGHT 6¼ INCHES)

VASES WITH INCISED DESIGNS
LOWER MISSISSIPPI VALLEY GROUP

a (LOUISIANA, HEIGHT 4½ INCHES)   *b* (MISSISSIPPI, HEIGHT 4 INCHES)

c (MISSISSIPPI, DIAMETER 6 INCHES)

e (MISSISSIPPI, HEIGHT 4¾ INCHES)

d (MISSISSIPPI, HEIGHT 6 INCHES)

VASES WITH INCISED DESIGNS
LOWER MISSISSIPPI VALLEY GROUP

St Francis river region, and may be regarded, it seems to me, as exceptional examples of the same general group of ware. The little bottle *e* contains a rather rudely engraved figure of an eagle, the head appearing on one side, and the tail, pointed upward, on the other. The particular locality from which the bottle came is not known. Ware closely related to the Middle and Lower Mississippi pottery is found in Texas, but its limitations on the west are not yet defined. Examples of the more elaborate incised designs belonging to this group of ware are brought together in plate LIII.

The vessels illustrated in plate LII are now preserved in the Museum of Science and Art in Philadelphia, and were kindly placed at my disposal by Dr Stewart Culin, of that museum. They form part of the Dickerson collection recently acquired and reported on by Dr Culin.[a] It is noteworthy that the designs engraved on these vases bear a striking resemblance to the scroll work of the middle Mississippi valley on the north and of the Gulf coast farther east, and it is to be expected that these designs will be found to affiliate closely with Mexican work, as do the forms of many of the vessels.

POTTERY OF THE GULF COAST

OCCURRENCE

Along the Gulf coast east of the delta of the Mississippi pottery is found in many localities and under varying conditions. The features most characteristic of the wares of the West recur with decreasing frequency and under less typical forms until Florida is reached. Features typical of Appalachian and Floridian wares make their appearance east of Pensacola bay.

The manner of occurrence of the ceramic remains of the Gulf region is interesting. In many cases several varieties of ware are intermingled on a single site. This is especially true of some of the kitchen-midden and shell-mound sites, which, it would seem, must have been the resort of different tribes, and even of distinct linguistic families, who visited the tide-water shores from time to time in search of shellfish. In the mounds, however, the conditions are simpler, and in cases we seem to have the exclusive product of a single people. This simplicity in the burial pottery may be due to the fact that only particular forms of ware were used for mortuary purposes. With some peoples, as has been already noted, certain kinds of vessels were devoted exclusively to culinary uses. Remains of the latter utensils will be found very generally in shell deposits, and it is in these deposits and not in the mounds that we would expect to find the wares of nonresident communities.

---

[a] Culin, Stewart, Bulletin of the Department of Archæology and Paleontology, University of Pennsylvania, vol. II, number 3.

Speculation as to the peoples to whom these wares should be attributed will for the present be practically unavailing. It is probable that the Muskhogean tribes occupied the coast rather fully between the delta of the Mississippi and Tampa bay, but several linguistic stocks must have had access to this important source of food supply. Even the Siouan family was represented (by the ancestors of the Biloxi of to-day), and it is not impossible that some of the ware, especially that embodying animal figures, may be due to the presence or influence of this people. Strangely enough, in the national collections from southwestern Alabama there is a lot of sherds exhibiting typical features of the peculiar pottery of New York state, which seems to belong to the Iroquoian tribes. It is possible, however, that the Museum record may be defective and that the association is accidental.

MOBILE-PENSACOLA WARE

The leading group of ware found along the great northern curve of the Gulf coast is well represented by the contents of mounds situated on Mobile, Perdido, Pensacola, and Choctawhatchee bays. The National Museum has a large series of vessels from a mound on Perdido bay, obtained by Francis H. Parsons and other members of the United States Coast and Geodetic Survey about the year 1889. Recent explorations conducted by Clarence B. Moore at several points along the tidewater shores of the Gulf have supplied a wonderful series of vases now preserved in the Museum of the Academy of Natural Sciences, Philadelphia. These collections have been very generously placed at my disposal by Mr Moore, and as they belong in the main to the same ceramic group with the Parsons finds, all will be presented together. The range of form in this group is quite wide, but not equal to that in the pottery of the Arkansas region. If the collections were equally complete from the two regions, this relation might be changed, yet it is still apparent that the western ware has the advantage in a number of essentials. In the Mobile-Pensacola district few traces of painted vessels have been found, and there is apparently less symmetry of outline and less refinement of finish than in the best products of the West. There are cups, bowls, shallow and deep pots, and a few bottles, besides a number of compound and eccentric forms, but the deep pot, the tripod vase, and the slender-necked bottles are practically absent. Such pots as occur show, as they do in the West, indications of use over fire, and it is worthy of remark that some of them correspond to western cooking vessels in being provided with handles and in having bands of crude ornamentation incised or relieved about the rim and neck, while others, occurring always in fragments, approach the eastern type, which is without handles and is characterized by an oblong body, somewhat conic below, and by stamp-finished surfaces.

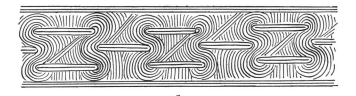

a

b

c

d

INCISED DESIGNS FROM VASES SHOWN IN PLATES LI AND LII

LOWER MISSISSIPPI VALLEY GROUP

VASES FROM A MOUND ON PERDIDO BAY
GULF COAST GROUP

The paste is fine and silicious, with but little distinguishable tempering; its colors are yellowish or brownish grays, rarely approaching black, and the surface is even, though seldom very highly polished. The walls are thin and of uniform thickness. Animals and animal features modeled in relief and in the round are attached to the vases or enter into their form in much the same manner as in the West, but with less frequency and freedom. They have, however, perhaps a greater interest on account of the peculiar and very definite correlation of the incised designs on the vases with the modeled life forms. This subject will receive attention separately farther on. The pottery is nearly all obtained from burial mounds, and it is observed that the vases in most, if not all, cases have been perforated or broken before consignment to the graves. This custom extended eastward through Georgia and Florida to the Atlantic coast, but it was practically unknown in the North and West.

The Parsons collection of pottery was obtained from a sand mound on Bear point, Alabama. Nearly all the pieces were broken, but otherwise they were so well preserved that many have been restored to much their original appearance under my supervision. Illustrations of a large number of the simpler forms are given in plate LIV.

From shallow bowls we pass to deeper forms and to globular vessels. A few specimens are cylindric, and occasionaly a wide-mouthed bottle is encountered. One specimen has a handle and resembles a ladle in form. The outlines are generally graceful, the walls thin, and the rims inconspicuous and neat. The incised designs are lightly and freely drawn, and include a wide range of formal figures, from simple groups of straight lines to widely diversified forms of meanders and scrolls. Life-form elements, often obscure, appear in numerous cases.

In plate LV three of the large bowls are presented. These exhibit characteristic varieties of form, and all are embellished with incised designs embodying life elements which are referred to later on in this section. Plate LVI a is a neat little jar with incised meander and step design from the Bear Point mound. It is also shown in outline in plate LIV. In b is introduced a bottle of northern type from Franklin county, Mississippi. It is of special interest, since it contains a painted design, c, embodying the most prevalent Gulf Coast life-form device, and is, at the same time, nearly duplicated by a similar bottle from near Nashville, Tennessee, illustrated by Thruston in his work, figure 40. Part of plate LVI and plates LVII, LVIII, and LIX are devoted to the presentation of life forms.

A rather remarkable piece, resembling middle Mississippi forms, is illustrated in plate LVI d. The head of a bird, probably intended for an owl, forms the apex of a full-bodied bottle, the funnel-shaped open-

ing being placed at the back of the neck. The wings and other features
of the body appear to have been depicted in incised lines. The little
vase shown in plate LVI *e*, from the Bear Point mound, is cleverly
modeled to represent a frog, and shows close analogies with the Mississippi valley work.

The builders of the sand mounds on Perdido bay seem occasionally
to have executed very elaborate engravings of eagles and serpents on
cylindric cups, which probably served as ceremonial drinking vessels;
illustrations are given in plate LVII. The first figure, *a*, represents
the base of a cup which is encircled by the engraving of an eagle; the
second figure, *b*, represents a fragment of a handsome cup of similar
shape, and serves to indicate the relation of the figure of the bird to
the rim of the cup. Part of the tail, talons, and wing are shown.
In *c* we have all that remains of the design on the cup *a* projected at
full length. The strange figure illustrated in *d* was obtained from
much shattered fragments of a well-made and neatly finished cup of
cylindric shape. It seems to represent the tails of three rattlesnakes,
the lines joined at the right as if to represent a single body.

In plate LVIII *a*, *b*, *c*, *d*, and *e*, we have examples of the modeling of
heads of birds and other creatures for bowl embellishments. The
treatment closely resembles that seen in more western work. Here,
as in the Mississippi country, the duck is a favorite subject. In *f* we
have a grotesque creature common in the art of the West. An eagle
is well shown in *e*, and what appears to be the head of a serpent or
turtle with a stick in its mouth is given in *b*. This feature appears in
the wares of Tennessee and Arkansas, the animal imitated being a
beaver. Additional specimens appear in plate LIX, three representing
the human head and one the head of a bird. These are not figurines
in the true sense, but are merely heads broken from the rims of bowls.

Mr Moore's collections from the Bear Point mounds furnish several
very well-preserved specimens of bowls and vases with wide mouths
and narrow collars, besides a number of heads of birds and mammals of
usual types, derived, no doubt, from the rims of bowls. All repeat
rather closely the finds of Mr Parsons, shown in plates LIV to LIX.
Specimens from Mr Moore's collections are presented in plates LX
and LXI.

POTTERY OF THE ALABAMA RIVER

Before passing eastward it will be well to notice the collections made
by Mr Clarence B. Moore in the valleys of the Alabama and Tombig-
bee. An examination of the superb series of vases obtained from
mounds at several points between Mobile and Montgomery makes it
clear that the Gulf Coast tribes extended inland well up toward the
middle of the state. Below Montgomery there is hardly a trace of

a (GEORGIA, DIAMETER 13¼ INCHES)

b (ALABAMA, DIAMETER 8 INCHES)

c (ALABAMA, DIAMETER 19 INCHES)

LARGE BOWLS WITH INCISED DESIGNS
GULF COAST GROUP

a (ALABAMA, HEIGHT 4⅞ INCHES)

b (MISSISSIPPI, HEIGHT 8 INCHES)

c

d (ALABAMA, DIAMETER 6 INCHES)

e (ALABAMA, DIAMETER 3 INCHES)

VASES VARIOUSLY DECORATED
GULF COAST GROUP

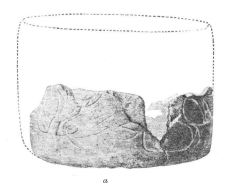

a

b

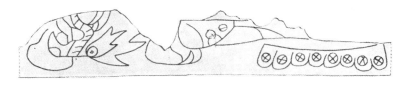

c

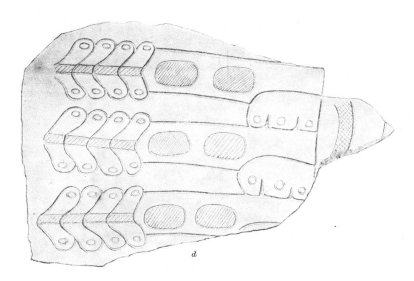

d

VASES WITH ENGRAVED FIGURES OF BIRDS AND SERPENTS, ALABAMA

GULF COAST GROUP

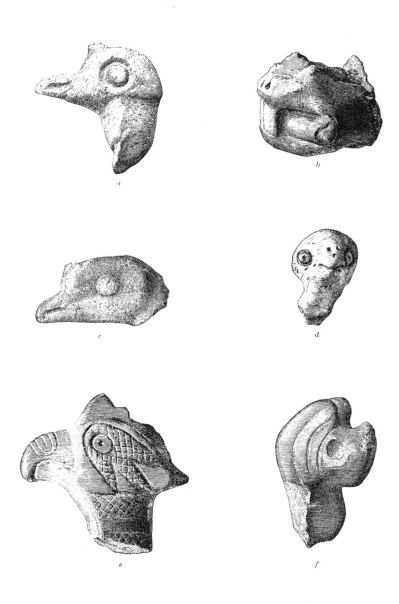

HEADS OF BIRDS AND ANIMALS USED AS VASE ORNAMENTS, ALABAMA

GULF COAST GROUP

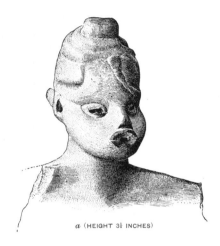

a (HEIGHT 3½ INCHES)

b (HEIGHT 4¼ INCHES)

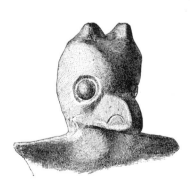

c (HEIGHT 3¾ INCHES)

d (HEIGHT 4¾ INCHES)

HEADS OF MEN AND BIRD USED AS VASE ORNAMENTS, ALABAMA

GULF COAST GROUP

a (DIAMETER 11¼ INCHES)

b (DIAMETER 5¼ INCHES)

c (DIAMETER 11¾ INCHES)

VASES WITH INCISED DESIGNS, ALABAMA

GULF COAST GROUP

(MOORE COLLECTION)

a (ALABAMA, MOORE COLLECTION, DIAMETER 13 INCHES)

b (FLORIDA, MOORE COLLECTION, HEIGHT 6 INCHES)

c (FLORIDA, MOORE COLLECTION, DIAMETER 14 INCHES).

VASES WITH INCISED DESIGNS
GULF COAST GROUP

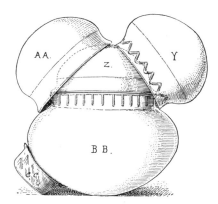

a (DIAMETER B B 17¼ INCHES)

b (DIAMETER 17¼ INCHES)

BURIAL VASES WITH COVERS, ALABAMA
GULF COAST GROUP
(MOORE COLLECTION)

the South Appalachian wares and only a trace of the Tennessee influence. The differences noted in passing northward from the coast are the larger size of the vessels, the more frequent occurrence of pot forms and bottle shapes, and the coarser and more silicious character of the paste. The decorations are almost wholly of Gulf Coast types. The use of some of the larger vessels in burial is well illustrated in plate LXII. Plate LXIII contains a large bowl with animal-derived incised designs, and below is a splendid specimen of pot or caldron, 18 inches in diameter. It is characterized, as are others of the same group, by a line of vertical ridges encircling the upright neck. In plate LXIV have been brought together a well-shaped bottle, of northern or western type, embellished with simple incised scroll work, and two tobacco pipes. One of the latter, *b*, is somewhat suggestive of Appalachian forms, and the other, *c*, is of the heavy southern type.

POTTERY OF CHOCTAWHATCHEE BAY

The next point east of Pensacola bay at which Mr Moore obtained collections is Waltons Camp, situated at the western limit of Choctawhatchee bay, Florida. In the main the ware repeats Perdido bay forms, as will be seen by reference to plates LXV, LXVI, LXVII. Three typical bowls are given in plate LXV, and two platters, one with plain circular margin and the other with six scallops, are shown in plate LXVI. The form is exceptional, and all the pieces have been perforated on burial. The incised designs of the scalloped specimen probably represent the fish. In plate LXVII have been assembled outlines of a large number of the Waltons Camp specimens. They serve for comparison with collections from points east and west. We are here within the range of the stamped ware typical of the Appalachian province, and a fragment with a simple angular type of filfot figure is shown in figure 53.

Among the animal forms obtained at this point are two strongly modeled heads of large size, apparently representing geese. Shell forms are common (see plate LXVII), and the engraved designs, treated farther on, are striking and instructive. From four sites along the northern and eastern shores of Choctawhatchee bay Mr Moore obtained large and very interesting collections. Perdido bay and western forms prevail, but there is a strong infusion of elements of Appalachian and Floridian art. A fragment of a cylindric bowl with the head of a duck modeled in relief at the top and conventional incised figures representing the body below appears in plate LXVIII *a*; and two views of a hunchback-figure vase are given in *b* and *c*.

Of special interest is a small jar or bottle from a mound on Jolly

---

bay, on which an eagle and an eagle-man mask are inscribed. These figures are shown in plate LXIX. Plate LXX *a* illustrates a curious dish with elaborate incised and indented designs representing conventionalized life forms. A rude bowl with highly conventional bird symbols appears in *b*. Both specimens were perforated before burial. In *c* we have the top view of a bowl with incurved rim, about the lip of which are engraved devices probably intended to represent the frog.

The most striking and instructive ware yet brought from the Gulf coast was obtained by Mr Moore from Point Washington, on the eastern margin of Choctawhatchee bay, just south of Jolly bay. Here the local group of ware prevails to a large extent, but two or three other varieties take a prominent place, not, apparently, as a result of the intrusion of outside peoples or of their ware, but through the adoption by local potters of the forms and symbols of neighboring districts. The exotics are the stamped ware of the Appalachian district to the north, and two or more varieties of somewhat well differentiated Florida pottery. Plate LXXI includes a large number of the bowls, ladles, etc., in outline, and specimens of exceptional interest appear in plates LXXII–LXXIV.

FIG. 53—Fragment of vessel with stamped design, from Waltons Camp, Choctawhatchee bay, Florida.

Plate LXXII illustrates three pieces which resemble the Mobile-Pensacola ware, but show rather exceptional forms and decorations. The deeply incised lines of the elaborate patterns have, in two of the specimens, been filled in with some white substance, giving a striking effect and reminding one of Central American methods of treatment.

These people had a marked fancy for embellishing their vases with animal forms, and birds and beasts have been much utilized. In plate LXXIII we have three fine bowls embodying the frog concept, partly in low relief and partly in very conventional incised lines. Plate LXXIV contains two delineations, probably of the owl. The interesting point

a (DIAMETER 14½ INCHES)

b (DIAMETER 17½ INCHES)

VESSELS OF LARGE SIZE WITH INCISED AND RELIEVED ORNAMENTS, ALABAMA

GULF COAST GROUP

MOORE COLLECTION)

a (DIAMETER 4½ INCHES)

b (ACTUAL SIZE)

c (ACTUAL SIZE)

BOTTLE WITH SCROLL DESIGN AND TOBACCO PIPES, ALABAMA

GULF COAST GROUP

(MOORE COLLECTION)

a (DIAMETER 15¼ INCHES)

b (DIAMETER 12¼ INCHES)

c (DIAMETER 15¼ INCHES)

BOWLS WITH INCISED DESIGNS, FLORIDA
GULF COAST GROUP
(MOORE COLLECTION)

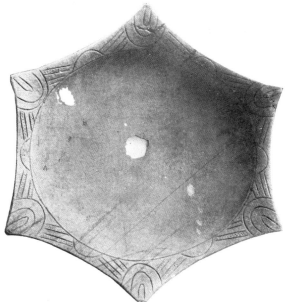

a (DIAMETER 14¾ INCHES)

b (DIAMETER 13 INCHES)

PLATTERS WITH INCISED DESIGNS, FLORIDA
GULF COAST GROUP
(MOORE COLLECTION)

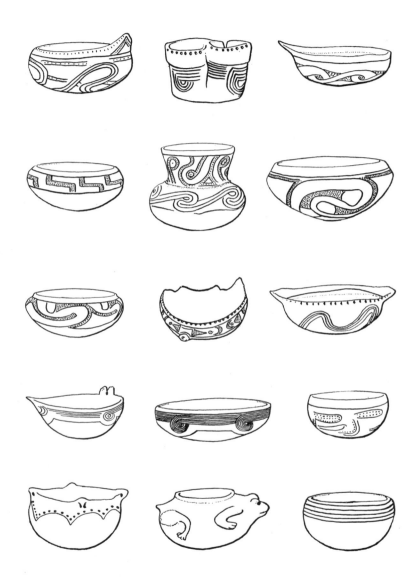

VESSELS WITH INCISED DESIGNS, FLORIDA

GULF COAST GROUP

(MOORE COLLECTION)

a (HEIGHT 7½ INCHES)

b

(HEIGHT 9 INCHES)

c

FRAGMENT OF VASE WITH A DUCK'S HEAD IN RELIEF AND VASE REPRESENTING A
HUNCHBACK HUMAN FIGURE, FLORIDA

GULF COAST GROUP

(MOORE COLLECTION)

a

b

c   *d*

(HEIGHT 4¼ INCHES)

VASE WITH ENGRAVINGS OF AN EAGLE AND AN EAGLE-MAN MASK, FLORIDA

GULF COAST GROUP

(MOORE COLLECTION)

a (DIAMETER 7¼ INCHES)

b (DIAMETER 4¼ INCHES)

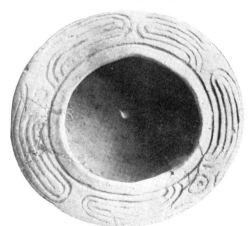

c (DIAMETER 9 INCHES)

PLATTER AND BOWLS WITH ENGRAVED DESIGNS, FLORIDA

GULF COAST GROUP

(MOORE COLLECTION)

OUTLINES OF VASES WITH ENGRAVED DESIGNS, FLORIDA

GULF COAST GROUP

(MOORE COLLECTION)

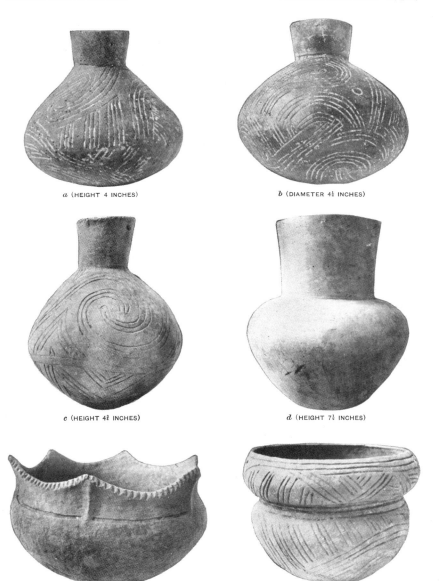

a (HEIGHT 4 INCHES)

b (DIAMETER 4½ INCHES)

c (HEIGHT 4¾ INCHES)

d (HEIGHT 7½ INCHES)

e (DIAMETER 5¼ INCHES)

f (DIAMETER 5¼ INCHES)

BOWLS AND BOTTLES WITH ENGRAVED DESIGNS, FLORIDA

GULF COAST GROUP

(MOORE COLLECTION)

a (DIAMETER 15¼ INCHES)

b (DIAMETER 10 INCHES)

c (DIAMETER 14½ INCHES)

BOWLS WITH RELIEVED AND INCISED DECORATIONS REPRESENTING
THE FROG CONCEPT, FLORIDA

GULF COAST GROUP

(MOORE COLLECTION)

a (DIAMETER 11¼ INCHES)

b (HEIGHT 5¼ INCHES)

c (DIAMETER 7¾ INCHES)

BOWL WITH RELIEVED AND INCISED DECORATIONS REPRESENTING THE BIRD CONCEPT,
FLORIDA

GULF COAST GROUP

(MOORE COLLECTION)

is that the conventional incised features representing the body and wings grade into the generalized ornament.

Plate LXXV represents a handsome bowl with engraved design, meant apparently for the frog, which was found by Mr Moore inverted over a skull in a grave at Point Washington, Florida.

APALACHICOLA WARE

It is interesting to note that here and there along the Gulf coast there are certain pieces of pottery that do not affiliate fully with the ordinary ware and that at the same time appear to present closer analogies with the wares of Yucatan and the Caribbean islands than do any of the other varieties; such peculiarities are more marked in the Choctawhatchee-Apalachicola section than elsewhere. The specimens brought together in plates LXXVI and LXXVII, belonging to Mr Moore's Point Washington finds, offer, to my mind, these hints of exotic influence. At the same time, they can not be divorced from their close affiliations with the ware of the Gulf coast to the west and with that of the Florida peninsula to the east.

Two vessels of rather rude shape are shown in plate LXXVI a and b. The upper part of the body is embellished with a wide zone of stamped figures, such as are common over a vast area to the north and east of Choctawhatchee bay. The most interesting feature of these designs is that, though typical of the South Appalachian stamped ware, they are seen at a glance to embody the commonest concepts of the Gulf Coast group—the conventional life elements, in which the eye, the teeth, and the body features of the creature are still traceable. Similar vessels are found toward the east, along the Florida coast, and appear in connection with a group of vases typically developed on Apalachicola drainage in Franklin county. The peculiar little vessel shown in c has an oblong, flattened body, rudely suggesting an alligator's head. The incised markings affiliate with the Mobile-Pensacola decoration. Vase d departs from western models, and approaches closely forms of ware typically developed on the peninsula of Florida. The remaining figure, e, is the top view of a small jar with a remarkable rounded lip. Although the engraved designs embody the Gulf Coast life elements, the method of execution departs radically from the normal treatment. The elaborate figures are traced over nearly the entire vessel, and are deeply incised, the channels being carefully carved out, leaving rounded ridges between them. The form and the material unite with the decoration in indicating a type of ware radically different from that of the Mobile-Pensacola district, yet represented by few other pieces in our collections. It affiliates most closely with the Apalachicola forms.

Equally distinct from the Mobile-Pensacola ware are the five pieces shown in plate LXXVII a, b, c, d, and e. In ornamentation their association is close with the pottery found at Tarpon Springs and other central and western peninsular sites. Their paste, color, and some details of form connect them with the Apalachicola ware. The frag· ment shown in *c* appears to represent a well-executed vessel corre sponding in shape to *c* of the preceding plate.

A characteristic and very interesting series of vessels was acquired recently by the National Museum from Mr C. H. B. Lloyd, who exhumed them from a mound in Franklin county. Ten of these are shown in plate LXXVIII. They represent a wide range of form and finish. The paste is silicious but generally fine-grained, and in some pieces flecks of mica are plentiful. The color is a warm gray, save in one case, where the firing has given a mottled terra-cotta red. In general they are South Appalachian rather than Floridian, as is indicated by their material, form, and decoration. Two pieces resemble the porous ware of Florida in appearance and finish. Three are decorated with elaborately figured stamps, and one is painted red. Incised lines appear in a few cases. Unstamped surfaces are finished with a polishing stone. All are perforated, a hole having been knocked in the bottom of each, save in one case, in which a circular opening about an inch in diameter was made while the clay was still soft. This vessel has a thickened rim, flat on the upper surface and nearly an inch wide. A rudely modeled bird's head is affixed to the upper surface of the rim. The surface is rather roughly finished and has received a wash of red ocher. A small fragment of another similar vase, supplied with an animal head, belongs to the collection, and a closely analogous specimen, now in the National Museum, came from a mound near Gainesville.

A remarkable vessel—a bottle with reddish paste, squarish cruciform body, as viewed from above, and a high, wide foot—is shown in plate LXXVIII, and on a larger scale in plate LXXVIII A1. A vertical view in outline is given in 2, and the engraved design encircling the base—partly broken away—appears in 3. The four flattish hornshaped wings that extend from the collar out over the body, ending in rounded projecting points, constitute a wholly unique plastic feature, although the engraved figures are repeated in sherds from northern and western Florida. The lines and figures are deeply engraved and almost certainly represent some graphic original, traces of the life features appearing through the mask of convention. Something in the general appearance and decorative treatment suggests Caribbean work, and in the shape of the base and the band of encircling decoration there is a hint of Yucatec treatment; still the piece is, as a whole, essentially Floridian.

Three vessels shown in plate LXXVIII, the largest pot and two smaller pieces, have collars of stamped figures, the remainder of the surface being somewhat rudely polished. In two cases the stamped

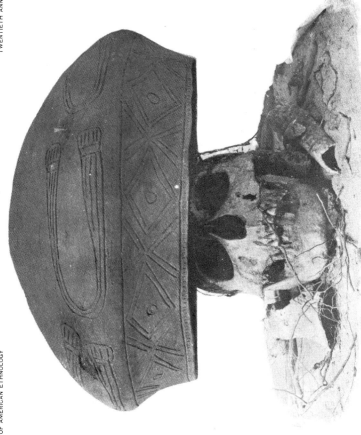

BOWL INVERTED OVER A SKULL IN BURIAL, FLORIDA

GULF COAST GROUP

(MOORE COLLECTION, DIAMETER 15 INCHES)

a (HEICHT 6 INCHES)

d (HEIGHT 3¼ INCHES)

c (LENGTH 6 INCHES)

b (HEIGHT 6¾ INCHES)

e (DIAMETER 6 INCHES)

VASES WITH ENGRAVED AND STAMPED DESIGNS, FLORIDA
GULF COAST GROUP
(MOORE COLLECTION)

a (HEIGHT 4¼ INCHES)

b (HEIGHT 3½ INCHES)

c (HEIGHT 4 INCHES)

d (HEIGHT 6 INCHES)

e (HEIGHT 3½ INCHES)

VASES WITH ENGRAVED DESIGNS, FLORIDA

GULF COAST GROUP

(MOORE COLLECTION)

GROUP OF VASES FROM A FLORIDA MOUND

GULF COAST GROUP

(DIAMETER OF LARGEST VASE 10¼ INCHES)

figures are sufficiently complete to permit a practical restoration of the full design. While I was observing the unique and remarkable nature of these designs and their dissimilarity to the ornamental designs of the surrounding areas in the United States, the idea of comparing them with the decorative conceptions of the West Indies occurred to me. The result of this study has been presented in a separate paper.[a]

Researches made by Mr Clarence B. Moore in 1902 among the mounds of the west coast of Florida, between St Andrews bay on the west and Cedar keys on the east, have brought to light a remarkable

Fig. 54.—Bowl with thick collar, Tampa bay. Diameter 8½ inches.

series of vases, a few specimens of which I am able to add at the last moment in plates LXXIX, LXXIX A, and LXXIX B. Several exceptional features appear, among which are certain compound and eccentric forms, bird shapes displaying most interesting treatment of wings and other features; and pierced walls, the openings representing the interspaces of the designs. The well-marked local characters grade off into western, northern, and eastern forms, so that no decided break occurs at any point. Stamp-decorated ware displaying a great variety of the highly elaborate figures occurs everywhere in association with the prevailing variety.[b]

MISCELLANEOUS SPECIMENS

Associated with the above-described ware along the Gulf shore are bowl-shaped vessels characterized by a peculiar thickening of the lip

Fig. 55—Sections of thick-rimmed bowls, Early county, Georgia.

or rim, and by the presence, in many cases, of red coloration. The largest collection of these vessels in our possession comes from a village site in Early county, Georgia, although specimens are found about Mobile bay and all along the west coast of Florida to Tampa and even father south. They are best illustrated by the collections of Mr A. S. Gaines and Mr K. M. Cunningham, now in the National Museum. These vessels, mainly in fragments, are not separable from the other

[a] Holmes, W. H., Caribbean influence on the prehistoric ceramic art of the southern states, in the American Anthropologist, vol. VII, number 1, January, 1894.

[b] Moore, Clarence B., Certain aboriginal remains of the northwest Florida coast, part II, Philadelphia, 1902.

forms of pottery associated with them, although they exhibit features so peculiar as to suggest that the type may have had a separate origin. They are associated, at different points, with the remains of nearly every variety of southern pottery. Although from the richest of shell-bearing districts, this ware, in common with the Appalachian pottery, is usually tempered with silicious matter.

The thickening of the margins of vessels in this group is a notable and peculiar feature belonging to the ware from no other region. A specimen from Tampa bay, Florida, is presented in figure 54, and a series of sections is given in figure 55. The surface retains but little of the red color. These bowls are symmetric in shape and were neatly finished with the polishing tool. Usually a thin

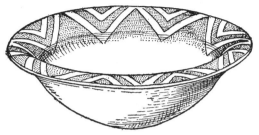

Fig. 56—Bowl from Mobile district, with patterns in color.

coat of red ocher has been applied. In a few cases the color forms simple patterns, as is shown in figure 56. The pattern in this example is executed in white paint on a red ground. This vessel has a flaring rim, only slightly thickened.

In specimens from Mobile shell heaps there is, as has been already mentioned, a certain suggestion of Mexican or Central American art, and it is not impossible that definite correlations with the ware of the South may in time be made.

LIFE ELEMENTS IN DECORATION

Before more eastern groups are treated, attention may be given to the interesting decorations of the Central Gulf Coast ware. The formal designs—the groupings of straight and curved lines, the meanders, the guilloches, and the scrolls—were at first treated independently of the life forms so variously embodied in the vessels; but as these studies advanced it came to be realized that the life idea runs through all the designs, and that the formal figures are connected by an unbroken series of less and less conventional forms with the semirealistic incised designs and with the realistic plastic representations as well. This is a very important matter to the student of the embellishing arts. The investigation was begun by assembling each variety of creature embodied in the ware—man, quadrupeds, birds, reptiles, batrachians, and fishes—placing the most realistic representations in both relieved and incised forms first, the others following in the series according to progress in conventional modification. The purpose was to ascertain whether there was general consistency, whether

20 ETH—03——8

1 (HEIGHT 6⅝ INCHES)

3

2

UNIQUE BOTTLE WITH ENGRAVED DESIGNS

GULF COAST GROUP

a (ONE-FIFTH)   b (ONE-FOURTH)

c (ONE-FIFTH)   d (ONE-THIRD)

e (ONE-FOURTH)   f (ONE-FOURTH)

BIRD-FORM VASES WITH INCISED DECORATIONS SUGGESTING THE ORIGIN OF
MANY CONVENTIONAL ORNAMENTS

NORTHWEST FLORIDA COAST

(MOORE COLLECTION)

1 (DIAMETER 8 INCHES)

2 (ONE-THIRD)

3 (ONE-FOURTH)

4 (ONE-THIRD)   5 (ONE-THIRD)

VASES WITH INCISED AND RELIEVED DECORATION
NORTHWEST FLORIDA COAST
(MOORE COLLECTION)

1 (ONE-THIRD)

3 (ONE-FIFTH)

5 (ONE-FOURTH)

6 (ONE-THIRD)

2 (ONE-FOURTH)

4 (ONE-THIRD)

VASES OF EXCEPTIONAL FORMS
NORTHWEST FLORIDA COAST
(MOORE COLLECTION)

each variety of creature passed down to the purely conventional forms through its own peculiar and distinctive series of variants. The conclusion reached is that there is at least a large degree of consistency, and that particular forms of creatures may be recognized far down the scale toward the geometric. Exceptions were noted, however. The symbols are occasionally intermingled, as if the significance of the particular forms had been lost sight of, the potter using them as symbols of the life idea in general, or as mere decorations.

As a rule, the incised designs are more highly conventional than the plastic, the eagle and the serpent being the only incised forms, so far as has been observed, realistically treated; but it was possible to recognize others through their association with the modeled forms. In vessels furnished with the head of a bird in relief, for example, the same kind of incised figures were generally found around the vessel, and these are recognized as being more or less fully conventionalized representations of wings. The same is true of the fish and its gills, fins, and tail; of the serpent and its spots and rattles, and of the frog and its legs. The relieved figures, realistically treated, become thus a key to the formal incised designs, enabling us to identify them when separately used. It will be seen, however, that since all forms shade off into the purely geometric, there comes a stage when all must be practically alike; and in independent positions, since we have no key, we fail to distinguish them, and can only say that whatever they represented to the potter they can not be to us more than mere suggestions of the life idea. To the native potter the life concept was probably an essential association with every vessel.

In plate LXXX is arranged a series of figures illustrating progressive variations in the bird concept, and in plate LXXXI the frog concept is similarly represented. The series are too limited to be entirely satisfactory, as it is only when a great number of these designs are before us that we see clearly the meaning of the transformations. Plates LXXXII and LXXXIII show some purely conventional designs, and many more or less fully conventionalized life forms copied from vessels of this group.

POTTERY OF THE FLORIDA PENINSULA [a]

Exploration on the peninsula of Florida has made such decided headway in recent years that archæologists may now reasonably hope to secure a firm grasp on the problems of Floridian prehistoric art. The general nature and range of the art remains are already fairly well understood, but little study has been given those details that must

[a] Acknowledgments are due to Mr Clarence B. Moore for a large part of the data embodied in this brief study of Florida pottery. Not only have his published works been drawn on but correspondence and frequent consultations with him have furnished valuable assistance. As an indefatigable worker, an accurate observer, a faithful recorder, and a prompt publisher, Mr Moore stands at the head of the long list of those who have undertaken personally to explore the ancient monuments of the eastern United States.

be relied upon to assist, first, in assigning these relics to particular tribes and stocks of people, second, in correlating them with culture features of neighboring regions, and, third, in determining questions of chronology. The extensive and careful researches of Mr Clarence B. Moore seem destined to fairly initiate this important work, and Mr F. H. Cushing has conducted very important excavations along the western coast, the results of which, although only half published, give us the first clear and definite insight into the life and habits of the prehistoric inhabitants of the Gulf coast.

HISTORIC ABORIGINES

The group of tribes occupying Florida during the period of Spanish discovery and conquest belongs to what is now known as the Timuquanan linguistic family. These people have now entirely disappeared, and little is definitely known of their arts or history. Other tribes have since occupied the territory, but none have been permitted to remain except a few Seminoles, some two hundred strong, who now occupy portions of the Everglades. There appears to be only the most meager record of the making of pottery by any of the historic tribes of the peninsula, yet pottery making was the rule with the southern Indians, and we may fairly assume that all of the tribes found in the peninsula by the Spanish were potters, and that much of the earthenware obtained from the mounds and shell heaps belonged to tribes of the historic linguistic stocks of the general region. The Timuquanan peoples are probably fully represented, but Muskogean influence must have been felt, and at least one of the principal varieties of pottery found in the northern half of the peninsula was typically developed in the region occupied by that stock. Traces of intrusive ideas are present, perhaps even traces of peoples from the West, and evidences of Antillean (Arawak) contact on the east have recently come to light. As the case stands, however, we have such slight historic knowledge of the native ceramic art of Florida that no part of its products can, with entire safety, be attributed to any particular tribe or stock of people.

The colored plate presented as the frontispiece of this paper is reproduced from a drawing by John White, of the Roanoke Colony, 1585–1588. It represents a native woman holding in her hand what appears to be an earthen bowl. This is one of the few authentic illustrations extant of a native of "Florida" in Colonial times.

The ware of Florida is extremely varied and presents numerous pronounced types of form and decoration, but it is found very difficult to separate it into groups other than regional. The various forms are intimately associated, the diversified characters grading one into another in the most confusing manner. It is very much as though the peninsula had been occupied by peoples of distinct origins, who had come together on common ground in such intimate relations that

ENGRAVED DESIGNS REPRESENTING THE BIRD CONCEPT, FLORIDA

ENGRAVED DESIGNS REPRESENTING THE FROG CONCEPT, FLORIDA
GULF COAST GROUP

ENGRAVED DESIGNS, ALABAMA AND FLORIDA

GULF COAST GROUP

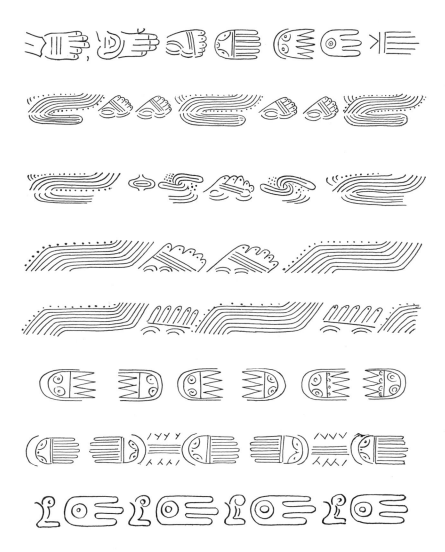

ENGRAVED DESIGNS, ALABAMA AND FLORIDA

GULF COAST GROUP

their respective cultures became in a large measure blended. This apparent intermingling of elements would seem to pertain to a late rather than to an early period.

CHRONOLOGY

Questions of antiquity naturally present themselves for consideration in this place, but very definite answers can not be given. We may reasonably anticipate that in time the ceramic evidence will materially assist in determining the succession of peoples and also in arriving at a somewhat definite chronology of events. The ware embedded in successive layers of midden refuse gives hints of change and progress, and the absence of sherds in the subordinate strata points apparently to a time when pottery was not used by the tribes represented. Then again the higher forms of ware appear well up in the strata and prevail over the surface of the country in general. Mr Moore refers to the topic in the following language:

When after a long and careful search in a shell heap no pottery is brought to light, it may be considered that the makers of the heap lived at a time when its method of manufacture was unknown. Pottery filled so great a want in the lives of the aborigines and was so extensively used by the makers of the shell heaps, where it is found at all, that it seems impossible to account for its absence upon any hypothesis other than the one suggested. One fact relating to pottery which Professor Wyman neglects to state is that in many shell heaps pottery is found to a certain depth only, after which it disappears. In other shell heaps, pottery plain and ornamented is found in association for a time, after which unornamented pottery alone is found. These points in connection with the pottery of the shell heaps have been noticed in so many scores of cases that the writer is convinced that many shell heaps were in process of formation contemporaneously with the first knowledge of the art of pottery making and its subsequent development. * * * It is well known that later Indians occupied the shell heaps as places of residence long after their completion, some doubtless cultivating them, and hence distance from the surface is a most important factor in determining the origin of shell-heap relics of all sorts.[a]

RANGE OF THE WARE

The pottery in our collections from Florida comprises a wide range of technic and esthetic characters. There are specimens rivaling the best work of the Lower Mississippi region, and others so rudimentary as hardly to deserve the name of earthenware. There are also numerous varieties resulting apparently not so much from differences in peoples and time as from the diverse uses to which they were applied. One group is wholly unique, consisting in the main of toy-like forms of rude workmanship, and exhibiting decidedly abnormal characters. There is good reason for supposing that it was manufactured exclusively for mortuary offerings, as it is associated almost wholly with burials. Again, the shell heaps furnish an inferior variety of ware quite peculiar to them. It is difficult to say just how much of this inferiority is due to antiquity and how much to the fact that midden

[a] Moore, Clarence B., Certain shell heaps of the St Johns river, American Naturalist, November, 1892, p. 916.

ware in general is rude on account of its manufacture for the preparation of food and its exclusive use in that process. The pottery of the burial mounds, except the peculiar ware mentioned above, and of the country in general is of a higher grade, often exhibiting neat finish, varied and refined forms, and tasteful decorations. Considered as a whole, the ceramic art of the Florida peninsula indicates a state of culture much inferior to that of the middle and lower Mississippi valley.

MATERIALS

The clay used, considering the whole peninsula, seems to have had a wide range of composition and to have been subjected to varied methods of treatment. The inferior pottery shows poorly selected materials and rude treatment, while the better product is characterized by finely prepared paste. Much of the ware is of unusually low specific gravity, as if rendered porous by weathering or decay of some of the denser ingredients.

The tempering materials are also varied. Much of the shell-deposit ware has been tempered with fibrous vegetal matter, such as pounded grass or bark, thought by Wyman to be palmetto fiber, which burned out in firing or has disappeared through decay, leaving the paste light and porous. This ware is rude and coarse in texture and is said to occur only in the older shell deposits. In many places the paste is exceptionally free from tempering ingredients, being fine-grained and chalky. These conditions may be due to the nature of the available materials rather than to any peculiar local ethnic conditions. The soft paste prevails in the St Johns river region and extends also to the west coast. The gritty paste of the Appalachian provinces reaches southward into northern Florida and is found, though quite rarely, down the east and west coasts. The use of pulverized shell is noted in a few cases along the west coast.

MANUFACTURE

The vessels were built up often of wide strips of clay, which, in many cases, were so poorly worked or welded together that the vessels fall to pieces along the joints. In the ruder pieces the lines of junction are still traceable, especially on the inner surfaces, where neat finish was difficult or unnecessary. The walls of the ruder ware are thick, clumsy, and uneven; those of the better varieties are thin, uniform, and evenly dressed. The finish is also varied, ranging from the roughest hand-modeled surfaces through those variously textured to well-polished surfaces. In many cases a thin coat of finer clay has been applied to the exterior to hide the coarse materials and render the polishing easy.

The baking or firing seems to have been of several grades or varieties; usually, however, the surfaces show the mottlings characteristic of

the open-air treatment common with the tribes of the United States.
The paste in the more porous wares is often somewhat whitened super-
ficially by volatilization of vegetal elements, the interior of the mass
remaining dark or black.   In some localities decided reddish and yellowish tints are seen, a result probably of oxidization of iron contained in the clay.   The improvised mortuary wares are generally
only slightly baked.

FORMS

The forms of the ordinary ware, as well as those of the "freak"
mortuary pottery, are much diversified.   Vessels of the culinary class
are apparently not numerous; but, being especially subject to breakage, they rarely appear in collections except as sherds.   Neither the
pot nor the deep caldron are common.   Cups and bowls, the latter
often of large size, are very numerous, a subglobular form with constricted lip being typically Floridian.   Bottles, or forms approaching
the bottle in shape, are rare, while eccentric and compound forms
occur in all sections.   Bottoms are rounded, conic, or slightly flattened.   Handles are not an important feature, while feet or added bases
of any kind are rarely seen in the normal ware.   Animal forms were
modeled with considerable freedom in later times, and occasionally
shells of mollusks and the gourd were imitated.   The shapes as a
whole are inferior to those in the districts to the north and west,
although, if we include the improvised mortuary pottery, they are far
more diversified.

DECORATION

Decoration is varied and heterogeneous, so much so that it can not
properly be described, except in connection with illustrations.   It
rarely includes fabric- and cord-marked surfaces, but the paddle stamp,
with varied designs, was used extensively in most sections.   Incising
and indenting were employed in working out designs of many classes,
and especially symbolic subjects.   In some varieties of ware the work
was very crude, in others it was extremely skillful.   The application of red ocher was general, and simple designs were executed in
this pigment.   Decorative effects were also secured by roughening the
surface in various ways, as by pinching up the soft clay with the finger nails, and by modeling ridges, nodes, and other forms in low or
high relief.   The lip or rim is often embellished by notching or scal-
loping.   The subject-matter of the designs ranges from the simple
geometric elements to somewhat realistic, although crude, delineations
of men and animals.   Conventional treatment of life forms is often
exceptionally refined and effective, but symbols of special or highly
developed types have not been identified.

USES

The uses to which the pottery of Florida was devoted were about
the same as among other native tribes.   There were vessels to serve

in the full range of domestic activities—cooking, carrying, containing, eating, and drinking—and others for ceremonial offices, and for burial with the dead. There were also miniature vessels, as well as figurines representing animals, probably intended to be used as toys. There were tobacco pipes, beads, and pendants, and other objects not assignable to any particular use.

The employment of earthenware in burial is of special interest. The dead were buried in ordinary graves and in sand and earth mounds, and, exceptionally, in shell mounds, and here as elsewhere it was customary to deposit various utensils with the bodies; but there are some curious and interesting features connected with the practice. Over much of the territory covered by this paper the vessels were deposited in the graves entire and are so recovered by our explorers, but in the Florida peninsula, and to some extent in Georgia and Alabama, a practice had arisen of breaking the vessel or perforating the bottom before consigning it to the ground. The most satisfactory explanation of this proceeding is that since the vessel was usually regarded as being alive and endowed with the spirit of some creature of mythologic significance, it was appropriate that it should be "killed" before burial, that the spirit might be free to accompany that of the dead.

The facts brought out by recent explorations of Mr Moore add new features of interest.[a] In cases it is apparent that the vessels were not only broken for burial, but that fragmentary vessels were used; and again that, as in the case of the Tick Island and other mounds, sherds were buried, serving probably as substitutes for the entire vessels. An exceptional feature of these phenomena is the presence in some of the burial mounds of sherds broken out to rudely resemble notched spear and arrow points. It would seem that the sherd was made to represent the vessel which was formerly buried entire, and that, possibly, extending its office to another field, it was modified in shape that it might take the place of such implements of stone and other materials as were formerly devoted to the service of the dead.

Still more remarkable is the practice, which seems to have become pretty general in Florida, of manufacturing vessels especially for burial purposes. Some of these pieces are in such close imitation of the real vessels that the distinction between them can not be drawn with certainty, while others are made with open bases, so that they did not need to be broken or "killed" when inhumed, having never been made alive. Others are of such rude workmanship and eccentric form that no ordinary use could be made of them. In seeking to explain these exceptional products two suggestions may be made: First, it is noted that the perforating of the vessels used in burial and the placing of sherds and toy-like vessels and figurines with

[a] Moore, Clarence B., Certain sand mounds of the St Johns river, Florida, Journal Academy of Natural Sciences, ser. 2, vol. x, Philadelphia, 1894.

the dead is confined, mainly at least, to Florida and the Gulf coast, and further that these practices pertain to comparatively recent times. It is also observed that articles of European make—Venetian beads, Spanish olive jars, articles of metal, etc.—are found in many mounds of this region, indicating the very general practice of mound-building during a considerable period following the arrival of the Spanish—a period extending over a hundred years or more. It is suggested, therefore, that possibly this whole group of extraordinary mortuary practices may have sprung up in post-Columbian times. The most prolific sources of gain known to the Spanish were the cemeteries of the aborigines, and the seekers of El Dorado and the Fountain of Life were the princes of grave robbers. It would be but natural that people possessing the ready resources of the southern Indians, finding the graves of their fathers ruthlessly desecrated by the invaders in their mad search for gold and pearls, should, while still preserving the spirit of their mortuary customs, cease to consign to the ground any articles of real value. It will be conceded that the inroads of hordes of avaricious and merciless strangers must have exercised a powerful influence on the habits and customs of the native tribes, and such phenomena as these mentioned might result naturally. The fact, however, that graves containing these objects are very numerous and often contain other articles of real value, as has been pointed out by Mr Moore, seems to render this theory untenable. Second, a somewhat more satisfactory explanation may be found in the idea of substitution for purely economic reasons; perhaps the demands of mortuary sacrifice grew burdensome to the people, or possibly the practice of the art in its normal phases fell into disfavor or gradually gave way to some other form of vessel-making art, while the practice of making ceramic offerings kept on in conformity with the persistent demands of superstitious custom. At any rate, the practice of hastily making sacrificial offerings of clay came into great favor and a study of the objects, many of which are illustrated in accompanying plates, shows that they embody in their rude way all varieties of form and decoration known in Florida, and shows, beside this, that the imagination ran riot imitating objects of many classes and conjuring up forms entirely new to the art.

The use of earthen vessels as receptacles for human remains has not been noted by Mr Moore in his extensive explorations on the Florida peninsula, although the practice was common in Georgia and other sections to the north and west.

EXAMPLES

MIDDEN WARE OF THE ST JOHNS

The shell mounds of the St Johns furnish varieties of ware said to be confined almost exclusively to these deposits, and supposed especially to characterize the middle period of their accumulation, the

earlier period being without pottery, and the later having several varieties of ware, which appear on the surface in great plenty. This
pottery has been recovered only in the shape of sherds, and can not
be studied to the best advantage. Among the fragments are found evidences of considerable variation in texture, treatment, and ornamentation. One variety exhibits a rather fine-grained paste preserving
the warm gray colors of the baked clay. The surfaces were finished
with a rubbing tool, and are plain or have been rather carelessly
embellished with patterns in
straight and curved incised
lines. Another, and the most
noteworthy variety, is characterized by the unusual appearance of the paste, which
has been tempered with a
large percentage of fibrous
matter, probably shredded
palmetto fiber. This tem-
pering substance has been
destroyed by fire or decay,
leaving the paste highly vesi-
cular and porous and of low
specific gravity. Generally
these sherds show clearly the

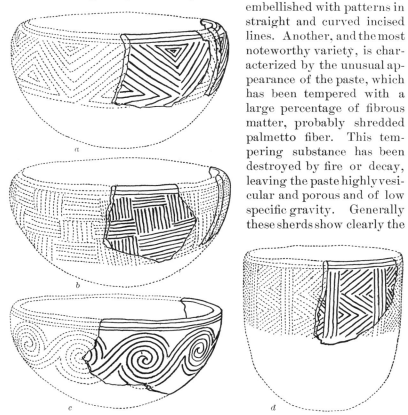

Fig. 57—Restoration of forms of fiber-tempered midden ware, St Johns river.

effects of use over fire. The walls are thick and uneven and the surfaces
are rudely rubbed down. The forms appear to have consisted mainly
of bowls with rims variously recurved, incurved, and otherwise modified, and with rounded or flattish bases. The diameter varies from a
few inches to a foot or more. Examples restored from fragments sufficiently large to indicate the shape and suggest the true character of the
ornament are shown in figure 57. They are from the Tick Island
mound, and appear typical of what is assumed to be the earliest pottery-

making period. The execution of the designs is decidedly rude, the incised lines being deep, wide, and irregular. The designs themselves, however, seem to comprise not only the archaic forms seen in *a* and *b*, but running scrolls such as occur in the most advanced grades of southern pottery, as in *c*. The angular interspaces in the latter designs are filled in with indentations, as in the Mobile-Pensacola and other wares (see figure 58). There is no absolute measure of the value of particular decorative motives in determining degree of culture progress, but elaborate scroll work can hardly be called archaic, and we must conclude either that this ware does not represent the earliest use of pottery among the shell-mound peoples, or that the more western tribes, already practicing this art, encroached on the original shell-heap people at a comparatively early date. It may be remarked further that the shapes, so far as observed, are nearly identical with the prevailing shapes of the best wares of Florida. This fiber-tempered pottery was found by Wyman at Old Town, Old Enterprise, Watsons

Fig. 58—Fragments of midden-ware bowls with incised scroll decoration, St Johns river.

Landing, Silver Spring, and Palatka,[a] but no details of occurrence are given. Mr Moore obtained specimens from Tick island, Orange mound, Huntingtons, Mulberry mound, and other localities, and his determinations of relative position and age have already been quoted.

Two sherds derived from hemispheric bowls decorated with running scrolls are illustrated in figure 58. There are pieces, however, that approach the better wares of later time in texture and finish, and it may yet be shown that the earlier pottery of Florida developed without marked interruption into the later and more highly elaborated forms. Additional sherds are shown in plate LXXXIV.

STAMPED WARE OF THE ST JOHNS

The use of the stamp or figured paddle in decoration was common throughout the peninsula, extending west into Alabama and north to North Carolina and Tennessee. It is not likely that it was characteristic of any particular people or culture group. That it is not of

---

[a] Wyman, Dr Jeffries, Fresh-water shell mounds of the St Johns river, Florida, Memoirs of the Peabody Academy of Science, Salem, Mass., 1875.

Mexican origin would seem to be proved by the fact that it does not occur west of Mobile bay. It is no doubt related to if not derived from the art of embellishing the vessels by impressing textile fabrics upon their plastic surfaces, practiced so extensively in the North. Mr Cushing expresses the idea, originating with his San Marco work,[a] that the use of wooden tools in which the grain of the wood gave rise to decorative surface markings might have led to the making of figured stamps or modeling paddles, but this idea requires confirmation. I have observed that some of the more elaborate stamped patterns employed are closely akin to designs used by ancient wood carvers and sculptors of the Antilles, thus suggesting some kind of connection between Florida and the islands.[b]

The ware of the St Johns shows the very common use of a modeling paddle the face of which was carved in checker patterns, consisting of shallow grooves crossing generally at right angles and numbering from five to twelve to the inch. Examples are shown in plate LXXXV. Occasionally we encounter more elaborate and artistic designs, such as prevail in the Appalachian province on the north. Various examples from the St Johns are brought together in plates LXXXVI, LXXXVII, and LXXXVIII. It would appear that the stamp paddle was not in use during the earlier stages of pottery making in Florida. According to Mr Moore the stamped ware occurs less frequently as we descend into the midden deposits, rarely appearing at any considerable depth.

ENGRAVED WARE OF THE ST JOHNS

The St Johns furnishes occasional specimens of ware of excellent make, seemingly not akin to the common pottery of the region, although apparently intimately associated with it in burial. An example is presented in plate LXXXIX a. It is a well-modeled globular bowl from a mound in Duval county, is 10 inches in diameter, and is tastefully ornamented with representations of a bird, probably the duck. The head of the bird is modeled in relief on opposite sides of the vessel. The bill points upward, and the wings, depicted in simple incised lines, extend around the upper part of the body of the vessel. A sketch of one of the heads appears in b. The duck is a prominent feature in the embellishment of Florida wares, but in many cases the forms are so highly conventionalized that only those who have traced the duck motive down from more realistic delineations can do more than guess at the original. An example of conventional duck design is presented in plate XC a. An equally conventional treatment, possibly of the vulture, appears in b. Other examples of this class are referred to in describing the pottery of western Florida. Much of the mortuary and midden ware is decorated with incised work, always carelessly executed.

[a] Cushing, F. H., Exploration of ancient key-dweller remains, Proceedings American Philosophical Society, vol. XXXV, p. 74.
[b] Holmes, W. H., Caribbean influence on the prehistoric ceramic art of the southern states, American Anthropologist, January, 1894, p. 71.

FRAGMENTS OF POTTERY FROM SHELL HEAPS

FLORIDA PENINSULA

(MOORE COLLECTION, ABOUT THREE-FOURTHS)

POTTERY WITH STAMP DECORATION

FLORIDA PENINSULA

(ABOUT THREE-FOURTHS)

a (DIAMETER 6¼ INCHES)

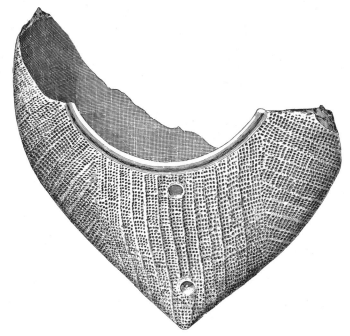

b (WIDTH ABOUT 9 INCHES)

POTTERY WITH STAMP DECORATION
FLORIDA PENINSULA
(MOORE COLLECTION)

a

b

POTTERY WITH STAMP DECORATION

FLORIDA PENINSULA

(MOORE COLLECTION, ABOUT THREE-FOURTHS)

a

b

POTTERY WITH STAMP DECORATION

FLORIDA PENINSULA

(MOORE COLLECTION, ABOUT THREE-FOURTHS)

a (DIAMETER 10¼ INCHES)

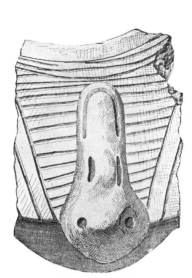

b (HEIGHT 4¾ INCHES)   *c* (DIAMETER 7½ INCHES)

VASES WITH RELIEVED AND ENGRAVED DESIGNS

FLORIDA PENINSULA

(MOORE COLLECTION)

b (ABOUT THREE-FOURTHS)

c (ABOUT ONE-HALF)

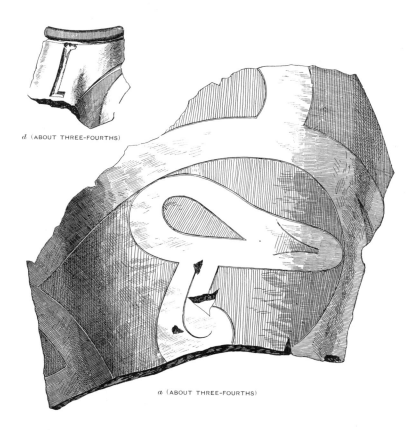

d (ABOUT THREE-FOURTHS)

a (ABOUT THREE-FOURTHS)

FRAGMENTS OF VASES WITH ENGRAVED DESIGNS

FLORIDA PENINSULA

(MOORE COLLECTION)

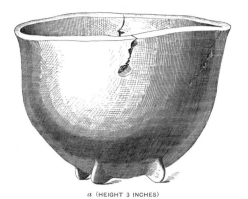

a (HEIGHT 3 INCHES)

b (HEIGHT 4 INCHES)

c (HEIGHT 4½ INCHES)

d (HEIGHT 4½ INCHES)

RUDE EARTHENWARE FROM GRAVES

FLORIDA PENINSULA

(MOORE COLLECTION)

IMPROVISED MORTUARY WARE OF THE ST JOHNS

Explorations on the St Johns have brought to light a form of earthenware having characters not heretofore observed in any locality, and likely to give rise to considerable discussion. The possible functions of this ware have already received attention. It has been found by Mr Moore and others at varying depths in the burial mounds, but never in the shell heaps. A few pieces were obtained from Mount Royal at a depth of 12 feet beneath the surface. It consists of vessels, vessel-like articles, animal figurines, miniature imitations of fruit, and various objects of eccentric shape, nearly all of rude construction and finish. As a rule these objects have the appearance of toys made by hands unskilled in the manipulation of clay and practically untrammeled by the traditions of the normal native art. The clay used was generally crude and untempered, the construction careless and hasty, and the baking very slight. Specimens worthy of being called vessels are mostly so crudely made that they would be of little service in any of the usual offices of a vessel. As a rule the bottoms of such specimens were perforated while the clay was yet soft, the opening being left rough as cut or punched, or dressed down rudely after the manner of the normal opening at the opposite end. They repeat, in a measure, the forms of the real pottery, but with many trivial variations. Decoration is in all styles, the incised, stamped, relieved, and painted, but in the main it is crude. The animal and vegetal forms are often so graphically suggested, however, that the idea of the modeler is intelligible. The panther, the wolf or dog, the squirrel, the turkey, the turtle, and the fish are more or less forcibly suggested. The size is usually small, and the clumsy forms, modeled with the unaided fingers, are solid or nearly so, the more massive portions having been in cases roughly perforated with a stick to prevent cracking and falling to pieces in the process of baking. Vegetal forms are extremely rare in the normal native art of the eastern United States, the gourd appearing in some cases as a model for earthen vessels; but in this mortuary ware various essays have been made to represent acorns, flowers, buds, ears of corn, and the like. A large number of unclassified forms, quite as rude as the preceding, resemble cylinders, cones, beads, spools, hourglasses, druggist's mortars, etc. On examination of the various ceramic collections in the United States, there are found occasional examples of small, rudely made, toy-like figures from other localities that may possibly fall into the same general class as these Florida mortuary fantasies.

The most satisfactory evidence of the close relationship of this pottery with the normal wares of Florida is its occurrence in a number of mounds at considerable depths and under varying conditions, and associated intimately with a wide range of relics. Besides this, there are many features of the ware that approach in appearance or manner of treatment the ordinary pottery, and, in fact, there is such a complete grading into vessels of normal character that in places no line can be drawn separating the trivial from the serious. We may therefore safely infer that all varieties were made by potters of the same period and linguistic family. In appearance these articles are rather new-looking, and, being found generally near the surface, may be regarded as representing a comparatively recent period. Examples of several varieties are brought together in plates xci–xcviii.[a]

PAINTED WARE OF THE ST JOHNS

The use of colors in decoration prevailed most decidedly in the Middle Mississippi Valley province, but in Florida color was in somewhat general use. Commonly the red color was spread over the entire surface and polished down, as it was in the West. When designs were used, they were always simple, and, in the main, consisted of broad bands in clumsy geometric arrangements. It is not known that color was confined to any particular class of vessels. A very large and remarkable piece of the painted ware is presented in plate xcix. It was obtained by Mr Clarence B. Moore from a sand mound near Volusia, Volusia county, and is 19 inches in diameter and 15½ inches in height. The base or smaller end is neatly perforated, as may be seen in the lower figure, the opening having been made when the vessel was modeled, and finished with the same care as was the mouth. It is possible that this vessel had some special domestic use in which the perforation was an essential feature, as in straining liquids, or it may have been a drum; but the practice of perforating vessels for burial and of making toy-like vessels with perforated bottoms for mortuary purposes offers an explanation of the significance of the whole class of perforate objects. It is surmised that the native theory was that a vessel which had only a supernatural purpose was properly perforate. It was never endowed with the powers and quali ties of a living thing. The red color is applied in broad bands encircling the apertures and in four vertical stripes connecting these. Fragments of a vessel of similar design are given in plate c. It also is from the mound near Volusia, and has been some 18 or 20 inches in length.

POTTERY OF THE WEST COAST

The several varieties of pottery described as occurring in the San Juan province, with the exception of the midden and mortuary ware, are found scattered over the state in mounds and on residence sites, but few examples have found their way into our museums. In the west, and especially along the west coast of the peninsula, other interesting

---

[a] Recent collections made by Mr Moore in the Apalachicola region show equally novel and varied shapes of this general class, the work being of much higher grade.

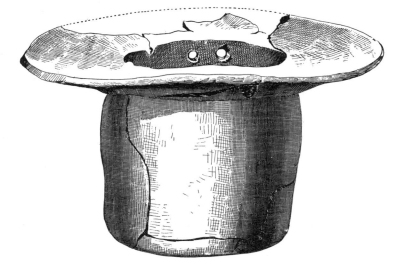

a (HEIGHT 4 INCHES)

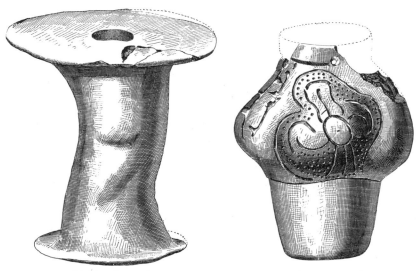

b (HEIGHT 4¼ INCHES)   *c* (HEIGHT 4 INCHES)

RUDE EARTHENWARE FROM GRAVES
FLORIDA PENINSULA
(MOORE COLLECTION)

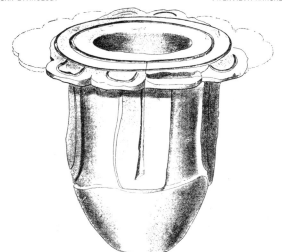

a (HEIGHT 4 INCHES)

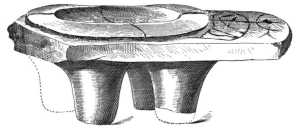

b (LENGTH 5 INCHES)

c (HEIGHT 3 INCHES)

d (DIAMETER 4 INCHES)

RUDE EARTHENWARE FROM GRAVES

FLORIDA PENINSULA

(MOORE COLLECTION)

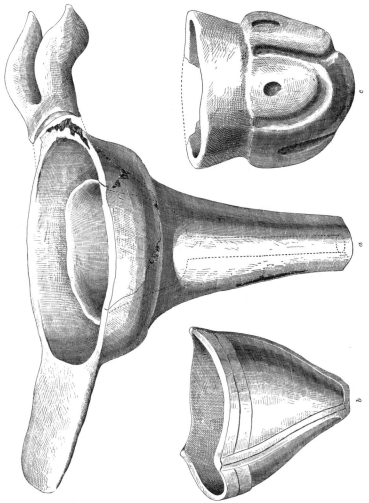

_a_

_b_

_c_

RUDE EARTHENWARE FROM GRAVES

FLORIDA PENINSULA

(MOORE COLLECTION)

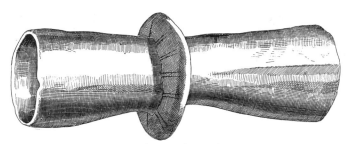

a (LENGTH 5¼ INCHES)

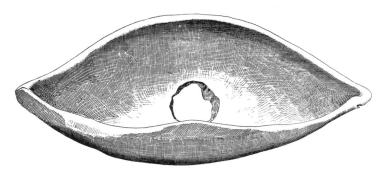

b (LENGTH 6 INCHES)

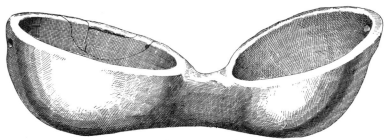

c (LENGTH 6½ INCHES)

RUDE EARTHENWARE FROM GRAVES
FLORIDA PENINSULA
(MOORE COLLECTION)

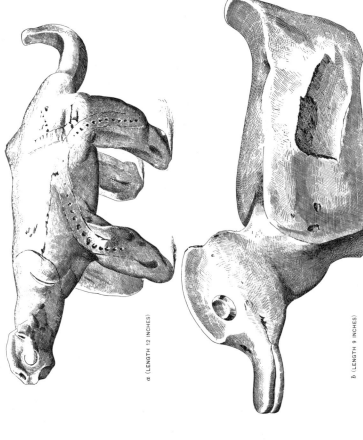

a (LENGTH 12 INCHES)

b (LENGTH 9 INCHES)

RUDE EARTHENWARE FROM GRAVES

FLORIDA PENINSULA

(MOORE COLLECTION)

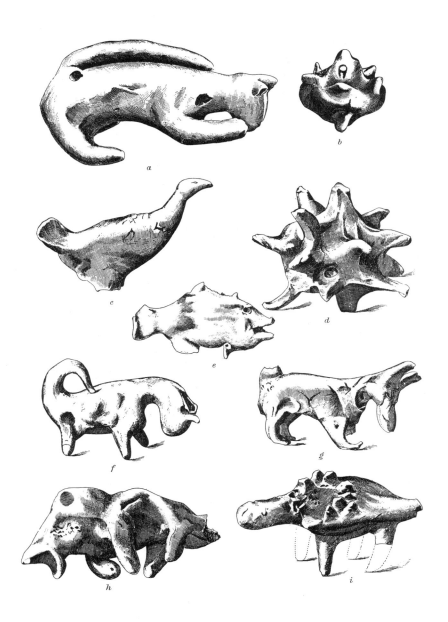

RUDE EARTHENWARE FROM GRAVES

FLORIDA PENINSULA

(MOORE COLLECTION, ABOUT THREE-FOURTHS)

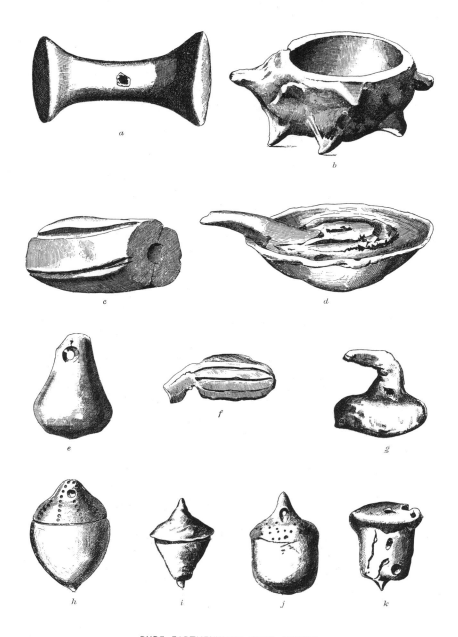

RUDE EARTHENWARE FROM GRAVES

FLORIDA PENINSULA

(MOORE COLLECTION, ABOUT THREE-FOURTHS)

a

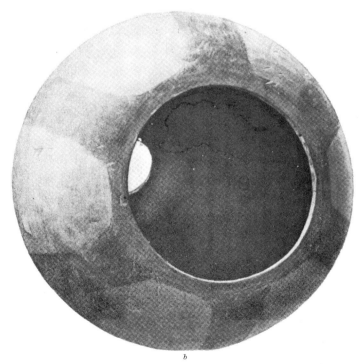

b

LARGE PAINTED VESSEL WITH OPEN BASE

FLORIDA PENINSULA

(MOORE COLLECTION, DIAMETER 19 INCHES)

varieties of products are encountered.   The most striking of these is characterized by its style of ornamentation, which consists of elaborate designs worked out largely with indentations or punctures instead of with plain incised lines, giving tattoo effects.   Specimens in the main fragmental have been found over a wide area, but the best preserved and most typical examples are those recently obtained from a burial mound at Tarpon Springs by Mr F. H. Cushing.   Some of these are presented in the accompanying plates, and the ornamental designs are projected at full length in plate CIV.   Notwithstanding the large degree of individuality displayed by these specimens, they by no means stand alone, being closely allied in paste, shape, and ornamentation to one or another of the varieties of Florida pottery.

The vase shown in plate CI is perhaps the most interesting and artistic of the group.   The lower figure gives a top view of the shattered vessel as it appeared when the various pieces were first hastily set together, while the upper shows it as restored by Mr Cushing, save in one respect, namely, that as in his restoration the base is more delicately pointed than seems warranted by any model found in Florida, the liberty of changing it has been taken, the bottom being given a gently rounded or slightly flattened outline, as if the vessel had been intended to stand alone.   The color is a yellowish terra cotta, the surface is even and well polished, and the walls are very thin.   The incurved rim is narrow and rounded on the margin and is embellished with four conic nodes placed at equal distances about the lip.   The decoration, which is applied and worked out in a very pleasing and artistic manner, appears in plate CIV*a*. Although it is highly conventional, it is undoubtedly significant and symbolic, and is based on some life form.   It is seen that the leading feature of the design is repeated four times above a broad meander band which encircles the body of the vessel, and that below the band a second and less elaborate feature is also four times repeated.   As we recall the usual association of animal features with vases in the general region, we examine the design to discover, if possible, some suggestion of a life concept.   It would seem that the leading elements of the design must represent the head of some creature, and by studying the four principal features, it is seen that they show decided analogies with more realistic delineations of the duck observed on other vessels, and the conclusion is reached that the device is a conventional treatment of this favorite concept and that the vessel was invested with appropriate life symbolism by the people to whom it belonged.

A second specimen from the Tarpon Springs mound is given in plate CII*a*.   It is quite equal to the other in delicacy of execution and in interest, and the exquisite design shown in full in plate CIV*b* may be looked on as of the same class as the preceding and as intended to symbolize nothing more esoteric or mysterious than the life idea associated with the vase in accordance with almost universal custom. It is instructive, however, to observe the graceful ways in which the esthetic instincts of a primitive people have taken hold of the crude elements of symbolism, making them things of beauty.

A third vessel of the same group, similar in shape and finish and embodying analogous elements of decoration, appears in plate CIII and the design is drawn out in plate CIV c. This specimen is shown also in the preceding plate, CII, in connection with a large plain pot, c, of symmetric shape and excellent surface finish. Two fragments decorated in this stipple style, one showing a graceful shield-shaped figure in relief, are shown in plate CV b and c. They came from a mound at Cedar Keys. The little cup shown in a of this plate is decorated with incised lines and punctures representing a crab-like animal, and also in color, certain spaces being finished in red. It is from Franklin county, Florida.

The same plate includes a remarkable specimen of compound vessel from a mound in Franklin county. It is a plain ware of usual make and has five compartments, four circular basins arranged about a central basin of squarish shape. One of the encircling basins has been broken away and is restored in the drawing.

One of the most novel forms is shown in plate CVI a. It is goblet-like and is open at both ends, reminding one of the Central American earthenware drums. It appears, however, from a careful examination, that the base was originally closed or partly closed, and that the end was broken out and the margin smoothed down so that in appearance it closely resembles the larger open end. The surface is embellished with broad bands of red and incised figures, all probably highly conventionalized animal features. A similar specimen embellished with unique incised patterns is shown in b and c of the same plate.

In plate CVII a bunch of four vessels, as exposed while excavating a grave in a sand mound at Tarpon Springs, is shown. Still other specimens of inferior size and make, also from Tarpon Springs, are similar in style to the pieces already illustrated, while some are small, rude, and quite plain or decorated with crude designs, and a few are modeled in imitation of gourds, seashells, and animals. In some cases compound and eccentric forms are seen. One medium-sized pot-like form, suggesting a common western type probably intended to stand for some life form, has a rudely incised design encircling the shoulder and four looped handles placed at equal distance about the neck. Occasional specimens are tall, and have the wide mouth and conic base so characteristic of the Appalachian region, and these are ornamented with the patterned stamp in various styles. Fragments from Tarpon Springs showing the florid stamp designs are given in plate CVIII, and griddle patterns appear in plate CIX.

The pottery secured by Mr Cushing at San Marco on the Pile-

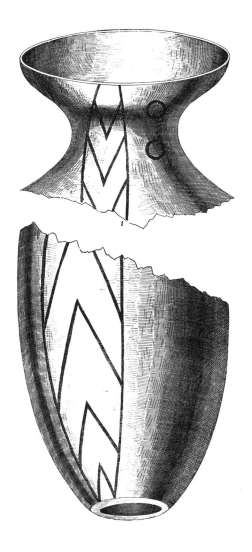

FRAGMENTS OF PAINTED VESSEL WITH OPEN BASE

FLORIDA PENINSULA

(MOORE COLLECTION, DIAMETER OF LARGE APERTURE 8 INCHES)

a

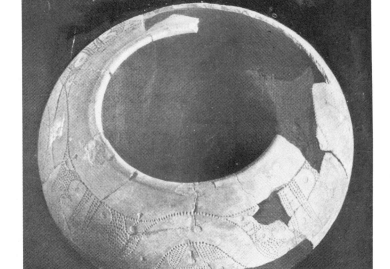

b

DECORATED VASES, TARPON SPRINGS

FLORIDA PENINSULA

(FREE MUSEUM OF SCIENCE AND ART, PHILADELPHIA, DIAMETER 13 INCHES)

c   *b*

a (DIAMETER 13½ INCHES)

VASES WITH ENGRAVED DESIGNS, TARPON SPRINGS

FLORIDA PENINSULA

(FREE MUSEUM OF SCIENCE AND ART, PHILADELPHIA)

a

b

VASES WITH ENGRAVED DESIGNS, TARPON SPRINGS
FLORIDA PENINSULA
(FREE MUSEUM OF SCIENCE AND ART, PHILADELPHIA, DIAMETER 8 INCHES)

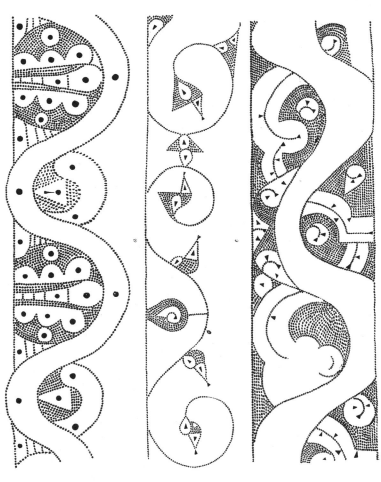

a

c

b

ENGRAVED DESIGNS, TARPON SPRINGS

FLORIDA PENINSULA

(SEE PLATES CI, CII, CIII.)

a (DIAMETER 3¾ INCHES)

c (ABOUT ONE-HALF)

b (ABOUT ONE-HALF)

d (DIAMETER 5½ INCHES)

FRAGMENTS OF DECORATED WARE AND COMPOUND CUP
FLORIDA PENINSULA

a (HEIGHT 10½ INCHES)

e (DIAMETER 5¼ INCHES)

d (DIAMETER 3¼ INCHES)

b   (HEIGHT 9 INCHES)   *c*

ENGRAVED AND PAINTED VASES, TARPON SPRINGS

FLORIDA PENINSULA

(FREE MUSEUM OF SCIENCE AND ART, PHILADELPHIA)

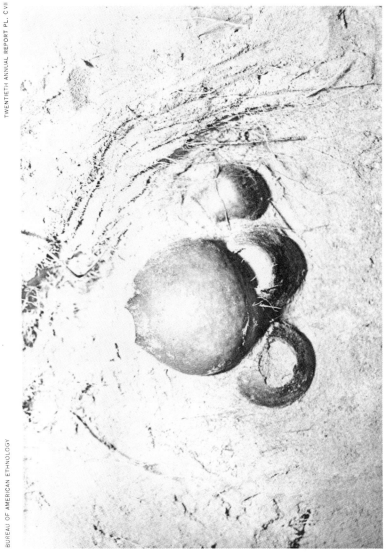

CLUSTER OF VASES IN SAND MOUND BURIAL
FLORIDA PENINSULA

POTSHERDS WITH ORNATE STAMP DESIGNS

FLORIDA PENINSULA

(ABOUT ONE-HALF)

POTSHERDS WITH GRIDDLE-LIKE STAMP DESIGNS
FLORIDA PENINSULA
(ABOUT ONE-HALF)

dwelling sites, and associated with remains and relics of the most remarkable kind,[a] is extremely simple in style, hardly excelling in its plastic and graphic features the gourd and wooden vessels found in such profusion in the muck-filled canals and, in many cases, it appears to be modeled in imitation of these vessels. It does not differ in kind from the ordinary West Florida ware, however, which indicates the practical identity of the Pile-dwellers with other occupants of the region in time and culture.

Somewhat common in the western and northwestern peninsular region is another variety of decorative treatment related to the delicate engraved work described above, but contrasting strongly with it. The designs in cases duplicate the peculiar scroll work of the Mobile-Pensacola district, and again are somewhat like the Tarpon Springs scroll work. The main peculiarity is that the lines are wide and are deeply incised, as is shown in plate cx a, b, c. In b, which is part of a large globular bowl, the figures are outlined in deep, clean lines, and some of the spaces are filled in with stamped patterns consisting of small checks, giving very pleasing results. In a and c some of the spaces are filled in with indentations made with a sharp point. Handled vessels—dippers, cups, and pots—are common, and it is not unusual to see the rim of a pot set with four or eight handles; e illustrates this feature and also a treatment of the scroll much like that prevalent farther up the west coast. There are traces along this coast of rather pronounced variations in composition, shape, and decoration. A number of sherds illustrating the varied decorative effects produced by pinching with the finger nails are illustrated in f, g, and h.

ANIMAL FIGURES

It is not uncommon to find in many parts of Florida, and especially along the Gulf coast, portions of fairly well modeled animal figures, mostly only heads, which originally formed parts of bowls and other vessels. These correspond very closely with similar work in the West, and are almost duplications of the heads found in the Pensacola region. The detached heads have been found as far south as Goodland point, San Marco island, where Mr Moore picked up two specimens that had evidently been made use of as pendants, probably on account of some totemic or other significance attached to them. Mr Cushing also found one of these bird-head amulets in the canal deposits at San Marco. All are of western types, and may have been brought from north of the Gulf. On the whole, the employment of animal figures in the art of Florida, as well as of the Atlantic coast farther north, seems a late innovation, and the practice of embellishing vessels with these features has probably, in a large measure, crept in from the West.

---

[a] Cushing, F. H., Exploration of ancient key-dweller remains, Proceedings of the American Philosophical Society, vol. XXXV.

TOBACCO PIPES

Tobacco pipes of earthenware are quite rare in Florida. The specimens figured in plate cxi are types, *a* being embellished with the imperfect figure of a bird resting on the bowl and perforated by the bowl cavity, while *b* is undecorated. Other specimens appear in *c*, *d*, and *e*. In general shape they correspond closely with the prevailing heavy-bodied pipes of the South and West. Only one entire specimen and two fragments have been reported from shell heaps.

SPANISH OLIVE JARS

From time to time collectors have reported the finding of pottery in Florida and other southern states bearing evidence of having been turned on a wheel, and also showing traces of a brownish glaze. Examination always discloses the fact that the ware is of Spanish manufacture. The

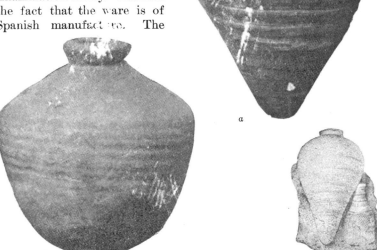

FIG. 59—Spanish olive jars, Florida.

paste is that of ordinary terra cotta, and in cases is burned quite hard, resembling stoneware. The forms are little varied, the short bottle neck and the long-pointed base being notable characteristics. The encircling ribs left by careless throwing on the wheel are often quite

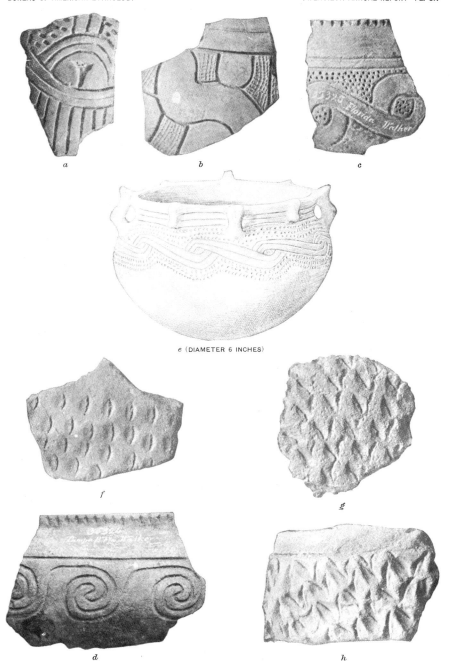

a

b

c

e (DIAMETER 6 INCHES)

f

g

d

h

HANDLED CUP AND VARIOUS SHERDS FROM THE WEST COAST

FLORIDA PENINSULA

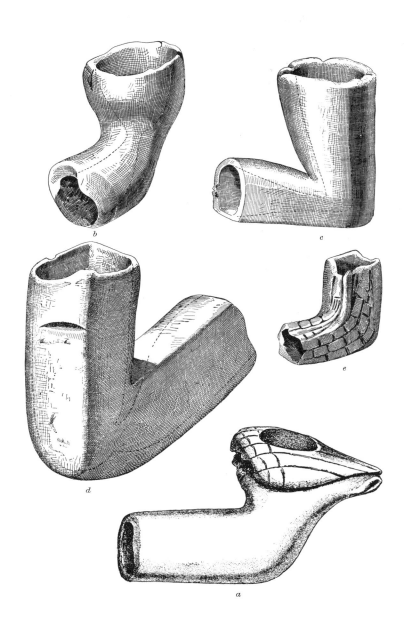

TOBACCO PIPES

FLORIDA PENINSULA

(MOORE COLLECTION, ABOUT THREE-FOURTHS)

pronounced. In numerous cases the inside of the lip has received a yellowish glaze. Occasionally these vessels are recovered from Indian mounds. In early times it was a common practice to ship olives to America in earthen jars of this class. Illustrations are given in figure 59. A very interesting specimen of this ware, figure 59 c, may be seen in the Natural History Museum at Boston. It is a jar with long, attenuated, conic base, which, with a glass bottle, was found embedded in a mass of coral obtained by dredgers from a coral reef off Turks island at the point where the British frigate Severn is said to have been wrecked about the year 1793. In a few instances very large and thick vessels of terra cotta have been reported, which are probably of European origin, and an antique bath tub of glazed earthenware was recently unearthed in one of the Gulf states.

POTTERY OF THE SOUTH APPALACHIAN PROVINCE

EXTENT OF THE PROVINCE

A culture province of somewhat marked characteristics comprises the states of Georgia, South Carolina, and contiguous portions of Alabama, Florida, North Carolina, and Tennessee. On the arrival of the whites a large portion of this area was occupied or overrun by the Creek Indians or their congeners, now included by Major Powell under the head of the Muskhogean linguistic family. The early explorers of this region referred to the tribes encountered as "Apalachee," and the name Appalachian has been given by our geographers to the range of mountains that extends into the area from the north. The designation of the culture area is therefore historically and geographically appropriate. The general area over which the pottery of this group is distributed is indicated in the accompanying map, plate IV.

PREVAILING TYPES OF WARE

The ceramic phenomena of this province include one great group of products to which has been given the name South Appalachian stamped ware, and also several less distinctly marked varieties, belonging, in the main, to groups typically developed in neighboring areas. Of these overlapping varieties the Florida and Gulf Coast groups on the south, the middle Mississippi valley group on the west, and other less striking varieties on the north and east may be mentioned. Tribes of at least three of the stocks of people inhabiting this general region continued the practice of the potter's art down to the present time. The Catawbas and Cherokees are still engaged to a limited extent in pottery making; and the Choctaws, Chickasaws, and Seminoles have, if the labeling of certain specimens now in the National Museum is correct, but recently abandoned the work. The manufacture of earthenware by the two first-mentioned tribes is described in the introductory pages of this paper, and illustrations are presented in this section.

Among the more noteworthy features of the ancient ceramic art of this province are the novel shapes of some of the vessels, the peculiar style of their decoration, the intermingling of local and what appear to be exotic forms, and, lastly, the very common use of vessels as receptacles for remains of the dead. A rare and exceptional feature of decoration, described by Colonel C. C. Jones and others, is the use of bits of shell and bright stones in inlaying. These bits were set in decorative arrangements into the clay while it was yet plastic—an art practiced to a limited extent at the present day by primitive peoples on both continents, but never rising to a place of importance.

The principal fictile product of the province was the large caldron or cook pot, although bowls were used and fancifully shaped vessels are sometimes encountered. Small figurines and tobacco pipes were made in considerable numbers, and potsherds were often cut into discoid shapes, perhaps for playing games of skill or chance.

The remains of what are supposed by some observers and writers to be primitive pottery kilns have been reported, but the evidence is not conclusive in any case.

The most striking variety of earthenware found within the limits of the Atlantic drainage is distributed very generally over Georgia and contiguous portions of all the adjoining states. For convenience of designation it has been called the South Appalachian stamped ware. Many of the more typical specimens in our collections came from the valley of the Savannah. The most strongly marked characteristics of this ware are its material, which is generally hard, heavy, and coarsely silicious; its shapes, the most notable of which is a deep caldron with conic base and flaring rim; and its decoration, which consists in great part of stamped figures of no little technic and artistic interest.

This stamped pottery is obtained from mounds, graves of several classes, village sites, and shell heaps. In some localities it is associated with remains of distinct varieties of ware, but in others it seems to occur alone. This intermingling of different varieties is not confined to village sites and shell heaps where accident could have brought the different sorts together, but is common in mounds whose contents appear to have belonged to a single community. Whether the different kinds of pottery originated with a single people, or whether the association is the result of the amalgamation of distinct groups of people, can not be determined. The area over which the sherds are scattered is so wide that we can hardly connect the manufacture of even the more typical forms with any single tribe or group of tribes. It is distributed over areas occupied in historic times by numerous stocks of people, including the Algonquian, Iroquoian, Siouan, Muskhogean, and Timuquanan. Of these groups the Muskhogean probably has the best claim to the authorship of this ware. The modern Catawbas (Siouan) and Cherokees (Iroquoian), especially the latter, make vessels corresponding somewhat closely to those of Musk-hogean make in some of their features, but these features may have been but recently adopted by them. In the region producing type specimens, the material, shape, and ornament are so distinctive as unitedly to give the ware great individuality; but in other localities less typical forms are found to occur. In some sections the material changes, and we have only the shapes and decoration as distinguishing features, while in others we must depend on the decoration alone to indicate relationship with the type forms.

Materials and Color

Usually the paste is hard and heavy, consisting of clay tempered with a large percentage of quartz sand or pulverized quartz-bearing rock. Occasional specimens from the Eastern Shore are tempered with shell. In color this pottery is of the normal gray and brownish hues of the baked clay.

Form and Size

The vessels of this group are well built, and have even, moderately thick walls and fair symmetry of outline. The shapes are not greatly varied as compared with other southern and with the western groups. There are bowls, shallow and deep, mostly of large size, having both incurved and recurved rims. There are pots or caldrons ranging from medium to very large size, the largest having a capacity of 15 or 20 gallons. The form varies from that of a deep bowl to that of a much lengthened subcylindric vessel. The base is usually somewhat conic, and in the bowls is often slightly truncated, so that the vessels stand upright on a flat surface.

Uses

As a rule the larger pieces show indications of use over fire, and it is not improbable that this stamped ware was largely the domestic or culinary ware of the peoples who made it; and that other forms less enduring, and hence not so frequently preserved, except in frag-ments, were employed for other purposes. This view would seem to be confirmed in some degree by the occurrence of smaller and more delicate vessels distinct in shape and decorative treatment along with the stamped ware on village sites and in some of the mounds opened by the Bureau of American Ethnology. Some of these vessels, how-ever, are so very distinct in every way from the stamped pottery, and are so manifestly related to groups of ware in which stamped designs, conic forms and quartz tempering were unusual, that we may regard them tentatively as exotic

The preservation of the culinary utensils elsewhere almost univer-sally found in fragments is due to their utilization for mortuary pur-poses. In no other province, perhaps, was the custom of burying the dead in earthen vessels so common as it was in the South Appalachian. Generally the bones are charred, and in many cases they belong to children. Apparently it was not customary to make vessels exclusively for burial purposes, although in some cases the bowl cover was constructed for the purpose. Generally the mortuary vessel stood upright in the grave, but in some instances a large wide-mouthed vase was filled with bones and inverted, and in a few cases bowls have been found inverted over skulls or heaps of bones.

In plate CXII we have illustrations of the manner in which these vessels were employed in burial. A bowl with incurved rim of a size to fit the mouth of the pot was set into it in an inverted position as a cover, as is shown by *a*. This specimen is from a mound near Milledgeville, Georgia. A vase of different type is shown in *b*. It was obtained from a mound in Chatham county by Mr E. H. Hill, and is covered with a small bowl exactly fitting the cone-shaped top of the vase. Colonel C. C. Jones[a] gives a careful description of the discovery in a mound on Colonels island, Liberty county, Georgia, of a burial vase with a lid of baked clay shaped to fit neatly. A smaller vessel containing the bones of an infant had been placed within the larger one. The larger vessel apparently differed from those found farther inland in having been covered with textile imprints, and in having a slight admixture of shell tempering. In these respects it resembled the typical pottery of the Atlantic seaboard, affiliating with the Algonquian wares of the Middle Atlantic province.

DECORATION

As has been mentioned, the remarkable style of decoration, more than any other feature, characterizes this pottery. Elaborately figured stamps were rarely used elsewhere, except in Central and South America. The exact form of the stamping tool or die is, of course, not easily determined, as the imprint upon the rounded surface of the vases represents usually only the middle portion of the figured surface of the implement. It is highly probable, however, that the stamp had a handle and therefore assumed the shape of a paddle, as do the stamps used by the Cherokees at the present time. Occasionally partial impressions of a small portion of the square or round margin of the stamp are seen. It was the usual practice to apply the stamp at random over the entire exterior surface of the vessel, and thus it happened that the impressions encroached upon one another, rendering an analysis of the design, where it is complex, extremely difficult. In many localities the design was simple, consisting of two series of shallow lines or grooves crossing the paddle surface at right angles, leaving squarish interspaces in relief, so that the imprint on the clay gave

[a]Jones, Charles C., Antiquities of the Southern Indians, New York, 1873, p. 455.

the reverse—that is, low ridges with shallow rectangular depressions in the interspaces. The lines vary from 3 to 10 to the inch, and, when covering the surface of a vessel, give a hatched or checkered effect closely resembling that made by imprinting a coarse fabric or a cord-wrapped tool. These figures have occasionally been regarded as impressions resulting from modeling the vessel in a basket or net, but close examination shows that the imprintings are in small, disconnected areas, not coinciding or joining at the edges where the impressions overlap, and that the arrangement of parts is really not that of woven strands.

The character of the work is fully elucidated by the Cherokee wooden paddles which are shown in plate CXIII a, b, c. One side of the broad part of the implement is covered with deeply engraved lines, carved no doubt with steel knives, but the work is not so neat and the grouping is not so artistic as in the ancient work. The effect produced by the use of such an implement is illustrated in d, a modern Cherokee pot, collected in 1889 by Mr James Mooney, and referred to already under the head Manufacture.

Where an intricate design was employed the partial impressions from the flat surface of the paddle are so confused along the margins that in no case can the complete pattern be made out. By a careful study of a number of the more distinct imprints, however, the larger part of the designs may be restored. For several years rubbings of such imprintings as came to hand have been taken, and some of the more interesting are presented in plate CXIV. They consist, for the most part, of curved lines in graceful but formal, and possibly, as here used, meaningless combinations. By far the most common figure is a kind of compound filfot cross, swastika, or Thor's hammer—that is to say, a grouping of lines having a cross with bent arms as a base or center, shown in a and b. The four border spaces are filled in with lines parallel with the curved arms of the central figure. The effect of this design, as applied to the surface of a fine large vessel from a mound on the Savannah river 10 miles below Augusta, is well shown in plate CXV a. Another excellent example is seen in plate CXVI.

An interesting result of my recent studies of the pottery of the region, referred to in the preceding section, is the observation that the designs stamped on the clay are in many cases closely analogous to designs used by the ancient insular Caribbean peoples. Many of the latter designs are engraved on utensils of wood, and the Appalachian stamps on which the designs were carved were likewise of wood, which suggests contact or intimate relationship of the peoples in ancient times. There can hardly be a doubt that Antillean influence was felt in the art of the whole southeastern section of the United States, or that, on the other hand, the culture of the mainland impressed itself strongly on that of the contiguous islands. A comparison of the stamped designs illustrated in plate CXIV with others of Florida and Guadeloupe island, given in a recent publication,[a] will make the analogies apparent.

The stamped ware is found plentifully throughout the state of Georgia and as far west along the Gulf coast as Mobile bay. Stamp designs constitute the prevailing decoration in the wares of Early county, southwestern Georgia. In eastern Tennessee, at a few points on the eastern side of the valley of the Tennessee river, examples varying considerably from the Savannah type have been observed. The vessels are generally intermingled with western forms of pottery. North Carolina furnishes some stamped ware, and in South Carolina stamped ware appears to be the prevailing variety. On the Florida peninsula this ware seems to have lost some of its most typical characters, the vessels having different shapes and the stamp designs consisting mainly of simple reticulations.

Although some of the peculiar designs with which the paddle stamps were embellished may have come, as has been suggested, from neighboring Antillean peoples, it is probable that the implement is of continental origin. It is easy to see how the use of figured modeling tools could arise with any people out of the simple, primitive processes of vessel modeling. As the walls were built up by means of flattish strips of clay, added one upon another, the fingers and hand were used to weld the parts together and to smooth down the uneven surfaces. In time various improvised implements would come into use—shells for scraping, smooth stones for rubbing, and paddle-like tools for malleating. Some of the latter, having textured surfaces, would leave figured imprints on the plastic surface, and these, producing a pleasing effect on the primitive mind, would lead to extension of use, and, finally, to the invention of special tools and the adding of elaborate designs. But the use of figured surfaces seems to have had other than purely decorative functions, and, indeed, in most cases, the decorative idea may have been secondary. It will be observed by one who attempts the manipulation of clay that striking or paddling with a smooth surface has often a tendency to extend flaws and to start new ones, thus weakening the wall of the vessel, but a ribbed or deeply figured surface properly applied has the effect of welding the clay together, of kneading the plastic surface, producing numberless minute dovetailings of the clay which connect across weak lines and incipient cracks, adding greatly to the strength of the vessel.

That the figured stamp had a dual function, a technic and an esthetic one, is fully apparent. When it was applied to the surface it removed unevenness and welded the plastic clay into a firm, tenacious mass. Scarifying with a rude comb-like tool was employed in some sections for the same purpose, and was so used more generally on the inner

[a] Holmes, W. H., Caribbean influence on the prehistoric ceramic art of the southern states, American Anthropologist, vol. VII, p. 71.

a (DIAMETER 12 INCHES)

b (DIAMETER 11⅜ INCHES)

BURIAL VASES WITH COVERS,
SOUTH APPALACHIAN GROUP

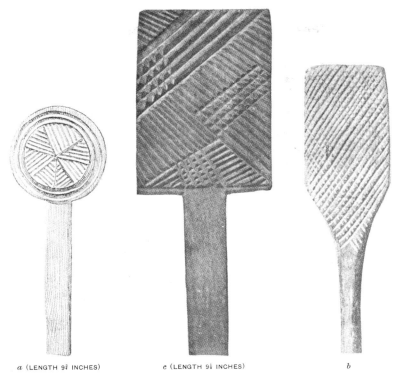

a (LENGTH 9⅞ INCHES)   *c* (LENGTH 9¼ INCHES)   *b*

d (DIAMETER 10 INCHES)

CHEROKEE STAMP-DECORATED POT, AND PADDLE STAMPS

SOUTH APPALACHIAN GROUP

STAMP DESIGNS RESTORED FROM IMPRESSIONS ON VASES

SOUTH APPALACHIAN GROUP

a (HEIGHT 16 INCHES)

b (DIAMETER 16¼ INCHES)

TYPICAL SPECIMENS OF STAMP-DECORATED WARE

SOUTH APPALACHIAN GROUP

surface, where a paddle or stamp could not be employed. That this was recognized as one of the functions of the stamp is shown by the fact that in many neatly finished vessels, where certain portions received a smooth finish, the paddle had first been used over the entire vessel, the pattern being afterward worked down with a polishing stone. However, the beauty of the designs employed and the care and taste with which they were applied to the vases bear ample testimony to the fact that the function of the stamp as used in this province was largely esthetic. It may be safely assumed, in addition, that in many cases the figures were significant or symbolic. The use of stamps and stamp-like tools in other regions will be mentioned under the proper headings.

EXAMPLES

VASES

The specimens shown in plate cxv may well be taken as types of the larger vessels of the Appalachian variety. The large vessel *a* is blackened by use over fire, and it not unlikely served the humble purpose of preparing food messes for the family, somewhat after the manner so graphically described and illustrated in Hariot's history of the Roanoke colony,[a] and shown in plate II. It is nearly symmetric, is 16 inches in height and the same in diameter, and has a capacity of about 15 gallons. The paddle-stamp has been carefully used, giving a pretty uniform all-over pattern; the design is shown three-fourths actual size in plate cxiv *a*. The rim is decorated with two encircling lines of annular indentations and four small nodes indented in the center, placed at equal intervals about the exterior.

From the same mound with the above several other similar vessels were obtained, two of them being larger than the one illustrated. Some fine, large bowls from the same mound have the entire exterior surface decorated with the usual compound filfot stamp. One of these is presented in the lower figure, plate cxv *b*.

The handsome vessel illustrated in plate cxvi was uncovered by the plow on Ossabaw island, Chatham county, Georgia. The negroes who discovered it at once reburied it. The manager of the place, learning of this, dug it up again. Within the vase were the bones of a child, with a few beads and ornaments. The bones were reinterred by the negroes, who feared that bad luck would follow wanton disturbance of the dead. A bowl, parts only of which were saved, was inverted over the top of the urn, and had prevented the earth from accumulating within. The specimens were acquired by Mr William Harden, of Savannah, who presented them to the Bureau of American Ethnology. This vase corresponds fully in material, shape, and finish with others from various parts of the Appalachian region. The stamped pattern

---

[a] Hariot, Thomas, A brief and true report of the new found land of Virginia, Frankfort, 1590, pl. xv.

is of the most usual type, but differs from others in having nodes at the center and in having the arms of the cross curved, as shown in plate cxiv *b*. The height is 15 inches, and the diameter at the rim 12 inches. The bowl cover is of the same kind of ware, and is well made and symmetric. The surface inside and out is finished with a polishing tool. The color, as in most of this ware, is a dark brownish gray, somewhat mottled by firing or by use over fire. Four S-shaped ornaments, with nodes placed within the curves, are set about the most expanded part of the body. The diameter is 12½ inches and the depth 7 or 8 inches.

The specimen presented in plate cxvii *a* was plowed up near Milledgeville, Georgia. It was engraved on wood for Dr. Charles Rau, and was published in his Collections of the National Museum, but the defects of drawing are such as to mislead the student with respect to the character of the surface finish. The stamp design was a very simple one, founded on the cross, the four inclosed angles being filled in by straight lines, as is seen in plate cxiv *c*. One arm of the cross was more strongly relieved than the other, and this gave rise, where the impressions happened to be continuous, to the heavy lines shown in exaggerated form in the Rau engraving. That the stamp was rigid and flat on the face is apparent from the nature of the impressions on the convex surface of the vase, and also from numerous deep impressions of the edge of the tool at the sharp curve of the vessel where the neck joins the body. The somewhat fragmentary vase presented in *b* was obtained from a mound in Georgia. The stamp design, so far as it could be deciphered, is given in plate cxiv *d*, and embodies as its main feature the guilloche or the imperfectly connected scroll.

The association of the stamped earthenware with ware typical of surrounding regions may be accounted for in two ways—first, through occupation of a single site by more than one group of people at the same or at different times, and, second, by the possession or manufacture of more than one variety by a single community. Two interesting illustrations of the intermingling of types may be presented. Explorations carried on for the Bureau of American Ethnology under the direction of Dr Thomas in the mounds and graves of Caldwell county, North Carolina, yielded many fine examples of pottery, among which were vases and bowls of southern type, bowls decorated with modeled animal heads and other relieved ornaments in western style, fabric-marked pieces, and rude, undecorated vessels, such as characterize the middle Atlantic tidewater region.

A striking example of the intermingling of separate types was brought to light by the opening of a small mound 10 miles below Augusta, on the Savannah river, Richmond county, Georgia, by Mr H. L. Reynolds, of the Bureau of American Ethnology. No mound has yielded finer examples of the stamped ware, two pieces of which have already been given (plate CXV), and along with them and intimately associated in the original interments were typical western forms. One piece, a long-necked bottle, with decoration in black paint, would, so far as its general appearance goes, be more at home in western Tennessee, or even beyond the Mississippi. This piece is shown in plate CXVIII *a*. It is neither as well made nor as neatly finished as its western prototypes, and the walls are unusually thick. The clay is tempered with quartz and mica-bearing sand, a strong indication that the vase is actually of Appalachian manufacture. Other bottles of western form, but undecorated, were recovered. One remarkable piece is shown in *b;* it resembles closely the famous "triune vase," *c*, from Cany branch of the Cumberland river, Tennessee, described by Caleb Atwater.[a]

Hardly less remarkable was the occurrence in this richly stocked mound of two cylindric cup-shaped vases, embellished with figures of rattlesnakes, combining in execution, materials, finish, and decoration most of the best features of the wares of the lower Mississippi and the Gulf coast. Unlike the ordinary vessels of the region, these vessels are of the finest clay, which in the interior of the mass is of a light gray color. The surface is blackened and well polished, and the designs, engraved with a fine sharp point, penetrate to the light paste, giving a striking effect. One of these vases appears in plate CXVIII *d*. Encircling its slightly incurved walls are figures of two horned or antlered rattlesnakes and a third serpent only partially worked out. Occupying one of the interspaces between the sinuous bodies of the serpents is a human face resembling a mask, connecting with lines apparently intended to suggest a serpent's body. The smaller cup contains the drawing of a single serpent extending twice around the circumference.

These rattlesnakes are drawn in highly conventional style, but with a directness and ease that could result only from long practice in the engraver's art. They are doubtless of symbolic origin, and the vases were probably consecrated to use in ceremonials in which the rattlesnake was a potent factor. The delineation of the serpent is not specifically different from other examples engraved on stone, clay, and shell found in several parts of the South and West. This remarkable design is illustrated one-third actual size in plate CXIX *a*. The part at the extreme right repeats the corresponding part at the left. The human head or mask is unique among pottery decorations, but it is not distinct in type from the heads stamped in sheet copper found in the mounds of Georgia and those engraved on shell in many parts of the Appalachian and Middle Mississippi regions.

That such a diverse array of ceramic products, inadequately represented by the illustrations given, should have been assembled in an

---

[a] Atwater, Caleb, Western antiquities, Columbus, 1833, p. 140.

obscure mound on the lower Savannah is indeed remarkable. Excellent examples of the pottery of the South, the Southwest, and the West are thus found within 100 miles of the Atlantic seaboard. Not the least interesting feature of this find was the occurrence of part of an old-fashioned English iron drawing knife and some wrought-iron nails, associated, according to the report of Mr Reynolds, with the various articles of clay, stone, and copper in the mound, thus apparently showing that the mound was built and that all the varieties of ware were made or assembled by a single community in post-Columbian times.

Mr Reynolds was firm in his belief that these vases and the diverse articles referred to were associated in the original interments in the mound, yet many will feel like questioning this conclusion. If a mistake was made by the explorer with respect to this point, the interest in the series is hardly lessened. If he is right, the mound was built by a post-Columbian community composed of distinct groups of people still practicing to some extent their appropriate arts, or by members of a single group which, by association, capture, or otherwise, had brought together artisans from distinct nations, or had from various available sources secured the heterogeneous group of objects of art assembled. If he is wrong, we are free to assume that the original stock which practiced the ordinary arts of the Appalachian province had built the mound and deposited examples of their work; that, at a later period, they had acquired and used exotic artifacts in burial in the same mound, or, that the mound was, after the coming of the whites, adopted by a distinct people who there buried their dead, together with articles of their own and of European manufacture. In such a case it would be reasonable to suppose that the earlier people were of Muskhogean or Uchean stock, and that the latter were the Savannahs or Shawnees. The report of Mr Reynolds on the opening of this remarkable mound is embodied in the work of Dr Thomas in the Twelfth Annual Report of the Bureau of Ethnology. A number of clay pipes obtained from this mound are shown in plate cxxiv. They are of forms prevalent in the general region.

The extension of typical Appalachian wares eastward toward the coast of North and South Carolina and Georgia is made manifest by recent researches of Mr Clarence B. Moore. From a mound in McIntosh county, Georgia, Mr Moore obtained the remarkable bowl shown in plate cxx, and a second specimen nearly duplicating it. It is quite eccentric in shape, as is well shown by contrasting the end view, *a*, with the side views, *b* and *c*. The color is quite dark, and the surface well polished. It is embellished with engraved figures in lines, and excavated spaces covering nearly the entire surface. The scroll border above is somewhat irregularly placed, and encircles, at opposite sides, a little node, the only modeled feature of the vase. The design, drawn at full length, is shown in plate cxix *b*, and is apparently a

LARGE VASE DECORATED WITH FILFOT STAMP DESIGN

SOUTH APPALACHIAN GROUP

(HEIGHT 15 INCHES)

b (HEIGHT ABOUT 9 INCHES)

a (HEIGHT 14 INCHES)

VASES DECORATED WITH PADDLE-STAMP IMPRESSIONS

SOUTH APPALACHIAN GROUP

b (HEIGHT 7¼ INCHES)

a (HEIGHT 9 INCHES)

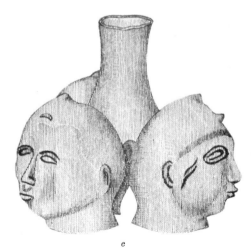

c

d (HEIGHT 5 INCHES)

VASES OF VARIED DESIGN AND EMBELLISHMENT
SOUTH APPALACHIAN GROUP

b

c

ENGRAVED DESIGNS FROM VASES SHOWN IN PLATES CXVIII AND CXX

SOUTH APPALACHIAN GROUP

rather crude attempt to depict a bird-serpent monster, some of the elements undoubtedly referring to the eye, wings, and feathers of the bird, while certain other features suggest the serpent; as a decoration it is very effective. It undoubtedly represents an important mythologic concept. The design from the companion vessel is shown also on this plate (c), and is a more simplified presentation of the same subject.

The large jar illustrated in plate cxxi a is unique in the shape of the neck, which is depressed, sinking partly within the shoulder. The form is graceful and effective, however, and the decoration is the typical button-centered filfot, applied with a paddle-stamp.

It appears also that vessels of the Gulf Coast type—at least with respect to the ornamentation—occur on the Atlantic coast, and one is shown in plate cxxi b. This is a tub-like specimen, 15 or 16 inches in diameter, with broken incised scroll work encircling the upper half of the body, which expands toward the base in a way seldom noticed in ware of its class.

In the collections recently made by Dr Roland Steiner in northwestern Georgia, we find another novelty in the shape of some terra-cotta figures. Some of these appear to have been derived from the margins of bowls or other vessels, while others are figurines pure and simple. The faces in some cases are modeled with exceptional skill, but the most notable feature is the flattening of the head, which gives to the specimens a striking resemblance to the flat-headed terra-cotta figures of Mexico. These objects are shown in plates cxxii and cxxiii. The associated vessels are all of South Appalachian type.

TOBACCO PIPES

It is difficult to say what forms the tobacco pipes of the southern Indians had taken in pre-Columbian times, the early writers having said little with reference to them. Their great number, the high degree of elaboration, and the wide differentiation of form indicate, however, a long period of tobacco pipe making. Stone was evidently the favorite material, and steatite, especially, being easily carved, handsome in appearance, and not affected by fire, took a prominent place. The historic tribes of the region, and especially of the Carolinas, have always been great pipe makers and have for at least a hundred years[a] practiced the art with much ardor, using the product in trade with neighboring tribes and with the whites. This commercial work has led to no end of fanciful elaboration of form, and to much that is strained and bad. We are led by this circumstance to question the age of all the more ornate forms of pipes not found in associations that prove them to be ancient.

The prevailing Algonquian clay pipe was a simple bent tube, and the Iroquois elaborated the same general form by various modifica-

a Lawson, John, History of Carolina, Raleigh, 1860, pp. 56, 338.

tions and additions. The same radical form is discovered in the clay pipes of the Appalachian country. As has been observed elsewhere in this paper, the groups or varieties of pipes are not so well marked as are the groups of vessels. Pipes are subject to free transportation, and no matter how distinctive the work of a given people, the presence of so many stocks moving back and forth must necessarily have led to much confusion.

Nothing more will here be attempted than the presentation of plates in which are brought together a number of the more usual clay pipe forms from the general region. The clay used was probably much the same as that employed by the same peoples in vessel making, but was left pure or was tempered with finely comminuted ingredients. The surfaces were usually well polished or were covered with various relieved ornaments. The colors were those of the baked clay. As a rule the fundamental shape was the bent trumpet; often, however, it was much modified, and was sometimes loaded with animal and conventional features in relief or in the round, as is shown in plates cxxiv and cxxv. Effigy pipes in clay are not common, but good examples are seen in our museums, and several are presented in plate cxxvi.

The heavy pipe with stem and bowl of nearly equal weight is a western and southern type found all the way from Florida to Arkansas. Two specimens of this variety were found in a mound on the St Johns river, Florida, by Mr C. B. Moore.

POTTERY DISKS

Pottery disks cut from sherds of ordinary ware are common in the South Appalachian region as well as along the Gulf coast, and it may be

FIG. 60—Small disks cut from sherds.

added that they are found to some extent over nearly the entire pottery-producing region. Some of these objects may have been used in

BOWL WITH ELABORATE ENGRAVED DECORATIONS (MOORE COLLECTION)
SOUTH APPALACHIAN GROUP
(LENGTH 9½ INCHES)

b (DIAMETER 11¼ INCHES)

a (DIAMETER 12⅞ INCHES)

LARGE VESSELS FROM EASTERN GEORGIA

SOUTH APPALACHIAN GROUP

(MOORE COLLECTION)

FIGURINES FROM NORTHWESTERN GEORGIA
SOUTH APPALACHIAN GROUP
(ACTUAL SIZE)

FIGURINES FROM NORTHWESTERN GEORGIA

SOUTH APPALACHIAN GROUP

(ACTUAL SIZE)

TOBACCO PIPES FROM BURIAL MOUNDS
SOUTH APPALACHIAN GROUP

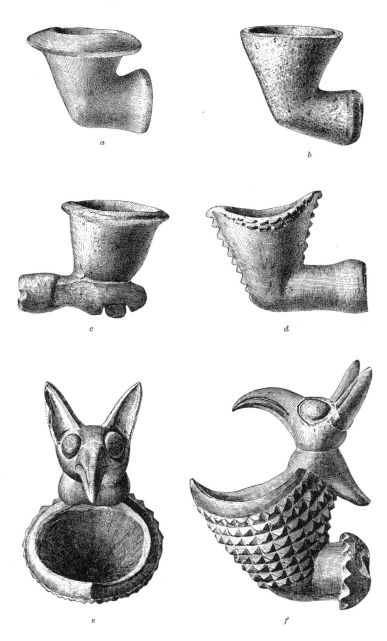

TOBACCO PIPES FROM BURIAL MOUNDS
SOUTH APPALACHIAN GROUP

playing games of skill or chance, but two pairs, found by Mr Moore in graves, indicate the use of the perforated ones as cores for copper ear-disks.   A few examples are illustrated in figure 60.

ORIGIN OF THE VARIETIES OF WARE

It is not yet possible to make a satisfactory analysis of the pottery of the Carolinas.   The presence here in pre-Columbian times of numerous stocks of people and the practice of the art by some of the tribes down even to the present day have led to great complexity of phenomena.   It happens also that the region has been but little studied, and no one has undertaken the interesting task of tracing the art of the modern tribes—the Cherokees and Catawbas—back through the many changes of the last three hundred years to its pre-Columbian phases.   The Cherokees and Tuscaroras are of Iroquoian stock.   The former people practice their art to-day in one locality in western North Carolina; the latter, who removed to New York to join the league of the Iroquois early in the eighteenth century, dwelt in central and eastern North Carolina, and probably left ware of somewhat marked peculiarities in this region, as well as in Virginia.   The Uchees, and the Yamassees, of Muskhogean stock, dwelt on the Savannah, but probably ceased pottery making at an early date, as they were among the first to come into familiar contact with the colonists.   The Shawnees, a tribe of Algonquian stock known in early times as "Savannahs," occupied part of Carolina and Georgia, and must have left numerous traces of their presence.   Two tribes of Siouan stock, the Tutelo and Catawba, and perhaps others not so well known, inhabited parts of northern Georgia and western Carolina, and a small area in south-central Virginia, and it is probable that much of the confusion observed in the ceramics of these sections is due to this occupation.   The stock was a vigorous one, and must have developed decided characteristics of art, at least in its original habitat, which is thought to be west of the Alleghenies.   Through the presence of the various tribes of these five linguistic families, and probably others of prehistoric times, the highly complicated art conditions were brought about.   Whether the work of the various tribes was sufficiently individualized to permit of the separation of the remains at the present day is a question yet to be decided, but there is no doubt that the task may be at least partially accomplished by systematic collection and study.

The first necessary step in this work is a study of the modern and historic work of the tribes that have kept up the practice of the art to the present day.   In the introductory pages, under the head Manufacture, the plastic art of the Catawbas and the Cherokees has been described at some length.   We naturally seek in the Siouan work in the West analogies with the work of the former tribe, as it was of

Siouan stock. But the Siouan peoples have not been pottery makers in recent times, and we have no means of making comparisons, save on the theory that the Middle Mississippi ware is wholly or partly of Siouan make. Moreover, the modern Catawban pottery has been so modified by post-Columbian conditions that few of the original characteristics are left, and comparison is fruitless. But an examination of numerous ancient sites and a number of mounds in the region occupied by the Catawbas in early historic time, and for an indefinite period in pre-Columbian times, yields forms of vessels distinctly western in some of their features, and in cases there appear also pretty well-defined characteristics of the historic Catawba work. A group of Catawban vessels collected between the years 1876 and 1886 is presented in plate cxxvii*a*. A number of pipes of this people of the same or a later period are shown in plate cxxviii.

Specimens found on the older dwelling sites of the people resemble the modern pottery in color and finish, but they are of better workmanship, and the shapes resemble less closely those of the whites. All are flat-bottomed, have the thick walls and peculiar color and polish of modern Catawba ware, and are well within the Catawba habitat, even if not from sites inhabited by them in historic times. One specimen labeled "Seminole" is identical with Catawba ware. It is probable that many other examples of old Catawban work exist, but only these few have fallen into my hands. Points of correspondence between this modern ware and the ware of the mounds in ancient Catawban territory, North Carolina, will be pointed out when the latter is presented.

A remnant of the Cherokee tribe now occupies a small reservation in Swain county, western North Carolina. These people were in possession of an immense tract of the South Appalachian region when first encountered by the whites, and there is nothing to indicate that they were not long resident in this region. An examination of their modern art in clay develops the fact that they are skillful potters, and what is of special interest is the fact that their ware has several points of analogy with the ancient stamped pottery of the South Appalachian province. Their ware retains more of the archaic elements of form than does that of the Catawbas, and the stamps they use in decoration are identical in many respects with those formerly used in the entire region extending from southern Florida to Virginia.

The question may thus be raised as to whether the Cherokees, rather than the Uchees or the Muskhogean tribes, are not the people represented by the ceramic remains of the Southeast. Such speculations are, however, in the present state of our knowledge, quite vain, and they may be misleading. All we can surely know is that these people retain well-defined features of the ancient art of the region, and that much of the ancient stamped ware of northern Georgia, western

Carolina, and eastern Tennessee is probably theirs, for it is found on the sites known to have been long occupied by them.

Specimens of modern Cherokee work are shown in plate cxxvii *b*. Processes of manufacture have been sufficiently dwelt on in the introductory pages.

In plate cxxix a number of vases from mounds in Caldwell county, North Carolina, are brought together. They display great diversity of characters—eastern, southern, and western—and, at the same time, bear evidence of recentness, and, in cases, of relationship to modern ware. All are tempered with silicious ingredients, and all seem, from the manner of their occurrence, to have belonged to a single community. Two specimens, the right and left in the lower row, are typically western in appearance. In the upper middle vase we see the handles and the side ornament in relief characters rare on the eastern slope but common in Tennessee; the stamped piece on its right affiliates with the southern ware, and the upper left-hand vase is a southern shape having incised designs like those of the Gulf coast. The remaining cup shown illustrates the use of fabrics in the construction and embellishment of pottery. The entire surface is deeply marked with a textile mesh, which at first sight suggests that of the interior of a rude basket, but close examination shows that it is the impression of a pliable fabric of open mesh woven in the twined style. It is seen that there is much lack of continuity in the imprinting, and also that the markings must be the result of wrapping the plastic vessel in fabrics to sustain it, or of the separate applications of a bit of the texture held in the hand or wound about a modeling paddle. This piece is more at home on the Atlantic coast of North Carolina and Virginia than it is in the South or West. From the Jones mound, in the same section, we have a series of vessels of still more modern look. So far as shape and finish go they are decidedly like the modern Catawba ware.

Over all this Carolina region there are indications of southern as well as western and northern influence, and vessels and sherds are obtained in many places that affiliate with the art of the South. The stamped varieties are intermingled with the other forms in the shell heaps of the Atlantic, on river sites back to the mountains, and, in places, even across to the heads of western-flowing streams.

There are also specimens of the peculiar florid scroll work of the Gulf province, and we may infer that southern tribes made their influence felt as far north as Virginia, beyond which, however, a scroll design, or even a curved line, is practically unknown, and the southern peculiarities of shape are also absent.

As we pass to the east and north in North Carolina it is found that the southern and western styles of ware gradually give way to the archaic forms and textile decorations of the great Algonquian area. From a kitchen midden on the Yadkin, in Wilkes county, within less than 25 miles of the Virginia line, we have a few specimens of very rude stamped ware and many pieces of large, coarse vessels that duplicate the shell-heap ware of the Chesapeake. This is about the northern limit of southern forms, but northern forms extend, with gradually decreasing frequency, to the western and southern borders of the state

POTTERY OF THE MIDDLE ATLANTIC PROVINCE

REVIEW OF THE ALGONQUIAN AREAS

As was pointed out in the introductory pages, a broad and important distinction is to be drawn between the ceramic products of the two great regions which may be designated, in a general way, as the North and the South. The former comprises that part of the great Algonquian-Iroquoian territory of historic times which lies to the north of a somewhat indefinite line extending from below Cape Hatteras, on the Atlantic coast, through southwestern Virginia, eastern Kentucky, middle Ohio, northern Indiana, northern Illinois, and middle Iowa to Nebraska, and beyond; the latter comprehends the territory to the south of this line. The ceramic art of the North is archaic and simple, that of the South is well advanced and complex. South of the line there are compound and varied forms; north of it all forms are simple. The pottery of the South has animal shapes; that of the North has none. The South has vessels with high, narrow necks, and stands and legs; the North has none. The South has painted surfaces and decorations; the North has no color, save the natural hues of the baked clay. The South has the fret, scroll, and other current ornaments, as well as symbolic and delineative designs; the North has little else than simple combinations of straight lines.

There are questions coming up for consideration in this connection, aside from those relating to the grouping and description of the ware, with which this paper is mainly concerned. We seek, for example, the meaning of the somewhat abrupt change of phenomena in passing from the South to the North. Is it due to differences in race? Were the southern tribes as a body more highly endowed than the northern, or did the currents of migration, representing distinct centers of culture, come from opposite quarters to meet along this line? Or does the difference result from the unlike environments of the two sections, the one fertile and salubrious, encouraging progress in art, and the other rigorous and exacting, checking tendencies in that dicretion? Or does the weakening art impulse indicate increasing distance from the great art centers in the far South, in Mexico and Yucatan? We are constrained also to ask, Is it possible to identify

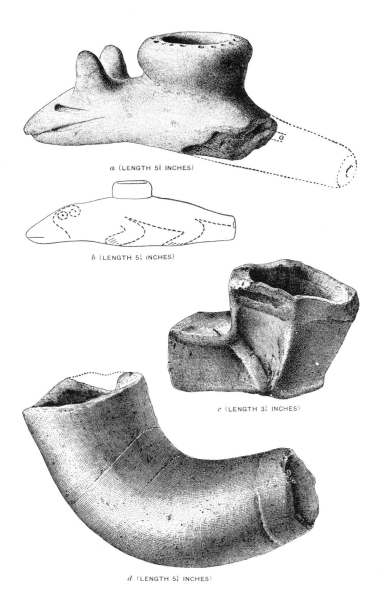

a (LENGTH 5¾ INCHES)

b (LENGTH 5½ INCHES)

c (LENGTH 3½ INCHES)

d (LENGTH 5½ INCHES)

TOBACCO PIPES FROM BURIAL MOUNDS
SOUTH APPALACHIAN GROUP

a (DIAMETER OF LARGE BOWL 10½ INCHES)

b (DIAMETER OF LARGE POT 10 INCHES)

MODERN POTTERY OF THE CATAWBA AND CHEROKEE INDIANS
SOUTH APPALACHIAN GROUP

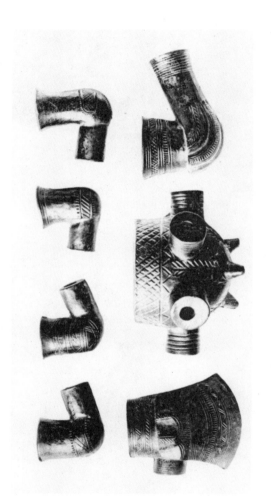

MODERN TOBACCO PIPES OF THE CATAWBA INDIANS
SOUTH APPALACHIAN GROUP
(TWO-THIRDS)

HELIOTYPE CO., BOSTON.

POTTERY FROM BURIAL MOUNDS IN NORTH CAROLINA

SOUTH APPALACHIAN GROUP

(ONE-THIRD)

the people or any of the peoples concerned on either hand, to follow their movements from place to place, to follow them back through the mutations of their history? These questions and others come up for consideration. Answers, or partial answers, to some of them will probably be forthcoming as investigation goes on.

Aside from these general questions, which are always uppermost in the mind of the ethnologist, there are others which pertain to the ceramic art in particular. What do these archaic northern forms teach of the beginnings and progress of art, and what can we learn from them of the inceptive stages of ornament? These queries have been considered to some extent in the introductory pages, and additional suggestions are made in presenting the various groups of ware.

To exactly what extent the Algonquian tribes are responsible for the northern types of pottery, aside from those definitely assignable to the Iroquois, may never be fully determined, but that these types are largely Algonquian may be assumed from the historic occupation of many sections by pottery-making communities of that family. There are complications in the Ohio valley and also, to some extent, in the northern Illinois-Indiana region, where the ceramic phenomena are complex, apparently representing successive occupations of the area by different peoples. It may in time appear that numerous stocks of people were concerned, for, though the ceramic remains indicate in general a primitive condition—a rather uniform grade of progress for the peoples represented—there is marked divergence in the other groups of products; art in stone, bone, and metal had reached a comparatively high degree of advancement in some sections. It may be remarked, however, that had the whole area now assigned to the Algonquian stock been occupied by that stock from the first, to the exclusion of all others, we could not expect uniformity in art remains over so vast an area. Communities of the same blood and culture grade, separated for a long period by great distances, and existing under distinctive environments, would acquire and develop activities and arts only a little less varied than would nonconsanguineous groups under like conditions. It is significant, however, that as we glance over the whole field we observe in the ceramic remains a marked family resemblance, not an equality of grade only, but close analogies in many features of treatment, form, finish, and decoration.

Beginning in the coastal districts of the Carolinas, we pass to Virginia, to New Jersey, to Connecticut, to Massachusetts, and to Maine through a series of groups exhibiting differences in detail, but having decided general likeness. If we pass from the east across the great highland to the Ohio valley, we find that the differences are more marked. There is a general resemblance, with here and there signs of stronger touches and more advanced ideas and practices, but as we pass beyond to the upper Mississippi and the Great lakes, the East is

seen to be repeated in a marked manner, and the merest details must
be relied upon to separate sherds from the two distant regions, if, by
accident, they become intermingled.

The Iroquoian group will be treated in a separate section, while the
northern and eastern Algonquian territory may be reviewed as carefully as the meager collections and incomplete observations at hand
will permit.

In the rather imperfect light of present knowledge, we may to best
advantage consider the ceramic work of this great province under
heads which express something of geographic culture grouping. First,
we have the Middle Atlantic province, which, for comparative study
of details, may be further separated into several subdivisions, the
principal being the Chesapeake-Potomac region, which presents a well-
defined unit, geographically, culturally, and ethnically.[a] Second,
there are the entire New Jersey and New England areas. The first of
these appears to be divided somewhat between the Delaware valley and
the coastal districts, while in the second collected data are so meager
that little can be done in the way of systematic technic or comparative
study. These Atlantic provinces are indicated approximately on the
accompanying map, plate IV. Third is the Ohio Valley province, in
which we shall have two or three subdivisions of fictile remains which
are not distinct geographic groups, one of them, at least, extending far
to the west in a succession of areas. Fourth, we have the Upper Mississippi and Missouri Valley provinces, so far little studied; and fifth,
the region of the Great lakes, of which we have only fragmentary bits
of information.

PAMLICO-ALBEMARLE WARE[a]

South Appalachian forms of ware prevail throughout Georgia and
South Carolina, save along the coast, where the simple textile-marked
wares of the North extend far southward, gradually diminishing in frequency of occurrence. Southern forms prevail largely in North Carolina, giving way farther north and in the region of the great sounds
and their tide-water tributaries to other forms apparently showing
Algonquian handiwork or influence. The change from southern to
northern types is rather gradual, which may have resulted from contact of peoples living contemporaneously in neighboring districts. In
some cases all varieties are found together, as in the Lenoir mounds in
Caldwell county, North Carolina, the village sites of the Yadkin, and
elsewhere. The intermingling does not consist exclusively in the
assemblage of specimens of separate groups of ware, as if people from
different sections had successively occupied the sites, but features
typical of these sections are combined in the same group of vessels,
or even in the same vessel.

---

[a] In the illustrations all the pottery of the Middle Atlantic province has been classed as of the
Chesapeake-Potomac group.

The northernmost advance of strictly South Appalachian features of the art so far observed is in the valley of the Yadkin in North Carolina, near the Virginia line; and the farthest advance of southwestern features is in the upper valleys of the Shenandoah and James, on the historic highway of the tribes between the North and South.

Particular attention may be called to the contents of village sites on the Yadkin in Wilkes county, North Carolina, just referred to. Here we have rather rude ware, mostly large, fire-blackened culinary utensils, manifestly of comparatively recent date. Among the sherds are a few pieces bearing stamped designs of southern type. We also have examples of the large, conic, net-marked vessels so prevalent in the Potomac-Chesapeake country. A wide zone of sites extending across the middle section of the state on the line of the Yadkin, and probably down to the sea in South Carolina, exhibits a remarkable intermingling of northern and southern elements.

In form the Wilkes county midden ware is limited almost exclusively to the wide mouthed caldron, with rather long body and somewhat conic base. The vessels are rudely treated, unsymmetric in shape, and thick-walled. The paste is tempered with a large percentage of gritty sand or coarsely pulverized steatite, the fragments of the latter standing out in high relief on weathered surfaces. The steatite in many cases forms one-half or two-thirds of the mass. In plate cxxx a series of outlines is given, restored from the many large fragments. which will convey a fair idea of the character of the vessels.

This ware exhibits great diversity of surface treatment. Aside from the few stamped pieces (which may be the work of a separate people. although akin to the prevailing type in everything save the surface finish), the vessels are nearly all marked with netting of about the weight of our finest fish netting (plate cxxx h). A superficial examination gives the impression that the vessels have been modeled or handled when plastic in a net, or that a net has been applied to the entire surface by wrapping, but a study of the markings shows that generally the texture has been applied with the aid of a net-covered paddle with which the plastic surface was beaten. In plate cxxxi a is photographically reproduced a fragment in which five facet-like surfaces, the result of that number of applications of the net-covered implement, are imperfectly shown. Certain heavier knottings are repeated in each impression, demonstrating the fact that the fabric was fixed to the tool and not applied to the vessel as a mold or wrapping. Had the latter been the case, the mesh impression would have been somewhat completely connected and continuous. In numerous cases parts of the surfaces have been scarified with a serrate-edged tool or comb, obliterating the net marks, as if in preparation for polishing and decorating. In a few cases very rude incised figures have been added, as is seen in the examples given in plates cxxxi a and cxxxii a.

The rim was smoothed down with the fingers, and the interior surface was finished with the scarifying tool, roughly applied. In a few cases rude ornamental effects have been produced by using the finger nail as a roulette, giving much the effect of fine net impressions. The nail was rolled back and forth as the finger was moved with rather strong pressure around the neck of the vessel. A specimen of this unique treatment is shown in plate cxxxi *d*, and some simpler finger-nail work is seen in plate cxxxii *a*. The use of a notched indenting tool is indicated in plate cxxxi *f*. Narrow fillets of clay were in cases rudely laid on and decorated with the nail in herringbone effects.

The surface treatment of a number of specimens is identical with that of the net-marked vase from Caldwell county, shown in the preceding section, plate cxxix. It appears evident that in finishing the rim of the vase a fillet of netting was wrapped about the neck to cause the desired constriction and hold the vessel together while the margin was pressed outward and finished.

The sherds shown in plate cxxxii *b* and *c*, the former from Wilson, North Carolina, and the latter from Clarksville, Virginia, illustrate the use of the cord roulette or cord-wrapped stamp in texturing and malleating the surface of vessels. The effect of rolling the tool back and forth is readily seen. The small fragment given in *d* shows the use of a wooden stamp with a neat design in curved lines in South Appalachian style. The clay retains the impressions of the grain of the wood. In *e* the surface has been textured with a wooden stamp or paddle the face of which was grooved, the effect being very like that of stamping with cord-covered tools.

PIEDMONT VIRGINIA WARE[a]

In northwestern North Carolina and in southwestern Virginia a somewhat marked local variety of pottery is developed which partakes to some extent of the character of the ware of the far Northwest, and probably represents some of the tribes which occupied the Virginia highland about the period of English colonization. Indeed, traces of this variety occur on the James in its middle course, and appear on the Dan, the Yadkin, and possibly on the upper Shenandoah. It occurs plentifully on New river, and will no doubt be found to extend down the westward-flowing streams, thus connecting with the little-known groups of northeastern Tennessee, eastern Kentucky, and western West Virginia. The pottery is always rude, and consists of simple pots, nearly always showing the soot-blackened surfaces of culinary utensils. Their strongest characteristics are the very general presence of rudely modeled looped handles, which connect the outcurved rim with the shoulder, bridging a short, slightly constricted neck, and the

[a] See footnote on page 147.

frequent occurrence of a thickened collar, sometimes slightly overhanging, after the Iroquoian style, but marked with cords and cord
indentings, characteristic of the rim decoration of the Upper Mississippi and Lake Michigan pottery. More extensive collecting may
enable us to separate these wares into two or more groups or varieties.
Pipes of the simple form common in the eastern Algonquian country
are found on some of the sites. A number of sherds illustrating this
pottery are brought together in plate cxxxiii. The people concerned
may have belonged to the Algonquian stock, for Algonquian features
decidedly prevail, but there is a possibility that they were Siouan.

Several sherds from a village-site burying ground 3½ miles north
of Luray, Virginia, are presented in plate cxxxiv. The simple but
extremely neat pots to which these fragments belong were buried with
human bodies in individual graves on the bottom land near a mound,
but this mound itself, though containing the remains of many hundred
bodies, did not yield any pottery whatever.[a] About Harpers Ferry
and Point of Rocks we have the same ware, but at Romney, West
Virginia, Iroquoian types prevail.

The pottery of upland Virginia and West Virginia is distinguished
from that of the tidewater provinces by the prevalence of handles,
few examples of which have been found in the latter areas, and the
ware of the general Piedmont zone also differs from that of the lowland
in the prominence given the neckband—a feature appearing frequently
west of the fall line, but rather exceptional east of it.

POTOMAC-CHESAPEAKE WARE

GENERAL FEATURES

The central ethnic group of the Potomac-Chesapeake province in
historical times was the Powhatan confederacy, seated for the most
part between Chesapeake bay and the James river. The art of this
district was probably, in the main, developed within the general region,
and was practiced in common by the confederacy and other tribes of
the same stock along the Carolina coast and throughout the Virginia-
Maryland tidewater province. It was probably practiced in more or
less modified forms by isolated tribes of other stocks coming within
the Algonquian influence. Possibly the conditions of existence along
the thousands of miles of tidewater shore line, where the life of the
inhabitants was largely maritime and the food was principally marine,
may have had a strong influence on the potter's art, tending to make it
simple and uniform. The shifting of habitation, due to varying food
supply, and possibly to the necessity of avoiding the periodic malarial
season, must have restricted the practice of an art which is essentially
the offspring of sedentary existence; or the exclusive practice of simple

a Fowke, Gerard, Archeologic investigations in James and Potomac valleys, Bulletin of the Bureau
of Ethnology, 1894, p. 49.

culinary phases of the art may have resulted from the absence of customs demanding vessels for mortuary purposes, ossuary burial at the end of a more or less prolonged period having prevailed to the exclusion of individual inhumation. At any rate, the elementary character and narrow range of the art are its most notable features, and it is remarkable that tribes cultivating maize and practicing several arts with exceptional skill should have been such inferior potters.

Whole vessels are rarely found in the region, and the archeologist must depend for his material on kitchen middens and village sites which furnish fragmentary remains exclusively. There is little trouble, however, in securing enough evidence to reach a correct estimate of the nature and range of the ceramic products. Only pots and kettles and a few simple pipes were produced. The ordinary forms are deep bowls and wide-mouthed pots of medium or small size. Save in remote sections where western and southern tribes are known to have wandered, we do not encounter such features as eccentric or compound forms, animal shapes, constricted mouths, high necks, handles, legs, or flat bases of any kind. Ornament is archaic, and curved lines are almost unknown. These statements are in the main true of the whole Atlantic Algonquian belt from Albemarle sound to the Bay of Fundy.

Though simple in form and archaic in decoration, much of the ware of the great tidewater province was well made and durable. The materials are the clays of the section, tempered with a wide range of ingredients, including pulverized shell, quartz, gneiss, and steatite, besides all grades of ordinary sand. The vessels were largely, if not exclusively, culinary.

Decoration is to a larger extent than elsewhere of textile character, though the Algonquian everywhere employed this class of embellishment. As a rule, the entire body of the vase is covered with imprintings of coarse cloths or nets or cord-wrapped tools, and the ornament proper, confined to the upper portions of the surface, consists in the main of simple geometric arrangements of impressions of hard-twisted cords. Details will be given as the wares of representative localities are described. Besides the textile designs, there are similar figures in incised lines, indentations, and punctures, or of all combined. In plate cxxxv *a* are assembled a number of the figures employed, and with them are placed some tattoo designs (*b*) copied from the work of Hariot,[a] whose illustrations represent the natives among whom the Roanoke colony was planted.

Rims are slightly modified for esthetic effect. Occasionally they are scalloped, and inconspicuous collars were sometimes added. Various indentings of the margin were made with the finger nails, hard cords, or modeling tools.

---

[a] Hariot, Thomas, A briefe and true report of the new found land of Virginia, Frankfort, 1590.

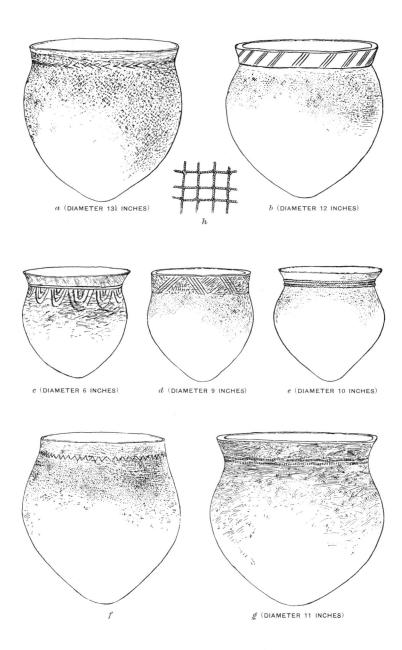

a (DIAMETER 13½ INCHES)

h

b (DIAMETER 12 INCHES)

c (DIAMETER 6 INCHES) d (DIAMETER 9 INCHES) e (DIAMETER 10 INCHES)

f

g (DIAMETER 11 INCHES)

KITCHEN MIDDEN POTTERY WITH VARIED MARKINGS

CHESAPEAKE-POTOMAC GROUP

KITCHEN MIDDEN POTTERY OF THE YADKIN VALLEY

CHESAPEAKE-POTOMAC GROUP

(ONE-HALF)

KITCHEN MIDDEN POTTERY OF THE YADKIN VALLEY
CHESAPEAKE-POTOMAC GROUP
(THREE-FOURTHS)

POTSHERDS WITH TEXTILE MARKINGS, NEW RIVER VALLEY, VIRGINIA
CHESAPEAKE-POTOMAC GROUP
(SLIGHTLY REDUCED)

POTSHERDS WITH TEXTILE MARKINGS, FROM LURAY, VIRGINIA

CHESAPEAKE-POTOMAC GROUP

(THREE-FOURTHS)

INCISED DESIGNS FROM POTTERY, AND TATTOO MARKS

CHESAPEAKE-POTOMAC GROUP

There is marked uniformity in the ware of thousands of sites scattered over the entire tidewater country, an area nearly 20,000 square miles in extent. The only distinction worth noting is that existing between the commoner variety of village-site ware and a coarser form found nearly everywhere associated with the ordinary variety, but prevailing over it in the great oyster-shell deposits. This latter ware corresponds to the net-marked pottery found so plentifully on the Yadkin in North Carolina, illustrated in preceding plates. In the Chesapeake country this pottery is not exclusively net-marked, other textile materials having been used. Whether or not this ware belonged to a distinct people dwelling at times in the region or whether it is a variety due to differences in function merely can not yet be fully determined, although analogies with the prevailing style are so marked that the theory of separate peoples finds little support.

MODERN PAMUNKEY WARE

Before we pass on to the ware of particular localities it may be mentioned that while the art practiced by the tribes of this province when first visited by the English colonists was soon practically abandoned, at least one community, a remnant of the Pamunkey Indians, residing on their reservation on the Pamunkey river adjoining King William county, Virginia, was practicing a degenerate form of it as late as 1878. At about that time Dr Dalyrimple, of Baltimore, visited these people and made collections of their ware, numerous specimens of which are now preserved in the National Museum. A few of the vases then gathered are shown in plate CXXXVI.

Professor O. T. Mason, referring to the work of Dr Dalyrimple, remarks that these people are "a miserable half-breed remnant of the once powerful Virginia tribes. The most interesting feature of their present condition is the preservation of their ancient modes of making pottery. It will be news to some that the shells are calcined before mixing with the clay, and that at least one-third of the compound is triturated shell."[a]

The modeling of these vessels is rude, though the surfaces are neatly polished. They are very slightly baked, and the light-gray surface is mottled with clouds of black. The paste lacks coherency, and several of the specimens have crumbled and fallen to pieces on the shelves, probably as a result of the slaking of the shell particles. Ornament is confined to slight crimping and notching of the rim margins. None of the pieces bear evidence of use, and it seems probable that in recent years the art has been practiced solely or largely to supply the demands of curiosity hunters. The very marked defects of manufacture and the crudeness of shape suggest the idea that possibly the potters were

---

[a] Mason, Otis T., Anthropological news, in American Naturalist, Boston, 1877, vol. XI, p. 627.

really unacquainted with aboriginal methods. It will be seen by reference to the illustrations presented in this and the preceding section that this pottery corresponds somewhat closely in general appearance with that of the Cherokees and Catawbas.

In 1891 these Indians were visited by Mr John G. Pollard, from whom the following paragraphs are quoted:

Mr Terrill Bradby, one of the best informed members of the tribe, furnished, in substance, the following account of the processes followed and the materials used in the manufacture of this pottery:

"In former times, the opening of a clay mine was a great feast day with the Pamunkey. The whole tribe, men, women, and children, were present, and each family took home a share of the clay. The first steps in preparing the clay are to dry it, beat it up, pass it through a sieve, and pound it in a mortar. Fresh-water mussels, flesh as well as shell, having been burnt and ground up, are mixed with the clay prepared as above, and the two are then saturated with water and kneaded together. This substance is then shaped with a mussel shell to the form of the article desired, placed in the sun and dried, then scraped with a mussel shell, and rubbed with a stone for the purpose of producing a gloss. The dishes, bowls, jars, etc., as the case may be, are then placed in a circle and tempered with a slow fire; then placed in the kiln and covered with dry pine bark, and burnt until the smoke comes out in a clear volume. This is taken as an indication that the ware has been burnt sufficiently. It is then taken out and is ready for use."[a]

SHELL-HEAP WARE OF POPES CREEK

The heavy, rude, net-marked or coarsely cord-rouletted pottery so common in this province has been found most plentifully at Popes creek on the Potomac, for the reason, no doubt, that the removal of the shells at this place for fertilizing purposes has exposed the pottery more fully than elsewhere. Typically developed, it is a coarse, heavy ware, having a narrow range of form, size, and finish. The paste is highly silicious, and is tempered very generally with quartz sand, some grains or bits of which are very coarse. The color is mostly somewhat ferruginous, especially on the surface, the interior of the mass being grayer and darker. The shapes are simple, and apparently without variations for esthetic effect. The vessels are deep bowls, wide-mouthed pots, or caldrons with conic bases, and are identical in nearly every respect with the midden vessels of Wilkes county, North Carolina, of which sherds are shown in plates CXXXI and CXXXII.

The walls rarely show constriction at the neck, and descend with slight even curves, at angles of from 30 to 50 degrees to the base, as is indicated in plate CXXXVII. The thickness varies from less than one-fourth of an inch to 1 inch, the greatest thickness being at the conic base. The diameter of the largest pieces was 20 inches or more, the depth averaging considerably less than this. The surfaces are

[a] Pollard, John Garland, The Pamunkey Indians of Virginia, Bulletin of the Bureau of Ethnology, Washington, 1894, p. 18.

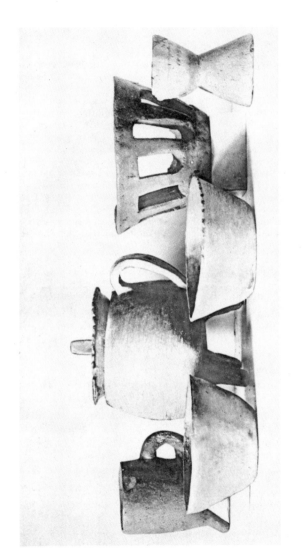

POTTERY OF THE PAMUNKEY INDIANS, VIRGINIA

CHESAPEAKE-POTOMAC GROUP

(TWO-SEVENTHS)

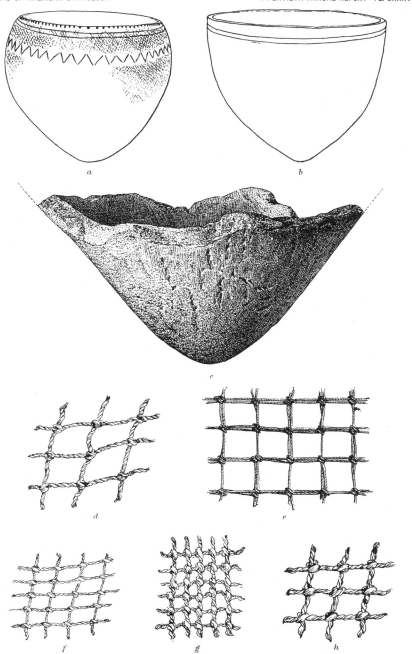

POTTERY FROM SHELL HEAPS AT POPES CREEK, MARYLAND

CHESAPEAKE-POTOMAC GROUP

uneven and roughly finished, but have received a large share of a rude kind of decorative texturing.   The exterior surface has usually received the imprint of an open-mesh net, applied by repeated paddling (plate CXXXVIII), and the interior has been scarified with a comb, or a serrate-edged tool, the teeth of which, occurring about ten or twelve to the inch, were blunt and not very even.   The original and principal function of this scarifying tool was no doubt that of modeling, but in cases it was drawn back and forth in such a manner as to produce simple, irregular, patterned effects, illustrated in plate CXXXIX.   These combs were probably notched bits of wood, shell, or bone, not over an inch or two in width.   The net-marked exterior and scarified interior are peculiar to this heavy ware, and give it a high degree of individuality.

Attempts at systematic decoration are rare.   In a few cases, when the rim was turned rather decidedly outward, a band along the inner margin received impressions from a bit of net.   The outer margin was rudely rounded or squared off, and, in cases, marked with a net, the finger nail, or an implement.   Rude, archaic patterns were some-times traced with the finger or a blunt tool over the net-marked exterior of the vessel.   The net was wrapped about the hand or an improvised paddle and applied to the plastic surface by paddling or rocking.   The object of this application was possibly threefold: first, to knit the clay together; second, to roughen the surface to facilitate heating, and, third, to give a pleasing finish.   It can not be determined whether the netting used in finishing the surface of these rude vessels was the same as that used in fishing nets, but it may fairly be assumed that it was the same.   Rather rarely here, but frequently elsewhere, this same style of ware was finished by applying other varieties of fabric, or by rolling cord-covered tools over the surface, as is indicated in plate CXXXVIII b.

By taking clay impressions from the fictile surfaces, numerous restorations of the netting have been made (plate CXXXVIII a).   The cords used were well twisted and varied from the size of a small thread to that, even, of coarse wrapping thread or twine.   The knotting is generally simple, the meshes ranging from three to seven to the inch. Illustrations are given in plate CXXXVII d, e, f, g, h.   One example, e, appears to have the threads arranged in pairs, but this effect, though often recurring, may be the result of duplicate imprinting.   In cases certain strands present the appearance of having been plaited.

As we have seen, similar pottery occurs on the Yadkin, in North Carolina; the materials are the same, the shape, size, degree of rude-ness, treatment of the surface, and decoration are the same, even the netting and the practice of partially obliterating the net impres-sions on the whole or a part of the vessels are the same.   This pottery is found in more or less typical forms intermingled with the ordinary varieties of ware on sites extending from the Yadkin to the Delaware.

The Popes creek shell-heap site, referred to above, is the best representative of its class in the province. It is located just below the upper limit of the oyster banks on the Potomac, which was possibly farther upstream in the period which witnessed the accumulation of the shells on these sites than it is to-day. It will be interesting and instructive to compare the ceramic remains of these deposits with those of a neighboring site on Potomac creek just above the oyster-producing limits, a stretch of nearly 20 miles of the lake-like Potomac intervening. The Potomac creek site, the seat of the famous Algonquian village of Pottowomeck, referred to by Smith, is still well supplied with fragments of the finer varieties of the ware of the region. Few coarse, heavy, carelessly made pieces are found, and net-marked specimens of the Popes creek type are rare, if not absent. It is observed, however, that the coarser wares are fragile, and that they disintegrate readily, as was observed at Popes creek, where the sherds taken from the shell deposits generally crumble on being handled. The two hundred years of cultivation to which the Potomac creek site, unprotected by compact layers of shell, has been subjected, must have gone far toward destroying all save the particularly durable pieces.

The clay used in the Potomac creek ware was usually very fine in texture, the sand employed increasing in coarseness with the size of the vessel. Weathered surfaces show the particles of white sand in relief, while shell is rare or absent. The paste is well baked, and of the usual warm gray colors, rarely approaching terra cotta.

The modeling was often skilful, and the surfaces of many of the smaller vessels were even and well polished. Most of the vessels were quite small, many being mere cups, holding from a pint to a quart. The walls of these vessels were thin and even, and the outlines approximately symmetric. The forms were well within the lines usual in the province, varying from that of a deep cup or bowl to that of a wide-mouthed pot with upright rim and slightly swelling body. The few bases preserved are slightly conic, the point being a little flattened, so that the vessel would stand alone on a hard surface. The finish is considerably varied within certain narrow limits. The prevailing body finish was given by some form of modeling tool covered or wrapped with fine, well-twisted threads, which was rolled back and forth, or was applied as a paddle. In some cases the textile markings were rubbed down for the application of incised or indented designs, and rarely the entire surface was polished.

a

b

POTTERY FROM SHELL HEAPS AT POPES CREEK, MARYLAND

CHESAPEAKE-POTOMAC GROUP

a (ABOUT TWO-THIRDS)

b   *c*

POTTERY FROM SHELL HEAPS AT POPES CREEK, MARYLAND

CHESAPEAKE-POTOMAC GROUP

Decoration was confined mostly to a zone about the rim, and consisted in the main of cord impressions arranged in lines encircling the vessel, or grouped in various ways to form simple patterns. The effect was varied, in cases, by series of indentations made by impressing a sharply folded cord of larger size. Rim-sherds are shown about one-half actual size in plate CXL b. The work was all, or nearly all, done by the application of cords singly, the cord having been wrapped about a wheel or some round surface so to be readily rolled back and forth. The rim-margins are simply treated, and are round or squarish, and either plain or indented with an angular tool or a cord. A few small pieces bear marks made apparently by very neat stamps

of chevroned lines, possibly some animal or vegetal form. There are other markings too obscure to be made out. It is evident that in cases a finely ribbed paddle was used, almost duplicating the textile effects.

Numerous fragments of the simplest form of tubular clay pipes have been found on this site. The best specimens are in collections made by Mr W. H. Phillips, of Washington, and are illustrated in plate CXLII.

DISTRICT OF COLUMBIA WARE

Generally speaking, the important village sites of the Potomac present a pretty full range of the two types of ware described above as the Popes creek and the Potomac creek varieties, although the latter may be said to predominate and to have the more general distribution. It will be unnecessary to examine other localities in detail, but, on account of local and national interest in the history of the site of the capital city, reference may be made to ceramic remains from the ancient village sites now occupied by the city of Washington.

FIG. 61—Rude earthenware figurine, Potomac valley (Phillips collection).

When the English first ascended the Potomac they found a small community of the natives occupying the terraces on the south side of the Anacostia river or Eastern branch, near its junction with the Potomac. Archeologists now find that the occupation was very general in the vicinity, and that relics of stone and clay utensils occur on nearly every available spot along the shores of both rivers, within as well as above and below the city limits.

The ceramic remains of these sites, as turned up by the plow and exposed by erosion and city improvements, are wholly fragmental, but restorations are readily made, and a few illustrations will serve to convey a correct idea of the art as practiced by the prehistoric Washingtonians. Outlines of several vases are presented in plate CXLI, and photographic reproductions of fragments are given in c, d, e, plate CXL. The fragment c is a part of the vessel outlined in a, plate CXLI. It was found on a village site which was partly destroyed in building the south abutment of the Pennsylvania avenue bridge across the Anacostia river in 1890. The shape was pleasing and symmetric, and the surface was well smoothed, though not highly polished. The simple ornament about the scalloped rim consists of cord imprintings arranged in a series of connecting triangular spaces. The mouth was about 9 inches in diameter.

It may be mentioned as a curious fact that as we approach the head of tide water on the Potomac and enter the district furnishing soapstone we observe the influence of this material on both the paste and the form of the earthenware. The sites about West Washington contain many sherds tempered with pulverized steatite, and the vessels to which they belonged were, in cases, supplied with rude nodes set a little beneath the rim, closely resembling the handles characterizing the steatite pots of the same section. From this circumstance it is clear that the making of pottery and the working of the soapstone quarries were contemporaneous events, a fact shown also by the intermingling of articles of both classes in the débris of many village sites.

In figure 61 a rudely modeled doll-like figure from the Phillips collection is shown. It is from one of the Potomac river sites, and is the only example of its kind so far found in the whole province.

WARE OF THE CHESAPEAKE AND EASTERN SHORE

A description of the sherds of an average Potomac river site could be repeated without essential change for those of an average site on the shores of Chesapeake bay. At Riverton, on the Nanticoke, for example, the general features of form, size, color, fragility, finish, and decoration are repeated. Minor differences are observed in many cases. Incised decoration takes the place, in a measure, of the cord-imprinted figures of Potomac creek. Shell tempering prevails, and the wrapped-cord paddling and rouletting takes the place largely of cord texturing. Net impressions are comparatively rare. The plain and indented rim, the conic base, and the combed interior surface observed in the Potomac wares are repeated here.

In advancing to the north we come to realize that gradually a change is taking place in the character of the ware, and that the change is toward the characteristics of the work of the Iroquoian province. The scalloped rim and the peculiar arrangements of incised lines take on northern characters. We have thus, as in other cases, indications of

POTTERY FROM POTOMAC CREEK, VIRGINIA, AND ANACOSTIA, DISTRICT OF COLUMBIA

CHESAPEAKE-POTOMAC GROUP

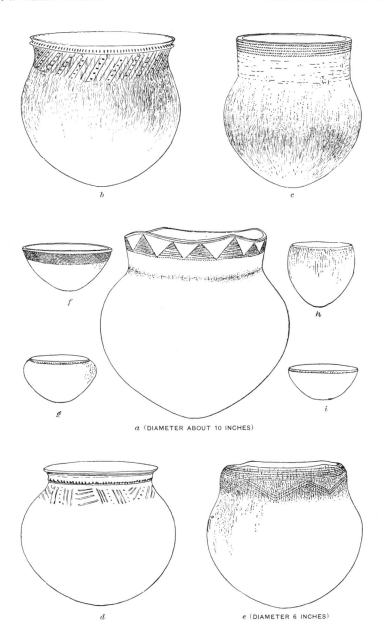

a (DIAMETER ABOUT 10 INCHES)

e (DIAMETER 6 INCHES)

POTTERY FROM THE VICINITY OF WASHINGTON, DISTRICT OF COLUMBIA
(RESTORED FROM FRAGMENTS)

CHESAPEAKE-POTOMAC GROUP

the close association in some way or other, peaceable or warlike, of the occupants of neighboring northern and southern provinces.

Collections from the upper Maryland and Delaware districts are extremely meager, and it is impossible now to trace in detail the transitions that take place between the drainage of the Potomac and that of the Susquehanna and between the latter stream and the Delaware.

TOBACCO PIPES

Although it was Virginia, possibly, that gave to England the form of tobacco pipe largely adopted there and most used by the whites generally throughout the three centuries that have elapsed since the founding of Raleigh's colonies, the clay pipes of the Virginia province are of the simplest possible type. They are slightly bent tubes from 4 to 6 inches in length, having gently expanding bowls less than 2 inches long, and stems that taper slightly to a neat mouthpiece. They are not unlike some forms of cigarette or cigar holders of the present period. The stem, in cases, is flattened so as to be held easily between the teeth or lips, as is indicated in the sections in plate CXLII *a* and *c*. The finish is of all grades between rude smoothing with the fingers and an excellent polish. The paste is usually very fine grained, the baking is often excellent, and the colors are the ordinary warm grays of the baked clay.

Ornament is seen only in rare cases; some specimens have a slightly relieved band about the bowl, and in a very few instances indented designs are observed. The bowl of the specimen shown in *d* has been decorated with an extremely neat design of the usual style of the region, applied apparently with a delicately notched roulette. The inside of the bowl and stem is usually blackened by use. It is a fact worthy of note that many of the sites yield fragments of pipes of much the same size and general style, which are made of pure white clay and bear indications of having been pressed in molds after the fashion of our ordinary clay pipes. This would seem to indicate that the whites took to making pipes for trade while yet the shores of the Potomac and Chesapeake were occupied by the native villagers. I will not enlarge on this subject here further than to present an illustration of a pipe and tobacco pouch, *f*, copied from a plate in Hariot's Virginia. The pipe is identical in shape with the clay pipes of the region as here illustrated, and we have the good fortune thus to be able to connect the historic tribes of the Roanoke province with the sites supplying nearly all of our archeologic material.

Pipes of this class are confined pretty closely within the South Algonquian province. The change from the wide rimmed, sharply bent clay pipe of the South Appalachian province is quite abrupt; but on the north the change is somewhat gradual into the more elaborate and elegant pipes of the Iroquois.

POTTERY OF THE IROQUOIAN PROVINCE

THE IROQUOIAN TRIBES

The group of tribes now classed, on the basis of language, as Iroquoian, constituted one of the most important grand divisions of the aborigines of North America. The central culminating event in their history was the formation of the league, which included at first five nations and finally six. The seat of this great group of communities was in New York, but their strong arm was felt at times from Nova Scotia on the east to the Mississippi on the west, and from the drainage of Hudson bay on the north almost to the Gulf on the south. There were several outstanding tribes of this stock not absorbed by the league—the Conestogas on the lower Susquehanna, the Cherokees in the Carolinas and Georgia, the Wyandots along the St Lawrence and the Great lakes, and others of less prominence in other sections. All save the Cherokees were surrounded by tribes of Algonquian stock. The cultural remains of this strongly individualized people constitute a well marked group of art products, fully identified and correlated with the makers. These remains are central in New York, in which state the types are found, but they extend out into the neighboring states, where they gradually lose their typical character. The tracing of the peculiarly Iroquoian art and art influence from center to circumference of the great province occupied, is a matter of very considerable importance to the historian of the aborigines, but little has been done as yet in a systematic way toward carrying out the work. Morgan, Schoolcraft, Hale, Boyle, Beauchamp, Harrison Wright, Perkins, Squier, Thomas, Cushing, and many others have contributed not a little, though most of the work has been fragmentary.

GENERAL CHARACTERS OF THE WARE

Pottery constitutes the most important feature of the Iroquoian remains. In general, it falls in with the simple ware of the northeastern states, but at the same time it presents numerous striking and distinctive characteristics of shape and decoration. Within the group there are many local variations in form, ornament, and composition, indicating the existence of somewhat marked tribal peculiarities, and it may be possible in time to segregate the work of some of the stronger tribes, such as the Onondagas and the Mohawks, who dwelt for a long time in limited areas. The Cherokees and Tuscaroras had for generations or perhaps centuries been completely isolated from their kin, and their work was thus highly distinctive.

The Iroquois did not dwell largely on the Atlantic seaboard, but occupied the shores of the lakes, especially Lake Ontario. Their favorite resorts, however, were along the rivers and on the banks of the hundreds of charming upland lakes in New York state. The question of the influence of the sea and of the lake environments upon their art, as distinguished from that of the great interior upland, has been raised by Mr Frank H. Cushing, who gives his observations and deductions with respect to this obscure but interesting matter in a paper published in Memoirs of the International Congress of Anthropology at Chicago.[a]   At present I do not feel qualified to discuss the question, lacking the necessary knowledge of the peoples and environments concerned.   It is possible that the Algonquian Indians may be responsible for most of the shore work, and the Iroquois responsible for the art of the inland and upland districts, which would account for most of the differences.   We are not able to determine the precise effect of environment on an art until we have made full allowance for peculiarities of peoples and difference in period.

Fig. 62—Bark vessel showing characters sometimes copied in clay by Iroquoian potters.

When the French entered the great St Lawrence basin the Iroquoian tribes were actively engaged in the practice of the plastic art, but its total abandonment was quickly brought about by the introduction of utensils of European manufacture. That these peoples had dwelt for a long period in this general province, and that their arts, as developed at the time of Columbus, were largely of local evolution, seems highly probable, and the stamp of local environment is especially marked in the potter's art.   The accompanying map, plate IV, indicates in a general way the distribution of the Iroquoian pottery.

In the various groups of plastic products previously examined, the vessel in its numerous forms is the leading feature, and in some cases it is almost the exclusive feature of the fictile remains.   In the Iroquois region it is different.   The art of tobacco pipe making shared the honors with vase making, and led to an elaboration of plastic forms and to a refinement of manipulation seldom surpassed within the area considered in this paper.   Life forms, rarely imitated by the surrounding Algonquian tribes, were freely employed by the Iroquois.

The strongest characteristics of the earthen vessels, and those which may best be relied on to distinguish them from all other like wares, is the pronounced projecting or overhanging collar—a frieze-like development of the rim—the outer surface of which was almost always ornamented with incised patterns.   A squarish mouth, with elevated

[a] Chicago, 1894, p. 216.

points at the corners and sagging margins between, is also a marked feature, and the sharp constriction about the neck and the gracefully swelling body, conic below, are hardly less pronounced and valuable group characters. It is possible that some of these features owe their origin to the bark vessels of the same region. This idea is presented by Cushing in the Fourth Annual Report of the Bureau of Ethnology,[a] from which figure 62 is reproduced. In the application of the human face or form in relief, we have another group index of the highest value. The angles of the frieze are very often emphasized by enlargments, projecting ridges, and raised points, and to these the plastic life features, mostly human, are added.

Besides the large percentage of vases presenting these characteristics, there are many of rather plain appearance that might not, if placed with vessels of Algonquian type, be easily distinguished save by the expert. Many are round-bodied and wide-mouthed, with inconspicuous lips. Some are bowls and others mere cups, the latter often quite minute. Leading features of form are brought out to good advantage in the numerous illustrations accompanying this section.

MATERIALS AND MANUFACTURE

The materials used were usually mixtures of clay and rather coarse tempering ingredients, in typical localities mostly silicious. The Iroquois occasionally used pulverized shell, as did their neighbors, the Algonquians, but they seem to have preferred pulverized rock of crystalline varieties. Respecting the securing and selecting of the ingredients, and the levigating, mixing, and manipulation of the paste, but little can be said. Evidences of the nature of the building processes are obscure, but there is no reason to suppose that other than the usual methods were employed.[b] The walls were probably built up of bits and strips of clay welded together with the fingers and worked down and polished with scrapers, paddles, and rubbing stones. The surface of the convex body of the vessel was sometimes finished by malleating with a textile-covered paddle or by rouletting with a cord-wrapped tool. The rim was added, and was then squared or rounded on the margin and polished down in preparation for the use of the graver and the tubular or pointed punch. The paste for large vessels was often quite coarse, but for the smaller pieces and for most pipes pure clay of the finest quality was employed.

The baking was conducted in shallow pits or on the surface of the earth, and in usual ways, no doubt, for the ordinary fire mottling is observed. No great degree of heat was applied.

---

[a] P. 520.

[b] For a very carefully made experimental study of this subject, see F. H. Cushing's article, The germ of shoreland pottery, in the Memoirs of the International Congress of Anthropology, Chicago 1894.

COLOR, FORM, AND SIZE

The colors of this ware are the colors of the baked clay; where it has not changed by use or age, grays of yellowish and reddish tones, rarely approaching a terra cotta, prevail.

In the matter of size these vessels have not the wide range of the more southern varieties. There are very few large pieces, and few very small ones. A height or diameter exceeding 12 inches is unusual. Small toy-like cups are occasionally found.

To the student of the many and varied ceramic groups of aboriginal America, a most notable feature of this, and of the Algonquian ware as well, is the marked simplicity of the forms. As the vessels were based on simple models and employed for a limited range of uses, there has been little tendency toward elaboration or differentiation of shape. The art as practiced here must have been still very near its origin—young as compared with the potter's art in the South. The only form prototypes that appear, and these are strongly suggested by the shapes of the vases, are the bark vessels and baskets in common use in the region. All are forms of use, yet a certain rude grace characterizes the outlines. The narrow limitations of form are indicated by the absence or rarity of bottles, bowls, plates, animal figures, compound shapes, flat bottoms, handles, feet, and pedestal-like additions.

ORNAMENT—PLASTIC, INCISED, AND RELIEVED

The decoration of Iroquoian earthenware is simple in execution, and limited in range of subject matter, indicating a people yet near the threshold of their esthetic career. This archaic simplicity is not so pronounced, however, in the treatment of plastic details as it is in the linear designs.

The forms of vessels are considerably varied within a limited range, and convey the notion, in many cases, that the makers had conceptions akin to our own with respect to proportion and grace; yet we are unable to say how much these qualities are due to suggestions acting within the art, and how much is the result of conscious appreciation of the esthetic in contour. Forms of tobacco pipes are often interesting and graceful. Nearly all are modifications of the trumpet shape, and the representations of living creatures so freely employed are generally added without serious detriment to the fundamental shape. The plastic additions to vases are also executed in a way to indicate the existence of restricting forces, traditional, esthetic, or otherwise, tending to hold the potter to simple, consistent models. This is in strong contrast with the employment of life features by the potters of the middle and southern provinces, where variety is endless and consistency is often disregarded. The rim-collar or frieze is often divided into two, three, or four parts by salients or ridges, and the modeled life-shapes are confined strictly to these features, adding emphasis to the form without reducing the simplicity or overburdening the vessel. Plastic ornaments comprise ridges, nodes, projecting points, medallion-like heads mostly or exclusively of men, and more or less complete figures of men. Mr Cushing has observed modifications of the ornamental ridges at the corners of the frieze which seemed to him to make them represent ears of corn. The modeling was done with the fingers, aided by modeling tools; the latter were used mainly in indenting, incising, and polishing. The fact that the life-forms employed in vase modeling are confined almost universally to the human subject is worthy of note, since in modeling pipes many varieties of animal were employed. The idea is thus emphasized that pipe making and vase making, though practiced by the same people, must have been carried on under somewhat different conditions or at periods not fully coincident. It is not unlikely that superstition gave rise to the use of these life-forms, and restricted them to the places on the vases and pipes to which they are so scrupulously confined. The women probably made the vases, but the pipes, it is surmised, were made by the men.

The archaic, rectilinear decorations of this pottery are in strong contrast with the graceful and elaborate designs of the South and West. So far but few curved lines have been observed, and the current ornaments, such as the scroll, the fret, and the meander, were wholly unknown. So elemental are the motives that they may safely be regarded as illustrating the first steps of these people in freehand ceramic decoration, though they were doubtless familiar with textile embellishment at a much earlier period. Textile texturing is not uncommon, and, in cases, nearly the entire body of the vase is covered with impressions of cords or coarse cloth applied by paddling or by some other method of malleating or imprinting. I am not certain that any specimen examined by me has markings made by handling the plastic vessel in a net or other inclosing fabric, as has been suggested by Mr Cushing's experiments already referred to.

The formal pseudotextile ornamental designs consist of straight incised lines and indentations arranged in simple combinations, forming encircling zones, generally around the frieze, but in cases around the body of the vase. The zones are usually bordered by parallel lines and marginal rows of indentations or notches, interrupted in the frieze by relieved features placed at intervals, dividing the space into two, three, or more sections. The margin or lip is rounded, square, or sloping, and is embellished with indents, punctures, or short lines, and the lower margin of the frieze is variously finished with a band of short lines, indented circlets, notches, indents, or relieved bead-like points.

The execution is varied. The lines were incised with an acute or rounded point, sometimes forced rudely through the clay, leaving a ragged line, and again trailed across the surface, giving a comparatively smooth channel. This, in the finer work, is gone over again and again to give it a smooth finish or polish. In cases, the effect seems to indicate that a curved edge was rolled back and forth, leaving linear indentations, and again that a notched or dentate edge, as of a wheel, was rolled along the line, being reset for each line, and not rolled back and forth in a zigzag, as the common roulette was. The skill exhibited in the use of the various decorating tools in the making of pipes is exceptional, and, in cases, remarkable. In rare instances the decorating tools took the character of small stamps, the figures being squares in relief, made by cutting cross grooves on the end of a stick or the face of a paddle.

The use of colors in ceramic decoration had not, so far as we can discover, reached the Iroquois country proper, and the very general use of intaglio and relieved decoration indicates that the plastic methods were exclusively employed.

In plates CXLIX–CLII a number of examples of the grouping of incised and indented lines and attendant plastic features in the decorated zones of the vessel are brought together. The combinations are essentially the same throughout the Iroquoian province, and the nature of local variations may be seen by reference to the plates.

DISTRIBUTION AND CHARACTERS OF SPECIMENS

SOUTHERNMOST OCCURRENCE

In passing up the Chesapeake and Potomac valleys, where Algonquian forms of earthenware are encountered on every village site, the archeologist begins to observe the occurrence of strange features in the ceramic remains on the Chesapeake about the head of the bay, and on the Potomac about the mouth of the Shenandoah. In the vicinity of Romney, West Virginia, the burial places have yielded numerous specimens of Iroquoian ware, not, however, wholly typical in every respect. These are intermingled, apparently, more or less intimately, with pieces that resemble in a general way the Algonquian vases. The scalloped expanding rim, with its frieze of groupings of straight incised lines, is present, and leaves no doubt as to the placing of most of the specimens. In plate CXLIII illustrations are given of finds at this place; they are from the collection of Mr Warren K. Moorehead, who visited the locality in about the year 1890, a period at which the freshets of South fork had exposed the contents of numerous graves. The general region is one likely to have been occupied, temporarily, at least, by the tribes inhabiting New York and Pennsylvania, and it is probable that the Tuscaroras passed this way on their journey northward to join their brethren of the League. The execution of the vases is rude, and the frieze is rather heavy for the weak body, but the lines are not, as a whole, ungraceful. Identical wares are obtained from Cavetown and other localities in northern Maryland.   The pipes, though resembling the south Algonquian forms, are like those of northern Maryland and southern Pennsylvania, and are distinctly Iroquoian.

LOWER SUSQUEHANNA POTTERY

The occupation of the lower Susquehanna by tribes of Iroquoian stock might be readily proved by the ceramic remains of that region, if history were entirely silent on the subject.   The peoples to whom this earthenware belonged were possibly the Susquehannocks of John Smith, but very probably were the Conestegas of later times, a people not connected with the League, and at war with some of the League tribes.   The last remnant of these people were the unfortunate villagers of Conestoga, who were massacred there and at Lancaster by the Paxton boys only a hundred and fifty years ago (1755).

From a village site near Bainbridge, on the Susquehanna, Mr Galbraith obtained a number of broken vases and sherds which came into the possession of the National Museum.   These are of familiar types of form and decoration, as will be seen by reference to plate CXLIV. Pulverized mussel shells were used in tempering the clay, and in cases the percentage of this ingredient is very large.   We have here, as elsewhere, the small body, the scalloped rim, the heavy overhanging collar, and the archaic arrangements of incised lines.   There are also the rather rudely modeled faces, two or four in number, projecting from the angles of the frieze (a, b, and c); and a somewhat unique feature is the enlargement of the notched lower margin of the frieze into pendant points, marked with incised lines, as is seen in d and e.   The diameter of this vase is about 10 inches.   The surfaces are imperfectly smoothed, as if rubbed down with the finger tips rather than with a polishing tool; and there are traces of textile imprints on the body and neck, as if a cord or fabric-covered tool had been used in malleating the surface.   The incised lines are rather carelessly drawn, and the modeled faces are extremely elementary.

The extension of this ware into eastern Pennsylvania and New Jersey has not been recorded, although Warren county, in northwestern New Jersey, has furnished examples of vases, preserved in the collections of the Academy of Sciences, Philadelphia, which have the overhanging upright collar, not, however, typically developed and not decorated in the Iroquoian style.   The tempering is silicious, the treatment rude, the walls thick, and the bodies long and conic below. The bodies are finished with textile-like impressions, and they have Algonquian rather than Iroquoian characters.

POTTERY OF NORTHERN PENNSYLVANIA AND NEW YORK

The Wyoming Historical and Geological Society of Wilkesbarre, Pennsylvania, located in the midst of the Iroquoian territory, has been

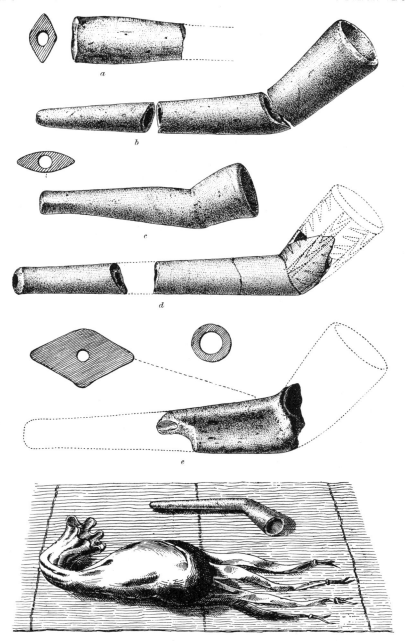

f (ACTUAL SIZE)

TOBACCO PIPES OF THE POTOMAC VALLEY
CHESAPEAKE-POTOMAC GROUP

a (HEIGHT 4¼ INCHES)

b

POTTERY FROM A BURIAL PLACE NEAR ROMNEY, WEST VIRGINIA

IROQUOIAN GROUP

(MOOREHEAD COLLECTION)

exceptionally fortunate in securing several specimens of these vases in an excellent state of preservation, and descriptions and illustrations have been published in the proceedings of the Society by Dr Harrison Wright. I have had seven examples reengraved from the Proceedings of the society, where they were published by Dr Wright, along with valuable descriptive matter.

The fine and unusually large specimen shown in plate CXLV a was found among the rocks at the Falls of the Wallenpaupack, Hawley, Wayne county, Pennsylvania, about forty miles northeast of Wilkesbarre, by Alonzo H. Blish, in 1847. The specimen shown in b was found by Weston Goss, July 12, 1879, under a rock, about one and a quarter miles from the Allen settlement, Lake township, Luzerne county, Pennsylvania. This is about fifteen miles west of Wilkesbarre. The striking little vase shown in c was taken from an Indian grave on the site of an extensive burying ground in Plymouth township, Luzerne county, Pennsylvania, about one mile west of Wilkesbarre, and presented to the Wyoming Historical and Geological Society by Mr John Kern. The symmetric pot illustrated in d was found by Asa L. Dana, in the year 1836, in a cave in Eaton township, opposite Tunkhannock, Wyoming county, Pennsylvania, about thirty miles north of Wilkesbarre.

The neat little vessel shown in plate CXLVI a is described as Tioga vase 1 by Mr Wright, and was obtained from a grave near Athens, Bradford county, Pennsylvania. It had been placed near the head of a body buried there, and had associated with it a "lapstone," and a rude arrow point of local type. The mouth of the vessel is elliptical, 4 by $3\frac{1}{2}$ inches in dimensions, the rim is carried up in rounded projections at opposite ends, and is embellished without by a simply modeled human face, signalized by a headdress or notched fillet, flowing gracefully to the right and left.

From another grave at the same place, and similarly placed with respect to the skeleton, we have the exceptionally interesting piece presented in b. It is notable for the abrupt battlement-like elevations placed at opposite sides of the rim, and also for the double zone of decoration. Several other vessels in a more or less fragmentary state, and less typical in shape, were recovered from graves at this point. It is interesting to note that these graves are on a tract of land purchased by the Susquehanna company from the Iroquois in 1754.[a]

The vases shown in c and d are from the general region under consideration, but the exact locality is not recorded.

In plate CXLVII a is given a handsome vessel with very unusual decoration. It is from the vicinity of Wilkesbarre and was found by Mr Jacob Cist in the early part of the nineteenth century. The decorative patterns resemble textile patterns, and have been worked out with great care with a pointed or notched tool, the form of which can not be determined.

The state of New York has furnished many examples of ware of the general type illustrated above, but, as a rule, it is in a fragmentary state. It is hardly necessary to present additional examples, save in two cases. The remarkable vessel shown in plate CXLVII *b* was obtained by Dr D. S. Kellogg in Plattsburg, New York. It is 11 inches in height, and is apparently very well made. The shape, which is especially notable, and the peculiar ornamentation take it out of the ordinary Iroquoian group and place it with the wares of the upper Mississippi valley. It has a long, conic body, slightly constricted neck, and simple expanding rim. The entire surface is decorated with roulette markings. A minutely notched wheel was used on the neck, and apparently a distinct and more coarsely notched wheel or tool was used on the body. This vessel is decidedly an exotic in the region.

Fig. 63—Fragments of decorated vase-rims from the Mohawk valley.

Two fragments of the very neat and quite typical ware of the Mohawk district are represented in figure 63. They belong to a small series of like sherds presented to the National Museum by Mr S. L. Frey. Reverend William M. Beauchamp, of Baldwinsville, New York, has made careful examinations of the earthenware of the state and has acquired an extensive series of drawings, some of which have been placed at my disposal. It is expected that Mr. Beauchamp will in the near future publish detailed studies on this and other branches of Iroquoian art.

EXAMPLES FROM NEW ENGLAND

Historically and traditionally we learn that the Iroquoian tribes occupied or overran the greater part of the New England province. They are known to have visited the Atlantic coast at many points between New Jersey and Maine, and, according to Leclercq, the Gaspeian Indians of St Lawrence gulf were three times defeated or "destroyed" by this bold and enterprising people. The Abnakis of

POTTERY FROM A VILLAGE SITE AT BAINBRIDGE, PENNSYLVANIA

IROQUOIAN GROUP

(ABOUT ONE-HALF)

c (HEIGHT 6 INCHES)

b (HEIGHT 6¼ INCHES)

d (HEIGHT 7 INCHES)

a (HEIGHT 13 INCHES)

VASES FROM GRAVES, NORTHERN PENNSYLVANIA

IROQUOIAN GROUP

(WYOMING HISTORICAL AND GEOLOGICAL SOCIETY COLLECTION)

b (HEIGHT 5¼ INCHES)

a (HEIGHT 4¾ INCHES)

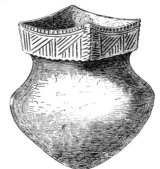

d

c

VASES FROM GRAVES, NORTHERN PENNSYLVANIA

IROQUOIAN GROUP

a (HEIGHT 8 INCHES)

b (HEIGHT 11 INCHES)

VASES FROM GRAVES IN PENNSYLVANIA AND NEW YORK

IROQUOIAN GROUP

Maine, in a treaty with the whites, claimed the land as far westward as the Connecticut river, which they spoke of as the ancient boundary between their people and the Iroquois.[a]   It is therefore to be expected that now and then remains or relics of the latter people will be found scattered over the New England states.

A number of earthen vessels approaching the Iroquoian type were recovered by Professor Putnam from a grave in Winthrop, Massachusetts (plate CLX).   They were accompanied by articles of European manufacture, leaving no doubt that pottery was in use after the coming of the whites.   During early colonial times this region was occupied by Algonquian tribes, and, though the Iroquois are known to have visited the vicinity of Boston bay, the question may be raised as to whether this variety of ware was not, in this section, common to the two stocks of people.   Its presence here is perhaps more reasonably accounted for by supposing that the Algonquians were subject to Iroquois influence, possibly obtaining the art of working clay from them.   The larger piece (c) has the pronounced overhanging collar, embellished with a frieze of incised lines grouped in usual ways, the shoulder being encircled by a line of indentations.   The small cup (b) is typically Algonquian, while the fragment (a) presents Iroquoian characters repeated in vases from Ipswich, part of which were obtained by Professor Baird from shell banks.   Good specimens of the same variety of ware are preserved in the museums at Salem, and an interesting specimen, belonging to the same subgroup, was found by Professor Wyman in a grave at Hingham, Massachusetts.   A rudely incised twined meander is the most remarkable feature of this vessel; it is the only example of its class, so far as my observation extends, found in New England.   The treatment of the rim and the lower margin of the frieze, as well as the pointed base, is Iroquoian rather than Algonquian.   In an interesting review of the antiquities of Connecticut, Mr James Shepherd illustrates a fragmentary vase from that state.[b]   The restoration is possibly somewhat inaccurate as to outline, for, judging by the many other specimens of its class, the body should be much longer and the base somewhat more conic.   The form as restored is not so much Iroquoian as Algonquian save in its rolled rim, but the zone of incised ornament is apparently Iroquoian.

The discovery of typical Iroquoian ware in the region of Lakes George and Champlain is to be expected, for the dominion of the eastern tribes of that stock certainly extended over much of this country at one time or other.   The collections and writings of Professor George H. Perkins, of Burlington, bear ample testimony to this.[c]

[a]Vaudreuil, Marquis de, letter of April 21, 1725, in Doc. Col. Hist. of New York, Albany, 1855, vol. LX, p. 943.

[b]Shepherd, James, New England Magazine, December, 1893.

[c]Perkins, George H., The calumet in the Champlain valley, in Pop. Sci. Monthly, New York, 1893, vol. XLIV, p. 238; some relics of the Indians of Vermont, in Amer. Nat., Salem, 1871, vol. v, p 14; on some fragments of pottery from Vermont, in Proc. Am. Ass. Adv. Sci., 1877, p. 325.

A typical example of this ware from Vermont was illustrated and described by Mr Perkins in the American Naturalist, vol. v, p. 14, and again very fully described in the Proceedings of the American Association for 1876. The specimen was found at considerable depth below the surface of the ground, in the town of Colchester, Vermont, in 1825. It is remarkable for strongly emphasized contours, symmetry, careful finish, and elaborate ornamentation, and is in every way typical of the group. An excellent cut of it appeared in Harper's

Fig. 64—Vase from a grave (?) in Colchester, Vermont.

Magazine, vol. LXV, p. 254. The illustration here presented, figure 64, is from a photograph of a cast of this vase, now preserved in the National Museum. The rim has been partially restored.

CANADIAN WARE

In historic times, and for an unknown period of pre-Columbian time, the Iroquoian tribes occupied a wide belt north of the St Lawrence river, Lakes Erie and Ontario, and their dominion extended at times over the Lake Huron region, and into the country about Lakes Superior and Michigan. As a matter of course the region is strewn with the fragments of their earthenware, which bears throughout the peculiar characteristics of Iroquoian art. There are many variations, however, of shape and decoration, as a number of tribes, the Hurons, Eries, etc., and, later, the Wyandots, occupied the region.

Ontario is especially rich in fragmental ceramic remains, and through the praiseworthy efforts of the Canadian Institute and other learned bodies of the Dominion, and especially of Mr David Boyle, of Toronto, many specimens have been collected and preserved, and numerous illustrations and descriptions have been published. I shall be able only to glance at these products, leaving all the details to those who have the opportunity for working personally in the various regions.

The earliest publication of illustrations of Iroquoian pottery was made by Mr W. E. Guest, in the Smithsonian Report for 1856, p. 274. Many fragments were found in or near an ancient earthen inclosure at Spencerville, a few miles north of Prescott, Ontario, and the cuts published by Mr Guest are restorations, a little defective in outline, perhaps, as the base is more nearly flat than is usual with this ware. In every other respect their features duplicate those of the typical wares of the Iroquois. Mr Guest also gives illustrations of three small disks made from potsherds, one apparently being perforated, as if for use as a spindle whorl or an ornament. The others are nearly identical with similar objects found plentifully in the southern states, and supposed to have served for playing some game of chance.

Village and camp sites in the Balsam lake region, Victoria county, have yielded to the intelligent efforts of the Laidlaw brothers, residents of the locality, numerous interesting sherds, of which a large series has been illustrated and described by David Boyle in the Fourth Annual Report of the Canadian Institute. In plate CXLVIII is presented a series of vases selected from his work. So typical are all of these in form and decoration that description is unnecessary. There is not a new element, beyond the simple variations to be expected in the art of a single people as practiced at different times or under changing conditions.

The island of Montreal, the site of the ancient Hochelaga, an Iroquoian resort of great importance, furnishes much typical ware of this class. Illustrations are given by Dr J. W. Dawson, in the Canadian Naturalist, volume v, page 435, and in his Fossil Men, page 91. In the latter work is shown also a well-preserved pot obtained from the upper Ottawa. It is not so typical as some others, but has the upright projecting collar somewhat developed, and is finished with vertical and horizontal incised lines. The line of indentations about the upper part of the body is rather exceptional in the central and southern Iroquoian regions, but is repeated in a similar piece from Bruce county, Ontario, and in many of the New England specimens. It is possible, since the

Algonquian tribes encroached at times on the northern margin of Ontario, that these vessels may have been modified in certain details by the art of that people.

Mr Boyle, in the Annual Report of the Canadian Institute for 1889, records the discovery of much fragmentary ware along and near the north shore of Lake Erie. It is stated that numerous unusual features of minor importance occur, but, from the descriptions and illustrations given, there is no reason for supposing it other than Iroquoian work. A number of exceptionally large pieces were observed, a diameter and height of 17 inches being noted.

In the same publication Mr Boyle presents a vessel of unusual shape, restored from numerous fragments found by Mr John McPherson on Mindemoya island, northern Lake Huron. This piece is shown in plate CXLVIII *f*. Attention may be called to the fact that it differs essentially from Iroquoian types, and resembles somewhat the Algonquian pottery of the Lake Michigan and Upper Mississippi regions. Since Algonquian tribes occupied this region more fully, perhaps, than the Iroquoian, the probabilities are that this vessel is of Algonquian make.

It is a remarkable fact that in the National Museum there are a number of fragments of typical Iroquoian ware entered as having been found in southern Alabama. Fearing that there may have been a mistake on the part of the curator or his assistants in placing this accession on the books, I will not venture to do more than mention the circumstance. Such an occurrence, if sustained, would be of much interest to students of stock distribution.

DECORATIVE DESIGNS

In plates CXLIX, CL, CLI, and CLII, a series of figures is presented to illustrate the nature and range of the incised and modeled decorations of this pottery. The example shown in plate CXLIX *a* is from a Romney, West Virginia, vase; *b, c, d,* and *e* are from fragmentary vessels procured from a village site on the Susquehanna, near Bainbridge, Pennsylvania, while *f* and *g* are from Mohawk valley sherds.

The designs shown in plates CL and CLI are mostly from vases in the Wyoming Historical and Geological Society collections, and belong in the Wilkesbarre region. The second figure, *b,* of plate CL, represents part of a zone of ornament encircling a Cherokee split-cane basket, and is intended for comparison with the incised design illustrated in *a.* There can be little doubt that the latter motive was derived almost directly from some similar textile ornament, the art of basketry having been universally practiced by the ancient tribes of the East.

The remaining figures of plates CL, CLI, and CLII serve to indicate the general uniformity and simplicity of the linear designs of the whole province. The employment of double zones of figures is illustrated in the lower figures of plates CLI and CLII. The design in the latter plate is from the Vermont vase shown in figure 64. The curved lines seen in these figures are not so by design of the decorator, but merely take the curves of the vessel margins with which they were associated.

The manner of introducing life forms is also clearly shown in four instances. The entire human figure, modeled in rather bold relief, is seen in plate CLII c. The face, with horizontal markings indicating the place of the body, appears in b, and a highly conventionalized treatment of the face is given in a. These conventionalized forms are present in great variety. One of the most realistic examples of figure presentation is shown in figure 65. Other figures and a number of rudely modeled faces are brought together in plate CLIII. These ornaments are in all cases attached to the angles of the frieze of square-rimmed vessels, or are placed beneath the elevated points of the round, scallop-rimmed variety. It is probable that these features are recent additions to the decoration, which consisted, originally, of archaic arrangements of lines and dots.

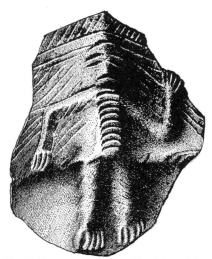

Fig. 65—Fragment of vase-rim with rudely modeled human figure, New York.

TOBACCO PIPES

THE PIPE A NATIVE PRODUCT

The American natives were a race of smokers, and the use of tobacco in political and religious ceremonials elevated the pipe to a place of unusual importance among the various products of the shaping arts. Much time, labor, and ingenuity were expended on the manufacture of pipes of stone, and nearly every section of North America has furnished to collectors excellent examples of this class of work.

Pipes were also made of wood, bone, horn, and other substances. It is highly probable that the antitype of the pipe was a vegetal form, such as a section of cane or other hollow stem, but, since smoking was practiced in widely separated localities, the earlier forms must have been divers. Clay was very generally employed in this art, and in some sections was in great favor. It is a notable circumstance that the Iroquois took a high rank as pipe makers, excelling all other peoples in the number and quality of these productions. With this people the manufacture of clay pipes was, no doubt, practiced pari passu with that of vase making, but it seems in many ways to have been a distinct and independent art. Pipes were not made of the same varieties of clay, or by the same hands, as were the vases. In all probability clay pipes were the work of men, as were the pipes of stone, while vessel making was the work of women. That pipe making was contemporaneous with vase making is shown by the repetition in pipe bowls of the form and decoration of vases, but it is apparent that the former art continued long after the cessation of the potter's art proper, extending down nearly or quite to Revolutionary times in the North, and down to the present day in the South among the Cherokees. In support of the theory of the later use of pipes of native make may be cited the fact that pipes are especially plentiful on the more recent town sites of the New York Indians. Metal pots were supplied plentifully by the earliest traders and colonists, but as smoking and pipe making were indigenous to America, it was probably many years before the intruders engaged actively in pipe manufacture. It is well known, however, that tobacco pipes of European make formed an important article of trade in colonial times, and we can not assume in all cases to distinguish the foreign from the native work.

DISTRIBUTION

Earthen vessels were made and used by women, and were little subject to transportation beyond the permanent settlements, but pipes belonged to the men, and were carried habitually about the person, thus reaching the farthest limits of the expeditions and forays of the people. They were also readily made on short notice at any point where clay could be secured. Since they were used in councils with neighboring peoples they were thus subject to still wider distribution by friendly or ceremonial exchange. It is observed, however, that the pipes of outlying communities are not wholly typical. The pipes of Romney, West Virginia, and Bainbridge, on the Lower Susquehanna, resemble somewhat the South Algonquian pipes, and those of the Lake Huron region vary equally from the types. This is the result, no doubt, of contact with neighboring peoples and the influence of their art forms.

MATERIAL, COLOR, AND FORM

In the manufacture of pipes by the Iroquois, fine clay, pure or mixed with very finely comminuted tempering ingredients, was used. Pulverized shell was used at times on the outskirts of the province.

So far as has been observed, the pipes have not been colored artificially. The varied hues of light and dark yellowish, reddish, and

a (DIAMETER 4½ INCHES)

c (HEIGHT 7 INCHES)

b (DIAMETER 3½ INCHES)

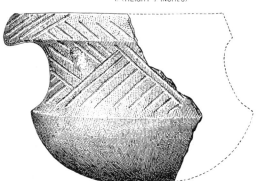

d (HEIGHT 5 INCHES)

f (HEIGHT ABOUT 9 INCHES)

e

VASES FROM THE PROVINCE OF ONTARIO CANADA

IROQUOIAN GROUP

(FROM BOYLE)

INCISED DESIGNS FROM VASES

IROQUOIAN GROUP

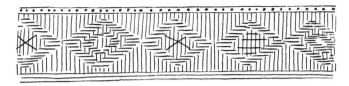

a

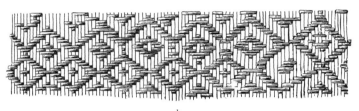

b

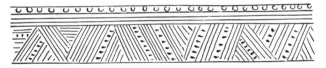

c

d

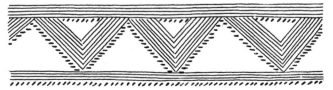

e

INCISED DESIGNS FROM VASES

IROQUOIAN GROUP

a

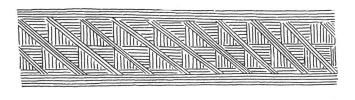

b

c

d

INCISED DESIGNS FROM VASES

IROQUOIAN GROUP

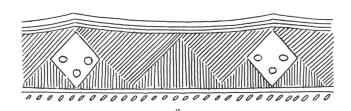

a

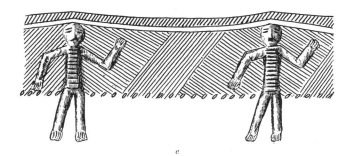

b

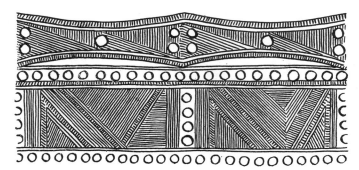

c

d

INCISED DESIGNS FROM VASES

IROQUOIAN GROUP

FACES AND FIGURES FROM VASES
IROQUOIAN GROUP
(ACTUAL SIZE)

brownish grays, the latter sometimes approaching black, are the result of baking, use, accident, or conditions of burial.

The simplest pipe form is a straight tube, with large enough opening at one end to receive the necessary bits of tobacco, and a passage small enough to permit the drawing of smoke without admitting particles of the ashes or leaf. The original forms must have varied with the diverse models at hand, and, if we take the whole country into account, there is considerable diversity in form, size, and material. Pipes of stone are much more varied in shape than are pipes of clay. The clay pipe of the East and North is based on the plain tube, the prevailing modification being the development of the bowl and the addition of a trumpet-like mouth. The tube is not straight, but is bent at the base of the bowl at angles varying from a few degrees to a right angle or even more.

The bowl was subject to varied and often extraordinary modification of form. The stem, as a rule, remained a plain tube straight or slightly incurved, often of uniform thickness save at the tip, or swelling gradually toward the elbow or curve. Very often the bowl did not begin to expand decidedly at the bend but beyond it, sometimes at the very rim, while in cases the expansion was gradual, the mouth being encircled by an inconspicuous band. In cases the lip was somewhat constricted. Description must fail to convey a clear and full notion of the varied modifications of this trumpet-shaped pipe, and four plates are introduced to serve this purpose. The bowl was the subject of much fanciful modification by the application of life forms, quadrupeds, birds, and men being freely employed. Occasionally the full figure of a man was represented, the feet forming the mouthpiece and the bowl opening in the top of the head. In cases animal forms were similarly treated, and serpents were made to coil about the full length of the tube. Generally, however, the upper part of the figure, the head alone, or certain features only were embodied in the bowl. Sometimes two creatures, or parts of two creatures, were affixed to one pipe, and a few specimens have been collected in which a number of heads or faces have been combined or knotted together in a grotesque cluster covering the whole exterior of the pipe. In very many cases a wolf-like head is modeled so that the mouth forms the bowl, the muzzle of the creature pointing upward. Generally when the head is placed on one side of the rim it faces the smoker, but pipes have been observed in which it looks to one side, or from the smoker. In one case a small face is modeled on the inner surface of the divided lip of the bowl. I have been able to recognize with reasonable certainty, besides faces of men, the features of the bear, wolf or dog, owl, eagle or hawk, crow or raven, and snake. Grotesque figures, combining features of men and animals, are rare, but fancy was likely to take almost any direction with these versatile potters.

In order that a fuller notion may be conveyed of the artistic ability of the pipe makers, and their plastic treatment of men and other creatures, a number of pieces are assembled in plates CLIV, CLV, CLVI, and CLVII.

POTTERY OF THE NEW JERSEY–NEW ENGLAND PROVINCE

GENERAL CHARACTERS

The pottery of the coastal districts throughout the middle and northern Atlantic states is uniformly archaic in its shapes and elementary in its decoration. Entire specimens are rarely found, as the custom of burying vases with the dead was not so generally practiced here as elsewhere, and the fragile culinary utensils found on the midden sites are always fragmentary. Sherds have been collected all along the coast and on the bays and tidewater rivers from the Chesapeake to Nova Scotia. They abound on countless ancient sites, and are especially plentiful in the shell deposits which line the shores. These wares are to a large extent Algonquian in type, although there is more or less blending with the Iroquoian wares of the interior districts along the fall line[a] and beyond in Pennsylvania and New Jersey, and somewhat nearer the ocean in New York and the New England states. The materials are, as in the Chesapeake country, clays of no great purity, intermingled with much coarse silicious tempering and, rather exceptionally, with pulverized shells and other substances. The paste is hard and is moderately tenacious where well preserved, but it crumbles rapidly when decay once sets in. The fracture is rough and uneven, and the colors are the usual brownish and reddish grays.

Manufacture was confined almost exclusively to vases and pipes; the former are simple utensils, and the latter are the small, bent trumpet tubes common to the Algonquian areas. In shape the vessels are extremely limited in range, extending to no other forms than those included between a deep cup or bowl and a wide-mouthed pot. Vessels of the latter variety were rarely more than 10 or 12 inches in diameter or in depth. The rims were usually carelessly rounded or squared off, and were seldom much thickened. Exceptionally they were supplied with exterior bands, which in New England expanded into a rounded frieze, resembling closely that of the Iroquoian ware. The rims were also occasionally scalloped, as in the Chesapeake country and in New York. The neck was never greatly constricted, the body swelled but little, and the base was often, especially in the New Jersey region, considerably lengthened below, and was decidedly pointed. Generally the walls were thin and the surfaces

---

[a] The term "fall line" is applied to the rather abrupt line of descent that occurs where the upland joins the lower tidewater districts. It passes through New York, Trenton, Philadelphia, Washington, and Richmond.

a (ACTUAL SIZE)

b

c (ACTUAL SIZE)

d

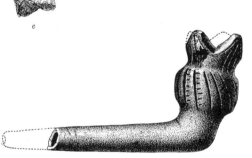

e

f (LENGTH 4 INCHES)

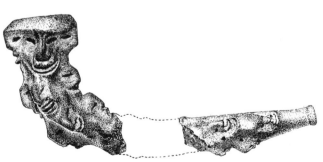

g (LENGTH ABOUT 8 INCHES)

h

EARTHENWARE PIPES

IROQUOIAN GROUP

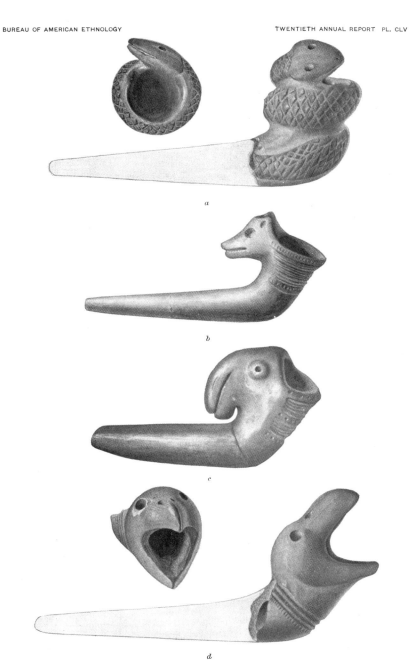

a

b

c

d

EARTHENWARE PIPES

IROQUOIAN GROUP

(THREE-FOURTHS)

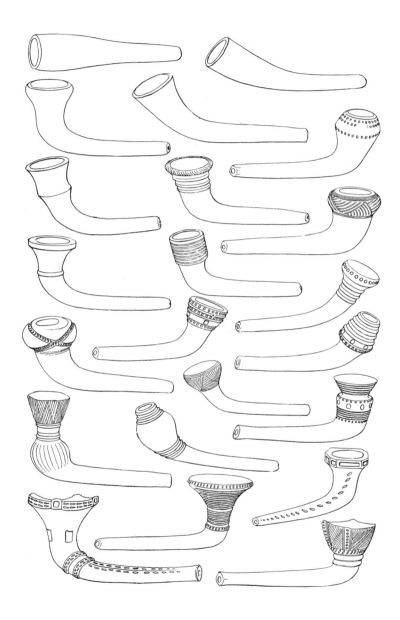

EARTHENWARE PIPES

IROQUOIAN GROUP

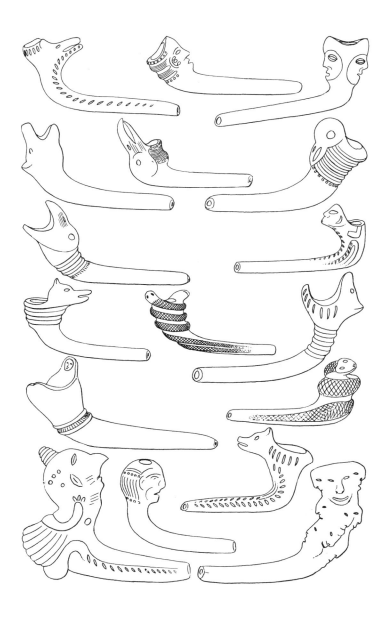

EARTHENWARE PIPES

IROQUOIAN GROUP

roughly finished. The polishing tool was used only to give sufficient finish to enable the decorator effectively to use his stylus or roulette. Details of decoration and finish may better be given when the varieties of ware are presented. The presence here and there of peculiar and apparently exotic types of decoration is quite puzzling; for example, in Maine and New Jersey are encountered occasional examples of rouletting exactly duplicating the style so common on the upper Mississippi. The peoples probably belonged to the same stock, however, and it is not at all improbable that migrations took place between these widely separated regions. The reticulated stamp, characteristic of Florida, appears now and then in Pennsylvania and New Jersey.

No attempt will be made in this place to cover the coastal districts in detail, and attention will be confined to a few localities chosen to represent the ceramic remains of the Northeast. The area considered in this section is included, in a general way, on the map, plate IV, accompanying a preceding section.

The Delaware valley is separated from that of the Susquehanna and Chesapeake by only a few miles of lowland, and it is not surprising that the forms of ware found on the village sites of the districts duplicate one another very closely. There is apparently no decided break in the characteristics of the art from Norfolk to New York bay.

DELAWARE VALLEY WARE

By far the most prolific of the pottery-producing sites in the Delaware valley is that on Pocatquissing creek, 3 miles south of Trenton, so thoroughly explored by Mr Ernest Volk for the Columbian Exposition. Here was found the largest, the best preserved, and the most highly elaborated pottery yet collected on the coast north of the Savannah river. Its relationship with the Algonquian wares of the Chesapeake and Yadkin is, however, very close, and is especially so in several minute details of form, elaboration, and decoration, thus enforcing the idea that the peoples were the same, or were very intimately related or associated. The forms and ornaments are somewhat more elaborate and graceful than those in the Chesapeake ware, and in some features it differs decidedly from that ware. Among these features of unlikeness may be mentioned the occasional much elongation of the bodies, the decided squaring off of the rim, the use of the roulette in decoration, and the addition of a line of indentations encircling the body low down and separated entirely from the main zone of embellishment about the neck.

Characteristic examples of the better ware of this locality are given in plate CLVIII. Large fragments appear in *a* and *b*, and the general shape is indicated in *c*. The diameter is 12 inches, and the height was probably a little more than this. The finish is excellent. The rim is flattened above and indented. The general surface is smooth, and the patterns, executed with a sharp point, are elaborate and unusually neat. The figures which cover the upper part of the body have little symmetry or continuity, a characteristic of Algonquian work, and consist of spaces and bands filled with simple lines, reticulated lines, and herring-bone patterns bordered by plain and zigzag lines. The prevailing outline of these vessels is given in *c*.

A smaller vessel, nearly complete, though broken, is illustrated in *d*, plate CLVIII. It does not differ in any essential from the preceding, but is smaller and much simpler in treatment, and its profile shows a decided angle separating the upper and lower slopes of the body. The stylus has been used from the inside of the margin to punch out a series of nodes about the exterior of the rim, and an isolated line of indents appears far down toward the conic base.

An additional example is presented in plate CLIX *a*, the outline restored appearing in *e* of the preceding plate. The diameter approaches 10 inches, and the height must have been a little more than that. The rim is turned sharply outward and minutely notched on the outer edge, the neck has been very slightly constricted, and, as in many better preserved specimens, the base was probably sharply conic. The paste is silicious, moderately fine grained, and yellowish gray in color. The surface is smooth, but without polish. The decoration consists of 22 lines of roulette markings, imitating coarse cord imprints, encircling the upper part of the body. A double line of like markings encircles the body quite low down.

The largest vessel of which any considerable fragments were recovered was originally about 25 inches in diameter and nearly the same in height. The surface was finished first with a net-covered tool, the meshes of the fabric being over half an inch in width. The upper part of the body was smoothed sufficiently for the addition of incised figures, but not so fully as entirely to destroy the deeper net impressions, and on the lower part and base the imprint is perfectly preserved. The rim is three-fourths of an inch thick, flattened, and sloped inward above, and is decorated, as in many other cases, with cord or stylus imprints. The use of the net and the manner of rubbing down the impressions more or less carefully, according to the needs of the decorator, are identical with corresponding features of the Chesapeake and Carolina net-marked wares. So closely do some of these specimens resemble those of Popes creek, Maryland, and Yadkin river, North Carolina, that the reader may be referred to plates CXXX and CXXXVII for details of shape and ornament.

A village site at Point Pleasant, on the Delaware, 25 miles above Trenton, has furnished numerous specimens of earthenware. It is a notable fact that some of the fragments gathered by Mr H. C. Mercer from the surface or from exposures made by floods are of a stamped ware, resembling very closely the checker-stamp varieties so

c (DIAMETER 12(?) INCHES)

d (HEIGHT 5(?) INCHES)

a

e (DIAMETER 8 INCHES)

b

POTTERY FROM A VILLAGE SITE NEAR TRENTON, NEW JERSEY

NEW ENGLAND GROUP

POTTERY FROM THE ATLANTIC COAST STATES

NEW ENGLAND GROUP

characteristic of Florida, Georgia, and parts of the Carolinas. It would seem that, if no mistake has been made in the identity of the sherds, colonists or visitors from the far south must have dwelt on the site long enough to engage in the practice of the potter's art.

Aside from these specimens, all the varieties of ware observed correspond very closely with those of the Trenton sites and with the typical tidewater Algonquian forms of the lower Delaware and Chesapeake regions. Higher up the Delaware we encounter vessels approaching the Iroquoian type, and finally, in the upper valleys, the ordinary Iroquoian wares prevail. It is stated by Mr Ernest Volk, and confirmed by Mr Mercer, that there were two successive occupations of some of the Delaware valley sites, and it is surmised from various reasons, one of which is the scarcity of pottery at the lower level, that a considerable period elapsed between the first and second occupations; but as these villages were situated on land subject to inundation, the change from the lower to the higher level may have been brought about in a single season. The greater number of relics in the upper deposits may have been due to longer occupation or to more thorough protection from floods. If there are pronounced differences in art, methods of burial, materials used, etc., it is quite as reasonable to suppose that the peoples changed as it is to assume that a period of such duration passed between the successive occupations that decided advances in culture status were made. It is a significant fact that, though there is less earthenware in the lower than in the upper deposits, there is no perceptible difference in the make. There appears, therefore, to be no sufficient reason for supposing that the earlier occupation of the valley, as shadowed forth in these remains, extends far back toward glacial times, or that the people in either case were other than the Algonquian inhabitants found in the Delaware valley by William Penn.

New England Ware

The ware of the region of New York bay, Long island, Connecticut, and Rhode Island indicates a closer affiliation of the makers with the Iroquoian potters than existed between the latter and the more southern Algonquians. A good illustration of the ware of the New York region is given in plate CLIX b. A similar specimen, found at Farmington, Connecticut, is illustrated in an article on Connecticut archeology by James Shepherd, published in the New England Magazine, 1893. If we judge by the examples of this ware known to me, the restoration given by Mr Shepherd makes the vessel too short in the body and without the usual conic tendency of the base. The indented designs in these specimens resemble a prevailing Iroquoian treatment.

The same ware is found throughout Massachusetts, and I have had the good fortune to find fragments of a small vase on the island of Nantucket.

The pottery of eastern Massachusetts is represented by a considerable number of pieces, some of which are entire, or nearly so. That the Algonquian tribes were making and using pottery on the arrival of the whites is made certain by numerous references to the subject in early writings. Thomas Morton, in Force's Tracts, volume II, page 30, says that "they have earthen potts of divers sizes from a quarter to a gallon, 2. or 3. to boyle their vitels in; very stronge, though they be thin like our iron potts." It seems, therefore, that notwithstanding the presence of apparently Iroquoian features in these vessels, we are warranted in attributing them to the historic Algonquians, since all the specimens are much alike in every essential respect.

The figures given in plate CLX will convey a good idea of the characteristics of this ware. Specimens *a*, *b*, and *c* were obtained by Professor F. W. Putnam from graves in Winthrop, Massachusetts. With them were associated glass beads, so that the date of their manufacture is probably somewhere between 1620 and 1650. The height of the larger vessel is about seven inches, and the others are shown on the same scale. Specimen *d* is from Hingham, Massachusetts, and the others given in outline are sketch restorations of small vessels recovered from a grave at Revere (*e*), and from a grave at Marblehead (*f*). In nearly all cases the surface has been worked down with textile-surfaced tools, and subsequently portions about the rim and neck have been rubbed down and rudely decorated with incised lines and indentations. The pipe *g* was found in Connecticut, and is decorated in a style corresponding closely to that of the Algonquian vases.

The village sites and shell banks of Maine yield considerable pottery of the simple styles common in the Algonquian areas. It is found in fragments, and but few specimens even of these have found their way to the museums. The vessels were mere pots, and the pipes, although sometimes ornamented with incised lines and indentations, are mainly the simple bent trumpet of the more southern areas. The clay is tempered usually with a large percentage of coarse sand, the finish is comparatively rude, and the ornament, though varied, is always elementary. The surfaces have, in many cases, been textured with cord-covered paddles, and over these, or on spaces smoothed down for the purpose, are various crude patterns made with cords, bits of fabric, roulettes, and pointed tools of many varieties. The use of the roulette would seem to link the art of this Abnaki region very closely with that of the Middle Atlantic states and portions of the upper Mississippi region. The simple notched roulette was used in the manner shown in plate CLIX *c*, and the compound roulette was quite common.

Prolific sites are found on the Kennebec and Penobscot rivers, and all along the shellfish-producing shore as far as Nova Scotia.

POTTERY OF THE APPALACHEE–OHIO PROVINCE

The pottery of a large area lying between the Appalachian ranges and the Ohio river is difficult of characterization. The ceramic conditions in certain parts are apparently such as might result from an intermingling of the work of peoples from the North, West, South, and East, while in other sections the ware of a single style prevails. Collections have not been made with sufficient care to enable us to say what is the nature of the association of the different exotic forms and features with products of more strictly local development. In many localities in East Tennessee we find together specimens of the stamped ware of the South Appalachian district, the polished bowls, pots, and bottles of the Mississippi region, vessels that resemble quite closely the ware of the valley of the Ohio on the north, and others almost identical with those of the Gulf province on the south.

FIG. 66—Vessel with animal-shaped handles, from a mound on Fains island, Jefferson county, Tennessee.

The stamped ware of the East Tennessee district does not always repeat the forms and patterns of the South Appalachian region with accuracy, but exhibits, in cases, decided individuality. In like manner pottery of western appearance is not typical of the West, but has a local flavor. The high-necked bottles, the humpback figures, the grotesque animal forms, and the red and white painted decoration are apparently wanting.

From mounds, graves, and dwelling sites over a large part of the province we have examples of a variety of ware, mostly shell-tempered, and consisting largely of culinary vessels, the strongest characteristic of which is the looped handles connecting the rim with the neck or shoulder. These handles are of many styles and vary in number from two to eight to a vessel. They are sometimes elaborated into animal figures, as is seen in figure 66, but generally they are less carefully worked out than in the West. Besides the two animal-shaped loops, placed on opposite sides of the rim of this vase, there are alternating comb-like ornaments, which probably represent some animal feature, set on the shoulder of the vessel. It is possible they stand for the hand or for a wing, and may thus be a conventionalized form of animal symbol common in the Central Southern states. This piece illustrates a prevailing form of culinary vessel, and exhibits the peculiar finish of the body produced by malleating with textile-covered modeling tools. A unique form of handle is shown in figure 67. This piece is not unusual in any other respect.

A small vessel of very unusual shape for eastern America is shown in figure 68. It exhibits the usual crude manipulation of the region, and is tempered with coarse shell. It is in every respect characteristic of the district, save in the prolongation of one side of the body into a rounded point, giving what may be likened to a shoe shape, but which also, as seen in profile, suggests the form of a bird. The two handles are

FIG. 67—Vessel with arched handle, from a mound in Sevier county, Tennessee.

placed as usual; one is normal, but the other extends out on the projecting lobe and is continued in three spreading notched fillets which connect with a notched band carried around the shoulder of the vessel.

FIG. 68—Shoe-shaped vessel, with incised designs, Loudon county, Tennessee.

The neck and shoulder are embellished with a pattern of incised lines rranged in alternating triangular groups. A similar vessel from n adjoining county is shown in figure 69. Especial attention is

called to these vessels by the fact that they are the only examples so
far added to our collections from the eastern half of the United
States exhibiting the peculiar shoe shape so frequently appearing in
the Pueblo country, and again as a prominent feature in the ware
of Central America. There can be no
doubt that the shape and the plastic
elaborations are significant and symbolic, but the exact nature of their
symbolism and the explanation of
their isolated occurrence are not yet
forthcoming.

FIG. 69—Shoe-shaped vessel, Monroe
county, Tennessee.

A small cup with three rows of nodes
encircling the body is presented in
figure 70.

Ware of the general type to which
the above specimens belong is found along the eastern slopes of the
Appalachian mountains in North Carolina, Virginia, and West Virginia.
It occurs along numerous streams entering the Ohio from the south,
and probably passes gradually into the well-known ware of the Miami
valley, where, at Madi-
sonville, we have the
most striking types of
handled pots. It is un-
fortunate that we must
pass so briefly over a
great area that ought to
furnish much material
for the history of arts
and peoples, but such
meager collections have
been made that we seem
to have warrant for the
theory that the absence

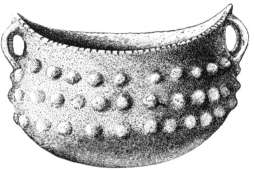

FIG. 70—Two-handled cup with rows of encircling nodes,
Tennessee.

of permanent residents, remarked of this region in early historic times,
may have, in a measure, characterized the eastern portions of the "dark
and bloody ground" from the very beginning of native art in clay.

OHIO VALLEY POTTERY

CULTURE GROUPS

The art remains of the Ohio valley occupy an important place among
the existing vestiges of our native races, and the relics of earthenware
pertaining to the region, although generally simple and inartistic, are,
from their associations, invested with exceptional interest.

The province is a vast one, having a width of from 200 to 400 miles and a length of nearly 800 miles. It is divided into numerous physiographic districts, more or less independent of one another, and furnishing boundless resources to peoples fortunate enough to occupy them. As a consequence, the ancient remains represent numerous important culture groups. The Allegheny river, heading far to the north in New York and Pennsylvania, was the home of the warlike Iroquois, and the region is strewn with the remains of their peculiar arts. The Monongahela drains part of the region occupied by the eastern Algonquians, and transiently by many hunter-tribes of other stocks, and it contains traces of their simple yet instructive handiwork. The main southern branches, heading along the Appalachian ranges, were overrun in their upper courses by the South Appalachian peoples, whose art has already been described; and in their lower courses they penetrated the very heart of the great culture province of the middle Mississippi valley. The northern tributaries drain a fertile region occupied in historical times by numerous tribes, mostly of Algonquian stock, but at earlier periods by tribes of mound builders whose affinities of blood are not yet fully made out.

I have already dealt briefly with the wares of the eastern and southern borders of this wonderful province, and have now only to review the pottery of the immediate valley of the river and its extensions to the north and west. The study of the pottery of this latter region is invested with especial interest, for the reason that it may be expected to assist in elucidating the much-discussed problems of the mound builders and the relations of these peoples to neighboring tribes and to the Indians of historic times.

Opportunities for study have not been wholly satisfactory, as the collections made by numerous explorers are much scattered, and, at best, are not rich. It has been possible to distinguish only two groups of ware that differ so decidedly from the surrounding groups, and that possess such individuality, as to warrant the predication of distinct groups of people or phases of culture. It is worthy of special note that although they represent regions furnishing evidence, according to many authorities, of exceptional progress in art and in general culture, few of the examples of earthenware utensils rise above the level of the average ware of the eastern United States which is assignable to historic stocks. Indeed, it may be said that as a rule the ware belongs to the archaic northern grand division of the art rather than to the more highly developed product of the South. A number of small terra-cotta figures found by Professor Putnam in one of the Turner mounds near Cincinnati[a], and referred to briefly in his report, seem to be an exception. The figures are said to be remarkably well modeled and wholly unique.

_____

[a] Reports of the Peabody Museum, vol. III, p. 173.

Professor Putnam's reference to these objects is as follows:

On another altar, in another mound of the group, were several terra-cotta figurines of a character heretofore unknown from the mounds. Unfortunately these objects, as well as others found on the altars, had been more or less burned, and many of them appear to have been purposely broken before they were placed on the altars. Many pieces of these images have been united, and it is my hope that we shall succeed in nearly restoring some of them. Enough has already been made out to show their importance in the study of early American art. The peculiar method of wearing the hair, the singular headdresses and large button-like ear ornaments shown by these human figures are of particular interest. The ear ornaments leave no doubt of the character of the spool-shaped objects referred to on a previous page.[a]

Occasional specimens of Middle Mississippi Valley type are found in Ohio, but I am not able to reach any conclusion as to the relation of the people concerned in their manufacture to the tribes referred to in the preceding paragraphs. Two excellent examples of this class are shown in plate CLXI. They come from a mound in Ross county, and are now preserved in the Ohio State Museum.

MIAMI VALLEY WARE

The pottery to be considered under this head does not include all the ware of the Miami district, but only that possessing characteristics peculiar to certain prominent sites located mainly on the Little Miami. This ware is not confined to the Miami region, for, as I have already indicated, it extends out with decreasing numbers of specimens and in less and less typical forms, even beyond the confines of the Ohio valley, especially into Kentucky and eastern Tennessee. The richest collections of the Miami wares are preserved in the Peabody Museum, and include a large series of well-preserved vases obtained from village sites in the vicinity of Madisonville. The Literary and Scientific Society of Madisonville made important finds in this region, and published descriptions and a number of illustrations.[b]

Some fine pieces obtained by Mr McBride, in Butler county, are preserved in the Museum of the Academy of Sciences in Philadelphia. Squire and Davis, in Ancient Monuments, figure 72, illustrate two vases of this class from near the surface of the ground in Butler county. From a village site at Fort Ancient, Warren county, Ohio, Mr W. K. Moorehead obtained numerous fragments of this pottery, illustrated in plate CLXII.[c]

The prevailing type of vessel is a round-bodied pot with wide mouth and flaring rim. Deep bowls are occasionally seen. The pots are strongly characterized by their handles, which connect the lip with the shoulder. As a rule these handles are thin bands, and lie close to

[a] Putnam, F. W., Sixteenth and Seventeenth Annual Report of the Trustees of the Peabody Museum of American Archæology and Ethnology, vol. III, numbers 3 and 4, p. 173.

[b] Low, Charles F., Archæological Explorations near Madisonville, Ohio, Archæological Explorations by the Literary and Scientific Society of Madisonville, Ohio, 1878–80, parts 1, 2, 3, and 4.

[c] Moorehead, Warren K., Fort Ancient, Cincinnati, 1890. plate XXVII.

the neck of the vessel. Their number is usually four, but two are sometimes seen, and occasionally there are more than four. In most cases they are wider where they join the rim, which is often drawn out to meet them. The outer surface of the handles is plain and flat in most cases, but examples occur in which it is concave, and in rather rare instances it is round. In no other section do handles form so important a feature of the ware as in southwestern Ohio. As a rule, in all sections, handles of this general type belong to vessels intended for culinary use, and it would appear from the signs of use over fire that many of the Miami vases were mere culinary utensils.

A number of specimens obtained from a mound near Madisonville, and referred to above, are shown in plate CLXIII. The first specimen, *a*, is supplied with two looped handles, alternating with which are two animal figures vertically placed. That the latter represent a quadruped is about all that can be said with safety, for they may have been intended for either a lizard or a mountain lion. In another case, a rudely modeled human head or face is attached to the upper margin of the rim. Nodes and low ridges take the place of handles in some specimens.

Examples of the average pot are given in *b* and *c*. Some peculiar modifications of the simple vessels are observed. One specimen, *d*, is mounted on a crudely made foot or stand; it has an awkward, topheavy appearance. The addition of this feature was probably an experiment on the part of the potter, who was possibly attempting in a crude way to copy the work of his southern neighbors. A double vase from the same site is shown in *e*. There is no doubt that, as our collections are enlarged, additional forms will be added.

Plate CLXIV is introduced for the purpose of showing the peculiar surface finish observed in this ware. The modeling implement was a paddle or a cylinder wrapped with twisted cords, and applied to the plastic surface; it was generally held so that the markings are approximately vertical. These markings are obliterated on the neck of the vessels by finishing with the polishing stone.

Decoration proper is confined to the lip and neck. The lip is plain, rounded, squarish or uneven on the edge, or has a narrow collar or band on the exterior; this latter is often indented in a rude and simple manner, a herring-bone arrangement of short incisions being common. The constricted zone of the neck is generally rather rudely but effectively embellished with an encircling design, based on the meander, scroll or guilloche. A series of these figures is shown in plate CLXV, and the impression given is that the makers of this ware have in some way felt the influence of more southern culture, and have, in a crude way, introduced into their symbolism and decorative art a number of borrowed elements. In some cases, the current scroll, composed of neatly interlocked units, is clearly drawn, but as a

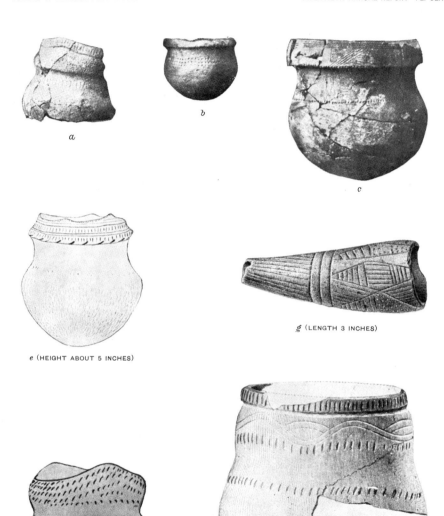

a

b

c

e (HEIGHT ABOUT 5 INCHES)

g (LENGTH 3 INCHES)

f (HEIGHT ABOUT 6 INCHES)

d (HEIGHT 4 INCHES)

POTTERY FROM NEW ENGLAND

NEW ENGLAND GROUP

a (DIAMETER 3¾ INCHES)

b (DIAMETER 7¼ INCHES)

VASES OF MIDDLE MISSISSIPPI TYPE
OHIO VALLEY GROUP
(OHIO STATE UNIVERSITY COLLECTION)

SHERDS WITH INCISED DECORATIONS FROM A VILLAGE SITE AT FORT ANCIENT

OHIO VALLEY GROUP

(MOOREHEAD COLLECTION, ABOUT THREE-FOURTHS)

a (HEIGHT 6 INCHES)

e (HEIGHT 3¾ INCHES)

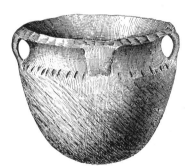

b (HEIGHT 4 INCHES)

c (HEIGHT 6¾ INCHES)

d (HEIGHT 10 INCHES)

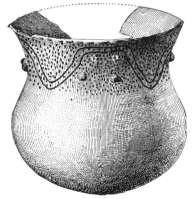

f (HEIGHT 7½ INCHES)

VASES FROM MOUNDS AT MADISONVILLE

OHIO VALLEY GROUP

b (HEIGHT 4¼ INCHES)

a (HEIGHT 4¾ INCHES)

VASES ILLUSTRATING TEXTILE IMPRINTINGS

OHIO VALLEY GROUP

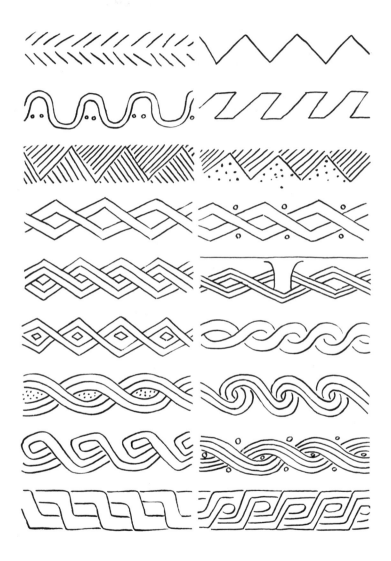

INCISED DECORATIONS FROM EARTHENWARE

OHIO VALLEY GROUP

rule the lines form a somewhat disconnected guilloche, apparently the result of careless imitation of intertwined fillets. In some cases the figures are angular, and in a few instances they have been somewhat carefully elaborated with a modeling tool, giving a relieved effect.

This pottery does not take a high place among the various ceramic groups of the mound builders, and, if we should assume to determine the relative culture status of the various peoples concerned in pottery making from this art alone, we should find the Miami tribes near the bottom of the scale. Judging by the poverty of shapes, there had been but little differentiation of use. The introduction of life forms had hardly commenced, and the esthetic features were treated in a very elementary way, as if but recently introduced.

Salt Vessels

One of the most notable varieties of earthenware found in any of the regions is that represented by what are usually referred to as "salt vessels." Two localities in the Ohio valley are especially noted for this ware; one is near Shawneetown, Illinois, and the other is near Nashville, Tennessee. A rather full account of the ware has been given in the introductory pages, and I do not need to dwell on it here, save to say that it is my impression that these utensils do not represent a peculiar people or culture, but that they were produced by the various tribes of the region for the special purpose of reducing the salt waters of the localities in which they are found.

POTTERY OF THE NORTHWEST

Family Distinctions

In a paper published in the Fourth Annual Report of the Bureau of Ethnology the ancient ware of the valley of the Mississippi was discussed with some care, but the ground was not entirely covered. It was shown, however, that the pottery of the upper valley belongs to a family distinct from that of the lower, and that the limitations of its occurrence appear to mark, with some degree of approximation, the distribution of peculiar groups of people and of particular phases of culture. The general distinctions between the earthenware of the North and that of the South have been pointed out in the introductory pages and in the section treating of the eastern Algonquian areas, and it may be added here that the very poorly defined zone of transition crosses southern Ohio and extends across the middle portions of Indiana, Illinois, and Iowa. The southern ware extends considerably to the north of this zone in numerous cases, and the northern forms are found in decreasing numbers as we pass across it to the south. In some sections the typical wares of both provinces are found together on one site. The correlations of either variety of ceramic products with groups of other classes of remains found in the same districts are not yet well made out.

In the West the contrasts between the ware of the North and that of South appear to be quite as pronounced as they are in the East. That of the South is highly differentiated and specialized; that of the North is pronouncedly archaic. That of the South exhibits variously tinted pastes, tempered principally with pulverized shells. The vases, as a rule, have full bodies, rounded bases, and, in very many cases, narrow and high necks. Animal forms are imitated with remarkable frequency and with much skill. The northern pottery shows a generally dark paste, tempered largely with coarse angular sand derived from pulverized rocks. The shapes are those of simple pots. The mouths are wide, the rims plain, and the necks but slightly constricted. Animal forms are rarely seen. The ornament of the South employs flowing as well as angular lines, varied colors, and a wide range of motives; that of the North is almost exclusively archaic, consisting of incised and indented geometric patterns. A comparison between the specimens brought together in the accompanying plates and those in the numerous plates of the Middle Mississippi section will prove instructive.

The pottery of the northern province is abundant, but is recovered for the most part in a fragmentary state. However, a sufficient number of well-preserved pieces have been collected to indicate pretty clearly the range of form and decoration.

This northwestern province includes the upper Mississippi valley, the Missouri valley, the region of the western Great lakes, and the valley of Red river of the North. The varieties of pottery are not confined to particular regions as decidedly as they are in the East. They may be classified for purposes of description under two heads, the rouletted and stamped ware and the cord-decorated ware, the latter including the work of the Mandans, the only tribe of the whole region known to have practiced the art in recent years.

This pottery occurs over large areas occupied in historic times mainly by the Algonquian and Siouan stocks. Much of it affiliates closely with the ware of the more eastern branches of the Algonquian, and, in some cases, in nearly all features of detail. One variety, however, shows decided affinities with the work of the South Appalachian potters. The Siouan peoples were probably potters in a limited way, especially where they were measurably sedentary in habits, and the same may be surmised of the Caddoan and other stocks. Mr A. J. Comfort, writing on this subject (Smithsonian Report for 1871, page 401), says that the Dakotas certainly practiced the art during the childhood of men still living. Dr J. Owen Dorsey, the well-known student of the Siouan tribes, informs me that Half-a-day, historian of the

Omahas, distinctly affirms that the art was practiced by his people as late as 1840, and the old lodge rings found on their village sites are well supplied with the usual cord-decorated and textured ware characteristic of the Missouri valley.

ROULETTED AND STAMPED WARE

A large part of the ware of the Northwest may be brought together in a single group, which may be called, from its most pronounced technic peculiarity, the rouletted group, but it is impossible to define with any degree of precision its geographic limits. The localities represented in the collections examined by me are indicated in a somewhat general way on the map accompanying a previous section (plate IV). The tribes by whom it was manufactured have evidently, at one time or another, occupied a large part of the Mississippi basin north of the mouth of the Missouri river. Parts of the states of Iowa, Wisconsin, Michigan, Illinois, Indiana, and Ohio are covered by this or by closely related ceramic groups, and traces of some of its peculiar characters are discovered far beyond these limits—as, for example, in New Jersey and Maine. There is some lack of uniformity within the group, and in time several subgroups may be distinguished, but the persistence of certain peculiar features in the widely separated localities goes far toward demonstrating a general unity.

The clay used exhibits no unusual features, but the tempering is always silicious and often coarse. The vessels have a narrow range of form and are such as were commonly devoted to culinary uses. There is, however, considerable diversity of detail, as will be seen by reference to the illustrations.

The decoration of this ware presents some striking features, the use of the roulette and the patterned punch stamp being especially characteristic. Cord-covered modeling tools were used in finishing the undecorated portions of the vessels, and pointed tools of various kinds were used in incising, trailing, and indenting patterns, as they were in other sections. In one locality a peculiar variety of patterned stamp was employed. Although the stamps were not quite the same as those used in the South Appalachian region, and were applied in a different way, taking the form of punches rather than of paddles, their use suggests a relationship between the art of the two sections, and this is enforced by the facts that features of ornamentation, shape, and material show unusually close analogies. Specimens of this class were obtained from mounds near Naples, Illinois, by Mr John G. Henderson and Mr M. Tandy.[a]

In plates CLXVI and CLXVII are reproduced a number of sherds illustrating the manner of applying the stamps, which must have been

---

[a] Henderson, John G., Aboriginal Remains near Naples, Illinois, in Smithsonian Report for 1882, Washington, 1884, p. 686.

mere bits of wood with the ends dressed in various simple, flattish-oval shapes, and divided by transverse grooves; they were but a step in advance of the ordinary punches and puncturing tools used in nearly all sections in decorative work. These stamps were not used to produce the mixed, all-over patterns characteristic of the South Appalachian specimens, but were applied in a systematic way, the separate impressions being preserved, arranged in neat order to embellish margins and fill in spaces. A number of the impressions are given in figure 71. In plate CLXVIII two of the cruder examples of the Naples vases which happened to be susceptible of partial restoration are given. Particular attention may be called to the larger vessel, which, although belonging to this locality and to this particular group of vessels, is remarkably like the Georgia type, duplicating specimens from the Savannah in appearance, material, outline, and some of the details of decoration.

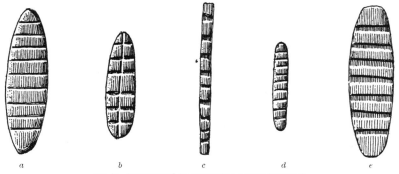

a   b   c   d   e

FIG. 71—Stamps used in decorating vessels (restored).

The pointed body has been textured with a cord-wrapped paddle or modeling tool, and the impressions have been partially obliterated in preparing the surface for the decoration. A punch was used to press out a row of beads encircling the rim; a stamp of the variety shown in figure 71a was applied to the outer margin of the rim; a roulette with irregular points was carried around the neck in a wide zone and below was crudely executed a design consisting of six sections, three of which are festoons of incised and indented lines, while the other three are carelessly traced coils produced in the same manner. The smaller piece, a, is also a South Appalachian shape.

Closely related in origin and effect to the stamped decorations described above is the work of the roulette, which especially characterizes this group of products. The implement, instead of being straight on the edge, like the stamps, took the shape of a wheel, or part of a wheel, with toothed edge. This was rolled back and forth over the surface to be decorated in the manner indicated in figure 72,

SHERDS OF STAMPED AND ROULETTED POTTERY, NAPLES, ILLINOIS

NORTHWESTERN GROUP

(THREE-FOURTHS)

b

a

SHERDS OF STAMPED AND ROULETTED POTTERY, NAPLES, ILLINOIS

NORTHWESTERN GROUP

(THREE-FOURTHS)

or was made to give broken lines, or to indent margins. A handle was probably used, as is indicated in the figure, the work being thus much more readily accomplished. Inexperienced observers would hardly be able to distinguish the markings made by the notched wheel from those made by the simple forms of notched or reticulated stamps, and by cords and fabrics, the general effect being much the same. In figure 73 is presented a small vase made by myself from ordinary potter's clay, and with it are the two tools, a notched roulette and a cord-wrapped roulette, used in finishing and embellishing its surface. The cord-wrapped stick served as a modeling tool to assist in shaping the vessel, in welding the clay together, and in rendering the surface even; at the same time it imparted the pecul-

FIG. 72—Use of the roulette or rocking notched wheel. This wheel is made of pasteboard and inked to show impressions on paper.

iar fabric-like texturing, which is not at all unpleasant to the eye. The band about the neck of the vessel was then smoothed with the thumb, and polished with a bit of smooth, hard wood. The rim or collar was smoothed also, and the notched wheel was run over it, reproducing the simple patterns characteristic of this group of vessels. A wheel with coarse notches was then rolled around the lower margin of the collar to give diversity and emphasis. The whole operation of building and decorating such a vessel need not consume more than half an hour. In many cases the potters of this and other northern groups, instead of notching the wheel, wrapped a hard twisted cord around it, applying it to the clay in the ordinary way.

In Indiana a number of localities have furnished examples of this ware, some of which may be considered quite typical. From a mound near Laporte Dr Higday procured several excellent pieces, described first by Foster,[a] and frequently illustrated in more recent works. I

FIG. 73—Vase made for trial of the roulette and cord-wrapped modeling tool.

have not had the opportunity of seeing these pieces, but base my interpretation of the various features on the illustrations, reproduced in figure 74 *a*, *b*, and *c*. It appears that a square punch rather than

a　　　　　　　　　　　　b　　　　　　　　　　　　c

FIG. 74—Vases from a mound near Laporte, Indiana (Foster).

a figured stamp or notched wheel was employed in the decoration of these vases, but the shape, the laying off of the decorated spaces, and the manner of filling these in with indentations is decidedly character-istic of the wares under consideration. From Michigan again we

[a] Foster, J. W., Prehistoric races of the United States of America, Chicago, 1873, p. 247.

have several other very fine examples of this ware, three of which are shown in plate CLXIX a, b, c and d. All have a number of plain bands and figures, which alternate with roulette-indented spaces. The thickened rim in b and in c and d is covered with reticulated incised or rouletted lines, and the body is lobed, as it is in several specimens owned by the Kent Scientific Institute, Grand Rapids, Michigan.

Similar in general style to the preceding is the handsome little vessel obtained from a mound at Albany, Whitesides county, Illinois, illustrated in plate CLXX a. The shape and ornamentation are somewhat novel. Four flattish lobes occur about the body, on each of which a figure, somewhat resembling a Maltese cross, has been made by incising or impressing broad shallow lines. The remainder of the body is covered with marks that resemble impressions of a coarse osier basket, but which may have been made with a blunt stylus.

Another fine specimen is shown in plate CLXX b. This is one of a pair of handsome pieces recently obtained by the Bureau of American Ethnology from a mound in Vernon county, Wisconsin. It is $6\frac{1}{2}$ inches in height, and in symmetry and finish it rivals the best work of the South. The paste is dark, compact, and fine grained, and is tempered with fine sand. The color of the surface is a rich, mottled brown. The lip is smooth and the margin rounded. The outside of the narrow collar is ornamented with oblique incised lines, and is crossed at intervals by lines made with a notched wheel. The neck is slightly constricted, and is encircled by a polished zone $1\frac{1}{4}$ inches wide having a line of indentations along the upper edge. The body is separated into four lobes by four vertical, depressed, polished bands about 1 inch wide. Two of these lobes are crossed obliquely by similar polished bands. These bands were all finished with a polishing implement and are slightly depressed, thus giving rise to the somewhat lobed shape. They are bordered by wide, incised lines. The intervening spaces or lobes are indented with a roulette, moved back and forth in irregular zigzag arrangement.

Specimens of this ware are found in Illinois as far south as Union county. On the west side of the Mississippi I know of no examples from localities farther south than Scott county, Iowa. Some of these were illustrated in the first volume of the Proceedings of Davenport Academy of Science. The vessel shown in plate CLXXI a was found in a mound near Davenport, closely associated with human remains and other relics, among which were several copper implements covered with coarse woven fabrics. Its height is 11 inches, the width of the aperture is $7\frac{1}{2}$ inches, and the diameter of the base is 4 inches. There is a broad, shallow constriction at the neck. The walls are from one-fourth to three-eighths of an inch thick, and the margin of the rim is squared off, showing the full thickness—a common feature in the northern pottery. The form is nearly symmetric and the surface is well smoothed, but is not polished. At present the paste is dark and crumbling and shows a rough fracture. A large percentage of sand was used in tempering. The color is a dark gray-brown, and the entire surface, with the exception of a narrow band about the base, has been covered with ornamentation. Two or three distinct implements have been used in the work. A part of the neck ornament was made by rolling back and forth a circular tool, the edge of which was notched. A row of indented nodes has been produced upon the exterior surface of the neck by impressing upon the inside the end of a reed or hollow bone about one-fourth of an inch in diameter. Patterns of bold lines, rather carelessly drawn, cover the body, and seem to have been made by trailing under pretty strong pressure the smooth point of a stylus— probably the bone or reed implement already suggested. Some of the large indentations on the lower part of the neck may have been made by the same implement, held in an oblique position and used as a scoop. This vessel and several others of the same group and section are flat-bottomed. I regard this as very good evidence that the work is recent, and it may yet be shown that this ware and the much-discussed engraved stone tablets of the same section are properly attributed to the tribes occupying the banks of the Mississippi long after the steamboat began its career on the Father of Waters. A similar vase, tastefully decorated with indented lines about the neck and a band of decoration consisting of broad, plain, sinuous bands on the body, comes from a mound in Buffalo township, Scott county, Iowa. A vase from Ross county, Ohio, copied from Squier and Davis's Ancient Monuments, figure 2, plate XLVI, is presented in plate CLXIX *f*. The ornament in this case is apparently treated in much the same manner as in the Laporte specimens, and the figure of a bird, quite conventionally drawn, is paralleled in a similar vase, plate CLXIX *e*, obtained in Michigan, the exact locality not being known. The parallel holds good with respect not only to the bird and its treatment, but also to other features of ornamentation, and the vessels closely correspond in shape. A third specimen decorated with bird figures was obtained by Dr H. F. Snyder from a mound in Illinois. The vase and design are presented in figure 75. In the museum of the Historical Society of Missouri at St Louis is still another vessel of this type, and another handsome vase of the same general class, copied from Squier and Davis, page 189, appears in plate CLXXI *b*.

It is a significant fact, in this connection, that the few pieces of pottery found by Mr Moorehead in the Hopewell mounds, near Chillicothe, Ohio, are of this general type. Illustrations are given in plate CLXXII. The large fragment *a* shows the usual incising and rouletting, and the shape is equally characteristic, resembling most closely, perhaps, that of the Iowa specimens already described. The restored shape appears in *b*, and the outline of a small piece with rouletted rim, cord-paddled body, and conic base is shown in *c*.

a (HEIGHT 4¼ INCHES)

b (HEIGHT 6½ INCHES)

VASES DECORATED WITH THE ROULETTE, ILLINOIS

NORTHWESTERN GROUP

a (MICHIGAN)

b (MICHIGAN)

c (MICHIGAN)

d (MICHIGAN)

e (OHIO)

f (MICHIGAN, FROM SQUIER AND DAVIS,
HEIGHT 5 INCHES)

EXAMPLES OF ROULETTE-DECORATED WARE
NORTHWESTERN GROUP

b (WISCONSIN, HEIGHT 6¼ INCHES)

a (ILLINOIS, DIAMETER ABOUT 4¼ INCHES)

EXAMPLES OF ROULETTE-DECORATED WARE

NORTHWESTERN GROUP

a (IOWA, DAVENPORT ACADEMY COLLECTION,
HEIGHT 11 INCHES)

b (OHIO, FROM SQUIER AND DAVIS, HEIGHT 5½ INCHES)

EXAMPLES OF ROULETTE-DECORATED WARE

NORTHWESTERN GROUP

It would seem that the builders of the great mound groups about Chillicothe, the enterprising people who gathered stores of shells from the Atlantic, copper from Lake Superior, flint from the lower Ohio valley, and obsidian from the Rocky mountains, Oregon, or Mexico, were identical with or closely related to tribes scattered over a large part of a region including parts of Ohio, Indiana, Illinois, Iowa, Michigan, and Wisconsin. Though the pottery of this group of peoples is not nearly so highly developed as is that of the southern mound-builders, as, for example, those of Cahokia, in Illinois, and of Etowah, in Georgia, there can be little doubt that their general culture was of an order equally advanced.

With respect to the origin of the great numbers of obsidian implements found in the Hopewell mounds, it may be well to note that there is no trace of Mexican characters in the pottery of these mounds; besides, the general trend of the group of ware here asso-

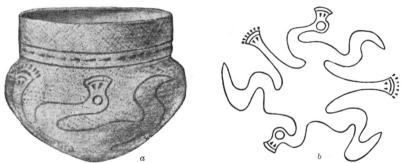

FIG. 75—Vase with conventionalized bird design. Drawings furnished by Dr H. F. Snyder.

ciated is from Chillicothe toward the northwest, suggesting the upper Missouri region or the valley of the Columbia as the source of the obsidian. The significance of this observation is emphasized by the discovery of fragments of rouletted ware in the Yellowstone National Park, where great beds of obsidian are found (see page 201).

Ccrd- and Textile-Marked Ware

Pottery of typical archaic form is distributed over a vast area in the Northwest. It connects with the corresponding wares of Virginia, Maryland, Pennsylvania, New York, and Canada, and its occurrence is very general and uniform over the Great lakes region, the upper Mississippi, the Missouri, and Red river of the North valleys, and it is found with decreasing frequency in the far-away Yellowstone country, and even, in rare cases, in the Green river valley and in Great Salt lake basin. In more or less typical form it extends over into the Middle Mississippi and South Appalachian ceramic provinces.

It is the product of peoples of the same general level of culture as those found in possession of the region, and is no doubt largely the work of the present inhabitants, the modern representatives of the great Algonquian and Siouan families. A number of these tribes continued to practice this art down to the period of English and French occupation, and the Mandans, the Grosventres, and possibly others, were making their simple ware until within the present generation.

Catlin describes the work of the Mandans (Siouan family) of sixty years ago, and his account is quoted in the introductory pages of this paper. Traditional accounts of the practice of the art are given by several authors. George Bird Grinnell, already quoted in the introduction, records definite traditions of the making of pottery by the Pawnees, and Mr A. J. Comfort states that—

Earthen vessels were in use by our Dakotas during the childhood of men still living (about 1870). I have interrogated separately and on different occasions the principal and most reliable men of the Sissiton and Wahpeton tribes, all of whom tell the same story of having seen earthen kettles for culinary purposes in use by their parents.[a]

An early explorer in the great Northwest, the Prince of Wied, speaking of the Mandans, Minitaris, and Arikaras, declares that—

These three nations understand the manufacture of earthen pots and vessels of various forms and sizes. The clay is of a dark slate color and burns a yellowish red, very similar to what is seen in the burnt tops of the Missouri hills. This clay is mixed with flint or granite reduced to powder by the action of fire. The workwoman forms the hollow inside of the vessel by means of a round stone which she holds in her hand, while she works and smooths the outside with a piece of poplar bark. When the pot is made it is filled and surrounded with dry shavings and then burnt, when it is ready for use. They know nothing of glazing.[b]

It is quite impossible to present this pottery in detail, and the wares of a few widely scattered localities may be chosen as typical of all. Wisconsin has many sites rich in sherds of this ware. Two Rivers, situated midway on the west shore of Lake Michigan, occupies an ancient and important village site, and large quantities of pottery fragments have been unearthed through the persevering efforts of Mr H. P. Hamilton, of the city; many of these specimens have been preserved and placed within the reach of students. The large vessel shown in plate CLXXIII was dug up in 1901, and is described as follows in a letter transmitting the photograph here reproduced:

I have just succeeded in restoring an earthen vessel—the first I have been successful with, and I have been trying for years. This vessel was discovered in the sand about four blocks from our office, near the lake shore, where innumerable vessels have been destroyed. The sand had thawed out for about 4 inches and the vessel was broken into some 200 pieces. Hot water and fire were resorted to and most of

a Comfort, A. J., Smithsonian Report, 1871, p. 402.
b Maximilian (Prince of Wied), Travels in the Interior of North America, p. 348.

c (DIAMETER 5 INCHES)

b (DIAMETER ABOUT 7 INCHES)

a (DIAMETER ABOUT 7 INCHES)

EXAMPLES OF ROULETTE-DECORATED WARE FROM HOPEWELL MOUNDS, ROSS COUNTY, OHIO

NORTHWESTERN GROUP

(MOOREHEAD COLLECTION, FIELD COLUMBIAM MUSEUM)

LARGE VASE FROM A VILLAGE SITE, TWO RIVERS, WISCONSIN
NORTHWESTERN GROUP
(HAMILTON COLLECTION, DIAMETER OF TOP 11 INCHES)

the vessel was finally secured. The fragments were so soft and easily broken while wet that they would easily crumble if held in the hand, but after being dried they became quite hard. It was quite a difficult task to join the pieces, especially toward the completion, when the restored large pieces had to be joined, but it was finally accomplished. The vessel is 13 inches in height and 4 feet in circumference. The weight is 10 pounds. The top opening is oblong, 10 inches the narrow way and 12 inches the wide way. Two pairs of holes have been bored in one side, probably for inserting cords for the purpose of checking an incipient crack. The ornamentation is not as elaborate as on some pieces I have found here, but still is very fair. A skeleton was buried with it, but nothing could be saved of this except some fragments of the skull.

The smaller vessel shown in this plate is about the size of an ordinary coffee cup, and is similar in character to the large piece.

The pottery of this site presents pronounced Algonquian characters, and if the sherds were to be intermingled with those of Atlantic coast sites it would be difficult to separate them. Plate CLXXIV contains fragments of rims of ordinary vessels. It will be seen that one of these has a sharp projection, such as is frequently seen in the Iroquoian ware of New York, and it is further noted that the mouth of the

FIG. 76—Sections of rims of vases from a village site at Two Rivers, Wisconsin

vessel was squarish, emphasizing the likeness to the Iroquoian work. It is not at all impossible that the influence of the powerful tribes of New York extended to the western shores of the Great lakes, but since this angular form is undoubtedly due to the influence of bark vessels, it may have had an independent origin in the West.

The paste of this pottery is not very fine grained, and it is tempered with silicious particles, sometimes rather coarse. The pot or caldron presents variants in form extending from deep bowl shapes, on the one hand, to rather tall jar shapes, on the other. In size the specimens vary from minute cups to vessels 18 or 20 inches in diameter. The base is rounded or conic, the shoulder is often slightly angular, and the neck is more or less sharply constricted. The rim is generally turned outward. The lip is much varied in form and embellishment. Profiles are shown in figure 76.

The surface is generally well covered with texturing and decoration. The body has been finished by paddling or rocking with textile-covered tools, or by cord-wrapped roulettes—usually, I believe, the latter—the implement having been rolled up and down from rim to base, leaving approximately parallel imprintings, as is indicated in some of the specimens illustrated. After the malleating process was finished, the neck and rim were smoothed down and decorated in various ways, most generally by impressing cords into the soft clay, producing patterns, or by merely repeating indentations of the cord laid on flat or doubled up, making deep indentations. This treatment extended to the margin of the lip and, in cases, to the interior surface. Trailed and incised lines and punctures are seen in numerous instances, and in the vessels suggesting Iroquoian relationships the patterns resemble those characterizing the Iroquoian ware.

The National Museum collections contain fragments of a well-made vessel from Lake Nipigon, western Ontario, 500 miles north of Two

Rivers. The ware is of much better make than the pottery south of Lake Superior, and has rather decided Iroquoian characters. The paste is silicious and

FIG. 77—Fragments of a large vase from Lake Nipigon, Ontario

heavy, the walls thick, the body well polished, and the neck and thickened collar decorated with strongly drawn patterns of incised straight lines. The fragments are shown in figure 77.

MANDAN POTTERY

It is fortunate for the student of primitive ceramics that at least one tribe continued the practice of the art down to the present period. The Mandans may even yet at times renew the work of pottery manufacture, but no record of this has been made for several decades. The work of this tribe is described by Catlin and is represented by several specimens preserved in our museums. It serves as a key to the great group of ware now under review, connecting it closely with the Siouan peoples—the buffalo-hunting tribes—the typical wild tribes of North America. To be sure, the Mandans lived in permanent villages composed of substantial earth lodges, were largely sedentary, and on account of their remoteness naturally kept up the practice of primitive industries longer than the equally sedentary tribes of the same family farther south.

Catlin's account of the pottery making of the Mandans is quoted in full in the introduction, and I need do no more here than present the illustrations, plate CLXXV. The vessel shown in *a* is 6 inches in diameter and 6 inches in height, about the average size, and strong and neatly made, of grayish-yellow clay tempered with sand or pulverized crystalline rock. Its characteristics of form are the wide mouth with rim developed into a wide collar, to which two handles are attached, alternating with two angular projections. The body swells but little, and terminates in a rounded cone below. The general surface was finished, first, with the usual cord-wrapped implement, traces of the imprintings being still seen about the neck. After this, the surface was finished by application of a tool producing impressions such as would be made by a paddle wrapped with straw or rushes; they are plainly to be seen in the illustration. Next, the neck and rim were rubbed down, obliterating the imprintings, and the collar and handles were embellished by impressing strong cords in simple, angular patterns. Triangular spaces at the top of the handles and over the alternating projections have received each three imprintings from a round-pointed stamp, probably the end of a stick, about one-fourth inch in diameter. Possibly these indentations may stand for the eyes and mouth of some animal, while the cord imprintings of the rim stand for the markings of the body. The specimen was received from Dr Washington Matthews, U. S. A., stationed at Fort Stevenson, North Dakota, in 1868. A very similar specimen is credited to the Grosventre tribe.

Specimen *b*, collected by General William B. Hazen, Chief Signal Officer, is recorded without assignment to any tribe. It was associated, however, with Sioux relics, and doubtless came from the Mandans, as it duplicates in nearly every particular the specimen described above. The body shows no traces of textile markings, but the entire surface is covered with impressions made by a paddling tool, and certain impressions about the neck suggest that this was possibly a bit of wood, carved with alternating low ridges and shallow grooves. The collar is without the three indentations seen in the other specimen. The color is terra-cotta, mottled with black cloudings, produced by the firing. Dried mush adheres to the inside and extends in lines— as if from boiling over—down the sides of the vessel. This latter feature and the presence of a buckskin carrying-band indicate recent origin and use.

The two specimens given in plate CLXXVI belong also to the Hazen collection, but, not being assigned to any locality or people, they should be referred to with caution. They possess, however, numerous features in common with Mandan work. Possibly they were obtained from village or burial sites at some point on the Missouri river. Specimen *a* has been finished by paddling with an implement wrapped with fine cords, and specimen *b* is tempered with shell, and has rude scrolls scratched on the four lobes of the body. These features would seem to connect the specimen with ware of the Middle Mississippi group.

Pawnee Pottery

The National Museum contains an interesting lot of fragments of earthenware brought in by Dr F. V. Hayden about the year 1867. A

Fig. 78—Outlines of vases from a Pawnee (?) village site, east-central Nebraska. Restored from large fragments.

few pieces are shown in plate CLXXVII. They are from a Pawnee village site on Beaver creek, Nebraska, in the east-central part of the state. They exhibit unusual variety of form and ornament, but nearly all appear to represent small pot-shaped vessels, a striking characteristic being the many handles. In this respect they suggest the handled pots of western Tennessee, illustrated in plate XII. The prevailing form is illustrated in outline in figure 78.

The fragment of a pipe (figure 79) found with these sherds is an unusual feature in the far Northwest.

Fig. 79—Fragment of a clay pipe from a Pawnee (?) village site, east-central Nebraska.

The paste of this ware is gray, with dark fire-mottlings, and it is not very hard. It is tempered with sand and, in cases, with grains of some dark crystalline rock. In general appearance the vessels are much like those of Mandan manufacture. The rounded bodies of the vessels, as a rule, have been finished with cord-wrapped or ribbed implements, and the necks, handles, and rims have been smoothed off to receive the decoration of incised lines and indentations. In some cases the body has been rubbed smooth and left plain, and in others the incised ornamental markings have been carried down over nearly the entire surface, as is shown in the middle left-hand figure of plate CLXXVII.

a

b

c

POTSHERDS FROM A VILLAGE SITE, TWO RIVERS, WISCONSIN

NORTHWESTERN GROUP

(HAMILTON COLLECTION, ABOUT ACTUAL SIZE)

a (DIAMETER 6 INCHES)

b (HEIGHT 7½ INCHES)

POTTERY OF THE MANDAN INDIANS, DAKOTA

NORTHWESTERN GROUP

a

b (HEIGHT 6½ INCHES)

POTTERY FROM THE MISSOURI VALLEY (?)

NORTHWESTERN GROUP

POTTERY FROM A PAWNEE VILLAGE SITE, NEBRASKA

NORTHWESTERN GROUP

(ABOUT THREE-FOURTHS)

The following paragraphs are quoted from Dr Hayden's account:

All along the Missouri, in the valleys of the Little Blue, Big Blue, Platte, and Loup Fork rivers, I have observed the remains of these old dirt villages, and pieces of pottery are almost invariably found with them.

But on a recent visit to the Pawnee reservation on Loup Fork I discovered the remains of an old Pawnee village, apparently of greater antiquity than the others, and the only one about which any stone implements have as yet been found. On and around the site of every cabin of this village I found an abundance of broken arrowheads, chipped flints, some of which must have been brought from a great distance, and a variety of small stones, which had been used as hammers, chisels, etc. I have gathered about half a bushel of the fragments of pottery, arrowheads, and chipped flints, some of which I hope to place in the museum of the Smithsonian next winter. No Pawnee Indian now living knows of the time when this village was inhabited. Thirty years ago an old chief told a missionary that his tribe dwelt here before his birth.[a]

OTHER NORTHWESTERN POTTERY

From a mound near Fort Wadsworth, North Dakota, Mr A. J. Comfort obtained much fragmentary pottery, and his descriptions, being detailed and interesting, are quoted:

The sherds were evidently from some vessels no larger than a small jar or goblet and from others whose capacity must have been 4 or 5 gallons. * * * The thickness of these sherds varies from one-eighth to three-eighths of an inch, according to the size of the vessel, though few exceed one-fourth. Sand has been the only substance used to give stiffness to the mass during process of molding and prevent the ware from cracking while burning, and has probably been obtained from disintegrated stones, some of which were found on the hearths elsewhere spoken of. I have been able to find no whole vessels, but from the fragments of the rims, sides, and bottoms it is not difficult to form a fair conception of their shape, which, for aboriginal art, was wonderfully symmetrical, gradually widening from the neck or more constricted portion of the vessel until it attains its greatest diameter at a distance of one-third of the height from the bottom, which is analogous, in curvature, to the crystal of a watch. To the neck is attached the rim, about 1 inch in width, though sometimes 2; this slopes outward at an angle of about 20 degrees from a perpendicular. * * * I have found no pieces containing ears or handles, though an Indian informant tells me that small vessels were supplied with ears.

That the aboriginal potters of the lacustrine village of Cega Iyeyapi were fond of decoration, and practiced it in the ceramic art, is shown by the tracings confined to the rims. Rim ornaments consist of very smooth lines about one-twentieth of an inch in width, and as deep, drawn quite around the vessels, parallel to the margin. These are sometimes crossed by zigzag lines terminating at the neck of the vessel and the margin of the rim. Lines drawn obliquely across the rim of the vessel, and returning so as to form the letter V, with others parallel to the margin of the rim, joining its sides, the same repeated as often as space admits, constitute the only tracings on some vessels. The inside of the vessels is invariably plain. . . .

The outside of the vessels proper, exclusive of the rim, which is traced, bears the impression of very evenly twisted cords running in a parallel direction and closely crowded together, the alternate swelling and depression of whose strands have left equidistant indentations in every line thus impressed. These lines run, on the sides of the vessels, in a direction perpendicular to the rim, and disappear within a half

---

[a] Dr F. V. Hayden, Smithsonian Report, 1867, p. 411.

of an inch or an inch of it, each indentation becoming indistinct near the end. I have counted from ten to fifteen of these casts in the space of a linear inch, and yet some of the sherds represent much finer cords.[a]

The ware of the Mississippi valley proper naturally extend far up the western tributaries, and a few fragments have been found in the Yellowstone Park, one of the most remote and inaccessible localities in the country. These fragments were brought in by Colonel P. W. Norris, Superintendent of the Park, in 1880. They represent a large jar or pot with upright neck. The material is coarsely silicious and the walls are thick. Just below the rim is a line of nodes made by punching with a round implement from within, and there are indistinct traces of roulette-markings. These pieces have a close analogy with the roulette-stamped ware of Naples, Illinois, and therefore with the whole rouletted group.

A few fragments of very archaic ware have been gathered in Idaho and on the site of Salt Lake City, Utah. These seem to be related to the primitive northern pottery, rather than to the Pueblo ware of the South.

---

[a] Comfort, A. J., in Smithsonian Report for 1871, pp. 400–401.

DATE DUE

JAN 0 3 1998			
MAY 0 6 1998			